SHIPS AND SEAMEN OF ANGLESEY 1558–1918
Studies in Maritime and Local History

Aled Eames

SHIPS AND SEAMEN
OF ANGLESEY

1558–1918

*Studies in Maritime
and Local History*

Aled Eames

First published in 1973
by The Anglesey Antiquarian Society
New edition: 2011

ISBN: 978–1-84527-352-1

Cover design: Eirian Evans

Published by Gwasg Carreg Gwalch,
12 Iard yr Orsaf, Llanrwst, Wales LL26 0EH
tel: 01492 624031
fax: 01492 641502
email: books@carreg-gwalch.com
internet: www.carreg-gwalch.com

Contents

Introduction to this new edition

The publication of *Ships and Seamen of Anglesey* in 1973 signalled the arrival of a maritime historian who was to have a profound impact on our understanding of Welsh maritime history. Aled Eames would go on to produce numerous titles on a range of maritime topics, in both Welsh and English, while his lectures, some of which were published, would attract appreciative audiences whether in maritime conferences or village halls. He would later be a founder/editor of Wales' only national maritime history journal *Cymru a'r Môr/Maritime Wales* which continues to provide a platform for all those interested in Welsh maritime history. His contribution to radio and television in Wales made him a household name and he successfully utilised both mediums to raise the profile of the maritime dimension's contribution to our understanding of Welsh history and of Wales' place in the wider world. Recognition was not confined to his homeland as exemplified in 1981 when he was elected to the Caird Fellowship at the National Maritime Museum in Greenwich and in 1986 when he presented BBC2's acclaimed series *Tradewinds*, in co-operation with Canadian and Finnish television. Thus it was that *Ships and Seamen of Anglesey* provided the springboard for Aled Eames to ensure that the study of Welsh maritime history received the attention of both the academic world and the general public, both within Wales and further afield.

Originally published as part of the Anglesey Antiquarian Society's 'Studies in Anglesey History Series' this was, in many respects, a bold move on the Society's part as very little had been published in Wales on maritime history at the time. The book's subtitle, *Studies in Maritime and Local History*, made its remit clear, and Aled Eames responded admirably to the requirement that the work provide source material for those wishing to delve deeper into the subject while also appealing to the general reader interested in the history of the island. Alongside David Thomas' *Hen Longau Sir Gaernarfon* and J. Geraint Jenkins' *Maritime Heritage: The Ships and Seamen of Southern Ceredigion*, this work stands out as one of the few regional studies in the field of Welsh maritime history. As with Thomas and Jenkins' studies, the title of Aled Eames' book is misleading, for it is not solely concerned with seafarers and ships but presents the significance and influence of the sea and maritime activity to the peoples of both the coastal and inland communities. On the other hand, it is also far from being an introspective, parochial study, for the island's story, through Eames' eyes, places its people's maritime experiences firmly in an international context. *Ships and Seamen of Anglesey* is much more than a study of local history with limited local significance.

On its publication *Ships and Seamen of Anglesey* was greeted with much critical acclaim and according to some experts in the field this remains his best work. It was praised for being 'a splendid mine of information', providing an insight into a range of maritime topics and 'a treasure-house of meticulous details'. It was described as 'a magnificent achievement within the limits set by its judicious author', for Aled Eames emphasised that this was not a narrative history of maritime Anglesey but a series of studies reflecting the varied nature of its people's relationship with the sea from Elizabethan times to the early twentieth-century.

Although *Ships and Seamen of Anglesey* is much more than the story of men and ships, the title does reflect the main focus of the study which has traditionally been at the heart of maritime history. Yet Aled Eames was also aware that, in order to fully appreciate the story of the ships that plied the world's sea routes, and of the men who sailed in them, a range of topics requires our understanding. Thus the reader is introduced to the variety and significance of maritime trade, to the business community so vital to the world of the ship and the seafarer and to the development of ports. In stressing the importance of Beaumaris, Amlwch and Holyhead Aled Eames was at the forefront in emphasising the specific contribution of small ports not only to our understanding of the economy of Wales and Britain, but also internationally.

By the 1970s it was clear that the scope of maritime history was expanding, and with it an appreciation of its significance to furthering our understanding of economic, social, political and even cultural history. *Ships and Seamen of Anglesey* reflected these new developments and these remain central to the book's success. Thus, for example, the final quarter of the twentieth-century saw maritime history paying far greater attention to the communities that were producing seafarers and that relied on the sea for their living, not only port towns and their immediate hinterland but also small, isolated villages and hamlets. The poverty of such communities, and their dependence on sea-related activities for their survival, was not lost on Aled Eames as his sympathetic portrayal of the island's smuggling heritage shows. Nowadays the significance of illegal maritime activity is no longer seen solely in terms of the romance of smugglers, wreckers and pirates but is a significant sub-topic of maritime history in its own right, and the attention given by Aled Eames to the nature of maritime communities, and illegal maritime activity, was certainly a significant development at the time.

The wider issue of political control of the seas is also an area which has seen great developments since the publication of this book, with naval history no longer regarded as solely concerned with the study of great men and great battles. This development is again reflected in the attention given by Aled Eames to the part played by the people of Anglesey, from all strata of society, in naval activity and in warfare. The naval dimension was obviously dear to him: the subject of his thesis after all was 'Sea Power and Welsh History, 1625–1660' (for which he had been awarded the Prince Llewelyn ap Gruffydd Prize), while he had also served in the Royal Navy during the Second World War. *Ships and Seamen of Anglesey* certainly gives due recognition to an aspect of Wales' relationship with the sea which merits further study.

The history of the role of the sea in terms of leisure is today receiving much more attention, not confined to maritime historians, and includes aspects such as aquatic sports, tourism and retirement. This certainly was not the case when *Ships and Seamen of Anglesey* first appeared, but the chapter on 'The Sea for Leisure' shows clearly that Aled Eames saw the significance of this area not only for our understanding of man's relationship with the sea but also in terms of its potential for future maritime historians. It is not surprising, therefore, that the sea for leisure in the context of this study is not confined to the experiences of the rich, but also draws attention to its wider social and economic implications.

Today maritime historians are increasingly aware of the concept of 'maritime notion' or 'maritime ideology'. This cultural significance of the sea – the sea as an inspiration to, and a reflection of, ideology and culture, permeating the lives of communities both directly and indirectly concerned with maritime activities – is present throughout the book. We might expect the inhabitants of Anglesey, as an island people, to be aware of the sea's penetration into all aspects of their lives, but this is not necessarily the case. Thus one of the successes of the book on a popular level in Anglesey was that it highlighted the sea as being not a backdrop to life on the island, but as being at its heart. In this respect *Ships and Seamen of Anglesey* reflected a growing awareness among the public that the significance of the sea was far greater than had previously been appreciated.

That *Ships and Seamen of Anglesey* should reflect so many facets of maritime history is no doubt due to the breadth of research, which can only be described as breathtaking. Coupled with this is Aled Eames' ability to draw out the human interest at every opportunity. 'Maritime history' sounds, to some, a dry topic, but all history, of course, is ultimately about people; Aled Eames successfully conveys this whatever the topic under discussion. He includes, for instance, 'long gossipy bulletins' sent by one Louisa Stanley to her Grandmama at Penrhos, recording the shipping she has seen on any particular morning; he interprets captains' log book entries so that they come alive to the reader; the small details, such as the finding of a South African ram and a ship's cat on a torpedoed German cargo steamer – all these create a picture of a lively and real maritime scene on Anglesey that we can all appreciate.

One of the interesting features of the book, regarded as being relatively innovative at the time of publication, is the successful use of oral testimony. Aled Eames interviewed numerous people about their seafaring experiences, thus preserving personal and intimate testimony which would otherwise have been lost for all time, and this at a time when 'oral history' was not generally regarded as 'admissible' by the academic world of which he was a part. Of course, for many of these old sea dogs Aled Eames was much more than a maritime historian, he was one of them and understood their world due to his service in the Royal Navy. It is not surprising that his first Welsh-language volume was the classic *Meistri'r Moroedd* (1978), which relied heavily on the oral testimony of a generation that would soon be lost. Central to this successful use of oral history was Aled

Eames' warm, engaging personality and these same traits are reflected in his style of writing, displaying an ability to tell the story in an interesting manner for both the specialist and non-specialist alike. His abilities as a great communicator are reflected in the readable manner of the book.

As Aled Eames himself emphasised, the book is not intended as a comprehensive study of Anglesey's maritime past; topics which had already received attention elsewhere, the history of Holyhead and of the Menai Ferries for example, were deliberately omitted. *Ships and Seamen of Anglesey* would itself lay the foundations for further studies on Anglesey and Wales' maritime past. Thus Aled Eames himself would go on to expand on many of the topics studied here – including the lives of women at sea in *Gwraig y Capten* (1984), the importance of the individual master mariner to north-west Wales shipping in *Shipmaster* (1980) and the experiences of ordinary men and women in the maritime world, often alien to many of them, in *Y Fordaith Bell* (1993). Others would go on to expand on Aled Eames's work to provide further insight into Anglesey's rich and varied maritime past, such as Bryan Hope's *A Commodious Yard: The Story of William Thomas & Sons, Shipbuilders of Amlwch* on the one hand, and on the other, *Ffarwel i'r Grassholm Gribog*, a study of the village of Moelfre, where Aled Eames lived for a while. It is in recognition of Aled Eames' contribution to maritime history, and due to the affection with which he is remembered in the village, that Darlith Goffa Aled Eames Memorial Lecture is held biennially in the village under the auspices of Partneriaeth Moelfre & Lligwy Partnership and MOROL.

MOROL (Sefydliad Astudiaethau Hanes Morwrol Cymru – Institute of Welsh Maritime Historical Studies) has been established with the aim of promoting Welsh maritime history. It owes its existence in no small measure to the work of Aled Eames and his fellow maritime historians in Wales and is designed to build upon the foundations laid by them. MOROL is not only concerned with publishing new works but on re-printing classic studies in Welsh maritime history. Over the years there has been a growing demand for *Ships and Seamen of Anglesey* to be published anew and MOROL, in conjunction with Gwasg Carreg Gwalch, is proud to make the volume available to today's students of Welsh maritime history, and to those interested in Welsh history in general – Aled Eames' reconstruction of a world that has passed but whose relevance has not diminished.

Robin Evans
Chair
MOROL (Sefydliad Astudiaethau Hanes Morwrol Cymru –
Institute of Welsh Maritime Historical Studies)

Foreword

In his introduction to his *History of England*, G. M. Trevelyan makes the following observation: 'In early times the relation of Britain to the sea was passive and receptive, in modern times active and acquisitive. In both is the key to her story'. Trevelyan's general statement could also be applied specifically to the history of Anglesey. In the previous volume in this series Miss Frances Lynch authoritatively described the archaeological background of the history of the prehistoric settlers on Anglesey. In the present volume we are given a fascinating insight into the lives of the maritime community of this island from Elizabethan times to the early years of this century.

The author is an acknowledged expert in the field of Welsh maritime history. He has used hitherto unpublished material from official sources, but he has also had access to the personal documents of seafaring families, and has, moreover, recorded oral material which would otherwise have been lost. This book, therefore, is not only the work of a specialist in this field, but one to which many people from Anglesey have made a valuable contribution.

In the forewords to the previous volumes in this series it has been my pleasant duty to thank the Anglesey County Council for financial support, and once more I express my committee's appreciation – but this is the last volume in which I shall be able to do so. When the Anglesey County Council initiated this project of publishing a series of specialist studies on the history of the island, it was regarded as a long-term undertaking which would embrace in course of time, every important aspect of the island's history. The Anglesey County Council has not survived to fulfil this laudable ambition, but the Publications Committee records its deep gratitude to the Council for initiating the series and for giving such generous and helpful assistance to the first four volumes.

Diolch i Gyngor Sir Fôn am gychwyn y gyfres, ac am ei chefnogi mor hael.

Helen Ramage,
General Editor

Preface

When I was invited in 1970 to contribute to this series of studies of Anglesey history, I readily accepted as it gave me an opportunity to return to some long-neglected transcripts of seventeenth-century documents made over twenty years ago. I recognized, however, that another twenty years and more of research by many students, and many monographs on specialised aspects, were necessary before a comprehensive maritime history of Anglesey could be written. What I have attempted, therefore, is not a narrative history but a series of studies to illustrate some of the ways in which the sea has affected the lives of the people of Anglesey. The Marquess of Anglesey, President of the Anglesey Antiquarian Society, indicated in his foreword to the first volume in this series that the aim of the Society was to provide source material for those who wish to conduct further research into specialist subjects and at the same time to appeal to the general reader interested in the history of the Island. I have tried to keep this in mind in writing the book and, in particular, to suggest that there is already much documentary material available in our local archives for the students of maritime history. If this book stimulates others to consult these records, I believe one of the original aims of the series will have been achieved.

Since I began this work, maritime records held locally have been considerably enriched by the recent acquisition of the mass of papers known to seamen as the 'Articles of Agreement', the original Board of Trade contracts of signing on for voyages, and many official logs for Anglesey and Caernarvonshire ships which had hitherto been stored in the Hayes Repository of the Public Record Office. Although I have only been able to skim the surface by reference to a few of the thousands of documents, I hope that I have been able to indicate the wealth of information that is now available to the student of maritime history. I wish to record my gratitude to the Anglesey and Caernarvonshire County Councils for their generous interest in the acquisition of these records, and in particular to Mr Dewi O. Jones of the Anglesey County Library, and Mr Bryn Parry, County Archivist of Caernarvon, and their respective staffs, for long days spent in the Hayes Repository extracting these records of

Anglesey and Caernarvonshire ships which otherwise might well have gone to the University of Newfoundland. Students of Welsh maritime history owe much to both Mr Dewi Jones and Mr Bryn Parry for their efforts to acquire documentary and photographic records of shipping, and I have reason to be very grateful to them both for many kindnesses and much thoughtful interest and encouragement. Another friend who greatly facilitated my work, Mr R. S. Wells, Registrar of British Ships for the Port of Beaumaris, allowed me to spend many days working through the Registers in a pleasant room overlooking Holyhead Harbour at Custom House, a gracious building erected in 1820, which has so many links with the maritime history of the county.

My indebtedness to many distinguished historians who are members of the Society for Nautical Research is great, both for the inspiration of their own writing and for much kindly encouragement. I have tried to acknowledge in the footnotes the many references to their work, but I wish to record my gratitude to Professor C. C. Lloyd and the Reverend J. R. Powell for their kindness twenty years ago when I was working at the Public Record Office and the National Maritime Museum, and, more recently, to Mr Robert Craig and Mr Basil Greenhill for their helpful suggestions regarding merchant shipping history in the last century. Dr Jürgen Meyer of the Altonaer Museum in Hamburg has kindly sent me photographs of Welsh ships at Hamburg, and both he and Mr Grahame Farr of Bristol have readily provided information. I have drawn heavily on the notebooks and papers compiled after years of patient research by the late Mr David Thomas of Bangor, and the late Mr Henry Parry of Nefyn, both of whom pioneered research into Welsh maritime history.

During the past two years I have been privileged to act as tutor to a number of WEA short courses in Anglesey, which gave me an opportunity to discuss aspects of the sailing ship era with master mariners and seamen, their descendants and those who remembered their families. I am happy to record my indebtedness to members of these courses at Amlwch, Beaumaris, Holyhead, Llangefni and Moelfre for their enthusiastic search for information. In many ways this is their book. Despite the kindness of several octogenarians who have allowed me to record their memories on tape, I have, sadly, all too frequently been reminded that had this work been carried out some thirty years ago there would have been much more oral material available regarding a way of life in Anglesey that has now gone for ever. It is in order to preserve what remains that I have recorded the last chapters of this book in more detail than would normally be permissible; I believe I owe the reader this explanation for what may appear to be a certain imbalance between the earlier and later chapters.

There are some obvious omissions; I have not discussed, for example, the Mersey pilot service based on Anglesey and staffed for generations by Anglesey men; this deserves a book for itself. On certain topics I have attempted to avoid the repetition of information which has already been provided by other writers and is readily available; H. R. Davies's history of the Conway and Menai Ferries, Henry Parry's history of the life-boat service in north Wales, and David Lloyd Hughes's history of Holyhead are examples of works in this context. I have followed the spelling of place names in *An Atlas of Anglesey* (edited Melville Richards, 1972) and I am grateful to Professor Richards for his scholarly advice whenever I have had any queries.

In a work which owes so much to others, there is a danger that this foreword might appear to be a catalogue of names, but it is appropriate that I should thank the following master mariners for the many hours that they have spent discussing their memories of sail with me, and for answering my questions so readily: Captain W. H. Hughes, DSC, Holyhead; Captain Henry Roberts, Moelfre; Captain R. K. Jones, Moelfre; Captain E. Griffiths, Bull Bay, and Captain W. Williams, Amlwch. Again I am much indebted to Miss Gertrude Thomas, Bryn Eilian, and the family of William Thomas, the Amlwch ship-builder; Miss Mamie Williams, daughter of Captain Ishmael Williams, Amlwch; Mrs E. K. Williams, Liverpool, daughter of William Thomas, the Liverpool ship-manager; Mr Hugh Farrell and the family of Captain Robert Jones, Garden Cottage, Amlwch; Mrs Dilys Humphreys and the family of Captain William Williams, Tynygongl, for granting me access to private papers and photographs in their possession. Mr Frank Bell of Holyhead and Mr R. T. Pritchard of Bangor, both local historians who have collected many valuable records and photographs over the years, helped me in many ways; the diary kept by Sub-Lieutenant A. Dutton, RNVR, following the sinking of HMS *Tara*, and other papers were kindly lent to me by Mrs M. Burke of Holyhead. The officers of the Royal Anglesey Yacht Club generously allowed me to consult their early records, and Miss M. Burton, whose family has long been associated with Anglesey yachting and life-boats, gave much valuable information. The contemporary Welsh artist, Kyffin Williams, allowed me to photograph the work of his ancestress, Frances Williams, founder of the Anglesey Association for the Protection of Life from Shipwreck, and very kindly lent me some valuable family papers.

The diagram of Amlwch Port was kindly prepared by Mr Douglas Hague and Mr Dylan Roberts of the Royal Commission on Ancient Monuments (Wales); Dr B. L. Davies of the Education Department, UCNW, and Mr R. G. Williams, of the Caernarvonshire Record Office, prepared the map indicating ports frequented by Davies and Thomas ships, and Mr Ifor Jones of the Department of Computing, UCNW, patiently advised on and prepared a computer programme to analyse the sailings of the Davies ships from 1843 to 1906. One of the most pleasant features of the work were the many 'voyages of discovery' with Mr Geoffrey Charles in search of paintings and photographs in various parts of the island; I am particularly grateful to Mr Charles for the expert way in which he reproduced many much-faded photographs, and for guiding me in the final selection of those which have been included in this book. It is appropriate that I should record my gratitude to the staffs of the libraries and record offices referred to in the footnotes; here at Bangor I am particularly indebted to the late Mr Emyr Gwynne Jones, Mr Alun Giles Jones and Mr Derwyn Jones for their ready advice and guidance at all times.

Several friends have read sections of this work, and Professor J. Gwynn Williams and Mrs Helen Ramage, the Honorary Editor of the series, have read it all. I am grateful to them for their valuable suggestions, and in particular to Mr Emrys Hughes, MBE, Llangefni, for carefully drawing my attention to infelicities of style, for reading the proofs and preparing the index. It is literally true that without the untiring devotion of Mrs Mary Price, who typed so many drafts and checked so many details, this work would not have appeared. To all who have helped me, I am sincerely grateful.

Aled Eames
Neuadd Reichel, Bangor.

Abbreviations

AC	*Archaelogia Cambrensis*
Add MSS	Additional Manuscripts
Adm	Admiralty MSS
Ad ML	*Additional Letters of the Morrises of Anglesey,*
	1735-1836 (ed. Hugh Owen), Y Cymmrodor XLIX
ARO	Anglesey County Record Office, Llangefni
B+A	Beaumaris and Anglesey Records
Bangor	Bangor MSS, General Collection
BCR	Register of British Shipping 1786 – Beaumaris,
	Custom House, Holyhead
BM	British Museum
Bod	Bodleian Library, Oxford
Cefn	Cefnllan MSS
CDH	*Caernarvon and Denbigh Herald*
CRO	Caernarvonshire Record Office, Caernarvon
CSPD	*Calendar of State Papers, Domestic*
CSP Ireland	*Calendar of State Papers, Ireland*
CWP	*Calendar of Wynn (of Gwydir) Papers*
DNB	*Dictionary of Welsh Biography, 1959*
DWB	*The Dictionary of Welsh Biography, 1959*
EHR	*English Historical Review*
HMC	*Historical Manuscripts Commission*
ML	*The Letters of Lewis, Richard, William and John*
	Morris (ed. J. H. Davies) 1907
MM	Mona Mine MSS
MM	*The Mariners Mirror*, the Journal of the Society
	for Nautical Research
NLW	National Library of Wales, Aberystwyth
NMM	National Maritime Museum, Greenwich
NRS	Publications of the Navy Records Society
NWC	*North Wales Chronicle*
NW Gazette	*North Wales Gazette*
PN	Plas Newydd MSS
PRO	Public Record Office
PYA	Porth yr Aur MSS

Parl Papers	Parliamentary Papers
Parl Debates	Parliamentary Debates
Raw	Rawlinson MSS
SB	*Sea Breezes*
SNR	Society for Nautical Research
SP	State Papers
TAAS	Transactions of the Anglesey Antiquarian Society and Field Club
TCymm	Transactions of the Honourable Society of Cymmrodorion
TCHS	Transactions of the Caernarvonshire Historical Society
TFHS	Transactions of the Flintshire Historical Society
TR	Tape-recorded interview
UCNW	University College of north Wales, Bangor
WT Liverpool	Letters and papers of William Thomas, Liverpool, Ship-Manager

Elizabethan and Early Stuart
Merchants and Seamen
1539–1641

Beaumaris in the spring of 1539 was the scene of much activity. For months past 'Roger ap John ap Atha', 'William Thomas', and 'Robert Voile' had been sailing boatloads of stone from 'Portaythewe', and from the quarry recorded in the accounts as 'Ogga Borde', possibly the old quarry later known as Porth Ogof, near Nantporth, a few miles down the Menai Strait from Beaumaris.[1] The stones were being taken to repair the town walls, and not before time in the eyes of Sir Richard Bulkeley who believed that 'if the king's enemies should chance to land here' they would overrun both town walls and the castle within the hour. In 1539 the King, Henry VIII, certainly had enemies. France and Spain had made peace at Nice in the previous summer, and the Pope's excommunication of Henry VIII brought with it the threat of invasion by combined Catholic powers. Thomas Cromwell, Henry's powerful minister, recently responsible for far-reaching political and administrative changes designed to bring Wales more effectively under the English crown by the Act of Union 1536, met the challenge of invasion by ordering a survey of military fortifications along the coasts of England and Wales. It was in response to this policy that Sir Richard Bulkeley, Chamberlain of North Wales, wrote to Cromwell reporting that beacons had been set and a vigilant watch kept, for 'the Isle of Anglesey lies open upon all countries; it is but a day's sail from Scotland, Breton lies open on it, and the men of Conquet know it as well as we do; so also the Spaniards know every haven and creek, and Ireland and other countries lie open on it'.[2] Bulkeley and his contemporaries were very conscious that Anglesey was an island, and therefore isolated, for even though the Menai Strait were comparatively narrow, 'there are but three passages between Caernarvonshire and Anglesey, the least of them further than a man can shoot over with a flyer'. There was little point in hoping for help from the mainland: 'the boats will carry but 12 or 16 men' so that the men of Caernarvonshire would be of no avail. The total of six or seven hundred men available for the defence of the island would soon be defeated should the enemy land there.

Gloomily Bulkeley reflected upon Anglesey's isolation: 'I would not give one grote for any help that they of Caern(arvon)shire cold do . . . although they were redy att the water side.'[3]

In accordance with Cromwell's demand for a survey, Bulkeley listed 'all havynes bays crickes within the Ile of Anglesey', and this document gives an indication of the places which he and his contemporaries considered worthy of attention, among them Malltraeth, Aberffraw, Cymyran, Rhoscolyn, 'Saint Bride is bay', Holyhead, 'The Roode of Cardinals betwext the Skerres and the Shores', 'The Crik of Saint Patrick', Cemais, Cemlyn, 'Amlogh', Dulas, Red Wharf, 'The Roodes all along and under the land of Gray Cote', 'the entering of the Sound of Prestholme', then the Penmon entrance to the Strait and the haven of Beaumaris.[4] The danger passed. Although Cromwell did not survive to see it, the next invasion was in 1545 when the French landed forces in the Isle of Wight, and the rapidly ageing Henry saw his *Mary Rose* sink, heeling over in a gust of wind before his eyes. Ill health, the scourge of so many naval expeditions, soon put an end to the French invasion, but a month earlier, Sir Richard Bulkeley in far-off Anglesey had been on tenterhooks as he wrote to his brother-in-law, John Wyn ap Meredith, Sheriff of Caernarvonshire, urging him to be ready to come to the 'rescue of Anglesey as soon as they shall see any beacons or fires'.[5] Bulkeley had had information from a Manx vessel that eighty French ships had passed the Isle of Man, bound for Scotland and he feared that 'It is not unlikely that they may visit this poor Isle of Anglesey on their return'.

Both in 1539 and in 1545 Bulkeley had stressed Anglesey's vulnerability, lying in the track of ships sailing between France and Spain on the one hand, and Scotland and Ireland on the other. Fear of invasion in Anglesey was nothing new. The windswept island had known ships of friend and foe for centuries: in the days when the sea united rather than divided, the early visitors to prehistoric Anglesey, and, later, the Celtic Saints had come this way. In more troublesome times the ships of Branwen, Gruffydd ap Cynan, Magnus Barefoot and a host of others had known the seas off Abermenai and Priestholme. So too had the fleet of Henry II and the ships sailing to supply Edward I's castles at Beaumaris and Caernarvon.[6] What was new in the Tudor age was that the English Crown and its officials,

Justices of the Peace, Sheriffs and Vice Admirals, were conscious of the need to review coastal defence and shipping resources on the basis of England and Wales as a whole. When Elizabeth I came to the throne the anxiety was still there, and the surveys continued. Anglesey, like the other maritime counties, was expected to provide information.

By 1566 deputies had been appointed to 'oversee the good ordre of all havens creeks boats vessells and maryners', at Beaumaris itself, from Beaumaris to Red Wharf, thence to Dulas, Cemais, and Holyhead. It was reported that there were 'three or four creeks that be apt landing places for shippes'; the only vessels belonging to Anglesey were three small 'pykards' belonging to 'John ap Res'.[7] The Port Book for Beaumaris, however, for the same year, 1565-6, recorded visits from eight vessels, none of them belonging to the port, two from Waterford, two from Chester, three from Brittany and one from Scotland.[8] The survey and the Port Books bear out Professor Ralph Davies's observation that during the early years of Elizabeth's reign, the shipping resources of England and Wales were very slight compared to the Dutch, French and Spanish; had the Armada come at the beginning of Elizabeth's reign instead of 1588, 'it would have attacked an England deficient not merely in naval strength, but even more in the supporting merchant ships and in the crews to man either'.[9]

Preoccupation with the vulnerability of the island continued to colour political and religious attitudes for generations; the sea and the dangers therefrom remain a constant theme in the papers of Anglesey families for the next two centuries. The fear of invasion from Ireland was inevitable; on the western coasts of the Irish Sea were good harbours whose names were densely packed on the early portolan charts,[10] in contrast with the sparsity of good harbours on the Welsh coast. The attractiveness of Ireland to the potential invader was naturally a threat to Wales, and the fears of Spanish and French landings in Ireland as a base for a subsequent attack against England were frequently expressed. The wise Elizabethan seaman Sir William Monson summed up the position: 'There are many choice and good harbours in Ireland . . . the more and better they are, the greater the danger to England because an invasion in Ireland does as much concern us as if it were attempted in England.' Monson, 'speaking like a seaman, for that their actions must be governed by the winds', realised that a favourable Southerly, or South Westerly wind which would assist the potential invader would at the same time keep English ships windbound in the Channel ports: 'a southerly wind which brings them for our coast, keeps our ships in harbour that we cannot budge.' It was impracticable to fortify the Irish harbours against possible attack, for the simple reason that there were too many of them. Therefore, Monson urged, the policy of the English fleet should be one of interception. 'My advice, therefore, is when an enemy is feared in Ireland that there be a case to keep our fleet at sea off Mizzen Head, as a place to take advantage of all winds.'[11] To keep a fleet at sea on a permanent station was no easy task, and it was essential to have a base from which to operate. The obvious choice here was Milford Haven, praised by Monson, and, nearly a century later, by Greenville Collins as one of the best harbours in Europe.[12] But if Milford was admirable as a base for defence, it was also attractive to an enemy. North of Milford there were many hazards for sailing ships, and it was unlikely that large men of war would be risked in such waters. Any large-scale landing postulated suitable harbours protected from foul weather, scourge of all invasions. Despite the alarms of landlubbers, if invasion was to come at all in Wales, seamen recognized that there were only two possibilities, Milford Haven in the South and, in the North, despite the mountainous hinterland of Caernarvonshire, the Menai Strait, and, more particularly, the haven of Beaumaris. Anglesey fears were not without some foundation.

The Port Books of Beaumaris provide evidence that the Menai Strait were well known to the seamen of France, particularly the Bretons, and to the men of the Biscay ports and Andalusia; the knowledge gained in the days of peace was to be put at the disposal of Philip II as war approached. A secret agent on the Continent, Daniel Rogers, reported in the 1580s that Philip II's captains in the Netherlands 'are full of cartes and descriptions of the West Coast of England, and have the Isles of Anglesey and Man so particularly painted forth that I doubt if you have seen the like . . . and all the discourses are of invading England'. A Welsh merchant at Antwerp, Richard Clough, introduced his friend and neighbour at Denbigh, Humphrey Llwyd, the physician and antiquary, to Ortelius,

'Cosmographer to Philip the Second', and Dr F. J. North has discussed the significance of Llwyd's provision of a map of Anglesey drawn more nearly correct and on a larger scale than the rest of Wales for Ortelius's atlas.[13] The scattering of the Armada of 1588 was not the end of the war, and in the Autumn of 1597 the largest of all the Armadas of the sixteenth-century sailed, only to be dispersed in raging storms off the coast of Brittany. Intelligently planned, its sailing orders were more flexible than those of 1588, and allowed the commander to head towards different areas, according to the circumstances in which he found himself. The Spaniards had with them a carefully prepared survey by a pilot who obviously had had previous experience of the Western and South Western coasts of England and Wales. Naturally enough, the unnamed pilot was most interested in deep ports such as Milford and Plymouth, but his report, now housed in the archives at Simancas, suggests that he had sailed in the Irish Sea.[14] After describing the dangerous entrances to the small harbours of Workington and Liverpool, and the sandbanks off Chester, he came to the approaches to Beaumaris where 'at low water at the mouth there are six or five fathoms, and within there is the same depth for one league'. The pilot was optimistic regarding an anchorage for a fleet: 'There is room for two hundred sails.' Whatever the first Sir Richard Bulkeley had done about repairing the fortifications of Beaumaris some fifty years previously, the Spanish pilot did not think much of them, for he wrote 'there is no fortress', but he had noted carefully the mountains of Snowdonia in the distance, stating that the land 'is the highest in England'. Moreover, there was 'water, meat, grain' available 'and cheaply'. Possibly most important of all, as far as a successful operation was concerned, he had high hopes of co-operation ashore from Welsh-speaking Catholics; 'They speak a language apart, there are many Catholics and they are very friendly to Ireland.'

The Spanish pilot shared the view of seamen regarding the inhospitable Welsh coast between Anglesey and Milford, 'a bad coastline, and on this account every year many of those fishing for herring are lost'. But, like Monson and Collins, he recognized Milford as 'the finest port in England', and here again he hoped for support from ashore, 'There are many Catholics and the people are naturally enemies of the English and do not speak their language'. As

Father Loomie, who has transcribed and translated this document, indicates, there is a note of caution about the pilot's written summary which is understandable; he alternates between obvious trivial details, and a more experienced appraisal of the strategic areas, and as a pilot is reluctant to share his knowledge extensively on paper, lest his unique usefulness to the Spanish war fleets be diminished. From the internal evidence of the document, however, it would appear that the pilot was much more certain in his descriptions of Western ports and conditions than of eastern England, and it seems probable that he was thinking in terms of what wind conditions and food supplies ashore would be like in the Autumn of 1597.

In the event, the Armada pilot did not get beyond Brittany. It must have been years since he had sailed to Chester and possibly Beaumaris, and, as the potential danger from Spain had increased, so had the persecution of Welsh Catholics. It was five years since Father William Davies, missionary priest, had been caught at Holyhead with four young men bound for Ireland. The officials who arrested him complained of the lack of co-operation of the Holyhead people, and his execution in July 1593, carried out before a crowd hostile to the authorities, made a deep impression.[15] Although the third Sir Richard Bulkeley, courtier and favourite of Queen Elizabeth, seemed to conform outwardly, particularly since the execution of his Denbighshire friend, Thomas Salusbury, it was rumoured that he had Catholic sympathies and his daughter married into one of the leading Catholic families in north Wales, the unyielding Pughs of Creuddyn. Here was an intriguing connection, for in a cave at Rhiwledyn, Little Orme's Head, within sight, on a clear day, across the sea from Beaumaris, was the secret printing press which prepared the first Welsh Catholic books for publication in 1586-7.[16] Although Llandudno bay itself was an uncertain anchorage with poor holding ground, it is likely that the cave could be approached by sea, and could have been used as a link in communication between the Pughs and vessels sailing by to Chester or Beaumaris in the 60s and 70s, before the stern measures against Catholics in the immediate pre-1588 period.

By 1598 invasion fears were high in Anglesey. In the previous year Anglesey had been granted immunities from levies of men and arms by the Privy Council, 'having a goodly haven to receive the enemy's shipping', and in November 1597 John Wynn of Gwydir, hard pressed to provide 'men and victuals for furnishing the Navy', thought it a 'gift of God that a man of war laden with corn is come aground in Anglesey'.[17] Two years later Sir Richard Bulkeley, writing to thank John Wynn for a basket of plums, expressed his own attitude (at least for official eyes) when he stated, with that dramatic intensity so typical of the Elizabethans, that 'so long as the Spanish navy is on the coast' he would not leave Anglesey, 'but would, with God's help, either keep it or make it his grave'.[18] Both he and John Wynn had done well out of the Tudors in Anglesey and Caernarvonshire, and years of service in Elizabeth's Irish wars had made many of the neighbouring Welsh gentry determined to maintain the Protestant settlement. The merchants, too, had a stake in the defeat of Spain.

The trade of Anglesey was linked most closely in the Elizabethan age with the port of Chester. Lewis, in his study of the Welsh Port Books, rightly suggested that 'Chester was the shopping centre which catered for the personal, household, and occupational requirements of the inhabitants of Anglesey and Caernarvon'.[19] The Port Books of Beaumaris show that at the beginning of the Elizabethan period, foreign vessels called at Beaumaris; in 1562 the *Saint Maire*, and the *Loche* of 'Bilbo' were there with Spanish iron, wine, pitch and resin, and in 1565 the 40-ton '*Kateryn* of Landermewe in Brittany' and the 30-ton *Anne of Brest*, brought salt, Rochelle wine and sack, whilst in the spring of 1566 the *Lyon of Conkett*, a 70-ton vessel, with a cargo of 500 barrels of bay salt, bore out the truth of the first Sir Richard Bulkeley's statement some twenty years earlier that Anglesey was well known to the seamen of Le Conquet, to the north of Pointe du St Mathieu on the rugged coast of Finisterre. After a two-month stay at Beaumaris, the *Anne of Brest* left for Brittany with '10c. Manchester cottons,[20] remnants containing half short cloth, 10 short cloths, 27½c. Manchester cottons'. Ten days before the *Anne of Brest* had sailed, the *John of Dumfreys*, commanded by 'Andrew Brun, Scotchman', arrived with a cargo of Rochelle wine and salt. Beaumaris remained a depot for the exchange of Manchester cottons and Northern cloths, but as the trade with Spain and Portugal declined owing to increasing hostilities, more goods went by way of Ireland, and in the 70s vessels from Carlingford, Waterford and Dublin brought a wide range of cargoes to Beaumaris including Rochelle wine, Irish linen cloth, wheat, barley, rye and salt. One of the arguments included in a petition for the improvement in the defences of Anglesey, that 'the Scots have but six hours sayling from Scotland to the Isle of Anglesey',[21] was borne out by vessels like the *Andrew of Kylkowberye*, 40 tons, the *Lyzarde* of Ayr, 30 tons, and the small *Margett of Kirkcowbrey*, 8 tons, and the *Gift of God*, 6 tons, of Glasgow, which brought rye, wheat and Gascony wines to Beaumaris in the 80s. The merchants of Glasgow, Liverpool and Chester found Beaumaris a convenient depot to exchange goods, but most of the Manchester cottons went to London in the later years of Elizabeth. Wine from Bordeaux and La Rochelle for Chester occasionally came to Beaumaris; in 1577 the *Margett Bonaventure* of Chester brought pepper, sugar, cinnamon, and wine from 'Andalozen in Spain', some of which was discharged at Beaumaris and the remainder passed to Chester.[22]

Apart from foreign vessels, however, there were an increasing number of vessels belonging to Beaumaris itself. The *Victory* of Beaumaris, a 44-ton vessel, was untypical: she sailed from Chester to Newfoundland in 1582 and was back in Beaumaris in June 1583 from 'Lisburne in Spain' with a cargo of 350 barrels of salt, '400 lbs. Castell soap' and six pecks of barley malt for a Manchester merchant at Beaumaris, Henry Hardie.[23] Most of the Beaumaris vessels were smaller, an average of about ten tons, and their main trade was with Chester and Ireland, particularly after 1580. Together with vessels from Chester and Ireland, they plied in a trade which brought a variety of cargoes to Beaumaris and exported slates in considerable quantities, mainly to Ireland: from October 1589 to July 1590, for example, 66,000 slates were taken to Carlingford, Dublin and 'Knockfergus' in four vessels, the *Elizabeth* of Beaumaris, 12 tons, taking the bulk of them, 50,000 in five voyages, 10,000 at a time.[24] Obviously, the slates came from the Carnarvonshire banks of the Strait, and at Caernarvon itself five small vessels were engaged in the trade, together with the *Michall of Ogwen* and the *Margaret of Bangor*. The organisation of the trade of Beaumaris that emerges from the Port Book is similar to development elsewhere: there is a certain elasticity, a man may serve as master of a vessel for one voyage, and he then appears as merchant for another vessel for another voyage, sometimes there is a combination of master/merchant, sometimes they operate completely separately and can be identified as merchants and masters transporting goods for others.[25] As the years go by one notes the concentration of certain trades in the hands of individual merchants, but in other years all are involved in the import of corn, for the fluctuations of harvests and abnormal circumstances affected Anglesey more than most areas, and at times the island had to replenish its corn supplies from ports in England, Ireland, Scotland, and the Isle of Man; in 1602-3 there were an unusually high number of corn shipments to both Beaumaris and Caernarvon.[26]

It was at Beaumaris that the clearest examples of north Wales merchants who became wealthy through sea-borne trade in the Elizabethan period emerged; Gabriel Roberts was the most successful of all. A Welshman who had married into the Johnson family, English merchants who had long controlled the commerce of Beaumaris as leaders of the privileged 'Englishry', Roberts concentrated his business in the Chester trade, buying a wide variety of goods in Chester and having them shipped to Beaumaris where they were then distributed to customers from Anglesey and its neighbouring counties. The Johnsons and other Beaumaris merchants had been involved in overseas trade, but Roberts appears to have become the leading merchant in the borough by the 1590s, hiring many Chester and Beaumaris vessels, particularly the *Harry of Heswall*, whose master, John Gryffith, acted as factor for other merchants as well.[27] Appendix I, an extract from the Beaumaris Port Book from Michaelmas 1595 to Michaelmas 1596, may be taken to illustrate the wide range of goods imported by Gabriel Roberts, from Gascony wine, gun-powder, to frying pans and a 'joynted bed'. Trade brought Gabriel Roberts sufficient wealth to enable him to buy, with his cousin Hugh Arthur (another merchant who features in the Port Books), the lands of Lord Herbert of Cherbury in Dindaethwy and thus found the Roberts family's estate of Castellior. His younger son, Lewis Roberts, entered the service of the East India Company, in the accepted fashion for younger sons of Welsh families to enter the commercial world of London.[28]

Another example of the new opportunities open to young men from Anglesey in the age of Elizabeth is illustrated in the career of

David Lloyd from Llaneilian who went to Chester and became one of its leading merchants.[29] David Lloyd was well established as a Chester merchant when he married the daughter of Richard Bavand, a prominent merchant retailer of Chester, among whose many commercial activities was the shipping of goods from Chester to Beaumaris in the *Harry of Heswall*, like Gabriel Roberts. Bavand probably employed John Gryffith as his factor in Beaumaris. Lloyd was one of a small group who had control of most of the trade between Liverpool and Chester in the 1580s and was a member of a similar group in whose hands the continental trade of Chester was concentrated; he was certainly trading with Spain up to 1582. So influential was Lloyd that he was entrusted by his fellow merchants in Chester with negotiating matters on their behalf in Hull and London; when the Queen required financial assistance for the provisioning of her army in Ireland in 1581, Lloyd was one of the merchants who loaned her most money. [30]

David Lloyd was wealthy enough to leave a number of legacies over £100, and his will[31] mentioned land which he farmed in England, but it appears that he had not forgotten his connection with Anglesey. He bequeathed 'to the Poore of the parish of llanellian where I was borne, the some of Fortye shillings to be distributed by the discretion of my loving Nephewe Rowland lloid, gent, my loving brother in law Hugh ap dd. Anwyll, my loving sister Ellen lloid, widowe, and the Church Wardens of the said parishe'. David Lloyd's name does not appear in the Beaumaris Port Books, although that of his father in law, Richard Bavand, does, but in his will he left money 'to make her a ringe' to his sister in law, Agnes Lloyd, and it may be that his deceased brother had been involved in Beaumaris trade. Certainly David Lloyd had a high regard for his Beaumaris nephew, Edward Lloyd, Agnes's son, for in addition to leaving him money, he wished to take the boy into his own house to ensure that he had a good career in typical Elizabethan fashion: 'my will and desire is that my loving wife shall bring him uppe untill such tyme as he shalbe able to goe to the unyversitye or to be put to be apprentice, at the discretion of my overseers.' He did not forget his brother 'Master doctor Lloid' and his wife, and in addition to bequests to a host of nephews and nieces he also decreed the cancellation of the debts of his Welsh relations: 'I doe forgive and release to my said brother in lawe Hugh ap dd. Anwyll all such money as he doeth owe me by my shoppbooke' whilst his 'old Unkell Jeuan Lloyd' was to have 'my Rydinge Clook, my Jurkyn, dowblet and Breches that I did use to were in the tyme of my sickness', perhaps referring to a period of convalescence at Llaneilian. Mayor of Chester, leading merchant, negotiator, financier, the Llaneilian boy who had gone to Chester had done well out of the sea and ships.

But it was a chancy business. The merchants of Chester claimed that between 1570 and 1580 they had lost more than £12,000 by piracy, and ten of their ships had been wrecked on the French, Irish and Welsh coasts during the same period.[32] The acts of piracy had not all been committed off the French and Spanish coasts: their largest vessel had been captured by pirates fronm St Malo in the Irish Sea. It was alleged that there were pirates nearer home; Beaumaris and the anchorage in St Tudwal's Roads off Pwllheli were already well established as rendezvous for pirates and merchants who were willing to purchase pirated goods. Not too many questions would be asked regarding wines and sugars which would soon find their way into the cellars of the gentry of north Wales, but as they themselves were not particularly wealthy, merchants from as far afield as Bristol were known to come to Pwllheli to barter, and at Beaumaris it was rumoured that the third Sir Richard Bulkeley had a network of contacts with the 'trade'. His brothers, Charles and Daniel, both seamen, were accused of selling pirated goods at Pwllheli in 1581 with the assistance of the Castellmarch family,[33] one of whom was Sir Richard's brother in law, and Recorder of Beaumaris: there were suggestions that Sir Richard's house in London was being used to sell powdered sugar and goods brought from Beaumaris, one of the contact men being another brother of Sir Richard's, a respectable counsellor of Lincoln's Inn.[34] Sir Richard Bulkeley was Vice Admiral of North Wales, an unpaid office out of which he was expected to make a profit, like every other Vice Admiral; from the Lord Admiral down to the humblest officials, corruption was normal routine.[35]

Although the Beaumaris merchants inevitably took part in the illegal trade, for they had the money to do so, both they and their Chester counterparts realised that the repercussions of piracy had effects upon their own trade. The Chester merchants were particularly concerned at the reprisals that might follow piracies carried out by men alleged to come from Beaumaris, and so adversely affect their increasing trade with the busey port of St Jean de Luz, which handled most of the exports of Northern Spain and South West France. They themselves had already suffered when pirates, who had had the effrontery to use Beaumaris as their base, had robbed vessels coming from Ireland. From the rough draft notes made at the examination of witnesses at Chester, it is possible to get some impression of one or two examples of this Beaumaris-based piracy.[36] News came to Chester in August 1581 that there were two pirate vessels in Holyhead Bay, and this was confirmed when one was seen cruising off Holyhead whilst the other went towards 'Mil baie' (Moelfre?). A Dublin merchant later deposed that he had been aboard the *Margaret* of Hilbre in the 'baie of holyhead' when, about nine o'clock in the morning a 'taule Barque' had fired at and boarded the *Margaret*. He estimated the pirate's crew to be about forty, 'some of them haveinge their faces covered with cipres or scars'; other witnesses confirmed the report and listed their losses in gold, silver, wearing apparel and other miscellaneous goods. These pirates then took the plundered cargo and sold it 'in divers partes alonge this Cooste to suche as came unto (them) with Bootes and so departed'.[37]

Another case, in 1586, concerned a number of men who admitted that they had come from Beaumaris where they had lodged after being discharged from a pinnace belonging to a Mr Leveson at Caernarvon. On arrival in Chester 'in a boote of Beaumaris' they had gone ashore and taken lodging at 'an old man's house nere the Church Stile' at Neston, and 'betweene one and twoe of the clock that night' had boarded a French ship. When one of the Frenchmen resisted, one of the boarding party 'ran the frenchman throwe with his dagger', and two others were wounded before they surrendered. With the Frenchmen 'bound and put under hatches', the pirates then appointed their own master and mate from among their company and decided to set sail for 'Rochell in France'. They panicked, however, when they discovered that the goods aboard the ship they had captured belonged to Chester merchants, and abandoned their plans, each man taking as much as he could of the loot with him ashore near Liverpool, where they scattered, 'every man and his waie to shift for themselves . . . and did not determine to meet again anye more'. The plundered vessel turned out to be the *Catherine* of St Vincente; the slain man, who had lived for three hours after being stabbed and then thrown overboard, was the steward, and had a wife, three sons and a daughter back in Sibora, the remainder of the crew coming from St Jean de Luz. The merchants of Chester had reason to be indignant again at the action of the petty pirates of Beaumaris for seizing the *Catherine* and attacking the men of St Jean de Luz, for it jeopardized their efforts to continue the export of Spanish iron through the Biscayan port so near to the Spanish border despite the outbreak of war with Spain in the previous year.

The pirates who had captured the *Catherine* had come from Beaumaris, but they were not Beaumaris men: in the instances where the home of the pirates who found themselves in prison is stated, one gets the impression that this was a very mixed crew that Mr Leveson had assembled aboard the pinnace which was paid off and laid up at Caernarvon.[38] This cosmopolitan type of crew was probably not untypical of the petty pirates of the coast; of the sixteen, one came from Wakefield, Yorkshire, one from 'Westmeyne' in Hampshire, two from Hull, one from 'furle in the Sussex', one from the Forest of Dean, two from Newcastle, one from Darmouth, and one from Waterford. How accurate and truthful the statements were is open to question, but by cross reference to the various examinations and confessions, it appears that they had all moved freely about Beaumaris for some days, all denied knowledge of which Beaumaris ship had brought them to Chester, and all conveniently forgot to say where and with whom they had stayed at Beaumaris. As a group they were probably fairly representative of the crews of ships in late sixteenth-century Beaumaris: coming from widely different parts of the country, one of them described as a gentleman (although he was not the captain or master of Leveson's pinnace), out to make quick gains by piracy if the opportunity presented itself, not averse to boarding a foreign vessel, 'purposing to give them a blow or two', as some earlier mariners had expressed it,[39] they considered themselves unlucky when the *Catherine* venture turned sour on them.

By the 1590s more than two hundred English vessels were engaged in privateering,[40] the legalised form of piracy against designated enemies which became so attractive to the Elizabethans. In an area like north Wales where the gentry were poor – those of

Anglesey notoriously so – where there was a chronic shortage of ready cash, it is not surprising that some took to the sea in the spirit poetically expressed by one of them, Tomos Prys, Plas Iolyn, 'tybio ond mudo i'r mor, y trowswn ar bob trysor' ('believing I had only to go to sea, to win vast treasure').[41] Dr K. R. Andrews has estimated that it would have probably cost over £200 to equip, man and victual a 30-ton vessel for a six-month voyage; a vessel of 100 tons would cost nearer £700.[42] It is unlikely that the younger sons of the Anglesey gentry could have financed such a venture on their own, but there were wealthy merchants in London like Thomas Myddelton, the Denbighshire merchant who was responsible for financing and sharing the prize cargoes of the 'ventures' of the Hawkins family as well as the smaller but still profitable enterprises of his own relatives, his cousin William and nephew John Myddelton.[43] Thomas Myddelton, a capitalist on a grand scale, was well known to the Welsh community in London as a money lender, and many of the young gentry mortgaged their little land in Wales to him. One of them was Pyrs Griffith, son of Sir Rhys Griffith of Penrhyn, across the Strait from Beaumaris, in Caernarvonshire. Griffith's career is shadowy: there is no firm basis for the tradition that he took part in the Armada campaigns and his name does not appear as captain of any naval ship or privateer, yet his contemporaries, such as Thomas Prys, another who borrowed money from Myddelton, refer to his many years as a seagoing man, and there is the suggestion that he was the 'Griffith, Welsh pirate', taken at Cork in 1600.[44] There is no doubt about one episode: a commission was given to the Mayor of Caernarvon and others to appraise the cargo of olive oil, earthenware and silks aboard the Spanish vessel *Speranza*, brought in by Pyrs Griffith 'in a certain man of war called the *Grace*' to the mouth of the Menai Strait at Abercegin in 1600.[45] There are references in the poetry of Tomos Prys to Griffith being away from the Menai for six years and more, and to Prys's mutual friendship with Sir Richard Bulkeley and Griffith, but all that is known for certain is that over the years Griffith so impoverished his estate that it was sold, eventually passing into the hands of Archbishop John Williams. Tomos Prys and Pyrs Griffith were 'amateurs'; Hugh Griffith, son of the Cefnamwlch family of South Caernarvonshire, was nearer the 'professional', a seaman, gun-runner to Toulon and Leghorn, Captain of the *Pendragon* and the *Phoenix*, accused of torturing the master of the *Peteryn* of Le Conquet, Griffith brought one of his prizes into St Tudwal's Roads whence she was brought round to Sir Richard Bulkeley at Beaumaris.[46] Another brother of Sir Richard's, Edward, was said to have been captured in Algiers where he had put in as captain of the *Bravado*, a vessel in which he had some success in the Mediterranean,[47] but little is known of him nor indeed of Hugh Griffith apart from the fact that the latter died at Algiers in 1602.

Undoubtedly one of the most intriguing figures is Sir Richard Bulkeley himself, the tall, fair-headed courtier and business man, who 'allwayes wore round breeches and thicke bumbast doubletts though very gallant and rich'.[48] On the one hand, there is the violent opponent of the Earl of Leicester, against whose attacks he was said to have 'stood upon his guard keeping allways 24 stout and lustie (men) with swords, bucklers and daggers to defend his p'son from attempts and assaults', who emerged from a skirmish with Leicester at Greenwich still secure in the Queen's favour, and on the other there is the business man, 'temperate in diet, not drinking of healths', ever increasing his holdings of lands, cornering the ready money in Anglesey to his own advantage, developing the quarries at Penmon, stocking his estates with timber, farming and a shareholder in the Virgina Company. Fifty years after his death a Beaumaris schoolmaster, William Williams, wrote the history of the Bulkeley family in which he noted Sir Richard's interest in 'marytyme affayres', and how 'he sent yearly a ship or two to Greneland for cod, ling, and other fish, which he did use to barter in Spayne for Malaga and sherrie wines'. The Port Books are strangely silent about Sir Richard's ships; perhaps it is not so strange! There are but shadowy references, and those in the form of accusations by his sworn enemies, to his brother Charles Bulkeley, of whom it was said that he 'was furnished and sett oute from the towne of Bewmares in Anglisey by the said Sr. Richard to the Sea' on piratical missions,[49] whilst his connections with his other brothers, David and Edmund, both said to be pirates, are enigmatically vague. The only certainty is that Sir Richard Bulkeley died a very rich man in 1621 at Baron Hill which he had built three years earlier, and no doubt his 'marytyme affayres' contributed to that wealth.

There were others who prospered in more orthodox ways. Gabriel Roberts, the Beaumaris merchant, died in 1614, a wealthy landowner who had proved how profitable coastal shipping and judicious local trading could be. His second son, Lewis, was then eighteen years of age: three years later he entered the service of the East India Company. He had inherited his father's business acumen. In 1623 he wrote to Beaumaris from Constantinople, where he was now acting on behalf of both the East India and the Levant Companies, as well as being a factor to the family of William Harvey, the physician. But Roberts was more than a successful business man – he became a Governor of the East India Company – he was interested in the theoretical basis of trade and commerce, and published in 1638 'one of the earliest systematic treatises in English', 'The Merchantes Mappe of Commerce'.[50] Drawing on his own experience in Constantinople, where he had seen the development of the exchange trade in English woollen cloths and Turkish and Persian raw silk, and his twelve years of travel in Europe, Roberts's book is a kind of reference book for traders, with details of the geography, products and currency of many countries. Although his work was aimed at 'all such as shall be imployed in the publique afaires of Princes in foraine parts', Roberts does not omit to include a reference to his native Anglesey which 'for its abundant fertility in all things is called by the Neighbouring shires Mam Cimbri, the mother of Wales'.[51] His description of the produce of the island, 'out of which is yearly sent 3000 head of cattel to supply the wants of other countries adjoining, together with a good quantity of corn, butter and cheeses', did not refer to the years when the harvests failed, some of which he must have known about as a boy in Beaumaris, when there were unusually large importations of corn. Although he admitted a decline in many villages, he was still ready to pay a tribute to the amenities of Beaumaris after all his wanderings in Europe: 'Beaumares, commodious for trade, as commanding a faire, safe and capacious haven and roads, to which, as being the place of my birth, I owe this grateful remembrance.' The 'Merchantes Mappe', prefaced by complimentary verses by his great friend, Izaac Walton, the angler, was a success, and Roberts published other works including 'The Treasure of Trafficke', in 1640, the year of his death.

Although his interests were world-wide, Roberts was not

unaware of the traffic in the Irish Sea, and commended the merchants of Manchester, 'who buy the yarne of the Irishe in great Quantity, and weaving it returne the same again in linen into Ireland to sell'.[52] One wonders whether his mind went to the Irish Sea as well as to the Mediterranean when he urged the state 'to keepe the seas, and streames, free and safe from all pyratts, . . . as the principall disturbers of the universall Trafficke of Kingdoms and Nations, and the greatest overthrowers of the Navigation and commerce of cities and countries'.[53] One of the legacies of Elizabethan privateering and a consequence of the decline of the navy in the early decades of the seventeenth-century was the infestation by pirates of all nations of the seas around Britain, and particularly the Irish Sea. The contrast between the over-romanticised exploits of the swashbuckling but bankrupt, anachronistic Pyrs Griffith and Tomos Prys, and the son of the Beaumaris merchant, breathing the spirit of a different age, is well illustrated in one final quotation from Lewis Roberts's 'Treasure of Trafficke': 'It is not our Conquests, but our Commerce: it is not our swords, but our sayls that first spread the English name in Barbary and thence came into Turkey, America, Moscovia, Arabia, Persia, India, China, and indeed over and about the world: it is the trafficke of their Merchants, and the boundless desires of that nation to eternize the English honour and name, that hath enduced them to saile and seeke into all the corners of the earth.'[54]

The cattle trade to which Lewis Roberts referred was an all-important factor in the economic life of Anglesey in the early seventeenth-century, and although 'the Spanish Fleet of North Wales',[55] as Archbishop John Williams so aptly described the cattle trade, swam across the Strait and then went overland with the drovers, much of the dairy produce went by sea, mainly from Beaumaris. Another example of a younger son of a wealthy Welsh family who went into the world of commerce was Maurice Wynn, son of John Wynn of Gwydir, and there are many letters from him from Hamburg where he was apprenticed to a merchant, urging his father to buy butter and cheese 'for which there is a good market in Germany'.[56] In 1624, after many years of apprenticeship both in London and Hamburg, Maurice Wynn had a good eye for business: he believed he 'could pick up a very good trade by bringing corn into Wales and exporting butter and lead ore to Germany. The best port from which to ship goods is Beaumaris'.[57] He was preaching to the converted as far as Sir John was concerned. He had for some years been shipping lead from Beaumaris to Spain, and occasionally to the Netherlands, and butter and herrings to France. His agent at Beaumaris reported in 1624 that he would have to store Sir John's lead until a vessel put in to the harbour, 'there were lately two that came from Biscay, laden with Spanish wool and iron for Chester; they stayed here only for a wind to take them to Chester water'.[58] But he promised to let Sir John know 'if any good French wines come hither'. Sir John also made use of London vessels trading to Chester; he wrote in 1622 to a Chester merchant asking him to arrange for a London vessel to call at Beaumaris for 20 tons of lead, if the master of the vessel could be trusted, 'for many fail when they have other men's goods in their hands'.[59] Sir John Wynn was not the only exporter, for there are many cargoes of butter and cheese to London, Bristol, Chester and Liverpool recorded in the Port Books. Chester shipped increasing quantities of coal and timber to Beaumaris, salt and tobacco came from Liverpool, only just beginning to develop its trade as a port; in return, Beaumaris sent herrings, leather, coal, more and more slates, which were also being shipped to Ireland. The hardware and crockery, occasional cargoes of walnuts, figs and oranges, wines, from overseas, and cider from Bridgwater, arrived at irregular intervals at Beaumaris, but perhaps the most unusual cargo was that brought by the *Hopewell* of London in 1618, for 'carefully shipped' in four chests came Sir John Wynn of Gwydir's 'tomb'.[60]

What a pirate would have made of the *Hopewell's* cargo is a matter of fascinating conjecture. That there were many pirates off the coast of Anglesey intercepting trade during the early Stuart period there is no doubt: between 1609 and 1616 a total of 466 merchantmen were taken by pirates,[61] mostly in the English Channel, but also in the Irish Sea, and by the 1620s near panic prevailed along the western coasts at the news of the approach of the 'Dunkirkers' or the 'Turks', the names given to pirates of whatever nationality, whether they came from Dunkirk, Sluys, Ostend, Nieuport, St Malo, the Biscayan ports, or Algiers and the Barbary coast. Sir Henry Mainwaring, himself a former pirate, writing in 1618, regarded Ireland as 'the Nursery and storehouse of pirates', an admirable base from which to draw supplies and attack shipping, where pirates could depend on other comforts, 'they have also good store of English, Scottish and Irish wenches which resort unto them, and these are strong attractors to draw the common sort thither'.[62] Whilst the main activities of the larger pirate vessels were in the open seas of the south-west approaches, Mainwaring stated that the smaller vessels used the Welsh coast: 'Within St George's Channel at Milford and the coast of Wales they may trim, but because the coast and channel are dangerous' it was only used by the 'small nimble ship.'[63] As the years passed, the decline of the Navy of James I, and the increased opportunities for piracy, led to the construction of many 'nimble ships', some of which plied off Anglesey.

Although there were allegations about supplies of butter and cheese being sold to pirate vessels, particularly off Pwllheli, the attitude ashore was changing. People ashore were afraid. Not only were there thousands of sailors prisoners at Salee, but the inhabitants of the sea coast were not safe in their beds. The news of the capture of another offshore island, Lundy, and the taking away of the inhabitants as captives in 1625, spread rapidly; the Deputy Lieutenants of Anglesey were quick to point out that 'their island was subject to the spoil of shipping bound for Ireland', and the Bishop of Bangor, Lewis Bayly, wrote to the king stating that the arms and powder at Beaumaris and Caernarvon were totally unserviceable, and that a hundred men 'would overrun the Isle of Anglesea', adding hopefully 'A king's ship would be great protection'. Bayly was not merely afraid of pirates. In a letter to Charles I shortly after the latter's accession, the Bishop recalled that a well-known Anglesey man, Hugh Owen, 'a most dangerous fellow, a Romishe recusant', who had left the island some years previously, 'and no man knew why', had returned in August 1625 'very gallant and full of gold' and all the papists in the area had flocked to him. At the time of Owen's brief visit, 'a ship of about 120 tons had sounded all the North East Coast of Anglesey, and sailed between a little island and the shore where no ship was known to go before', and Bayly concluded that the Catholic sympathisers in Anglesey 'are heare so audacious that they never durst be so bold if they knew not of some invasion or conspiracie intended'.[64] Soon after Owen's departure, two other known Catholics left the island, William Wood of Talyllyn, Malltraeth, and David Lloyd of Bodedern. To Bishop Bayly and his contemporaries it was all very sinister. A sharp look-out was kept for suspicious vessels which might herald the return of these native Catholics with their Spanish, French, and Irish allies.

In the event, it was the pirates who caused trouble, not an enemy invasion. In 1633, John Griffith, of Cefnamwlch, the Lleyn lawyer who was now Vice Admiral of North Wales, wrote to the Admiralty emphasising the dangers to 'commerce betwixt Wales and Ireland by pirates which rove in the St George's Channel' and threatened to impoverish and 'strike terror into the inhabitants not without fear that they will surprise them in their own houses'.[65] His predecessor, Sir Richard Trevor, had reckoned that in the counties of Caernarvonshire, Anglesey, and Flintshire there were about forty seamen in all, and few that could handle a boat as far as Land's End,[66] so that there was little opposition locally to the pirates. The demand from merchants and the dwellers on the coast was that they should be protected by the king's ships.

The task of the Navy in the 1630s was not easy. In 1618 it had been revealed that half of the ships on the Navy's list existed on paper only, and there were grave charges of maladministration and corruption against Sir Robert Mansell, the Treasurer of the Navy, and Sir John Trevor, the Surveyor, both Welshmen and protegés of Lord Howard of Effingham, the Elizabethan Lord Admiral. Together with Phineas Pett, the shipbuilder, they were alleged to have been paid three and four times over for timber which was supposed to have been used for building vessels for the State but which had in fact been used for their own purposes, including fitting out a vessel, the *Resistance*, in which they each had a third share, which was furnished, and 'sailed with the king's sails and rigged with the king's tackling'.[67] Despite efforts to remedy the situation after 1618, it is not surprising that the Navy was short of ships in the 1620s and 1630s, and nowhere was this felt more acutely than in the Irish Sea.

In command of the king's ships on the Irish station since 1615, Sir Thomas Button, a Glamorganshire man, had seen many years of service at sea. He was an Elizabethan seaman, first distinguishing himself when in command of the pinnace *Moon* by his single-handed efforts at Kinsale at the time of the Spanish invasion in 1601,[68] and then sailing in a ship owned by Mansell and Trevor who had bought the *Wylloby* and sent 'Tom Button to the Indys in her to exercise his picoring'.[69] In the Caribbean he appears to have joined forces with the most successful and experienced of the 'professional' privateers, Captain Christopher Newport, and although the Venetian ambassador's report in 1603 was no doubt wildly exaggerated, there is little doubt that it was a profitable venture: 'Captains Newport and Button and other men of war have taken two or three frigates from the West Indies with three millions of gold, and are in Milford Haven, or at some port in Ireland: however to please the Queen she is made to believe it is in a harbour in Wales.'[70] The search for a north-west passage was a matter of great commercial, as well as navigational, importance to the men of the early seventeenth-century, and when Button was selected to lead the expedition in 1612 after Henry Hudson's failure in the previous year, he took with him special instructions from Edward Wright,[71] tutor to Prince Henry, a mathematician whose work was of great significance to navigators, and also the hopes of the 'Company of the Merchants of London Discoverers of the North-west Passage', shrewd men like Thomas Myddelton. Button did not find a way to China and India, but he did survive a harsh winter and surveyed the coasts of Hudson's Bay, and named the Nelson River after the master of the *Resolution* who died there, and New Wales and Button's Bay where he wintered.[72] On his return Button was appointed to serve on the Irish station, distinguished himself again by his skill in combined operations with the army ashore in the difficult waters of the Sound of Jura in 1615,[73] and was one of the few to emerge with credit from the unsatisfactory expedition led by Mansell against the pirates of Algiers in 1621.[74]

It was a weary Sir Thomas Button who sailed into the anchorage off Holyhead in mid-June 1631 and penned a letter to report his actions to the naval authorities in London: 'being nowe in Holyhead road having chast a Biscayan piratt yesterdye and last night but could do no good and this tyde am goinge for Dublin to wafte over the fleet that comes thence for Chester faire and the rest of my tyme will spend as well as I can.'[75] He had served at sea for nearly forty years and the *Ninth Whelp* was a much smaller vessel than those he had previously commanded. The ten *Whelps* were almost identical, the naval administrators having at last realised that large, cumbersome, 'prestige' vessels were useless against the Dunkirkers, for as a contemporary Welshman, who had seen many pirate ships, put it succinctly, they were often chased but seldom taken, 'for a great ship following one of them may be said to be a Mastiff Dog running after a hare'.[76] The *Ninth Whelp*, built in 1627, was 62 foot in length, 25 foot beam, approximately 9 foot from the upper gunwale to the upper edge of the keel, about 190 tons, mounting up to twenty guns,[77] and probably like the other Whelps 'in foul weather she, being very floaty, rolls and tumbles so much that they are not able to make use of the ordnance now belonging to her'.[78] Her complement of sixty men must have led to the appalling overcrowding which was true of all these ships; large crews were regarded as necessary in the case of action with an enemy as well as to work the heavy gear of the seventeenth-century ship. Angered at being 'unhorsed of the ship in which I have so long served', caught up in endless wranglings about arrears of pay, and accusations against him that he forced the other ships under his command 'to victuall day by day hand to mouth', 'leaving the baker and butcher unpaid',[79] old Sir Thomas had taken to sending his nephew, Captain William Thomas, to sea in his place. But on this occasion at Holyhead Captain Thomas was not aboard: he had been accused of torturing the commander of a captured Dunkirker and the embezzlement of prize goods, much to Sir Thomas Button's chagrin, as he believed his sister's son to be 'an honest man and knows he had some honest men with hym that would not be Actors of so dishonest things'.[80]

However disgruntled Sir Thomas Button might have felt, the people of Holyhead and the Anglesey coast were glad to see the *Ninth Whelp*, for they had been much troubled at the news of the Dunkrikers' activities and were even more horrified when the news came that, about two o'clock one morning, ten days after Button's letter from Holyhead, over two hundred pirates had landed at Baltimore, ransacked houses, and taken more than a hundred men, women, and children to be sold as slaves.[81] Inevitably, Button, as senior officer, was held responsible, whilst Captain Hooke, who had been at Kinsale in the *Fifth Whelp*, the only other vessel in Button's anti-piratical force, blamed Button that he had not been able to put to sea because of lack of victuals. Charles I was alarmed at the incident and wrote sharply to the Lords Justices and Council in Ireland: 'You shall inform us where responsibility lies. You blame the two captains appointed to guard the coast, and they blame each other, but we are not satisfied with these recriminations.'[82] The incident was made much of and represented as an insult to the English crown, and alarmist exaggerations were spread abroad in the coastal areas regarding future raids, a convenient justification for Charles's Ship Money Tax which was ultimately to have far-reaching political and consitutional repercussions.[83] A fortnight before the Baltimore raid, Button had written from Dublin: 'I am now off to the Isle of Man to scour the northern parts, whilst the *Fifth Whelp* will scour the Western.'[84] The events which had overtaken him meant that he had to sail to the south, leaving the northern waters exposed: 'in going I shall leave behind me a pirate, who is between the Isle of Man and Ayr, who may do much harm between Dublin and Chester during my absence.'[85] That month Button was proved right, for the Lords of the Admiralty had to record in July that 'now the postbark to Holyhead has been robbed'.[86]

Button was made the scapegoat, but easily cleared himself of all the charges brought against him as he had twenty years and more earlier when he was accused of collusion with known pirates. There is a curiously pathetic quality in the testy old seaman's letters, now housed in the Public Record Office, for he had an impossibly wide area to defend, and when ordered to reduce his crews said bluntly to the armchair sailors in London: 'I will say to the last that they that first proposed those abatements never purposed to be themselves employed, and little knew what they did.'[87] The September before the Baltimore raid, Button described in one letter how he had been sailing all that summer of 1630 between Dublin, Chester, and the Isle of Man, and he must have come to anchor in Holyhead, Moelfre and Beaumaris often. One wonders whether any Anglesey people looking out to sea saw just one of these incidents he describes: 'would have caught a good Spanish ship, but she got from me with rowing when the wind 'dollred'. I could not work oars, sails, and small shot at once, being undermanned.'[88] When the new expeditions to the North-west Passage by Luke Foxe and Thomas James were being planned, Sir Thomas Button was consulted at the king's command: he gave detailed instructions and observations, particularly about the setting of the tides and the 'darke and longe continewed mistes', and the 'ilands of ice'. But he was confident that ultimately someone would find the passage to the North-west, 'which I doe as confidently beleave to be a passage as I do there is one either between Callis and Dover or betweene holy Head and Ireland'.[89] After a lifetime at sea, over half of which had been spent in these very waters, if any man knew the seas between Holyhead and Ireland, it was Thomas Button.

Ironically enough, the next naval captain to sail the *Ninth Whelp* into Holyhead and Beaumaris was another explorer and leader of an expedition to search for the North-west passage, Captain Thomas James, also a South Walian, who came from Wern y Cwm, near Abergavenny.[90] Perhaps sailing to the North-west passage was considered appropriate training for anyone who ventured with a king's ship to the north Wales station, no doubt equally remote to the administrators in London. Whatever the reason for the curious coincidence, some eight months after his arrival in Bristol following an eighteen month voyage in search of the North-west passage, Captain Thomas James sailed into Holyhead in command of the *Ninth Whelp* in June, 1633.[91] Whereas the details of Thomas Button's early career are uncertain, Captain Thomas James was admitted to the Inner Temple in 1612, and although it is not known whether he practised law, he was certainly at sea in a Bristol privateer in the 1620s. James was a scholarly man who was in close touch with the scientists of Gresham College, centre for much of the intellectual life of early seventeenth-century England.[92] The route to the north-west had considerable commercial implications, and the Bristol merchants who sponsored him hoped that Captain James would break the monopoly of the London-based East India Company. Of greater significance to posterity, as Christopher Hill has pointed out,[93] was the way in which the search for the north-west brought together scientists, practical navigators, and seamen, merchants and financiers. To a certain extent this was true of Button, for he was the friend of Edward Wright and Henry Briggs, the mathematicians, of Wolstenholme and Myddelton, the financial patrons, but Thomas James moved even more easily, intellectually at least, in this company, linking scientific, nautical and commercial enterprise, a man of the scientific renaissance, part of the intellectual movement based on Gresham College, London.[94]

The watchers ashore as the *Ninth Whelp* sailed in to Holyhead in

June 1633 would hardly have been aware of any of this, seeing the familiar vessel coming to an anchor, and wondering whether old Sir Thomas Button was aboard. But to James it was a rather special occasion for it was probably his first visit to Anglesey and his mind may have gone back to his own wintering in the far-off north-west where he had named landmarks after his native Wales and, as his journal records, had celebrated 'the first of this month being St David's Day, we kept holiday and solemnised it in the manner of the ancient Britons'.[95] A week after James's arrival in Holyhead, Captain Richard Plumleigh, in another old command of Sir Thomas Button's, the *Antelope*, a 34-38 gun vessel, sailed into Beaumaris Roads.[96] Plumleigh, an experienced naval officer, who had fought many actions against the Dunkirkers, including one in which they 'had fought with them board and board from ten at night till seven in the morning',[97] had come to Beaumaris to await the Lord Deputy of Ireland, Wentworth, later Earl of Strafford, to take him over to Dublin. Strafford was soon to establish that stern and efficient rule which proved too successful and 'thorough' as far as the Parliamentary leaders were concerned, a policy which eventually led to his own downfall and execution, a preliminary to the Civil War. Plumleigh had already spent one summer in the area, and in September 1632 had written from 'Stidwales Bay' describing a vain chase of Nutt and other pirates whom he later described as 'an hot potch of all nations in Europe'. Although Plumleigh, writing from Beaumaris in June 1633, reported that 'the Biscayners have made great spoil on this coast',[98] so efficiently did he and Thomas James hound the pirates that this marked the turning of the tide as far as piracy on the Welsh coast was concerned. Gradually the pressure on Nutt, Norman and their fellow pirates exerted by the harassing tactics of Plumleigh and James compelled them to seek other areas for their activities, and Thomas James's letters give a detailed account of a highly successful summer cruise. His regular reports from Beaumaris, Chester, Dublin, Carrickfergus, the Mull of Galloway, the Isle of Man and Holyhead indicate the pattern of his sailing, with occasional cruising to Milford and Bristol convoying ships – he escorted fifty of them for Bristol Fair in August. The letters are full of evocative detail: writing from Holyhead he writes that he had heard there was a pirate between there and Dublin which had seized Dutch and other ships, so he came up, 'contrary to my orders, hoping to catch him. I tided it up the Channel, stopping during the ebb. I chased the pirate for a day, but lost him in the dark': requisitioning additional guns for the *Ninth Whelp* 'to scour her decks if she be boarded', reporting a broken main-mast, 'it being a deceitful tree', and setting sail in a stiff north-easterly wind in March 1634 to be on his station early as Strafford had requested.[99] In June 1634 James, writing from Chester, explained how he had sailed on the western coasts, leaving 'no creek . . . unseen', and had now arranged with the Deputy Vice Admirals ashore to have 'Flags placed in different positions on the hills' which were to give him intelligence of shipping in the area; instead of putting into harbours in which he might be windbound, he had arranged for boats to be sent with news and provisions. 'This is better than having to go into harbour . . . as the direction of the wind often makes it difficult to get out.'[100] Aware of the strategic importance of the Isle of Man, so ideally suited as a base for pirates to pillage the trade between Chester, Liverpool and Dublin, Captain James made frequent visits to the island where he suspected the Governor, Captain Christian, was in league with the pirates, and had no hesitation in reporting to Strafford: 'unless this island is governed by an honest man it will be a real danger to trade. It affords shelter from all winds, and pirates may easily lurk there. It is not twenty leagues from Dublin and commands a view of England, Scotland, Wales and Ireland.'[101]

Apart from routine calls at Holyhead and Beaumaris, and occasional urgent visits to transport messengers to and from Holyhead, neither Plumleigh nor James had much to say about Anglesey, but the Vice Admiral, John Griffith, had earlier reported that Plumleigh's 'great industry, care, vigilance, and diligence' gave 'great contentment to the people of these parts. He omits no possible part of his duty, loses no time, is constant to his ship, governs well and his mind is always upon his business'.[102] For his part, Plumleigh occasionally became exasperated, as Button before him had done, at the sheer impossibility of his task, having with him 'two ships only, above 400 leagues of water to guard from pirates', he was still expected 'to give an account of every fisherboat that is pillaged within that circuit'.[103] He had reason to feel the situation was much better than when he had first come into these waters, when he had reported that 'Egypt was never more infested with caterpillars than Land's End with Biscayners'.[104] Thanks to an able commander like Captain James, and the energetic support of Strafford, the *Whelps* were now better victualled, armed and manned, and early in 1635 an attempt was made to improve their sailing qualities. It was recognised that they had been so undermasted 'as it hindered their sayling'; their main masts were, therefore, removed and 'sett in place of ye foremasts . . . and, bigger and better mayne mastes prepared and fitted'.[105] Both Plumleigh and James were highly thought of by Strafford, not a man who was easily pleased or content to tolerate mediocrity.[106] The passage to Ireland assumed increasing significance in the minds of politicians as the Civil War approached. As rumours of Strafford's bringing over an army of Protestants and Catholics to support the king and to subdue Parliament spread, so the uneasiness increased in Anglesey, always a sensitive barometer of national opinion. There were grave suspicions of Strafford's demands for more ships to be put at his disposal to wipe out piracy, yet in Anglesey there would have been many, particularly the merchants of Beaumaris, who would have agreed with him when he wrote 'The Channel between England and Ireland must be kept as His Majesty's Chief port'.[107] One who would have had much to contribute in a better management of naval affairs, Captain Thomas James, had already died in 1635.

During the hundred years since the first Sir Richard Bulkeley had expressed his concern regarding the exposed nature of Anglesey's position, the two most skilled seamen who had used its harbours as bases in its defence were Sir Thomas Button and Captain Thomas James. Button had his roots in the Elizabethan period, a seaman who knew the Caribbean and the north-west as well as the Irish Sea, a fine seaman and navigator: James had none of Button's flamboyance, but he also was a most skilful navigator, a commander whose care for his men emerges refreshingly in an age when letters relating to naval ships make sad reading. In some ways, James was nearer to Lewis Roberts than he was to Button. Both James and Roberts had a reputation for scholarship, both were connected with the intellectual movement which had much backing from the world of commerce, both were Welshmen who had migrated into that world, both had literary interests. Whether the strong tradition that Thomas James's narrative formed the basis for Coleridge's 'Ancient Mariner' is true or not,[108] it is certain that both Captain James and Lewis Roberts made a contribution to the history of Anglesey in the age of the Early Stuarts.

[1] Douglas Knoop and G. Peredur Jones 'The Repair of Beaumaris Town Wall, 1536-38'. *TAAS*, 1935, 59; quoting from PRO Exchequer K. R. 489/12. 'Gr. ap John Rowlyn' and Richard Goch also received payments for boatloads of stone.

[2] B. E. Howells (ed.), *Calendar of letters relating to north Wales* (Cardiff 1967), 37. For Bulkeley family, Glyn Roberts, *Aspects of Welsh History* (Cardiff, 1969), 11-22; D. C. Jones, 'The Bulkeleys of Beaumaris', *TAAS*, 1961, 1-20.

[3] *ibid.*, 38; *Letters and Papers Henry VIII*, XIV, I, 381.

[4] E. A. Lewis, *Welsh Port Books, 1550-1603* (London, 1927), 305.

[5] *CWP* 9.

[6] Frances Lynch, *Prehistoric Anglesey* (Llangefni, 1970). Melville Richards (ed.). *An Atlas of Anglesey* (Llangefni, 1972).

[7] Lewis, *Welsh Port Books*, 308.

[8] *ibid.*, 240.

[9] R. Davies, *The Rise of the English Shipping Industry* (London, 1962), 2.

[10] F. J. North, 'The Map of Wales', *AC* 1935, 2-70.

[11] M. Oppenheim (ed.), 'The Naval Tracts of Sir William Monson' (*NRS*, 1913), v. 16, 17.

[12] E. Gwynne Jones, 'Anglesey in Invasion 1539-1603', *TAAS*, 1947, 26.

[13] F. J. North, '*Humphrey Llwyd's Maps of England and Wales*' (National Museum of Wales, 1937), 11-63.

[14] A. J. Loomie, 'An Armada Pilot's Survey of the English Coastline, October 1597', *MM* 49. 4 (1963), 288-300. Michael Bouquet in an interesting note in *MM* 51, 3, 210 (August 1965), points out that the name given to Chester River, 'Aguas Chester', by the Armada pilot, was also the name given to the Dee by coasting seamen, and his description of 'the shores called of Wales and England' for the English and Welsh Grounds, confirm Father Loomie's suggestion that the Spanish pilot was on very familiar ground in certain areas of his report. For general background to the post-1588 Armadas, Admiral Sir H. Richmond, *Statesmen and Sea Power* (Oxford, 1946), 20-21.

[15] E. Gwynne Jones, *Cymru a'r Hen Ffydd* (Caerdydd, 1951), 31.

[16] R. Geraint Gruffydd, *Argraffwyr Cyntaf Cymru, Gwasgau Dirgel y Catholigion Adeg Elisabeth* (Caerdydd, 1972), 8-11; 'Gwasg Ddirgel yr Ogof yn Rhiwledyn', *Journal of Welsh Bibliographical Society* (1958) ix, 1-24; G. Bowen, *Efrydiau Catholig*, ii, II; *DWB* 818-9. At high water, the floors of both caves at which Professor Gruffydd and I landed in a rowing boat were

Vessels off the Anglesey shore of the Menai Strait and the approaches to Caernarfon: William Daniell's engraving 1814
(Gwynedd Archives Service)

The crew of the Afon Alaw *at San Francisco, c. 1900*
(Gwynedd Archives Service)

The schooner Wyvern *passing under Menai Suspension Bridge*
Engraving by Hay, 1848

An early engraving of Holyhead harbour

The Irish Mail Steamers at Holyhead

The New Harbour of Refuge at Holyhead, 1840
(Anglesey Archives Service)

Survivors of H.M.S. Tara at Alexandria after their ordeal in the desert, 1916
(Anglesey Archives Service)

Dr Jones reading the Admiral's address at the presentation to Seaman William
Williams, V.C., D.S.M. and Bar, M.M., at Llangefni, 31 Oct, 1918.
(Anglesey Archives Service)

Borth-wen brickworks with its own quay

William Thomas' shipyard – Iard Newydd – at Amlwch, 1872

Porth Amlwch, c. 1900

The steam flat Temple (*alongside*) *believed to be at Mostyn on the Dee,
known to Welsh seamen as 'Afon Gaer' (Chester River)*

Workers at Iard Newydd, Amlwch

Captain William Thomas, Amlwch,
1822-93, in his younger days
as a master mariner.
Photographed by C. Bvisson, Cannes.

His son, William Thomas, Amlwch,
the designer and shipbuilder

Porth Amlwch harbour entrance

Eilianus *crew from Amlwch*

Black Rock *across the harbour entrance at Amlwch*

*The Gaelic, captain Ishmael Williams on her launch day.
The ship was wrecked on Egremont Beach, August 1909.*

Maggie Williams *on her launch day*

The Euphemia

William Cox-Paynter's 3-masted schooner Camborne *built at Iard Ochr Draw, Amlwch in 1884. Painting by Reuben Chappell.*

The 3-masted schooner Eilian, *last of the younger William Thomas's* Amlwch-built schooners

The Cymric, *built at Amlwch by William Thomas, 1893, and commanded by Captain Robert Jones, Amlwch, at Jersey harbour*

Moelfre fishing boats

The Earl Cairns *crew from Moelfre, 1914*

Moelfre lifeboat station

*Captain William John Hughes
from Moelfre*

Cox'n Dick Evans' tribute, Moelfre

Beaumaris lifeboat station

A steamer passing by Beaumaris pier

Herring fishermen at Moelfre, early twentieth century

Slate Schooners in Porth Penrhyn, c. 1890

under water; the cave which housed the printing press was on higher ground. According to tradition it was from seaward that the smoke was seen which betrayed the position of the cave, and it may be that it was by sea that the conspirators escaped.

[17] *CWP* 186. Wynn wrote to Bulkeley's deputy: 'Therefore good cousin, being sole Lieutenant in the absence of Sir Richard, see the same safely kept and conveyed to land to some safe place, lest other shipping, coming thither, carry it away by force.'

[18] *ibid.*, 205.

[19] Lewis, *Welsh Port Books*, xxxvii.

[20] *ibid.*, 238-40.

[21] *ibid.*, xxvii.

[22] *ibid.*, 244.

[23] *ibid.*, 247

[24] *ibid.*, 262.

[25] T. S. Willan, *The English Coasting Trade* (Manchester, 1938), 46-54.

[26] Lewis, *Welsh Port Books*, 293-301.

[27] *DWB* 871; Lewis, *Welsh Port Books*, 264-288.

[28] *infra.*

[29] D. M. Woodward, *The Trade of Elizabethan Chester* (Hull, 1970, 49-122. *passim.*

[30] *ibid.*, 117. £2,540 was loaned by the merchants and citizens of Chester and Liverpool; of this £340 came from David Lloyd, and £200 from Richard Bavand, his father-in-law.

[31] B. M. Harl. MSS 1991, 176-9. The will was dated November, 1599, and his wife Alice was named as his executrix.

[32] Woodward, *The Trade of Elizabethan Chester*, 45.

[33] Carys Roberts, 'Piracy in Caernarvonshire and Anglesey', *TCHS* 21 (1960), 50.

[34] Geraint Dyfnallt Owen, *Elizabethan Wales* (Cardiff, 1962), 136.

[35] K. R. Andrews, *Elizabethan Privateering* (Cambridge, 1964), 22-31.

[36] These examples are based on transcripts made by the late T. Charles Jones at the Chester Record Office of notes in rough draft of the examination of witnesses. I am deeply indebted to Mr Jones for many kindnesses over the years; unfortunately most of his papers have disappeared; these transcripts are from a notebook of his in my possession.

[37] *ibid.* Examinations 'touchinge a piracy lately comitted betwene dublin and hollyhed', 14 August 1581. One of the witnesses described the pirate vessel as of 40 tons, with a crew of 40 men. Woodward, *The Trade of Elizabethan Chester*, 46.

[38] *ibid.* Examinations taken at Chester 31 July 1586. For the connection with St Jean de Luz, Woodward, *The Trade of Elizabethan Chester*, 38-39.

[39] G. V. Scammell, 'Manning the English Merchant Service in the Sixteenth-Century', *MM* 56, 2 (1970), 135.

[40] K. R. Andrews, *Elizabeth Privateering*, 32-50.

[41]   This line is from Prys's poem 'Cywydd i ddangos yr heldring a fu i wr pan oedd ar y mor' (The troublous life of a man at sea). This poem, written in a curious mixture of Welsh and English, bears some resemblance to Captain John Smith's *'An Accidence for All Young Sea-Men'*, 1626, 18-20, particularly where both describe actions at sea.

[42]   K. R. Andrews, *Elizabethan Privateering*, 49.

[43]   *ibid.*, 113-118; A. H. Dodd, 'Mr Myddelton the Merchant of Tower Street', in *Elizabethan Government and Society* (*Essays presented to Sir John Neele*, ed. Bindoff, Hurstfield and Williams (London, 1961), 249-82.

[44]   *DWB* 298; *DNB* 678; *CSPD* 28 Feb. 1603.

[45]   UCNW Penrhyn MSS 88. The *Speranza* is described in the document as 'of Aymounte in Spain', 'lately seized by Perseus Griffith . . . and taken to Cegin Creek'.

[46]   Owen, *Elizabethan Wales*, 139-43.

[47]   *ibid.*, 143-144.

[48]   The information on Sir Richard Bulkeley derives from the account by William Williams, 'History of the Bulkeley Family' in NLW MSS 9080 E. An edited version by E. Gwynne Jones appeared in *TAAS*, 1948.

[49]   *ibid.*, It was alleged that Sir Richard 'had Canare Wynes and other things and receaved to his house and to other places to his use the same and soche like stuffe of the said Charles being Piratts goods, and taken by the shipps which Sr Richard dyd vyttele at the towne of Bewmares'. It should be added that this was evidence given by sworn enemies of the Bulkeley family, the Wood family of Rhosmor.

[50]   *DWB* 871; *DNB*.

[51]   Lewis Roberts, *The Merchantes Mappe of Commerce, Necessarie for all such as shal be imployed in the publique affaires of Princes in Foraine portes . . . 1638.* 219. If NLW Wigfair MSS 2851 and 2852 refer to this Lewis Roberts, then in 1624 he was described in a safe conduct offered to him by the Turkish authorities as 'about the years of Twentie eight, haveing a ruddie Countenance, with light yellowish long haire, a small blacke spotte on the left side of his nose and of midle stature'. M. Griffiths, 'A seventeenth-Century? Welsh-man Abroad', *NLW Journal*, XVIII, 4, 1972, 415-24.

[52]   Lewis Roberts, *The Treasure of Traffike or a Discourse of Forraigne Trade*, London, 1641, 66.

[53]   *ibid.*, 46.

[54]   *ibid.*, 92.

[55]   *CWP* 1748. W. Ogwen Williams, 'The Anglesey Gentry as Business Men in Tudor and Stuart Times'. *TAAS* 1948, 100-114, has examples of imports and exports as recorded in PRO E/190, 1335, 1336.

[56]   *CWP* 1205, also 1078, 1132. In 1623 Maurice Wynne described the scarcity of food at Hamburg and in Germany and suggested that 'were a man to bring beef and tallow from Ireland he would make good store'. In another letter he urged his father to 'purchase at each Chester Fair 100 barrels of butter, weighing 100lbs. a piece, to be sent to London in the ship that brings

goods to that fair', Maurice himself taking the responsibility to see that it was shipped from London to Lisbon 'where butter is very scarce'.

[57] *CWP* 1205.

[58] *ibid.*, 1255.

[59] *ibid.*, 1021.

[60] *ibid.*, 621.

[61] H. Richmond, *Statesmen and Sea Power* (Oxford, 1946), 26.

[62] G. E. Mainwaring and W. G. Perrin (ed.), *The Life and Works of Sir Henry Mainwaring* (NRS, LVI), II, 40.

[63] *ibid.*, 39.

[64] PRO SP Chas., I, xi, 37, quoted E. G. Jones, 'Hugh Owen of Gwenynog', *TAAS* 1938, 42; *CSPD* 1625/26, 172, 236; E. G. Jones, *Cymru a'r Hen Ffydd*, 55-7.

[65] *CSPD* 1633/4, 84. Griffith admitted that there were only two pirates annoying the coasts at the time of his letter, June 1633, 'a Biscayner and an Englishman, one of that breed which had trespassed upon them these two or three years'. According to Griffith one of the pirates had a vessel of 300 tons burthen, 'furnished with some 26 pieces of ordnance', and had taken 'a Scottish bark in the harbour' at Pwllheli, where the inhabitants and Roberts, 'a merchant of Bristol', had bartered with the pirates.

[66] A. H. Dodd, 'Wales in the Parliament of Charles I', *TCS* 1945, 34.

[67] W. G. Perrin (ed). *The Autobiography of Phineas Pett* (NRS c 1) lviii, lxi, 25. The evidence of the witnesses in the 1608 Commission of Enquiry reveals the extent of Mansell and Trevor's corruption. The depositions are recorded in full in A. P. McGowan, *The Jacobean Commissions of Enquiry 1608 and 1618* (NRS, 116, 1971), 7-255.

[68] *CSPD* Eliz., 1601-3, 299.

[69] W. J. Smith (ed.), *Calendar of Salusbury Correspondence* (Cardiff), 140-1.

[70] *CSPD* Eliz., 1601-3, 293.

[71] D. W. Waters, *The Art of Navigation in Elizabethan and Stuart Times* (London, 1958), 276.

[72] For Button's voyage and its significance, Waters *op. cit.*, and *DWB, DNB*, and the present writer's note on his career in the *Dictionary of Canadian Biography*. Phineas Pett, the shipbuilder, recorded in 1612 in his *Autobiography* that he accompanied 'Captain Thomas Button to make choice of a ship for the North-West Passage, in which journey he was to be employed by the appointment of the Prince'. Pett, *Autobiography*, 95.

[73] *CSP Ireland*, 1615-25, 7.

[74] J. Corbett, *England in the Mediterranean*, 1. 110; Monson, 111. 98-118. The journal kept by Button's nephew, John, is in PRO SP 14/122/106.

[75] PRO SP 16/194/15. Button to Nicholas, 'Holyhead this 16 of June 1631'. A contemporary Anglesey diary confirms that the weather at this time was fair and 'raynie'. Hugh Owen, 'The Diary of Bulkeley of Dronwy, 1630-36', *TAAS*, 1937. In light airs, Button would have had little hope of catching a Biscayner.

[76] James Howell, *Epistolae Hoelianae*, 110.

[77] R. C. Anderson, *List of English Men of War, 1509-1649* (SNR Occasional Publication, 7, London, 1959), 19.

[78] *CSPD 1627-1628*, 560.

[79] *CSP Ireland*, 1625-32, 623, 628. PRO SP 16/228/119.

[80] PRO SP 16/215/80: For the charges against Sir Thomas Button, SP 16/228/119: SP 16/215/43. Thomas was eventually released, served in merchant ships until the outbreak of the Civil War, then like many of his fellow seamen from the Thames, served Warwick in the Parliament's fleet. As captain of the *Eighth Whelp*, and later the *Warwick* and the *Nonsuch*, William Thomas had a distinguished career and became one of the most successful of the Captains in the Parliamentary Fleet; his imprisonment and unhappy experience at the hands of the Stuarts strengthened his determination and zeal for the victory of Parliament. A. Eames, 'Captain William Thomas, a naval captain of the English Civil War', in *MM* 47, 2 (1961), 145-149.

[81] *CSP Ireland*, 1625-32, 617, 621. The list of those carried away captive indicates that whole families were taken: 'Abraham Roberts, wife and children,' 5, 'Evans and boy, his cook, his cook's wife, and maid,' 5, 'Old Osborne and maid,' 2, 'Bessie Flood and her son,' 2, 'William Gunter's wife, maid and 7 sons,' 9.

[82] *CSP Ireland*, 1625-32, 627. Henry Barnby, 'The Algerian Attack on Baltimore, 1631', *MM* 56, 1, 27, discusses the circumstances of the raid, but is mistaken when he states that Button was at home in Glamorgan at the time of the raid; the letter from Holyhead would seem to invalidate Barnby's point. In the charges later made against Button the reference is to the *Fifth Whelp*: 'That Sir Thomas Button having all the charge of victualling the king's pinnace, the 5th Whelpe imployed for guard on the Irish coast, tooke so little care . . . that she was kept in harborough at Kinsale from ye 23 of May 1631 to ye 27 of June.'

[83] In October 1635, Robert Bulkeley of Dronwy, Anglesey, noted in his diary: 'I pd yestday xs mise towards ye king's ship.' Hugh Owen, 'The Diary of Bulkeley of Dronwy, 1630-36'. *TAAS*, 1937, 30.

[84] *CSP Ireland*, 1625-32, 612, June 6, 1631.

[85] *ibid.*, 620. July 5, 1631.

[86] *ibid.*, 622-3. July 14, 1631.

[87] *CSPD*, 1631-3, 330. The charges against Button alleged that he was guilty of corrupt victualling, irregular and careless disposal of prize goods, the employment in his crews of 'divers gents and idlers', and complicity with Captain William Thomas, accused of torturing the commander of a captured Dunkirker. PRO SP 16/228/119. In an age when naval pay was hopelessly in arrears, Button claimed that the Navy owed him thousands of pounds; he was however probably no stranger to independent, if unorthodox, ways of financial survival. In 1609 it was alleged that he had acted with Jennings and Ford, pirates, in selling sugar captured from

Spanish ships illegally. A. P. McGowan (ed.), *The Jacobean Commissions of Enquiry, 1608 and 1618* (NRS, 1971), 249-51.

[88] *CSP Ireland*, 1625-32, 577.

[89] The full text of this letter is printed in G. T. Clark, *Glamorgan Worthies* (Dowlais, 1883), 82-85.

[90] C. M. MacInnes, *Captain Thomas James and the North-west Passage* (Bristol, 1967), 4.

[91] *CSP Ireland*, 1633/47, 13.

[92] 'When James went in search of the North-west passage, his instruments were those of Edward Gunter, the notable mathematician at Gresham College, he discussed his voyage with mathematicians and astronomers, and when he sailed he took with him a chest full of the best "mathematicall bookes", books on travel including the works of Hakluyt and Purchas, and a wide range of navigational aids.' D. W. Waters, *The Art of Navigation in Elizabethan and Stuart Times*, 499.

[93] Christopher Hill, *Intellectual Origins of the English Revolution* (Oxford, 1965), 46-47.

[94] Commander D. W. Waters, the outstanding authority on the subject, has stated that James's observations on longitude were 'not being bettered a hundred years later'. James had arranged with Henry Gellibrand, professor of Astronomy at Gresham College, to observe an eclipse of the moon which Gellibrand at Gresham also observed, 'with the result that they determined the longitude of James's position to within 15', making it to have been 79° 30' W of Gresham College instead of the actual 79° 45' W.' Waters, *Art of Navigation*, 500.

[95] *The Dangerous Voyage of Captain Thomas James . . . as related in his Journal* (London, 1633). Miller Christy (ed.), *The Voyages of Captain Luke Foxe of Hull and Captain Thomas James of Bristol in search of a North-west Passage in 1631-32* (Hakluyt Soc., 1894). C. M. MacInnes, *Captain Thomas James and the North-west Passage* (Bristol, 1967).

[96] Button had been very attached to the *Antelope* in which he had weathered many storms, one of which is recorded in the shipbuilder, Phineas Pett's *Autobiography*, as his son John was aboard, 'a wonderful great storm, through which many ships perished'. Pett, 133. The *Antelope* was 92 feet long, with a 31' 9" beam, and mounted between thirty-four and thirty-eight guns, and was a ship of about 500 tons.

[97] This action had taken place some years previously when Plumleigh, leaving his own ship at Plymouth, had taken passage in a small pinnace which had met a much larger Dunkirker. In his letter to Buckingham, Plumleigh reported: 'We hailed one another after the custom of the sea. They said they were of Flushing, but presently offered to lay us on board.' The attack was repulsed, and when the Captain of the pinnace was killed, Plumleigh took command, and successfully withstood a second assault, 'We finding ourselves fairly overmatched brayled up our mainsail and went before the wind and fought with them board and board for ten at night till

seven in the morning', when Plumleigh reached Studland Bay. PRO SP 16/86/77.

[98] *CSP Ireland*, 1633/47, 99 PRO SP 63/254/65.

[99] *CSP Ireland*, 1633/47, 13, 54. *CSPD*, 1633/34, 407, 510. PRO SP 63/254/36.

[100] *CSP Ireland*, 1633/47, 54.

[101] *CSP Ireland*, 1633/47, 23, 24. In October 1633, James wrote a letter from Milford Haven which typifies the work of the *Ninth Whelp*. 'I have been to the Isle of Man, but the Lord Deputy has already sent you an account of my doings there. I then went along to the Moulde (*sic*) of Galloway in Scotland looking for pirates. However I found none, and when I landed at Carrickfergus I was assured by a great assembly of the nobility of Northern Ireland and Scotland there collected that these parts were free of pirates and that the traders were trading in peace. After voyages to Dublin, Holyhead, and Dublin again I was ordered to waft three Hollanders to Scilly, whose cargoes were worth 10,000 *l*. Had a very tempestuous jounry, and finally brought the ships in here. I hope I shall soon get my four small pieces of brass ordnance.'

[102] *CSPD*, 1632, 416. In 1633, Griffith had to answer many difficult questions about cases of bartering with Norman, the pirate at Pwllheli. *CSPD*, 1633/4, 133, 175.

[103] *CSPD*, 1634/5, 225.

[104] *CSPD*, 1629-31, 296. In the same letter Plumleigh had reported that '20 sail of sloops' had attempted to land on Lundy but were repulsed by the inhabitants.

[105] PRO SP 16/264/77A, 7 f. 1635.

[106] Of Plumleigh, the Lord Deputy wrote in September, 1634: 'Sir Richard Plumleigh is now going back to winter quarters. He has done excellent service.' *CSP Ireland*, 1633-47, 76. As early as October 1633, Strafford had recommended Captain James to the Admiralty. 'I must give the Captain the testimony of (being) a very diligent attendant upon his charge, a very civil man in his conversation and able man in his profession.' C. M. MacInnes, *Captain Thomas James and the North-west Passage*, 26.

[107] *CSP Ireland*, 1633-47, 25. Despite the improved situation there were still stories that caused a shiver of apprehension among Anglesey men interested in shipping; when Plumleigh seized a Spanish vessel in 1634 witnesses claimed that the Spanish Captain had previously captured a Plymouth ship 'and tortured the mate and his boy by burning matches between their fingers to say what money was aboard the ship'. *CSP Ireland*, 1633-47, 68, 9. The activities of Sir Beverley Newcomen and Captain Thomas Kettleby, who succeeded Plumleigh and James in the late 1630s in the guard of the Irish seas, may be similarly traced in their letters in *CSPD* and *CSP Ireland*.

[108] C. M. MacInnes, *Captain Thomas James and the North-west Passage*, 27.

War at Sea Off Anglesey
1642–60

Sea power decided the Civil War. Admiral Sir Herbert Richmond defined sea power as 'that form of national strength which enables its possessor to send his armies across those stretches of sea and ocean which lie between his country or the country of his allies and those territories to which he needs access in time of war: and to prevent his enemy from doing the same'.[1] The Civil War was a struggle between a divided country, but throughout there was the fear on the part of Parliament that the king would receive assistance by forces brought by sea, either from the continent of Europe, or, more particularly, from Ireland. There the nucleus of a well-drilled English army formed by Strafford, to say nothing of the Catholic forces, and any foreign troops that might be landed there, could be brought to upset the balance of the war in England. In the terms of Richmond's definition, the stretch of sea which was important was the Irish Sea. To Richmond, and Mahan before him, sea power meant control of the sea, and for this they postulated three fundamentals, ships, bases, and shipping, a term which included merchant shipping, a seafaring population, and a shipbuilding industry. In the case of the English Civil War, whichever side, king or Parliament, possessed most of these fundamentals controlled the seas around Britain.

The Civil War in Wales was, in effect, an invasion of Wales by opposing forces, both of whom saw the strategic importance of the country once the war moved into its more vital phases. To the king, Wales was a source of supplies, a base from which his forces from Ireland, and his infantry from Wales were to be drawn for the battles on English soil. To Parliament, Wales was a thorn in the flesh, a country whose coasts would have to be patrolled to prevent the landing of recruits for Charles: a country which would have to be captured, not for its intrinsic importance, but for the two bases which might be used by Royalist ships, Milford Haven in the south, recognized by contemporaries as one of the best harbours in Europe, and the only other base available where ships might 'lie or ride very securely', the Menai Strait.[2] Sea power exercised a decisive influence upon the course of events in remote and poverty-stricken Wales. It

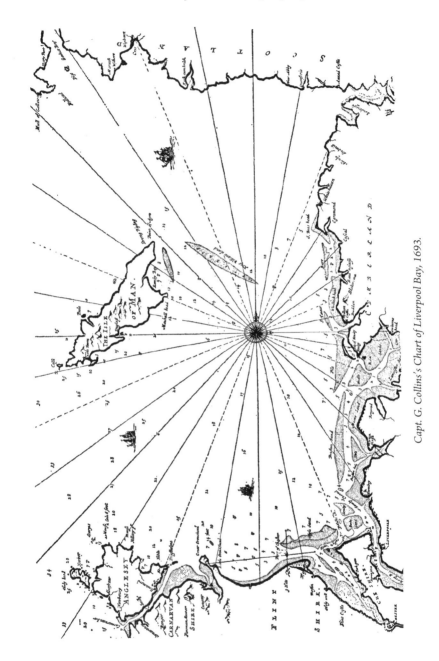

Capt. G. Collins's Chart of Liverpool Bay, 1693.

was sea power that enabled Parliament to secure the main base, Milford Haven, which they used both as a bridgehead from which they eventually conquered south Wales, and as a base from which their ships were able to operate and blockade the Irish coast, thus preventing any large-scale invasion from Ireland. It was sea power that in the early years of the war enabled the Royalists to continue the campaign in north Wales and the border counties with supplies drawn from their bases at Beaumaris and Chester, and enabled the latter to withstand seige for so long. But when once Parliament was able to divert more of its ships to the Irish Sea and Liverpool Bay, and when one by one the ports were seized, it was sea power that finally crushed the hopes of the king's party in the north. Parliament's forces invaded Wales overland from England, and by sea through the main base at Milford. The only hope that the Royalists had was to invade through the bases they possessed in the north, through Chester in particular, which, although its sea approaches were difficult, was situated near to the fighting in the Midlands, and Beaumaris, with better sea approaches, but the disadvantage of being more remote from the main fighting and with difficult mountainous hinterland intervening. But the Royalists did not possess the shipping to carry out any large-scale seaborne invasions, and the stranglehold which the ships of Parliament eventually exerted upon them prevented their making the most of a situation which had initially promised well and proved a vital factor in the Civil War.

This, then, was the background to the war at sea off Anglesey, a country dominated by the Bulkeleys, although since the death of Sir Richard, the great Elizabethan, somewhat torn by their feud with the Cheadles. Domestic issues were overshadowed by the only matter which roused the Anglesey gentry, coastal security, and the fear of invasion, recently renewed by the outbreak of the Irish Rebellion in 1641. The King, in response to the county's loyal address, replied in August 1642 from York with a promise to 'protect them from the invasion of any other assumed Arbitrary Power';[3] the Civil War was at hand, but the war in Ireland was of more immediate concern to Anglesey – on the route to the fighting, the importance of communications from Holyhead to Dublin assumed new significance. Inevitably the loss of the *Phoenix*, 'cast away at Ormes Head in Caernarvonshire'[4] early in 1642, and the rumours upon which the Vice Admiral of North Wales based his report that in the same area, 'the recusants of Creuddyn . . . Uncle Pue of Penrhyn, are preparing their arms and mean ill toward the town of Conway'[5] made the inhabitants of Anglesey aware of their lack of naval protection.

The *Phoenix*, lost on passage between Chester and Dublin, was one of the two hired merchantmen that had been pressed into service at Dublin to support the English forces in face of the Irish rebellion. Dublin and the ports of Carrickfergus, Cork, and Youghal, remained in English hands, but they depended upon the support of the Navy. When the main body of the Fleet in the Downs had taken the decisive step of siding with Parliament at the outbreak of the Civil War, one of the hopes left to the King was that the Irish Squadron, strengthened to meet the threat of the Irish rebellion, would remain loyal to him. Commanding the *Bonaventure*, largest vessel in this squadron, was Sir Henry Stradling, an experienced naval officer and son of the influential St Donat's family in Glamorgan. In late June the King sent secret orders to Stradling which he was 'to perform . . . in as private a way as you may, with as much expedicion and as little Noyse'.[6] Taking with him the *Swallow*, commanded by Captain Kettleby who had for some years been engaged in the same kind of duties as Captain Thomas James in the 1630s, Stradling was to sail at 'the first opportunity of winde to come about by Scotland for Newcastle' as there was 'att present a very pressing occasion for your repaire into the Northern parts of this Kingdom for a service much importing the safety of our person'. At Newcastle, still in Royalist hands, Stradling revictualled his ships before sailing to Holland to join the convoy being assembled there by the Queen, Henrietta Maria, to bring over munitions and forces to support her husband's cause. The Earl of Warwick, Commander of Parliament's fleet, had been quick to recognize the potential danger of Stradling's ships and had sent Captain Batten with six ships to prevent them from leaving Newcastle; in October it was reported that Batten had captured the *Swallow* and the *Bonaventure* 'when they were taking in provisions with an intent to go over to Holland to the Queen, but Captain Stradling with his long boat made escape and is gone to Ireland'.[7] The English authorities in Dublin knew nothing of the secret orders, only that the *Bonaventure* and *Swallow* had vanished from Kinsale, leaving the Irish coast open to the attacks of Irish rebels and Dunkirk and Spanish privateers. Wexford had already been taken by rebels and pirates who had 'set up the Spanish colours on their walls . . . where they profess openly they will make another Dunkirk, and infest us in all parts of this Kingdom, and so intercept the passage between Chester and Dublin, as to hinder all intercourse between that place and this'.[8] Lord Bulkeley at Baron Hill had received false news in a letter in August that the *Swallow* and other ships 'have forsaken the Earl of Warwick and have come over to the king, with 12,000 foot and 5,000 horse'. The rumours surrounding all these events naturally heigthtened the nervousness of the inhabitants of Anglesey who had a few months previously reminded the Council of State 'how contigous these counties of Anglesey and Caernarvon are to Ireland, being within 8 hours sail, and that these are weak, unprovided of powder, shot and ammunition'.

Following the departure of the *Bonaventure* and the *Swallow*, the most powerful vessel of the Irish Guard, certainly in northern waters, was the king's pinnace, the *Swan*. On July 8, 1641, a warrant to the Lord High Admiral had stated that 'The king is pleased that his new pinnace, the *Swan*, now in Ireland, shall be employed for the guard of the Irish Seas'.[9] A vessel of about 200 tons, mounting 20 guns, she was manned by a crew that had been increased from forty to sixty in January 1642: the *Confidence*, the other merchant-man hired at the same time as the ill-fated *Phoenix*, was a vessel of 100 tons, mounting 'ten pieces of ordonance', and she had her crew increased to forty. The commander of the *Swan* was Captain John Bartlett, whilst his brother, Captain Thomas Bartlett, commanded the *Confidence*.[10] The absence of the Bartletts' names from the list of captains of the 1625-42 period, and John Bartlett's subsequent history (his request at the Restoration was to be given command of the post barques plying between Holyhead and Dublin) suggest that their experience was largely confined to the coastal waters of the Irish Sea: they may have been connected with the 'John Bartlett, merchant, of Dublin' who delivered herrings to the Royalist Stores in 1643.

In February 1642, John Bartlett put in a demand for stores 'for such shipping as are employed and may be employed in the St George's Channel which must be speedily sent to Dublin'.[11] He ordered a supply of masts, ready made, for the *Swan*; the mainmast was to be '63 feet long and sixteen inches through', the foremast '52 foot long, 14 inches through' and a 'bowsprit of the same cantling'.[12] In addition, Bartlett wanted 'a boatbuilder sent over with the material for building of boats, to say cliff boards for here is none to be had. We having lost our boats are fain to take away other men's boats for His Majesty's service which causeth many complaints and is the undoing to many poor men'. This is an indication of Bartlett's wisdom and discretion, his awareness of the sensitive political situation, and also of the shortage of shipwrights and timber in the ports which he visited regularly. His other requirements are indicative of the type of stores ships like the *Swan* and *Confidence* used: 'cables of 5, 6, 7, 8, 9, and 10 inches of each sort three, and hawsers of 4 inches and 4 inches and ½ six, rigging answerable to vessels that such cables will serve, with anchors answerable to the cables, with flags, ensigns, pennants, prop lanthorns, hamborrow lines, tarred lines, spun yarn, and howsing, marling, canvas for sails, bolt rope and twine for sails, blocks of all sizes,' together with ammunition to serve the different types of guns.

It is important to stress the dimensions and fire-power of the *Swan*, as there has been a tendency to romanticise her role as that of a small vessel gun-running against great odds. In fact she was the most powerful ship in the area, and was not much threatened by Parliament's ships in the first two or three years of the war. The Bartletts plied regularly between Ireland and Chester and Beaumaris. During 1642 and 1643 their task was two-fold; on the one hand they maintained communication between the king's forces on the mainland and Ormonde in Ireland, whilst on the other they assisted the land forces in the campaign against the rebels in Ireland. At the outset the latter was most important, and the Marquis of Ormonde, the English commander, reported that the Bartletts had served with distinction and 'have with much faithfulness and industry served here in these troubled times, and with hazard of their lives gave us good assistance towards the relieving of Drogheda several times when it was straightly beseiged by the rebels'.[13] The armistice between the king and the rebels in the autumn of 1643 left the Bartletts free to concentrate on their other role, the maintenance of communications between Ireland and the king's forces on the mainland, and also to assist in the transport of any forces which the king wished to bring over from Ireland to relieve Chester and to supplement his armies in the inland campaigns in England.

Anglesey received the news of the armistice with mixed feelings. In July 1643 they had heard with much concern that Sir Thomas Myddelton had been commissioned by Parliament to lead forces to invade north Wales to prevent the king from drawing men and supplies from the area, and particularly to seize the ports through which supplies were to pass to the king from Ireland. The prospect of armies of English Royalists, Anglo-Irish Catholics, and even Irish landing in Anglesey to support the king was not much more attractive than a Roundhead invasion. Troops of whichever side would make heavy demands on the food stocks of the island, whose trade had already been much disrupted by the war. It was about this time that the Commissioners of Array for Anglesey wrote to the king stressing their position: 'wee are an Island scituat betweene Ireland and Lancashire, lyeinge open subiect to invasion on all parts, beinge dayly robbed on our coasts by the rebells of Ireland and parliamentary shipps, which are many in number att this time in Liverpoole, and threaten dayly to invade and possess themselves of this island.' As always they stressed the importance of the island's potential as a haven for shipping: 'there is no other haven butt this of Bewmares nearer than Milford where theire Shipping can finde any salfe (*sic*) harbours to wynter.' They alleged that information had come to them that Myddelton and Brereton, the Parliament's commanders in the drive to the north-west, had designs to take Beaumaris; suspects had already been arrested and 'confessed that they were imployed and offered great sumes of money by them for the surprizinge and betrayinge of the castle and town of Bewmares and the haven'. If this plan should succeed, the men of Anglesey pointed out, 'if they can be masters of this haven, they may with their shippinge stoppe all passage and intercourse between all parts of England northward of us, and Ireland'.[14]

The reference to the Liverpool shipping underlines another factor which now concerned the inhabitants of Anglesey. In April 1643 Parliament had secured Liverpool and there were rumours of Parliament ships based there under a Captain Danske intercepting 'all vessels that offered to pass between Chester and Dublin'. Earlier in the year, in February 1643, the Commissioners of the Admiralty who were responsible for the administration of the Parliament Fleet, had contracted with Captain Ralph Danske, master of the *Charity*, for sea service of eight months at an estimated cost of £1087.4s;[15] the *Charity* was a 120-ton ship carrying six guns, and manned by thirty-six men. In June, in an exciting action off Morlaix, Captain William Thomas, Button's nephew, in the *Eighth Whelp*, and Captain Danske in the *Charity* captured the Royalist *Mayflower*, and later joined Warwick's fleet attempting the relief of Exeter. In July Bristol was taken by Royalist forces under Prince Rupert, and a number of vessels captured there were put under the command of the elderly Sir John Pennington. Although the latter's attempt to secure Milford Haven was foiled by Parliament ships commanded by Captain Richard Swanley, Royalist shipping and the Irish-Dunkirk privateers posed a serious threat to Parliament in the Irish seas. In particular, the Parliament forces, who had driven a wedge through Royalist country and captured Liverpool in April 1643, needed support.

Hard put to it to find ships to meet all the calls of the summer of 1643, Warwick sent the *Charity* north as part of a small squadron of ships based on Liverpool to intercept any forces from Ireland. Among the Baron Hill manuscripts is an undated letter[16] from Dr William Griffith of Carreglwyd, who lived on the north-west of the island, to Thomas Bulkeley, the High Sheriff at Beaumaris, in which he described how he and his neighbours were 'shrewdly affrighted in these naked parts by three men of warre, whereof two anchor'd neare land all day yesterday and last night at a place called Yr Wylfa three miles from mee, the third at Holyhead, where it still remaineth, but that being farther from mee and come in since the other two, I cannot give you any certain account of it, but that it is a tale vessel bearing diverse pieces of ordinance, and I am told declines to discover what she is'. Dr Griffith could give no further details of the vessel at Holyhead, but he made it his business to know what the two others were up to, particularly as they had anchored 'in a place unusual for ships of that burthen'. His curiosity was matched by his neighbours, and all that night they kept a watch: there was no need to muster men, they were all already there, 'truly I believe all the musketts of these parts attended there last night'. Some brave and curious Anglesey men went out in a boat and were invited aboard, and reported to Dr Griffith on their return that both ships were 'men of warre full of men and ammunition: in the greater were seen 6 peices of Ordinances ready mounted, and 8 unmounted'. There then follows a vivid picture of the motley crew jostling around their mess deck tables, suddenly confronted with the raw Anglesey ambassadors half frightened, half curious, who found to their delight one of the crew who could speak their own language, but who, unfortunately, declined to furnish either his compatriots or the historian with a key to the dating of this document, namely, the identity of the Captain. Aboard the larger vessel the Anglesey men:

> Saw some 40 or 50 men in one room at two tables at dinner; what further company there were in the ship they could not see. There was one Welshman of their company with whom our men conferr'd and who told them they were sent into these parts by the Earl of Warwick to secure these coasts from some Dunkirkers that lye in these Irish Seas. I fear what you will soon apprehend, their errant concearns us more nearely: . . . I may add that they were inquisitive to learn of our men how matters stood between king and Parliament, which I conceave was but to fish their disposition towards them. The Welshman that was of their company would not tell of which County of Wales he was, neither would he tell their Capt's name. They were seen yesterday before they came to their aforesaid place of Anchorage to sound our shores as they went for 6 or 7 miles.

Dr Griffith estimated that the ships were 'guess to be' 120 tons and 100 tons, and 'the lesser seemed to be as full of men as the other'. Bulkeley or someone else had added a marginal note to the letter which confirms that the ships then sailed towards Chester: 'Word was brought hither last night by some employed to watch on coasts, yt 3 ships such as are here described passt towards Chester Water about 3 o'clock in the evening: but whither they may not come back is uncertain.' The ships were probably Danske's *Charity* and other vessels on their way to Liverpool, and the date of the document is probably late July or August 1643: the tonnage tallies with the *Charity*, the 40 or 50 men may have been correct or simply over-estimation, which was an understandable error, for a number of men in the confined space between decks might well have appeared more

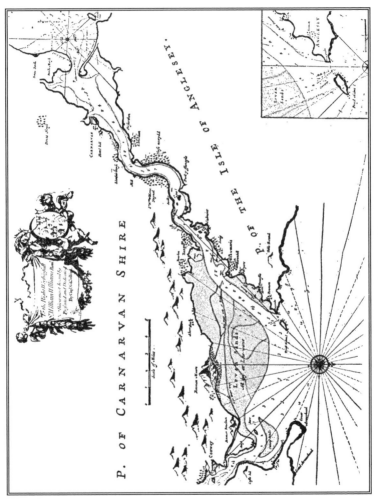

Capt. G. Collins's Chart of the Menai Strait, 1693.

than were actually there: the one Welshman in the crew would be in keeping with what is again fairly certain, that the crews of naval ships were mainly recruited in the ports of the south of England, and the careful soundings were what Mainwaring and contemporary mariners would have expected of the master of a hired merchantman in the naval service.[17] Whoever they were, the Parliament ships were sufficiently impressive to cause considerable unease in Anglesey and the letter reflects accurately what the dwellers of the coast must have felt at the approach of unfamiliar ships, whether they were of Parliament or the king, Irish or Dunkirk.

The war was coming nearer. Towards the end of August the king, 'hearing of the infinite mischief which both Wales and Chester have suffered from the piratical ships of Liverpoole' which were said to have seized 'all vessels moored or outward bound' for Chester, and now threatened Beaumaris, ordered that his Caernarvonshire supporters should send guns for the Bartlett ships to Chester.[18] The Welsh Royalists were naturally reluctant to part with guns that they might need themselves, but Charles sent word that they would be better protected if they helped to arm a Royalist vessel 'than if they had all those pieces on shore' for his intention was that ships should be based in the Principality: 'her stay will be mostly at Beaumares,' and it was predicted that other Royalist ships from Bristol were soon due to arrive there. Despite the loss of the Navy to Parliament, the king now had more ships to challenge his opponents at sea; the Confederate Catholic forces were granting commissions to men like 'Captain Francis Oliver, native of Flanders', in a 120-ton ship, the *St Michall the Archangel*, and although they were not as yet his open allies, the Irish-Dunkirk privateer fleet at Wexford presented a much more serious threat to their mutual enemies, the ships of Parliament. Whilst Parliament held Milford Haven and Liverpool, the former excellent, the latter a poor enough base for sailing ships, the Royalists had a string of potential island bases which stretched from the Isle of Man and Anglesey to Lundy, the Scilly Isles, Jersey and Guernsey. Following his armistice with the Confederate Catholics on 15 September 1643, Ormonde made ready to implement the king's order sent to him in the previous April 'to bring over the Irish Army to Chester'.[19] With the approaches to Chester threatened by Parliament ships from Liverpool, Anglesey havens assumed greater significance.

The Edwardian castles of north Wales were still regarded as strong-points, and at Beaumaris, Caernarvon and Conway there was a new urgency regarding defensive preparations by Royalist sympathisers. At Conway, Archbishop John Williams, who had fled from York in 1642, was fortifying the castle out of his own considerable fortune for the king. Williams was a remarkable man. On his return to Conway, some sixty years since his birth there in 1582, Williams looked back on a career which had taken him from Ruthin School by way of St John's College, Cambridge, to high office under James I, as Bacon's successor as Lord Keeper of the Great Seal, and as Dean of Westminster and Bishop of Lincoln. His fortunes had waned under Charles I, and he had been imprisoned in the Tower, largely due to the enmity of Buckingham and Laud; when he was released in 1640 his power was still considerable. A moderate in politics and ecclesiastical matters, Williams was closely associated with the followers of his friend Bacon, and, as a patron of scholars, had recently been responsible for bringing to England the great Moravian educator, Comenius, whose ideas and those of his friends, Hartlib and Dury, formed, in Professor Trevor Roper's telling phrase, 'the intellectual cement of the English country party'.[20] Their mutual interest in, and support of, Comenius brought Williams into association with those who were eventually to lead the opposition to the king, John Pym and the Earl of Warwick, and with the 'modern' supporters of scientific and mathematical studies; his superior intelligence and generally moderate attitude goes a long way towards explaining Williams's eventual disenchantment with many of the king's soldiers. A civilian and an intellectual, John Williams had great drive and energy and a certain impatience with the military mind; his letters reflect his own clarity of thought and his enthusiasm, his ability to see to the heart of a problem, but they also betray sometimes his lack of understanding of the technical aspects involved. He clearly appreciated the importance of sea power, as his letters bear witness, but he was probably over-sanguine about the ability of early seventeenth-century ships and seamen to carry out large-scale landings in shoal waters and on open beaches such as 'Abergele, Ruthland, or Rhyl or Vorud', which he suggested. It is equally true, however, that he recognized the possibilities of the Menai Strait: he urged Ormonde to send troops 'And the vessels that transport them maye for 8 or 10 days lie or ride very securely in that Sleeve between Anglesey and Caernarvonshyre'.[21]

Ormonde and Williams both recognized the vital importance of control of the sea passages between Dublin and Chester and Beaumaris, but by 1643 Ormonde admitted 'the main difficulty I find in the work is shipping to transport and safely to convey' troops across the Irish Sea.[22] The *Swan* and the *Confidence* were able to transport ammunition and maintain communications, but there was an urgent need for ships to bring the troops across from Ireland. Even the transport of guns presented problems, and Ormonde's frustration was evident when he wrote in October to Archbishop Williams informing him that Captain Thomas Bartlett would have brought 'two whole culverin . . . but that the mast of his ship would not bear them'. As it was, 'Captain Bartlett hath aboard him 14 barrels of powder, and some small proportion of match for the use of the ordnance which he carries with him: which are four demi culverin mounted with all appurtenances, and 400 shot for them'. The ammunition was for Bulkeley at Beaumaris; 'The pieces are consigned to Mr Bulkeley at Beaumaris and so is the poweder, except one barrel, which is for Captain Bartlett's own provisions.'[23] Short of money and ammunition, and with several thousand infantry and at least '300 horse' waiting for transport vessels, Ormonde looked desperately for more ships. Apologising to Williams that he had not consulted him beforehand because of the difficulties in getting letters across, due to the uncertainty of winter passages and possible interception by Parliament ships, Ormonde in October promised any Irish or foreign ships at Wexford 'if they go to Beaumaris . . . with powder, arms, or any other necessaries for war, that they shall receive ready money for such wares, and free liberty to depart when they have sold them'.

Nearly a month later, Williams was still scanning the horizon for the long-awaited ships. He indicated his fears in his next letter to Ormonde: 'Alass! we growe dayly in more uncertaintye of the landynge of the forces from your partes than we were, somme giving out that they are not for these partes but for Bristol.' If the troops did not arrive, then Williams was convinced that north Wales was lost to the king, and Welshmen would be pressed into the service of the Roundheads; 'beginninge allready to levye forces of our nation, whereof they never hadd any before.' As an immediate measure, Williams asked that at least '100 able souldiers well commanded for officers' should be sent over with the assistance of one of the Bartlett ships to garrison Conway; 'I do not care of what country they are, soe as they come with armes and competencye of ammunition, which shall be payed for or returned.'[24] Any large-scale landing of troops, Williams had to concede, might cause severe problems, and Ormonde had been honest enough to admit that the condition of the troops was such that they might readily desert: 'the greatest danger I fear when they are landed on the other side is that if provision of shoes, stockings, clothes, and money be not instantly made to them it will be easy to seduce them with likely promises.' Gloomily Ormonde had confided to Williams that unless adequate preparations were made to receive the troops, 'this part of the army will not only be useless to his majesty, but perhaps be drawn in a great part to fight against him'. Even the enthusiastic Williams, who was not himself bothered what nationality or religion the troops sent were, had to recognize the sensivity of his neighbours to excessive demands for money to support hordes of rugged, ill-equipped troops who could easily be branded 'Irish' or 'Papist' and cause much trouble in Anglesey and Caernarvonshire.

At this low ebb in the Royalist fortunes, the tide turned. The Earl of Castlehaven, despairing of ever getting enough small craft to risk sailing across with troops, at last succeeded in hiring three large vessels, each of 400 tons, and having 'mounted sixteen or fourteen pieces of ordnance' aboard them, sent two of them to Dublin early in November 1643.[25] They arrived on the very day that Captain Baldqin Wake arrived there from Bristol with 'two ships and five barks to transport them away'. The capture of Bristol had meant that at last the king had been able to respond to Ormonde's repeated requests for shipping. Pennington, the King's Admiral who had seen service with so many of his present enemies in the Ship Money Fleets, sent the experienced Captain Baldwin Wake, one of the five captains who had remained loyal to the king when the Fleet had sided with Parliament at the beginning of the war. He had been compelled to leave his ship, the *Expedition*, in 1642 as his crew chose to enter the service of Parliament; there is no indication of his new command in 1643, but it was as captain of the *Proud Black Eagle* that he took Prince Charles and his retinue to safety towards the end of the Civil War.[26] Beaumaris was soon to know Baldwin Wake well.

In mid-November, 1643, Wake set sail for Beaumaris, with about two thousand effective troops aboard his convoy of ships. The weather was bad, and they were driven before a gale to the entrance of the Dee, anchoring off Mostyn; it was another two days before they could land the troops because the weather was so stormy. It must have been an unpleasant experience, the ragged sea-sick troops, crowded aboard improvised transports which rolled and pitched so much that they felt ready to die, Wake trying to keep his scratch force together as they ran before the gale off Anglesey, unable to make the Menai Strait, and apprehensively approaching shoals and sands of the Dee estuary. When the wretched troops got ashore, away from the stench between decks, they were hardly in a state to attack the enemy, but the Roundheads for their part seem to have believed some exaggerated reports: Sir Thomas Stanley reported that 'eleven ships laden with Irish soldiers are discovered near our coast', that eight more were to follow, bringing ten thousand troops in all. Brereton, in command of the Parliament troops, was much frustrated by these landings 'on the Welsh shore about sixteen or twenty miles below Chester'; he believed that if these forces from Ireland had 'stayed but ten days longer, it is conceived the city of Chester could not have subsisted.'[27] As it was, Brereton and Myddelton had to withdraw their forces from Wales, abandoning their encircling movement, as they feared further landings, and also Roundhead troops moving down from the north of England. It was now Brereton's turn to ask for ships, underlining the importance of sea power in the minds of the men who fought these campaigns, 'unless speedy aid be sent by sea to prevent landing of more forces the preservation of these parts may be much endangered'.[28]

The weather having moderated a little, Wake appears to have sailed with another convoy from Dublin and then put in to the Menai Strait in early December. But the strong winds that had carried him over from Ireland persisted, and may be one of the reasons for his inaction for the next weeks; John Williams admitted that he was not surprised that Ormonde was not getting all his letters at this time, 'consideringe howe obstinately the wynde hath remayned fixt, in one point, these six or seven weeks to the admiration of the very seamen'.[29] If the weather was bad, so too was the situation in the eyes of the people of Beaumaris. Wake's demands on them increased as the weeks went by: eight tons of salted beef (to be paid for later), almost as soon as he arrived, '£100 in cash and £10 worth of fresh victuals for immediate use to be followed by a weekly supply of thirty five hundredweight of bread, forty hundredweight of beef, seven and a half hundredweight of cheese, five hundredweight of butter and £12.13 in cash'. A claim was later made against Lord Bulkeley regarding the 70 barrels of beef he provided for Wake; Michael Lewis was said to have bought for him on behalf of Wake and Bartlett 'twentie oxen or steares which were some of the best the country afforded at 30s a beast'.[30] These excessive demands brought protests from the gentry of Beaumaris, and even the Bulkeleys and the Cheadles were moved to join together in the letter of protest, which stressed the ways in which the war had already disorganized the island's economy, particularly the cattle trade. Wake was not easily satisfied, and almost immediately demanded more money to prevent his crew from mutiny, and more and more victuals.

At this distance in time one can see the inevitability of the tension that arose between Captain Wake and the Anglesey gentry. Swinging to an anchor in appalling weather, he needed money and food for his disillusioned crew, who had no hope of prize money whilst unable to put to sea, and had probably had more than their fill in transporting and convoying just one batch of troops over from Ireland. On the other hand, in an island so chronically short of money, with its trade disrupted in a war the rights and wrongs of which had seemed remote from their own immediate interests, the Anglesey gentry could hardly be blamed for wishing Captain Wake and his ships miles away. Ruefully they contemplated which were the worst evils: the Royalist ships sent to protect them, the Roundhead ships, their alleged enemies, or the Dunkirkers. The end result was the same; inordinate demands on the island's economy and little hope of compensation.

On their passage to Chester in November, Wake's ships had taken an ammunition ship which had been intended for the Roundhead armies both in Cheshire and Lancashire, and this underlined the potential of his force: Orlando Bridgeman, the Royalist lawyer from Chester, writing from Beaumaris at the end of November,[31] urged that Wake should use his ships to take Liverpool from the Roundheads, thus depriving them of the only port they had 'to bring in a new store of arms or ammunition' in the north-west. Bridgeman recognized that together with the Bartletts' ships, 'Captain Bartletts ship and the king's pinnace, the *Swan* now at Chester, excellently fitted of all things', and his own vessels, Wake had a force which was infinitely superior in fire-power to the small Parliament squadron, still probably commanded by Danske, which was based at Liverpool. Indeed, Bridgeman felt that the Bartletts' ships themselves, 'joined to 2 or 3 others, are able to master all the ships in Liverpool water'; Bridgeman for his part would make certain that the *Swan*, 'one of the best as they say in these seas', was made ready for the operation. The all-important task in the minds of the great seamen has always been to seek out the enemy fleet and to destroy it; Bridgeman was stating this view, although obviously Ormonde thought that the first task was to get the troops across without delay. In the event, whether because of the unfavourable weather or because of the uncertain morale of his men, Wake frittered away the next two months at Beaumaris, and ultimately when Liverpool was taken again by the Royalists under Prince Rupert in June, 1644, the Royalists' failure to blockade that port was underlined, as the Parliament's ships sailed out, 'richly laden and well furnished with ammunition . . . with the Governor and the wealthiest inhabitants'.[32] It was a mistake that Parliament did not make when they eventually recaptured Liverpool.

By March 1644 Wake was back in Bristol; he explained his failure to return to Dublin in terms which echo his problems whilst he lay in the Menai Strait: it was reported that 'he having endeavoured to pass over again to Dublin with his ships, he found them in so ill case, and his men so disobedient that he was fair to tack about, and return to Bristol'.[33] It had not been a good cruise for Captain Wake, and Anglesey had no reason to remember his visit with pleasure. But Beaumaris, Holyhead and the Royalist communications between Chester and Dublin could still depend on the Bartletts. The refrain in the letters from Williams and Ormonde in 1644 is constant: no ships or money to transport troops over. Towards the end of April, Ormonde wrote from Dublin what must be taken as a typical example of many such letters: 'I have been so often forced to press barques for the transport of men without paying the owners, that now, ater a long easterly wind, the harbour is empty; soe I cannot send Colonel Trafford with 300 men for Anglesey for want of shipping.'[34] But it was not merely shortage of Royalist shipping. Parliament's own ships were becoming more plentiful: Ormonde heard with dismay in the spring of 1644 that 'ships imployed by Parliament . . . as it were block up these coasts, some nowe rideing (as I heare) upon the point of Aire, neare Mosson betwixt Beaumaris and Chester'.[35] And it was not only off the Dee that they were active; Anglesey was startled when the news came that Roundhead ships had 'with much scandal and insolency' taken seven barques full of provisions bound for Dublin and Chester, 'out of the very port of Hollyhead'.[36]

The growing recognition of the strategic importance of Beaumaris as a base was reflected in the appointment of Sir John Mennes to be 'governor of north Wales' based at Beaumaris. At the outbreak of the Civil War, Mennes had been appointed to the command of the *St George*, 792 tons, and Rear Admiral of the Summer Guard, but had refused to obey Warwick's orders in July, and, with Wake and the other three captains who remained loyal to the king, was deprived of his command. Sir John Mennes was an experienced seaman and highly thought of by the king. As a young captain in 1629 he had been chosen to bring the court painter Rubens across from Dunkirk in the *Adventure*, and, just before the outbreak of war, it was Mennes who had been entrusted with taking Queen Henrietta Maria and her daughter to Holland in the *Lion* in February 1642. Twelve years earlier, Mervyn, one of the ablest of the Stuart naval officers, complained that in his fleet he had captains 'who knew neither how to command nor how to obey', and asked that Mennes might be given a command so that he might have some captains 'who have passed their a.b.c.'[37] As Samuel Pepys was later to discover, Mennes was an incompetent administrator but 'most excellent company'.[38] The Anglesey gentry soon had doubts even about his company. Sir John lived in part of the house at Friars, between Beaumaris and Penmon, and it was alleged after the war that he had converted to his own use much plate and rich apparel. In June 1644 forty-six trunks were brought by sea to Anglesey and left at Friars; Mennes, it was alleged, took charge of them stating they 'were in danger of being taken away by Wexford pirates', and 'converted great store of the said goods to his own use'. More immediately serious to the Royalist cause was that Mennes was soon on bad terms with Archbishop John Williams, who wrote angrily to Prince Rupert early in 1645 that 'Sir John Mennes and his men spread abroad in ale-houses up and down the country' rumours that Prince Rupert was displeased with Williams. The Archbishop was further incensed when he was superceded at Conway by Sir John Owen, who had fought in Rupert's cavalry at Bristol and Newbury. The constant bickering between the military commanders, who were strangers to Beaumaris, Caernarvon and Conway, on the one hand, and the local gentry and Williams on the other, did much harm to the Royalist cause. Williams had heard that the negotiators sent by Charles to Ireland had not reached Dublin; although he feared they were 'cast away in that bark they took at Carnarvon or . . . taken by the Parliament ships, concealed under hatches, to let the king still go on with his treaty at London, and not think of any new means of recruiting from Ireland', he still had hopes that they might 'have put into some remote creek in Ireland'. Some weeks later, Sir John Owen had an urgent message from Chester informing him of a plot to surprise Caernarvon by the ships of Parliament from Liverpool who intended to sail into the Menai Strait flying the king's colours 'upon pretence of coming from Ireland to serve his Majesty' and land troops.[39] There is no evidence that these vessels ever sailed, but in such a tense situation the wildest rumours gained some credence. Despite his wide experience of naval matters, Sir John Mennes, without ships, could do little, if anything, more than the Bartletts, and in helping himself to various 'pickings' at a time when the Royalist cause seemed already lost, he was only guilty of what several of the local gentry stood accused. Thomas Cheadle having already survived a murder trial in the pre-war period, when he was accused of poisoning Bulkeley and marrying his widow, and pardoned for 'piracies' in his youth, made hay during the wars, being later accused of 'seizing barks and boats in the harbour of Beaumaris', establishing a corner in salt and charging extortionate prices for it, and seizing goods and money from another vessel, 'on dry land near Lleiniog'.[40] It was at Lleiniog that he took the opportunity to fortify the outworks of the old Aberlleiniog castle on the shore, which was to have significance when the war came to the Strait.

By August 1644, the Admiral of Parliament's fleet, Warwick, urged that merchant ships should be prepared to prevent the Royalists from making use of the 'inlets' on the Welsh coast, and in the same letter recommended that Captain Stephen Rich be appointed 'master of some good ship for the winter's service'.[41] He was retained in command of the *Rebecca*, a 255-ton ship, which, according to the list of the Summer Guard of 1644, had a crew of 102 men;[42] Rich served in her in the Irish squadron for the next few years. The commander of this force, Richard Swanley, formerly an East India captain, had achieved not only distinction in the South Wales campaigns based in Milford, but also some notoriety. There were already many 'atrocity' stories abroad: Royalists were said to have committed 'unheard of outrages and cruelties' on the Pembrokeshire coast, but the one that caught the imagination in 1644 was Swanley's interception of some ships bound for Bristol from Dublin. Ormonde had sent from Dublin a hundred and fifty men, who had formerly served with the English forces in Galway at the time of the Irish rebellion, to supplement the king's forces in Bristol in the early summer of 1644. A vessel transporting the troops was caught by the ships of Captain Swanley, who, according to a Royalist account, 'was so inhuman' that he ordered the captured troops to be bound and thrown overboard. The ruthlessness of the action did much to dissuade other ships from transporting troops across to Beaumaris and Chester, and spread terror among the troops to be transported. For these were men who had shared their army quarters with them in Ireland, seventy of them, and two women, thrown overboard, and called 'Irish rebels', when they were in fact troops who had fought for the king against the rebels in Ireland. The restrained way in which Ormonde reported the incident to Archbishop Williams was not echoed in the popular press: 'one sayes that Captain Swanley tooke six score English, Irish, and sent them a fishing to the bottome of the sea: Another sayes that Captain Swanley made those Irish drinke their bellies full of water.' Captain Rich was to emulate Swanley at the taking of Conway castle two years later when the Irish troops captured were delivered to Rich 'who had undertaken to set them swimming towards the place whence they came'. Small wonder, then, that Ormonde found the troops reluctant to be shipped across, 'the men (are) fearful to venture upon the voyage'.[43]

The defeat at the battle of Naseby in June 1645 meant that, if the king was to survive, he had to have help from Scotland or Ireland; the capture of secret correspondence revealed that he was negotiating through the Earl of Glamorgan for Catholic forces from Ireland and Europe to land in Wales. This disclosure lost him so much support in the south that almost all that was left to the king was north Wales, where he still hoped to land troops. New emphasis was placed upon the importance of Anglesey and it was given out in public (even if there were secret reservations) that the king might make for Beaumaris, either to make a stand there or to sail from there to join up with Montrose in Scotland.[44] In the depths of an exceptionally cold winter the king wavered in desperation from one design to another; in the hope of hastening forces from Ireland he offered to send his youngest son, the Duke of York, over to Ormonde. In December 1645 the latter received orders to 'send over Captain Bartlett's ship to Beaumaris as soon as may be, with ten barrels of powder to be left there for the use of Chester'. However welcome the powder might have been, this was merely 'a pretence', for Bartlett was to remain at Beaumaris 'to stay and expect there some directions from the king' . . . 'in order to the duke of York's transportation'.[45] All the designs were doomed to fail. By the time further forces were ready to be sent over from Ireland, Chester had fallen. In February 1646, the Royalist commander, Byron, surrendered the now hostile, desperate city to Parliament's forces, and, following secret instructions in cipher, made his own way to Beaumaris and Caernarvon.[46]

The morale of the defenders of Chester had suffered a severe blow some months previously when, pressed as they were on all sides, they heard that the *Swan*, which had throughout been a symbol of hope of relief from Ireland, had been captured. The manner of the capture symbolised the hopelessness of the Royalist position, for she was not taken at sea but stolen surreptitiously out of harbour whilst John Bartlett was ashore. At the court of enquiry, Bartlett explained that he had not gone aboard the *Swan* at anchor in the Bay of Dublin that day in early November 1645 'as he had no money to pay the sailors'.[47] Captain Robert Clarke, in command of the *Jocelyn*, had sailed from Milford Haven in late August or early September for the north of Ireland, taking with him two small ships and Captain

Willoughby of the *Globe*, who knew the coast well.[48] After service at Carrickfergus, which as Captain William Penn, another of the Parliamentary squadron at Milford, said, was 'to them that know it, no place to winter in', he had sailed for Dublin Bay, where he had captured some fishermen, whom he had 'shut down in the hold'. One of the captives later told the story: about 5 o'clock in the evening he heard Captain Clarke calling for volunteers asking 'who would serve the turn'? The master of the *Jocelyn*, Banks, volunteered, and set out with a score of the crew in the *Jocelyn*'s longboat for the *Swan*, Captain Clarke calling to them as they pulled away from the ship's side, 'Blades, be true one to the other, the lights will do you service'. A little after midnight they were back aboard, reporting that the *Swan* had been captured, her crew offering little resistance, saying that they had 'waited for cessation after cessation'.[49] Banks had also captured a 'Flemish' ship, and in no time Clarke was sailing for the Welsh coast with his captured ships, manned by skeleton crews; sails had been taken from the *Jocelyn* for the *Swan*, another indication of the care with which this exploit had been planned. The news was received with much pleasure by the Parliament's commanders and there are many reports in their letters of the capture; in South Wales, Laugharne, commander of the Parliamentary forces who had worked with the Milford squadron in several combined sea and land operations, reported to London: 'I heard from Anglesey that Captain Clarke had taken a Fleming worth £3,000, and Captain Berkley's ships with 18 guns, some brass culverins.'[50] Little wonder that Clarke was 'very gratified' at this exploit: within a short time he had obtained command of the *Swan* himself and sailed her for the next two years at least[51] on patrols against Royalist and pirate shipping in the very waters that she had made such a name for John Bartlett.

The news caused dismay in Anglesey, and this was heightened when, after the surrender of Chester, Captain Stephen Rich in the *Rebecca* sailed into the Menai Strait in May with secret instructions for the gentlemen who were prepared to assist the Parliament's forces now driving forward for Caernarvon and Beaumaris. The king himself was in the hands of the Scots; Archbishop John Williams, anxious to avoid further ruin to north Wales, and heartily sick of the way in which he had been treated by the military wing of the Royalist forces, was ready to go over to Parliament. So were many others.

When he had returned to the area at the outbreak of war, Archbishop Williams had received a warm welcome in Anglesey, with 'many visits and feasts at Tom Bulkeley's'.[52] Now, in time of adversity, it appeared that men of Lord Bulkeley's generation, like the Archbishop, saw the wisdom of treating with the enemy, who recognised for their part the possession of Anglesey as 'a design of great consequence, and which being affected would much facilitate the reduction of the rest of those parts, and hinder the bringing in of any Irish into the north-west'.[53] Rather than risk an assault across the Menai Strait, which might be costly, General Mytton was empowered to promise 'a sum not exceeding £2,000' to any of the Anglesey gentry who could bring about a peaceful surrender of Beaumaris Castle. Byron, the Royalist Commander, after his experience of the long seige of Chester, was preparing Caernarvon for a similar last-ditch defence, but soon began to have doubts whether Lord Bulkeley was similarly resolute concerning Beaumaris. On 18 May he wrote angrily to Lord Bulkeley, expressing astonishment at his apparent co-operation with Captain Rich, and regret that he was being deceived by friends like Sir Robert Eyton, 'who is employed on the island as a spy'.[54] Lord Bulkeley had connections with the Navy of Parliament, for his wife Blanche was the sister of Robert Coytmor, the Caernarvonshire man who was secretary to the Earl of Warwick, Admiral of the Parliament fleet.[55] Captain Rich may well have known Bulkeley's brother-in-law and Captain Rowland Coytmore, an important member of the merchant community of Wapping.

Whatever Lord Bulkeley's views were, however, his son, young Colonel Richard Bulkeley, and the experienced Lt. Colonel John Robinson, now living at Mynachdy on the north-east of Anglesey, appeared determined to resist the forces of Parliament. As the tension increased, the old feud between the Bulkeleys and the Cheadles again came to the surface. When the *Rebecca* and Rich's other vessel, the *Rupert*, anchored in Friars Road there was naturally much speculation regarding their intentions. Young Richard Bulkeley wrote an angry letter to Rich accusing him of landing men 'in the dead of last night' at Lleiniog to supply the Cheadles with arms and ammunition.[56] He went further, stating that in daytime Rich's seamen had, in the town of Beaumaris, 'behaved very uncivilly threatening the people with burning of houses, cutting of throats and other words of dangerous consequence, to the great terror of the inhabitants'. His final charge was that some of Rich's officers had come 'to Friars House and abused a gentlewoman of very good quality'. Two days later, Rich replied denying all the charges and suggested that 'if any gentlewoman has suffered abuse' from his officers, she should 'come aboard and show the party' so that he, Captain Rich, could make certain that she should receive 'such satisfaction as she shall require'.[57]

On the same day, General Mytton at Caernarvon wrote to the younger Bulkeley urging Anglesey to send 'one two or more gentlemen . . . to Parliament to procure the best terms they can for the island', so as to save 'their country from a bloody war'.[58] The gentry of Anglesey recognised the inevitable, and, within a few days of the surrender of Caernarvon, they too made peace, asking in the negotiations with Mytton's representatives, 'that there may be free intercourse of trade and commerce, by sea and land between this island and all other parts of the king's dominions'.[59]

The war was over, but now troops had to be sent to Ireland where Ormonde had also recognised the inevitable and come to terms with the English Parliament. Beaumaris was nominated as one of the ports from which men were to be embarked: the soldiers who volunteered for service again were to be paid 6d. per day subsistence whilst they waited to be embarked at Beaumaris; on going aboard they got an advance of one month's pay. Rich, who, like the other Parliamentary officers, had found young Bulkeley intolerably arrogant, was soon on good terms with his father, but had to apologise in November for not being able to help with his ships in supplying corn to the island as he had to transport eighty cavalry, men and horses, to Holyhead en route for Ireland. Now that the period of the emergency was over, Rich looked for, and obtained, a peace-time appointment, 'to be commander of the ordinary packet boats passing betwixt Holyhead and Dublin'.[60] His appointment dated from November, 1646, at a contract rate of eleven pounds per month for each of his two boats, 'he covenanting to set sail upon receipt of any packet too and from the state, and that one of the packet boats shall for that purpose be constantly attending at Dublin, and the other at Holyhead'. It was not until December 1647, however, that he received his money, a grant of £319.8.5. being approved. Thus Parliament rewarded a faithful servant, and ensured that the communications between Holyhead and Dublin were in the hands of a skilled and experienced war-time seaman.[61]

It was no sinecure. A contemporary list in 1648 gives the names of thirteen ships operating from Waterford alone with commissions which enabled them to seek booty on the Welsh and English coasts for two or three weeks before making for specified destinations in France, one of them claimed to be 'one of the best sailing vessels in the world'.[62] A year previously 'two papists' had been arrested in a barque held at Holyhead, one of them having a secret letter, written in French, containing messages for a French agent in London. One of the suspects was said to have confessed to a knowledge of plots by French and other Catholic forces, 'and saith for certain there are 6 frigates ready to be landed at Washford for some design'.[63] Lord Bulkeley, alarmed at these 'bloody and desparate intendments', asked Parliament to 'order some shipping for these coasts to fright away these pilfering rascals and to prevent invasions'.[64] Parliament was soon faced with more severe crises; in 1648 the revolts in Kent, Essex, South Wales, a threatened invasion in Scotland, and the revolt of more than half the fleet, made their situation extremely difficult. The north Wales revolt in 1648 was therefore part of the general disaffection, but, as elsewhere, consisted of comparatively local and isolated risings; the Caernarvonshire revolt had in fact been defeated on the seashore at Y Dalar Hir, near Llandygái, at the eastern entrance to the Menai Strait, before the Anglesey gentry declared for the king in July 1648.[65]

The conquered stragglers from several risings made their way to Anglesey where the over-confident and arrogant young Richard Bulkeley took command, ignoring Archbishop Williams's advice that the Welsh should not be led into turning their island into a battleground. Lord Bulkeley, himself sympathetic to the revolt in the Navy, and disillusioned by the excessive demands of men like Colonel Carter, the ruthless Roundhead soldier now governing Conway, was alleged to have been involved 'in correspondence and intelligence with the rebels in Ireland, Isle of Man and Scotland'.[66] Although outwardly co-operating with Parliament, Lord Bulkeley was accused of being 'a great contriver' of the revolt and sending information and messengers to the exiled Stuart princes in Holland to whom Captain Batten, Jordan and other experienced naval commanders had sailed with part of the fleet.[67]

General Mytton, having successfully defeated the Caernarvonshire risings, bided his time and wrote to London asking for 'a pinnace or two . . . for the reducing of Anglesey to the obedience of Parliament'. They were not necessary. Again the Cheadle-Bulkeley vendetta proved to be a decisive factor. Major Richard Cheadle, who was serving with the Parliamentary forces, used his local knowledge to find sufficient small craft to transport Mytton's soldiers across the Menai Strait, landing them at Cadnant, and within a matter of hours the Royalists were again defeated. For his part Cheadle was awarded £2,000 out of the money levied as a punishment on the island. He did not live to enjoy it. Some four months later, in February 1650, Richard Cheadle and Richard Bulkeley met in a duel on the Lavan Sands; Bulkeley was slain and Cheadle hanged for murder at Conway.[68] The vendetta was over. It was also the end of the war in Anglesey. Despite all the consternation, the fears and threats of invasion, the actual fighting on the island had amounted to nothing more than a few hours of skirmishes.

The war at sea was not over. The revolt of part of Parliament's fleet in 1648 and its presence at Kinsale early in 1649 under the command of Prince Rupert, was a threat which Parliament could not afford to allow to go unchallenged. The execution of the king and the ending of the Thirty Years War in Europe meant that more attention might be expected from a continent which had sympathy with Rupert and his rebel fleet. Rupert's Vice Admiral was Sir John Mennes, Beaumaris's erstwhile governor, who no doubt heard with approval of a dramatic incident in March 1649 which caused much consternation on the Welsh coast. It was Captain John Bartlett, again, who was involved. Anchoring in St Tudwal's Roads, Bartlett sent about twenty of his men ashore in two longboats, and with all the speed of a carefully planned exploit, they made their way to Castellmarch, seized Griffith Jones, a prominent Roundhead supporter, and plundered his house 'of plate, money, apparel and linen'.[69] Within a few hours Griffith Jones was aboard Bartlett's ship, a prisoner bound for Wexford. Jones must have ruefully contemplated his premonition of such an event some six years previously, when he had urged that he should be allowed to retain guns and ammunition in self-defence because of the exposed situation of his house in Lleyn: 'being the utmost end of the country and more maritime than any other part, and so more subject to invasion and danger'. For good measure he had emphasised in his letter that he lived 'nearer than any other man of his quality to the road of best reception for ships of burden ... from the Land's End of England to the Mule (*sic*) of Galloway, Milford Haven excepted'.[70] The raid in 1649 by Bartlett was apparently intended as a reprisal for the sentencing of the Caernarvonshire Royalist leader, Sir John Owen, to death for his part in the Second Civil War, and may have earned him his reprieve. Some weeks later, Griffith Jones's brother-in-law, Richard Griffith, wrote to him confirming that the raiders 'had left hardly any clothes for his wife, and what his daughter and son in law had there is all gone'; the two raiders left behind would have been put to the sword but for the womenfolk of the raided house who had begged for quarter for their assailants despite their own losses, and 'if Captain Bartley comes again to the country he will find a different reception'. It was little comfort to the wretched Griffith Jones languishing at Wexford to hear that the raid had had the salutary effect of putting the dwellers on the Welsh coast 'in a better position of defence than it ever was', nor could it have made other 'collaborators' with Parliament, dwelling near the coast in Anglesey, sleep more easily in their beds.[71]

1649 proved to be a year, however, when there emerged a new and powerful weapon which was to have long-term effects upon British history, the Navy which under Blake was to achieve greatness. The Irish Sea became a centre of much activity; in March 1649 Sir George Ayscue was appointed to 'command in the Irish Seas' with Captain William Penn as his Vice Admiral. Both had already seen much service in the Navy of Parliament, and they were soon in action providing convoys for shipping in the Chester-Dublin area, whilst Blake mounted a highly successful blockade of Rupert's fleet at Kinsale. On 5 June 1649, Ayscue was at Beaumaris, in the *St Andrew*, probably the largest naval vessel that had been in these waters, a 42-gun ship built at Deptford in 1622, with a length of keel of 110 feet, a beam of 36 feet, and nearly 800 'tons and tonnage'.[72] Whilst the inhabitants of Anglesey were no doubt impressed at this expression of strength, Ayscue had no wish to linger in the Menai Strait as Wake had done, and whilst he was at Beaumaris orders came for him from the Council of State 'to leave some small vessel about Beaumaris or Holyhead that may give you advertisements; meantime we leave it to you to ply up and down on those seas, and do such service as you judge best'. It seems likely that Popham, one of his fellow Generals at Sea, was with Ayscue aboard the *St Andrew* at this time; he wrote in June from the *St Andrew* that 'in going from Bewe: Morris . . . I was forced into Dublin Bay' and thus assisted Michael Jones's campaign there.[73] Ayscue's original appointment had been to the *St George*, also built at Deptford in 1622, a sister ship of the *St Andrew*, but it is unlikely that there would have been two such large ships at Beaumaris at the same time. One or two, it was to Anglesey people a powerful 'showing of the flag' which, incidentally, since February in that year, had been flown in accordance with the decree 'that the ships at sea in the service of the State shall only bear the red cross in a white flag'.[74]

In July Ayscue was ordered to divert all shipping in Liverpool Bay to Milford to transport the forces under Cromwell for Ireland; the pressed ships were not to receive 'their orders for the place until they are out at sea, so that the enemy may have no notice of their transport'.[75] Early in August, Cromwell sailed with a convoy of thirty ships, and had a rough passage to Dublin, 'the Lord Lieutenant was as sick as ever I saw a man in my life'.[76] Another eighty ships sailed under the command of Richard Deane, the third of the 'Generals at Sea', a few days later; the operation was carried out successfully without any significant interruption by Rupert's fleet or anyone else. The contrast between the successful invasion of Ireland by Cromwell's forces, and the failure of the Royalists to invade Wales provides a compelling illustration of Admiral Richmond's definition of sea power quoted at the beginning of this chapter.

Cromwell made a rapid recovery from his sea sickness. The gentle letter he wrote from aboard the *John* in Milford Haven to his daughter Dorothy, the advice regarding his son Richard's education, and his kindly letter supporting a claim that his fellow Lincolnshire-man, Ayscue, should not be at a financial disadvantage because of his sea service, are in sharp contrast to his actions during the weeks that followed.[77] Persuading himself that 'this is a righteous judgement of God upon these barbarous wretches, who have imbrued their hands in so much innocent blood',[78] first Drogheda and then Wexford were put to the sword, whilst to the north Carlingford was taken with the assistance of some ships of Ayscue's fleet. At Wexford Cromwell reported the capture of 'some very good shipping, one of them of thirty-four guns, which a weeks time would fit to sea', and three other vessels, including a fine frigate of twenty guns which he had found upon the stocks, but was so impressed with her lines that he ordered the workmen to complete. The irrepressible Bartlett escaped the slaughter, and as the Irish ports were taken by Cromwell's forces, Bartlett, and others like him, moved to the Isle of Man. Rupert and the Royalist fleet took the opportunity of Blake's temporary absence to sail south for Lisbon in the autumn of 1649, and as both the eastern Irish coast and the Welsh coasts were held by Parliament and no large enemy ships left in the area, the centre of naval activity moved elsewhere, to the blockade of Lisbon, to the Mediterranean, and eventually to the bloody struggles with the Dutch in the English Channel and the North Sea.

Whilst the Isle of Man remained in Royalist hands, however, raids on shipping could be expected, for it was an excellent base from which to mount quick attacks and intercept ships sailing between Dublin, Holyhead, Chester, Liverpool, and the ports of Northern Ireland, Scotland and to the Cumberland coast. In November, 1649, a request came from Liverpool for a frigate for service 'upon the coasts of Lancashire and north Wales' to prevent piracy against coastal ships 'which are thence carried into the Isle of Man, and then sold'; the Cumberland and Scottish ports complained of a loss of trade, and in north Wales it was Mytton's alertness that forestalled the taking of Bardsey as another island base to attack shipping in the piratical tradition which echoed Elizabethan days.[79]

But there was a difference. Whereas in the years of Elizabeth and James I there had been obvious collusion with the pirates, the 'New Model Navy' and the military rulers ashore viewed their enemies in a much harsher light. In 1650 the Council of State ordered 'the sending some ships into the Irish seas for preventing the piracies of Bartlett in those parts'; his days were numbered. Thomas Sparling, commander of the *President*, and John Sherwin, captain of the *Hind*, were given orders to ply between Carrickfergus, Dublin and the English, Scottish and Welsh coasts 'for the protection of merchant vessels, and the surprising, beating and destroying of all Irish men of war', and in the autumn Sherwin reported the capture of Bartlett's ship, 'also a parcel of letters which I took from Bartlett's vessel at the Isle of Man'.[80] In the following year the Commonwealth's Governor of Anglesey was warned that there was a plot afoot to land troops in north Wales; 'of surprising those counties upon landing some forces for the Isle of Man, with whom they expect a conjunction of old and new malignants in those parts'.[81] So concerned were the Committee of Admiralty in March 1651 that Blake himself was ordered to take a fleet into the Irish sea, and 'to have special eye to the Isle of Man where . . . there are great preparations and many Designes now afoote to disturb the peace of the Commonwealth'.[82] His orders stressed the need to intercept any forces transported or any communication between the Isle of Man and the neighbouring coasts, and Anglesey just a few hours' sailing away was naturally one of the danger points. In April a Caernarvon vessel was seized and taken to Liverpool as a prize, and there was much concern at the delay in getting the *Truelove* and *Convert* out to sea 'to prevent the coming of ye Earle of Derby out of the Isle of Man'. But nothing came of it all; Blake was himself occupied with the arrival of Admiral Tromp and the Dutch fleet off the Scillies, ships were needed in the North Sea to support Cromwell in his campaign against the Scots, and Blake was therefore ordered to postpone the taking of the Isle of Man, leaving some ships there on guard 'until you can be at leisure for that service'.[83] In October, 1651, the Isle of Man surrendered.

The enemies at sea were soon to be drawn from amongst the finest seamen in the world; the war with the Dutch was desirable in the eyes of Cromwell and the city merchants, whose financial support sustained him, and it was popular with the trading community in almost every port. Between 1649 and 1660 over 200 vessels were added to the British Navy, over 80 of them built by English shipwrights.[84] The energetic and effective shipbuilding programme formed the new Navy, which in turn created the conditions which enabled English commerce to develop in the late seventeenth and early eighteenth centuries. All this was but dimly realised in 1650 when, surprisingly, there is a reference to Dutch ships at Beaumaris. On 8 February 1650 the Council of State ordered that the 'generals of the fleet (be) sent to, to come to the council, to confer with them about the ships of De Witt that are now in the water of Beaumaris'.[85] William Williams, Rector of Llansadwrn, writing some twenty years later, had good reason to remember the occasion well. He recorded how De Witt and 'Capt. Joost Van Colster had beene att Brazil in America to endeavour to settle the Holland Plantations which the Portuguez had disturbed'.[86] They had fared ill in an encounter with the Portuguese, and on their return voyage had been driven off course by a storm and 'rov'd in St George's Channell, not knowing on what coast they were'. Meeting a Liverpool vessel at sea, 'he had conducted them into the harbour of Bewmares'. The Dutchmen, much relieved to have an opportunity to revictual, spent some time repairing their storm-damaged vessels. Young Richard Bulkeley, recently returned to Beaumaris from exile in Europe, having made his peace with Parliament, was soon on good terms with the Dutch admiral and his officers; 'and during their abode there, the sayd Richard Bulkeley was very familiar with them and delighted much in their companie'. It was after coming ashore in a wherry from the Dutch ships that Bulkeley, riding his horse towards Penmaenmawr, overtook Richard Cheadle: 'some high words passing betweene them they both drew, the sayd Richard Bulkeley having only a short bawble of a sword by his side, and Major Cheadle a very long tucke, by which he ran the sayd Richard Bulkeley into the heart soe that immediately he fell down dead'. Ironically De Witt and his officers, the future enemies of the regicides, were the last companions of the young Royalist killed on the desolate Lavan Sands.

This was an isolated incident of vessels driven by stress of weather into Beaumaris; two years later the Dutch were busy in the Channel and the North Sea. Despite all their other commitments, from 1649 to 1660 the naval guard convoyed merchant ships in the Irish seas and maintained effective communications between Scotland, Ireland, Wales, and the English ports. Out of the mass of naval papers relating to this period one can trace the activities of many of the ships in detail, from their building to their ultimate fate; seldom has a navy been so well served by those ashore, from shipbuilders to victualling agents, and the orders to, and letters from, the captains reflect the devotion and sense of duty which was fostered. The orders to captains of ships regarding convoy were simple and clear cut: sometimes there was a division of responsibility, the convoyed ships being passed from one squadron to another. In 1649, Captain Baddiley, the senior officer in the Downs, was ordered 'to appoint a convoy to bring six or seven ships now in the Thames, five of which are laden with corn, and bound for Chester, Liverpool, Wales and Dublin, to the Commander of the northern squadron, to be conveyed thence to their respective ports, and your convoy ship is to return to you for further orders'.[87] Within the Liverpool Bay area the convoys were usually provided by individual ships: the *Marigold*'s captain, Humphrey Felstead, was ordered to provide a convoy in 1652, meeting the vessels laden with provisions for the forces in Ireland at their rendezvous off 'Highlake in Chester Water' . . . 'and the first wind after two or more are ready, sail with them for Galway, wait for their unloading, but no more than 20 days, and convoy them back in sight of the Welsh coast'.[88] The usual format of the letters of instructions to captains followed the pattern: 'with the first opportunity of winde and weather you sett sayle and plye'[89] on whatever station they were allocated. In the 1640s vessels were given clear instructions regarding lights to be shown as signals when sailing in company, and 'how, in case fowle weather seperate us, to meet again';[90] the Commonwealth convoys must have employed similar methods. The Commonwealth shipbuilders, avoiding the early Stuart policy of building large, ornate ships, strove to emulate the Dunkirkers by designing vessels with clean deck lines, longer keels and shorter overall length, thus avoiding excessive rake; the peak building year was 1654, but for the first years of the Commonwealth most of the ships employed in Welsh waters were vessels captured from the Royalists or privateers. Towards the end of the 50s, however, many Commonwealth-built vessels visited Beaumaris and Holyhead during the course of their patrols in the Ireland, Isle of Man, Scotland, Chester area. At the close of the Commonwealth period, the *Dartmouth* and the *Oxford*, built in 1655 and 1656, were engaged in patrols off the Isle of Man and Anglesey.[91]

Captain John Sherwin, who had taken Bartlett's ship at the Isle of Man, had already had reason to doubt the seaworthiness of his 200-ton *Hind*, taken from the Royalists in 1648. Early in 1651 she was described as being so old and unserviceable that 'those who have the charge of transporting ye States Treasurie for Ireland will not adventure to transport it in her'; another letter described her as 'old and crazy' and suggested removing her guns to another vessel, but in June she was ordered to convoy vessels from Chester Water to Connaught and later in the month to convoy a vessel laden with provisions from Chester 'to Dumbarton Firth'.[92] Shortly afterwards Sherwin took Bartlett's vessel at the Isle of Man, but the *Hind* was then wrecked in July on the Irish coast. In the autumn a number of widows petitioned the Admiralty; one of them, 'Roberta Fryth widdow', stated that 'William Fryth her late husband being chirurgeon in the Hynd frigott of the States, under the command of Captain John Sherwyn was drowned when the said frigott was cast away upon the coast of Ireland, and hath left her with two small children in greate wante'.[93] Her petition was supported by Captain Sherwin, himself one of the survivors, and she and the widows of the Gunner and two Quartermasters all received £6 pension, as well as the widow of another mariner from the *Hind* who had been 'commanded ashore upon service on the Isle of Man in which service he was slaine'. Sherwin himself was given another command, this time one of the new vessels built at Wapping in 1651, the *Primrose*, a vessel mounting between 24 and 32 guns, of about 280 tons. In October 1654 the *Primrose* was at Beaumaris, windbound, and Sherwin wrote to the Navy Commissioners requesting a refit, revictualling and pay for his men 'who have been out for some time and are badly off for clothes'.[94]

The Commonwealth had made valiant efforts to cope with victualling the rapidly expanding navy, and, recognizing that seamen served the best pay masters, had increased wages so that at least their seamen did not share the opinion of their fellows in the neglected navy of 1629 when 'foul weather, naked bodies, and empty bellies make the men voice the king's service worse than a galley slave'. By 1656 it would seem that 'slop' clothing (first introduced in 1628 to give seamen a change of clothing 'to avoid the nasty beastliness which many of the men are subject to by the continual wearing of one suit of clothes') was being sold at cheaper prices to the seamen,[95] and it is likely that despite the inroads made into all supplies by the First Dutch War, Sherwin's men were much better off than their predecessors had been. The following year found Sherwin and the *Primrose* chasing two men of war from Brest off Holyhead; they got away much to Sherwin's annoyance.[95] It had been a difficult year for him for he had a large area to patrol and occasionally he gave vent to his feelings of frustration, as he had done a few months earlier when he wrote to the Navy Commissioners for 'orders for disposal of his frigate and men, and not to hang, like Mahomet's tomb, neither relating to heaven or earth'.[97]

Inevitably with such a long coastline to patrol, occasional pirates acting independently slipped through any protective cordon. Four vessels were attacked in June, 1656, 'two being taken at Holyhead and the others run on shore', and Thomas Swift of Holyhead was compelled to pay £50 to the pirates: Swift 'hearing we had a frigate at Beaumaris, sent out after her, but it was like shutting the stable door after the steed was stole'.[98] Swift, a member of the Commission for the Propagation of the Gospel in Wales, was the most powerful man in Holyhead during the period; no doubt he was aware that, should there be landings or piratical raids, he was a marked man, as indeed Griffith Jones of Castellmarch had been. Five years previously, at the time of the 'scare' regarding the Isle of Man, it was reported that 'a Post barque belonging to Thomas Swift of Holyhead hath lately been taken by the enemy' and it was suggested that Swift's crew and passengers 'now in the Isle of Man' should be exchanged for any Royalist prisoners in Chester or Anglesey, 'man for man, and quality for quality'.[99] Shortly after Swift's unfortunate encounter with the Holyhead pirates in 1656, Captain Robert Bowen of the *Mayflower*, lying in Caldey Road, off Tenby, reported that he had earlier in the summer transported a Major Morgan to Beaumaris from Dublin and had then cruised about, chasing a San Sebastian pirate 'which had taken a vessel from Dublin bound for West Chester', and had taken two other prizes. Whether these had anything to do with the Holyhead incident is uncertain: Bowen reported that he had also 'relieved 14 other sail which would have been taken had not providence ordered it otherwise'. Whether Captain Bowen regarded himself as 'Providence' or not, he was certainly beginning to feel the strain of his work; his ship needed careening, and he needed another officer, 'having been employed in the *Mayflower* since Feb 1653, and having no master or mate, she being a 6th rate'.[100]

Convoy work had a dual effect: it gave confidence to the merchants, thereby assisting the development of trade generally, and although the Beaumaris Port Books have been lost, as indeed have most of the Port Books for the Civil War and Commonwealth period, it would be true to say that this was a formative period for the growth of coastal trade which culminated in the late seventeenth and eighteenth-century development of commerce. The other effect was upon the Navy itself, by giving its seamen that most valuable of all experience, 'sea time'. At Cadiz in 1625 the English Navy had shown great incompetence, 'officers losing spars and sails from ignorance of the elementary principles of their art', and the crews had been guilty of 'utter incapacity in the mere everyday work of a sailor's duties'.[101] The ships and seamen on the Welsh coast in the 1650s were far removed from such scenes: they presented a contrast in their very numbers to the days of Thomas Button and his solitary ships. The experience gained by the men of the 40s and 50s off the Welsh coast was put to good use elsewhere; Penn, a great exponent of sea time, 'I not being inbred to lie in harbour',[102] Ayscue, Robert Clarke, Robert Bowen, all distinguished themselves in other campaigns in the West Indies, the Mediterranean and the Dutch wars. This was as true of the crews as it was of the captains. For the most part the ships were manned at the main naval ports in the south of England where they commissioned, and it is virtually impossible to say how many Welshmen served in the Navy of the Commonwealth. Occasionally, in times of emergency such as the Dutch Wars, or when there were powerful privateers operating in an area, the crews of the already crowded vessels were increased. Captain Robert Bowen in 1656, when he brought the *Mayflower* to Beaumaris, had been ordered at Dublin, 'in view of the extraordinary numbers of men' carried in enemy ships, to increase his crew from sixty to seventy men. In recruiting the additional crew, which would have to be done locally in the Liverpool Bay area where he was operating, he was told 'to take care that they be able and stout men, fitt to pforme seamen's labour, and also that noe unnecessary number of boyes be kept on board yr shipp to the prejudice of the service'.[103] There was considerable insistence on seamanship: 'to be an able seaman is not to be gained by learning of words (as a parrot which can speak words but understand them not) but by laborious and hazardous experience'.[104] This was the experience that the convoy work of the Commonwealth Navy gave; the captain was no longer 'a gentleman that hath been on a voyage or two at sea (who in fowle weather is sicke, or if not sick, yet he cannot stand on his leggs for the labouring of the ship at sea, and therefore is forced to keep in his cabbin)', but rather a man who was a 'seaman bredd, whose bodie hath been accustomed to sea stormes and night watchings', a captain who could speak to his seamen

> 'in their own language and can correct by his own experience every mans errors or ignorance, from ye boy that carries the frittle at his girdle to the First Commander under him, that as well in the darkest stormy nights and greates dangers (as in ye fairest daies) is abroad amongst them, as well to behold everyman's forwardnesse or sloth, Thereby to encourage and cherish the best deserving and to reprove and punish the sloth and base cowardize of others . . . '[105]

How many Welshmen there were in the Commonwealth Navy is impossible to assess; certainly there were a number with Welsh-sounding names,[106] but, hazarding a guess, the one Welshman seen amongst the crew of the ship off Wylfa by Dr Griffith of Carreglwyd and the Anglesey coastal watchers of the Civil War period, may be fairly near the typical percentage of Welshmen in the naval service in mid seventeenth-century. The naval tradition, and, indeed seafaring generally, was a later growth in Wales. To the majority of Anglesey people the sea had been something to be feared, a source of danger from invaders and pirates; the achievement of the Commonwealth Navy was that it made the seas around the coast safer for legal trade. At a time when it was estimated that a vessel of 30 tons carried as much cargo as 100 horses[107] this became very important to the Welsh economy, particularly in view of the wild, impassable roads that remained a hazard for another hundred and fifty years. It was in the 1650s, too, that Welsh men and women began to venture 'beyond seas', as servants in the foreign plantations of Virginia, Maryland and Barbados, an incidental consequence of Ayscue's reduction of Barbados in 1652. Among the first to sail from Bristol were Seth Williams 'from Kemmis', John Williams of 'Tregard', and

Evan Ellis of 'Landeiniolen', all bound for Barbados.[108]

The death of Cromwell and the restoration of Charles II in 1660 caused no violent change in the lives of the majority of Anglesey people, grown accustomed to shifts in government and only too glad to be rid of heavy taxation and 'fanatical' sermons. Shortly before Charles's return, an agent of Parliament had written from Beaumaris warning that 'Captain John Bartlett of Tuttle Street, Westminster, should be watched. He is counted the father of all pirates, and is a great favourer of the common enemy. He will speedily put to sea at his old trade'.[109] But the day of the captain who had served the Stuarts so faithfully was at hand, and he did not need to take to piracy. As the Roundheads had rewarded Captain Stephen Rich for his services at the end of the Civil War, so Captain John Bartlett was allowed to return to his old haunts as captain in charge of the post barques plying between Holyhead and Dublin. In the dark days of the wars, Orlando Bridgeman, the distinguished Chester lawyer, who at the Restoration became Lord Keeper, had obtained from, Charles I 'the Pattent of the Post Barkes betwixt Holyhead and Dublin' for John and Thomas Bartlett, his brother, following the death of the holder, Captain Longford, in the early 1640s. But 'by reason of the then distracted tymes', and the Bartletts' preoccupation with Royalist naval service, they had been unable to take up the appointment. John Bartlett had reason enough to hate Thomas Swift, who appears to have taken over from Captain Rich in 1649; Bartlett in his petition stated that 'the post barks have been for 12 years past in the hands of a fanatick who at this present tyme calls your petitioner piratt, whereas of right he is your Majesty's Admiral of the Irish Seas'.[110] The last payment in cash appears to have been made to Captain Stephen Rich on March 31st, 1649, when he received payment for '6 months, 2 weeks and one day';[111] as they then cease, it may be that Rich, like many other naval captains who had given good service to Parliament in the Civil Wars, went out of favour or actively disapproved of the execution of the king and the ascendancy of the Army. Swift, who seems to have acquired many offices at Holyhead during the Interregnum (he was postmaster, contractor for the post-barques, as well as being variously described as governor and Mayor of Holyhead), knew which side his bread was buttered and was willing to come to terms with the new government, but he had made too many enemies. Bartlett petitioned that he should be granted two vessels in place of those which he had lost in the late king's service, and that he be paid the £340 that Swift had been allowed, and an additional £160 'to be paid out of the postage', at the rate of £125 per quarter for his vessels and sixteen men.[112] September 1660 found him busily fitting out the *Swallow* and the *Rose* for the new service, and complaining somewhat testily to the Navy Commissioners that they were 'short as to the delivery of two boats and four seamen to each vessel for rigging. The vessels are much desired by Lord Ormond and the Irish Commissioners'.[113] The wheel had come full circle.

[1]   H. Richmond, *Statesmen and Sea Power* (Oxford, 1946) ix.
[2]   *AC 1869*, 336. Williams to Ormonde, January, 1645.
[3]   A. H. Dodd, 'Anglesey in the Civil War', *TAAS* 1952, 8. The political implications and the relationships between Anglesey families during the Civil War are dealt with in Professor Dodd's article; this present chapter is an attempt to supplement Professor Dodd's work by relating the affairs of the county to the general background of the war at sea.
[4]   *HMC Ormonde*, II, 77. There had been much bad weather – the Wynns of Gwydir received a letter written on 29 December 1641 referring to 'the great wrecks that have lately occurred upon this coast'. A Dutch ship was lost at Porth Neigwl, a British ship aground at Dinas Dinlle, and 'on Friday a Dutch convoy came aground at Porth y llonge'. John Bodwrda to Owen and Maurice Wynn at Gwydir, *CWP* 1701.
[5]   *CWP* 1695. For the Puw family and their loyalty to the Roman Catholic cause, see articles by Geraint Bowen in *DWB* 818-819; *Efrydiau Catholig*, ii, 11, *TCHS* 1946; R. Geraint Gruffydd, *Argraffwyr Cyntaf Cymru* (Cardiff, 1972), 8-10, and 'Gwasg Ddirgel yr Ogof yn Rhiwledyn', *Journal of Welsh Bibliographical Society*, IX, July 1958, 1-24.
[6]   Glamorgan Record Office, MSS D/DTD 10. The *Bonaventure*, built in 1621 at Deptford, a 32-gun vessel, 418-557 tons, 96' keel, 32.5' beam, had been considered 'needlessly large and expensive' for antipiratical work by Wentworth as early as 1634, *CSP Ireland*, 1633/47. Captain Kettleby had served in the *Swallow*, another Deptford built ship, 96' x 32.2', 357-478 tons,

for some years on the Irish Station. In 1638 Charles I had sent a letter to Wentworth appointing Kettleby 'Admiral of the Fleet to Guard the Irish Seas' and underwritten it 'I recommend this man the more seriously to you, because I assure you that he is of my own choice'. *CSP Ireland*, 1633/47, 8 Feb. 1638, 180. In 1642 the *Bonaventure* was victualled for a crew of 170 men, the *Swallow* for 150. Bod Raw MSS A 223/5.

[7] BM E.240, 35; J. R. Powell, *The Navy in the English Civil War* (London, 1962), 27.

[8] Carte, *Life of James Butler, Duke of Ormonde* (Oxford, 1842), iii, 268.

[9] M. L. Baumber, 'The Navy and Civil War in Ireland, 1641-3', in MM 57, 4 (1971), 385-397, is a general account of the Irish campaigns 1641-3. *CSPD* 1641-3, 46, 8 July 1641.

[10] *HMC Ormonde* II, 213. Ormonde recognised the worth of the Bartletts: 'their abilities in their places and their knowledge of these coasts and harbours are such as give us good satisfaction upon all occasions'. The activities of the *Swan* and *Confidence* are described in more detail in A. Eames, 'Sea Power and Caernarvonshire, 1642-1660', in *TCHS* 1955, 29-45, and in A. Eames, 'The King's Pinnace, the *Swan*, 1642-45', in *MM* 47 (1961), 1, 49-56.

[11] *HMC Ormonde*, I, 69.

[12] This was in accordance with contemporary practice, the foremast and bowsprit were both to measure four-fifths of the mainmast. In a paper presented to Buckingham, Henry Mainwaring gave the formula for measuring masts: the mainmast was to be reckoned as four-fifths the breadth of the ship multiplied by three, the foremast four-fifths of the mainmast, and the mizzen mast half the length of the main-mast, the 'bigness of all masts to be 1 inch to a yard in length'. H. Mainwaring, 'The Seaman's Dictionary', in *The Life and Works of Sir Henry Mainwaring* (NRS, vol. LVI), II, 186-7.

[13] *HMC Ormonde*, II, 213.

[14] NLW Carreglwyd MSS 1714.

[15] *CSPD* 1641-43, 567. Feb. 11, 1643. For the action by Captain Thomas and Danske, B. M. Thomason Tracts, E56/1; A. Eames, 'Captain William Thomas, a naval captain of the English Civil War', *MM* 47, 2 (1961), 145-149.

[16] UCNW, Baron Hill, 5368.

[17] The 'deep sea line' used by mariners in the early seventeenth-century in deep water was marked at twenty fathoms, thirty, forty, etc., but the 'sounding line' for shoal waters was marked 'at two fathom next to the lead it is marked with a piece of black leather put into it betwixt the strands; at three fathom the like; at five a piece of white woollen cloth, at seven fathom a piece of red cloth; at ten a piece of leather, at fifteen fathom, either a white cloth or a piece of leather, and so it is marked no farther'. Mainwaring, 'The Seaman's Dictionary', 1644, in Mainwaring, VI, 229.

[18] NLW Llanfair-Brynodol MSS 58, 30 Aug. 1643. Howells, *Calendar of*

Letters relating to North Wales, 59.

[19] Carte, V, 153.

[20] H. R. Trevor Roper, 'Three Foreigners: the Philosophers of the Puritan Revolution', in *Religion, Reformation and Social Change* (London, 1967), 255-275. Williams was also related to John Hampden; C. V. Wedgewood, *The King's War* (1958), 39.

[21] *AC* 1869, 336.

[22] J. R. Powell and E. K. Timings (ed.), *Documents relating to the Civil War, 1642-1648* (Navy Records Society, CV, London, 1963), 97.

[23] *ibid.*, 98. J. R. Powell, '*The Navy in the English Civil War*' (1962), states that it was in the *Employment*, a 20-gun ship, that Thomas Bartlett brought the guns and powder to Beaumaris on this occasion. There was an *Employment*, a 30-gun merchant ship, in the Irish guard for the summer of 1643, but this must have been another ship. When Bartlett moved from the *Confidence* is uncertain.

[24] *Carte*, V, 514-5.

[25] *ibid.*, IV, 469.

[26] *Mainwaring*, I, 312. Wake had commanded the *Tenth Whelp* in 1640; he was one of the captains exempted from mercy in 1649. D. E. Kennedy, 'Naval Captains in the English Civil War', *MM* 46, 3 (1960), 185.

[27] R. Morris and P. H. Lawson, 'The Siege of Chester', *Chester and North Wales Archaeological and Historical Society*, XXV (new series), 1922, 48; *Documents Civil War*, 103, 104.

[28] Morris and Lawson, *Siege of Chester*, 49.

[29] *AC* 1869, 310. It may have been adverse weather conditions that kept the Liverpool based Parliament ships in harbour when Wake made his original landings on the Flintshire coast.

[30] Dodd, *Anglesey in the Civil War*, 11-12; UCNW, Baron Hill MSS 5367, Bartlett was said to have paid £30 for beef to Wake. NLW MS 9080E.

[31] *Documents, Civil War*, 106.

[32] *Carte*, IV, 474.

[33] *Documents, Civil War*, 126.

[34] *Carte*, VI, 102.

[35] *ibid.*, VI, 83.

[36] *ibid.*, VI, 83.

[37] *Mainwaring*, II, 44. *The King's War*, 69; *MM* 48, 3 (1962), 227.

[38] Arthur Bryant, *Pepys, The Man in the Making* (London, 1948), 229, 235.

[39] *CWP* 1748, 1917; NLW Brogyntyn MSS 566.

[40] *CWP* 1873. It was also alleged that Cheadle had seized a 'Scotch ship laden with wines for the merchants of Chester, valued at £5,000, the factor whereof John Preston was by him imprisoned, whereby the king lost £200 custom and the merchants their goods'. *CWP* 1874.

[41] *CSPD* 1644, 557, August 1644.

[42] BMTTE 669, fo. 9, 8, 36, 58, Bod Raw Bodleian MSS A 223, 15.

[43] Carte, *Life*, iv, 60; *Mercurius Aulicus*, May 18, 1644. Some fifteen hundred

troops were eventually transported towards the end of June across to Scotland, coming to anchor in 'a bay of Isla'. Carte, *Life*, iv, 62. But the fear of interceptions increased the demand for 'danger money' from the owners of merchant ships, and it was claimed that Swanley's actions had 'struck a great terror into all neighbouring coasts, and scarce a ship durst stir out of harbour'. Carte, *Life*, iv, 60. For Captain Robert Rich's action at Conway, letter from Mytton to Lenthall, 12 August 1646, printed in *The Tanner Letters*, Original Notices and Letters of Irish Affairs, extracted from the collection in the Bodleian, C. McNeill (ed.), Dublin, 1943, 226. For Swanley, M. L. Baumber, 'An East India Captain, The Early Career of Captain Richard Swanley', *MM* 53, 3 (1967), 265-279.

[44]   *CSPD* 1645-7, 160-1. The king was at Denbigh where he met Sir John Owen and Archbishop Williams in September 1645, and it was from Denbigh that Lord Digby wrote to Nicholas: 'I have nothing to add but to tell you in private that whatever face we make towards Anglesey, or discourse we raise of the king's taking ship for Scotland, His Majesty's resolution is with 500 choice horse presently to steal or break through to Newark from whence by God's blessing we make no doubt of joining Montrose'.

[45]   Carte, VI, 330. C. V. Wedgwood, *The King's Peace*, 532-38.

[46]   *CSPD* 1645/7, 174.

[47]   *HMC Ormonde*, I, 101.

[48]   G. Penn, *Memorials of the Professional Life and Times of Sir William Penn*, I, 138-9. Captain (late Sir William) Penn, father of the Quaker who gave his name to Pennsylvania, and Captain William Thomas, Button's nephew, were among the most successful commanders in the fleet of Parliament.

[49]   *HMC Ormonde*, I, 305. The *Jocelyn* was victualled for 59 men. Bod Raw MSS A 223/34; 78.

[50]   *HMC Portland*, I, 315.

[51]   In August 1646 he was 'near Chester River' writing from aboard the *Swan*, giving details of the 'papists' at the Isle of Man, and two years later he was there again, this time after capturing 'two small barks betwixt Carrickfergus Bay and the coast of Scotland'. *HMC Portland*, I, 385, 495. Clarke remained in command of the *Swan* until 1650 and then followed steady promotion to command more powerful naval vessels: the *Reserve*, 1650-3, the *Drake*, 1653, *Bristol*, 1655, *Unicorn*, 1656, *George*, 1657, *Triumph*, 1659, and *Speaker*, 1660, Dr R. C. Anderson's notes, NMM 57/043.

[52]   *CWP* 1719.

[53]   *CSPD* 1645/6. Cttee. of Both Kingdoms to Colonel Mytton, March 11, 1646.

[54]   *CWP* 1771.

[55]   J. E. Griffith, *Pedigrees of Anglesey and Caernarvonshire Families* (1914), 42. Robert Coytmor remained as first Secretary of the Admiralty Committee when the Earl of Warwick's office was taken over by them in 1649. For further details of Coytmor's career, A. Eames, 'Sea Power and

Caernarvonshire' in *TCHS* 1955, 47-50, where extracts from his letters, and sources are given.

[56] *CWP* 1783-1788, 1796.

[57] *CWP* 1788, June 10, 1646.

[58] *CWP* 1789.

[59] *CWP* 1792. Proposition made by the gentry and inhabitants of Anglesey to General Mytton at Llangefni, June 12, 1646.

[60] *CSPD* 1647, 612.

[61] He was still being paid at £11 a month for his packet-boats up to May, 1649. Bod Raw MSS, 224, 56.

[62] *HMC Ormonde*, I, 121, *Tanner Letters*, 223. For details of the contract made between Ormonde and Swart, master of one of these vessels, *HMC Ormonde*, I, 119.

[63] *Tanner Letters*, 228-9.

[64] The arrest of another spy near Flint with secret letters found hidden in his left boot added to the general concern. *ibid.*, 250-53.

[65] A. H. Dodd, *History of Caernarvonshire*, 131-5; A. Eames, 'Sea Power and Caernarvonshire, 1642-1660', *TCHS* 1955, 39-42.

[66] *CWP* 1910. It was alleged in the charges against Lord Bulkeley that he had sent 'one Major Phillips' to 'Charles Steward ... and had it not been for the said Thomas and Richard (Bulkeley) there had been no revolt or War against Parliament in the Isle of Anglesey'.

[67] For letters relating to the events of 1648, *Documents Civil War*, 300-408. The *Swan* sailed from Rainsborough's fleet with a convoy for Dublin three days before the revolt. *ibid.*, 330. One of the grievances of the Navy was that Parliament were suspected of 'a design of introducing land-soldiers into every ship, to master and overawe the seamen'. *ibid.*, 355.

[68] *infra*. Dodd, 'Anglesey in the Civil War', TAAS, 1952, 26-27; B. Dew Roberts, 'Cheadle against Bulkeley', TAAS, 1945, 25-37, *The Island Feud (1947)*.

[69] *CSPD* 1649-50, 30.

[70] NLW Llanfair Brynodol MSS. Griffith Jones to Falkland, 25 Jan. 1642/3. The 'road' referred to was probably St Tudwal's Roads.

[71] NLW Llanfair Brynodol MSS 96; 83-89, 91, 93 all refer to the attempts made by Richard Griffith to release Griffith Jones.

[72] R. C. Anderson, *Lists of English Men of War, 1509-1649* (1959), 18. J. R. Powell (ed.), *The Letters of Robert Blake*, NRS, Vol. LXXVI, and G. Penn, *Memorials of the Professional Life and Times of Sir William Penn* (1833) contain many letters relating to the activities of the fleets in 1649-50. R. C. Anderson, 'The Operations of the English Fleet', 1648-52, *EHR* 31 (1916), 406.

[73] *CSPD*, 1649-50, 175, 209; *Tanner Letters*, 311.

[74] Penn, *Memorials W. Penn*, 1, 288.

[75] *CSPD* 1649-50, 218.

[76] J. Buchan, *Oliver Cromwell* (London, 1934), 336.

[77] T. Carlyle, *'Oliver Cromwell's Letters and Speeches'* (London, 1908), II 35-39.

[78] *ibid.*, 51.

[79] Whitelock, *Memorials, iii,* 160. *CSPD* 1650, 4, 30, 31. Colonel Robinson of Mynachdy, Anglesey, had been given a commission by Ormonde to garrison the island, but when his men landed, Mytton's troops seized them.

[80] *CSPD* 1650, 395, 435, 91-2. *HMC Leybourne Popham*, 78. The *President*, a 26-gun, 220-ton ship had been bought in 1646; after 1650 she was known as the *Old* or *Little President* to distinguish her from the new vessel named *President*, built in 1650. The *Hind* had been bought in 1643, a vessel of between 140 and 200 tons, mounting 13 guns. R. C. Anderson, *List of English Men of War*, 1509-1649, 21, 22.

[81] *CSPD 1651*, 89, 91, 108.

[82] In the month that the Isle of Man surrendered, Bartlett was alleged to have raided the harbour at Carrickfergus, 'taken vessels out of harbour, landed men on shore, and taken men out of their houses'. *Tanner Letters, 342.*

[83] *CSPD* 1651, 124, 318, 307. Bod Raw MSS A 225/104; 226/10.

[84] For lists of ships added to the fleet see R. C. Anderson, *Lists of Men of War, 1649-1702* (NRS Occasional Publications, 5), 1935; Oppenheim, *EHR* XI, 46.

[85] Penn, *Memorials*, 295.

[86] NLW MS 9080E., transcribed E. G. Jones in *TAAS* 1948, 75.

[87] *CSPD* 1649-50, 172.

[88] *CSPD* 1652-3, 26.

[89] PRO ADM 2/1731/70. Orders to Captain Rooth at Milford, 12 March 1659.

[90] NMM WYN 2/2. 9711/2/2.

[91] The *Dartmouth* had been built at Portsmouth in 1655 and the *Oxford* at Deptford in 1656; both were vessels of between 200 and 260 tons, mounting between 23 and 32 guns.

[92] Bod Raw MSS A 225, 149, 127.

[93] Bod Raw MSS A 226, 22.

[94] *CSPD* 1654. Oct. 24, 1654.

[95] In 1628 cotton waistcoats were sold for 3/ each; in 1656 their fixed price was 2s. 2d.; stockings which had been sold at 1/4d. were 10d. per pair, canvas drawers at 1s. 8d., whereas in 1628 cotton breeches were 2/8d. Oppenheim, *Administration of Royal Navy*, 329.

[96] *CSPD* 1655, 527. One of the vessels was 'Capt. Swart in his new frigate of 18 guns' who escaped in the darkness.

[97] *CSPD* 1655, 462.

[98] *CSPD* 1656-7, 67.

[99] Bod Raw MSS A 225, fo. 123, 2 June 1651.

[100] *CSPD* 1656-7, 404.

[101] Oppenheim, *Administration of Royal Navy*, 226.

[102] Penn, *Memorials,* 142.

[103] PRO ADM 2/1729/57. Another Commonwealth naval captain, Bartholomew Yate, of the *Falcon*, pressing men on the north-east coast of England, writing in May 1653, had to confess he had had to let 50 keelmen go 'on account of the mighty clamour of their wives'. *CSPD* 1653, 353.

[104] Bod Raw MSS A 192, 339.

[105] Bod Raw MSS A 192, 341. The writer of this document was clearly conscious that seamen have their own jargon: 'in the darkest nights sometymes when the eye can afford small helpe, then the hearing must supply that defect, which a man that hath not learned ye sea phrases and gibberish can neither understand nor give directions in'.

[106] Meredith Price, cook of the *Nightingale* in 1654, must have been one Welshman in the fleet; he was dismissed his ship as he was 'much given to drink, swearing and railing, and his unhandsome ordering of meat has much disturbed and prejudiced the ship'. *CSPD* 1654, 582.

[107] F. Mathew, *A Mediterranean Passage by Water from London to Bristol* (London, 1670), 7. Vessels driven to take shelter by stress of weather were sometimes welcome at Beaumaris; in 1659 Sir Owen Wynn's agent bought from a Dutch ship laden with Spanish wines for Dublin 'two dozen lemons and two dozen Seville oranges at one shilling per dozen and two pomegranates at 6d. apiece, and 2 pomecitrons at 9d. apiece'. *CWP* 2206.

[108] D. Bowman, *Bristol and America*, a record of the First Settlers, 1654-85, 19.

[109] *CSPD* 1659-60, 353.

[110] PRO SP 29/6/122; SP 29/8/34.

[111] Bod Raw MSS A/224, fo, 56.

[112] PRO SP 29/8/34.

[113] *CSPD* 1660-61, 264. In 1661 Bartlett was paid £458 for the services of the two vessels, 'from the first of October to the 24th June last'. *HMC Ormonde*, III, 415. Swift was still hoping to regain favour, according to Bartlett, who alleged in September 1661 that Swift had sent up his wife 'who was the most wickedest woman against His Majesty and his restoration in the world'. Bartlett hoped to have two vessels built for him by midsummer 1662, but in the meantime had had to hire two vessels from the hated Swift, 'he that signed the petition in north Wales for taking away the king's life', as Bartlett reminded Secretary Nicholas in London. Bartletts's claim for payment was based on the fact that Swift had been paid 'in Oliver's days £500 a year for the same two old vessels which I have hired from him'. *CSP Ireland*, 1660-62, 428.

Legal and Illegal Shipping
1660–1786

Two years after starting his survey of theWelsh coast at Beaumaris in July 1737[1] Lewis Morris, son of Pentre-eiriannell, Penrhosllugwy, poet, scholar, and Searcher to the Customs at Holyhead, was still hopeful of obtaining 'a good sloop of about 30 tons'[2] with a mate and a crew of five men which he required for his marine survey. He wrote to his friend William Vaughan, M.P. for Merioneth, and first President of the Cymmrodorion, not only inviting his support but also suggesting that if his request was granted, Vaughan might like to sail with him to the Isle of Man, Whitehaven and Dublin, as he had set his mind on visiting these ports.[3] His choice reflects the centres to and from which, in addition to Chester and Liverpool (which he had obviously visited), most local trading vessels plied in mid eighteenth-century, ports which were familiar to Anglesey seamen. Despite many frustrations with the 'Amralti', vigorously expressed in his letters over the next few years, Lewis Morris eventually produced his charts and plans of harbours which were much in demand; in the 1760s his brother Richard asked him to send to William Vaughan 'a parcel of your charts of St George's Channel, being often asked for then by shipmasters'.[4] Lewis Morris's 'Observations relating to improvements that might be made in harbours' contain a contemporary description of Anglesey trade which was true for most of the period under discussion in this chapter.

Lewis Morris, possibly deliberately in order to enlist sympathy and support, took a gloomy view of Beaumaris's trade, 'a place of good trade formerly, and might be so still, if the inhabitants pursued it, it being an excellent harbour, well situated and well supplied with the gifts of nature'.[5] Corn, butter, cheese, oysters, mussels, cockles were available in plenty, and at Penmon 'there are several Quarries of Mill-Stones, of the grit kind, of which great Quantities are shipp'd off there'. Red Wharf, where he advocated that a pier should be made under Porthllongdy, was 'a noted place for the Limestone Trade' with 'black and grey Marble in abundance, which bears a good polish'. The sand at Red Wharf was particularly valuable in the days before fertilisers such as guano, 'here is a rich sand for manuring,

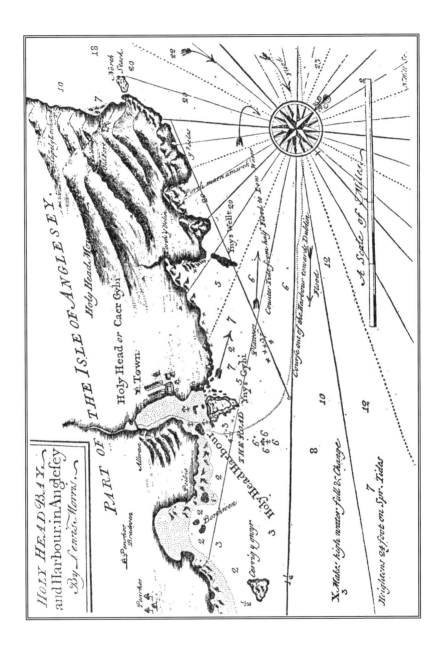

which is carried in small sloops to all parts of Anglesey'. Morris claimed for Red Wharf sand that 'no Manure yields greater crops of Oats and Barley which are the chief natural Commodities of this Island, in general, for Exportation'. Herring 'in plenty', and 'large loose Planks of sound grey marble, thrown out of their beds by the Sea' which would be most suitable, when sawn, as 'fine columns for public buildings' and 'Quarries of Mill-Stones, of the Grit-kind, which are shipp'd off here' were other attractions at Red Wharf. Along the coast, Dulas, where the entrance was narrow, with many 'large loose stones, which makes it dangerous going in and out', was again a 'Place much frequented on Account of the Corn and Butter trade, and Herring fishery': Morris noted here a cargo which appears in the Port Books from time to time, 'upon all this coast they make Fern-ashes, which is sold to Soap boilers, Glass houses, Smelting houses, Refiners, etc.' The small creek of Amlwch, 'no more than a Cove between two steep Rocks', a place of refuge 'provided the Mouth of the Harbour can be discovered, which is now difficult for a Stranger', had some trade in corn, butter and cheese, and Lewis Morris noted that 'here the Liverpoole Pilot-Boats lie afloat, to be ready to meet any Vessels in the Offing', work which they have carried out with distinction ever since. And so Morris went round the coast of the island, favouring Cemlyn as 'a convenient place to make a small Dock, Nature having laid the lines of one ready to our hands', particularly as here again there was, nearby, a quarry of 'the stone *Asbestos*, a beautiful marble'. Holyhead, where Morris himself worked, was obviously given considerable attention: in addition to noting the sailing of the three Packet-Boats, he advocated repairing the harbour and building warehouses 'for the Irish to import their goods that pay English Duty'. Morris anticipated the later development of Holyhead as a harbour of refuge: 'A Pier might be run out to the S.E. from the Salt-house, on the South Point of Salt Island within which large vessels might lie afloat; Also the North Sound, and the Sound of Parry's Island ought to be walled up, which would prevent the swell in the Harbour'. Even without these improvements, Morris noted that in 1747 'there was shipp'd off here of different kind of Grain, Twenty two thousand Bushels'. In addition to supplies such as butter, cheese, bacon, 'Wild Fowl in abundance', and fish, Morris recorded that much profit was made from burning 'a Plant growing on the Sea Rocks, called by the natives *Gwymmon* . . . into a kind of salt, called kelp; one of the Ingredients in making Glass, and used also in Allum works'. The two small ports of Aberffraw and Malltraeth were used by coasting sloops to load corn, butter, cheese, fish. Lewis Morris, in concluding his survey, drew attention to the changes in the cattle trade since Lewis Roberts's day and the suitability of Anglesey beef for victualling 'ships for long voyages'.

> '*Roberts*, in his Map of Commerce, published about One Hundred Years ago, says, that *Anglesey* sent then to the *English* Markets about Three Thousand Head of Cattle yearly. But they have improved so much in Husbandry, since his Time, that they amount now to about Fifteen Thousand; besides, at least Five Thousand Hogs, and a great Number of Sheep: And after the Fairs are over yearly, it is computed that the Stock of the Island is at least Thirty Thousand Head of Cattle.
>
> The Beef of this Island is found more solid and sweet than that feeding on Ranker Grass, and it is probable would be found in the End to be cheaper to victual Ships for long Voyages, than more flabby Meat, which is subject to be destroyed by Salt, and to shrink in the Boiling'.[6]

It is significant that whilst he mentioned the export of 'Four Million One Hundred Thousand' slates annually from Caernarvon, Morris does not consider the export of slates from the Caernarvonshire shores at the Bangor entrance to the Strait, at Abercegin or Aberogwen, worthy of mention. Prophetically anticipating tragedies such as the loss of H.M.S. *Conway* some two hundred years later, Morris warned that the passage of the Swelly, 'called by the Welsh, Pwll Keris, a name borrow'd (it is likely) from the Roman Charybdis', should not be 'meddled with but at slack Tide . . . this nick of Time must be carefully observ'd by large Ships, taking the advantage of a fair wind, and a good Pilot'. Whilst he recognized the possibility of building a bridge across the Strait near the Swelly rocks, Morris's main concern was that 'a better Passage for Ships' should be made there by blowing up rocks and widening the channel, 'which would be of infinite Service to the Trade of Cheshire, Lancashire,

Cumberland, Scotland, Ireland and Wales, as is well known to the Inhabitants of these Maritime Parts'. The Menai Strait, in Morris's view, was 'but one continued Harbour, where Thousands of Vessels may lie secure'.

By mid eighteenth-century, Anglesey's export trade, therefore, was largely agricultural produce and stone, carried in small sloops from a number of places which were hardly more sheltered than open beaches. It had changed little in a hundred years and more, except that as the demand for agricultural produce and slate from the Strait increased, so did the number of sloops. Before the end of the eighteenth-century it is not easy to say how many there were of these vessels. Professor Ralph Davies has warned that the pathway through the shipping statistics of the seventeenth and eighteenth centuries is slippery, and often misleading,[7] and R. C. Jarvis has indicated the need to understand the reasons for, and the background to, the statistics collected in the eighteenth-century.[8] With all their limitations, and having due regard to the distortions in the recording in the war years, both Davies and Jarvis have used the tables known as 'Dalley's Tables',[9] prepared by J. Dalley for the Registration of shipping to show the tonnage of the ports of England and Wales 1709-1782; the statistics for Beaumaris, reproduced in Appendix III, follow the general trend. Here, as elsewhere, the acceleration in the growth of the shipping industry was particularly noticeable in the years from the mid eighteenth-century to the outbreak of the American War of Independence when the figures were again distorted by war-time conditions. The 1786 Act, which required the careful recording of details relating to all ships belonging to a port, naturally provided more accurate local records: by 1787 it is possible to see how Beaumaris ranked in relation to the other Welsh ports. Ports were put in order according to their total tonnage; in this national rating in which, naturally enough, London, Newcastle, Liverpool and Whitehaven led the way, Beaumaris was easily the first of the Welsh ports, fourteenth in the national rating; Cardigan was twenty-third, Swansea twenty-fifth, Milford thirtieth, Aberystwyth thirty-eighth, Chester forty-ninth, and Cardiff sixty-sixth.[10] It should be remembered that 'Beaumaris' at this time included virtually all the north Wales ports from Barmouth, apart from a few creeks near Chester, but nevertheless this does indicate how north Wales shipping had developed within the late seventeenth and the early eighteenth centuries. In 1787 Beaumaris was said to have 191 vessels registered under 50 tons, 70 between 50 and 100 tons, 9 between 200 and 300 tons, and one over 300 tons.[11] Two years later Beaumaris had a total of 298 ships belonging to the port, 207 under 50 tons, 82 between 50 and 100 tons, and nine over 200 tons. The number of seamen, 'usually on board when in actual employment', estimated to belong to the port, amounted to nine hundred and sixty-three.[12] From the evidence of the Custom House Register Books it is evident that a very large number both of vessels and men belonged to Caernarvon, Pwllheli and Barmouth, but the Anglesey ports, and particularly the Menai Strait, were frequently visited by ships from the other ports under Beaumaris's jurisdiction, and they were part of Anglesey's maritime tradition.

To give some brief indication of the nature of Anglesey's trade, it is necessary to look in more detail at the inward and outward cargoes for representative years. In the 1680s trade had seen some twenty years of development since the Restoration, and Anglesey's maritime community had no doubt already felt the benefit of the five-fold increase in Liverpool's coasting trade during this period.[13] The import of salt and earthenware from Liverpool and coal from Chester and the export of agricultural produce and fish from Anglesey had been undertaken by ships from Chester, Liverpool, Whitehaven, Dublin and Anglesey itself. The Port Books for coastwise trade for Beaumaris from Xmas 1680 to Xmas 1681 record forty-eight different inward cargoes to Beaumaris, in eighteen different vessels, ships from Lancaster, Chester, Greenfield, Mostyn and some obvious Anglesey vessels such as the *Hopeful Bettie* of Holyhead.[14] Nine cargoes entered Holyhead itself: the vessels came from Chester, Conway, Greenfield, Mostyn and Dublin. There were thirty-one outward cargoes coastwise, almost all for Chester, many of them slate cargoes and therefore from the Caernarvonshire shore; the *Hopeful Bettie*, for example, took 20,000 slates on the 10th August for Chester. One of the busiest vessels was the *Wheel of Fortune* of Chester, which brought miscellaneous cargo from Chester to Beaumaris, including 4 tons of iron, hardware, hops, tobacco, starch, one trunk of books, 40 tanned hides, window glass, vinegar, glass bottles in an April cargo, then more tobacco, four dozen frying pans, four dozen hand bellows, 300 tanned hides, four boxes of tobacco pipes, two boxes 'apothecar ware' and one parcel 'linen paper' in July, and two more miscellaneous cargoes including gunpowder, iron and sack in August and November. On her return voyage, the *Wheel of Fortune* took 40,000 slates, corn, skins, barley, rye, malt, household goods, a 'parcell of matting', bacon, and herrings.[15] In the following year, 1682-3, Chester imported five cargoes in the *Wheel of Fortune* alone, whilst a number of small vessels like the *Austin of Portinlleyne* which took 4,000 red herring, the *Margaret* of 'Delas', which took 12 barrels of herrings, cheese and butter, and the *Speedwell* of Caernarvon with a cargo of slate, also brought cargoes to Chester. During the same period the *John and Margaret* of Chester, the *Blessing* of Mostyn, the *Dolphin* of Beaumaris, *Peter* of Beaumaris, *Mary* of Greenfield, *Wheel of Fortune*, *Mayflower* of Chester, *Nightingale* of Liverpool, *Abraham* of Dublin, *Hopwell* of Coleraine, were among the vessels which took sixty-eight cargoes, most of them coal, for Beaumaris, not including those for Barmouth and Caernarvon. The overseas trade of Beaumaris was largely with Ireland:[16] at the turn of the year 1680-81, for example, the *Assistance* of Whitehaven brought 58 Irish cattle and 85 sheep from Dublin. In the month of January 263 cattle, 288 sheep, and 2 'nags' were imported, whilst the *Wheel of Fortune* was one of the eight vessels that took 158,000 slates to Dublin during 1680-81. Holyhead also received vessels transporting 'nags', one or two at a time, whilst in 1683 Beaumaris imported six bullocks 'of the groathe of said Island' from the Isle of Man in the *Royal Charles* of Ramsey.[17] The Cattle Acts passed in the 1660s to eliminate Irish cattle imports did not become effective until the 1680s; after 1681 these cattle imports diminished considerably. The pattern of importing salt from Liverpool and coal from Chester continued: sixty-nine cargoes of coal were taken to Beaumaris in 1682-3, and twelve for Caernarvon in the same period. The tonnage of the vessels engaged in the trade is not available, but the nature and size of the cargoes suggest that they were, for the most part, small local vessels whose sailing was confined to the Liverpool and Chester trades.

Many of the Beaumaris Port Books for the early eighteenth-century are missing, but fortunately the record kept by a Customs Official for his own use from July 1729 to December 1730 has survived.[18] During this eighteen month period 226 cargoes were imported into or exported from Beaumaris; 285 to and from Caernarvon, and 88 to and from Holyhead. The average tonnage of the vessels involved in this trade was a little over fifteen tons.[19] The portrait of Anglesey's trade that emerges is of a wider range of cargoes being imported, with the export trade remaining largely agricultural produce, stone, and slate from Caernarvonshire. Much of the trade was carried out in small local vessels like the *Golden Apple* of Red Wharf, 14 tons with a crew of 2 men, the *Hopewell* of Amlwch, 16 tons, 2 men, the *Mary* of Holyhead, 20 tons, 4 men, the *Fox* of Dulas, 12 tons, 2 men, and the *Betty* of Cemais, 15 tons and a crew of 2. These small vessels carried a variety of cargoes, largely from and for Liverpool and Chester; in July 1729, for example, the *Golden Apple*, with Owen Davies as master, brought a box of tallow candles and empty glasses from Liverpool and 36 bushels of salt, and two days later the *Hopewell* of Amlwch, William Petters master, brought 2 casks of wine, tobacco, 20 fir planks and molasses, also from Liverpool. The *Squeril* of Beaumaris brought two cargoes in the same month, one of coal and paving stones, and the other of coal and crates of earthenware. In August the *Golden Apple* took 15 'peggets' of oats to Liverpool, and the *Friendship* of Dumfries, a small vessel of 20 tons with a crew of three, which had come from Dublin, took 20,000 slates to Dumfries, one of three vessels from Dumfries which took 52,000 slates there between July and December 1729. In October fourteen vessels brought cargoes which included wine, tobacco, salt, bricks, window glass, allum, cloves, household goods, '1 old Bedd and Bedstead', coal, empty casks, leather, 'Irish sope'; the exports in the same month consisted of slates, barley and '29 boxes and trunks wearing apparel', the latter cargo being taken by the *Bullshead* of Beaumaris. Predictably, July and August were the busiest months, November the quietest; twenty-one vessels were at Beaumaris in July 1729, only six in November. Occasionally a larger vessel arrived to disturb the routine visits of small local sloops: in May 1730, the *Unicorn* of Woodbridge, a 50-ton vessel with a crew of seven, which took a cargo of 450 quarters of corn to London from Beaumaris, and two months earlier the *Kent* of Ramsgate, 60 tons, seven men in the crew which embarked 800 'peggets' of oats for London, also from Beaumaris.

The export of agricultural produce naturally varied according to the success or failure of crops, but the slate trade continued uninterrupted in the early part of the eighteenth-century, and the late David Thomas calculated that 3,612,000 slates were exported from the Menai Strait in the eighteen-month period recorded by this unknown Customs official,[20] two hundred and ten shipments, mainly to Ireland and to the Chester area; the great demand from Liverpool came later. Anglesey itself was receiving slate across the Strait in small vessels like the *Garth Boat*, the *Glane i Gallon* and the *Cymwynas*, unusual in having Welsh names, even if one was misspelt.

The eighteenth-century saw much building work on the Anglesey estates of the wealthy: timber came by sea to Cemais for the Meyrick rebuilding at Nanner, near Cemlyn, and by a Liverpool flat for the Bodorgan mansion of Owen Putland Meyrick.[21] Timber also came to Cemais for Edward Wynne's building operations at Bodewryd; there were others, the Pantons' house, Plas Gwyn, Pentraeth, and Carreglwyd near Llanfachreth for the Griffith family.[22] They all needed slate, and the slate, like so much of the timber and the stone, came by sea. Among the busiest of the slate boats was the *Blessing* of Beaumaris whose master for some of her voyages was unusual in that he is described as 'Robert Pritchard, Poet',[23] it is likely that he was the 'Robert Pritchard of Pentraeth, Anglesey', who in 1738 wrote a long religious poem which was included in 'Blodeu-gerdd Cymry', published in 1759.[24]

Although these vessels of the eighteenth-century were small, it must be remembered that they were being increasingly used not only to transport slate or agricultural products, but also for importing furniture such as the 'great chair' for which Elizabeth Morgan paid 'to the sailor for carriage' soon after her arrival at Henblas in 1733.[25] Everyday tools and equipment also came by sea: William Bulkeley went in November 1734 to Cemais to the 'boat with timber' that had arrived there, and bought spades, shovels, 'thirteen Joyces about 6 foot long for 7d. a piece', 'ten plough bearers' and other timber for agricultural implements.[26] The Welsh Bibles which were despatched by the S.P.C.K. for distribution in Anglesey came by ship to Caernarvon in 1755,[27] and the Morris letters abound in references to goods being sent by sea to London, Liverpool and Chester from

Holyhead. In the 1720s, when the curate of Bodewryd reported to Chancellor Edward Wynne at Hereford regarding the latter's affairs in Anglesey, he gave an account of coal and timber delivered at Cemais.[28] In the same letter he gave a shocked account of an all too familiar occurrence, the anger of the poorer inhabitants of the island at the exportation of corn in times of near famine. Apparently the mob had refused to allow corn to be shipped at Beaumaris, and 'all ye town Women flocked together and hurraed' their leaders: 'They were well armed with stones and broken glasses yt one of 'em hitt Jack Hughes of Glan yr Afon upon ye Head yt he bled very much'. After a chase in which he 'pursued ye Jade' a number of the crowd were captured and the riot quelled. The sea could be the means of bringing goods that were welcome, but it could also take away essentials in time of need; this proved a source of social unrest throughout the years. On such occasions the islanders were very conscious of the role of the sea in their life.

Wars brought back fears of invasion, and the sea was regarded with apprehension. The presence of many men-of-war at the time William III was in Ireland must have been viewed with mixed feelings by a community who had seen trade develop slowly but steadily, and were now threatened not only by the enemy's privateers, but also by the dreaded 'press' which took so many seamen away from the coastal trade. Long shadows have been cast by the events of 1689 and 1690 in Ireland, when the Protestant north stood firm for William of Orange against the exiled James II, newly landed and supported by the Catholic provinces. Most of the inhabitants of Holyhead doubtless felt more secure in 1690 when the *Monk*, commanded by Sir Cloudesley Shovell, one of the great seamen of the age, sailed into the Bay.[29] The *Monk* and the *St Alban's* did not stay long, but their presence was a counter to the alarm caused by the yacht reported to run 'almost every week over to the Welsh coast for news, and carries intelligence back to Dublin', putting in 'for the most part to a place called Scallocks, near Holyhead'. This was the vessel which was reported as 'an armed Ketch' commanded by the son of 'a man named Thomson living at Armshead (Ormeshead) between Chester and Beaumaris to whose house letters are sent by those who are in correspondence with the enemy in Ireland'.[30] Apparently the younger Thomson sailed every week with this correspondence, thus maintaining communications for the Stuart sympathisers on both sides of the Irish Sea. William's victory at the Battle of the Boyne relieved the Protestant fears, but although the British naval victories at Harfleur, Cherbourg and La Hogue dispelled the fears of a French invasion, the French 'guerre de course' continued and vessels off Anglesey in 1693 were on their guard for the eleven French privateers reported to be waiting for the ships going to Chester Fair. The depredations continued spasmodically; in July 1696 four small vessels arrived at Dublin, 'three from Liverpool laden with salt and one from Mostyn with coal, who the day before were taken by a French privateer near Holyhead, but were ransomed again'.[31] In 1703 the *Primrose*, carrying the first cargo of pig lead shipped for London from Flintshire, was captured by a French privateer as she came 'out of Bleau Morris, with another vessel in company, ye convoy being at some distance before them'.[32] It was alleged that increased insurance rates and delays in waiting for convoys adversely affected the development of the trade of the London Lead Company's mines in Flintshire.

When Lewis Morris was engaged in his survey of the coast nearly forty years later, war was again in the air, and, like his brother John before him, Lewis Morris had ideas of a naval career once his survey was complete: 'I want to be upon my watch if a french war comes, to consider timely of another post, for this business will then be at an end, and suppose I applyd for a Birth aboard a Cruizing Man of War in ye Channel?'[33] In the event Lewis was shrewd enough not to serve in the Navy, and so outlived his relatives who did. Both Welsh literature and the survey of the coast benefited. But the letters of the Morris brothers reflect the concern regarding privateers and their effect upon Anglesey's trade; twenty years later, during the Seven Years War, William Morris at Holyhead wrote to Lewis reporting the presence of a French privateer of eighteen guns taking ships on the Menai coast, and frightening the 'old women' among his neighbours.[34] Naturally enough, these privateers in northern waters were not as numerous as those in the English Channel, and the long wars with France which had started in 1689 had had the effect of encouraging the transatlantic tobacco and sugar ships to discharge their cargoes in the ports of the north-west, away from the main haunts of the privateers. Whilst the growth in the shipping of

Liverpool and the Clyde continued unabated following this initial impetus, the wars brought considerable temporary activity to other north-western ports, including Beaumaris and Holyhead. William Morris had reason to be grateful for the tobacco and sugar ships.[35]

The advent of 'foreign' ships coincided with increased activity in the coastal trade, and by 1770 there were over twenty vessels engaged in the transport of copper ore from the as yet undivided Parys Mountain estate. Between March 1771 and 1772, 2,475 tons of copper ore were taken from Amlwch for the Warrington Copper and Brass Company, the cargoes ranging from 16 tons in the *Seahorse* to 70 in the *William and James*, and in the years 1769-1772 vessels belonging to Beaumaris, Pwllheli, Caernarvon, Aberystwyth, Aberdovey, Cemais, Cemlyn, Dulas, Liverpool, Conway and Amlwch itself were engaged in the trade.[36] The stage was set for Thomas Williams, Llanidan. The slate trade, in decline since the 1740s, awaited the new owner of the Penrhyn estate who was to change all this in the 1780s, but there were many little slate vessels that sailed from the Menai Strait, and the evidence is that new ones were being built to join the fleet each year. A very faded and battered account book (almost undecipherable because of the writer's habit of crossing out items once they had been completed, and also writing across in the current fashion to save paper space) records the activities of some of these slate vessels.[37] The sloop *William and Mary*, John Edwards, master, on her first voyage in July 1781, took slates to Gosport, whilst the sloop *Aurora* took slates to London in March 1783, and to Chester in 1784. In 1782 Captain John Williams, master of the *Aurora*, was receiving 28s. per month in wages, but this was later increased to 32s. during the same year, and his crew were paid 30s., 20s., and 15s. per month. Also recorded are the advance payments made at different ports from which the ports of call on the voyages can be traced. Gruffydd Jones, the boy who sailed in the *William and Mary* on her maiden voyage, was paid at the rate of 15s. per month, and was given an advance of 10d. at Pwllheli, 2d. at 'Milfort', 4s. for shoes, 'am scidia' – either at Milford or Portsmouth, 6d. at Portsmouth, 3s. 8d. at London, 2s. 3d. at 'Dofar', and then he left the ship. The balance of his wages were received and signed for by his grandfather when the *William and Mary* returned to the Strait.

By the 1780s the shipping off Anglesey had increased both in the tonnage of individual vessels and in numbers. The dramatic development of Liverpool during the preceding forty years meant that not only were there vessels sailing past Anglesey to thriving Liverpool, but to the meet the needs of this ever-expanding town and its hinterland there were Anglesey vessels carrying cargoes which Lewis Morris had described, agricultural produce and building materials. Copper and slate were soon to be exported to an extent beyond Morris's wildest dreams. This, then, was the legal trade, but as with all coastal communities, there was an illegal trade, which engaged the attention of some of the inhabitants of Anglesey.

The eighteenth-century has long been recognized as the age of smuggling, and much romantic fiction has been based upon what in reality was bitter, unromantic and unpleasant. Since the thirteenth-century representatives of the Crown had been appointed to collect customs duties on both coastwise and foreign trade, but the late seventeenth and the eighteenth-century wars accentuated the problem; not only was trade with France supposed to be stopped, but the highly protective duties imposed in peacetime to meet national expenditure encouraged all sections of the community to break the law and avoid high prices by black market dealings with smugglers on an unprecedented scale. Additional duties were levied on a wide range of goods, and the rates and duties on various goods changed so frequently that even the honest master of a ship was so confused by them that he might unwittingly break the law. Towards the end of the seventeenth-century, moreover, the more widespread adoption of the fore and aft rig in place of the square rig had enabled ships to sail much closer to the wind, and coastal ships were so designed that they were able to sail faster and were more manoeuvrable. There was therefore 'a great financial inducement to smuggle and also a means to do it easily'.[38] Collusion between customs officers and the smugglers was not unknown; luxury goods, small in bulk in proportion to their value, such as brandy, fine lace and linen were much in demand, but more commonplace commodities such as tea and salt were subject to such high duties that they were smuggled into the country in large quantities. Where the stakes were high, men were willing to risk violence in an age of violence; the Act of 1736 authorised the death penalty for dangerously wounding a Customs or Excise Officer, or for hindering them in the execution of their duties by force of arms. This was the Act which authorised a wide range of punishment for offences such as assisting smugglers, signalling to them or in any way defrauding the law, whilst at the same time authorizing rewards to 'informers' in the form of free pardons and money payments.

Inevitably the English Channel afforded smugglers their greatest opportunities because of its very proximity to the Continent, the shortness of the passage by sea, and its nearness to the great city of London, the haven for so many criminals.[39] There were disadvantages on the South Coast. The ports and coastline were carefully watched for the landing of French spies or potential invaders, and by mid-century many smugglers preferred to 'break Bulk' on approaching the Channel and transferred their smuggled goods to smaller vessels which could find some more deserted and less carefully guarded strip of coast. Whilst smuggling was practised throughout the eighteenth-century in the St George's Channel and the Irish Sea, it was probably in mid-century that it was at its height. Until 1765 the Isle of Man was constitutionally independent of the English Crown;[40] it was privately owned and not subject to the Customs duties or laws of England. As taxes on the mainland increased under the pressure of continental wars, so the Isle of Man became more and more popular as a storehouse for high duty goods, tobacco, rum, brandy and gin, in particular, which were distributed as convenient to the mainland. All the smugglers had to do was to wait for their opportunity for sailing with a favourable wind, making preferably for a quiet strip of beach. One has only to look at a chart to recognize how suitable Anglesey and the north Wales coast were for the smugglers' purposes, coming from the Isle of Man or Ireland, as indeed the pirates of the sixteenth and seventeenth centuries had done before them. On 30 April 1765, the Isle of Man was purchased with £70,000 of Customs money, and became subject to the same laws as the rest of England and Wales. The letters which had passed between the Collector of Customs at Beaumaris and the Board of Commissioners of Customs between January 1763 and March 1767 are, therefore, of considerable interest, and form the main source for the paragraphs which follow.[41]

The letters tell the story of smuggling as seen through the eyes of those who tried to prevent it: the Collector, in charge of the port, a post of considerable antiquity and ever-increasing complexity; the Comptroller, who although otherwise subordinate to the Collector, had joint responsibility with him for the cash and accounts of the port; the preventive service afloat; the Commanders of the Revenue cruisers who had to battle against both the smugglers and the elements, for the smugglers often operated in foul weather hoping to evade detection; and finally the shore-based Tide-Surveyors, Tide-Waiters, Land-Surveyors and Land-Waiters, the riding officers and the boatmen. Captain William Gambold, master of the Revenue cutter *Pelham*, based for most of this time at Beaumaris, outlined in a letter to the Board of Commissioners in May 1763 some of the problems which confronted him and his men.[42] He alleged that the smugglers got passage to the Isle of Man from Liverpool 'or the first place they can find boats bound there'; at the Isle of Man, 'several of the smugglers joyn together and hire an Irish wherry of thirty or forty tons with 9 or 10 hands on board, in which they bring over their prohibited goods, and do not come near the shore till about twelve o'clock at night'. Once they approached a beach, they had rapid co-operation from the dwellers ashore: 'in less than an hour's time (they) will land and carry the whole cargo into the country, as there are several farmers concern'd with them, which have their carts and horses ready for that purpose'. Gambold stated that some of the Irish vessels which plied between the Isle of Man and the Welsh coast were not engaged in any trade but smuggling, and were built 'slight and sharp' so that they were 'remarkable fast sailers'. Moreover, when his Revenue cutter approached the places where he suspected the smugglers were landing their goods, 'the smugglers on shore make fire on the hills for a signal to the wherrys that we are on that coast, so that they may avoide us'.

Gambold felt that the only way to intercept the smugglers was to 'man our own Boat with ten or eleven hands, and surprise them in the Night, when they are going to land their cargo'. The undermanning of his cutter prevented his being able to do this, for 'our whole crew consists but of ten hands Including a Boy'; Gambold requested that he should be allowed four additional men, 'which will enable me to man the Boat properly, and be able to work the Cutter at the same time, by which method I hope to be able to make very considerable seizures, which cannot be done without a proper number of hands'. The Revenue cutters were fast, they were free of the legal limitations regarding the length of bowsprit, and they had a good spread of canvas, but this called for a fairly large crew of good seamen. Whether Gambold received the additional hands is not clear from Custom House records, but when the *Pelham* was caulked, graved and painted, and therefore unable to be on her station, provision was made to guard the coast: 'during the time the Cutter was under Repairs we sent both her Boats along the coast, the Commander in one and the Mate in the other, in this case we were oblig'd to hire three additional hands to man the Boats properly'. The refit of the *Pelham* was long overdue, for Captain Gambold had complained that she had 'become very leaky Especially in her upper works and decks, so that the Mariners do not lye dry in their Beds, therefore he prays your Honrs order to have her thoroughly overhall'd, graved and painted'.[43] Although originally the intention was to have the *Pelham* refitted at Liverpool, it was decided a month later, in May, to carry out the repairs locally in Anglesey.[44]

It was as well for Captain Gambold and the crew of the Pelham that she had received this refit, for in October she ran into very heavy weather. Gambold described how, 'being apprehensive of a Hard Gale coming', he took the *Pelham* 'into Amlough Creek' where he moored her 'in the best manner he was able, to prevent her being drove on the rocks'. Although she was safe enough at first, 'the wind being N.N.E. occasioned a very great sea to come in, which stove the Cutter's Boat to pieces, broke the cutter's bowsprit, the pall of the windlass, several handspikes and both the Cutter's Leggs (or shores)'. Gambold reported that it was with very great difficulty that they saved the *Pelham* from being driven on to the rocks.

On another occasion, a couple of weeks before Christmas, 1764, Gambold had left Moelfre Bay about eleven o'clock at night bound for Liverpool when 'it came to blow very hard and thick weather at W.S.W.'[45] As an experienced seaman Gambold took all the steps necessary, reefing and reducing sail, but the gale worsened, 'by this time the sea run so very high, and ship'd so many seas that we could hardly keep her free with our Pump', and he eventually decided 'to wear ship and stand inshore in the hopes of smooth water'. As visibility improved he realised he was 'about a league to leeward of the Ormes head', and after vainly trying to stand out to sea again, he decided in view of the 'most violent gale' that it was 'high time of saving our lives if possible by fetching this bay which we did with the utmost difficulty, and come to an anchor half past three in the evening'. His next decision was a difficult one; after 'putting the vessel in the best condition we could to ride out the gale, the night coming on, and fearing that the wind would come to the northward, we resolved to get out the boat and venture in her to try for the shore'. The wind was too strong for them to pull to windward and they were forced to run the boat on to the beach 'where there was a very great surfe', and the boat filled and was smashed to pieces, two of the crew being drowned. When morning came Gambold must have had mixed and troubled feelings as he saw the *Pelham* riding safely to her anchors, and trudged back wearily to Tŷ Gwyn, nestling under the Great Orme, to write to the Collector at Beaumaris asking one of the other Revenue cutters to bring replacements for crew and sails, and sadly counted the cost of the previous twenty-four hours.

The commander of a Revenue cutted had other problems, though, besides decisions taken in adverse weather conditions. In the spring of 1765, Gambold was taken to task for not 'seizing the Manx boat, out of which he took a considerable quantity of prohibited goods'. Gambold argued that he had seen two other vessels 'coming from the Isle of Man and standing for the Welsh coast having the looks of smugglers', and he could not afford to put any of his men on board the first vessel to take her as a prize as he wished to come up to the other vessels. Gambold had claimed two years previously that 'the nine or ten men belonging to the Wherrys are exclusive of the Smugglers that hire them, so that when they come on this coast they are frequently sixteen or twenty men on board', and the Collector at Beaumaris urged that Gambold should have a larger crew, particularly as savings could be made by cutting down allowances when the *Pelham* was at Beaumaris, for 'as she is stationed at this port all the men on board who have Familys, reside in the town'. Moreover, 'in order to keep the Commander constantly cruizing on the coast', the Collector proposed the cutter was to be allowed no provision money at Beaumaris 'except the Day she sails and the day she arrives'.[46] The usual allowance given if a smuggler was seized was ten shillings a ton; Gambold claimed this allowance for seizing the 'William and Mary cutter for importing brandy from the Isle of Man' in 1765. Occasionally there were disputes when two or more Revenue cutters were working in the same area: in 1763 Captain Robertson of the *Lord Howe* asked Beaumaris officials for a ruling 'in case the *Pelham* cutter or any other cutter sho'd be in sight when he makes a seizure, are the crew on board such a cutter to have a share of the seizure'?[47]

Another cause for appeals was the dispute regarding the distance from the shore the suspected smuggled goods were seized. A little before dawn on 12 May 1765, Gambold and the crew of the *Pelham* sighted 'a boat with her sails down, lying Hull to within two leagues of the Skerries Island on which stand the Skerryes Light House in St George's Channel'. On sighting the vessel, Gambold ordered that the cutter's boat should be lowered, 'and that the mate and six men should go in pursuit of her'. The crew of the *Pelham* later testified that they saw 'the said boat hoist sails and at the same time make use of their oars standing a N.N.E. course towards the Isle of Man'. After a chase of over three hours, in which both the cutter and the boat she had lowered took part, the stranger was boarded, 'where we found her laden with thirty half anchor casks of Brandy, two casks with wine in them 846*li* Tea 224*l* of liquorice, and 40*l* Tobacco'. The crew of the *Pelham*, in evidence, claimed that the 'Master and hands on board the Boat declared that they came the Day before about 10 o'clock from the Isle of Man with the above goods, and would have smugl'd them on the coast of Anglesey the same night, but the wind died away so that they could not reach the shore before daylight'. John Hinds told them that he was 'their pilote to bring them on the coast of Wales, for which he received one Guinea besides the privilege of carrying a small venture of Tea' which was found on board by the *Pelham*'s crew and pointed out that 'Skerries Island on which stands a Lighthouse is about one mile from the Anglesey shore, in the port of Holyhead where duty is paid for coal landed at Skerries'.[48]

Although the Isle of Man, chief base for the smugglers, came under the jurisdiction of the Crown after its purchase in April 1765, there were still some vessels with tempting cargoes aboard off the Anglesey coast in the following year. Captain Robertson of the *Lord Howe* seized three hundred and fourteen gallons of brandy in small casks in the brig *Nicholas* in May 1766, and 'in another vessel loaded with Chees from Chester bound to London ten gallons Brandy'.[49] In the following month Captain Gambold requested that the *Pelham* should have a major refit as her hull and standing rigging were over ten years old, and she required sails, ropes and repainting before the next winter. By implication, Gambold's letter underlines the fact that he felt the danger from the Isle of Man was over, for he stated his cutter could be best spared in the spring when the hours of darkness were few, 'as the Chief smugling on the coast is either from Guernsey or France, and the smuglers do not choose to run the risque of coming through the Channel these short nights'. In the closing decades of the eighteenth-century and at the beginning of the nineteenth-century, Lawrence Banks, an agent for the Carteret Priaulx family of Guernsey, admitted that he was spending '£400 a year to keep things as quiet as possible' for smuggling goods on the north Wales coast, and in 1804 one of the Carteret Priaulx captains, John Phillips, in the Fowey cutter *Lion*, was stated by Banks, writing from Caernarvon, to have been chased up and down the Welsh coast by the Revenue cruiser *Speedwell* of Milford.[50] Other smugglers from the Isle of Man moved, after its purchase by the Crown, to north-east Ireland, and it was the many Port Rush smugglers who maintained links with France, particularly with such convenient smuggling markets as Belle Île, Lorient, and Roscoff. Captain Gambold took the *Pelham* to London for her refit in 1766, but in 1770 she was captured in Beaumaris Bay by one of the Rush smugglers, John Connor, nicknamed Jack the Batchelor, who, after plundering the *Pelham*, ran her on the rocks at St David's.[51] Connor then settled at Roscoff where he continued to organize smuggling to Ireland and Britain; in the late 70s the Collector at Carlisle alleged that there were at least fifty large smuggling vessels sailing out of Port Rush. As far as Anglesey was concerned, however, these larger Irish vessels do not appear to have frequented the Welsh coast as much as the earlier Manx smugglers, which were, of course, smaller and probably made the voyage to the isolated beaches and back to the Isle of Man in a very short time. When they did, as in the case of the *Pelham* in 1770, they were too strong to be tackled by a single small Revenue cutter. Indeed, it would seem that the Beaumaris officers had had a premonition of the fate of the *Pelham*, for in the previous year, 1769, they had pointed out to the Board that 'the present mode of smugling is quite different to what it was before the Isle of Man was sold to the Crown, for the vessels now made use of are much larger and a much greater number of men, which renders the Pelham cutter unfit for this Station, being too small and her crew only ten in all are too few very unequal to attack one of the present smuglers'. The Collector and his colleagues at Beaumaris suggested that a seventy ton vessel which had been built two years previously at Rhuddlan 'for the smugling trade' and since seized at Whitehaven, should be put on the Beaumaris station, with Captain Gambold, who was 'well acquainted with this coast and done good service to the Revenue', in command of her, manned by twenty mariners. One reason for their obvious alarm was that on that very day they had had reports of a vessel off Amlwch sailing 'towards Orms Head reported to be loaded with Prohibited goods and has got a false Boltsprit and appears like a sloop when sailing in daytime but her real boltsprit is to be seen under that'. Gambold in the *Pelham* had put to sea, but Lieutenant Cross, commander of the *Hornet*, was not aboard to join in the search, and when the *Pelham* anchored in Moelfre Bay, Gambold had already decided that the smuggler was too powerful for him to tackle alone. The weather deteriorated, and when eventually the *Hornet* and the *Pelham* sailed in pursuit, keeping company all day and night, they failed to find their quarry, described as 'a cutter Deep wasted and a great number of men seen on board'. The *Hornet* returned to Beaumaris and the *Pelham* 'cruized along shore to Holyhead' as the news was that one of the smugglers' agents was at Amlwch arranging for the disposal of the goods of another vessel due to arrive shortly.[52]

Although there were smugglers who had the confidence to land their goods in the Menai Strait area under the noses of the officials at Beaumaris, and Bangor was described in 1757 as a 'great thoroughfair for smuglers', there is reason to believe that many preferred not to risk the hazards of the Lavan Sands and Caernarvon Bar, making instead for places like Moelfre and Amlwch where there was plenty of sea room. In 1765, when replacing the 'boatman at Traethbuchan', the Collector pointed out 'that there is no boat at or near Traethbuchan, this officer's business is to act as waiter and searcher and coal meter and prevent smuggling', and as 'there are three creeks in his district that several small vessels frequent', it was the opinion of the local Customs officers that he should be allowed 'ten pounds a year additional salary towards keep a Horse, and oblige him to keep a journal'.[53] Occasionally there came an opportunity to gain a reward: Owen Owens 'Boatman at Traith Bach' seized an open boat called the *Speedwell* for importing eight gallons brandy and eight gallons Geneva from the Isle of Man' on 23 May 1763; the *Speedwell* was eventually burnt and her 'small boat Tackle and Furniture all sold and accounted for in the Midsummer Quarter 1764', and, as she was said to be eighteen tons burthen, Owen Owens claimed 'the usual allowance of Ten shillings per Ton for his service in seizing the said vessel'.[54]

The officers based ashore had a difficult task for they had to cover much territory; in 1714 an attempt had been made to allocate districts to the riding officers: one at Dulas to patrol the coast 'from the Sound to Dulas, 11 miles'; another 'from Dulas to Cemmaes 10 miles, and to keep a Journal and to reside at Amblwch', another to reside at Cemlyn, 'and his station to be from Cemaes to Trevadog, ten miles'; and so round the coast, six of them in all. Unlike officers in some other parts of north Wales, however, they do not appear to have been subjected to physical violence from the smugglers and their accomplices, and in the 1760s nothing worse is recorded than the chapter of accidents that befell one Lewis William, Tidesman and Boatman at Holyhead, who 'as he was going out of the Customs House on his duty, was met by a Boar, which bit him on his knee, and hurt him in such manner that he was disabled from Duty'. The unfortunate Lewis was accident prone, for on the very day that he resumed work 'he had the misfortune to fall as he was Mounting his Horse which hurt him in the same knee in such a manner that he has every since been unable to do duty'.[55] He was superannuated, as were his other colleagues, after long periods of service which suggests that they had learned how to survive and, perhaps, to turn a blind eye; one of the casualties was a certain Robert Thomas who was prone to fall victim to the hazards and temptations of boarding vessels – 'piercing a puncheon of rum on board the *Perky* from Antigua', 'intoxicated with Liquor' aboard the *Lovely Match*, and reported as being 'Commonly Disguis'd in Liquor and very incapable to take care of the Trust reposed in him'.[56]

There was a darker side to the smuggling. If there is little evidence of actual violence ashore, there is plenty to underline the poverty which made smuggling attractive. Frequently charges were not pressed because the smuggled goods had been found in houses of people who could not possibly pay, 'from the best account they are all very poor people' – these were the small fry, the wealthy were usually safe enough. Customs officers had to work through 'informers', and although whole communities obviously co-operated in smuggling, there were inevitably those who were tempted by monetary reward for information. In April 1766 two minor officials 'seiz'd in a Garret in the house of Dr Francis Lloyd four chests containing 339 li wt. Tea and paid the Informer by agreement one guinea each chest with a promise his name sho'd not be mentioned';[57] they similarly seized 'eight chests containing 640 li wt. Tea sunk underground in a Field', on the same conditions. Some weeks later the officers had 'seized twelve chests and one bag containing 1025 *li*. wt. Tea in a stable belonging to John Griffith, Esq.' and paid the Informer 'fifteen pounds with a Promise his name sho'd not be mentioned'. Although they had been successful in tracing the large quantities of smuggled tea, the officers found it extremely difficult to prosecute any person 'for want of evidence', and they were therefore out of pocket: 'these officers have discovered everything they know relating to these seizures and have paid for the information at a high rate out of their own share', and they therefore asked that they should be paid a share of the value of the goods seized. Sometimes the 'informers' were not paid but given a free pardon for their own part in the smuggling; one of the *Pelham*'s crew, John Jones, had served in a spell in Caernarvon gaol for smuggling wine and brandy, but had been eventually released, on his own petition, to serve aboard the Revenue cutter where, no doubt, his previous experience as a smuggler was used to advantage on the principle of 'set a thief to catch a thief'.[58]

The heavy duty on tea inevitably led to considerable smuggling. Two examples out of many cases recorded in the letters of the Anglesey Collector to the Board must suffice. Early in 1764, at Beaumaris, a pilot boat called the *Young Tom* was seized by Captain Metcalfe and the crew of the *Hornet* Revenue cutter. The Customs officers reported that 'Young Tommy was a boat of ten tons burthen, and a very remarkable smugler for some years past, and had been in this harbour about 10 days before the 710 cwt. of Tea was seized on board, and the Master says he took in the same tea from ashore in this harbour'.[59] Thomas Hughes, the Tide Surveyor at Beaumaris, stated in evidence that he had 'Board'd and Rumag'd the Young Tom in the harbour on the 24 Feb. last and found her in ballast', and that she had remained at Beaumaris until the 5 March when the Revenue cutter's men made their coup. The *Polly and Nancy* from the Isle of Man had already been seized on the suspicion that 800 pounds of tea had been landed from her, although no tea was actually found aboard her. It was thought that the tea had been put ashore, and that the *Young Tom* was being used to transport the tea for distribution at a more convenient spot than Beaumaris, where they were under the eyes of Customs officials. A fuller account emerged from the cross-examination of Robert Ruddell by the Collector at Beaumaris. Ruddell stated that he was in the Isle of Man on the 29 February when he 'agreed with a certain Richard Scarisbrick to carry him twenty one Bags of Tea to be landed anywhere in the Port of Leverpoole', for which he was to pay freight of eleven guineas; 'that same day he bro't the said Tea on the Key at Douglas in the Isle of Man'. Scarisbrick, according to Ruddell's evidence, assisted him and four other 'passingers' to stow the tea aboard the *Polly and Nancy* and 'the same day they sail'd from the Isle of Man, and on their passage met with a contrary wind which drove them into Beaumaris Harbour, it being then Duskish they landed all the said Tea, and Richard Scarisbrick Assisted and lodg'd the same in an Out House at the Sign of the Coffee where it remained till the 5th March'. Having successfully concealed the tea, 'about 2 o'clock in ye Morning they carr'd seven hundred and ten pounds wt. or upwards of the said Tea on board the Young Tom Pilot Boat'. Accoring to Ruddell there were only two men aboard the *Young Tom* at the time, and the bags of tea were stowed aboard when Thomas Young, the master, was ashore, that Young was not party to this arrangement, that the four 'passingers' who had assisted them to move the tea were now returned to the Isle of Man, and that he, Ruddell, had paid Scarisbrick six guineas for landing the tea at Beaumaris. Within ten hours of the tea being loaded aboard the *Young Tom*, it was seized by the *Hornet*'s crew, and in view of the *Young Tom*'s reputation as 'a very remarkable smuggler for some years' it is not surprising that, despite her master's protestations of innocence, both the *Polly and Nancy* and the *Young Tom* were seized by the Customs officials, who were also anxious to arrest those who had landed and stored the tea in the outhouse of the Sign of Coffee, Beaumaris.

Another example of tea smuggling concerned a certain David Saice,[60] master and part-owner of the boat *Windsor* of Aberystwyth. According to the evidence of Hughes, the Tide Surveyor, he had boarded the *Windsor* on the 18 August 1764, 'and found her loaded with limestone which the master said he took on board at Red Wharfe and on searching the vessel he found two potts of butter upon the Limestones which the Master said belonged to a passinger who was on shore'. A further search of the vessel revealed 'one pot of butter under a Bed in the Cabbin which the Master said belonged to the Vessel, and upon the Bed one small pot of butter'. The master of the *Windsor* was unable to produce documentary evidence regarding the butter, so Hughes seized it. On carrying the butter ashore to the Watch house, Hughes noted that the large pot of butter which he had discovered under the bed was lighter than the other pots, and therefore 'ordered the Top to be taken off, and in this pot was found eleven pounds wt. of Tea, and in the little pot was found upon the bed four pounds weight Tea'. Hughes immediately returned to the *Windsor* and seized her 'for running the said Tea and as more care was taken of the two pots in which the tea was found in', he suspected that the master knew all about the matter, although the latter denied this strenuously and insisted that the pots belonged to the 'passinger'. David Saice, in his own defence, stated that he had sailed from Aberystwyth in May in ballast to a place which he called 'Black and Blue' (Dulas?). He had been carrying limestone to Liverpool until the 15 August: 'when (my boat being loaded with limestones as usual at Red Wharfe in the Isle of Anglesey and bound for Liverpool) a Stranger who called himself Wm. Richard came and desired me to carry him with four mugs of Butter to Liverpool which I agreed to do for two shillings and no more'. On the following day they had set sail, but 'the wind being very contrary', they had had to put into Beaumaris, 'there to wait for fair wind for Liverpool'. Two days later, a Saturday, Hughes and his men had come aboard and seized the butter, but Saice strenuously denied having any knowledge of the contents of the tubs, saying that 'William Richard told him the butter was indended to be put on board a sloop that was loaded with limestones and Butter for Liverpool, who had a proper clearance for her loading but had sailed a Tide before the said William Richard came to Red Wharfe'. The Aberystwyth master's evidence presents a lively picture; he and his crew protesting their innocence as Mr Hughes, the Surveyor, suspiciously eyed the mugs of butter, and, finding that one of them was lighter', put 'his tuck into the Butter and found it was not three inches deep'. Wm. Richard had disappeared, and David Saice pleaded his innocence and the return of his boat 'which is all that a poor man, his family and self have to get our Livlyhood by'. To support his plea of innocence and the return of his boat 'which is all that a poor man, his family and self have to get our Livlyhood by'. To support his plea of innocence, the master of the *Windsor* obtained a testimonial signed by the Collector, Comptroller and Surveyor at Aberystwyth to the effect that 'David Saice of this Town, Mariner, is well known to us and has been so for these four years last, and that during that time he has not been concerned in any illicit Trade to the best of our knowledge and belief'.

There were other commodities subject to duty which were smuggled into the island: soap, 'India silk handkerchiefs', silk stockings – the customs officers acknowledged receipt of 'three stamps and a Pott of colour to be used in stamping silk handkerchiefs and silk stockings, either imported or seized'. Occasionally there would be appeals such as that of Edward Dougherty, who pleaded ignorance of the laws regarding the importation of Irish poplin and stated that he had intended to buy Irish linen in Dublin, 'but meeting therewith some designing persons who persuaded him that it would prove to his advantage to lay out his money in woollen stuffs, He yielded to their advice and bought a few pieces of Irish poplin which he sent over in a vessel to Holyhead where they were immediately seized by the officers of the customs and condemned as contraband'. Dougherty alleged that this action had reduced him 'from a state of independence to which long course of Labour and Industry had raised him, to the lowest point of poverty and Distress', and begged that he might send back the goods to Ireland and there recoup his losses to some degree. The officers were, however, suspicious of his story for they had rummaged several houses 'and in a garret belonging to Mrs Mary Arthur, Innkeeper', had found eight pieces of Irish woollen stuff or poplin containing 'seven hundred sixty four yards', which they had seized. The goods were marked for John Edwards, Chester, and the officers believed that Dougherty was only a go-between and that 'the goods belonged to John Edwards of Chester'.[61]

The very complexity of the system of claiming duty on such a wide range of articles inevtiably led to many appeals. Mark Coghlan, Master of the brigantine *Perry* of Limerick, petitioned the Commissioners in October 1764 on the grounds that 'being bound from Limerick to the West Indies' early in the year 1764, he was caught in a violent storm, 'dismasted and put on shore on the coast of France, and all the sails destroyed'. In order to proceed he therefore had to buy new sails in France, and bought the cheapest canvas he could for £24.10.0. When, however, on his return journey from Antigua he put into Holyhead laden with rum, the officers at Holyhead insisted that duty should be paid on his sails as they were French, 'tho' they are above two thirds worn, being made very slight'. Surprisingly enough, he then adds 'as there are no sailmakers at this port' (i.e. at Holyhead), his sails were valued by two masters of ships and the Tide Surveyor, but Coghlan protested that the duty was very high and as he wished to complete his voyage 'and no sails to be bought here', he requested that he be allowed to proceed to Dublin and granted a refund of the duty paid.[62]

The smuggling of spirits was common throughout the century; William Bulkeley of Brynddu noted in his diary on September 21, 1741, 'Paid a Flintshire smuggler that was Come to Cemaes from the Isle of Man 25/- for 5 gallons of French Brandy, which I think is right good'. In 1760 William Morris, writing to his brother Lewis, reported that a couple of Manx wherries had gone to pieces on the rocks near Holyhead, and added as an afterthought that brandy was the common drink of the inhabitants of Anglesey, a drink called 'todi', made of brandy with a little water and sugar.[63] In the 1730s a Customs officer at Greenock on the Clyde who had just visited the Isle of Man reported 30 'sail of vessels' loading brandy to run to neighbouring coasts,[64] and in 1788 the Tide Surveyor at Liverpool reported that he had 'boarded a sloop called the *Blessing*, John Morris master, who said he was from the coast of Wales with limestones'.

On examining the hold, the Tide Surveyor 'found 53 kegs containing 339 gallons of foreign brandy and geneva, stowed among the limestones'.[65] There was considerable smuggling of small amounts of brandy and spirits in vessels carrying legitimate cargoes, but Sir Llewellyn Turner, in his 'Memories', had a story of a certain Boaz Pritchard, a Caernarvon shopkeeper, who as late as the 1820s and 1830s was smuggling very large quantities of brandy in the Channel Island fruit schooners, using the familiar technique of transporting the prohibited goods by means of a ghostly hearse through the streets of Caernarvon.[66]

One of the obvious problems for customs officials was the mercantilist policy adopted by Britain whereby plantation products could not be shipped direct to foreign ports but first had to be brought to a British port. Tobacco and sugar were two commodities affected by this policy; when duty had been paid, the tobacco, for example, was reshipped ostensibly to a port where a rebate of duty could be claimed, but, instead of going far, the tobacco was put ashore in some quiet haven, sold at a good price and the repayment of duty claimed. There are many references to attempts at salvaging tobacco cargoes in the letters of the Morris brothers, who were Customs officials themselves. Lewis Morris was given leave of absence to make his survey of the coast, but William Morris, as Deputy Comptroller at Holyhead, saw much of the day-to-day problems.[67] There were the West Indian sugar ships to be dealt with. 'Here's a ship arrived from Antigua laden with rum to be warehoused and exported and nothing can be done . . . until an anser be had from London', and he adds that he wonders how he has stayed alive he is so busy, watching the myriad tricks of the merchant Vickers, the Manxmen and the Irish to defraud the Customs, like 'a grey cat watching a hundred mouse holes' at once.[68] Frustrated that he could not go to the Fair at Llannerch-y-medd (perhaps not for quite the same reasons as his younger brother John as he lay dreaming aboard the *Torbay* the previous year), he amusingly listed to his brother Richard the many-sided nature of his activities, 'deputy customer, Collector, deputy comptroller, comptroller of the coal duties, deputy searcher, coast waiter and searcher, water bailiff, deputy vice-admiral, collector of Skerry lights, surgeon, florist and botanist to the Garrison of Holyhead'![69] William Morris reported that in between

April 1759 and April 1760 fourteen large vessels bringing sugar had arrived at Holyhead; their cargoes were put ashore and re-embarked on smaller vessels, two or three of them taking one cargo of the original larger vessel. Some weeks later his brother Lewis wrote to him on the subject of sheep on Plynlimon in Cardiganshire where he now lived: William Morris ruefully stated that he had not even a lamb, let alone a sheep, but there were many sugar ships at Holyhead he could see from his doorway and there were more to come, and they, after all, were his sheep and cattle![70] And here William Morris was being both honest and realistic, for despite the trouble involved, whether it was dealing with sugar, or tobacco cargoes, seizing contraband goods, attending wrecks and seeing to the disposal of their cargoes, all services brought in fees to augment the salaries of the Customs officers, who worked very much on a basis of payment by results. It was with some satisfaction, therefore, that he wrote to his brother Richard in London on the following day that American ships were arriving in twos and threes at Holyhead, bringing him the odd penny![71]

Time and time again William Morris refers to wrecks and his duties in going aboard wrecked vessels to supervise the salvaging of cargoes of sugar, rum, salt and tobacco; sugar vessels from the West Indies, several Chester ships, a Chichester brig, and many others before his very eyes off Holyhead. Whether employed in legal or illicit trade, it is obvious from reading the Morris Letters that the casualties were high; the wrecks were not regarded as a calamity by people ashore but often enough as some kind of heavenly manna. This was understandable in an age when poverty and famine stalked the land; the crops failed in 1757 abnd 1758 and hungry mobs marched from Beaumaris and Llannerch-y-medd to Holyhead to attack the warehouses there. William Bulkeley wrote in his diary in February 1758: 'Mobbing has been so frequent this winter in this county and several shiploads of corn butter and cheese have been publicly Stole and carryed away, and the Greatest part of it never sold at all and what was sold was next to nothing, Barley at 1s a Pegget, Butter at 1d and Some for ½d a pound and the cheese at the same time'. Twenty years earlier William Morris had written of the mobs robbing the warehouses at Red Wharf of corn, butter and cheese, and they had ample reason to complain that high prices were being charged when there was plenty to be had on the island.[72] In 1757 his niece, Margaret Owen (sister of John and William Owen who went to sea), writing from Pentre-eiriannell, expressed her concern as to the safety of a friend's vessel as it was dangerous for vessels carrying foodstuffs to approach the Anglesey shore because of the mobs who would seize their cargoes.[73] There are many references in both the Morris letters and the Custom House papers to wrecks on the Crigyll rocks, near Holyhead; the *Young Dirk* bound Liverpool to Ostend in 1766 with a cargo of tobacco and rock salt, wrecked there, was but one of many. She presented problems to the Customs officials for she was wrecked 'on a ridge of rock where no sort of carriage can come within three hundred yards of her in order to unlaid her'. It was also stated that the cargo was rapidly deteriorating, but no boat would 'ventur to lye alongside being so dangerous a place this time of year'.[74] There were those, however, who were willing to venture on most occasions at Crigyll: in 1774 three men known as the thieves of Crigyll rocks, were found guilty of plundering the wreck of the *Charming Jenny* stranded at Crigyll[75] and thirty years earlier in 1740 the *Loveday and Betty*, a Liverpool vessel, was similarly plundered; both Lewis Morris, who wrote a poem about it,[76] and William Bulkeley, who was present at the trial, testify to the impression the 'Lladron Creigiau Crigyll' trial made.[77] There does not appear to have been much deliberate 'wrecking', and, as with smuggling, as conditions ashore improved and the bitterness of famine conditions died away, the nineteenth-century saw a change in attitude. Whilst high taxes had made attempts at evasion inevitable, once the slate and coal taxes had been removed, and particularly the salt tax which had weighed particularly harshly on the poor, legal trading became the normal way of life, although isolated cases of smuggling occurred until the middle of the nineteenth-century.[78] One positive discouragement during the eighteenth-century had been the likelihood that those engaged in smuggling might be 'pressed' into the service of the Royal Navy: the Collector at Liverpool had recognized this as early as 1727 when he asked for a press warrant for the sloops in the vicinity of the Isle of Man so that they could 'press some few fellows out of the barks and boats that trade to the Isle of Man from the coast of Scotland and Wales who are the principall if not sole traders now to that island'.[79] He believed this 'would terrifie those people so' that it would do more to discourage smuggling than all the sloops employed in the preventive service. The ending of the Napoleonic Wars made many naval men available for the coastguard service, but the most effective deterrent to smuggling came with the removal of duties which thus made the trade no longer profitable.

In 1786 the first general ship registration act came on to the Satute Book,[80] an act which attempted to ensure correct identification of ships by making owners register their ships so that their 'Certificate of Registration' became a kind of passport for the ship. The certificate contained an accurate description of the vessel so that there would be no confusion regarding its legal ownership, but it also provided a ready means of identification in cases of illegal actions such as smuggling. One of the fortunate by-products of eighteenth-century smuggling was this boon to maritime historians, for from 1786 the Custom House Ship Registers record every ship registered belonging to the port of Beaumaris, where and when they were built, their rig and tonnage, and the names of their owners. The specimen lists of ships contained in Appendix IV and much of the detail relating to late eighteenth and nineteenth-century shipping would not have been as easy to come by but for the activities of the eighteenth-century smugglers.

[1]   A. H. W. Robinson, 'Lewis Morris – An Early Welsh Hydrographer', *TAAS* 1968, 40, and *Marine Cartography in Britain, A History of the Sea Chart to 1855* (Leicester, 1961).
[2]   UCNW Mostyn MS 7578, E. G. Jones, 'Llythyrau Lewis Morris at William Vaughan, Corsygedol', *Llên Cymru*, 10 (1968), 12.
[3]   *ibid.*
[4]   *ML*, ii, 327
[5]   Lewis Morris, *Plans of Harbours, Bays and Roads in St George's and the Bristol Channels*, 1748, 2-7.
[6]   *ibid.*, 6.
[7]   Ralph Davies, *The Rise of the English Shipping Industry in the Seventeenth and Eighteenth Centuries* (London, 1962), 395.

[8]   R. C. Jarvis, 'British Ship Registry: the quantification of source material', *Exeter Papers in Economic History*, 4 (1970), 149-165.

[9]   BM Add MSS 11255-6.

[10]   BM Add MSS 38, 429 (Liverpool Papers CCXL).

[11]   *ibid.*, Beaumaris had a total of 271 vessels, 10,670 tons, all British built; Liverpool had 353 British and 76 foreign built, 445 in all, 72,731 tons. Cardiff at this time had 19 vessels, 744 tons. Cardigan, the next largest of the Welsh ports, had 225 vessels registered in 1789, Aberystwyth 112, Chester 27, Cardiff 21.

[12]   BM Add MSS 38430.

[13]   T. S. Willan, *The English Coasting Trade*, 184.

[14]   PRO E190, 1343/18. Professor J. Gwynn Williams kindly allowed me to use his transcripts of the 1680-1683 Port Books in the Public Records Office.

[15]   PRO E190, 1345/17.

[16]   PRO E190, 1343/7.

[17]   PRO E190, 1346/3.

[18]   UCNW Bangor MS 484.

[19]   The total tonnage entering and leaving Beaumaris from July 1729 to December 1730 was 3,387 tons in 226 vessels, an average of 14.9 tons. For Caernarvon, for the same period, 4,514 tons in 285 vessels, average 15.8 tons, whilst at Holyhead, where the packet boats were naturally larger and heavier, and brought occasional cargoes, the tonnage is 2,454 in 88 vessels, an average of 27.8 tons.

[20]   On the basis of UCNW Bangor MS 484.

[21]   I am indebted to R. B. White for the references in the Meyrick papers, UCNW Bodorgan MS 1326; Mr White intends to publish an account of 'Fflott Bodorgan' in *TAAS*.

[22]   UCNW Penrhyn MSS 1643, 1968, 1971.

[23]   UCNW Bangor MS 484, Penrhyn MS 1642.

[24]   *DWB* 799, *Blodeu-gerdd Cymry*, 1759, 402. According to UCNW Penrhyn MSS 1642, 1643, Robert Prichard, Poet, carried 337,000 slates in ten cargoes in the *Blessing* between 9 September 1730 and 15 December 1732.

[25]   Lady Nesta Evans, *Social Life in Mid Eighteenth-Century Anglesey* (Cardiff, 1936), 33.

[26]   Hugh Owen (ed.) 'The Diary of William Bulkeley', *TAAS* (1931), 45.

[27]   *Add ML*, i, 258. The freight charge from London to Caernarvon for the 50 Welsh Bibles and 56 Welsh New Testament Common Prayers was 11/-. 3/6 was paid for their carriage from Caernarvon to Dulas.

[28]   UCNW Penrhos MSS, i, 367. William Morris in March 1757 reported that prices were high on the island, the farmers exporting their corn and not enough for the inhabitants: 'y ffermwyr yn cael Prisiau da am eu hydau i fyned i'r Mor, ac heb gadw digon i ddiwallu'r wlad'. *Add ML*, ii, 895.

[29]   *CSPD* 1690-91, 19.

[30] *CSPD* 1690-91, 552. The reports in May 1690, when Shovell was at Holyhead, were that 'Tomson is coming from Dublin in a large sloop of two masts, eight guns, 16 oars, and 40 men, with some passengers on board'. *ibid.*, 19. Requests were made later for the 'small yacht that is now in Chester water to cruize near Holyhead' to intercept the vessel.

[31] *CSPD* 1696, 278. 'Geography was no longer so kind to us as when we fought the Dutch. The English Channel was also the French Channel: our back doors on the Irish Sea were much more vulnerable from Brest than they were from Helvoetsluys'. M. Lewis, *The History of the British Navy* (London, 1957), 118-122.

[32] Quoted in M. Bevan Evans, 'Gadlys and Flintshire Lead Mining', *TFHS*, 1960, 18, 92, 4. J. N. Rhodes, *The London Lead Company in North Wales, 1693-1792* (unpublished Ph.D. thesis, University of Leicester, 1970), 45. An Irish merchant reported 'a small three masted vessel' chasing other ships off the Skerries. *CSPD* 1702-04, 48.

[33] UCNW Mostyn MSS 7596.

[34] *ML*, ii, 204.

[35] *infra*. For the re-export of tobacco to Ireland from Whitehaven, and the Clyde ports, L. M. Cullen, *Anglo-Irish Trade 1660-1800* (Manchester, 1968), 90, 161.

[36] UCNW MM MSS 3540, 3541.

[37] UCNW Cefnllan MS 8.

[38] R. C. Jarvis, *Customs Letter-Books of the port of Liverpool, 1711-1823* (Manchester, 1954), xx.

[39] J. A. Williamson, *The English Channel* (1959), 272-276. For an account of the work of the Collector, Isle of Wight, D. Arnold Forster, *At War with the Smugglers* (London, 1970). The quantitative importance of smuggling is discussed by W. A. Cole, 'Trends in Eighteenth Century Smuggling', *Econ. History Review*, 2nd series, vol. X, 1958.

[40] R. C. Jarvis, *Customs Letter-Books, Liverpool*, xx, xxi.

[41] UCNW Bangor MSS 12199. The late David Thomas transcribed these letters whilst they were still held locally. The originals are now deposited at the Custom House Library, London.

[42] *ibid.*, 19.

[43] *ibid.*, 14.

[44] *ibid.*, 18.

[45] *ibid.*, 124.

[46] *ibid.*, 162. If the *Pelham* put in to any other port, Gambold was to give reasons for so doing to the satisfaction of the Collector, otherwise no provision allowance would be given.

[47] *ibid.*, 35.

[48] *ibid.*, 194.

[49] *ibid.*, 226.

[50] C. H. Ward Jackson, 'The ships of the port of Fowey at the turn of the 18th century'. *Exeter Papers in Economic History*, 4 (1970), 57; Margaret

White, 'The Carteret Priaulx papers – the influence of the Napoleonic Wars on Guernsey', *Transactions of La Société Guernesiase*, XVII (1963), 460.

51 L. M. Cullen, *Anglo-Irish Trade, 1660-1800*, 153.

52 UCNW Bangor MSS 19060.

53 UCNW Bangor MSS 12199, 139.

54 *ibid.*, 132.

55 *ibid.*, 38. In 1761 a mob had stoned officers who had tried to arrest a wherry unloading goods at Llandrillo yn Rhos, near Llandudno. D. Thomas, *Hen Longau Sir Gaernarfon*, 72.

56 *ibid.*, 203.

57 *ibid.*, 217. Dr Francis Lloyd was not much of a doctor according to William Bulkeley: 'Mr Frances Lloyd (whom they call DOCTOR because he was about 6 weeks in Guy's Hospitall under cure for an ailing he had)'. Diary of William Bulkeley, June 24, 1742. But he was sufficiently respectable to be High Sheriff of Anglesey in 1761-2.

58 D. Thomas, *Hen Longau Sir Gaernarfon*, 77.

59 UCNW Bangor MSS 12199, 71-6. For a discussion of the amounts of tea smuggled and estimates of prices in the eighteenth-century, W. A. Cole, 'Trends in Eighteenth Century Smuggling', *Econ. Hist. Review*, 1958.

60 *ibid.*, 104-8. Was 'Saice' an 'Englishman'? (Welsh word *Sais*.)

61 *ibid.*, 180.

62 *ibid.*, 117.

63 *ML*, ii, 263.

64 Cullen, *Anglo-Irish Trade*, 146.

65 Jarvis, *Customs Letter-Books, Liverpool*, 140. Any brandy or geneva imported in any cask or container of less than 60 galls or in any vessel of less than 100 tons (except for the use of seamen not exceeding two gallons per man) was forfeit.

66 Ll. Turner, *The memories of Sir Llewelyn Turner* (London), 483-4.

67 William Morris's letters relating to the 'press', and naval matters are discussed more fully in the chapter 'The Beginnings of a Naval Tradition', p. 149.

68 *ML*, ii 599. 'Fe balla'r amser imi fanegi iwch y triccia a'r castiau mae'r Ficws a'r Gwyddhelod a'r Mancsmyn yn ei ddyfeisiaw i gogiaw ein Harglwydd Freyenhin, a minnau ac nid arall yn eu gwarchod, mal y gwelwch'i gath lwyd yn gwylio cantwll ar unwaith rhag llygod'. William Vickers was postmaster at Holyhead, and a prominent merchant. The customs had their suspicions regarding his activities. UCNW Bangor MS 12199, 138-9.

69 *ML* i, 50.

70 *ML*, ii 227. 'Wale hai nid oes yma gymaint ac oen, chwaethach dafad. Ond y mae y llongau siwgr yn dda iawn. Mi welaf bedair or drws; mae digon etto i ddyfod. Ond y nhw druain yw fy nefaid am gwartheg i!' In *ML* ii, 145, William Morris, again writing to Lewis in December, 1759, reported that a large number of sugar vessels, many from New York, had come to Holyhead,

all paying duty, whilst a ship of Danzic had put in on her way to Liverpool, more duty for William! 'Dyma yn y borth long o Ddantzick, mi a wranta ei bod yn 5 cant o dunelli, troi i mewn wrth fynd i Nerpwl i dalu i Wilym 6s. a 8d.'.

[71] *ML* ii 228.

[72] *Add ML*, i, 35.

[73] *Add ML*, ii, 888-9.

[74] UCNW Bangor MS 12199, 258.

[75] Hugh Owen, 'The Anglesey Quarter Sessions Records, 1768-88', *TAAS* 1925, 81.

[76] Hugh Bevan suggests that this is Lewis Morris's best satirical poem. Hugh Bevan, 'Lewis Morris' in *Gŵyr Llên y Ddeunawfed Ganrif*, ed. Dyfnallt Morgan (Llandybie, 1966), 177.

[77] Dafydd Wyn Wiliam, 'Lladron Crigyll', *Môn*, iii, 2, 1-5.

[78] For a discussion of the unwritten rules understood by both smuggling communities and the preventive service, E. P. Thompson, *The Making of the English Working Class* (London, 1970), 64.

[79] Jarvis, *Customs Letter-Books, Liverpool*, 30.

[80] 26 Geo. iii. cap. 60.

The Beginnings of a Naval Tradition

The Navy of the seventeenth and eighteenth centuries was closely based upon Chatham, Portsmouth and Plymouth, 'the dockyard towns in which the seamen congregated and to which men came or were 'pressed'. They lived by and fed the Navy; it was to their narrow, teeming alleys that the seamen returned'.[1] By the nineteenth-century, Wales, far removed from these southern bases, contributed fewer per capita of naval officers than England and Scotland: Professor Michael Lewis, basing his estimates on the biographies prepared by Marshall and O'Byrne in the first half of the nineteenth-century, has stated that, of the forty-five Welsh naval officers mentioned, the two leading counties as far as numbers are concerned, according to the percentage of population, were Pembroke and Anglesey.[2] This is not surprising; Pembroke, with the fine base of Milford Haven for all types of shipping, and strong English influences in the county, and Anglesey, on the main sea routes to Ireland and to the increasingly important port of Liverpool, were counties where the fears and dangers of invasion had been recognized. In the seventeenth-century the war at sea off Anglesey had been waged by English officers and crews drawn from the southern ports, but in the eighteenth-century, alongside the considerable development of locally owned and built coastal shipping, there are indications that a naval tradition was beginning to develop. Both the gentry, who saw the possibilities of a naval career for their sons, and the seafaring population, some of whom may have first come into contact with the Navy through being 'pressed', found in the sea service an alternative source of employment which, when compared with the precarious existence ashore, had certain attractions of the adventurous. It should be emphasised that only a minority were involved, but by the end of the long French wars in 1815, there was some evidence of a 'naval interest' in the county, a recognizable strand in the history of Anglesey.

Any attempt to trace the fortunes of all Anglesey's naval men during the period would be beyond the scope of this present work; the individual histories selected to illustrate the general theme have been chosen simply because they are the best documented. Anyone interested in the history of eighteenth-century Anglesey must inevitably turn to the monumental collection of letters of the Morris brothers and to the vivid diary of William Bulkeley. Lady Nesta Evans, in her detailed study of these sources, came to the conclusion that 'The Diary, supported by the evidence of the *Morris Letters*, makes it abundantly clear that, both in matters of detail and questions of general policy, the attention of the people of Anglesey, when their interest in political matters could be roused at all, was centred on the sea and the fortunes of our sailors, and that they were passionately eager to match our Navy against that of Spain in open warfare'.[3] The long years of peace under Walpole's government had brought this reaction from William Bulkeley as he wrote in his diary at the year's turning: 'Thus Ended the Year 1735, famous for nothing remarkable in England but for the daily depredations of the Spaniards upon the English Merchants, and no redress to be hoped for – the English Ministry being held in every Court in Europe in the utmost contempt; and tho they have as great a Fleet now, as ever England had, in time of war . . . yet no use are made of all these to right the Merchants and retrieve ye glory of Old England'.[4] Mr Bulkeley and those who thought as he did had to wait for a further four years before war was declared against Spain, and it is in that year, 1739, that the first reference to John Morris's career at sea occurs. The fortunes of John Morris, as reflected in the letters of the Morris brothers, for a little over one year, may be taken to provide some impression of an Anglesey man's life in the Navy in mid eighteenth-century.

In 1739, John Morris was already an experienced seaman, in his early thirties. Little is known of him before this: it is probable that he was with his brother Richard in London in 1735. A few days after Christmas 1738 John Morris wrote to his brother William from Gibraltar, and early in February he wrote again from the *Mary* of Liverpool, this time from Marseilles, giving him an account of his voyage from Gibraltar to Barcelona.[5] John, the youngest of the Morris brothers, shared their literary interests, and at Gibraltar had been inspired to write an 'englyn' describing the Rock; a fair wind had taken them to Ibiza and Majorca, where in light airs John had spent some hours sketching headlands and mountains (he probably shared Lewis's interest in surveying), and attempting an occasional englyn, such as:

Heb wynt war helynt i'r hwyl – ar gefnfor
    Gwag ynfyd yw'r gorchwyl;
   Hwyra dasg, hir yw disgwyl,
   A sala gwaith Sul a gwyl.

John Morris's letter to his brother Richard from Liverpool, dated 5 July 1739,[6] describes the difficulties he has as a seaman in regularly communicating with his brothers. He had written from Holyhead and again from Portin-llaen where they had been loading corn for Lisbon. At Lisbon, due to his brothers' connections, he had had a 'grand entertainment' in the company of many masters of ships, and had given them the news of his brothers' activities. On the last trip he had been away for five and a half months, and promised himself that on his return he would 'take a jaunt to Anglesey', but fate had ordered otherwise and he had found himself at Dublin in a ship loading salt, again for the Mediterranean. John was anxious to see something of the world before taking a shore job: 'I wish you would enquire what's become of Mr Weston, him that was our Chief Mate in ye *Harrington*. If he's a Captain I should like it in my heart to take another trip to India, however, I design to visit both Guinea, West India and North America before I leave off rambling, if God spares my life so long'. He took his profession seriously and asked his brother Richard about the most recently published books on navigation, as he had failed to come across any that suited his purpose 'although I have at present by me six or seven epitomes'. He was ambitious to qualify as a master mariner, and had little time for incompetent masters. It was mid-July 1739 and John Morris had 'unluckily strained my knee' and his ship had sailed for Dublin without him.[7] He found the enforced stay in lodgings tiresome and expensive; he was not sorry to leave his previous ship as he reckoned the pay poor, and had high hopes that he might get a berth as a second mate aboard a vessel soon to sail for the Guinea coast. 'It's certain that Guinea is the best place for a young fellow of my learning to go out of this place, for if he lives, he's undoubtedly preferred ye next voyage if he keeps the same employ, for the captain and officers dies so often that there's continually new ones sent out, but never a chief mate hardly but what has been before upon that coast, so I am actually resolved to venture one trip please God to give me health'. This preoccupation with death and ill health in seamen, particularly in hot climates, was not unusual, for the appalling conditions aboard ships had been notorious for centuries and Morris was aware of the risks he ran aboard a slave ship. 'If I die in the prosecution, God's will be done; I have neither wife (nor children to my knowledge) to cry after me, and if I don't go abroad now while I'm free I am sure I never shall if I alter my state, except it be through some other means more than ordinary that I should be obliged *perforce* to go. So much for that'.[8]

By October of 1739 the war fever against the Spaniards had affected John Morris; no longer was he content to look for a berth aboard a merchantman, his ambition was now to serve aboard a man of war, 'I am resolved now to be one amongst them i ladd Ysbaengwyns'.[9] Bu he was wise enough not to be drawn in as a pressed man, and quickly wrote to his brother Lewis Morris to see if the latter could obtain an exemption for him, for he had already heard of good seamen being pressed from some Liverpool-bound ships. Whilst he was happy enough in his lodging in Liverpool with his cousin William Hughes, the latter's wife made his life more than uncomfortable, particularly resenting his Welshness.[10] By 6 November, however, he had good news; he had a letter that the *Torbay* was soon to be put in commission, and that he had a good chance of becoming master's mate aboard her.[11] Appointment as Master's Mate, the understudy of the Master who had responsibilities for navigation, was the normal way of entry into the naval hierarchy 'for the clever, ambitious or well-backed young merchant seaman'.[12] The Morrises were great 'fixers'[13] with many contacts in the naval 'Establishment' and it was therefore not surprising that this was the route by which John Morris, who was clearly a clever and ambitious young merchant seaman, entered the Navy. John wrote to his brother Richard that, although he himself might not be able to board a 'cheeseman' bound from Liverpool for London because of the danger from the 'press',[14] he would put his chest aboard her, directing it to Ben Jones, his London friend's house. War had been formally declared against Spain, and a man of war's tender had already pressed many men out of Liverpool ships, 'but is now gone for Beumares, as some says, where there lies wind bound ships bound for this place, gwae Fon ac Arfon'. The war fever had hit Liverpool and John Morris himself longed to be in the fray. 'I hope I shall soon be at 'em, ag yno, either a golden chain or a wooden leg'.[15] It was the seaman's philosophy, age old, past and future.

Some weeks later John was still kicking his heels at Liverpool; he had sent some butter he had from Anglesey to London and a copper mug by the *Recovery*, Captain Coates, and his chest in the *John and Martha*, Captain Nevill, together with his bed clothes.[16] He was particularly anxious that the chest and case should not have too rough handling 'for fear of breaking ye bottles that there is in both, with some liquor in, that may make us merry when we meet, but would make me full if the bottles were to break, and ye liquor spillt about my books and cloaths'. Alas for his longed-for celebration, the *John and Martha* only got as far as Hoylake because of heavy seas, where, to make matters worse, the crew fled ashore to avoid being pressed by the *Bonetta* sloop, although he had the reassuring news that the *Recovery* had arrived at London with his butter and cheese. This was small comfort, John Morris was still at Liverpool writing on the 19 January 1740 in a chastened mood; no news of the berth aboard the *Torbay*, and in the meantime he had 'refused several mate's berths out of this place, both to Guinea, West Indies, and Virginia'.[17] To add to his low spirits, it was icy cold in Liverpool, he had heard from his brother William at Holyhead that their sister had had two still-born children, and his mother was seriously ill according to his brother Lewis. Occasionally he got news from Anglesey by the Anglesey-Liverpool packet which he described as *'yr hen Brins Llywelyn gynt'*, but his position in Liverpool was becoming desperate, for he had to lodge at an ale house belonging to 'Mrs Partis Scipio at ye Dock Side',[18] where he paid 3/6d. a week, 'victuals and lodgings and obliged by the custom of the town to call for a pint of ale every dinner and supper, which amounts to sixpence within twopence every week, besides what I spend when I meet here and there my countrymen (whom I can't shun for the sake of news!)'. One gets the impression that John Morris was not averse to the occasional pint of ale with the many Welshmen whom he found in the dockyard taverns awaiting a berth, but he was conscience-striken that he might soon have to borrow money that his aged parents could ill afford. He had had news that John Pritchard of Rhoscolyn, 'after he had lost his vessel on ye coast of Ireland', had left in a ship for Virginia where he was to have a vessel built for his new employer, Mr Cunliffe.

John Morris enjoyed a little gossip in his letters; two days after the said John Pritchard sailed, contrary winds had driven them back, and Pritchard, according to John Morris, had immediately gone to St Asaph to meet a girl from Holyhead 'that had come there with Mr Vickers, her brother in law, of purpose to be married. So at Llanrhaeadr, Jack and she were joined fast, stay'd with her one night, so parted, he here, and she home again. So he got a fair wind again as soon as he came, and away he went and will not return in less than two years'. At this point even John Morris's gossip ran dry. 'Now I'm quite aground', he added humorously. He still had his sense of humour but it was wearing thin. It is perhaps with something of a shock that the modern reader takes in the next sentence, for here is the younger brother of the much-revered Morris brothers of Anglesey wrting: 'I've a black lad about sixteen years old to sell for a friend, and I can't get any body to buy him. I wish I had him in London, I'd sell him under £30, only a little above £25'.[19] The days of the abolition of slavery were yet far off and this sentence would not raise an eyebrow in the contemporary eighteenth-century world.

At long last, in April 1740, John Morris arrived at Chatham; his brother Lewis writing from Holyhead to Richard in London somewhat piously hopes that all will go well with their younger brother: 'I wish he may keep sober – dyna wendid y mab'.[20] Lewis Morris was himself very interested in the progress of naval affairs and asked his brother to write to him with 'a catalogue of ye Men of War, their force, etc. and where stationed'. On 16 April 1740 John wrote from aboard the *Torbay*,[21] complaining of rheumatism in his hands, and also some irritation which caused him to be bled. Each night he had to sleep in another mate's hammock as his own belongings had not arrived, and he complained bitterly of the difficulties of having but his one best suit of clothes for all occasions. He shared his brothers' literary tastes and felt deprived of books to read and even had to borrow pen, paper and ink to write his letters. One of the reasons for his discomfort was that the tender that bore his belongings was held up by contrary winds, as indeed was the progress of the fleet down to the Nore, and he was aghast at the thought of the fleet sailing before the tender arrived. Coming aboard the *Torbay* he had been stiff with cold, and had not ventured ashore since: he complained, moreover, that on first joining his ship he had been twenty hours without food or drink. A fortnight later he was in a happier mood; his brother Richard had sent him money and the Captain of the *Torbay* had praised his work, particularly as the ship's master was ashore and there was only one other mate to supervise the storing of the food and drink in the hold before they sailed for the Nore. Either for reasons of naval security or indeed sheer incompetence, no one seemed to know how long the ships were to remain at their present berths, and John Morris suggested to his brother Richard that he should send him some quires of paper for him to keep a journal by the packet that sailed from Irongate or Wapping New Stairs.[22]

Writing from aboard the *Torbay* at Blackstakes on 18 May to his brother Richard, John was able at last to give some account of movement in the fleet with the hope that they would soon be sailing for Portsmouth; John himself made ready by writing to all his friends, 'Ive writt to Anglesey, Liverpool, Creuddyn and to all friends since I came down to here, but can't get a line from anybody'.[23] Four days later John Morris wrote a letter to his brother Richard which, in the light of subsequent history, is somewhat ironic. Apparently Lewis Morris had written to John asking him to use his best influence to help the career of an Anglesey lad, Ned Edwards. John was scathing in his reply, 'I told him that I thought it would be of no service to ye lad to come here except he had recommendations to some commissioned or warrant officer, or another, if he expects to get any post; and told him that I did not know one office aboard the ship that he could execute'. Here was the fully fledged naval man pouring scorn on the local boy in a way that boomeranged, for Ned Edwards eventually became a successful and wealthy captain – but at this point John Morris's comments were forthright, 'How should he when he has never been at sea in his lifetime, only in little boats about Holyhead Bay'? John Morris confessed he had little liking for the talk of taking the youngster under his wing, yet he went as far as to say, 'I'd willingly do any service to the lad if he had any knowledge of the sea; but as it is, one may as well take a prentice to teach him, as he that knows nothing'.[24]

John Morris had cause to be irritable. Although they had had their sailing orders for three days past, the wind continued easterly, and the fleet swung to their anchors, and each day the health of the crews deteriorated. Three hundred men had recently been pressed from the *Edinburgh*, just back from Lisbon, and transferred to the *Torbay*, and John Morris in June wrote of his ship, 'Our ship is very sickly, and has been for some time. My messmate is not come on board yet, I wonder what makes him stay. It's hard for me myself to act, having so many men to look after. The other mate that came down from the *Rendezvous* is a mere novice yet, worse than I was at first'.[25] It must be remembered that in those years the Navy was poorly manned and conditions of health aboard had improved little in a matter of over a hundred years. Dr James Lind, the pioneer of nautical medicine, witnessed at first hand the way in which pressed men were sources of infection, some of them 'deeply tainted with the scurvy and other disorders, which break out upon a long confinement and fatigue at sea', others, men 'picked from the streets or the prisons . . . communicating infection to the whole fleet', making the guard ship at the Nore, where they were first received, 'a seminary of contagion'.[26] The strain was already telling on John Morris; he complained that he was almost too fatigued, since he had reached Spithead, to 'hardly lay pen to paper yet to write to anyone'. He longed for a letter from his friends and relations in Anglesey, and heard that a once-fancied bride, Sioned, in Anglesey, had married another man. At last security measures were being taken regarding the fleet. 'We are kept aboard so strictly that there is not one allowed to go ashore for fear we should not be ready when we get our orders to sail'. Short of money as he had been for some time, John Morris looked forward to the possibility of some advance money – 'Our fore topsails have been loose this two days, and we expect to receive two months tomorrow. I was flung out of the bounty money, and conduct money too'. As he was a petty officer, John Morris was unable to visit his friend and neighbour Dick Owen, though the latter was aboard Sir John Norris's ship which was lying close to them, but he had plenty to occupy him, for in the anchorage in St Helen's Road a gale sprang up on 17 July and the *Lyon*, a 70-gun ship, ran foul of the Admiral's ship, adding to the chaos in an already ill-organized fleet. Ned Edwards had arrived aboard, and Morris was less prejudiced against him: 'I don't doubt but shall make something of the lad if we go a cruize.'[27]

By the 14 August 1740, the fleet had arrived at Torbay. John, writing to his brother Richard, was already disillusioned:[28] 'I wish we may return from this cruize (if we are to return) before the heavy winter comes on'; his complaints about the food were commonplace but nevertheless very real; he longed for a warmer climate such as he had experienced in his days in the merchant fleet in the Mediterranean, to 'refresh our wearied bodies with a coque of wine or a swingeing bowl of good punch, which necessaries (of all things most necessary to a seaman) we are debarred of and not allowed to get upon any account; nothing allowed to be brought on board our ship but eatables, no manner of drinkables, even plain ale and cider is prohibited. Fish we have plenty brought to us: some fresh meat now and then, and fruit'. Occasionally there was the rare bounty that some 'few kind good natur'd country lasses brings us a little fresh butter and milk when the weather permits. But what benefits all this without liquor? Good humming beer, or stiffning for a can of phlip, or a bowl of good punch! We can't drink Saturday night's health after this rate'! One can imagine John's parched throat as he penned these words. John Morris reported much sailing to and fro by pacquet boats, shipping stores and the myriad rumours that have spread before the sailing of any fleet, before or since, but the strongest 'buzz' was that they were eventually bound for the West Indies.

Inevitably the long wait aboard within sight of the shore proved too much for some who had been pressed to serve with the fleet, and in this same letter John Morris gives a vivid picture of the cruelty of the age. Morris writes to his brother in a matter-of-fact fashion, but it indicates vividly the lot of the poor wretch who had felt he could stay aboard no longer and had decided to swim ashore.

'One of our people the other day was try'd by Court Martial on board Sir John Norris for swimming away from the ship, and he was sentenced to receive one hundred lashes with a cat. Accordingly this forenoon the Admiral made a signal to all ships' boats in the Fleet to attend the prisoner, arm'd etc. We had a pair of gallows erected in our longboat, and the prisoner was order'd into her and there bound to the gallows, where the Provost

Marshal of the Fleet read his orders and gave the prisoner twenty lashes. From thence they were tow'd on board the three Admirals, where he received twenty lashes on board each, attended by upwards of thirty boats, and then returned on board here, and received twenty more which made up the complement'.

Witnessing this bloody sight, John Morris's mind strayed to his native Anglesey, and his *hiraeth* was increased as he remembered that that day was in fact Llannerch-y-medd Fair day. It was not a far step from that to dream of his pretty Morfudd and the thought of holding her in his arms there on Fair night. Sleepily enough he concluded his letter with the somewhat cynical thought that perhaps by now his pretty Morfudd was the wife of some lucky shore-bound farmer! To make matters worse, the weather was so bad that the fleet attempted several times to set sail, only to be forced to return to its anchorage because of the tempestuous weather and any element of surprise in its movements must have been long since lost. Some days later they were back from Torbay at Spithead, and the news was that they were to sail with Sir Chaloner Ogle as Admiral for the West Indies.[29] Ogle has a place in Welsh history as the destroyer of the famous pirate Bartholomew Roberts, Barti Ddu; his campaign this time was not so successful. John Morris himself did not look forward to the prospect of life aboard a three-decker in hot climates and he confided to his brother Richard that if it was to be his fate to go to the West Indies, he wished he were in a smaller ship for his health's sake. Already he sounded a tired and sick man, and in his next letter confessed that he was 'very much fatigued'. He had already fallen out with the Irish First Lieutenant aboard his ship, and was saddened to hear that his Captain, whom he much admired, was soon to be moved to another ship. Again he reports on the health of the fleet. 'All the Fleet sickly, which I believe in a great part is owing to our having so many soldiers on board'.[30] By October he was obviously showing signs of strain, the constant movement of the fleet from mooring to mooring was taking its toll. 'We un-moor'd last Wednesday and last night moored again, and this night the Captain says we must unmoor again in the morning. I am sadly tired, having been upon hard duty all day, and am to be like so all this night, having three vessels alongside with beer and water which we must take in all this night. Rwyf fi fel dyn o'i gof. Am obliged to do everything myself, the rest of the mates being sickly and some ashore, ag os na chaf air da y Cadben rwan ni chaf byth'.[31]

In the same letter there are indications that John Morris was thinking seriously of his naval career: he recognized that his time in the merchant service might not stand him in as good stead as a similar period in the Royal Navy, and he realised that in many ways this was an easier berth than master of a small merchant vessel. He felt that he should set his sights on a 40-gun ship based preferably on Liverpool. 'Ond gwych fyddai gael mynd yn feistr ar un ohonynt hwy, ah? A master of a 40 gun ship is a good birth, but enough of this'.[32] Of such are men's dreams made – the sad reality was that he had hardly made a penny out of all his seafaring and now it was 'past one on a Sunday and at two I go to stow the hold. I've hardly the senses about me to write anything, and am afraid shan't get time to write to my father, therefore I desire you to acquaint him we are just sailing'. He had been delighted to meet Mr John Bodvel, the brother of Mr Bodvel of Madryn, and was certain that the old people, his parents, would be delighted to know that he had met such a close friend of the family. Perhaps he had a premonition of his fate, for he bade all his family adieu 'hoping shall live to see 'em all well again'. It was his last letter. Neither he nor John Bodvel returned to the shores of Wales.

Admiral Vernon had long been awaiting the promised reinforcements from England and had been only able to maintain a limited force off Cartagena: when the large naval escort force for Cathcart's expedition, under Sir Chaloner Ogle, eventually left England on 26 October, all Vernon could do was to await their arrival in Jamaica, intercepting enemy cruisers whenever possible. Ogle's ships had come out undermanned, and their stay in Jamaica had further depleted their crews by sickness, so that John Morris may well have been a sick man before ever reaching Cartagena. The Navy Board, writing to the Secretaries of the Admiralty from the Navy Office on 3 March 1741/2, accepted Vernon's criticisms of some of the ships sent out: 'their lower battery lying too low, and that they were crank ships, and believes that the Chichester and *Torbay* may be the worst of them'.[33] As these papers were written from the Navy

Office, it may not be too fanciful to regard Richard Morris, who worked there, as having seen them. It could not have brought him or his brothers comfort to know that their promising young brother John had been lost on what a distinguished naval historian has described as 'the most disastrous expedition in history. An untrained force was sent to the unhealthiest part of the world at the worse season of the year, with the maximum delay and the minimum secrecy'.[34]

The news of John's death filtered through but slowly: William Morris, writing from Holyhead to his brother Richard, found the 'fatal truth confirmed by all hands', and reported that his aged parents were grievously stricken by the bad news, and that their aged mother was almost inconsolable.[35] To add to the brothers' anguish, the more they heard of the ill-starred, ill-organised, and ill-fated expedition to Cartagena, the more they realised their poor brother might as well have died in his own bed. Ironically, the nearest account they had of their brother's death was from the same Ned Edwards whom John had had doubts about taking to sea with him: William wrote at the end of May on a Sunday evening: 'Ned Edwards gave but a lame account of brother's death, didn't mention the time or place. He says he was taken ill and recovered a little: then taken ill a second time and died of convulsions: says his things will be sold before the mast: had made no will: had about 40s. in his chest which he owed aboard'.[36] In a letter of the 15 July 1741 William informed his brother Richard that he had since heard that Captain Bodvel and Captain Morris, son of the Dean of Bangor, had also died in the Cartagena campaign, and the last link with John Morris came some time later when William wrote to Richard informing him that Ned Edwards had promised to call upon him in London bringing with him John Morris's ring, and any remnants still in his possession.[37]

The Morris letters refer to other Anglesey men who went to sea. The War of the Austrian Succession (which lasted until 1748) and The Seven Years War (1756-63) meant that there was a continuing demand for men to man naval ships, and the letters not only reflected the concern of people ashore for the outcome of distant battles, but also contain many allusions to men from Anglesey who had either volunteered or been pressed into the naval service. In an age when connections and patronage were important, it is not surprising that the Morrises with their wide circle of friends, with Richard at the Navy Office, and Lewis and William with their Customs service experience, should have encouraged young Anglesey men to enter the Royal Navy. They entertained high hopes at one time for their sister's boy, William Owen, 'a stouter, stronger-made lad than his brother John'. The latter had gone to live with his uncle, Lewis Morris, at an early age and was regarded as a promising poet and scholar. William Morris, in arranging in 1753 for his nephew William to be apprenticed to the captain of the Dublin yacht 'now abuilding at Deptford', recommended him as a 'lusty, ingenious lad, writes a good hand, casts accounts well'.[38] The intention was clear. William was to be prepared for a naval career: 'The birth is a good one, for the Captain's apprentices attend the cabin, and as they carry so many nobility to and fro Dublin, they get a good deal of money'. But this, envisaged William Morris, was but the first stage; his brothers, who were nearer to positions of influence in London, could then further his career, 'Perhaps, after he's been awhile aboard, some of you may do something for him'.

Four years later, Lewis Morris took up his brother's suggestion, writing to William that Admiral Boscawen's secretary, who was a friend of Richard Morris, was willing to advance William Owen's career, 'and has promised to speak to ye Admiral to get Wil Owen made a midshipman in the Admiral's own ship, which he can certainly do, and if W. O. was now here he would be entered in pay directly'.[39] Everything was arranged for William Owen to go down to Portsmouth where Boscawen would be for at least a month, and Richard Morris at the Navy Office was to obtain 'a ticket for him to go safely there'. Lewis Morris could see no problems apart from fitting the lad out, 'here lies the great difficulty – the money to fit him out, for he must have a suit of what they call *uniform* and a gold lace hat, before he is fit to appear on ye quarter deck'. Morris realised that his sister's family might not be able to foot the bill, but he advised, 'If he is *thoroughly bent* on this affair, let them stretch all they can and send him up directly. By answering for his character we can get him a twelve month's credit here for some cloaths and be besides of some little help to him'. His mind inevitably went back to Cartagena, the *Torbay*, and his long-dead brother, 'My brother John formerly would have jumped at such an offer as this'.

Little wonder, then, that Lewis Morris, in particular, was infuriated at his sister and her husband for their lack of enthusiasm: 'Of all the mothers and fathers in ye world I don't believe you can pick out a pair so simple as poor Will Owen has', and he had little patience with the young man himself, for the Owens had decided that he should stay in Holyhead rather than join the Navy. Lewis Morris could barely contain himself: 'Here Admiral Boscawen is in town, and the midshipman's place applyd for and granted . . . The recommendation from his own secretary, a man in great friendship with my brother. I am positive he would soon have been made a lieutenant and very probably a captain if he had any spirit to drive through the world. Such a step to preferment is uncommon. Good Gods! And so he is to be a negro like Mwcc mawr and people of that class, to carry coals to ye old woman of Holyhead, and to have a mammy's *didy* now and then'![40] Within a few months Morris was reporting the departure of Admiral Boscawen and his secretary, Macpherson, who had obtained the midshipman's place for Will Owen, with the fleet for the Bay of Biscay and could not resist adding 'Dyna lle buase'r ffwlcyn gan W. Owen rwan ped fuase ras'.[41] In the light of subsequent events, it might have been as well for William Owen if his mother had agreed to his joining the Navy at this time, for Boscawen was a new type of naval officer who was interested in the welfare and the health of the men under his command, and it was due to men like Hawke and Boscawen that an attempt was made to remedy the worst features of life in the Royal Navy.

William Owen did not stay at Holyhead for long, however, and whilst his more scholarly brother John eventually served under Boscawen, William threw in his lot with that other 'Holyhead Bay sailor', as John Morris had slightingly called him, Captain Ned Edwards, who had had a chequered career since his visit to the Morrises with their brother John's belongings. A prisoner of the French, he wrote to William Morris in December 1745 from Bordeaux, but by the following May he was free again and in Bristol by the autumn waiting for another ship. His sister 'Nel' kept a public house at Rhydbont, Holyhead, and William Morris saw her often, there are frequent references to the over-anxious sister's worries about Ned Edwards, 'He uses his poor sister ill in not writing to her, and she is so foolish as to be doating fond of him and fretts herself to pieces' – so much so that William thought she loved her brother far more than her husband, 'a millwright of good business'.[42] In March, 1747, she was more than ever concerned for Edwards had married in Boston on one of his voyages to North America, whence he used to bring seeds of plants and trees for the keen naturalist William Morris. By 1753, Ned Edwards 'had got to be master of a ship of 150 tons, to trade from Boston to Jamaica, thence to London, thence to Portugal, thence to Boston', and Lewis Morris grudgingly admitted that he 'may possibly do tolerably, for he doth not want spirit, though he wants learning'.[43] Two years later Edwards had been promised a letter of marque ship 'of 22 guns on one deck', and Lewis Morris had bought some excellent rum from him, which he sent by ship from the Thames to Aberdovey. 'Duw wnel na chyffwrdd y Ffrancod a hwynt, . . . rwy'n eu hofni yn dost, mae yno 32 gallons or rum gorau a brofais erioed, a brynnias gan Ned Edwards'. Privateering was a risky business and Edwards was again captured by the French: Richard Morris arranged for his release in exchange for a French captain, and, if Lewis Morris reported accurately, Edwards was none the worse for his experiences: 'Here is Ned Edwards just come to town, having grown as fat as a hog in ye French prison: and his owners are for giving him an armed ship of 18 or 20 guns'.[44] In his next letter to Holyhead, Lewis sent news that Ned Edwards was to have a much larger ship, and admitted that if only he had more intelligence he would have a bright future: 'If Ned had ye luck to have a head fit for preferment he might have been made a great man'. This reluctant compliment followed information which Edwards had given Boscawen: 'He has given Admiral Boscawen an account he took when in prison of the French privateers and their stations, etc. which will be of great service'.[45]

The summer of 1757 brought Captain Ned Edwards his new command, and Lewis Morris wrote to his brother William at Holyhead in August with the details: 'Ned Edwards is captain of a ship of 650 tons, mounting 24 guns, 12 and 9 pounders on one deck – a new ship (the *Superbe*) taken from the French with stores and 300 soldiers for North America (and now called *Viscount Falmouth*)'.[46] There were prospects 'for Welsh sailors thick and three fold' with Edwards, and their nephew William Owen was assured of a berth, 'he'll be some officer aboard, I don't know whether he's capable of being mate or second mate or gunner or what: he shall have what he merits'. Lewis Morris, who was in London at this time, was much interested in Captain Edwards's vessel and had heard from his other nephew, John Owen, the nature of her next assignment: 'Here is John Owen just from the Navy Office and tells me that he saw Captain Edwards who informed him that his owners have contracted with the Government to carry 320 soldiers to New York, and not to tell anybody, and that he must sail in 14 days'. Later that evening Edwards called on Lewis Morris to invite him 'to go on board at Deptford to reconnoitre his ship'; Lewis Morris himself responded enthusiastically to Edwards's invitation to prepare a notice inviting Welshmen to join the ship, a notice of the type not uncommon in recruiting crews for privateers, but this was unusual for it was to be written in Welsh: 'He is to have a letter of marque and just now I am about writing an advertisement in Welsh to put in ye papers on Monday or Tuesday to invite the Welsh sailors to enter on board their countryman. Llong *yn chwythu tan oi thin ai phen* a llawer o hylldod gida hynny – the first advertisement of the kind that ever was seen'. One of the first to join Edwards's ship was Griff. Griffiths, who had been Lewis Morris's clerk at Aberdovey, and was now entered aboard the *Viscount Falmouth*, 'as Captain's clerk and ship's clerk'.[47]

The party at Deptford went well. Lewis Morris reported to his brother William at Holyhead that 'she is a charming vessel and well found, . . . we went to Deptford with him yesterday, dined there and drank punch aboard'. After dry docking for inspection at Gravesend, she was to sail for Ireland on 5 September, there to take soldiers aboard, all in great secrecy, at which Morris snorted cynically: 'Dyna bobl gyfrwys! A phawb yn gwybod. However, we must keep it a secret'.[48] His nephew, William Owen, and his friend, William Parry, another Holyhead boy, determined to join Captain Edwards, arrived safely in London, but were afraid of being taken up by the press gang before they found their way aboard the *Viscount Falmouth*, and sent this note, presumably to Richard Morris:

'Dear Uncle – I have arrived here safe from the Press, but I am a stranger in town and afraid of being taken up. I should be very glad if my brother was to come here with some security for me and the other lad at the Sign of the Crown in Old Cock Lane – Your humble servant, William Owen'.[49]

His brother, John Owen, must have found them, for when the *Viscount Falmouth* sailed they were both aboard, with a number of other Welshmen, although not as many perhaps as Lewis Morris had hoped for as he admitted in one of his letters, 'I am afraid the Anglesey lads will be silly enough to stay behind'. Although he was happy enough to drink punch with Captain Ned Edwards, Lewis Morris could not resist adding, somewhat maliciously, in another letter to William, a comment about the Captain's appearance, 'anaml y gwelsoch i wr fwy, ai glustogau *velved* yn ei Barge, ag ynteu yn aur drosto fel pry'r *Lindys*. I suppose *Lindys* is ye old Celtic word for those lines of gold colour on that animal'.[50]

About a year later John Owen heard from his father that the *Viscount Falmouth* was at Louisburgh and that William had written saying that he had seen the French firing on the British as they landed 'hyd nad oedd y mor yn wyn fel pedfasai gafod o gesair dros ei holl wyneb'[51] and that Captain Edwards was so pleased with him that he had promised to make him master of a prize ship before the end of their voyage. But when they came home eventually it was without William Owen; it was the captain's clerk, Griff. Griffiths, who wrote to the Morris family from Bluefields Bay, Jamaica, in July 1759 telling them that William had died on the 17 June of that year, 'a burning fever carried him off'.[52] The *Viscout Falmouth* arrived back in the Thames after a voyage of two years and eight months: William Owen was the only man lost, which speaks highly for the efficiency and cleanliness of Edwards's ship. Griff. Griffiths, the clerk, was sickly, but William Parry, the Holyhead boy who had joined with William Owen, had come home a boatswain, with 'a Rigger's Protection to keep him from the Press; a good lad and he has saved all his wages about £80'.[53] No one had a good word for another Anglesey boy with the unlikely name, De la Hoyde, for he had proved to be both an inefficient sailor and a fool ashore. Captain Edwards was secure in the favour of the owners, who intended to sell the vessel and put him in command of another; in the meantime, Richard Morris ruefully nursed a thick head after dining aboard, for the first and, he swore, the last time, with Captain Edwards and half a dozen of his shipmates, with much revelry, drinking a wide variety of wines, the best of all being the 'bottled port' which had travelled from the Thames to Jamaica and had come back tasting even better.

Revelry in harbour was one thing, but at sea much had happened which brought sorrow to the Morris family. At about the same time as William Owen had died in Jamaica, his brother John died aboard the *Edgar*, a 60-gun ship, in the Mediterranean. John Owen was a protégé of the Morris brothers as well as their nephew; he was a poet whose work they respected, the friend of that most famous of Anglesey poets, Goronwy Owen, and a member of the Welsh literary circle which was to remain an abiding memorial to the Morris brothers. John Owen was probably born at Holyhead in the early 1730s, went to live with Lewis Morris in Cardiganshire as a young boy, and later moved to London where he assisted Richard Morris in the preparation of Goronwy Owen's work for the press. It was probably through the influence of his uncle Richard at the Navy Office that John Owen obtained a place as clerk aboard the *Edgar*, commanded by Captain Francis William Drake.[54] The office of clerk aboard men of war went back several centuries, gradually emerging as 'Purser', the man who looked after the stores of the ship, sold 'slops' and, in the case of 'pursers of talent and approved character', became Secretary to an Admiral.[55] John Owen obviously was a young man of talent, and according to his uncle Richard had attracted the attention of Admiral Edward Boscawen, 'Old Dreadnought' or 'Wry-necked Dick' as the sailors called him, Commander of the Mediterranean squadron. They had sailed from England in early April and had blockaded part of the French fleet at Toulon whilst Hawke's squadron kept watch off Brest. When Bosacawen's fleet put in to Gibraltar for water and refitting, De la Clue with the French fleet put to sea, and there followed the engagement of Lagos Bay where Boscawen did not hesitate to chase the French into neutral waters and destroy them. John Owen did not live to see this victory, for he, like many others of the crew of the *Edgar*, died of a fever at Gibraltar.

Richard Morris, at the Navy Office, gradually pieced together the circumstances of his death: 'a parcel of prest men were put on board the *Edgar* from the *Princess Royal* guardship at ye Nore, who brought the jail distemper with them and infected the whole crew, of whom abundance died, being taken with fevers and sore throats which killed them by wholescale'. Captain Drake and John Owen were smitten: 'The quinsey broke in the captain's throat when he was just a dying, so he recovered when it was in doubt whether he or his clerk would dye first'. It was John Owen who died. Richard Morris had seen the letter which Captain Drake had sent to his agent, Dickson, which indicated the good impression John Owen had made, 'The captain complains greatly of the distress he was in from the loss of the best clerk he ever had in his life and declares that he had rather have lost half his ship's crew, and says that though the admiral had promoted him he would not have parted with him this voyage'. With avuncular pride, Richard Morris wrote: 'Admiral Boscawen had actually appointed John purser of a prize ship, and had sent for him aboard to take his warrant at the very time he lay ill'; adding piously, 'but God was pleased to forbid it, and no doubt promoted him to a better place'. On a more mundane note, Richard Morris reminded brother Lewis that John had lived 'a whole year at my house as one of the family', and Richard had advanced him £12 'towards fitting him out suitable to his place', whilst there were some outstanding debts: 'Roberts ye taylor, has his note for £7.7s. for cloaths, and owes Evan Williams £6.16.6d. for his harp, which I think are all his debts. But I hope his wages and cloaths bill will near pay the above, especially if I can get the harp back again for Williams'.[56]

A little over two years later, Dr James Lind, physician at the naval hospital at Haslar, published his important essay 'on the most effectual means of preserving the health of seamen in the Royal Navy', in which he paid particular attention to the 'Jail Distemper'. He claimed that in 1759, when the fleet had been freed from fever, and 'infected vessels . . . properly purified . . . The *Conqueror* and the *Edgar* two new ships of the line . . . arrived at Spithead. They had been manned partly with pressed men from the *Princess Royal* at the Nore, and from jails'. He then gave a careful description of the fevers which raged in the ships which were subsequently infected by men from these ships, and his account bears out the circumstances of John Owen's death described by Richard Morris: 'The *Edgar* sailed soon after for the Mediterranean, where the contagion in a few months acquiring great vigour, together with a superadded scurvy, destroyed sixty of her men'.[57] The Morris brothers with their general interest in scientific matters would no doubt have been aware of Lind's treatise and may well have discussed its contents with the several naval surgeons who were members, or corresponding members, of the Cymmrodorion Society, men like Elis Hughes of Merionethshire, Evan Jones of Flint, both named as members in the 1762 list. At this time, the Cymmrodorion Society, due no doubt to the Morrises' own interests and circle of friends, had a fair sprinkling of members with naval associations, such as Henry Williams and John Williams, the one from Glamorgan, the other from Carmarthenshire, both listed as 'At sea, Purser in the Navy', several lieutenants either in the Navy or the Marines, clerks in the Navy Office, Charles Evans of Rotherhithe, a ship-chandler, and, not surprisingly, Captain Edward Edwards whose address was now given as Boston, New England. Another Anglesey member of the Council for the year 1762 was Wheldon Jones, whose address is given as 'Shad Thames', described as a sailmaker, an old friend of the Morrises. By 1762 the Cymmrodorion had been meeting for over ten years, first at the London Stone Tavern, in Canon Street, and then at the Half Moon in Cheapside; the naval men felt at home among these 'good tidy' Welshmen who liked a pot and a pipe and a gossip in the 'large room' of the *Half Moon* or the *Queen's Arms* (in St Paul's Churchyard, where they also met).[58] A naval surgeon who is not listed among the members of these first Cymmrodorion but who was no doubt welcome in this convivial society when he returned home from sea, was another friend of the Morris family, Herbert Jones, son of Tynewydd, Llanengan in Lleyn, brother of the long-lived rector of Llanfaethlu, Humphrey Jones; both Herbert and Humphrey Jones were well known to the Morris family and there are many references to them in the correspondence. Born in 1720, Herbert Jones served as an apprentice to Dr Evans of Llannerch-y-medd; there is no evidence regarding how or when he went to sea, but it is likely that he first went as a surgeon's mate, probably in the early 1740s. By 1746 he was ashore on leave at Llannerch-y-medd and William Morris described his uniform as covered in gold; 'He, it seems, is surgeon of the *Swan*, man-of-war, built at Chester'.[59] Tobias Smollett's 'Roderick Random', drawn from his own experiences as a surgeon's mate in Ogle's expedition in which John Morris had lost his life, has been praised as a classic of English literature, presenting 'a series of pictures of contemporary naval life which in vigour and sharpness of drawing have never been excelled ... Smollett is doing with his pen what Hogarth was doing with his brush'.[60] Inevitably there are many harsh and bitter caricatures of men in Smollett's pages, but he was probably drawing from life when he presented his sympathetic portrait of the irascible yet kindly Welsh surgeon's mate, Morgan, and it is interesting to speculate which of the Welsh naval surgeons provided him with the material for this lively character. The Morrises themselves found Smollett's writing both amusing and infuriating, but 'Roderick Random', published in 1748, certainly gives a valuable insight into the Navy in which members of the Morris family and their friends served.

By 1760 Herbert Jones was a wealthy man and William Morris reported that his brother, the Llanfaethlu parson, was buying part of the Presaddfed estate on his behalf. In September, 1760, Richard Morris had a letter from Herbert Jones, newly-arrived in the Downs, and forecast that he would soon be one of the leading men in Anglesey, for he had about ten thousand pounds in prize-money due to him. Richard, a month later, writing to his father in Anglesey, gave a more precise account of the naval surgeon: 'Llyma Mr Herbert Jones feddyg wedi dychwelyd o'r Dwyreiniol India, yn gawr penllwyd, ar ol saith mlynedd o bererindod: mae'n ddigon cul ei fochau, sudd y corph wedi sychu gan ormod gwres y fan, ond gan iddo roi heibio gwell na mil o bunnau bob blwyddyn mae popeth o'r goreu. E fydd yn sieri Sir Fon ar fyrder'.[61] From other scattered references in the Morris Letters, it appears that Herbert Jones had served in Admiral George Pocock's squadron in the East Indies and had taken part in the actions against the French fleet off Fort St David and Pondicherry in 1758 when there were heavy casualties on both sides; Herbert Jones was surgeon aboard Pocock's flagship, the 64-gun *Yarmouth*, and Richard Morris wrote to his brother Lewis soon after the East Indian squadron returned to the Downs that 'Herbert Jones Feddyg (Sierri Sir Fon yn y man) is at your old lodgings at Prestwood's till ye *Yarmouth* is paid off'.[62] Generous as always (unlike Lewis), Richard did not begrudge the surgeon his good fortune: 'rwy'n deall fod yr Harbad wedi anfon adref rai miloedd o bunnau, ac fe'i haeddai, nid oes ond tri'n fyw o holl Swyddogion y llong yr aeth ynddi'.[63] Herbert Jones, with his new-found wealth, bought the estate of Llynon in Anglesey, where he died in 1767.[64] His nephew, one of the Vicar of Llanfaethlu's sons, succeeded to Llynon and in due course became High Sheriff in 1791; it was his son, Humphrey Herbert Jones, who became Comptroller of Customs at Holyhead at the end of the century.

Prize money was very much a matter of being in the right place at the right time; Richard Morris recognized this when he reflected that whereas Herbert Jones had his thousands of pounds, George Williams, who had started out on a similar career, 'ei gyd brentis gynt', had recently written to him pleading great poverty, with a wife and seven children to keep. 'Dyna fel y mae cwrs y byd, rhai yn llwyddo eraill yn methu; diau fod y Siors yn llawer amgenach meddyg na'r Harbed, ond nid un o anwyliaid ffortun yw ef'.[65] Richard himself at the Navy Office was frequently asked by his brother William to have searches made on behalf of relatives of Anglesey seamen to whom prize-money and wages were due; the very fact that the requests became increasingly numerous suggests both that there were more Anglesey men in the Navy as the years go by, and that the casualties among them were also mounting as the wars dragged on, even though many more died through fever than were killed in action. The letters to and from Richard provide interesting glimpses of mid eighteenth-century Anglesey men in the Navy, although here it is only possible to refer to a handful of cases into which Richard was asked to institute searches: Owen Roberts, a Holyhead sailor, writing home from the *Dreadnought* at Port Royal, Jamaica, in 1758, that another Holyhead man, Richard Williams, 'was killed by a cannon ball in the engagement with the French on 21st October last in the West Indies'.[66] John Williams, midshipman on board the *Cumberland* in 1759, the son of Dafydd Williams, formerly solicitor at Beaumaris,[67] William Hughes of the *Revenge* about whom nothing had been heard for a year, Thomas Michael who had also served aboard the *Revenge* for eighteen months, and John Pritchard of Rhoscolyn who had written to a relative, Martha Jones, telling her that he was due to have some prize-money 'soon after Christmas' and asked her 'to employ a proper person to receive the same'. Pritchard had been a member of the crew of *St Albans* 'when she and others took the *Modeste*, *Temeraire* and *Centaur* and destroyed the *Redoubtable* and *Oursin*', and was now one of the prize crew aboard the *Centaur*.[68] Often enough it was not greed for money but sheer anxiety that caused William Morris to be plagued by his neighbours to write to Richard for news: 'Pray where is the *Hercules* ship of war? A young man of this place belongs to her and I am often teazed by the mother of him'.[69] Not all was sad news; Richard wrote to Lewis Morris on one occasion that 'Sion ab Ifan Edwart y Saer ar gyfer Bodorgan' had called on him, with an air of prosperity about him 'came home captain's steward in the *Buckingham*, and had been at taking of Guadaloupe, etc. and is worth money. His Irish wife is in service here, but he intends to put her into a shop: formerly kept divers alehouses about town and failed'.[70]

There was much haphazardness regarding the payment of prize-money, for this was some fifty years before Nelson wrote his famous memorandum to Earl St Vincent stating that 'Prize money to be as regularly paid in London, Portsmouth, Plymouth as Seamen's wages'.[71] Richard Morris, in the midst of personal tragedy, the sudden death of his son 'Dicie' in September, 1760, wrote to his brother Lewis outlining a plan which had been much in his mind for some time past.

'I have in the course of this war had a great deal to do with receiving seamen's wages, and prize money, which puzzled me confoundedly, for want of keeping a proper account thereof. I have now completed a scheme which will be of infinite use for ye future, where I have all before me, at one view, from 1st January 1766 and to be continued on the same plan, under the heads of Chatham, Plymouth, Portsmouth, a pay office in Broad Street for wages, and a head for prize money, agents, where paid, etc. I return about £5,000 a year in these articles, and get a small matter by commission etc. which helps dyn cloff a little; ond nid yw'r oll ond gwagedd'.[72]

Another task, adding to the hated mountains of paperwork which he alleged would bury him alive, was the frequent request for 'protection' for men and ships from the 'press'. As Liverpool became a more prosperous port, so the press gangs paid more attention to the waters frequented by Anglesey seamen, as in the case of John Morris, who had actually wanted to serve in the Royal Navy, but in the role he had cast for himself, and not as a pressed man. Naturally enough, the Navy wanted seamen and not landlubbers: equally merchant ships did not wish to be deprived of their most valuable seamen. The very nature of the coastal trade demanded a certain number of ships and seamen – Trinity House was allowed 200 persons employed in laying buoys – and the Customs officers at the various ports could request protection for vessels which were essential to the economy of their area. Thus William Morris at Holyhead wrote innumerable letters to his brother Richard at the Navy Office for 'protection' for certain ships and seamen of Anglesey. A few examples must suffice: on 17 June 1762 William wrote to Richard asking for protection for 'the *Elizabeth* of Holyhead, Watkin Thomas, master, burthen forty tons, in the Irish and coasting trade, three men beside the master'; two months later he was writing for a further protection for this vessel as 'the old protection expires the 2nd September'.[73] In October he wrote for protection for three Holyhead vessels, the *Hopewell*, *Speedwell* and *King's Fisher*, commanded by John Roberts, Rowland Butler and William Hughes respectively, each of them 'burthen six tons, three men besides the master, in the pilote and fishing trade'.[74] Occasionally a sloop carrying corn would seek shelter in a quiet retreat like Cemlyn in order to avoid the press; William sometimes sent urgent requests for protection for such vessels as the *Darling* of Holyhead, 'burthen of 40 tons, employed in the Irish and coasting trade, whereof William Williams is master, the former protection being taken out tomorrow'; there were problems when protection was delayed, for vessels with urgent cargoes were afraid to put to sea, 'protection is desired for four men belonging to the *Nancy* brigantine, John Forcer master, eighty tons, in the Irish and coasting trade. As the ship must be detained here, with he loading of sugar until her protection comes, you are desired to procure and send it as soon as is possible'.[75] Others that sought protection were the boat belonging to 'Sion William ab Sion Owen, gerllaw Figin gynt', for two men in the '*John of Kemlyn* in this port, Edward Jones, burthen about 30 tons in the coal and coasting trade'.[76] Not only do these letters give us an indication of the fears of the coastal seamen and of the activities of the press, they also indicate, albeit in a somewhat fragmentary way, the nature of the coastal trade of Anglesey before

1786 when the Registration of Shipping gives us a fuller and more accurate record.

Richard Morris worked hard at the Navy Office as a Chief Clerk to the Comptroller at a time when naval administration was complicated both by the increase in the size of the Navy and by the ill-defined relationship between the Comptroller and the Navy Board on the one hand, and the First Lord and the Admiralty on the other. From 1763 until his death in 1779 he lived in a house within the precincts of the Tower to be near the Navy Office; his work in connection with the Cymmrodorion Society, the Welsh School in Grays Inn Road, and his literary interests have been described elsewhere, but the same qualities of energy, industriousness and kindness which he showed in his dealings with his fellow Welshmen, were also given to the seamen who served in the Royal Navy.[77] Occasionally the quiet routine of his paper work was disturbed by more dramatic happenings: in February 1764 he was 'in a pack of troubles about the death of my friend, a Navy Surgeon, to whom I was agent, who was killed last Sunday seanight in a Duel in Hyde Park; I buried him and must attend the Old Bailey Sessions on ye Murderer's Trial, which gives me much trouble and conern'.[78] There were happier occasions; helping a Holyhead boy who had been apprenticed to a sailmaker in Dublin to establish himself in the trade in London, dining with such captains as Ned Edwards, who in his later years appears to have brought over North American vessels, one a year, to be sold in the Thames. There were the sadder occasions, such as the night he met Griff. Griffiths who had first sailed with the same Ned Edwards but was now a very sick man; 'angau yn cropian ar wyneb y ddaear',[79] going home to Wales to die. Richard Morris himself never went home to his native Anglesey, but his fifty years and more in London had a considerable impact on Welsh life, and upon the fortunes of Welshmen who served in the Navy.

One of the corresponding members of the Cymmrodorion Society in the 1762 list was Robert Lloyd, of Tregaean, Anglesey. There must be many thousands of visitors who have climbed to that simple yet dignified memorial to the Morris brothers overlooking Dulas Bay, near the Pilot Boat Inn, and gazed at ships sheltering in Moelfre Bay or sailing for Liverpool, with Mynydd Parys and Holyhead Mountain in the distance on the one hand, and, on the other, the magnificent Snowdon range. Fewer visitors will have been privileged to visit Plas Tregayan, a pleasant seventeenth-century house situated in the parish of Tregaean, some two miles north of Llangefni. Robert Lloyd of Gwynus Pistyll in Caernarvonshire came to live at Plas Tregayan when he married Margaret Edmunds, the daughter of a well-to-do clergyman, and it was here, on 24 March 1765, that his son, Robert, the future Admiral, was born. Robert Lloyd was the eldest son, and at the age of fourteen was entered as Captain's servant aboard the *Valiant*, a 74-gun ship, commanded by Captain Goodall. This was the acknowledged route for young gentlemen who wished to make a career of the Navy, for since Samuel Pepys's day there had been an attempt to provide a professional corps of officers for the Navy, to ensure that the 'tarpaulin' became something of a literate gentleman, and that the gentleman had an adequate training in seamanship and navigation.[80]

The year that Robert Lloyd joined the *Valiant*, another Anglesey man, in command of the privateer *Juno* with a crew of forty, was causing considerable havoc in the West Indies: Robert Beaver, son of an Aberffraw schoolmaster, John Beaver, had gone to sea at an early age, and during the American War of Independence gained much wealth through the prizes he took first in the *Juno* and later in the 28-gun *Hero*.[81] His health suffered and he returned to live at Maes y llwyn, Amlwch, but it is perhaps not too fanciful to suggest that young Lloyd, now starting on his career in the Navy, had heard of the Aberffraw captain who had made such a reputation for himself in the Caribbean and was to return towards the end of the war to his native Anglesey where he became Governor of the lighthouse at Point Lynas. But to young Lloyd the exploits of such privateers as the famous Fortunatus Wright, who had married Mary, the daughter of the diarist William Bulkeley, earlier in the century, and Robert Beaver must have seemed very remote as he languished in a French prison shortly before his sixteenth birthday. He had been promoted to midshipman aboard the sloop *Fairy*, but was wounded and captured shortly after joining her, and it was 1781 before he was released, not a particularly auspicious start to his career. After a brief period aboard the *Medway*, a 74-gun ship, Lloyd, in May 1782, joined the frigate *Hebe* in the English Channel.[82]

It was in 1783 that Lloyd's career took a new turn, for it was then that Captain Edward Thornborough took command of the *Hebe*. Thornborough had first gone to sea at the age of seven as a servant to his father, the first lieutenant of the *Arrogant*, in the Mediterranean. His career is remarkable for the very exceptional and continuous nature of sea service, for during a period of nearly sixty years he was only twice unemployed for more than a year; contemporaries recognised that he had few rivals as a practical seaman. Still in his early thirties when Lloyd joined the *Hebe*, Thornborough made her one of the most efficient of the Navy's frigates,[83] and it must have been an admirable training ground for the young Anglesey midshipman. Prince William Henry, later William IV, also served part of his sea apprenticeship aboard the *Hebe* at this time, and Robert Lloyd had reason to be well satisfied with his own prospects when he passed for lieutenant, a critical hurdle in the naval officer's career in November, 1790. Moreover, he had obviously made a favourable impression upon that 'remarkably powerful man with a pleasing countenance', Edward Thornborough, for when the latter took command of the *Latona*, a 38-gun ship, he received Lloyd aboard as one of his lieutenants.

In November 1793 Thornborough, in the *Latona*, engaged a squadron of French ships, endeavouring to delay them until the British line-of-battle ships could be brought into the action, and he was publicly commended by the Admiralty in a letter to be read to all ship's companies. When the mists off Ushant cleared, and gave way to sunshine on that Sunday morning known afterwards as the 'Glorious First of June, 1794', Thornborough took the *Latona* into the heart of the action to support the *Bellerophon*, which was being heavily attacked. It was a measure of Thornborough's high opinion of Lloyd that when he was appointed a few weeks later to the command of the *Robust*, a 74-gun ship, he took Lloyd with him as his first lieutenant; when his journal was delivered to the Admiralty Office, Thornborough certified 'that Mr Robert Lloyd served as first Lieutenant under my Command on board His Majesty's ship the *Robust*'. The Journals which Robert Lloyd kept are now among the Lieutenant's logs housed in the National Maritime Museum at Greenwich and describe in detail the activities of the *Robust* from the day in July 1794 that Thornborough as Captain, Lloyd as his First Lieutenant, and the three other Lieutenants had their commissions read on board, and Lloyd saw to it that the crew 'scrubbed Hammocks, washed and scrubbed the Decks above and below', to early in December 1796, when the *Robust* came safely to her anchorage at Spithead.[84] These journals of the *Robust* reflect the nature of life at sea during a crucial period of British naval history, and also indicate the range of duties of an individual vessel as recorded by her Anglesey First Lieutenant; cruising off Ushant, Scilly or Cape Clear, intercepting enemy vessels, 'at 10 made all possible sail in chace of three French frigates', or larger fleet actions, 'the van of our fleet well up with the enemy. Cleared ship for action at 6 the Headmost ships up with and engaging the rear of the enemy, we continue gaining on the Fleet'. This was six miles off the Ile de Groix, in June 1795, and the *Robust* was one of the expedition sent to support the émigré Royalists and their supporters ashore. Some weeks later, at anchor in Quiberon Bay, Lloyd records having to send 'all the Boats Manned and Armed . . . to the Beach', and, a little later, 'all the launches in shore to cover the Retreat of the Royalists keeping a constant fire at the enemy . . . at 8 the Boats returned the Royal Army having retreated to the Fort'. The next day it was an evacuation exercise, for in the afternoon 'at ½ past 5 perceived the Republicans had stormed and Taken the Fort. Sent all our Boats on shore to take the people off. The Frigates and gunboats weighed and ran inshore to cover the embarkation of the Troops'. But not all was excitement of this nature; there were the long weeks blockading the French coast, escorting convoys, swinging to a mooring at Spithead or to a single anchor in Quiberon Bay, the inevitable 'make and mend', 'sailmakers employed repairing the Foretopsail' and Robert Lloyd, like many a First Lieutenant both before and after him, followed the time-honoured device for employing idle hands, 'people employed scrapping (*sic*) the ships side'. That there were occasional discipline problems aboard the *Robust* is evident from his journal, particularly at Spithead before they sailed, and the defaulters were dealt with in the contemporary brutal fashion, 'Punished Peter Tomley, Mariner, with 13 lashes for Mutinous Behaviour at noon', 'Punished Thomas Horton, Mariner, with 12 lashes for bringing Liquor into the Ship without Leave', 'Wm. Paine and Peter Murray with 12 lashes each for Neglect of Duty'. 'John Gilbert Soldier for being Drunk when Centinel with 12 lashes'. A year later the conditions of service in the Navy led to the mutinies at Spithead and the Nore. There are references to the health of seamen in Lloyd's journal – on a Sunday in August 1795, after cleaning ship fore and aft, and mustering the ship's company, he 'sent the launch on shore with the Scorbutick men to gather herbs' in Quiberon Bay. There is evidence from another source which explains Lloyd's action in this case. Dr Thomas Trotter, who was Physician of the Fleet and had a genuine concern for the health of the common seaman, recorded that the scurvy was gaining ground among the ships, and when the *Robust* returned to Spithead in September after three months at Quiberon Bay, Trotter noted the course of the sickness aboard her: 'as long as the fruit and lemon juice were served, the scurvy was kept under control: but these being done in July, she landed 69 at Haslar in the last stage of the disease'.[85] One is tempted to reflect upon what went through the Anglesey First Lieutenant's mind as he entered in his journal on 5 October 1796 at anchor off the Ile d'Yeu, 'The Duke of Bourbon and all the French officers left the ship – Employed cleaning ship fore and aft'. From the sunny, though boisterous waters around Belle Ile and Quiberon Bay they sailed in 1796 for the Downs, and eventually cruised in the rather different waters off Texel and Camperdown, the scene of Duncan's victory in 1797.

On 15 December 1796, a week or so after leaving the *Robust* and being promoted to the rank of Commander, Robert Lloyd went aboard the *Racoon*; 'succeeded Capt. Roe, read my Commission to the Ship's Company, and took Command'.[86] Two days later, having taken aboard 482 lbs. of fresh beef, in light winds and hazy visibility, Lloyd sailed quietly from the Downs, and within a few hours in his first command at sea he was in action off Dungeness, firing his six pounder and bringing-to the *Vigilance*, a lugger. For the next two years the *Racoon*, under Lloyd's command, waged war on French vessels and intercepted and boarded ships of all nationalities plying in the English Channel. It is as well to remember that these were the years when British ships had been moved to the Mediterranean, despite the fact that this meant withdrawing them 'from home waters at a moment when the country lay under a threat of invasion and strong enemy fleets still lay in Brest and Cadiz in spite of the victories off St Vincent and Camperdown'.[87] In March 1798 French sources indicated that there were at least eighteen French frigates and corvettes and two hundred and twenty-six 'gunboats' distributed between the Dutch ports, Antwerp, Ostend, Dunkirk and Le Havre, and over seventy thousand troops encamped near the coast, and although Nelson's victory at the Battle of the Nile in August 1798 brought new hope to the English government, it is against a backcloth of invasion fears and constant threats to British shipping that Lloyd's journals of his activities in the English Channel from December 1796 to December 1798 must be read. The climate of crisis and anxiety in which Lloyd performed his duties will be familiar to the generation which one hundred and forty years later knew the fears of invasion, strained their eyes to look for enemy vessels looming out of the darkness, and followed the exploits of the 'little ships', the motor launches and motor torpedo boats of the 1939-45 war in the very same waters as Lloyd and the *Racoon*. And at home in Anglesey, Lloyd's contemporaries prepared themselves for the worst; at Beaumaris, not only the able-bodied made themselves ready, 'Robert Walters will sound his Trumpet being the only warlike Instrument he can use to Inspire his Neighbours to defend this County in case of an attack from its enemies as being an Infirm person, occasioned by a Rupture since his infancy which the Surgeons in this Town and Country can testify'.[88] Across the Menai Strait, the Headmaster of Friars School, Bangor, the Reverend Peter Williams, had preached a sermon at Caernarvon at the Assizes in 1797, and a footnote to the printed version to his sermon illustrates how he and many of his contemporaries regarded 'this hour of peril . . . Be it always remembered that this Sermon was preached in the middle of the French Revolution, when we were troubled on every side – without were fightings, within were fears – Buonoparte *without* threatened to invade and annihilate us: and *within* a factious Opposition encouraged his threats. At this time also the awful Mutiny at the Nore, and many other ominous events prognosticated ruin'![89] Captain Robert Lloyd in the *Racoon* in the Channel was a heroic front-line defender in the eyes of his Anglesey neighbours.

Here it must suffice to quote one or two extracts from Lloyd's journals to indicate the nature of the activities of the *Racoon*. On 20 April 1797, about four leagues off Beachy Head, on a night of moderate breezes and fair weather, 'at 2 a.m. made sail and gave chase . . . fired several shots and brought to *Les Amis* French privateer belonging to Bulougne and the *Good Intent* of Sunderland which she had taken'; early in 1798 in the same area the *Racoon* saw a cutter to the southward of her, and 'made sail in chace . . . came within Musquet Shot of her when she hoisted French colours and commanded a heavy Fire of Musquetry and of Grape from her stern chase guns by which the Master was killed and four men wounded'. But Lloyd was not yet beaten, and two hours after first sighting the enemy, he 'bore up and gave her our Starboard Broadside by which her topmast went', and when the French tried to board the *Racoon*, 'Brot too under her Lee and gave her another Broadside at which time (½ past nine) she sank, and proved to be Le Policrate french privateer of 72 men and 16 guns, five of which she threw overboard in chace'. Despite the loss of the master of the *Racoon*, George Kennedy, and some of his crew, Lloyd captured a small Fench privateer, *Le Parmé*, eleven days later, and on 29 October 1798 his journal records 'at 6 a.m. saw 3 sail in N.E. at ½ past made them to be three Luggers, made sail and after a running fire of two hours, brought too and captured *La Vigilante* of 14 guns and 50 men'. The *La Vigilante* was so damaged in the action that she sank and 'while assisting to take the men out of the other Two escaped to windward'. The frequent references to the 'chace' are in keeping with Lloyd's attitude throughout; not for nothing was he a prominent member of the Anglesey Hunt.

Occasionally the vessels captured were not French but British smugglers; on 1 September 1797 'at 4 a.m. saw a lugger in the N.N.W., made sail and gave chace, fired several shot and brot too the chace. She proved to be the *Princess of Wales* smuggling vessel laden with 200 tubs of spirits and 20 Baggs of Tobacco. Took possession and sent her into Dover'. In February 1798, the *Racoon* 'gave chace to a cutter in the Eastward, boarded her, she proved to be the *Peggy of Folkestone* laden with spirits, took possession of this and sent her into Dover'. A measure of the number of vessels sailing in the Channel in September 1798, for example, is indicated by the fact that Lloyd records in his journal either baording or speaking to ships bound from Cronstad to Lisbon, Flushing to Faroe, 'Newfoundland laden with fish', from Dundalk to Lisbon, a Hamburg vessel bound for New York, a sloop from Guernsey, and a galliot in distress in a strong gale, all in the course of about ten days. Not all the time was spent in boarding or chasing other vessels; every Sunday, when it was possible, Lloyd 'mustered the ship's company in clean cloathes and read the Articles of War', other days were spent in routine tasks, 'carpenters employed painting ship's side, people about the rigging', 'Gunners been fiting new Britchings to the Guns', 'people scouring the hold' after an action, and there were many frustrating days when having chased a suspicious sail for some hours they had to abandon their quarry just off the French coast, 'hauled our wind off the chace being too near in shore', 'chace of a Lugger close under the French land', and another 'close in St Vallery'. Occasionally there were cases of mistaken identity; an English gun brig, the *Biter*, was attacked in the dark and suffered casualties, and the journal for June 11, 1798, recounts a similar chase: 'Fresh gales and cloudy, at 9 a ship to the southward made a private signal, which we did not understand, at ¾ past 9 we tacked in his wake, beat to Quarters and made clear for Action. At 11 hoisted English colours, at 10 minutes past he hailed us and proved to be H.M. Sloop *Inspector* one of Admiral Duncan's squadron, whose private signal did not correspond with the Admiralty signals'. It was not the first nor the last time that mistaken identification signals have led to near tragedy.

Successfully intervening in an action by a French lugger against two English West Indiamen, attacking French shipping off Calais, Boulogne and Dieppe, Robert Lloyd had a particularly profitable December in 1798, for within two days he captured *Le Vrai Decide*, a 14-gun privateer, and *L'Intrepide*, of 16 guns and manned by a crew of sixty. Lloyd himself was wounded in this action; later in the same month he handed over the command of the *Racoon* in which he had proved himself to be one of the most successful captains of the smaller British vessels at a critical time in the English Channel.

At home in Anglesey, Robert Lloyd nursed his wounds and waited for his next command. He had married Elizabeth Charlotte Gibbs, the daughter of Henry Gibbs, Surveyor General of Customs, in 1789, and in December 1799 he attained post captain status, the most crucial point in a naval officer's career.[90] It was not until 1801 that he received his next appointment, but this time it was in command of a large ship, the *Mars*, a 74-gun ship, and again it was his old commander, Thornborough, now Rear-Admiral Thornborough, with whom he served, for the *Mars* was Thornborough's flagship in the Channel Fleet.[91] Among his letters from aboard the *Mars* is one dated 24 Feb. 1801[92] in which he recommends a certain Henry Roberts to replace John Prichard as Master at Arms, but it is not possible to say whether these were Welshmen, although there is some evidence that Lloyd encouraged his young countrymen. It will be recalled that Lloyd had shown concern for the health of his seamen during the difficult days in the *Robust* in Quiberon Bay, and there is striking contemporary testimony to this aspect of his career whilst serving as Captain of the *Mars*. Despite the encouragement of Earl St Vincent, the Admiralty had been slow to implement the plan first suggested by John Markham, Captain of the *Centaur*, to convert part of the forecastle of the 74-gun ships into a sick bay and dispensary where wounded and sick men could be treated in a clean, well ventilated space. Dr Thomas Trotter, in his *Medicina Nautica*, describing the medical history of the Fleet in the Revolutionary Wars, enclosed 'a draught of the Markham's Sick Berth' drawn specially from one of the ships which had adopted the plan.

> It is taken from the *Mars*, the flagship of Rear-Admiral Thornborough; Captain Lloyd, in the construction of this berth, gave every joiner in the *Mars* to the disposal of Mr Peter Blair, the surgeon, till it was fitted in the first style for elegance and accommodation. The Decks of the *Mars* at this time perhaps exhibited, above and below, the finest appearance of any ship in the British Navy. Captain Lloyd had even been at the expense and trouble to paint all his lower decks white, which gave the cheerful look of a drawing room to a battery of thirty two pounders.[93]

Captain Robert Lloyd was ashore again in Anglesey from 1802-1807, taking an active part in the affairs of the island, particularly the Beaumaris Book Club, later to become the Royal Anglesey Yacht Club, and it is likely that it was during this time ashore that he agreed to take with him to his next command Valentine Herbert Jones, son of Herbert Jones, Llynon, Anglesey, and grandnephew of another Herbert Jones, the naval surgeon, who had bought Llynnon out of his prize money. On 29 March 1807 Captain Robert Lloyd wrote from Beaumaris acknowledging receipt 'this moment' of the

Admiralty letter appointing him 'to the command of His Majesty's Ship *Hussar*, and am sorry to say that I am prevented from setting off this evening to join her for my being on the Grand Jury, and the Judge will not discharge me till the business of the County is finish'd'. Lloyd thought this would only mean a delay of a day or two, but he then planned to 'proceed without a moment's loss of time' to join his ship.[94] For the next month, Lloyd's letters relate largely to the problems of bringing his crew to its full strength; he asked for certain individuals whom he wished to have transferred from other ships, 'Mr Geo. Read, Carpenter of His Majesty's Ship *Cyclops* having been recommended to me in the strongest manner as a sober and diligent officer', 'Mr William Mc Dougall, Mster's Mate of His Majesty's ship *La Nymph*, late of the *Juno*, having been recommended to me, and the young man very particularly wishing to sail in the *Hussar*, being requested by his friends to take him under my protection', are among those for whom Lloyd applied to the Admiralty. And Valentine Herbert Jones went to the *Hussar* on 19 May as a volunteer 1st class, and so started a naval career which took him to serve aboard at least two more ships under Captain Lloyd during the next four years.

The *Hussar* took part in the bombardment of Copenhagen in 1807 and after further service in the Baltic was ordered to the American station. By January 1810 Robert Lloyd had transferred to the command of the *Guerriere*, another 38-gun ship taken from the French and now on the Halifax station, and in February 1811 he took command of the *Swiftsure*, also on the West Indian and North American station. Young Valentine Herbert Jones, now a midshipman, served with him aboard both ships. By June 1811, however, Robert Lloyd was back in Beaumaris, for the *Swiftsure* was paid off on the 11 April[95] and young Jones went to another 74-gun ship, the *Edinburgh*.

In less than a year, in February 1812, Lloyd was appointed to command the *Plantagenet*, 74 guns, and wrote to the Admiralty requesting that James Perkins, coxswain, Andrew Shoal, cook, Andrew Lamby and Michael Beasdon, servants, all of whom had served with him aboard the *Hussar*, *Guerriere* and *Swiftsure* in their respective capacities, should be transferred to the *Plantagenet*.[96] From his letters written aboard the *Plantagenet*, one gets the impression that Lloyd genuinely cared for the welfare of his crew and took trouble to recommend various members for promotion[97] or to justify compassionate leave. Moreover, he was not unmindful of his Anglesey tenants and their families; 'Richard Chambers private Marine serving on board His Majesty's Ship under my command is the son of a Tenant of mine, and was, when very young, bound an apprentice to the Master of a coaster sailing between Liverpool and London'. Apparently young Chambers had deserted the coaster after a disagreement with the master and had enlisted as 'a Marine Boy'. He had, when Lloyd wrote from aboard the *Plantagenet* in Jamaica, already served six out of his seven years as a Marine Boy, but 'it being the young man's wish to return to his former profession of seaman, joined with the very earnest desire of his parents and myself to the same effect', Lloyd requested that he should be discharged from the Marine Corps so that he should serve as a seaman entered on the Ship's Book of the *Plantagenet*.[98]

The first sphere of operations for the *Plantagenet* after Lloyd had taken command in February 1812 was the Baltic, where the British fleet maintained unobtrusive control and countered Napoleon's attempt to deny Britain cargoes of essential naval stores. The commander of the British fleet, Admiral Sir James Saumarez, used his ships effectively in a campaign which had vital consequences, eventually encouraging Russia to resist Napoleon's pressure. Among the Saumarez papers there are letters which refer incidentally to Lloyd's activities; writing from aboard his flagship the *Victory* in Wingo Sound, on 10 May 1812, Vice Admiral Sir James Saumarez reports the arrival of the *Plantagenet* which had taken ten days to come from the Downs, 'having had constantly easterly winds which account for the non arrival of the packets'. In August, and again in October, there are orders for Captain Lloyd of the *Plantagenet* to take charge of convoys or to escort Russian ships through the Belt.[99] In one of his own letters to the Admiralty, Lloyd complained of the unsatisfactory performance of his guns 'when attacked by the Danish gunboats' . . . 'the short guns were not equal to the services expected from a ship of the line'. Apparently even half and hour's action had proved their inadequacy and unsuitability for a long engagement, and he therefore requested that 'the *Plantagenet* be supplied with her proper long 16 pounders to enable me to support my own Character as well as the Honour of the British Flag entrusted to my care'.[100]

The outbreak of the war with the United States in 1812 demanded that many ships serving in European waters should be transferred to the American station, and among them went Captain Robert Lloyd and the *Plantagenet*. The task of the British Navy in American waters was a difficult one, for although the American Navy itself was comparatively small, there were hundreds of American privateers who were in a position to attack British shipping if once they had the freedom of the seas. The British had to blockade the Chesapeake and the Delaware, protect their own convoys and attack American shipping wherever and whenever possible. The American privateers harassing British commerce had had much success, particularly in the Irish Seas, and insurance rates, a sure indication of the perils of navigation, were higher than they had been during the worst years of the French wars. The British, freed, at least temporarily, from the commitments of the European theatre of operations, were determined to take a tougher line with the Americans, and proclaimed a strict blockade of the whole American coast from Canada to Florida. Among the significant items which appeared in the British press, according to C. S. Forester in his *The Naval War of 1812*, was 'a pitiful list of the captures effected by a single ship, H.M.S. *Plantagenet*, during three months off the American coast – twenty-five names, sloops and schooners of thirty or fifty tons, with total crews of two hundred men, brought prisoner to Bermuda'.[101] The London *Gazette* published extracts from Captain Lloyd's letter to his Admiral, Sir John Warren (Appendix VI[102]); the names of the twenty-five vessels and their proposed destinations give a telling illustration of the nature of the work of Captain Lloyd and his vessel in the context of a blockade which caused much hardship along the American seaboard. Lloyd's ship was a large warship, the vessels captured were small craft. There was nothing heroic about this work, but it was highly profitable and essential in the slow strangulation of American shipping. More significant to Anglesey, it was one of the sources of income, the prize-money, which enabled Robert Lloyd to build the walls of Plas Tregayan.

However profitable in prize-money the American War proved to Captain Robert Lloyd, it was in 1814 that his most controversial action as a naval officer occurred. On the night of 26 September

1814, Lloyd in the *Plantagenet,* with other vessels including the *Carnation* and the *Rota,* put into Fayal Roads to replenish his stores prior to his return to Jamaica.[103] Inshore he could see a suspicious vessel at anchor, so he ordered Captain Bentham of the *Carnation* 'to watch her movements,' and ordered the *Plantagenet's* cutter and pinnace to assist the *Carnation.* Bentham, observing that the suspicious vessel was under way, ordered Lieutenant Robert Fawcett in the pinnace to observe her movements more closely; this was at eight o'clock in the evening. When the pinnace approached the schooner, he was ordered by them 'to keep off or they would fire, upon which the Boat was immediately backed off, but to his astonishment he received a broadside of round, grape and musquetry which did considerable damage'. Despite Fawcett's repeated requests that they should cease fire, the 'enemy still continued their destructive fire, until they had killed two men and wounded seven without a musquet being returned by the boat.'

Lloyd's response to this was unequivocal. 'This conduct in violating the neutrality of this port I conceive left me no alternative but that of destroying her.' He ordered Bentham to tow the brig *Carnation* into harbour and all the boats of the *Plantagenet* and the *Rota* were put at his disposal. Much to Lloyd's annoyance, Bentham was somewhat slow carrying out this order; the reason for the delay was the jamming of a cable and slip-rope in the hawse, which caused the *Carnation* to swing round against the helm until the cable was cut outside the hawse. Meanwhile the American privateer schooner, the *General Armstrong,* for so she proved to be, was being warped 'under the Fort very fast' so Bentham decided to send the boats into the attack without delay in case she should escape. This attack was extremely costly, for although the privateer was on the rocks (which the British did not realise at the time), the men in the British boats suffered not only from the privateer's guns but also from a murderous cross-fire from Americans whom Lloyd alleged were hidden in the rocks immediately above the *General Armstrong,* 'every American in Fayol . . . being armed and concealed in these rocks'.[104] Eventually the *Carnation,* helped at last by a favourable breeze, anchored close to the privateer, 'and in a short time after she was a perfect wreck and then burnt.' In this second phase of the attack, the *Carnation* suffered few casualties. The *General Armstrong,* Lloyd later discovered, a schooner of about 360 tons with a complement of ninety men, had left New York sixteen days earlier and had in recent months caused a great deal of damage to British commerce and shipping. A valuable and hitherto successful raider had thus been destroyed, but the carnage in the British boats had been appalling, and Lloyd had now to count the cost of his actions.

Firstly he had to record the loss of many valuable members of the crews of his ships. His anger and grief are reflected in his letter reporting the action, 'so many of my brave crew being murdered in the most flagrant manner, without the shadow of pretence, by the privateer firing on them in a neutral port, and when the conduct on the part of my Boats did not evince anything like hostility'. But there was also the diplomatic crisis which he might have precipitated, for the Portuguese Governor of Fayal had sent Lloyd a note at ten o'clock, two hours before the midnight attack, in which he had reminded him 'that the English Commander of His Majesty's Navy ought to respect the vessels under my protection', and had ordered that he should abstain from any further action against the *General Armstrong*. Lloyd had answered that he had intended to respect the neutrality of the port, but as men from one of his boats had been killed and wounded 'without the least provocation', and as this was 'certainly breaking the neutrality of the port', he was determined to capture the *General Armstrong* 'in consequence of the above outrage.' He had then proceeded to order the capture or the destruction of the American privateer, whether the Portuguese Governor liked it or not.

Unfortunately for Lloyd, it would appear that it was not only the Portuguese who did not like it, for in the bundle which contains Lloyd's letters to the Admiralty is a note, in a different hand, unsigned but obviously the comments of a secretary either prior to or after a meeting of the Admiralty Board, and this roundly condemns 'the injudicious attack of the ships under the command of Captain Lloyd'. Lloyd's actions are then analysed and he is condemned for sending in a boat late in the evening, for it was unnecessary and was bound to provoke and 'produce the effect which followed'; he should not have attacked at night but should have complained to the Portuguese Governor: 'It would have been time enough to take the law into our own hands when proper redress had been refused';

finally, 'The honour and character of our Navy would not have been in the least degree impaired if, with a 74 gun ship, a large Frigate, and three smaller vessels opposed to a privateer, we had deferred till daylight any hostile measures against her, supposing such measures to have been justifiable'. The last straw was that Lloyd had weakened his force by sending home to Britain two vessels with the badly-wounded seamen, when there were still many privateers in the area, and the unknown commentator, comfortably removed both in time and space from the heat of the action, concludes 'The whole proceeding deserves strong animadversion'.

Such is the lot of a naval commander. Had the *General Armstrong* escaped under cover of darkness, Lloyd would no doubt have been blamed and regarded as a laughing-stock; had there not been a delay in bringing the *Carnation* to action, due to no fault of his but to the jammed cable, the loss of life would not have been as great, for it was the action of the boats which proved so costly in the lives of British seamen. But Lloyd was the Senior Officer who naturally took full responsibility, and had the sad task of informing the Admiralty that, in the boats belonging to the *Rota*, twenty-one men had been killed, three had since died, and forty-six wounded, whilst of his own crew in the *Plantagenet's* boats, eleven had been killed and thirty-nine wounded, many of them severely.

Captain Lloyd remained in command of the *Plantagenet* until she was paid off in April 1815. He did not serve at sea again, for with the final defeat of Napoleon the long wars with France were at end, and Robert Lloyd, like very many other naval officers, retired to his country estate, made prosperous by the prize-money of his campaigns at sea. He was fortunate, for once the wars were over, there were severe problems of officer unemployment, and between eighty to ninety per cent of the post Captains were virtually redundant. Lloyd lived until 17 January 1846, so that he had twenty-four years on full pay, on active service, and forty-three years on half pay, years which he spent for the most part in his native Anglesey. The promotional ladder for a post captain was slow, but comparatively sure; Lloyd became a Rear-Admiral on the 22 July 1830, and Vice-Admiral of the Fleet on the 10 January 1837 – halfway up the Flag-Officer's Ladder, the rank which Nelson had attained by the time of his death. Ashore there was much to interest

Lloyd: he was Deputy Lieutenant of Anglesey at the time of his death, had been High Sheriff of Anglesey in 1820, and took an active part in the social life of both Anglesey and Caernarvonshire. When he was seventy-two, Robert Lloyd married his second wife, Ellen, the daughter of Thomas Roberts, Surgeon, of Garth View, Bangor; his grandson recalled that Miss Roberts was then a lady of twenty-seven who 'took care of him, limited his grog, and checked his swearing'. Apparently old Lloyd once told the Bishop of Bangor that his swearing was 'a bad habit he had acquired since he came on shore'. Seen through the eyes of his small grandson, Lloyd was an impressive figure, rough and brusque with others, but gentle and kind to the small boy whom he called his 'man Friday', who was allowed to help him dress, and never ceased to marvel before the old man put on his wig, at 'the fearful gash that ran from end to end of his skull – a French delicate compliment paid him as he boarded *L'Intrepide*; also an ugly red mark on his side which probably dated from Quiberon'.[105] Visiting Plas Tregayan today one recognizes the still pervading power of Robert Lloyd's personality; his portrait stands out in a dining room full of portraits of naval and army officers, the farm and outbuildings and walled gardens are always referred to as the work of the Admiral; in the shade of the fine old trees, looking down at the Plas, there is the carefully measured Admiral's Walk, which Lloyd used to pace, the exact length of the quarter deck of one of his ships, probably the *Plantagenet*, his last command, and the unusual 'Admiral's Bath' which he had constructed at the side of the Pump Tower, in the wood to the south of the house, where he used to run for a shower in all weathers, even in his old age. The Lloyd's only daughter, Margaret, married Captain Thomas Parry Jones-Parry, R.N., who, like his father-in-law, served in many of the actions of the French wars, including Camperdown 1797, commanded the sloop *Musette* on the West Indies station, and went on half pay in 1814.[106]

Throughout this chapter there have been incidental references to Anglesey men who served on the lower deck of naval ships, and it is fairly certain that their numbers increased in ratio to the demands of the Navy for men. There were men who volunteered and there must have been many who were pressed into service, as the Morris Letters indicate. But with the Revolutionary Wars there came a sudden and vast demand for naval manpower which could not be met through the normal channels of volunteering or pressing, and the Quota Acts of March and April 1795 were introduced. These Acts were intended to provide manpower by giving geographical regions, whether in the country or in seaside towns, the responsibility for raising an additional quota of men, who, although conscripted, rather than genuine volunteers, would receive a bounty for serving in the Navy. Unlike the pressed men, who had for the most part in the past been seafaring men, these 'Quota men' were not of necessity seamen at all, and were viewed with great suspicion by the existing crews of ships, who resented them both because they were 'land-men' and also because they were being paid a much larger bounty than had been paid to the genuine volunteers, who had joined the Navy in 1793 at the outbreak of hostilities. The resentment was increased as it was felt that the local authorities in town and country who were responsible for the administration of the Acts had merely found in the Quota System an opportunity to rid themselves of as many 'undesirables' as possible, thieves and pickpockets from the towns, vagrants and idlers from the country areas, 'a sort of minor gaol delivery . . . It suited the Justices of the Peace to conclude that the local poacher would be as destructive to French sailors as he was to English birds – and possibly they were right, though there was no shred of evidence to prove it.'[107]

How far the Anglesey Justices recruited men by presenting them with alternative of 'Quota or Quod' is impossible to say, but the list of 'Lord Mayor's Men', as they were known in the Fleet, indicates that they had to cast their net widely in their attempt to produce the quota of men expected from them. At a meeting held on 27th March 1795 by the owners and masters of vessels within the port of Beaumaris,[108] it was stated that they were expected to produce one hundred and ninety-six able-bodied men; the meeting decided that the Lords Commissioners of the Admiralty should be informed that 'owing to the great extent of coast within the Port of Beaumaris', they had decided to appoint Commissioners to select men at Beaumaris, Amlwch, Holyhead, Bangor, Caernarvon, Conway, Pwllheli, and Barmouth, as all these places were within the jurisdiction of the Port, and that meetings should be held during the third week in April at the following places to ensure that all members of the shipping community were given an opportunity of recognizing their responsibilities under the new Act – at the Bull's Head, Beaumaris, at Tŷ Mawr, Amlwch, at Mrs. Lewis's, Barmouth, at Tŷ Eiddaw, Pwllheli, at The Eagles, Holyhead, and at the Harp, Conway. The Commissioners elected were for the most part men who knew the seafaring population well, shipowners like Jonathan Roose, Amlwch, Jared Jackson of Holyhead, Benjamin Wyatt of Lime Grove, closely connected with the slate trade ships, Wm. Sparrow, Collector of Customs at Beaumaris, and merchants like John Parry of Beaumaris and John Price of Amlwch. Commissioners and masters of vessels were of the opinion that within the port of Beaumaris 'able-bodied seamen cannot be had for a less Bounty than £30 per man, and Ordinary Seamen for less sum than £25 per man, and Landmen for a less sum than £20 per man.' This brought a somewhat shocked letter from the Admiralty disapproving these rates and pointing out that they were all about five pounds higher than the rates paid in the Port of London. Moreover, the Admiralty strongly disapproved of the suggestion that each assistant to the Commissioners should be paid an allowance of 'Two guineas per head for each man each assistant may be able to procure, besides sixpence per mile conduct-money, from such place is employed at to the place where the Man must be produced to the Regulating Officer for approbation'. A scandalised secretary wrote to the Commissioners that their proposals were absolutely inadmissible, that the usual allowance everywhere else did not exceed 5/- per man, 'and no other expense but those of paper, printing and other incidental disbursements'. Another of the problems of the Commissioners was that once the men were recruited there was no tender at Beaumaris, or the other ports, to transport them to a naval port, and they were ordered to get them to Chester in the best way they could. It was alleged that the presence of a recruiting party of the Cheshire Fencibles in Caernarvon was further seriously retarding the attempt to get men for the Navy, despite the handbills explaining Naval bounties which they had distributed throughout the limits of the port. Recruitment was indeed complicated through disagreements between the Beaumaris and Caernarvon Commissioners and the Admiralty letters drew their attention to these 'unpleasant altercations' which was impeding the work. Although the Beaumaris Commissioners appear to have defied the Admiralty and paid a higher rate of Bounty, the volunteers were very slow in coming forward, and in May, in desperation, it was decided that the relevant clauses of the Quota Act should 'be Translated in Welsh and got Printed and distributed at the expense of the Commissioners in different parts of this Port'.

With the minutes of the meetings of the Commissioners and the Owners and Masters of Vessels for the Port of Beaumaris in 1795 are a bundle of forty-seven separate sheets upon which are written the name and the amount of bounty paid to each of the men recruited for the Navy; these are listed in Appendix V. Some were seafaring men and were recruited as Able Seamen, men like John Tyrer of Beaumaris, John Owen of Amlwch, and John Williams of Holyhead, but many of them were labourers from the inland parishes, Llangefni, Llandyfrydog, Llangaffo, and Llantrisant. There were also men from further afield, a miner from Cornwall, a shoemaker from Blackburn, a gardener from Waterford, a seaman from London, and out of the forty-seven recruited, just over half came from Anglesey. There may have been others who were recruited whose record sheets have disappeared, but it would seem likely that the target figure of one hundred and ninety-six was not reached. It should, moreover, be borne in mind that Beaumaris had more ships and seamen at this time than any other port in Wales, and although the statistics of the eighteenth-century are notoriously misleading, it is as well to remember that nine years previously it had been estimated that, in all, two hundred and ninety-eight ships belonged to the several ports which were included in the limits of the port of Beaumaris, and these ships were reckoned to be manned by nine hundred and sixty-three seamen.[109]

When John Morris joined the *Torbay*, the Navy consisted of about thirty thousand men, but by 1796 the total was over a hundred thousand, and by the end of the wars in 1815 it was about one hundred and thirty thousand.[110] At the outset of the French Wars in 1793 the British Navy was still very much the Navy of the eighteenth-century, but by the end of the wars in 1815 it was much transformed and, as Professor Michael Lewis has suggested, began 'to look like a modern navy'. The clash had been between French land power and British sea power, and it was 'those far-distant storm-beaten ships upon which the Grand Army never looked' which 'stood between it and the dominion of the world'.[111] The peace brought immediate problems of redundancy, and Anglesey men who had thought of a lifelong naval career had to seek alternative employment.[112] One outlet for their services was the recognized preventive service of the Customs and Excise in their long war against the smugglers, the newly established Coastguard Service, and it was to this service that Lieutenant Valentine Herbert Jones turned. Together with Edward Owen, who had joined the Navy on the same day,[113] and had served under Captain Lloyd's command in the *Hussar*, the *Guerriere*, and the *Swiftsure*, Jones left Captain Lloyd in 1811 and went aboard the *Edinburgh 74*, commanded by Captain Robert Rolles; after service in the Mediterranean and the North American stations the young men found themselves unemployed at the end of the wars in 1815, but whereas Owen then remained on half pay, Jones served for six years on the Cape of Good Hope and Newfoundland stations, aboard the *Orontes, Sir Francis Drake*, and *Favourite*. In 1813 he joined the Coastguard Service, and in addition to responsibilities ashore he had command at various periods during the next eight years of the Revenue cutters *Rose* and *Sprightly*.

Lieutenant William Jones, third son of the Prebendary of Penmynydd, the Reverend Hugh Wynne Jones, of Treiorwerth, and Rector of Llantrisant, had followed a more chequered career, having first served in East Indiamen before joining the Navy as an Able Seaman on board the *Romney* in 1801, when he was about eighteen years of age. In the following year he had the harrowing experience of being wrecked in the *Sensible* and cast away on a quicksand off Ceylon, where he miraculously survived for several weeks until rescued by the sloop *Trincomalee*. William Jones then became a Midshipman aboard the *Victorious 74*, moving in 1803 to the *Windsor Castle* in which he served in several actions off the French coast and in the Mediterranean. He took part in the boat actions against the Turkish squadron and was wounded at the Dardanelles in 1807, but after further service in the *Sybille 44* off Ireland, he was promoted to Lieutenant in May 1809, and served in that capacity in the sloops *Espiegle, Jalouse* and *Stork* of which he was First Lieutenant in 1813. But here his naval career comes to an end, possibly shortened because of the wounds he had received in the Dardanelles, a service for which he received a grant of money from the Patriotic Society.[114]

Another Lieutenant who went on half pay in 1815 was Meyrick Bodychen Sparrow, whose uncle was Collector of Customs at Beaumaris; entering the Navy in 1804 as a third class volunteer aboard the *Endymion*, commanded by Captain the Hon. Charles Paget, son of the first Marquis of Anglesey, Sparrow had, like William Jones, served in the passage of the Dardanelles 1807, and reached Lieutenant's rank in April 1813. He was serving aboard the *Phoebe*, a 36-gun vessel, in 1815 when the peace put an end to his naval career, and compelled him, like the others, to return to his native Anglesey.[115]

The impetus given to the economy by the industrial advances of the eighteenth-century, only temporarily halted by the wars, meant that there were sources of employment for experienced naval officers who wished to remain at sea. The considerable developments in commerce and communications, in industry and transport, the massive emigrations in the first half of the nineteenth-century called for increased shipping and experienced mariners to man those ships. There were more immediate needs nearer home in Anglesey: Lieutenant Thomas Evans, R.N., surveyed the harbours at Holyhead and Beaumaris; Lieutenant Charles G. Robinson, R.N., produced his sailing directions for the North and North East Coast of Anglesey; the increasing number of packets and steamships plying daily from and to Liverpool from Anglesey like the *Albion* and the *Prince of Wales* needed commanding officers, men like Commander Emmerson, R.N.; whilst seamen who had served in the wars now found employment in the merchant service. One of them, Captain Evans of the Mona Mine vessel *Hero*, sailed regularly from Amlwch, whilst others sought employment ashore, men like William Francis, who taught navigation at his school in Amlwch. The men who had seen service in the Navy were now not only sufficiently numerous to suggest the development of a naval tradition in Anglesey, but they also had an important part to play in the economy of the island in the long peace that followed the wars of 1793-1815, the hard school in which they had learned their seamanship.

[1]   David Mathews, The Naval Heritage (London, 1945), IX.

[2]   Michael Lewis, *A Social History of the Navy 1793-1815* (London, 1960), 68-9.

[3]   Nesta Evans, 'The Political History of England in Mid Eighteenth Century Anglesey as seen by William Bulkeley of Brynddu'. *TAAS* 1935, 114.

[4]   *ibid.,* 115.

[5]   *ML,* I, 5.

[6]   *ML,* I, 6.

[7]   *ibid.,* 8. He added, 'I keep as regular a journal as any Captain that sails out of town, and far preferable to many who can hardly work a day's work, ay, some that does not know how to make a right handed triangle gets to be captains of good ships here, as more than one or two of our dear countrymen hath, the more the shame for them that trusts their ships and cargoes with 'em'.

[8]   *ibid.,* 9.

[9]   *ibid.,* 11. ':ladd Ysbaengwyns' – 'to kill Spaniards'.

[10]   *ibid.,* loc. cit. 'Mae bob amser yn groesawus i mi ond cythraul ydi'r wraig weithiau. Ye letter came to her hands first (he being at ye shop); she openet it and seeing Welsh and English mixt thought it had been some other language, and was frightened out of her wits almost, sent ye girl to fetch him home, and said there was a letter from his brother about some mischief or other'.

[11]   *ibid.,* 12.

[12]   Michael Lewis, *The Navy of Britain* (London 1948), 175.

[13]   T. J. Morgan in *Gwŷr Llên y Ddeunawfed Ganrif,* ed. Dyfnallt Morgan (Llandybie, 1966), 180.

[14]   For discussion and descriptions of the Press Gang, Christopher Lloyd, *The British Seaman* (London, 1970), Chapters 7 and 8; Lewis, *The Navy of Britain*, 310-12; Peter Kemp, *The British Sailor* (London, 1970), 98-102.

[15]   *ML,* I, 13.

[16]   *ibid.,* 14.

[17]   *ibid.,* 15.

[18]   *ibid.,* 20.

[19]   *ibid.,* 21. A recent study of the Slave Trade is Oliver Ransford, *The Slave Trade, The Story of Transatlantic Slavery* (London, 1971).

[20]   *ML,* I, 22. 'that's the lad's weakness'.

[21]   *ibid.,* I, 23. The *Torbay* was an old ship, originally built at Deptford in 1693, and subsequently rebuilt there in 1719 by Richard Stacey; she was 156.8' long, with a beam of 43.9' and 17.8' depth of hold, mounting 74 guns, and a crew of up to 600 men.

[22]   *ibid.,* I, 25. In his letter to his brother Richard, John describes the flags worn by the ships at Sheerness.

[23]   *ibid.,* I, 26.

[24]   *ibid.,* I, 27.

[25] *ibid.*, I, 29.

[26] 'In the commencement of the late war, the seeds of infection were carried from the guardships into our squadrons, to all quarters of the world, and particularly to North America, by the large fleets which sailed thither'. James Lind (1716-94), in C. C. Lloyd (ed.) *The Health of Seamen, NRS*, cvii (1965), 234, 303.

[27] *ML*, I, 30, 31.

[28] *ibid.*, I, 32-34.

[29] *ibid.*, I, 35.

[30] *ibid.*, I, 36.

[31] *ibid.*, I, 41. 'Rwyf fi fel dyn o'i gof – I am like a man out of his mind . . . and if I do not get a good word from the Captain now I never shall'.

[32] *ibid.*, I, 42. 'Would it not be great to go as master of one of them, eh!'

[33] ADM/B/117 quoted in B. Mcl. Ranft (ed.), *The Vernon Papers, NRS* XCIX (London, 1958), 348.

[34] Christopher Lloyd, *The Nation and the Navy* (London, 1954), 92.

[35] *ML*, I, 47.

[36] *ibid.*, I, 55.

[37] *ibid.*, I, 57, 74.

[38] *ibid.*, I, 231. William Morris was a great admirer and friend of Captain Weller of the *Dorset Yacht*, the yacht built at Deptford, and when Weller was promoted to a larger ship in 1755, Morris felt that he would not see his like again.

[39] *ibid.*, I, 449.

[40] *ibid.*, I, 468.

[41] *ibid.*, I, 487. 'There the young fool W. Owen would be, had he had the grace' (sense, i.e. to accept the midshipman's berth).

[42] *ibid.*, I, 74, 92, 128, 142, 154. In 1770 a correspondent wrote: 'An arm of the sea divides Holyhead from the rest of Anglesey, but except in very high tides is generally passable. At the end of the sand and tide road is a very long stone bridge, called Rhyd Pont, with a cluster of houses. Small vessels come up hither'. *A Short Account of Holyhead* in the *Isle of Anglesea*. Bibliotheca Topographica Britannica (London, 1783), 15. This where Captain Edwards's sister kept her Inn.

[43] *ibid.*, 241.

[44] *ibid.* 365, 376.

[45] *ML*, I, 477.

[46] *ML*, II, 4. Lewis Morris still had reservations: 'Captain Edwards is the biggest captain that trades to Jamaica, he is an important man, a pity there isn't more in his head'.

[47] *ibid.*, II, 4-6. 'A vessel firing forrard and aft, with much offensive power.'

[48] *ibid.*, II, 8. 'Such clever people! and everying knowing!'

[49] *ibid.*, II, 9.

[50] *ibid.*, II, 18. 'Rarely have you seen so great a man, with velvet cushions in his barge and he himself covered in gold like the Lindys fly'.

[51] Add *ML*, II, 952. 'so that the sea was as white as with a shower of hail on its surface'.

[52] *ML*, II, 136.

[53] *ibid.*, II, 206.

[54] Add *ML*, II, 958. The *Edgar,* launched at Rotherhithe in 1758, was 154.6' x 43.10' x 18.3' and 1,297 tons. She was at the reduction of Havana in 1762 and was broken up in 1775.

[55] Lewis, *The Navy of Britain*, 182-186; Lloyd, *The British Seaman*, 90.

[56] *ML*, II, 123; Add *ML*, II, 424, 428.

[57] James Lind, 'State of Infections in the fleets at Spithead in the years 1758 and 1759, C. C. Lloyd (ed.), *The Health of Seamen.*

[58] R. T. Jenkins and Helen Ramage, *A History of the Honourable Society of Cymmrodorion, 1751-1951* (1951), 66.

[59] 'Dr Herbert Jones a glywais fod dydd arall yn Llanerchymedd wedi ymdrobaeddu mewn aur hyd nad oedd (na bo ond ei grybwyll) wedi glynu rhyd ei ddillad, fel prin y gwyddechi o ba beth y gwnaed hwynt'. *ML*, I, 89.

[60] H. W. Hodges (ed.), Tobias Smollet, *Roderick Random*, v-xiv.

[61] Here is Mr Herbert Jones, surgeon, having returned from the East Indies, a grey-haired giant, after a seven year pilgrimage; his cheeks are thin enough, and his body seems dried (shrivelled) up with the heat, but as he has put aside more than a thousand pounds a year, all is well. He will soon be sheriff of Anglesey. *ML*, II, 261. *ibid.*, II, 245.

[62] *ML*, II, 265. In another letter Richard Morris states that Herbert Jones had admitted to him that he was worth more than £8,000, *ML*, II, 268.

[63] I understand that Herbert has sent home some thousand of pounds, and he deserves it, there are only three alive of all the officers who sailed in her'. Add *ML*, II, 962.

[64] The memorial tablet in Llanddeusant parish church is inscribed 'many Years one of His Majesty's Royal Navy Surgeons died June 30, 1767, aged 47'. Herbert Jones's nephew, also named Herbert Jones, who succeeded to the estate at Llynon, put forward an interesting project for the settlement of 'a colony of at least a Thousand people which shall consist of Artificers of different sorts' in North America in a letter which he wrote to Benjamin Franklin on 6 April 1783, almost immediately after the American War of Independence had ended. David Williams, 'An Anglesey Emigration Project', *TAAS* 1946, 51.

[65] 'That is the way of the world, some succeed, others fail: no doubt George is a better surgeon than Herbert, but he is not one of fortune's darlings'. *ML* II, 268. Dr Richard Evans of Llannerch-y-medd, to whom both Herbert Jones and George Williams had been apprenticed, was highly regarded by the Morrises and William Bulkeley, and when he died in 1742, Anglesey lacked a doctor for many years. There are references to George Williams's promise as a surgeon, and there were hopes that he would return to Anglesey to practise, but in the 1760s the Morrises were still commenting on the lack of a surgeon on the island. Dr Wheldon of Holyhead, who was

related by marriage to the Morrises, died aboard the *Experiment*; 'being surgeon of the *Experiment* man of war died in the Cuba expedition', according to a letter from William Morris in September 1749. ML, I, 145. G. Nesta Evans, *Social Life in Mid Eighteenth-Century Anglesey* (Cardiff, 1936), 100-104.

66 *ML*, II, 71.

67 *ibid.*, 112. John Williams was said to have died in the East Indies.

68 *ibid.*, II, 285; II, 249; II, 103.

69 *ibid.*, II, 484.

70 *ibid.*, II, 268.

71 Lloyd, *The British Seaman*, 146.

72 *ML*, II, 252, 'but all is but vanity'. Richard Morris had to pay 1/- for every search at the Ticket Office and he was much out of pocket as a result of his enquiries on behalf of Anglesey men whose relatives did not always 'think fit to reimburse me'.

73 *ibid*, II, 487, 505.

74 *ibid*, II, 510, 511.

75 *ibid*, II, 115, 131.

76 *ibid*, II, 438. A farm called Figin still exists, at Traeth Bychan, not very far from the Morris brothers family home.

77 R. T. Jenkins and Helen Ramage, '*A History of the Honourable Society of Cymmrodorion*', 29-36.

78 *Add ML*, II, 611.

79 *ML*, II, 222, 'death stumbling along the ground'.

80 Lloyd, *The British Seaman*, 81, 179; Lewis, *The Navy of Britain*, 250-4.

81 'Hugh Beaver, An Anglesey Sea Captain', *TAAS*, 1928.

82 Details relating to Lloyd's career are based on John Marshall, *Royal Naval Biography* (London, 1825), William O'Byrne, *A Naval Biographical Dictionary* (London, 1849), *DNB*, and letters, logs and journals referred to in the footnotes and housed with the Admiralty papers at the National Maritime Museum and the Public Record Office.

83 See article in *DNB* XIX (1909), 767-9, on Edward Thornborough by Sir J. K. Langton.

84 NMM ADM/L/R 168. The *Robust*, a 3rd rate, was built at Harwich in 1764, 168.8' x 47' x 19.9', 1,624 tons; she was eventually broken up in 1817.

85 Thomas Trotter, *Medicina Nautica* (1796-1803), edited by Professor C. C. Lloyd in *The Health of Seamen*, Navy Records Society, cvii (1965), 234, 303.

86 NMM ADM/L/R 109. Journal of the proceedings on board His Majesty's Ship *Racoon*, commanded by Robert Lloyd, Esq., 15 Dec., 1796 – 31 Dec., 1797; 1st January – 31 December, 1798. The *Racoon* was an 18-gun brig, built at Deptford in 1795.

87 Richmond, *Statesmen and Sea Power*, 196.

88 UCNW B + A MSS, ii, 310.

89 Peter Williams, *A Clerical Legacy* (Caernarvon, 1831).

[90] Lewis, *A Social History of the Navy*, 186.

[91] *Steel's Navy List*, 1801; *Mars 74*, R.Ad Thornborough, Captain R. Lloyd.

[92] PRO Adm 1/2068, written from the '*Mars* off Ushant, 24 Feb. 1801'.

[93] Thomas Trotter, *Medicina Nautica*, in C. C. Lloyd, *The Health of Seamen*, 264.

[94] PRO Adm 1/2076. The *Hussar*, a 5th rate, had been built at Buckler's Hard in 1807 and was therefore a new ship; she mounted 46 guns, 154' x 40½ x 13.6', 1,077 tons.

[95] PRO Adm 1/2080. Lloyd wrote on 5 June 1811 from Beaumaris regarding one of his crew aboard the *Swiftsure* which he had left on 9 April 'two days before the ship was paid off'.

[96] PRO Adm 1/2080. The *Plantagenet*, 3rd rate, 74-gun ship, had been built at Woolwich in 1801, 181' x 47' x 17', 1,777 tons.

[97] In March 1812 Lloyd wrote that the *Plantagenet* was without a Master-at-Arms, but recommended that Mich. Biarden, Ship's Corporal, who was acting in that capacity 'is perfectly qualified in every respect' and should be confirmed in the appointment as Master-at-Arms. In December of the same year he recommended John Miller, Carpenter's Mate, for promotion: 'It is with great satisfaction I am able to say he is a very deserving man, has been nearly twenty years in the service, is sober diligent and attentive, can read write and account and from every information I can obtain is perfectly qualified for a Carpenter in His Majs. Navy'.

[98] PRO Adm 1/2081, written aboard 'His Majesty's ship *Plantagenet*, Jamaica, 10 June 1814'.

[99] A. N. Ryad (ed.), *The Saumarez Papers, Selections from the Baltic Correspondence of Vice-Admiral Sir James Saumarez 1808-1812*. NRS CX (1968), 243, 263.

[100] PRO Adm 1/2081, Letter written aboard *Plantagenet*, Jan. 1, 1811.

[101] C. S. Forester, *The Naval War of 1812* (London, 1958), 174.

[102] *Gazette*, 1814, 512; Appendix.

[103] All the extracts and details that follow are from the bundle of letters in PRO Adm 1/2081.

[104] Lloyd, in his letter of 28 September 1814 reporting the action, praised the boats' crews: 'Never were there any officers or men that behaved with more bravery, coolness and resolution.'

[105] S. H. Jones-Parry, *An Old Soldier's Memories* (London, 1897), quoted by E. G. Wright in *TAAS* 1938, 91-2. Lloyd was buried in Tregaean Churchyard in 1846. I am indebted to Colonel Roger Lloyd for permission to photograph the painting of Robert Lloyd at Plas Tregayan, where the Admiral's Blue Peter and his sword when he was a cadet are still carefully preserved.

[106] O'Byrne, *Naval Biographical Dictionary*, 865.

[107] Lewis, *Social History of the Navy*, 118; Lloyd, *The British Seaman*, 179, 181.

[108] UCNW PYA MSS 33075 – minutes of meetings held 27 March – 6 June

1795.

[109] *ibid.*, letter dated Admiralty Office, 6 April 1795.

[110] Lloyd, *The British Seaman*, 261-4.

[111] A. T. Mahan, *The Influence of Sea Power upon the French Revolution and Empire* (London, 1893), II, 118.

[112] For a discussion of the redundancy problem among naval officers after 1815, Michael Lewis, *The Navy in Transition* (1965), 58-71.

[113] O'Byrne, *Naval Biographical Dictionary*, 845. O'Byrne does not give any details regarding Edward Owen's background.

[114] O'Byrne, 595.

[115] O'Byrne, 1101.

Copper, Slate and Shipping
1786–1840

Louisa Stanley, grand-daughter of Sir John Stanley of Alderley, was fond of sending long gossipy bulletins to 'Grandmama Owen', her grandmother living at Penrhos, near Holyhead, full of stories of the valour of the British guards at Williamstadt, of the fortunes of French émigrés (to whose relief Margaret Owen had been pleased to contribute), and exciting news about privateers. On 5 November 1794, writing from 'High Lake', where she had been staying, she told her grandmother that the weather had been so good that 'we bathed in the sea, as late as yesterday, and if we staid here longer would bathe again, the sea is so fine'; the weather had been fine enough 'some part of every day to allow us to take our walk,' and then she adds an unforgettable little picture: 'Yesterday and today we counted near a hundred sail of ships, most of them coming out of Liverpool. It was a beautiful sight, the sea seemed quite crowded with them.'[1] It was a familiar sight, too, for 'Grandmama', for by the closing decades of the eighteenth-century there had been a massive increase in the shipping off the coast of Anglesey, plying to and from Liverpool as that port's trade in imported tobacco and sugar, and exported salt and coal developed, not to mention the 'slavers' bound for the African coasts. Between 1785 and 1810, Liverpool's annual imports of sugar rose from 16,600 to 46,000 tons, and those of tobacco from 2,500 tons to 8,400 tons;[2] as early as 1770 Liverpool was exporting 48,000 tons of white and rock salt, most of it going to America and Ireland, whilst in 1791 it was estimated that 79,000 tons of coal were being exported, '57,000 tons going to foreign ports, and the remainder by coastwise shipping'.[3] Although the opposition within the port of Liverpool itself was increased because of the activities of men like William Roscoe and William Rathbone, in 1790 one hundred and thirty-eight ships were engaged in the slave trade, with a tonnage of 24,330, employing 3,716 seamen.[4] The 'hundred sail of ships' which Miss Stanley had seen and which were a familiar sight to her Anglesey contemporaries, were, however, not merely interesting in a picturesque, remote sense, for they were fundamental to the dramatic and far-reaching changes which took place in the economy of the island and of the hinterland of the Menai Strait during the 1780s and 1790s.

The wealth with which Richard Pennant transformed the quarries of Cae Braich-y-cafn into what was eventually to become one of the largest slate quarries in the world, and created at Port Penrhyn a base for shipping which would employ increasing numbers of Caernarvonshire and Anglesey seamen, was derived from the sugar plantations of Jamaica.[5] And even more directly involved with shipping and commerce was the copper industry in Anglesey, which coincided with the development of the slate industry across the Strait. War and slavery were both essential ingredients in the demand for copper. The British Navy, engaged in a series of far-ranging wars during the eighteenth-century, needed copper sheathing for its ships; as the naval captains recognized, copper-bottomed ships were more readily answerable to the helm, they were much faster, tighter, and manoeuvrable than 'uncoppered ships', and needed to spend much less time in the dockyard for repairs. The need to protect the hull of a vessel from attacks of worm, particularly in tropical waters, and to prevent the fouling of the ship's bottom, was also very necessary to the slavers, and Thomas Williams was as ready to meet their demands as those of the British Navy, and, indeed, the navies of France, Holland, and Spain as well.

The spectacular career of Thomas Williams, the Anglesey solicitor who became the virtual dictator and monopolist millionaire of the late eighteenth-century copper industry, has been described in detail by Professor J. R. Harris in 'The Copper King', and the story of the Amlwch mines by John Rowlands in 'Copper Mountain', the first volume in this present series,[6] here it is relevant to draw attention to the implications of Williams's enterprise as far as the seagoing population was concerned. At the risk of oversimplification, Williams's problem in the yearly stages was a matter of transport; having been called in by Edward Hughes of Llysdulas to act on his behalf regarding land in which copper had been found, he had within ten years become the key figure in two companies, the Parys Mine Company in conjunction with Hughes and John Dawes, a London banker, and the Mona Mine Company, in partnership with the Earl of Uxbridge. The nearness of Anglesey copper to the surface made it cheap to extract, but Anglesey lacked coal in the quantities required for large-scale smelting. Williams's nearest source of coal was the South Lancashire coalfield, made accessible through the construction of the Sankey Brook Canal; he could take the ores from Anglesey and smelt them in Lancashire near the coalfield, or he could bring the coal to Anglesey to carry out the smelting on the Parys Mountain site. Whichever policy he adopted, the tax on the coastwise shipment of coal would increase costs. His solution was a compromise: the copper ore was partially smelted in Anglesey, so as to reduce the cost of freightage, and was then sent to two smelting works at St Helens, the Stanley works, owned by Thomas Williams, Lord Uxbridge, John Dawes, and John Wilkinson, the famous ironmaster, and the Ravenshead works, owned by the Parys Mine Company. Both works were managed from 1780 by Michael Hughes, an Anglesey man born at Lleiniog, youngest brother of Edward Hughes, Llysdulas.[7] In the 1780s Williams extended his interests by acquiring key works in the copper and brass industries at Holywell and Greenfield in Flintshire; alternative copper smelting works at Upper Bank, Swansea, to which he later added those at Middle Bank and Penclawdd; a Birmingham warehouse; the Temple Brass Mills in Buckinghamshire; further warehouses in Liverpool and London; and a chemical works, the Garston Vitriol Works. As Professor Harris states, 'It is obvious that he had grasped the essential principle of cartel working – that of mastering a sufficient part of the industry to dominate the whole'.[8] Although nominally independent, all the concerns were in fact run by Williams, and from 1788 to 1792, in particular, he was virtually 'dictator of the national copper trade'.[9] One example of his enterprise must suffice: when the British and French navies at the end of the American War of Independence realised that three large ships had been lost with much loss of life because of the 'ships being copper sheathed upon iron bolts and other iron fastenings', it was Williams who set about finding a solution in 'providing copper bolts and sheathing nails of sufficient hardness, and to abandon the iron ones, so avoiding galvanic action', and it was to Williams that the British Admiralty had to turn for copper patent bolts. Before long Williams was simultaneously supplying the navies of France, Holland and Spain.[10]

As the scale of the copper mining operations in Amlwch increased, so did the need for vessels to transport the ores to the St

Helens and Swansea smelting works. The vessels used in the first place were naturally those already sailing in the trade; the registers of Beaumaris and Liverpool for 1786 and 1787 indicate that there was a considerable number of vessels built in the 1770s which must have been available. Some of them had been carrying ores destined for the Warrington Copper and Brass Company from Amlwch in the pre-Williams period. The *Speedwell* of Pwllheli, the *Morning Star* of Conway, the *Molly* of Cemlyn, the *Providence* of Caernarvon, the *Blessing* of Aberystwyth, the *Blessing* of Aberdovey, the *Jenny* of Amlwch were among those that took cargoes of thirty tons or less in 1770 and 1771; in 1771 twenty-three different vessels took a total of 2,236 tons of ore from Amlwch, some of them making several voyages, the heaviest cargo being that of the *William and James*, which took ten cargoes of 70 tons, and at the opposite end of the scale, the *Sea Horse*, which carried three cargoes of 16 tons each.[11] In 1775 two hundred and two tons of 'raw copper ore' were shipped for Sir Nicholas Bayly for Neath in five vessels, the *William and Jane*, the *Peggy*, the *Providence*, the *Happy Return* and the *William and Mary*.[12] When the first register of ships was made in 1786, there were one hundred and ninety-eight vessels registered in the port of Beaumaris,[13] a large number of these vessels would have been employed in carrying slate in the 70s, but they would certainly have included some vessels which had also carried copper ores and coal; these were the vessels which were immediately available to Williams and his partners.

By the late 80s Thomas Williams was so involved in the large-scale undertakings that he did not have a personal interest in more than two vessels, both registered at Liverpool. The *Green Linnet*, a 76-ton sloop, was owned by him, his partner John Dawes, the London banker, and Michael Hughes, the manager at St Helens; the *Raven*, a 73 tons galliot, built at St Helens in 1788, was owned by Williams, Dawes, and the Reverend Edward Hughes of Greenfield, Flintshire.[14] But Williams was anxious to encourage both owners and masters of ships at Amlwch, and some sixteen years later James Treweek, the Amlwch mine agent, reminded Lord Anglesey's agent that in Williams's day there was a clear appreciation of the mutual interest of the mine owners and the shipping community: 'we can venture to affirm that if the persons here interested in shipping are once so far discouraged as to be made to sell of their vessels, the Proprietors of the mines will find much difficulty in getting their goods carried so cheap and regular as at present. Of this fact the late Mr Williams was well convinced, and in order to induce experienced mariners to settle in the place he allowed masters of vessels a gratuity in addition to the freight paid.'[15] It was not only masters of vessels that were encouraged by Thomas Williams: the ownership of vessels built in the 1780s suggests that men in managerial positions in the copper and allied industries saw the financial possibilities of investing in Amlwch shipping. Professor Harris gives 1788 as the date of the formation of the Amlwch Shipping Company, but the evidence of the 1786 Register indicates that it was already in existence in that year, with interests in the following vessels:

> *Eagle*, Owen Mathias, master, built Rhuddlan 1786, 54' x18.4' x 10', 76 tons, Brig.
> *Mona*, James Eyres, master, built Liverpool 1786, 59.8' x 19.3' x 11.8', 94 tons, Brig.
> *Eleanor*, William Williams, master, built Red Wharf 1786, 53' x 19.2' x 10.6', 81 tons, Brig.
> *Mary*, James Roose, master, built Caernarvon 1784, 53.4' x 18.7' x 10.6', 77 tons, Brig.
> *San Pareil*, William Hughes, master, built Pwllheli 1783, 47.9' x 17.8' x 9.7', 61 tons, Sloop.
> *Amlwch*, Rowland Owen, master, built Beaumaris 1786, 54.5' x 18.2' x 11', 76 tons, Brig.
> *Kitty*, John Kackay, master, built Liverpool 1785, 54.10' x 19' x 11', 83 tons, Sloop.
> *Portland*, John Pritchard, master, built Pwllheli 1778, 54.10' x 19' x 10', 83 tons, Sloop.[16]

These comparatively new vessels, larger than the usual run of local vessels, suggest that the Amlwch Shipping Company, in which John Price, the Mona Mine Agent, Stephen Roose of the Parys Mine, John Stephens of the Liverpool Copper Office, and Michael Hughes, manager of the St Helens Works, were prominent members, had responded quickly to the new demands for copper ore carrying vessels. There were also a number of private ventures in larger vessels in which this group and their associates were involved: the Rooses, Price, and Howson of Amlwch, Jackson, Percival and David Jones, all Liverpool merchants; Samuel Williamson and a Greenfield group; Michael Hughes of St Helens and David Richards of Swansea were members of the group who owned the brigantines *Maria*, 95 tons, built at Portinllaen in 1786; the *Uxbridge*, 124 tons, built at Liverpool in the same year; the sloop *Sally*, 41 tons, built at Barmouth in 1785; and the brigantine *Jane*, 102 tons, built at Chester and later captured in the French Wars.[17] Between 1786 and 1789 over seventy vessels were engaged in the carrying trade to St Helens and Swansea from Amlwch, many of them small vessels owned by local farmers, mariners, and small businessmen, all of them benefiting from Amlwch's boom-town conditions with its population increased to nearly five thousand by 1801.[18]

The nature of the work of these vessels may be illustrated by one or two examples from the Port Books. The Beaumaris-built brig, *Amlwch*, commanded by a local man, Rowland Owen, took six separate cargoes of 70 tones of copper ore from Amlwch to Liverpool in the six month period from July to December 1789, four for Lord Uxbridge, and two for Hughes and Company. During this period she also brought coal and cast-iron plates from Swansea and Cardiff to Amlwch, and 20 barrels of white salted herrings along with one of the copper ore cargoes to Liverpool from Amlwch.

Whilst the *Amlwch* was making these voyages, the *Uxbridge*, a 124-ton brigantine, commanded by another local man, Robert Roberts, took four freights, one of 60 tons, the others of 100 tons for Parys Mine, to Liverpool, and brought three cargoes of coal, one from Swansea and two from Liverpool, to Amlwch. The *Portland*, an 83-ton sloop, another of the Amlwch Shipping Company vessels, made eight voyages to Liverpool during the same period, three cargoes of copper for the Mona Mine Company and five for the Parys Mine Company; she brought back four cargoes for different merchants: tobacco, rum, brandy, timber, flour, earthenware, iron, and coal; the details of the remaining four inward cargoes are not recorded.[19] A final example: the *Mersey*, a flat owned by John Jackson, the Liverpool merchant, and Michael Hughes, the St Helens manager, took four cargoes for the Mona Mine and two for the Parys Company, each of 60 tons of copper, from Amlwch to

Liverpool, but as there is no record of the inward cargoes she may have returned in ballast. Hughes and Jackson owned a number of flats, the *Happy*, the *Union* and the *Miner*, all newly-built, with a similar beam of 16' 7", no doubt specially designed to be used on the Sankey Canal as well as in the open sea. When the *Union* was sold to the Amlwch Shipping Company in 1790 Hughes, who had a third share in her, received £187. He was also part-owner, with associates and neighbours in St Helens, of the flats *Nancy*, *Anne* and the *Friends*. Michael Hughes was an enterprising man, in the mould of Thomas Williams himself; it is not surprising to find that in addition to his copper and shipping interests he was a shareholder in canals, the Amlwch Brewery, the Bootle Bottle Company; the friend and associate of the Greenalls, the brewers, and John Wilkinson, the ironmaster; lent money to the first Sir Robert Peel, was a considerable landowner and a very active magistrate in the St Helens area.[20] The Amlwch Shipping Company, of which he was a prominent member, still had three brigs, one sloop and a galliot sailing regularly for them in 1823, but their accounts indicate that a year after Hughes's death in 1825 all except the brig *Mary* and the flat *Union* had been sold.[21]

With such men as Thomas Williams and Michael Hughes involved, it is not surprising that there was dissatisfaction with the harbour at Amlwch, described by Lewis Morris as 'a small creek, two miles to the West of Eilian's Point' which he did not consider worth a plan, as it was 'no more than a cover between two steep rocks, where a vessel hath not Room to wind even at High Water.' Some defensive works had already been carried out in the 1780s, but there was clearly a need to improve the harbour to avoid delays for the scores of ships now using it, and in 1793 an Act of Parliament was passed 'for enlarging, deepening, cleansing, improving and regulating the Harbour of Amlwch.' The undated watercolour by John Smith who toured Wales in the 1790s shows two piers forming the entrance with two small white houses on them, both of which probably displayed lights. These were later replaced by a small lighthouse which was built at the end of the 150-foot pier which was completed in 1816, projecting out in a north-westerly direction from the east side of the harbour. Danielle's well-known view of the harbour, engraved in 1815, does not therefore show this pier, but it does show the eight large ore hoppers 'contrived against the rock-face on the east side and filled from the upper-level road.'[22] The improvements to the harbour were welcome, not only because of the improved facilities which by 1797 were said to enable thirty vessels to enter the harbour, but also because 'in cases of strong North and westerly winds' it would 'be very useful as a place of retreat for ships and vessels navigating the North, English and Irish Channels'. The sad record of vessels lost shown in the registers from 1786 bears silent testimony to the need for places of refuge; the voyages from Amlwch to Swansea and Liverpool in the winter months took a heavy toll.

Not all the vessels lost were engaged in the copper trade; there were many more now carrying slate from the Menai Strait following the development of the Penrhyn quarries. In addition to the examples quoted in the copper trade in the six month period July–December 1787, there were many slate and general cargoes among the two hundred and more shipments recorded in the Port Book of Beaumaris. Here, again, only one or two examples can be given: the *Thomas and Jane*, a 21-ton sloop owned by Dean Thomas, mariner, and Jonathan Roose, merchant, both of Amlwch, and Jane Roberts of Bangor, took 15,000 slates and empty casks to Liverpool on July 6th, 1789, returning to the Strait with 'geneva', brandy, earthenware, coal, and 32 barrels of white salt. A week later she took another 14,000 slates and empty casks to Liverpool, again returning with a miscellaneous cargo, coal and 34 barrels of white salt. This was the pattern of her trade, four more voyages to Liverpool with slates, empty casks, old iron and rags, returning with miscellaneous cargoes, mainly coal and salt. The *Pennant*, a 30-ton sloop, owned by Owen Williams, mariner, Llanallgo, and Shadrach Williams, Llanrhwydrys, farmer, with two other farmers from Llandysilio and Llechgynfarwy as non-subscribing owners, made voyages with 13,000 slates and 10 tons of kelp to Liverpool, returning with timber, flour, groceries and coal, whilst the *Morning Star* made voyages to Conway and Whitehaven with slates, and with potatoes to Chester, and a number of vessels, including the *Harriet Elizabeth*, the *Lady Bulkeley*, the *William and Mary* and the *Lord Bulkeley* made voyages to Irish ports, Dundalk, Dublin and Newry, outward with slate, inward with cattle and horses.

The years 1789-94 were years of considerable building activity in Britain, and these were prosperous years for the slate industry. The outbreak of war with France was a severe setback to the trade with London, insurance charges on freight increased alarmingly, and some of the slate vessels refused to go further than Milford. The slate tax also seriously affected the trade from 1795, but the demands of Liverpool and the northern counties were such that there was still a good market there, and naturally these were regarded as much safer waters in which to sail than the English Channel in wartime, as already indicated in the account of Captain Lloyd's activities there. Between 1794 and 1798 there was a drastic cut in the output of the Penrhyn quarry and the number of employees was reduced from over five hundred to a little over a hundred. The improvement in the market after this date, and the fact that Penrhyn could get their slates to the vessels at Port Penrhyn so much more cheaply than the Nantlle and Ffestiniog quarries could get their produce to Caernarvon and Portmadoc meant that the Strait was still busy with slate vessels at the turn of the century, and within the next three decades this activity increased dramatically, particularly after the development of Felinheli, later called Port Dinorwic, by Assheton Smith.[23] As early as 1783 vessels had been built at Moel-y-don, the *Earl of Uxbridge*, a 120-ton brig, two small sloops, the *Little John* and the *Lady Caroline* (built in 1786).[24] In 1791 another comparatively large vessel, the *Countess of Uxbridge*, was built at Moel-y-don, whilst a number of other vessels were built at Pwllffannog, Beaumaris and Bangor, all in response to the increased activity in the slate trade in the early 1790s.

The Beaumaris register from 1789 contains evidence that as in the copper trade, so in the slate industry, men in managerial positions ashore saw the possibilities of investing in shipping. Lord Penrhyn's agent, Benjamin Wyatt of Lime Grove, Bangor, had shares in a number of slate vessels: the *Albion, Lord Bulkeley, Lady Penrhyn*, Thomas Williams's old vessel the *Green Linnet*, sold in 1799 a little before his death, the *Raven, Friendship*, the *Bangor and Liverpool Packet*, the *Penrhyn Castle*, and the *Olive*. His relatives, James and Arthur Wyatt, similarly had interests in fourteen vessels, whilst Samuel Worthington of Llwynon, Llandygai, who owned a mill for grinding flint stones 'which are brought from the coasts of Kent and

Cornwall and reduced here to an impalpable powder and then conveyed to the pottery at Liverpool' had shares in at least seven vessels.[25] But as with the Amlwch copper vessels, local merchants, druggists, drapers, as well as farmers and quarrymen, also invested their savings in the slate vessels, and the late David Thomas noted that in addition to the above groups, men like John Elias, 'Minister of the Gospel', Llanfechell, Evan Richardson, a well-known Caernarvon schoolmaster, and John Jones Talysarn, another well-known preacher, held shares in local ships. He also estimated, in the absence of the relevant Port Books, on the basis of shipping returns in the local *North Wales Gazette* in 1808, that 268 vessels sailed from Port Penrhyn, 106 from Hirael, and 237 from Caernarvon with cargoes of slate during just one year, with over eighty vessels leaving the Strait in both March and June of that year.[26] It is too early to have accurate records of the crews of these vessels, but it may be safely assumed that a fair proportion came from Anglesey as well as Bangor, Caernarvon and Lleyn.

In view of the heavy traffic of sailing ships through the Menai Strait there was much evidence given in opposition to the building of the Suspension Bridge and, later, to the Tubular Bridge. Although both Telford and Stephenson were eventually proven to have been justified, the opposition was genuinely and generally held by many of the master mariners who gave evidence. It was argued by more than one of the Menai pilots that a bridge would impede navigation; that the baffling winds in the Swellies would be made even more treacherous, particularly as square-rigged vessels needed their highest sails to counteract the high land on either side of this most difficult part of the Strait, and one witness stressed that he would wish to use 'topgallant sails, royals and topgallant studding sails if I could carry them,'[27] More relevant in this present context is the evidence presented by the pilots that not only did coasting vessels beat through the Swellies, 'from 15 to 20 together,' but vessels of three to four hundred tons were known to pass through, such as the American ship bound from Liverpool to New Providence in Rhode Island: 'in consequence of the wind coming to blow from the Northward, she could not weather Lynus Point; the Captain being an Englishman, he knew the Strait of Menai, and bore up to make his passage through these Strait, and consequently made his passage through St George's Channel into the Western Ocean.'[28]

This evidence was given in 1811; a few years later vessels from the Menai Strait were sailing regularly with slates to America. Within a month of each other, in 1816, the 'new and fast sailing brig *Mount Pleasant*' sailed from Caernarvon for Charlestown, South Carolina, with slates and accommodation for six passengers in the cabin, and for an unstated number of others in the spaces between the stacks of slates; similarly, the brig *Dispatch* of Workinton was loading slates at Port Penrhyn, bound for Boston with similar accommodation.[29] In the meantime, however, some of the Strait vessels were to suffer at the hands of the American privateers just as, indeed, American sloops were being captured by Captain Lloyd in the *Plantagenet*. As long ago as 1777, at the time of another war, two American privateers had appeared off Anglesey and captured a vessel believed to be carrying the furniture of the Bishop of Bangor,[30] but in the war of 1812 it was off Land's End that one of the most successful of the American commerce raiders, the fast *Argus*, commanded by William Allen, captured Richard Williams, master of the *Eleanor* of Caernarvon and ordered him to take 53 passengers, captured from Bristol and St Ives ships, into Bristol.[31] A few months later, two other Menai Strait vessels, bound for London, were captured off Folkestone,[32] but by this time many vessels were risking the Channel voyage as freights were high. The *North Wales Gazette* carried a fairly typical notice in September 1813: 'Now loading, Pickle Harring Wharf, London, Brig – *Lady Bulkeley*, for Caernarvon and Amlwch, to sail in 14 days. For freight or passage apply Captain Griffith Jones at the said Wharf.'[33]

The enemy were not the only reason for losses at sea in these years, for news of casualties by shipwreck continued to occupy many columns in the north Wales press. Fifteen captains of ships in the Menai Strait contributed subscriptions ranging from 10/- to 2/6 towards the 'relief of widows and orphans of men drowned near Great Orme's Head' in October 1812; the same edition of the *North Wales Gazette* carried the text of a passionate speech made by the poet Shelley at a public meeting at Beaumaris in support of Mr Madocks's Tremadoc Embarkment which had been damaged by bad weather, the conclusion of which no doubt sent the citizens of Beaumaris home inspired, 'How can any look upon that work and hesitate to join me when I publicly pledge myself to spend the last shilling of my fortune, and devote the last breath of my life to this great, this glorious cause.'[34] Building embankments, piers, jetties, harbour works was very much in fashion, and the stones from the quarries of Anglesey provided another freight for vessels in the coasting trade. Tenders were invited for transporting 12,000 tons of large stones from Red Wharf Bay for building works at Holyhead Harbour in 1811; Anglesey marble became very fashionable for chimney-pieces during the Napoleonic wars when foreign supplies were unavailable; limestone was required both for agricultural and building work, and lime kilns were dotted about the island, whilst the Penmon quarries provided stone for a number of projects ranging from Holyhead pier and the Marquis of Anglesey's column, to the two bridges across the Strait and the new Birmingham Town Hall.[35]

The post-Napoleonic War period saw an increase in shipping as the slate industry extended its markets. The Liverpool firm of Worthington, already established at the flint mill at Llandygai,[36] developed the contracts which since 1803 they had established in the handling and shipping of slates, manufacturing writing slates and preparing by-products of the Penrhyn quarries, whilst other Lancashire men, the Casson brothers and William Turner, increased their interests in slate and shipping from Caernarvon. But it was not only local shipping that was increasing: at a public meeting in 1818 held at the instance of the various shipping interests of Liverpool, with John Gladstone, M.P., a prominent speaker, it was emphasised that as 'the trade carried on from the Ports in the St George's and North Channels' had expanded 'until it is now become of great magnitude and National Importance,' and as there was no refuge between Milford and Belfast Lough, and many vessels lost and unnecessarily delayed, that Holyhead was 'admirably calculated to form an excellent Asylum Port for this General Trade.' The mercantile interests at Liverpool considered that, 'at a comparatively moderate expense,' a wet dock could be constructed at Holyhead which would 'contain from two to three hundred ships . . . with sufficient water to admit Merchant Ships of the large classes, as well as those of the small of His Majesty's Navy, without being attended with interruption to the Packets.' Moreover, the meeting stressed the strategic importance of developing Holyhead, for the war had shown that whilst vessels bound for the westward from the Irish and St George's Channel had to join their convoys at Cork, and those for the Baltic and Northern Europe at Long Hope in the Orkneys, these long distances, and the 'open exposed nature of the passages to them' had led to the capture of many fine vessels, which would be avoided if Holyhead were developed into a convoy rendezvous, 'and a most desirable outlet for departure established.' The meeting was firmly of the opinion that Holyhead should be developed as a naval base, as 'from the want of a naval station on the east side of these Channels during war, the Enemies cruizers have frequently made many important captures close to our ports'; future enemies would be deterred from approaching 'were those ships of His Majesty's known to be stationed at Holyhead in the centre of Navigation, Inwards and Outwards.'[37] It was 1818, and the enemy was still France, or America; Germany, not yet a nation state, was not in any way considered as a threat. The century of peace which followed in home waters meant that it was not until 1914 that there was any fear of war, but for the early decades of the nineteenth-century the post-war thinking, after a century of wars with France, was a valuable asset in the development of Holyhead as a port, and enabled its supporters to enlist the financial aid of those who saw its strategic significance as well as its role in the postal packet service, and as a harbour of refuge for merchant shipping.

One of those who did much to establish Holyhead as a port was Captain Hugh Evans. Son of Hugh Evans of Gwyndy, who had conveyed the mail between Gwyndy and Holyhead for many years, Captain Evans, in November 1807, submitted a sketch he had drawn of Holyhead Island, 'shewing the coast commonly called the Back of the Head, with the Courses of several vessels steering in the Night with a fair wind, and the sails as actually set at the time they severally struck, or went on shore, all which have happened at this spot within the last Twelve months.'[38] Captain Evans's sketch has a number of delicately coloured drawings of vessels to support his claim regarding 'the propriety of erecting a distinct Light on the South Stack,' and also contains further drawings of vessels which got into difficulties in Holyhead Bay. At the Back of the Head he depicts nine vessels, and 'one of H.M. Packets, standing out, after running by the Head, and falling in with a Schooner, who was steering for the rocks, but followed the Packet out,' whilst in the Bay there are four vessels which 'drove on shore' and were lost, two dismasted vessels being towed into harbour, and two brigs which 'having slip'd their Cables in the Road, with pilots on board got safe into Penrhos river.' The South Stack Lighthouse, 1809, the purchase of Salt Island in 1810, the construction of a new pier, opened in 1821, known as Admiralty Pier, where the new Custom House, and Harbour Office were built, near the site of the granite archway erected to commemorate the visit of George IV in 1821, all serve as monuments to the efforts of Captain Hugh Evans, appointed Holyhead's first Harbour-master in 1811.

There were other changes at Holyhead during these years. After much consideration of the evidence regarding steam boats in other services: 'The *Rob Roy* plied two winters between Greenock and Belfast, and last winter between Dover and Calais: the *Eclipse* plied the whole of last winter between Glasgow and Belfast, and the *Cambria* between Liverpool and Bagillt: a Steam Boat has plied regularly through all seasons between New York, the Havannah and New Orleans': and the considered opinions of Captains Goddard, Skinner and Davies, the Holyhead masters, regarding the performance of steam packets through 'the heavy seas and desperate gales which frequently prevail for weeks together in the Irish Channel,' the Holyhead service went over to steam, and from the 1st of June 1821 to 1st June 1822 it was reported that the 'average length of the voyages of the Holyhead Packets . . . has been about seven hours and a half: the average of the Sailing Packets was fifteen hours.' The age of steam had arrived. The fifteen man crew of the steam packets were well satisfied with their ships in 1822 and one captain reported, 'I never read a novel before I was on board a steam packet, and I go down now frequently and read for an hour or two; if a man works hard in the day he has his night's rest . . . I have not the anxiety now which I used to have being up night after night.' The same captain reported that Holyhead was very much crowded with vessels, 'I have seen 120 or 130 vessels there.'[39]

The account books, log books and papers of the vast majority of these vessels have disappeared for ever, many lost with the vessels, others destroyed in various well-meaning salvage and 'tidying' operations. Some, fortunately, remain, in private possession and in collections such as the large Porth yr Aur collection housed at Bangor, and they provide glimpses of life at sea in the same vessels of the early decades of the nineteenth-century. The sloop *Jane and Betty* of Holyhead was owned in 1812 by four Anglesey farmers, Owen Roberts of Bwlan, John Owen of Fferam in the parish of Llangwyfan, John Jones of Bodfeiriog and Thomas Pierce of Cefn, and commanded by Owen Jones, a mariner, of Parlwr Gimach, also in Anglesey, but after a dispute regarding the accounts of the vessels, which was amicably settled, Richard Pierce, possibly the son of one of the owners, became master.[40] In October 1813, Richard Pierce made a sworn statement before the Reverend H. Wynne Jones, one of the Justices of the Peace at Holyhead, that he had been delayed by stormy weather on his passage from Drogheda with cargo of oats for Liverpool, and having encountered 'a very heavy sea' and a north-easterly gale off the Great Orme's Head, had borne away for the shelter of Holyhead with a reefed mainsail when the wind came round to the south-east.[41] His 'protest' against the weather conditions was recorded as the normal procedure to explain his non-arrival at Liverpool with his cargo at the expected time. The victualling accounts of the *Jane and Betty* from December 1815 to December 1816 indicate that the cost of victualling the sloop's crew of three, including the master, for a whole year amounted to £43.11.2d, and this included eleven guineas for lodgings for the crew in harbour, and £6.7.4d for a woman who cooked food for them in Liverpool; the wages bill for the same period was £25.4.0 for Captain Pierce (42/- a month), Robert Roberts was paid £14.4.3d and Thomas Hughes £7.7.8d, her total cost for wages and victualling amounting to £100.7.1d. Captain Pierce's wages were increased to 50/- a month, and he was given back-pay for the year, and as a result of all the *Jane and Betty*'s expenditure over the year, a one-fifth share of her profits for the Anglesey farmer-owners amounted to £10.4.10¾d.[42] During this period she was frequently employed carrying slate; two cargoes of 44 tons to Liverpool in 1813, 43 tons to Chester and 42 tons to Dublin in 1815, and in 1816 two of 44 tons to Runcorn, two similar amounts to Liverpool, and a further two with 43 tons again to Liverpool. During the year 1818 the *Jane and Betty* earned £300 and her expenses were £249, with £106 of this for victualling and wages, so that her profit on the year's working was about £51. Her account book for 1818-19 shows that she sailed fairly regularly between Caernarvon and Liverpool or Runcorn, with occasional passages to Bristol, Neath, Pwllheli, and, on one occasion, she put in to Malltraeth to discharge culm.[43]

In August 1821 Captain Pierce bought a one-fifth share in the *Jane and Betty* from one of the original owners, probably his father, Thomas Pierce, blacksmith, of Trefdraeth, for £16.0.0d.[44] A year later the *Jane and Betty* took 55 tons of slates from Caernarvon to Ostend at a freight of 20/- per ton, returning with unspecified freights including oak boards at 31/- per ton to Wexford, and thence to Liverpool with beans and barley at 10/- per ton.[45] From Liverpool she then took cargoes to Mostyn, Conway, and 'Velinhely'. Earlier that year Pierce had paid at Liverpool 2/7d for washing and 'cooking for 9 days at 6d per day, and 4 at 9d per day,' and 7d for a loaf of bread.[46] Captain Pierce often made purchases for his Anglesey friends at his ports of call: Miss C. Williams may have been a very close friend, for she wrote to him from Bodafon just before he left for Ostend with his slate cargo asking him to make some rather special purchases. Her letter is worth quoting in full for the liveliness of the portrait it presents of the simple every-day relationship of the captain of this little Anglesey sloop and his friend so long ago, a token of countless errands of a similar nature undertaken by sailors for their friends ashore.

'As you are going to Ostend I shall be extremely obliged to you if you will and can conveniently without putting yourself in danger buy me as much black silk as will make me a Dress – I must have nine yards – I should like to have a good one now I am about it either plane or figured. I have seen some spoted – I dare say they will be higher in price so that I will leave them to your choice – have the goodness to remember me kindly to your Mother and I'll thank you to present my duty to my Mother, my best love to my brother and Sister and I hope they are all well – we often talk of you Jane and Elin beg to be kindly remember'd to you I still regret you did not stop until Monday . . . the Bangor steamer packet went through the Bay this morning and took some passengers from our neighbourhood for the first time it looked Beautifull but the tackls made a dreadful noise I wish you a

pleasant voiage and a happy return – Dr. Captain Believe me very
Truly yours very respectfully
C. Williams.[47]

The papers of the *Jane and Betty* include many accounts of
payments made as dues when passing lighthouses: these were paid at
a Custom port, for example, Captain Pierce paid at Wexford the dues
of 3/6d for the Skerries and 1/9d for South Stack, and at Penzance
he paid as follows: Forelands 3/6d, Goodwin 1/9d, Dungeness
3/6d, Owers 1/9d, Needles 1/9d, Portland 1/9d, Caskets 1/9d,
Eddystone 3/6d, Lizard 1/9d, Longships 1/9d, Scilly 1/9d, Lundy-
Milford 3/6d, Smalls 3/6, Bardsey 10½d, a total of £1.12.4½d on his
voyage from Ostend to Wexford. There are also many papers relating
to his expenditure on clothes, and shoes: between January 1821 and
January1823 he paid £3.11.0 for new shoes, six pairs at 9/- a pair and
for soleing and heeling at 3/- a time.[48] He continued to collect books
and parcels for Anglesey people – in 1823 a Holyhead correspondent
thanked him for some books he had brought and added: 'The old
woman has delivered the Book of the Laws and the bundle
containing my wearing apparel quite safe but your kind son has not
sent me John Bull.'[49] What became of Miss Williams and Captain
Richard Pierce is not revealed in the ship's papers, but six years after
his Ostend voyage, whether he managed to get the dress material or
not, he must have still been an attractive man, for there is a
provocative note from a lady writing from Liverpool to him in 1829,
reminding him now 'that you are at Beaumaris without a sweetheart
and I am still in hopes to have your company when you will return to
Liverpool again, Now I am alone the Cat . . . left the house, and the
mise has room to play.'[50] In June 1836 the *Caernarvon and Denbigh
Herald* reported that 'the sloop, *Jane and Betty*, Pierce, master,'
loaded with slates, had struck the South Bank Caernarvon Bay, and
sank 'when she was got into deep water.'

Although there were risks in war-time, there were
compensations, for freight rates remained high, but in the 1820s
there was a considerable reduction in the rates paid, and many of the
small Anglesey and Caernarvonshire sloops began to find it difficult
to pay their way in the face of competition from steamboats.
Occasionally a master was tempted to augment his earnings by some

quiet ventures into the smuggling market. The sloop *Cilgwyn*, owned
by John Evans, a Caernarvon solicitor (and a prominent shareholder
in the Cilgwyn quarry), Thomas Jones of Bryntirion, Caernarvon,
and John Price of Cadnant, Anglesey, was employed in carrying
slates coastwise and to Ireland in 1823 when it was found she was
bringing home illicit cargoes in addition to the normal ballast taken
in for her return voyage from Dublin to Caernarvon. The owners
indignantly denied that they had knowledge of the master's action in
taking on board 'some Whiskey soap paper and glass though he was
always particularly enjoined . . . to be careful not to permit any
contraband goods to be shipped aboard the said sloop.' They
proposed to dismiss the master forthwith, although they stated in his
defence that they believed his story that 'he intended the Whiskey for
the ships use, the crew consisting of 4 men and the soap was
intended for himself and some of the crew,' and that the 'glass was
put aboard against his will.'[51] The *Cilgwyn* was one of the vessels
which switched from one trade to another, carrying both slates and
copper ores. She was one of sixteen vessels which made fifty-four
voyages between them to Swansea with copper ore from Amlwch
between June 16th, 1828, and March 19th, 1829, carrying a total
tonnage of 4,587 tons, worth £11,873.17.2d according to the Mona
Mine papers.[52]

The letters which passed between James Treweek, a Cornishman
who had come to Amlwch in 1811 as manager for the new Mona
Mine Company (now controlled by the Earl of Uxbridge and the
Vivians, Cornishmen who had close connections with the south
Wales copper industry), and John Sanderson, principal agent of the
Plas Newydd family, give a valuable picture of the problems
besetting the shipping which carried copper ores from Amlwch. The
industry had suffered something of a decline since Thomas
Williams's death in 1802, and by the 1820s there was an excess of
vessels looking for freights and crowding Amlwch harbour so that
there were delays in discharging cargoes. There were by this time
some good sailing vessels in the fleet, particularly the *Dublin*, which
Treweek described as 'a very fine vessel of about 120 tons' which
'frequently made her passage when others could not'[53] and had an
experienced captain, Captain John Jones, who had been years in the
London trade, as had his predecessor, William Francis, who had

considerable experience during the Napoleonic Wars and had since become a successful teacher of navigation at Amlwch. The Mona Mine Company had themselves departed from all previous policy by acquiring a Colchester-built schooner of 90 tons, the *Hero*, in 1823, and had placed Captain John Evans in command of her, another experienced seaman who had been captured in the French wars and served with and been recommended by Captain Hugh Evans, the distinguished Holyhead Harbour Master. The many letters of Captain John Evans to Treweek and Sanderson give a vivid description of conditions at sea in this type of vessel from the time he sailed with her for Amlwch from the Thames with a cargo of old iron for ballast in June 1823 until his death some seven years later. The vessel was 'so well manned and fitted, and also sails so well' that she was not insured, and Treweek reported soon after her arrival in Amlwch from Llanelli in July 1823 that 'Captain Evans of the *Hero* and Captain Jones of the *Dublin* had a fair chase home by agreement before they started, but the *Dublin* beat, got in about 2 hours and ½ before the *Hero* – most are of the opinion that she would not be able to do it again for the *Hero* sails remarkably well.'[54] In January 1824 the *Hero* beat out of Milford 'against a S. W. wind accompanied by about 40 sail.' The others had soon had to turn back and Captain Evans described his battle against gales, rain, lightning, before he got into Dublin Bay where he rode out further gales; despite a long passage of seven weeks from London he wrote confidently to Sanderson: 'I met with no accidents whatever on the passage and the vessel is now in excellent order fitt to proceed to any part of the world.'[55] The *Dublin* was not so fortunate: in November 1824 she was lost with all hands on her return voyage from Pembrey to Amlwch. A pathetic note from Owen Rowlands, who had attended to the weighing machine at Amlwch Port for over twenty years, to John Sanderson stated: 'I had a Boy about sixteen years of age attending with me (my son) he went with a vessel called the *Dublin* from Amlwch to Pembrey for one voyage he never was from home before and by coming home the vessel went down with them and none of them was found,' and asked that his daughters should be allowed to help him attending the machine and 'keeping things clean' at the same wages 'as I had before with the Boy.'[56]

A few days after the *Dublin* was lost, the *Hero* also ran into difficulties which started when she was sailing with close-reefed topsails about five miles off the Smalls Light, in a heavy westerly swell which, combined with a strong south-easterly wind, 'made the ship very laborsome occasioned by the cargo.' Visibility worsened, the gale increased, and Evans hove to off Lundy for the night. At daybreak he shaped his course for Mumbles Head, but 'at the time I expected to see it the atmosphere became so very thick with rain and blowing a strong gale with a tremendous sea that obliged me to run as I considered myself on a lee shore.' The wind eventually went round to the N.W. with squalls and the *Hero* beat into the roads and came to an anchor on a black evening. The sea was running so high that the pilots could not get aboard and it was not until late afternoon on the following day that they got safely into Swansea.[57]

Freights were low in the 1820s for the copper ore vessels, much lower for the voyage to Swansea than they had been in Thomas William's day, and inevitably masters had to take risks in order to earn a precarious living. Captain Evans had reason to feel frustrated, for the *Hero* had to have several extensive repairs; other vessels, far too many for the trade, choked up Amlwch Harbour so that he was inevitably delayed; as a vessel belonging to the Mine Company, he did not receive as favoured treatment by the carts used to unload vessels in Amlwch harbour, and he had always to take copper freights in wintry weather on the southerly voyages whilst the other vessels sought alternative cargoes in more sheltered waters.[58] Treweek and Sanderson decided to reduce the number of vessels at the port in 1829 by only employing those that were willing to take cargoes through the winter, but it was almost too late as far as Captain Evans was concerned, for in the spring Treweek reported to Sanderson that 'I'm afraid Captain Evans of the *Hero* is in a bad way – he has not been able to go to sea with the vessel that last two trips.'[59] There was much canvassing of possible replacements for him as master of the *Hero*; Treweek's letters on the subject of the various masters' suitability reflect the care with which the appointment was made – he was concerned lest the master should be too young, for he had seen the consequences at Amlwch, 'the running of many promising young men in placing them too soon' in command, but there were others who, although experienced and excellent mates, were not suitable for command: 'I am compelled to say that many men, wile answerable under others, are not fit to take command.' He had advised an employee to 'put his son before the mast in one of our coasting vessels that he might be better prepared to become a captain'; another young man should only be appointed if a 'proper sailing master' went with him until he was much more experienced. Captain Francis Madren had taken temporary command of the *Hero* at the request of Captain Evans when he was taken ill, and Treweek had to admit that he was 'considered to be one of the most active and I believe he is one of the best coasting sailors belonging to the port of Amlwch, he really is a first rate man.' Treweek had some reservations because of past experience in dealing with Madren in the latter's younger days as master of a small vessel, but realised that the Captain had settled down now that he was married, 'he is very much altered in his appearance and conduct.'[60] And so it proved; Madren was appointed master of the *Hero* and retained command of her for at least the next twelve years until she was sold in 1842.

Treweek had a very real interest in the *Hero*, for her frequent and often costly repairs were carried out at the shipbuilding yard which he had established in conjunction with his sons, Nicholas and Francis, at Amlwch Port. An examination of the *Hero*'s account books reveals that several hundred pounds were paid to the Treweek brothers over the years: it was they who supplied her sails, cordage, spars, planks, oil, oak, oakum, shrouds, repaired her iron and timber work; their bill for the period July-December 1837, for example, being £129.9.8d, and again for July-December 1842, £177.5.4½d.[61] In 1854 it was estimated that an expenditure of £332 was necessary after which 'she would be a good serviceable and handy little coaster.'[62] The regular income, for so it certainly appeared, which the Treweeks received for carrying out work on the *Hero*, must have been a welcome asset, particularly in the early years, to the rapidly increasing shipbuilding business. From 1825 approximately one sloop a year came from their slip; in 1825 the *Unity*, 1826 the *Marquis of Anglesey*, 1827 the *Margaret*, 1828 the smack *Eleanor*, 1830 the brigantine *James and Jane*, thus forming a firm base for their future activities in the 1830s and 1840s and preparing the way for the further expansion which took place under Captain William Thomas, who eventually bought the yard from Nicholas Treweek. Moreover, the Treweeks and the other mine agents, together with the families who had prospered from services to the copper mines, continued to invest money in shipping, and when the Amlwch copper trade declined, both the investors and those who sailed the ships shifted their interests to more general trades, providing the transport for the building materials, stone, slate and allied product, so important to the Welsh builders of Merseyside, and harbour works such as those at Holyhead.

The age of improvement was at hand. Despite its reputation as Môn Mam Cymru, the granary of north Wales, there had often been violent protests at the export of foodstuffs from the island in times of famine on the island itself, and in 1817 a mob at Amlwch removed the rudder of a vessel to prevent her sailing.[63] The flight of agricultural workers from the land, many to the copper workings at Amlwch at the end of the century, enclosures early in the nineteenth-century, and the formation of the Anglesey Agricultural Society in 1808 to encourage more scientific farming, all brought about changes in the methods of work on the island; so, too, did the efforts of the Rev. James Williams of Llanfair-yng-Nghornwy, who is not only remembered for his lifeboat work but also as the first to use the iron plough on the island.[64] The sea-weed and sand of Red Wharf Bay, and manure brought back in slate vessels from Ireland, were used as fertilizers, and in 1843 Messrs. Hills started an artificial fertilizer works at Amlwch which was in later years to receive very many cargoes of guano in the ships of Amlwch. In the 1830s the railways had not come to Anglesey and both exports and imports still depended on shipping; in keeping with the spirit of progress and 'improvement' it is not surprising that shipbuilding and the construction of improved facilities for landing cargoes, affording shelter to shipping and the provision of navigational aids received a considerable impetus.

The Lighthouse at South Stack, erected by 1809, was followed by a number of other lights and beacons: a perch and beacon on the West Mouse, Point Lynas, Amlwch pier, Llanelian Telegraph, Colonel Hughes of Llysdulas's tower of refuge on the Dulas rocks, and the Trinity House Lighthouse being built at Penmon, were among those mentioned by Lieutenant C. G. Robinson in his 'Sailing Directions for the North and North East Coast of Anglesey' in 1837.[65] Another naval lieutenant, Thomas Evans, had had long disputes regarding his charges earlier in the century for laying buoys in the channel approaching Beaumaris,[66] as the officials of that ancient borough had long and acrimonious correspondence with very many owners of vessels who regularly used the Strait but refused to pay dues to the Port authority. In 1821 it was alleged that 'several vessels which are the property of private individuals employed in the carriage and conveyance of stone for the Bridge now erecting at the expense of the Government across the Strait of Menai at Bangor Ferry which constantly sail and navigate within the limits of the Port of Beaumaris' refused to pay, and in 1835 George Evans, innkeeper of the Sportsman Hotel, Caernarvon, one of the owners of the *Vale of Clwyd*, steam packet, wrote to the Town Clerk of Beaumaris indignantly refusing to pay, 'I shall be glad to know (why) 3/- each time is demanded for, as there is not a single lamp in the Town to guide a vessel into the river or is there one Buoy that can be seen even on a moonlight night, and neither Harbour or Pier to Shelter a vessel.'[67]

Whatever the indignant innkeeper might say, there had been an improvement in the provision of places of shelter. At Cemais, Lieutenant Robinson noted that 'there is now a small stone pier, lately built by local subscription, which affords good shelter for ten or twelve small craft at tide time,' although he regretted that the pier had not been extended a little more so that it 'would then have rendered the harbour safe and capacious, and could have been accomplished for no great sum, as every facility for building is at hand.'[68] At Red Wharf Bay, 'where vast quantities of excellent limestone are shipped,' he found the small jetty at Porth Llongdy adequate, but recognized that the bay was much exposed to north-easterly winds;[69] in the Strait, Wyatt's improvements at Port Penrhyn and the landing quay for steam packets at Ynys Faelog, near Cadnant, were of considerable assistance to the mariner.[70] At Llanddwyn the 40-foot landmark erected in 1819 was replaced by a lighthouse in 1846, an important step forward, for the vessels wrecked attempting Caernarvon Bar had been numerous in the 1830s and 1840s.

The Register of 1836, the year when there was a large re-registering of ships, gives some idea of the way in which shipping had developed in the fifty years since the first registration. Of the two hundred and thirty-six vessels belonging to Beaumaris, a very large number still, of course, were Pwllheli and Caernarvon ships: the late David Thomas listed nearly three hundred vessels built at Pwllheli alone between 1786 and 1836, mainly small sloops. The vessels with Anglesey connections, either built or owned by people on the island, during the fifty years decreased in numbers, but it is noticeable that there are many larger vessels in the late 20s and 30s reflecting the need for greater carrying capacity and also, no doubt, a more ambitious range of ports visited.[71] The smaller vessels registered were used for coastal work and fishing; Owen Williams of Llanidan and later Craigydon, son of Thomas Williams, the copper magnate, had encouraged trawling in Caernarvon Bay, and off Red Wharf since the early years of the century, and Arklow vessels regularly visited the Menai Strait for mussels for the Liverpool market.[72] The larger vessels recorded in the register books traded further afield, not only in copper, slate and stone, but also in any trades that had high freights. In 1822 quite a small vessel, the *Caernarvon Packet*, 53 tons, was chartered by London Merchants to load at St Michael's in the Azores: 'a cargo of Green Fruit in boxes which are to be stowed in the usual way, say the two ground tiers on their sides ... With a well hole down each hatchway to Kelson which is to be kept clear of all incumbrances in order to allow a free circulation of air.'[73] Oranges and lemons were a special Christmas treat in early nineteenth-century Britain, and the cry 'Ripe St Michaels' was a familiar sound from the street hawkers; the *Caernarvon Packet* sailed at the end of November, so she was one of the 'ships of Christmas' as Michael Bouquet has so evocatively described them.[74] The use of small vessels in the fruit trade was deliberate policy as it was believed that vessels of larger tonnage filled the market too rapidly, whereas smaller vessels were less subject to delay on passage, thus avoiding the danger of spoiling the fruit.[75] The fruit schooner trade to the Azores was but one of the alternatives offered to the enterprizing owner; the register-books recording the fate of vessels lost suggests that by the 1830s and the 1840s many of the larger vessels were venturing into long-distance trades. The Treweeks' brigantine *James and Jane*, built at Amlwch, foundered in the Bay of Biscay in 1840, the *Stanley*, 143 tons, owned by William Owen of Holyhead was 'lost at Florida' according to information provided by the British Consul at New York, and the largest vessel registered at Beaumaris up to 1836, the 246-ton snow, *Arion*, built at Sunderland but owned by three Holyhead merchants, William Roberts, Robert Spencer and William Bulkeley Jones, was wrecked at the Cape of Good Hope in 1842.[76] The *Lady Robert Williams*, a 168-ton snow, built at Red Wharf Bay in 1821 and owned by a Beaumaris merchant, a Llanallgo farmer, a Pentraeth shopkeeper and a widow from Llanbedrgoch, was lost near Wick on an unrecorded date, and the dismal entry 'Foundered at sea' without any further indication of the exact position occurs in several cases. The 'Liverpool and North Wales Steam Packet Company' registered the *St David*, built at Liverpool in 1824 by the well-known builders, Humble and Hurry, and another steam vessel, the *Prince Llywelyn*, built at Liverpool in 1822, was registered in the names of a large number of shareholders: druggists, drapers, wine merchants, grocers and landed gentry from Beaumaris, Liverpool, London, Shrewsbury, Caernarvon, Amlwch and Llangefni. The steam packet *Cambria*, which had been running from Liverpool to Bagillt since 1821, joined the *Prince Llywelyn*, and soon there was a regular service to the Menai Strait throughout the summer months. By 1837 Lieutenant Robinson, describing Cemlyn Bay, was able to say 'the trade is comprised in a few coasters visiting it with coal, there is also some grain exported, though this branch of trade has much decreased of late, being so facilitated by steamers from Amlwch, Menai, etc.; and indeed the same exists around Anglesey, for the small bays and harbours where vast quantities of produce used to be shipped is now totally monopolised by steamers from the principal ports.'[77] But the days of sailing ships were far from over and, for the next fifty years and more, both sail and steam vessels came to the quays and beaches of Anglesey. The tall ships Miss Stanley had seen continued to delight the eye, but the noisy steamer recorded by Miss Williams, Captain Pierce's friend, had also come to stay.

[1]   UCNW Penrhos MSS II, 230, 222, 223.

[2]   F. E. Hyde, *Liverpool and the Mersey* (Newton Abbot, 1971), 26.

[3]   *ibid.*, 30.

[4]   *ibid.*, 34.

[5]   *DWB*, 744.

[6]   J. R. Harris, *The Copper King, A Biography of Thomas Williams of Llanidan* (Liverpool, 1964); John Rowlands, *Copper Mountain* (Llangefni, 1966).

[7]   J. R. Harris, 'Michael Hughes of Sutton – the influence of Welsh copper on Lancashire business, 1780-1815'. *Trans. Hist. Soc. of Lancs. and Cheshire*, 101 (1949).

[8]   *ibid.*, 142.

[9]   Harris, *The Copper King*, 88-103.

[10]   According to Williams, the shock of the loss of one English and two large French warships had caused the British and French navies to consider abandoning copper sheathing, despite its great advantages, in 1782, but by 1783, with the assistance of 'two ingenious artists of Birmingham', he had solved the problem of 1783, and Mathew Boulton, writing to his fellow-industrialist James Watt in 1785, reported that Williams's 'Rolled bolts are sold to all the naval powers in Europe as well as their (the Parys Co.) sheathing; they have travelling agents abroad negotiating the France, Spain and Holland and workmen to show these states Experiments with the Bolts, etc.' quoted Harris, *Copper King*, 49.

[11]   UCNW MM MS 3540.

[12]   UCNW MM MS 3543.

[13]   BCR, 1786. Many of these vessels belonged to Barmouth, Pwllheli, Caernarvon and Conway as well as to Anglesey ports, but they all came under 'Beaumaris' until the nineteenth-century.

[14]   Robert Craig and Rupert Jarvis, *Liverpool Registry of Merchant Ships* (Chetham Society, Manchester, 1967), 47,51.

[15]   UCNW MM MS 1317.

[16]   BCR, 1786; Harris, *The Copper King*.

[17]   BCR, 1786. In 1822 the 'mast, spars, Ropes, Sails, Rigging, Anchors, Timber and Iron work of the Flat called Sally of Menai Bridge, lately wrecked' at Penmon, were advertised for sale by auction, *NWG* 30 May 1822.

[18]   Rowlands, *Copper Mountain*, 160, 137.

[19]   UCNW Bangor MS 19084, cf. PRO E 190/1447.

[20]   J. R. Harris, 'Michael Hughes of Sutton', *Trans. Hist. Soc. of Lancs. and Cheshire*, 167 (1949). In 1823 the Amlwch Brewery Company were advertising Cognac Brandy at 25/- per gallon, all at 45/- per barrel, and Amlwch Porter at 45/- per barrel. *NWG* 9 Jan. 1823.

[21]   UCNW Bangor MSS 17127.

[22]   I am indebted to Douglas Hague of the Ancient Monuments Commission for this information, and to him and Dylan Roberts for the

map of Amlwch Port. UCNW Bangor MS 19084.

[23]   Dylan Pritchard, *The Slate Industry of North Wales* (unpublished thesis, Bangor, 1935), 15-46; UCNW PYA MSS 29077, 2760.

[24]   UCNW Bangor MS 19064.

[25]   UCNW Bangor MS 19063, BCR.

[26]   D. Thomas, *Hen Longau Sir Gaernarfon* (Caernarvon, 1952), 84.

[27]   Evidence of John Thomas, Menai Strait pilot, 20 May 1811, to *Committee on Holyhead Roads and Harbour. Parl. Papers, Appendix to Second Report*, 1811, 78.

[28]   *ibid.*, Evidence of Captain John Jones, 10 May 1811.

[29]   *NW Gazette*, 11 April 1816, 2 May 1816. In 1815 it had been reported that the Trustees of the Caernarvonshire Harbour had 'expended from four to five hundred pounds in blasting some of the rocks at the Swillies, to low water mark which has rendered a most free passage for ships and vessels of large burthen coming from the eastward of the harbour or sailing through the Strait of Menai.' *NWG* 6 April 1815.

[30]   A. H. Dodd, *A History of Caernarvonshire*, 1284-1900, 311.

[31]   *NW Gazette*, 19 August 1813. For Allen's activities in the *Argus* in the English Channel and Irish Sea in 1813, C. S. Forester, *The Naval War of 1812* (London, 1958), 134-136; A. T. Mahan, *Sea Power in its relation to the War of 1812* (London, 1905), ii, 216-220.

[32]   *NW Gazette*, 31 March 1814. The vessels were the *Agenoria* and the *Ann*; the former was recaptured and taken into Deal, with her master, Captain Jones, badly wounded. The *Ann* was taken by her captors to a French port.

[33]   *NW Gazette*, 16 September 1813.

[34]   *ibid.*, 1 October 1812.

[35]   *ibid.*, 31 January 1811, 1 April 1811,L. T. C. Rolt, *Thomas Telford* (London, 1958), 121. Buckley received 6d per ton from the Government for all stone quarried on his land at Penmon.

[36]   Edmund Hyde Hall, *A Description of Caernarvonshire*, 1809-1811, ed. E. Gwynn Jones (Caernarvon, 1952), 107.

[37]   UCNW B+A MSS iv, 321.

[38]   Mr Frank Bell drew my attention to this sketch map which is now in the possession of the Anglesey County Library.

[39]   *Parl. Papers: Fifth Report of Select Committee on Roads from London to Holyhead, and into regulations for conveying His Majesty's Mail between London and Dublin: Steam Boats, June 1822*. Evidence of Captain William Rogers, 145. Rogers pointed out that they had had a number of north-westerly gales, but the worst were the easterly gales as 'there is always a heavy sea upon the shore, the gale does not last so long, but leaves a very disagreable short sea. Many times after an easterly gale, we have been two days beating over in a sailing packet, which a steam vessel will perform in eight or nine hours.' (Evidence given 30 March 1822.)

[40]   UCNW PYA MSS 31571.

[41]   *ibid.*, 31578.

[42] *ibid.*, 31593. In July 1816 the *Jane and Betty* took a cargo of coal to Aberffraw, and her expenses include 'sistance to Aberffraw, 3s.'

[43] *ibid.*, 31594.

[44] *ibid.*, 31618. 25 August 1821. Bill of sale. The Pierces may have been relatives of Charles Pierce who became such a wealthy member of the Davies Menai Bridge Shipping Company. *infra.*

[45] *ibid.*, 31621. The cargo from Ostend oak bark, 2 parcels of books, and 1 hamper of roots. *ibid.*, 31630.

[46] *ibid.*, 31651.

[47] *ibid.*, 31627.

[48] *ibid.*, 31642, 31639, 31653, 31616.

[49] *ibid.*, 31649.

[50] *ibid.*, 31603.

[51] *ibid.*, 31158.

[52] UCNW MM MSS 2641.

[53] *ibid.*, 432.

[54] *ibid.*, 1540.

[55] *ibid.*, 589.

[56] *ibid.*, 492.

[57] *ibid.*, 599.

[58] *ibid.*, 600. A fairly typical letter from Evans is that dated 10th May 1825. 'Since I wrote to you from Flint I took a cargo of Coal to Amlwch – discharged all the cargo on 5th April and engaged carpenters to caulk the flat of the bottom where we found 54 feet elm planks totally decayed – which was then renewed – on the 9th discharged the carpenters and took in ballast for Pembrey, the wind at the time blowing strong from the S.W. I engaged to go to Conway to load copper ore for Llanelly at 10/- per ton, – on the 23 a.m. it blew a strong gale from the Eastward with a tremendious sea – at 9 the weather cleared up – North Bishop bearing SE distance about 4 miles was pooped by two waves the first of which took the jolly boat off the stern – fortunately before the second came we had got the boat inboard over the lee quarter . . . I was much alarmed the vessel had suffered by the blow – until I sounded the pump – I found she made no water – from Llanelly I proceeded to Pembray to load coal.'

[59] UCNW MM MSS 939.

[60] *ibid.*, 948, 953, 954.

[61] The total earnings of the *Hero*, according to her account book during the period July 1836 to June 1860 amounted to £4,939.2.5d. During the same period the total bills paid to the Treweeks for repairs and supplies amounted to £1,941.16.2d. John Hughes, Amlwch, the Surveyor, recommended the following repairs: 'Outside, considerable number of planks in the bottom, and from Bilge to Bends – of pitch pine, cost including labour, Trenails, Pitch and Oakum £110.0.0, Stern Posted Dead Wood £15, Rudder Irons and Spindles £3, Inside, Oak Floors now visible £30, Refixing Iron knees for the purpose of placing down floors £5, Beams £8, Quarter Deck £15:

Ceiling and Stringers £40, New Sails £26, New Wrap £6, Running Rigging £10, Iron Work and Bolts £20, Sundry articles about the Deck, winch, windlass, Partners of Masts £12, Lifting up Masts, dismantling rigging and replacing same £15, New Pumps £10, Beams £7.

[62]   UCNW MM MS 3609.

[63]   D. V. Jones, 'The Amlwch Riots of 1817', *TAAS*, 1966, 94. The vessel was the *Wellington*. Some of the accounts of the *Wellington* are among the Bangor MSS at UCNW.

[64]   E. A. Williams, *Hanes Môn yn y Bedwaredd Ganrif ar Bymtheg* (Cymd. Eisteddfod Môn, 1927), 125.

[65]   G. C. Robinson, *Sailing Directions for the North and North East Coast of Anglesey* (Liverpool, 1837).

[66]   UCNW B+A MSS ii, 187, 190, 191.

[67]   *ibid.*, 277. The Trustees of Caernarvon Harbour had since 1815 made considerable efforts to improve its facilities, and charts of Caernarvon Bar and Harbour were published weekly in the *North Wales Gazette. NWG*, 6 April 1815.

[68]   Robinson, *Sailing Directions*, 14-15.

[69]   *ibid.*, 31.

[70]   Benjamin Wyatt of Limegrove, near Port Penrhyn, agent to the Penrhyn family, was the brother of James Wyatt, the architect who designed among very many other eighteenth-century buildings, Plas Newydd, for the Earl of Uxbridge. Benjamin Wyatt played an important part in the development of the Penrhyn slate industry; his designs for tenants' houses and employees 'set a new standard for the whole neighbourhood' and his development of the port at Abercegin, which was now named Port Penrhyn, indicate that he too had architectural ability. Dodd, *History of Caernarvonshire*, 246.

[71]   In 1786 there were at least 45 vessels from Anglesey under 50 tons, 17 between 50-100 tons, and 3 between 100-200 tons; in 1836 there were 16 vessels under 50 tons, 4 between 50-100 tons, and 3 between 100-200 tons. But the pattern is more clearly illustrated if ten-year periods are taken:

	under 50	50-100	100-200	200-300
1786-1795	136	31	10	1
1796-1805	70	19	8	–
1806-1815	48	22	8	–
1816-1825	61	30	10	–
1826-1835	51	21	11	1

I have tried to avoid counting vessels registered *de novo* more than once, but as I have only extracted the vessels which seemed to have definite Anglesey connections, either having been built on the island or with predominantly Anglesey owners, and as these vessels frequently changed hands, the figures should be taken only as a general indication of the pattern. Vessels under 15 tons were not included in the later registers.

[72] E. A. Williams, *Hanes Môn yn y Bedwaredd Ganrif ar Bymtheg*, 172.

[73] UCNW PYA MSS 31918. Charter party between the owners of the *Caernarvon Packet* and Messrs. William Burnett and Company, of London, merchants.

[74] Michael Bouquet, *No Gallant Ship* (London, 1959), 70-80.

[75] Captain Griffith Jones, master of the *Caernarvon Packet*, was to be paid '£7.7.0 per ton of 20 boxes, and a £5.5.0 gratuity to the Master with an extra 5 guineas provided he pays that attention to the ventilation of the cargo as is necessary for its preservation and use all diligence in the prosecution of his voyage without calling at any port except through absolute necessity. The vessels hatches to be kept open at all times during the homeward voyage when the weather will admit thereof, in order to give ventilation to the Cargo.' UCNW PYA MSS 31918.

[76] BCR.

[77] Robinson, *Sailing Directions*, 12.

An Anglesey Ship-owning Family
in the Age of Victoria

There was much prosperity and even more poverty in early Victorian Britain. Anglesey had seen both as a result of the rise and decline of the copper industry created by the genius of Thomas Williams. Reference has already been made to the widespread investment in the small ships built in Anglesey in the opening decades of the nineteenth-century. Vessels were owned by family groups, farmers or shopkeepers who had shares in ships commanded by relatives; by neighbours, particularly in villages like Moelfre and Cemais, and groups with mutual business interests, as in Amlwch and Holyhead. Sometimes the link came about through working together on a common project such as the engineers of the Menai bridges; there were also those who had been brought together by membership of the same religious denomination. Puritanism had long accepted wealth and its acquisition as a sign of Divine Blessing, to be ploughed back both into industrial and philanthropic investment, from which there should be, in both cases, good dividends.[1] In Anglesey, the Calvinistic Methodists owed much in their early years to substantial farmers[2] and shop-keepers; their first chapel was built at Llangristiolus in 1764 and from this district came the most successful of all shipowners (and philanthropists) with Anglesey-based offices.

Richard Davies, born in 1778, son of a yeoman, at Capel, a farm in the parish of Llangristiolus, married Ann Jones of Coed Howel, of the same parish, and started a general store in nearby Llangefni.[3] In the early decades of the nineteenth-century there had been a rapid increase in the population of Anglesey[4] and although by-passed by Telford's London-Holyhead road, Llangefni had been transformed from a cluster of a few houses into a thriving little market town. In its main street stood a new inn, the Bull, owned by Lord Bulkeley,[5] and Richard Davies's store where each year an ever-wider range of goods was sold, giving it on market day something of the appearance of the 'general stores' in romanticised 'Wild West' films. Davies was a man of authority in the Calvinistic Methodist community on the island; he had the confidence to deal with quiet dignity and firmness with his somewhat overpowering and temperamental minister, the leader of the Calvinistic Methodists, John Elias. Richard Davies's flair for business and his staunch support for the Calvinistic Methodist cause, was shared by his sons, John, Robert and Richard, all of whom had naturally come under the influence of John Elias at their chapel at Llangefni.[6] Educated at the local National School (there was as yet no Nonconformist British school at Llangefni), and then at a private school in Chester, the Davies brothers were given responsibility at an early age. With a shrewd eye for business, Richard Davies had seen a market for selling goods at 'cost' price at two places on the Anglesey coast where goods could be landed and where new industrial undertakings brought together a concentration of workers. At Red Wharf, the stone quarries employed many workers in the 1820s and 30s, and here Richard Davies began to sell goods brought at sea from Liverpool at low prices for ready cash.[7] There was another landing place with greater possibilities. On 25 April 1828, Richard Davies leased from the Marquess of Anglesey some land, 'formerly a part of a certain common called Cerrig y Borth, . . . Together with the warehouse, Timber yard and appurtenances.'[8] Towering in the sky only a few hundred yards away was Telford's magnificent new Menai Bridge, completed two years previously. The timber yard had been the site of much activity during the building of the bridge, and Davies saw its potential in the rapidly developing community on the Anglesey side of the bridge. For the first two years, one of his fellow-Methodists, William Hughes of Llandrygarn, was put in charge of the yard and warehouse, but by 1830 they were taken over by John Davies, Richard Davies's eldest son,[9] then aged 21. Robert Davies, his second son, was sent as soon as he was old enough to Caernarvon to manage a newly-acquired iron foundry, whilst the youngest son, Richard, was put in charge of the store at Red Wharf Bay, where there was an increasingly brisk trade for sloops and smacks carrying stones for the building industry in Liverpool and north Wales, and sand for both agricultural and building purposes. The Menai Bridge branch flourished to such an extent that it was eventually decided to concentrate upon this business and dispose of both the Caernarvon and Red Wharf Bay concerns.

At Menai Bridge a small Methodist community had been established at the 'Warehouse'. A number of young men came to stay under John Davies's roof, not all of them actually working there, but building up businesses of their own in the village, such as John Edwards, grocer, and Morris Williams, draper.[10] Both they and the employees of John Davies shared the religious atmosphere of the warehouse where family prayers and temperance meetings were held; the register of the new Methodist chapel in Menai Bridge in 1838 had 'John Davies, merchant' at the head of the list of members.[11] Until 1838 the Methodists met in stable lofts and the parlour of the Cambrian Inn, and it was the inn-keeper, David Hughes, who 'gave up of the lease held under Lord Anglesey for building a chapel at Menai Bridge' in a document witnessed by John Davies, obviously the chief negotiator for the Methodists.[12] Much assistance was given to the growing Methodist cause at Menai Bridge by Richard Davies, Llangefni, and his fellow-elder, Samuel Dew. The connections were not merely religious. John Davies decided to extend his interests by taking shares in a number of the small vessels which brought general goods, such as sugar, flour and hardware, as well as timber and iron, to Menai Bridge. He started in a small way, and had shares along with Samuel Dew of Llangefni, described then as 'carrier', in the *Eliza and Catherine*, built at Bangor, and launched on 16 December 1836 by Edward Ellis, who built many vessels for the coastal trade. Dew and John Davies had shares in another of the vessels built by Ellis in the following year, the *Mona*, whilst John Davies had 8 of the 64 shares in the *Lady Bulkeley*, a 56-ton smack launched at Beaumaris, also in 1837.[13] As John Parry and Edward Ellis at Bangor, Ishmael Jones at Cemais, and the Treweeks at Amlwch built more and more ships for the coastal trade, so the demand for timber for ship-building increased. Timber was scarce on the island, and, in addition to ship-building, there were also the demands for timber and lathwood for household building and, across the Strait, for the expanding communities associated with the slate quarries. John Davies recognized that investing in small local shipping was not enough. Like timber merchants in other British ports, he decided to buy his own North American-built ship.[14]

Timber had traditionally come from the Baltic countries, but Napoleon's Treaty of Tilsit 1807 and the subsequent economic blockade had led to desperate shortage of a commodity which was of fundamental importance to Britain. The vast forests of North America were an obvious alternative source of supply, and in order to give this trade permanent encouragement, heavy duties were placed on all Baltic timber once Napoleon's embargo was lifted. The first half of the nineteenth-century thus saw a dramatic increase in the British timber imports from North America. From Upper and Lower Canada, Nova Scotia, New Brunswick, Prince Edward Island, the timber came across the Atlantic; by 1839 there were over a thousand ships a year carrying timber from Quebec.[15]

Alongside the timber trade in the maritime colonies of North America there developed a rapidly-expanding shipbuilding industry, and Robin Craig has established the hypothesis that 'British North American shipbuilding was well suited to the volatile nature of the freight market in Britain . . . the product of the British North American yards was particularly useful to the new kind of shipowner who had become characteristic in Britain after the Napoleonic wars.'[16] In Anglesey, 'the new kind of shipowner' was represented by the Davies family. John Davies recognized that the British North American vessel was a cheap product which could easily be purchased at Liverpool and, as it was 'a more or less standardised product in response to a generalised rather than a particular demand situation,' it could easily be adapted to any fluctuations or change in trade. Moreover, the fashionable view was that these colonial-built vessels were faster at sea and that they delivered their cargo in better condition than comparable British vessels. In addition to their more plentiful and, therefore, cheaper timber, the North American shipbuilders had affected a compromise between older and newer methods of constructing ships, with a wooden hull on iron frames and ties, which enabled them to build longer vessels. Their sharper bows and longer flare gave them an improved hull which enabled them to be handled more easily; they responded more readily, a deciding factor in clawing off a lee shore. As timber merchants, the Davieses may have been particularly attracted to the argument that, as these vessels were built of timber whose specific gravity was less than that of the British timber used in building British vessels, they 'drew less water for a given amount of cargo, were much easier in a seaway, and could consequently sail faster.'[17] A hard-headed business man like John Davies saw that factors such as manoeuvrability and shallower draught could be of particular significance to him, as he intended to bring these vessels into the somewhat restricted waters of the Menai Strait.

Another factor influenced John Davies in his decision to buy a vessel built in North America. There had been a sprinkling of Anglesey people among the Welsh emigrants to the New World in the seventeenth and eighteenth centuries, some of them 'apprentices' or servants for the tobacco plantations, others, like the best-known of Anglesey poets, Goronwy Owen, professional men looking for a new start in life. The bleak years of economic recession, poverty, famine, and increasing bitterness between Anglican landlords and Nonconformist tenants in Wales led to a dramatic increase in the number of emigrants in the nineteenth-century. During the Napoleonic Wars, in 1796, a vessel had sailed from Caernarvon to America 'with about three hundred emigrants, all inhabitants of Caernarvonshire, Anglesey and Denbighshire.'[18] Twenty years later the *Gomer*, a 160-ton snow, built at Traeth Bychan, Merioneth, in 1821, and owned by her master, Captain Richard Pritchard of Tremadoc, three London Welshmen and some Merioneth farmers, was sailing regularly from Portmadoc, Caernarvon and Beaumaris with slates and emigrants to the New World.[19] Other slate ships which carried passengers from the Menai Strait were the barque *Hindoo*, owned by an Anglesey man, Mr Humphrey Owen of Rhuddgaer, and commanded for several years by Captain Richard Hughes, who was said to have crossed the Atlantic in her at least twenty-five times without the slightest mishap,[20] the brig *Marquis of Anglesey*, and the *Royal William*, owned by William Turner, the proprietor of the Dorothea slate quarries. These vessels had a high reputation, but earlier slate vessels had been notorious for their lack of food and comfort; one much-quoted Merioneth emigrant, writing from America, warned his family dramatically that the Caernarvon slate ships sailing from Liverpool were by far the best even if it meant walking all the way to Liverpool.[21] It would be unwise to generalise from the comments of one disgruntled emigrant, and over the years the conditions were probably much worse aboard overcrowded vessels from Liverpool than in those from the smaller western ports. The conditions aboard one of the early nineteenth-century emigrant vessels sailing from the Strait are described in an account in Welsh of the brig *Albion* from Caernarvon in May 1818: as they sailed past Llanddwyn heading for

Portin-llaen a committee was elected from the passengers to decide upon the rules to be observed aboard, among them penalties for swearing, lack of cleanliness, interference with the sailors in working ship, indiscipline on the part of children, and arrangements for the distribution of food. Anyone found guilty of lying was to be punished by being made to clean out the 'heads' or toilets for three days.[22]

By the 1840s the number of emigrants had developed into 'a desperate outrush of economic refugees'. Between 1840 and 1860 nearly 150,000 left Liverpool, the chief port of emigration, each year, and very many of these were Irish who had come over to Liverpool on the cattle boats, sometimes for 1/- or 1/6d per head.[23] When they got to Liverpool the thousands of emigrants shipped aboard overcrowded vessels, and many of them died either on passage or on arrival, thousands of them on the quarantine island, Grosse Isle, in the St Lawrence, near Quebec. Each year the number of vessels arriving with emigrants and taking away timber cargoes increased. Aboard the timber ships, conditions were grim.[24] For an outward passage shipowners put in temporary decks which were laid on the lower beams, sometimes as little as 5½ feet below the upper deck, and on 'this temporary deck, tiers of rough wooden berths were constructed along the sides of the ship with a row down the middle.'[25] As there were no portholes, the only ventilation and light came through the open hatches. In bad weather the hatches were battened down. Once they arrived in America, the temporary decks were removed so that the timber could be shipped aboard.

The appalling conditions aboard emigrant ships, reflected graphically in the letters of some of the more literate emigrants,[26] did not deter scores of Anglesey and Caernarvonshire families from emigrating; over 500 from each county in the thirties and over 2,000 from Caernarvonshire and 600 from Anglesey in the forties.[27] Among them were many quarrymen, and it must be remembered that John Davies's timber yard had close working relations with the slate quarries whose products were exported from the Menai Strait. In 1843 John Davies decided to purchase a North American-built vessel which could transport slates and emigrants to the New World, and bring back timber for his own yard at Menai Bridge. Years afterwards one of his nephews described how the family gradually encroached on the land between their yard and the Menai Strait, having 'leased some property from the Anglesey estate (they) took the old coach stables and yards and proceeded . . . to squat upon and enclose certain of the lands which had been reserved for the ferry. After a few years they built the wharf, which is now the Princess Pier, and during the thirties their own and other ships began to trade to Menai Bridge.'[28] The obvious success of the barque *Hindoo*, built at Pictou, Nova Scotia, sailing to New York, Quebec and New Brunswick from Caernarvon since 1839, and the ease with which she negotiated what had hitherto been alleged to be the difficult approaches to the Strait,[29] were other factors which influenced Davies.

In 1843 the Davies brothers and their father bought the *Chieftain*, at Liverpool, each having a quarter share in her, and after one voyage from Liverpool to Quebec, she arrived at Menai Bridge on 1 October 1843. Built at St John's, New Brunswick, and launched there in September 1841, the *Chieftain*, 795 tons, was quite a big ship by the standards of the early Victorians; she was 137' long, with a beam of 29' and a depth of hold of 22', and had one deck and a poop deck. The intention was to make room for the emigrants in the hold with the slate cargo, and it is likely that the spaces between the stacks of slate were well within the terms of the Passenger Acts which had been passed in 1835 and 1842.[30] John Davies could hardly offer worse conditions than existed in the Liverpool ships, overcrowded as they were with Irish refugees, and as he proposed to sail the *Chieftain* from Menai Bridge he eliminated the expenses incurred at the hands of rapacious lodging-house keepers who had grown fat on the wretchedness of emigrants at Liverpool. The appeal of the *Chieftain* was immediate: here was a ship owned locally by widely respected Methodists which would enable Nonconformist emigrants to cross in an atmosphere far removed from the densely-packed Liverpool ships, full of 'Papists'. But it was not mere altruism on John Davies's part, it was good business. There was a market for slate in North America, a demand from emigrants, and he was a timber merchant. The *Chieftain* was a sound investment.[31]

The *Chieftain* remained at Menai Bridge loading her cargo of slate and emigrants and then sailed for New Orleans, where she arrived on 12 January 1844: after a month at New Orleans the *Chieftain* returned to Liverpool by 5 June 1844. In John Davies's timber yard at Menai Bridge a clerk with copperplate writing had entered into a blue notebook[32] the details of the *Chieftain*'s first two voyages; the notebook was found among the papers of Henry Rees Davies, John Davies's nephew, and is invaluable because it contains all the sailings of the Davies family's ships from the days of the *Chieftain* to the sale of their last ship, the very successful *Merioneth*, a little before the death of Robert Davies, the last of the Davies brothers, in 1905. The following table, extracted from the entries in the Sailings Book, gives an indication of the way in which the *Chieftain*, the first of the ships, was sailed over the next five years, the Hungry Forties.

The *Chieftain* was well thought of by north Wales emigrants; the local press contains references to 'this fine vessel' in which seventy emigrants as well as slates left Menai Bridge in April 1846, and a further two hundred in the following August, nearly all from Caernarvonshire and Anglesey 'whose destination is the Wisconsin territory.' After a 'very long boisterous passage' they had arrived safely in Quebec and had written a letter to 'Messrs. Davies (Borth or Menai Bridge) in which they highly praise the ship and officers.'[33] Westward passages across the Atlantic in sailing ships were frequently very different experiences from passages to the east because of the prevailing wind system, the former taking on an average at least twice as long; often enough vessels sailing for America had to beat to the westward for six weeks or more in foul weather and frequent gales. However 'fine' the vessel, an Atlantic storm must have been a chastening experience for the *Chieftain*'s emigrant passengers.

John Davies had competition in the Menai Strait not only from locally-owned ships, but also from American ships. Only a few days before the report of the *Chieftain*'s safe arrival, the new American ship *California* had sailed from Bangor with passengers for New York,[34] and a couple of months earlier another American ship, the *Bertrand*, had sailed to Boston: in both cases, anyone desiring 'cabin or steerage passage' was to apply to the Captain on board or at Mr Wyatt's office at Port Penrhyn, a sure sign that they were slate ships. The navigation of the Strait appeared to pose no problems for they were usually towed out to sea – the *North Wales Chronicle* reported 'The *Chieftain*, Williams, master, was towed out to sea on

Wednesday last by the steam tug with slates and about 70 passengers for Quebec.'[35] Occasionally an American came in with a flourish and the Caernarvon paper reported enthusiastically: 'On Tuesday last the splendid American ship *Oneco*, Joshua Drew commander, English measurement 738 tons and actual burthen between 900 and 1,000 tons, came over the Bar in Gallant style and anchored in the Strait. To those who cavil about the obstructions of the bar entrance to the port, we would remark that this large ship came over at half flood, without the slightest difficulty or damage, the wind at that time being northerly, and consequently very bad for the Channel.' The *Oneco* was to load slates, but she also had accommodation, 'her commodious 'tween decks present an unusually favourable opportunity for emigrants to embark for the American continent.'[36]

The Welsh American newspaper, *Y Cenhadwr Americanaidd*, reported regularly the departure of the *Chieftain* from the Strait and her arrival in North America, together with reports of the intended destinations of her Welsh emigrants.[37] Much attention was given to the very good opportunities available in many areas for quarrymen and their families, and the local Welsh press also contained letters from emigrants encouraging their relatives to follow them to North America. The *North Wales Chronicle* in July 1848 reported that 'the Wisconsin territory in the United States is likely in course of time to become a Welsh colony, from the number of natives of the Principality who gave that remote but fertile country the preference.' Despite the human tragedies, there was an air of optimism; a Caernarvonshire man, Daniel Williams, writing from Glyn, Wisconsin, still felt deeply the loss of his wife on the voyage out, but rejoiced to see that his sons were succeeding as

'regular Americans . . . we have built a large log chapel in this district; the congregation is very numerous; the members in the society are near two hundred persons . . . I have seen no poor people in this part, for in fact they are all freeholders residing on their own land. This is an excellent locality for young women. The Caernarvonshire women are well thought of by the English settlers – they get from 6/6 to 8/- a week with their board, etc. The women are not required to do any outdoor work of any description, not even to milk; the men do all. An active young woman will finish her work by twelve o'clock and then she goes to school in the afternoon. There are two schools within a short distance of our house… We have 360 acres of wood, meadow and arable land. The house is beautifully situated on a slight eminence, and commanding an extensive view of the vale of Wisconsin. Our forest trees at the back of the house surpass anything I ever saw in my old neighbourhood (Glynllifon) and I can scarcely at times bring my mind to bear to think the lads have a right and privilege to cut down their choice trees without committing offence, and further to think it is all their own.'[38]

John Davies was happy to see that his countrymen were transported to this new Utopia in his expanding fleet of North American ships.

By 1846 the Davieses had acquired a further three vessels for the Atlantic trade: the *Enterprise* had a very brief career, for after her first voyage for them, from Liverpool on 3 July 1844 to Quebec, and back again to Menai Bridge with a cargo of timber by 12 October, she sailed from Caernarvon on 30 November, arrived safely in New Orleans in January 1845, but was wrecked on her return voyage in the Bahamas. The *Agnes*, another New Brunswick vessel, built on the Miramichi in 1844, was bought in the year that the *Enterprise* was lost and made four successful round passages to Quebec and New Orleans between April 1845 and August 1846; on 11 September she sailed from Menai Bridge but was wrecked on the Pillar Rocks near Quebec on 9 October 1846. The *Courtenay*, built at St John's, New Brunswick, a six hundred ton ship, was bought at Liverpool in June 1845, made her first voyage for Davies from Liverpool to Quebec that summer and arrived back in Menai Bridge with a cargo of timber on 2 October 1845. Three weeks later she sailed from Menai Bridge with emigrants and arrived at St John's, New Brunswick, on 2 December. Her return voyage, leaving St John's on 24 January, was a nightmare, and it was not until 17 June that she was back at Menai Bridge. The sailings book simply records 'waterlogged and got to Killybeggs' but the local press had a fuller version, including a letter from 'a person on board' who told of the frightening winds which caused the *Courtenay* to leak so badly that despite pumping night and day she became waterlogged, 'we were completely overpowered by the rush of water. From that time we were a wreck, daily expecting to

Sailed	From	Arrived	At	Sailed	Arrived	At	Length of voyage mths. days	
17 May 1843	Liverpool	14 July	Quebec	11 Aug.	1 Oct.	Menai Bridge	4	14
9 Nov.	Menai Bridge	12 Jan. 1844	N. Orleans	March	5 June	Liverpool	6	27
22 July 1844	Liverpool	1 Sept.	Quebec	28 Sept.	29 Oct.	Liverpool	3	7
7 Dec.	Liverpool	28 Jan. 1845	N. Orleans	1 March	11 May	Liverpool	5	4
22 May 1845	Liverpool	25 June	Quebec	1 Aug.	29 Aug.	Menai Bridge	3	7
11 Sept.	Menai Bridge	20 Oct.	Quebec	14 Nov.	19 Dec.	Menai Bridge	3	8
15 Apl. 1846	Menai Bridge	20 May	Quebec	24 June	29 July	Menai Bridge	3	14
12 Aug.	Menai Bridge	28 Sept.	Quebec	26 Oct.	26 Nov.	Menai Bridge	3	14
3 Feb. 1847	Menai Bridge	10 Mar.	Mobile	7 May	21 June	Liverpool	4	18
3 July	Liverpool	23 Aug.	Quebec	20 Sept.	24 Oct.	Menai Bridge	3	22
9 May 1848	Cork		S. Island and Quebec		30 Aug.	Menai Bridge	3	21
23 Oct.	Menai Bridge	10 Dec.	N. Orleans	16 Feb.	8 Apl.	Liverpool	5	16 SOLD

be swept away, but hoping to see some vessel which might deliver us; in this we were disappointed.'[39] With their sails torn or carried away, much of their provision washed overboard, they drifted helplessly for forty-one days; their plight was desperate, but they survived and were towed to Menai Bridge for a refit which kept the *Courtenay* in the Strait for nearly three months.

The details of the Davies Sailings Book and the press reports are further supplemented by the simple narrative verse written by Margaret, wife of Captain Robert Jones, master of the *Courtenay*. She was the daughter of William Thomas, a saddler at the 'Eagle and Child', Holyhead, a prominent Methodist, and she had met Robert Jones when he was mate of a vessel that put in to Holyhead.[40] On his return from his next voyage, which had taken him to the Far East, they were married at Holyhead in 1842. The wedding, the stay in Liverpool before his vessel left for Sydney, her own feelings when she returned to Holyhead, her relief when he arrived home safely in January 1844, and her anxiety when he made a further voyage to Calcutta are described in simple unaffected verse. Robert Jones was then given command of the *Courtenay* and, according to Margaret, John Davies, Menai Bridge, paid him £10 a month.[41] The first voyage lasted little over three months from Liverpool to Quebec and back to Menai Bridge, and Margaret ruefully recorded that her husband had little time at home before he was off on a similar voyage; the Davies Sailings Book indicates that the *Courtenay* arrived at Menai Bridge on 2 October and sailed twenty days later.

The return passage from New Brunswick was that in which the *Courtenay* took such a buffeting. Captain Jones had told his wife that it was freezingly cold whilst they were taking their timber cargo aboard at St John's.[42] The *Courtenay*, like the other early Davies vessels, had one deck, but she also had beams for a second deck, which was used for emigrants and slates on the outward passages, and then removed when the timber was taken aboard. The stowage problems presented by timber cargoes were always a headache to masters, and the extremely cold conditions may have been responsible for some hurried wedging and securing of cargo, so that when the storm hit them the timber may have shifted. Deck cargoes of timber were an additional hazard, and although it was illegal after 1840 to carry deck cargoes in the North American trade between

September and May, there were many evasions. If the *Courtenay* had a deck cargo, the ice forming on it would have made the vessel unstable. Whatever the reasons, with seas sweeping the deck, and the pumps fighting a continuous but losing battle, they had to cast much gear overboard and pass a chain around her hull. Captain Jones carefully rationed the bread and water for all aboard, and after forty-one days of drifting helplessly they made their landfall at Killybeggs. After an eventful voyage herself in the steam packet from Holyhead to Dublin, Margaret Jones joined her husband in Ireland; they remained there with the *Courtenay* for three months and Margaret much enjoyed the Irish hospitality.[43] A steam tug was sent from Menai Bridge to tow the *Courtenay* back to the Strait; she was unloaded at Menai Bridge and then went to Caernarvon where she had a three month refit.

Margaret Jones gives a lively description of this period in her life; Captain Jones going with Davies to Liverpool in a steam packet in rough weather, and returning with 'pounds worth of furniture,' the *Courtenay* going through the Swellies to Caernarvon, the captain and his wife living in comfortable, but expensive, lodgings there, with Margaret enjoying every minute of the obvious deference shown to her husband as master of such a big ship, and so highly thought of by the Davies family. In mid-August Margaret was delighted to show off the *Courtenay* to her mother who had come from Holyhead to spend a fortnight with them 'i edrych amdanom a gweled Cortni.'[44] A month later, in mid-September, the *Courtenay* was towed out again over Caernarvon bar and sailed for St John's, a safe and uneventful three month voyage, arriving in the Mersey on a foggy New Year's Eve, 1847. Margaret Jones was there to meet her husband. During the three weeks they had together in Liverpool, Margaret recorded that they had their photographs taken, so that if they lived to a ripe old age they would know what they looked like 'when we were twenty-six.'[45] She was dead herself within five years, but at the time it seemed that it was her husband who was in the most danger, for not only were the seas to battle with, but on his next voyage, in March 1847, six of the 243 emigrants died of cholera aboard the *Courtenay* bound for New York.[46] Captain Jones, however, received high praise from his passengers, and when he sailed from New York to Quebec for the inevitable timber cargo, he was promoted to command a larger vessel acquired by Davies, and his mate took command of the *Courtenay,* which was sold in 1848, John Davies probably recognizing shrewdly that she would never be quite the same after her service trails in the Atlantic storms two years previously. Robert Jones's new command was the *Tamarac,* built in New Brunswick in 1846; Margaret Jones again recorded with obvious pride the impression the new ship made on her arrival at Menai Bridge, and when Captain Jones's trunks arrived at Holyhead from the ship, the finest and most admired present was a Bible which he had bought for £3 in a New York shop.[47]

Captain Robert Jones's *Tamarac* was one of the dozen North American vessels which John Davies and his family had purchased in the years 1843 to 1847. The brig *Ann Davies,* named after his sister, was a smaller vessel than the others in the fleet, but she was engaged in the same trade, slate outwards and timber back to the Menai Strait. She made six quick voyages, mainly to the smaller North American ports from Menai Bridge, and was then sold. The nature of her trade and the close mutual interest of Penrhyn slate and the Davies ships may be illustrated by one of them. In March 1848 she sailed from Menai Bridge for Boston, where she arrived on 16 May. The agent for the Penrhyn slate quarries had written to Asa Wilbur, of Boston, on 22 March stating that a cargo of slate had been put aboard the *Ann Davies,* and on the same day had informed Davies Menai Bridge that as this slate cargo was worth £453.18.8d and 'bills you have sent against us for timber as sent to me amount to £530.3.10' the balance in their favour was £76.5.2; if they called in soon to exchange receipts 'I will allow you on this invoice for cash £5.13.6 and pay you this balance, £81.18.8.'[48] A few days previously a testy letter from the Penrhyn agent indicated that the slate trade was flourishing: 'as the *Ann Davies* has been loading since Thursday I wish you would send the Capt. Here to sign bills of loading and take the vessel out from the Wharf as our Harbour Master complains of her occupying the berth so long, it being wanted for other vessels.'[49] The *Ann Davies* sailed from Boston for St John's, New Brunswick, collected her cargo of timber, and arrived back in Britain, at Maryport, on 28 July. A fortnight later she was again sailing for Quebec where she arrived at the end of September, returning to New Quay in late November, and was then sold.

In the autumn of 1847 John Davies inserted a notice to emigrants in the local press that the 'fine, fast sailing ships *Tamarac*, new ship, 1,400 tons burden, *Peltoma*, new ship 850 tons burden, *Northumberland*, 700 tons burden, were 'to sail about 15th November from the Menai Strait to New Orleans.'[50] Davies was well aware of the spectre of cholera and ill-health in the American ports, and no doubt he had this in mind when he advertised that 'New Orleans is as healthy as any town in the States from October to June; This is mentioned to give emigrants a true knowledge of the place.' Moreover, by sailing to New Orleans, Davies pointed out that the emigrant could save money, 'as steamers proceed direct from New Orleans to Wisconsin, Missouri, Iowa, Indiana, Illinois and Ohio, which makes the expense less than from any other port in the states.' The appeal to Welsh sentiment was not overlooked for, as John Davies emphasised in his advertisement, 'the commanders being well-known Welshmen, is a guarantee to passengers their comforts will be attended to.'[51] There must have been keen competition between these vessels, which sailed and arrived at their destinations within days of each other. The *Peltoma* left Caernarvon on 21 December 1847, the *Northumberland* sailing from Menai Bridge the same day, and the *Tamarac* sailed after Christmas on 30 December.[52] The Peltoma arrived at New Orleans two days before the Northumberland on 15 February, and the *Tamarac*, under Captain Robert Jones, although she had sailed later, arrived at Savannah a week later. The *Tamarac* made the fastest return passage of the three; she left on 12 April and was at Liverpool on 22 May, six days after the *Peltoma*, which had, however, left over three weeks earlier. All three vessels sailed to Quebec again in June and were back in the Menai Strait in the autumn for further cargoes for New Orleans as in the previous year. The *Oregon*, the largest so far of John Davies's fleet, commanded by Captain David Evans, was engaged in a similar trade in 1847-8 to Quebec, Mobile and New Orleans, and was at Menai Bridge in August 1848 whence she sailed for New Orleans, returning on 31 March 1849 to Liverpool. Leaving Liverpool in May 1849 the *Oregon* was at New York by the 13 June; *Y Cenhadwr Americanaidd* noted the deaths of Robert Charles of Blaenau Ffestiniog and his wife, both of whom died shortly after disembarking from the *Oregon*.[53]

Death had also come to the Davies family. John Davies had gone to Torquay for a change of air in the early spring of 1848, and there in April he died, aged 39.[54] Half a century later, his contemporaries, then very old people in Menai Bridge, still held their breath and spoke in awe of the far-reaching plans that John Davies had had for his ships,[55] and it was generally acknowledged that he was the most able member of his family. His shares in the ships were transformed to his father and brothers Richard and Robert. Charles Pierce, John Davies's young cousin and protégé, to whom he had taught much at Menai Bridge, moved to Llangefni to look after the store,[56] whilst Richard Davies, senior, came to Menai Bridge, where he also died in 1849.

At the time of John Davies's death the nature of the shipping trade was changing: the vast exodus of emigrants to British North America had reached its peak in 1847, when over 30,000 from England and Wales, and over 54,000 from Ireland, had arrived in Quebec alone, and although the numbers remained high for a further decade, there was now a shift to Australia, particularly after the discovery of gold in 1851, and to other countries in the Southern Hemisphere.[57]

This change is reflected in the Davies Sailings Book. In 1848-9 the *Eliza Caroline*, the *Infanta*, *Chieftain*, *Tamarac*, *Peltoma*, *Northumberland* were all sailing from Menai Bridge on voyages which took them to North America and back in three or four months. Henceforth the Davies vessels were to engage in trade which took them on voyages of a year and more, for they now entered the Indian and Australian trades and started to carry nitrates from Chile and guano from Peru. These were the trades of the sailing ships in the second half of the nineteenth-century: Bombay, Calcutta, Melbourne (which increased its population dramatically in the years 1851-61)[58] and Sydney were boom towns, and the Davies ships were part of the vast fleet that traded to and from them carrying goods from, and for, an increasingly prosperous industrial Britain. The tonnage of ships entering and leaving British ports more than doubled between the mid 1840s and 1860, and rose by another 50% by 1870: as Asa Briggs has pointed out – 'it is impossible to understand international economic interdependence in the nineteenth-century without devoting considerable attention to the merchant navy.'[59] This is the background to the development of the

Davies shipping interests and it is as well to recognise that it was due to John Davies's vision in the 1840s that they were in a position which provided them with a springboard into the rapidly developing and highly profitable era of the next decades.

Following John Davies's death and in consequence of the changing pattern of trade, a number of vessels were sold and newer North American-built ships bought. The *Chieftain, Ann Davies, Tamarac* and *Northumberland* were sold, the last two on their return from voyages to Quebec which had started form Menai Bridge a few days before Christmas 1848. The barques *Lord Stanley* and *Highland Mary*, built in 1849, and the ships *Carlton, Caroline, Mersey, Amidas, Olivia*, all built in 1850, and the *Lady Louisa* and *John Davies* in 1851, were acquired during the period 1850-51, all of them built in New Brunswick, Quebec and Nova Scotia. The two barques *Peltoma* and *Infanta* continued their sailings from the Menai Strait to Boston, New Orleans, New York and Quebec;[60] another ship, the *Eliza Caroline*, sailed from Plymouth on New Year's Eve 1849 for Port Phillip and Melbourne, where she arrived three months later on 31 March 1850. Captain Rowlands, her master, who had previously commanded the *Infanta*, took her from Melbourne to Callao, and then to Chincha Island, Peru, and back to Cork, a voyage of twelve months twenty-two days. Managed after John Davies's death by his brother Robert, the *Eliza Caroline*, which had been built with beams for a second deck, made over a score of voyages, details of which are given in Appendix VII (i). The *Eliza Caroline* is an example of the second phase in the development of the Davies fleet, as the *Chieftain* represented the earlier North American phase. The *Lord Stanley*, a barque of 714 tons with two decks and a poop deck, commanded by Captain E. James, sailed for Sydney from Plymouth on 4 May 1850, arriving there on 26 August, visiting Callao on her return voyage and arriving back in Liverpool on 16 June 1851, a voyage of thirteen months' duration. Her second voyage was longer, taking in Melbourne and Bombay and lasting nineteen months: between 1850 and 1868 the *Lord Stanley* made over twenty voyages to North America, the Mediterranean, Australia and the west coast of South America. Another good investment, owned by Robert Davies, was the *Highland Mary*, a 500-ton barque built at Sheet Harbour, Nova Scotia, and commanded in 1850 by Captain Peter Griffiths. On 12

September 1851 she sailed from Liverpool for Singapore, arriving there on 17 March 1852; before she was wrecked off Portness in the St Lawrence on 14 October 1864, she had completed seventeen voyages in which she had visited Singapore, Mobile, Callao, Dundee, Savannah, Boston, Bahia, Pensacola, Quebec, Miramichi, Montevideo, Antwerp, Flushing, Buenos Aires and Coquimbo. She was at Menai Bridge a few months before she was wrecked in the St Lawrence.[61] Two new ships of similar dimenions, both built at St John's, New Brunswick, the *Caroline* and *Carlton*, sailed from Liverpool to Adelaide within a few weeks of each other in 1851, calling at Callao on the return passage. The *Caroline* took just two days longer on a complete voyage of 14 months and 7 days.[62]

Not all the North American vessels owned by the Davies family in the fifties had a long life: the *Lord Ashley* was lost on her second voyage when she tried to tow a derelict and was herself wrecked on Havana Bar, the *Amidas* was lost when she caught fire on her third voyage in the South Atlantic, and the *Carlton* on her fifth voyage on Cape Craysfort, Falkland Islands. The *Ebba Brahe*, built at Quebec in 1852, became leaky when bound for Bombay and had to put in to Port Louis, Mauritius, and was sold there in 1861; she was later owned by a Calcutta merchant. But the *Olivia*, which first sailed from Liverpool for New York in 1851, remained in the Davies fleet until 1868; in the fifties she sailed regularly from London for Melbourne, returning via Callao, and in the sixties she made a number of voyages to South America and the West Indies interspersed with shorter trips to Quebec for timber. The *Caspian, Exodus,* and *De Salabery* were other vessels of the mid-fifties and sixties engaged in the Australian and South American trades, whilst the *John Davies*, named after the real founder of the family's fortunes, a 900-ton New Brunswick-built vessel, made twenty-one voyages between 1850 and 1870, largely in the South American and Quebec trades. The *William Wright*, another New Brunswick vessel, sailed in the Australian-South American trade in the late fifties and early sixties and then appears to have been largely confined to voyages from Hamburg, Antwerp or Cardiff for Callao and the guano islands until she was sold in 1877. During the sixties over a hundred visits were made by vessels of the Davies fleet to Callao, and of the best anchorages on the west coast of South America,[63] but described some years earlier by Charles

Darwin as a 'filthy, ill-built small seaport.'[64] The *Ajmeer, Caspian, Etta, Magnificent, Minnehaha, Superior, Glenmonarch,* and *True Briton* took guano aboard at Guanape Island off the coast of Peru to the north of Callao, and some of them, together with the *De Salabery, Conway Castle, Lady Louisa, British Empire* and *Curlew* also called at Chincha Island to the south, near Pisco Bay. Others called at Mollendo and the Chilean ports of Coquimbo, Iquique and Valparaiso, whilst in the seventies and eighties Davies ships, including those already mentioned, and the *Arizona, British Empire,* and the *Edinburgh* made visits to Huanillos and offshore islands such as Lobos de Afuera and Macabi Islands. The loading of guano was a slow process: at Lobos, for example, the vessels remained at anchor for months whilst the crews toiled from dawn to dusk working the cargo by hand. One watch in the ship's boat would pull a lighter to a position near the rocky shore from which it could be filled with guano from a canvas chute from the cliff above, fending the lighter off the rocks as well as keeping her under the chute. Once full, they would tow the lighter alongside their own vessel where the other watch would heave the guano aboard by dolly-winch in tubs filled by the watch in the lighter below. Whilst the latter was then towed back for another load, the watch aboard went below to stow the guano in the hold, and so it went on, day in day out, week after week.[65] The crew of the *Ajmeer, Magnificent, Conway Castle, Edinburgh, British Princess, Arizona, British Empire, Superior, William Wright* and the *True Briton* all spent long months in this backbreaking work at Lobos in the seventies. Generations of Anglesey seamen knew only too well the stench of the guano islands, the flies and the insects, crawling and biting, between their fingers, on the backs of their hands, on their necks and faces, as persistent as the smell was pervasive. Peruvian guano, six to ten times as concentrated as the liquid manure advocated by Chadwick in the 40s, was imported into Europe on a vast scale; by 1875 one Anglesey farmer alone, John Hughes of Llyslew, in the parish of Llanidan, was said to be spending £300 annually on guano. Davies ships brought guano to Antwerp, Hamburg and St Nazaire, as well as to the British ports; the Sailings Book records their arrival at Belle Ile where they often waited several days before proceeding to St Nazaire.

The sixties had also seen the development of the trade with the

Far East: the *Royal Visitor*, a 1,200-ton wooden ship built in Quebec in 1860, sailed for years from Liverpool, London, Antwerp and Cardiff for Calcutta, Bombay, Rangoon, and Moulmein, from 1861 until 1875, when she was transferred to the Callao, Coquimbo, Chinchas trade for a final three years before she was sold. The *Minnehaha, Glen Monarch, Edward Allison, Cilminar* and *British Empire* were other wooden North American-built vessels similarly employed in the Far East trades; the Davies ships were now known in shipping circles as the *Windmill Line*, after one of their overlookers, John Griffith, had insisted on each of their wooden vessels having a windmill pump of which he was the inventor. Although the majority of their ships were engaged in world-wide trade, the original timber trade with North America had continued in the fifties and sixties. In addition to more demands from shipbuilders in Anglesey and Caernarvonshire there were calls for timber from the rapidly developing seaside resorts of north Wales. Looking back to the days when new hotels and terraces of large houses were being built on the promenade at Llandudno – the St George's and the Queen's Hotels opened in 1854 – an elderly inhabitant recalled at the beginning of this century that a 'vast amount of timber was used in erecting the hotels and large houses. Much of the timber was brought to Llandudno from Menai Bridge by sea; a number of timber baulks would be chained together and towed by a steamer to the bay, and left on the beach, whence they were hauled up by manual labour, while bricks and other materials were brought in sailing smacks and landed on the beach.'[66] The timber came to Menai Bridge in Davies ships. The *Avon* sailed regularly in the fifties from Menai Bridge to Quebec for timber, each round trip taking a little over three months. The *Eliza Caroline*, which had first sailed from Menai Bridge to Quebec in the forties and had then moved to the Australian and South American trade, was brought back to the Menai Bridge-Quebec run in the sixties, and made some swift return passages of a little over two months. Appendix VII (ii), in which some specimen pages of the Davies Sailings Book are reproduced, and Appendices Vii (i-iv) give some indication of the range of the trade of the Davies fleet.

Following the death of John Davies, the shipping business was administered by his brothers, Richard and Robert Davies, and their cousin, Richard Hughes, son of Jonet, their father's sister. To distinguish it from their other interests, the shipping company was registered as R. Hughes and Company, but although the *Lloyd's Registers* for the sixties and seventies indicate that the vessels belonged to this company, the *Mercantile Navy Lists* for the same years give Robert and/or Richard Davies as the managing owners of nearly all the vessels; the *Olivia*, managed by Richard Hughes of Menai Bridge, and the *Glen Monarch*, managed by Charles Pierce of Bangor, are exceptions in the 1865 list. In the previous summer, in August 1864, Robert Davies had transferred 24/64 shares in the *Highland Mary*, that hard-working Nova Scotia barque, to his brother Richard Davies, 10/64 to Richard Hughes, 'ship owners' of Menai Bridge, and 6/64 to Charles Pierce of Bangor, 'ship owner'. Both Hughes and Pierce were already closely connected with the shipping business, but in the fifties and sixties it is likely that the Davies brothers had the major share, both managerial and financial.

Richard Davies, tall, handsome, of dignified bearing, and his brother Robert, an energetic, eccentric little man, quick in all his movements, were different not only in appearance and manner but in their interests. During the lifetime of John Elias, the conservative leader who had dominated the Methodist movement in the Anglesey of their youth, the Methodists had for the most part shunned political action, apart from opposing Catholic emancipation, but after his death in 1841, and the publication of the Blue Books on education six years later, this mood of political quietism changed. Richard Davies broke new ground when he was adopted as Liberal candidate in the 1852 election, contesting the seat for the Caernarvon boroughs, an old Tory preserve. Although Davies was defeated in this election, he was a new type of candidate, a Welsh-speaking Calvinistic Methodist elder who had been educated at a local elementary school. He represented the challenge of Welsh Nonconformity to the older English Tory and Anglican supremacy, and Welsh historians have regarded his candidature in 1852 as 'a landmark in the political history of Wales in the nineteenth-century.'

Despite his supporters' claim that he came 'from the ranks of the long-maligned people of Wales',[67] it must be remembered that the success of the shipping interests had already made Richard Davies a wealthy man. Mere wealth was not enough, however, in mid nineteenth-century Britain; in order to obtain Plas Newydd support, the Marquess of Anglesey was reassured that men of Davies's stamp were often 'softened by being in decent company'.[68] Sir Richard Williams-Bulkeley of Baron Hill, whose family tradition would normally have led him to support a Whig or anti-Tory candidate, was, however, in no doubt that the 'parading' of Richard Davies by the Caernarvon Liberals marked 'the introduction into Wales of a direct religious warfare . . . Mr Davies or Davis is started not because he is a fit and proper man, not because he is conversant with trade and is a large shipowner, not for any qualifications of any sort or kind, but simply because he is a Dissenter'.[69]

In 1855 Richard Davies married Anne, daughter of Henry Rees, a remarkably powerful preacher and acknowledged leader of the Calvinistic Methodists in Wales, although his chapel was in Liverpool, where he was very closely connected with all matters relating to the Welsh community. Davies's marriage into the Rees family strengthened both his political and shipping connections. If her father's wishes were followed, it also gave him a paragon of a wife: 'If trials came to Mr Davies, let them come from his tenants, or his ships, and not from his dear Annie' was Henry Rees's advice to his daughter soon after her marriage.[70] Although he was defeated in the 1852 election, Richard Davies and his wife had the benefit of the wealth brought by the ships for holidays in Switzerland, winter in Ventnor, a home in the Conway valley, and, later, a well-appointed mansion at Treborth. Henry Rees's letters to his daughter indicate that in the fifties and sixties her husband was still very much preoccupied with his ships. In 1855 Rees wrote to console them: 'I am very sorry that the bad news about the ship has turned out to be true,' and later, to congratulate them about the safe arrival of another: 'I am glad to hear that the *Exodus* is yet in the land of the living and I should like to hear of her safe arrival in Liverpool . . . what a wonderful distance that vessel must have travelled since last April! What work she has done, what storms she has suffered . . . I have often observed that oceans are crossed and high walls built before I can make one good sermon.'[71] In another letter, Rees gently sounded a warning to the Davieses regarding worldly values: 'I fear the news about the ship is too likely to be true. But they tell me the loss of property will not be so great as one would have imagined. But oh, the loss of life! It may be that it will require some care for us to keep ourselves more alive to the one than to the other, at least to obtain such apprehensions of the infinite importance of the one so as to forget the other as nothing.'[72] When the extension of the franchise brought a new election in 1868, Richard Davies was such a powerful figure locally that the Bulkeleys decided it was not prudent to oppose him in the election of that year. He was the first Nonconformist to be elected to Parliament to represent Anglesey, as he was the county's first Nonconformist J. P., and, in 1884, its first Nonconformist Lord Lieutenant. Sir Richard Bulkeley, speaking in support of Richard Davies at the time of the 1868 election, referred to him as a wealthy man who 'had a strong faith in the stability of things' and 'would not lend himself to any violent changes, to any ultra Radical changes. That was a virtue in itself and it was a sign also that he liked a full enjoyment of the privileges of property'.[73] Richard Davies did not disappoint his supporters among the landed gentry. A Whiggish Liberal rather than a Radical, he was always present to vote when matters obviously aroused his Nonconformist conscience, denominational issues such as the disestablishment of the Anglican Church in Wales, Irish Home Rule, and the Endowed Schools Act Amendment Bill, but he was not present nor did he vote at the reading of the Merchant Shipping Bill. It is difficult to find grounds in his parliamentary record to exonerate this acknowledged leader of Welsh Nonconformity of the 'heartbreaking indifference' to the lot of seamen of which Plimsoll accused Gladstone and his fellow-Liberals.[74] The rigours of a Cape Horn passage to Callao or across the Indian Ocean were far-off matters; nearer home, Mrs Richard Davies paid the costs of transport and a week's accommodation in Liverpool for all the Nonconformist ministers of Anglesey, so that they could hear the evangelist Mr Moody preach in 1876.[75]

Richard Davies died at Treborth in 1896. Professor R. T. Jenkins summed up the significance of his career: 'As he (and his family) exemplified the new free trade economic order, so also in politics he became an almost legendary symbol of the new Liberal Nonconformist middle class whose ascendancy in Wales was to last into the present century.'[76] It was the wealth derived from shipping that created the opportunity for Richard Davies to become that symbol.

Whilst his brother was thus involved in politics, Robert Davies moved to Caernarvonshire in the 1850s to live in the gracious house, Bodlondeb, on the banks of the Menai Strait, looking directly across at the timber yard and quay where the ships, sources of the family's wealth, were berthed. Robert Davies shunned politics and confined his attention to the shipping business and his private hobby of chemistry; a brief incursion into public life, apart from his chapel activities, was as High Sheriff of Anglesey in 1862 and this brought him great anxiety of mind, for he was much moved by his public responsibility at the last execution at Beaumaris in that year.[77] Already the eccentric behaviour so characteristic of his later years was apparent. He was already wealthy enough to donate £1,000 to the fund being collected by John Phillips to establish the Normal College for training teachers at Bangor; the donation appeared princely compared to the sum from £5 up to £50 promised at the Rhyl meeting addressed by Hugh Owen and Robert Foster in September 1856, and Robert Davies was hailed as the man who had laid the foundation for the new college. But John Phillips quarrelled bitterly with Davies and later stated that 'it would have been infinitely better not to have taken a shilling from him.'[78] When the suggestion was made, following the Endowed Schools Act, 1869, that the ancient grammar school at Beaumaris might be amalgamated with the Friars School, Bangor, opinion in Anglesey was much incensed; Robert Davies, an ardent Methodist, strongly disapproved of any alliance with the Anglican-dominated Bangor school. Ten years later, Richard Davies, M.P. for Anglesey, referred to the matter in his evidence to the Aberdare Commission in 1880,

'this proposal caused great excitement in Anglesey. Numerous meetings were held in opposition to it. My brother at this time took great interest in the matter and finally laid the following proposal by the county, that proposal is contained in this letter:

My dear Sir,
I am anxious, I believe, in common with all the inhabitants of Anglesey, to secure this charity in the county for which the donor intended it, and to see the school so established that it may be, as he wished, a real boon to the county. I should be glad if I could do something to assist in this matter. With this

intention I have drawn out a few conditions, which, if acceptable to the county, I intend submitting to the Endowed Schools Commissioners, with an offer that, should they approve of them and decide upon Beaumaris as the best place for the school, I will subscribe £200 towards the expenses needed to repair and enlarge the present buildings; but should they decide that it would be more advantageous to remove the school to another locality, and so require a new range of buildings, and consequently more funds, I will increase the amount to £5,000.'[79]

The proposals by Robert Davies received much support in Anglesey, but there followed a difficult period of negotiations and the scheme ultimately fell through, much to the Davieses' disgust. Robert Davies appears to have lost interest in the matter and retire to his frugal existence, concentrating on his business interests until about 1885 when he finally retired from the firm. As the years went by, with Richard Davies becoming more involved in politics and Robert Davies more eccentric, obsessed with a quite imaginary eye complaint, more and more of the work of the firm passed into the hands of other members of the family, and managing clerks. Richard Hughes now lived at Min-y-don, Menai Bridge, previously the home of the Davies family. He died in 1873, but his son, also named Richard Hughes, made certain of a close interest in the business by marrying his cousin, Beatrice Conway Davies, daughter of Richard Davies, the M.P. It was, however, Charles Pierce who was cast in the mould to emulate the role which John Davies had played. His mother, Margaret, sister of Richard Davies, Senior, had married Owen Pierce of Trefeilir in the parish of Trefdraeth, some miles to the south-west of Llangefni. It is possible that he was thus related on his father's side to Captain Richard Pierce, master of the *Jane and Betty*, whose activities have been mentioned in an earlier chapter.

Charles Pierce had little schooling; he briefly attended the school at Capel Mawr, Cerrigeinwen, where the master was the poet Robert Parry (Robin Ddu Eryri).[80] Neither Robin Ddu nor Charles Pierce stayed long at Capel Mawr, and at the age of thirteen Pierce was apprenticed to his cousin, John Davies, at Menai Bridge. This was in 1835, and Pierce saw John Davies expand his monopoly business as a timber merchant and ironmonger at Menai Bridge, importing general goods in small coastal smacks, to the days when four or five large North American-built ships arrived at Menai Bridge with consignments of timber. Young Pierce not only learned to read and write under John Davies's guidance, he learned a great deal about the shipping business, and when John Davies died in 1848, and Richard Davies, Senior, in 1849, it was Charles Pierce who was promoted to take charge at Llangefni. Here again Pierce was very successful and judiciously invested all his savings in shipping: he was also shrewd enough to marry Margaret, the daughter of Samuel Dew, the prominent Llangefni Methodist businessman, friend and partner in many of John Davies's enterprises.

The name of the shipping firm, R. Hughes and Company, operating from the Packet Road yard, near the Liverpool Arms, Menai Bridge, was retained until the end. It is safe to assume, however, that from the 1870s Charles Pierce's role became increasingly important in the determination of policy. Between 1875 and 1884 one after another of the ships previously managed by one or both of the Davies brothers was taken over by Charles Pierce, and by 1884 he was listed as managing owner of all eighteen of the company's ships. He remained in control of the firm until his retirement when Henry Rees Davies, Richard Davies's son, took over the responsibility. The expansionist phase in the firm's history, when new British-built iron ships and barques were purchased to replace the wooden North American ships, was no doubt due to Charles Pierce's initiative and direction. In the sixties he moved to Bryn Dinas, overlooking the Menai Strait, but nearer to Bangor than Robert Davies's Bodlondeb, and became prominent guiding Bangor's development – a member of the Board of Guardians, then Mayor and Alderman of the City Council, Chairman of the Bangor Bench of magistrates, and one of the spokesmen for the city in the negotiations to establish the University College. Unorthodox in his religious views, he was never a church member, but nevertheless was a generous supporter of the Twrgwyn Welsh Calvinistic Methodist Chapel and contributed very considerably to the building of the English Presbyterian Church at Princes Road, Bangor, and to the Borough Hospital for Infectious Diseases, Minffordd, Bangor. Radical in his political views and an admirer first of Gladstone and then an active supporter of Lloyd George, to whose election campaigns he made generous financial contributions, Charles Pierce, the erstwhile apprentice of John Davies, died a wealthy man.[81]

The building and opening of the Suez Canal, the development of iron-built sailing ships and the changing nature of the trade of sailing ships in the face of competition from steam ships, had their inevitable effect upon the Davies shipping interests. They had continued their policy of buying wooden North American ships after a temporary lull during the Crimean War period; between 1857 and 1862 six vessels were bought, and in the 1863-66 period a further twelve, seven of them built in Quebec during these years by the firms of Valin and Dinning.[82] But the Davieses and Charles Pierce also now turned to British yards. Long-distance voyages and heavy cargoes such as railway iron, coal, ores and phosphate rock strained the hulls of wooden ships and caused shipowners to think about investing in iron vessels. Between 1860 and 1890 British shipbuilding, challenged in the first half of the century by the North Americans, drew dramatically ahead of the rest of the world with the building of iron and steel ships.[83] Robert Davies bought a new wooded ship, built at New Brunswick in 1866, the *Conway Castle*, but in the same year he also acquired the *Dolbadarn Castle*, an iron ship, built by T. R. Oswald at Sunderland three years previously. This policy continued for some years: new North American-built wooden vessels, *Canute, Curlew, England* and *Edinburgh*, were added to the fleet, and so, too, were the iron ships *Bacchus*, built at Birkenhead in 1867 by Glover, and the *Sarah and Emma*, built at Liverpool in 1860 by Vernon. It was in the seventies that the Menai Bridge firm, in common with many other British shipping concerns, expanded their fleet of iron ships by having a group of sister ships specially built for them by one of the booming shipbuilding yards. In the days when the speed of sailing-ships had been all-important, designers had always tried to improve on their previous models, but in the seventies and eighties shipbuilders recognized that, with carrying capacity as important as speed, it was more economical to build iron 'sister ships' of similar specifications and dimensions, on lines that had already proved satisfactory. Minor improvements and modifications were still attempted with each ship, of course, but a glance at the registered dimensions of the sailing ship fleet listed in the Appendices will illustrate this point. It was at this time that Welsh shipowners developed their working relations with particular shipyards. William Thomas of Llanrhuddlad and Liverpool went to R. & J. Evans of Liverpool and to Doxfords of Sunderland for his shipbuilding programme; the Davieses went to Thomas Royden[84] and Sons of Liverpool, in whose yard at Baffin Street, near the Queen's Dock, iron sailing ships were being built in rapidly increasing numbers. The *Malleny*, built in 1868, was the first of the Royden vessels purchased by Robert Davies, but the crucial phase in the relationship with the Liverpool shipbuilders was between 1875 and 1877 when the Menai Bridge company had seven iron vessels built for them by Roydens, all named after north Wales counties. The *Anglesey* and *Merioneth* were completed in 1875, the *Caernarvonshire, Denbighshire* and *Flintshire* in 1876, the *Cardiganshire* and *Montgomeryshire* in 1877; they were all obviously built to similar specifications, between 1,200 and 1,400 tons, with the *Caernarvonshire* and *Flintshire* almost identical, as were the slightly larger *Merioneth* and *Denbighshire*, whilst the last two to be built, the *Cardiganshire* and *Montgomeryshire*, were a little larger still. The first to be built, the *Anglesey*, was shorter and proportionately beamier than the other vessels; she was larger than William Thomas's *County of Anglesea*, built two years later, but shorter than his ship-rigged *County of Caernarvon*. Another Anglesey shipowner, David Morgan of Bryn Gwyn, Dwyran, who, according to Lloyd's Registers, already owned five wooden North American-built barques, went to another yard in the Baffin Street area, Potter's next to Royden's, for his first iron ship, the *Allegiance*, 1,180 tons, in 1876, and in 1883 Potter's built the *Bryn Gwyn* for him, an iron barque of identical dimensions to the *Allegiance*. It is a measure of the short-lived sailing ship boom of the later seventies and early eighties that the Davies brothers and Pierce had the seven north Wales 'shire' class built for them at the time that William Thomas, Llanrhuddlad, was having the 'County' class built, W. E. Jones, Portdinorwic, and the Gwynedd Shipping Company the *Moel Eilian* and her three sister ships, the North Wales Shipping Company the *Gwynedd* and the *Eivion*, and the Eryri Shipping Company the *Glandinorwig* and her three sister ships.[85] By the eighties the *Lord Cairns*, an iron ship built by Harland and Woolf at Belfast in 1877, and the *Dunnerdale*, an iron barque built at Birkenhead in 1867, had been added to the Menai Bridge company's fleet, all of them now managed by Charles Pierce.

Iron barques such as the *Dunnerdale* were good investments, more economic in manpower than the ship-rigged vessels, yet still capable of carrying heavy cargoes, and engaged in trades which earned good dividends where sail was not threatened by the steamship. Unable to compete with the latter in the passenger trades, there was still a call for sailing ships in the Calcutta, Rangoon, Chittagong jute and rice trade, the San Francisco grain trade, the Australian wool trade, in the South American trades, particularly nitrates and guano, and in the export of heavy machinery, rails, coal and salt.[86] Time was not as important as carrying capacity. The late Professor J. Glyn Davies, himself at one time manager for Thomas Williams, the Liverpool 'Cambrian' Line, described the sailing ships as floating warehouses for grain and wool cargoes. 'If they came by steam in one avalanche at the beginning of a season, there would be no available storage. The warehouse would be swamped under. The sailing ships warehoused the cargoes for the cost of low freight, a very big saving.'[87] The Davies Sailings Book indicates, however, that their vessels were driven hard, and some of the voyages were regarded as particularly successful, winning admiration from the sternest critics among the seafaring community. Such was the voyage of the *Merioneth* in 1887; she left Cardiff on 16 October with a cargo of coal, arrived in San Francisco on 20 January 1888, a 96-day passage.[88] As if to confound the experts still more, Captain Robert Thomas and the crew of the *Merioneth* then brought her back from San Francisco to Cardiff in 94 days, leaving on 4 April and arriving on 8 July. This was a record passage, but others of the fleet, the *Caernarvonshire, Flintshire, Dolbadarn Castle, Lord Cairns, Bacchus, Dunnerdale, Cardiganshire, Anglesey* all made good passages to San Francisco during the same year, whilst the *Montgomeryshire* and the *Sarah and Emma* went to Rangoon, and the *Chinsura* to Sidney. In 1888, the year that Joseph Conrad sailed the Gulf of Siam in his first command, the barque *Otago*, from Bankok to Singapore,[89] the *Montgomeryshire* went to Singapore, the *Merioneth* sailed in September for Bombay, Akyab and Bassein, the *Bacchus* and *Sarah and Emma* to Rangoon, the *Denbighshire* to Coquimbo and Iquique, whilst the *Flintshire, Lord Cairns, Dolbadarn Castle, Anglesey, Chinsura, Cardiganshire* and *Dunnerdale* all sailed for or from San Francisco during the year.

From the 1870s the Sailings Book had carefully noted not only the total length of voyage but also the number of days at sea; to the shipowner, time in harbour was wasted time unless cargo was being loaded or discharged, and the sooner this was done the better. Each port presented its own problems to the master, and there were inevitable delays, particularly in the South American ports where vessels had to discharge their cargoes into lighters which came alongside. The *Dunnerdale* had sailed from San Francisco at the beginning of September 1889 and put in to Holyhead in January 1890, remaining there for eight days before she proceeded to Dublin to discharge her grain cargo. She sailed again, on St Patrick's Day, from Cardiff and arrived at Coquimbo on 7 July 1890. There she remained for a month discharging her coal cargo. In a photograph of her taken shortly before she left for Pisagua, one of the lighters into which her coal cargo had been discharged can be seen alongside her, with the hoist rigged directly above, and the bowsprits of the next vessels in line waiting to complete discharging their cargoes are just visible. It is a scene which must have been familiar to many thousands of seamen who visited the South American ports in sailing ships. From Coquimbo the *Dunnerdale* sailed for Pisagua, one of the Chilean nitrate ports; *Lloyd's Register*, 1894, indicates the procedure at Pisagua: 'vessels anchor close in-shore in 20 to 30 fathoms. Good anchorage. Vessels are loaded and discharged by launches, which are themselves loaded and discharged by smaller boats.' The *Dunnerdale* sailed for Hamburg in October, arriving at the German port in mid-February 1891. The *Dolbadarn Castle* had started sailing in the Davies fleet in the sixties, making voyages to Calcutta and Rangoon, then in the seventies to Ceylon, Melbourne, South America, Singapore, Akyab, to Rangoon, Yokohoma, San Francisco, Sydney in the eighties, completing six further annual voyages to San Francisco and one to Iquique before she was finally sold in 1894. The voyages of the *Anglesey* and *Merioneth* outlined in Appendix VII (iv) may be taken to illustrate the pattern of activities of the Davies ships in its post-1875 phase.

The last vessels to be built for the Anglesey shipowners were named, appropriately enough, after two Anglesey rivers: they were both fine steel four-masted barques, the *Afon Alaw*, 2,052 tons, completed in 1891, and the *Afon Cefni*, 2,066 tons, in 1892, both built by A. Stephen and Sons, Glasgow. There was a wide gulf between the first and the last of the Davies ships: the *Chieftain* of 1843 was a wooden full-rigged ship with wooden masts and rigging made of natural fibres, the *Afon Cefni* was a steel barque with steel masts and yards, with most of her rigging made of wire rope, with steam-powered winches for her heavy gear, and therefore a smaller crew proportionately even though she was almost three times the tonnage of the *Chieftain*, which, as a wooden vessel, was probably a much drier ship. The builders' spar and rigging plan of the *Afon Cefni* gives some impression of the complexity of these fine vessels in the last days of sail. The undated photograph of the deep-loaded *Afon Alaw* under full sail in the mouth of the River Elbe is from the valuable collection of Dr Jürgen Meyer of the Altonaer Museum in Hamburg. The *Afon Alaw* was in Hamburg in October 1896 following a voyage from Cardiff to Singapore and Bassein, and she was there again in the 1904-1914 period when she was owned by William Thomas, Liverpool, and commanded by Captain Evans Jones, who made fast return passage to Mejillones for nitrates in her in 1907-8.[90]

Several of the North American-built ships such as the *Magnificent, Canute, William Wright* and *Royal Visitor* had been sold in the seventies, others lost, the *Victory* wrecked off Spurn Point in April 1876, the *Conway Castle* lost at Huanillos in May 1877, and the *British Empire* burnt off Alleppy in January 1883.[91] But the most severe setback was the early loss of the *Afon Cefni*. She had left the builder's yard in Glasgow in April 1892 and was towed to Barry. On 7 May she sailed from Barry, arrived at Rio in mid-June, and sailed from there in mid-August. In February 1893 she was at Rangoon and left there again in April, arriving in Hamburg on 19 September. She finished discharging her cargo on 21 October, sailed for Swansea five days later, and arrived there in mid-November. The *Afon Cefni*, having taken general cargo and coal aboard, left Swansea on 5 January 1894, and the Sailings Book then contains the melancholy note 'Lost, ship never heard of again'. Coal in iron and steel hulls was a cargo which called for very careful ventilation, and in 1894, six other coal-laden vessels were lost and a further eight in 1895.[92] Whether the *Afon Cefni* was burnt at sea with her coal cargo alight, whether she was wrecked in collision, or a victim of a violent storm at sea remains a mystery.[93] Not so the fate of the *Caernarvonshire*, which had sailed from Swansea in May 1895, arriving in San Francisco in late October; a fortnight later she left on her return voyage, on 11 December, and was wrecked at 12.30 a.m. on 11 April 1896 on Yohane Point on the west coast of Ireland. According to Captain D. T. Williams, later of the Blue Funnel Line, who was a young seaman aboard the *Caernarvonshire*, they had not sighted land since leaving San Francisco and there had been no opportunity of checking the chronometers. Earlier on the fateful day the Caernarvonshire had been carrying full sail, 'our vessel was under such pressure of canvas that she was heeling over and scooping seas on board over the lee rail,' and despite shortening sail during the dog watches, she was still proceeding at a good rate of knots when she struck the rocks shortly after midnight. The crew launched a boat and managed to keep off the lee shore till daybreak, and eventually all were safely ashore in the village of Castletownshead. Apparently those on watch between eight and midnight had seen several fishing boat lights, but had not identified the Fastnet light; 'what had happened was that we had over-run our distance. Not seeing the Fastnet, the master knew that by this time he must have passed it, and decided to haul off the land until daybreak. However, it was lucky that we went ashore where we did; if we had gone a little further we would have run on the cliffs'. At the Court of Inquiry the master was criticised for approaching the land without using the lead, but his certificate was not suspended, and he later became master of the *Flintshire*.[94] Over the sixty years of the Davies fleet, fifteen vessels were lost at sea.

By the turn of the century the ships, now managed by Henry Rees Davies, were almost all in the San Francisco trade: the *Bacchus, Lord Cairns, Merioneth, Flintshire, Afon Alaw, Cardiganshire, Montgomeryshire* all visited 'Frisco', as it is entered in the Sailings Book, between 1896 and 1898.[95] The *Afon Alaw* made three more visits before she was sold there in 1903, although she later passed into the hands of other Anglesey owners, the firm of William Thomas, Llanrhuddlad and Liverpool. The photograph of the *Afon*

Alaw's crew (page 50) was taken about 1900 when she was at San Francisco: it is as alive today as it was when caught in a moment of time seventy years ago. It is evocative of a whole era of sailing ship history, and, if studied carefully, speaks more about life aboard these ships than many thousand words. The master, immediately impressive as a man of authority, the keen-eyed mates, the experienced craftsmen, the carpenter and sailmaker, the young fresh-faced apprentices and the international crew, also young men for the most part, even the ship's dog and the two ship's cats, belong to the *Afon Alaw*, but they represent a whole generation of seafarers.

The Boer War brought higher freights, so the *Lord Cairns* sailed from Barry for Capetown in 1901; the Russo-Japanese War was in the offing, and the *Merioneth* sailed for Nagasaki and then on to San Francisco where she remained for a year, finally returning to Dublin in November 1904. The *Montgomeryshire* sailed in mid-June 1898 from Antwerp for Yokohoma, arriving there on 20 October, sailing again in late November across the Pacific to Tacoma, thence to Sydney, Newcastle N.S.W., back to San Francisco with a coal cargo, and, early in 1900, home for Dublin with grain, the total length of the voyage being just three days over two years.[96] She then joined the others of the Davies fleet in annual voyages to San Francisco; in the race home from 'Frisco in 1902, of the eight ships that left in the last weeks of December, only the *Muskoka*, said to be the fastest sailing vessel afloat and commanded by the redoubtable Nova Scotian Captain Albert Crowe, made a faster passage than the *Anglesey*.[97] In 1902 the *Anglesey, Flintshire, Montgomeryshire, Lord Cairns, Merioneth, Afon Alaw* and *Cardiganshire* were all at San Francisco, but the end was in sight. Freights were fewer, spells in harbour longer. In the spring of 1903 the *Flintshire, Montgomeryshire, Cardiganshire*, and *Lord Cairns* were sold; the *Afon Alaw*, which had remained idle at 'Frisco for over a year, was sold there in November, passing into the management of William Thomas, Liverpool, and, finally, the *Anglesey* and *Merioneth*, last of the fleet, which had both returned to Liverpool in the autumn of 1904, were both sold on 10 April 1905. A few months later Robert Davies died.

In the early days John Davies had reassured prospective emigrants by informing them that they were sailing in vessels commanded by 'well-known Welshmen'[98] and a cursory glance through the names of the masters of the Davies ships confirms that the majority of them were of Welsh origin. As early as 1847 there is an interesting sidelight on the Welsh masters of the Davies ships. There was much indignation throughout Wales following the reports of the Commissioners on the State of Education in Wales in 1847; an irate 'Master of a Coaster', writing from Holyhead to the *Caernarvon and Denbigh Herald* on 13 December 1847, drew the attention of his readers to the fact that there were many Anglesey-owned ships captained by Welshmen, which gave the lie to the suggestion that the masters 'know nothing of navigation'.[99] His nationalist pride shows how bitterly Welshmen felt about the misrepresentations in the Report, but it also indicates how the Davies fleet had already made an impression on the minds of their contemporaries. 'Messrs Davies and Sons of Menai Bridge have ten or twelve ships sailing to all ports of the Globe; of the burthen of about 8,000 tons register, and the commanders, officers and crews are Welshmen except one English commander and what is very remarkable is that they never lost a ship commanded by a Welshman, but their English commander lost two. I do not mean to insinuate that this occurred by neglect or misconduct, only it happened.' He continued indignantly: 'Have we not a *Hindoo*, a *Royal William* and others trading foreign? Is it supposed that Messrs Davies, Owen's, Turners, and others would trust their property to the charge of commanders not knowing navigation?' Having studied carefully the Davies Sailings Book and recalling the local reputation which still survives about their thrift, one cannot but agree with the correspondent from Holyhead that they would have been unwilling to trust the wealth involved in their sailing vessels to incompetent masters and seamen. Moreover, the correspondent insisted that morale aboard the ships was high: 'It is worthy of remark, with respect to the six or seven vessels which arrived in Menai Bridge the last fall voyage from Quebec, that not a man deserted his ship . . . the same crew have been for the last two or three years sailing on board the *Hindoo, Chieftain* and others.'

Inevitably, as the Davies ships moved from the North American trade to Australasia, South America, and India, and as their immediate link with Menai Bridge became more limited, their voyages commencing in larger ports, Liverpool, London, Cardiff, Swansea, Hamburg, so the crews became more international, as indeed was the case with all British ships. But, as the names of the masters of their vessels indicates, the Davieses cultivated the Welsh connection: Captains Thomas, Jones, Roberts, Williams, Hughes, Lewis, Davies, Pugh, Griffiths, Rowlands, Edwards, Morgan and Pritchard appear frequently, and it is safe to assume that a number of young Caernarvonshire and Anglesey seamen started their careers in the ships belonging to this Menai Bridge firm. Others who had already served in Anglesey coastal vessels or in the Portmadoc schooners moved to them confident that they had already learned their seamanship the hard way; Evan Jones, writing in 1950, recalled that he had gone to sea in 1882 in the Portmadoc schooners before he made his voyages in the *Bacchus, Merioneth, Denbighshire, Lord Cairns* and *Dolbadarn Castle*.[100] Representative of an earlier generation was Captain William Williams of the Caernarvonshire village of Rhiw; it has been possible to reconstruct the outline of his career from notes kindly contributed by his grandson, Mr Riby Williams, of Weymouth, and from the records of the Davies ships and the Beaumaris Registers.

After some years before the mast in the Portmadoc brig *Mystery*, William Williams was promoted mate and then master, commanding her on three highly successful voyages to the West Indies, Brazil and the River Danube, 'to the greatest possible satisfaction' of her Portmadoc owner, who wrote to the young captain's father in December 1845 stating 'He is a good honest young man, and you should have every reason to be proud of such a son'. In October 1848, at Liverpool, Captain Williams took command of the *Ann Grant*, a 378-ton Whitby-built barque, owned by Edward Ellis and John Phillips, described in the register as 'Shipowners of Bangor'. (Edward Ellis, shipbuilder, and John Phillips, Calvinistic Methodist preacher and fund-raiser for Nonconformist schools and the Normal College, who had now moved to Bangor, had shares in several ships; Ellis also held shares with John Davies of Menai Bridge, their fellow Methodist, in several other coasting vessels.) The *Ann Grant* was engaged in the slate trade from the Menai Strait, and it is likely that it was during this period that Captain Williams first came to the notice of the Menai Bridge Davies family. When the new full-rigged ship *John Davies*, built in New Brunswick, made her first voyage for the Menai Bridge shipowners, from Liverpool to New Orleans in

December 1851, William Williams sailed in her as first mate, and in the following year he took command of the *Carleton* when, as already indicated, Captain Robert Jones had to come ashore, following the maiden voyage to Adelaide, owing to the fatal illness of his wife, Margaret Jones of Holyhead. Captain Williams joined her in May 1852, a few days before she sailed for Callao, and remained her master until she was wrecked in the Falkland Islands in September 1855.

After a spell in the *Sulway*, which he joined as master at Port Stanley not long after the loss of the *Carleton*, Captain Williams was appointed by Richard Davies to command the new ship *William Wright* (built New Brunswick 1856) when she sailed early in 1857 for Melbourne and Callao. On his return to Bristol, in April 1858, Captain Williams must have told Richard Davies that he wanted to take his wife with him on his next voyage; writing from Menai Bridge, the shipowner informed Captain Williams, 'We are glad you sent to us at once your decision as we should have been highly annoyed if it had been left to the last moment,' and acidly pointed out that it was impossible: 'You are aware that on that point our decision has been taken long since.' A fortnight later Davies again wrote to Captain Williams asking him to take the *William Wright* from Bristol to Newport as he had chartered her 'from Newport to Caldera for Irons and Coals the former not exceeding 100 tons at 55/- and the latter as much as she likes at 32/6, with guano home.' Obviously Richard Davies hoped that Captain Williams would change his mind: 'I hope by this time you have reconsidered your determination.' Davies could be as high-handed as he liked, but Captain Williams was not a man to be browbeaten; Davies had to appoint Captain Jones of the *Highland Mary* to take command of the *William Wright*.

Captain William Williams did not sail again for the Davies family. A few months later, in 1859, he was appointed to command the *Simla*, a new iron ship built at Birkenhead, and in the following year received the congratulations of the Meteorological Office.

'I am directed by Admiral Fitzroy to inform you that your observation and remarks on the influence of the Simla magnetism are peculiarly valuable. None superior have come under his notice since Scoresby's investigations in the Royal Charter. These registers have been placed with Mr Evans, Superintendent of Compasses to the Admiralty, who will discuss them in the appendix to a paper for the Royal Society.'

There then followed years of commanding well-known vessels like the *Commodore Perry*, formerly of James Baines's Black Ball Line, and by the 1870s Captain Williams was listed in *Lloyd's Registers* as a ship-owner, with offices at 36 Fenchurch Street, London. In 1873 he was the registered owner of the American-built *Light Brigade*, and in 1875 the even better known *Donald Mackay*, 2,408 tons, also built in the United States and at one time owned by James Baines. In command of her Williams placed a Captain T. Williams; he may have been a relative and possibly Captain Thomas Williams of Criccieth, who had been marine superintendent for Baines's Black Ball Line, and, eventually, himself took over several of Baines's vessels, establishing the *Cambrian* line of Liverpool sailing ships in which so many Anglesey men served. Their story is told in a later chapter. It is certain, however, that Richard Davies had lost an outstanding man when Captain William Williams decided to put his wife and his own interest before those of the Menai Bridge shipowner. At least one of Williams's eight children followed him to sea, whilst another received the CMG after serving as Treasurer of the Gold Coast Colony. It was a far cry from the village of Rhiw and those early years serving before the mast in the Portmadoc brig *Mystery*.

Some of the Davies captains lost their lives in shipwrecks, others died at sea, like Captain Morgan of the *True Briton*, whose death is noted in the Sailings Book. The *True Briton* had sailed from Cardiff in March 1867 for Callao and 'passed the equator 17th April per Mate's letter received by Breton Castle advising of Captain Morgan's death.'[101] Arriving at Callao in June, where she remained until August, she sailed again from Chinchas in October with a cargo of guano, and docked safely in London in February 1868. Her voyage had taken five days less than a similar voyage by the *Ajmeer*, which had had to put in to Holyhead when outward bound for three days, but it was a month longer than the *Conway Castle*, which had sailed from Liverpool in May of the same year. In the sixties and seventies the majority of the Davies ships visited Callao regularly and there is a local tradition that the body of at least one of the captains was brought home for burial many months later along with the guano cargo.

There were many fine seamen in the crews of these ships. The late Commodore Gerald N. Jones, in his reminiscences, has a moving account of an Amlwch man, Harry Hughes, who served with him as an A.B. and was lost overboard from the *Ladye Doris*, on passage home from San Francisco. Running with the wind aft and yawing badly, with mountains following seas breaking over the rails as she yawed, the master bitterly regretted that he had not hove to before nightfall, and called Hughes to take the wheel, although it was his watch below. Everyone in the ship realised the difference when Harry Hughes was at the wheel, and there he remained throughout the worst hours of the storm. But the next day his refusal to give in to his tiredness told its tale, for when the hands were aloft furling the mainsail, Harry Hughes fell from the footrope at the lee yardarm, dropping clear of the ship. Despite their frantic searching, the hands in the boat that was lowered, and all the crew, knew their search was hopeless, for Hughes had oilskins and sea boots on, and the weather was bad. Commodore Jones remembered vividly the sadness of the following Sunday morning, when, as was customary, Hughes's belongings were placed on the main hatch-cover and sold by auction by the second mate.[102] The lid of Hughes's wooden sea chest was open so that the painting of a ship under full sail on the inside could be seen; using ship's paint and some small brushes he had bought whilst they were at San Francisco, Hughes had painted the *Merioneth*, the vessel managed by Charles Pierce, which had made such a fast passage out to San Francisco in 1888. Harry Hughes had sailed aboard the *Merioneth* and was proud of her record voyages. Amlwch had lost another fine seaman.

The ships which Commodore Gerald Jones knew were the later ships of the Davies fleet; in order to get some impression of what it was like to be a member of the crew of one of the ships it is necessary to look at the log kept just one hundred years ago by a certain Robert Thomas who, in his later years, was secretary of the Caernarvon Shipwrights Association.[103] On 20 June 1872, Robert Thomas left Liverpool aboard the *British Princess*, bound for Valparaiso, and fortunately decided to record his voyage. Not only does his log give a valuable account of a sailing ship voyage on a route which many thousands of ships experienced throughout the last century, but it also provides internal evidence regarding the accuracy of the entries in the Davies Sailings Book. The *British Princess*, a 1,400-ton ship built in New Brunswick in 1864, was almost 200' long, with a beam of 29.8' and a depth in the hold of 23.9'; she was, therefore, a new ship when the Davieses acquired her, and was not old when Thomas made his voyage in her in 1872. She was certainly not an unseaworthy vessel of the type that Samuel Plimsoll was campaigning about and collecting evidence at this very time for 'Our Seamen', yet the work which Thomas had as carpenter and his matter of fact record of her voyage, of which only very limited extracts can be given here, give some idea of the strain of Cape Horn voyages on both the ships and their crews.

Between October 1866, when she made her first voyage for the Davieses, and May 1872, the *British Princess* had made four passages to India, another from Aden to Bombay, and another voyage to the west coast of South America. She had arrived back in Liverpool from Bombay in April 1872 and had finished discharging her cargo on the 6 May. A little over a month later, on 20 June, with a cargo of coal for Valparaiso aboard, she left her berth in the Liverpool docks at nine o'clock in the evening and anchored in the Mersey overnight. Towed out by a steam vessel next day, Thomas noted in his log that they had sighted the Great Orme's Head at 6 p.m. as they battled into a heavy head sea, and next morning 'the steamboat left us at 8 a.m. not being able to tow us any longer'. As the *British Princess* sailed out into the Atlantic, Thomas carefully recorded, in a good clear hand, courses, sail changes, the state of the weather, his own activities, 'carpenter fitting up the Captain's State room', 'carpenter making Chronometer stand', 'carpenter repairing long boat', and the ways in which the crew were occupied, 'people employed as yesterday mat making', 'people employed scrubbing paintwork', 'people employed scraping the bulwarks outside', all obviously fine-weather occupations. But on the ninth day, when they were in 45°12'N 10°45'W, the sea and wind increased, 'ship pitching very heavy and taking large quantities of water on board.' A week later 'at daylight sighted the island Madeira . . . the sun is very warm today, 35°24'N 16°51'W Course S.W. wind N.E.' Occasionally the normal routine was disturbed: 'cook and stewart went aft to fight but were prevented by the Captain,' and the next day 'cook refused duty and was put in irons,' where he remained for a couple of days.

Forty days after leaving the Mersey, they crossed the Equator, and, as if to celebrate, three hours later, '9 p.m. cook steward fighting'; fifty-five days out, 14 August, 'today we saw a Cape Pigeon, the weather is getting cold'. Two days later, in heavy thunder and lighting, 'Handed the Fore and Mizen Top Gallant Sail, called all hands to shorten sail', but some days later Thomas recorded a much more worrying hazard, 'great steam and heat coming up from the hould'. The overheating of coal cargoes and consequent fires destroyed many sailing ships throughout the century. But the danger passed; eleven days later, on the seventy-seventh day out, they encountered a 'heavy gale and a tremendous sea. 4 a.m. shipped a heavy sea, stove in the main hatches, washed away midship port. All hands employed securing the main hatches with new sails, ship labouring very heavily washing everything moveable about the decks'. At 8 a.m. the captain decided to 'wear ship', a difficult enough manoeuvre, but not as difficult as tacking in bad weather in these ships; this brought some of the strain off her whilst the crew trimmed the coal cargo and the carpenter carried out temporary repairs.

The *British Princess* was now in the vicinity of Cape Horn and her master and crew knew what to expect. There was little time to repair the damages of one storm before the next gales came. This is how Robert Thomas recorded the next two days:

78 days out Thursday 5 Sept
Comes in with more moderate weather sea gone down considerably people employed making new darbaulin for the main hatch
Carpenter employed making new hatched
4 p.m. called all hands to shorten sails wind and sea increasing
12 p.m. handed the lower mizen Topsail and Wore ship
79 days out Friday 6 Sept
Comes in with heavy Gale of wind from SW and heavy sea ship labouring heavey ship large quantities of water wash away peice of the starboard Galan Bulwark smashed the starboard side
Light and washed the Gally scuttle over board passed a barque hove to set the lower Mizen Top sail
Pumping ship regular every 4 hours
Long spell each time One hand Laying up with bad hand

The following day the *British Princess* 'pooped a heavy sea wetting the Cabin and Capts stateroom' and all the time she was rolling heavily in the freezingly cold weather, 'snowing very heavy and bitter cold'. The weather moderated slightly for the next two days and they were able to tack and come up with Statten Island again, 'all covered with snow' and making the most of the better weather, eighty-three days out, they 'made all sail – sighted Cape Horn Spoke an American ship snowing heavy People trimming coal Carpenter making screens for the side Lights in the Mizen Riggin'.

So the entries in Robert Thomas's log continue day by day, gale following gale, with every advantage being taken of the slightest improvement in the weather to press on with all sail and the carpenter himself repairing the damages as rapidly as possible before the next gale hit the *British Princess*. Although the entries in the log are briefly and barely stated, one should try to imagine what they meant in terms of physical effort on the part of the crew; on the ninetieth day Thomas's log reads: 'Blowing a moderate gale and heavy sea 2 a.m. Called all hands to shorten sail hove ship to under the Lower Main Topsail.' Consider what it must have felt like to turn to in the pitch darkness of an icy cold night, to handle heavy gear with one hand for oneself and one hand for the ship, with seas constantly washing over the decks and then going below, exhausted and soaking wet to damp, confined quarters. The *British Princess* remained hove to for two days, then when the weather moderated they set the lower fore topsail, but by evening again it was 'blowing a strong gale from the N.W. with tremendous sea ship labouring heavy.' Next day was much the same and Robert Thomas recorded in his log: '10 p.m. shipped a heavy sea smashing in the windows and doors of the Port Forecastle and the half deck flooding bouth rooms wetting the men's beds and clothes.' Another day of repairing damage, 'Carpenter nailing blanks over the doors of the Forecastle and windows'; his craftsmanship was soon put to the test for the next morning there was a 'strong gale increasing in force to a Hurricane the sea running like high mountains the heaviest gale and sea we have met'. Day after it was the same, winning their way a little, then hove to or having a shorten sail considerably, and one senses Thomas's concern on the 107th day out as he wrote: 'ship labouring heavy and shipping large quantities of water keeping the decks constantly full of water washing from side to side dangerously.' But the *British Princess* was winning the battle, and as they sailed NW by N the weather as last began to improve and by the 118th day they began to smell the end of the passage. As the crew got the anchors and chain-cable on deck and scrubbed the paintwork, Thomas was busy overhauling the cable shackles and making coal tubs for use in discharging their cargo; on the 120th day they sighted land and 'the light of Corrobana Point, Shortened Sail and lay to till Morning'. The pilot came aboard at 5 a.m., the second mate went ashore for orders, returning with the news that they were to make for Callao, not Valparaiso, and with all sail set the *British Princess* headed north. The rest of the passage was in comparatively good weather, the crew scrubbing paintwork, varnishing masts, the poop, and the deck house, the carpenter, possibly ominously, 'altering the weighing machine,' and on Sunday, 27 October, 130 days out from Liverpool, Robert Thomas wrote with evident relief in his log, '12 a.m. Tacked ship, 4 p.m. came too in 18 Fathoms water with the Port Anchor. Capt. went on shore to report the ship We arrived safe Thank God'.

The *British Princess* remained at Callao and the Maccabi Islands from the end of October until the 27th April: Thomas's log indicates how the time passed, the crew employed discharging coal, the carpenter 'making trucks for to run the coals out the tween decks', and then caulking the ship: 'one hand refused duty was took before the Consul and from there was send to gaol because he would not turn to his work.' In December they sailed for the Maccabi Islands. Off the Maccabi they ran into more fog than usual, and drizzling rain; as they approached the land they took soundings: '7 a.m. took a cast of the lead, 27 fathoms black sand, 9 a.m. sounded again, Black Mud. Fog cleared sighted the land and a large paddle steamer bound to the Island.' There was little to report for the next weeks, the crew working day after day loading guano in the tubs the carpenter had made. They remained there for four months and two days, loading the foul-smelling guano, whilst the carpenter not only carried out work on his own ship but also aboard the *Etta*, another ship owned by the Davieses and built a year earlier than the *British Princess* at Quebec. The *Etta* had sailed from Newport about a month after the *British Princess* had left Liverpool, and arrived in and sailed from the Maccabi Islands about a month after her, her total voyage of sixteen months nineteen days lasting three days more than that of the *British Princess*.

On 24 April 1873, Thomas recorded the start of their voyage homeward to Falmouth for orders: the *British Princess*, despite all his caulking, leaked badly on this voyage, and he had to keep watch for some time in the mate's watch as one of the crew was ill, but his log is as interesting and as carefully kept as ever. On the 113th day, Friday, 11 August, they ran in for Falmouth, the captain going ashore for orders, 'and took one of our crew on shore to pay him off nearly dead with the Dysentry. Ship dodging in the bay waiting his return. 4 p.m. Captain came on board with orders to proceed to Antwerb'. Such are the bare bones of a voyage which was another routine voyage in a sailor's life, sixteen months sixteen days, 424 days of his life at sea, a record which happens to have survived. In the Davies Sailings Book, which confirms the dates exactly, this voyage occupied just one line.[104] It may serve to remind the reader what each one of the other 872 lines must have meant to the men who sailed in these ships and bought, sometimes with their lives, the wealth which came to the Davieses and Charles Pierce, and through them to many movements and institutions of which they were benefactors. It was certainly not achieved without losses; on the same page as the line recording this particular voyage by the *British Princess* are the losses of the *England*, which left Cardiff on 15 April and was wrecked 19 miles off Bombay on 6 July 1872, and the *Minnehaha*, which sailed from the Tyne early in 1873, arrived in Callao in May, loaded at Guanape in June, sailed in September, and then, as she left Falmouth having called for orders to proceed to Dublin, was wrecked at 3 a.m. on Pennines Head, the Scillies.

Apart from wrecks like these and the dramatic loss of a whole crew in a vessel never heard of again, like the *Afon Cefni*, there were the everyday hazards. Harry Hughes, of Amlwch, who had served aboard the *Merioneth*, did not lose his life aboard one of the Davies ships, but the manner of his death, falling from the rigging, recalls authentically what must have been a fairly commonplace occurrence. Individual deaths by accident were frequent in these sailing ships; glancing through the returns of seamen whose deaths were reported to the Registrar General of Shipping for just one year, 1881, the bare sentences evoke the human tragedies recorded. In that year alone, over a thousand seamen from British ships were drowned in accidents other than wrecks: 'fell overboard,' 'knocked overboard in taking in mainsail and drowned,' 'jumped overboard while in a state of delirium'; another two hundred or more men were killed in accidents, 'struck on head by block falling from aloft'; these are the causes of death. Here are some which relate to men aboard the Davies ships during the year 1881:[105] Elias Williams, A.B. aboard the *Flintshire*, outward bound from Liverpool for Rangoon, who was drowned soon after passing the light vessel at the entrance to Liverpool, 'fell overboard while setting jib guys; moderate gale blowing'; William R. Evans, 3rd mate of the *Dolbadarn Castle*, who was drowned when a dinghy capsized in Singapore Roads; Harry I. Munday, apprentice aboard the *Cardiganshire*, who was drowned at sea on passage from Liverpool to Singapore, 'fell overboard, supposed drawing a bucket of water'; and Carl Hartmann, Ord. Seaman, of the *Denbighshire*, Hamburg to Rangoon, killed when he 'fell from aloft when stowing upper main topsail'. The wages of an able seaman in 1881 in the South American or Far East trade averaged fifty-five shillings a month; in 1848 the average had been forty-five shillings.[106]

Some of the seamen aboard his ships had their lives cut short at an early age, but Robert Davies himself lived until he was nearly ninety. For many years he had lived 'a somewhat eccentric and parsimonious life, letting his share of the business accumulate';[107] during his last fifteen years he devoted himself to philanthropic work. This was not haphazard charity; every case was carefully investigated, and if a chapel had benefited from his gifts, he wanted to receive their annual reports to see that the money had been well invested. He built an English chapel for the Methodists at Menai Bridge at a cost of over £5,000, restored the Welsh chapel there, gave £10,000 to start the Methodist orphanage at Bontnewydd, Caernarvonshire, £10,000 to the British and Foreign Bible Society, and over £170,000 to endow the Welsh Methodist Mission in India. A difficult man in committee, obsessed with minute details, he was much tortured by the problems presented by his wealth; in order to endow the Missionary work, he had to invest his money, but if he invested in railways, did they not run on Sundays, and was it right to give money earned on a Sunday to support missionary work in

India?[108] This concern did not overflow into the world of seamen, their work on Sundays was accepted as a necessary fact of life. Although he donated considerable sums to various causes anonymously, his wealth and reputation for philanthropy made him the target of hundreds of begging letters on all kinds of subjects, such as the request of a Manchester wheelwright who wanted financial assistance to publish his *Telyn a Cherdd Dannau y Cymry*, claiming 'I am not asking you for help for a common and every day book, but the first and only complete work on Welsh Minstrelsy that was endeavoured to be published'.[109]

A brief examination of the Davies papers indicate in some measure the wealth which had been derived from the shipping business. During 1904-5, in the last year of his life, he gave £21,557.1.0 to private individuals, towards the reduction of chapel debts, and to various religious institutions.[110] It would appear from the detailed record of the cheques and cash involved in these transactions that he had a sliding scale of gifts: £5 to Congregational, Wesleyan and Baptist chapels in England and Wales that asked for his assistance, and £100 to £400 to Calvinistic Methodist chapels, many of them in the north of England and south Wales. Then there are the many personal gifts, simply entered against the initials of the recipient, sometimes with the phrase 'son's education' or 'daughter's medical'.[111] Robert Davies led an austerely frugal life; it is said that he gave away nearly £500,000 in the last years of his life, and when he died his estate was valued at £446,383.14.7d.[112] Taken in conjunction with the obvious wealth of his brother Richard Davies's descendants, and that of Charles Pierce, the Bangor tycoon, this gives some measure of the wealth that sprang from the shipowning business that had had its beginning in the little sloops and smacks of the Menai Strait; over £400,000 in 1905 was no mean fortune. Robert Davies also left about four thousand acres of land in Anglesey (as well as an estate in Ireland); the farms on this land were in 'a shocking state of dilapidation . . . the late owner simply let the land as grazing land, and would not allow the tenants to live in the house, or the outbuildings at all, with the result that they have become ruinous.' At the time of his death none of Robert Davies's money was invested in shipping, his shares now being in the North British, the Caledonian, the Great Central, and Great Eastern Railway

Companies, and the Gas Light and Coke Company of London, the South Metropolitan Gas Compnay, the Brentford Gas Company, and the Commercial Gas Company. In the Bodlondeb cellars of this lifelong supporter of temperance causes, the wines and spirits, valued at a little under a thousand pounds, had been long neglected and were in poor condition, 'although in almost every instance the corks were sound enough at the necks, there were a good many that were somewhat decayed at the lower end, and . . . most of the samples that we tested had to be strained through a muslin.' Robert Davies died, as he had lived, a lonely man. In earlier years he had loved nothing better than attending open air meetings of the Salvation Army in London: he had been happy to be a Sunday School teacher in Menai Bridge. Despite all his wealth, there is a pathetic quality about the small payments made for services rendered in the last few weeks of his long life: to Samuel Williams, workman at Bodlondeb, 'for sleeping at Bodlondeb 5/- a night' and 'For reading to Mr Davies, 4 Sunday mornings 2/6 each morning'; similar payments to John Williams, workman at Bodlondeb, John T. Jones, his coachman, R. J. Owen, gardener, and William Williams, another workman, who took it in turns to sleep at the house, or were involved in extra duties because of Robert Davies's last illness. Two days before Christmas 1905 his secretary distributed 'copper among children in accordance with Mr Robert Davies's custom,' and also paid the eight shillings 'which Mr R. Davies gave every Saturday to a number of people in Menai Bridge.' For many years one of Robert Davies's eccentricities had been a weekly distribution of flour to dozens of people who were willing to observe the condition that the recipient should personally fetch this dole from Bodlondeb on Tuesday in each week.

The sale of the last of the ships and Robert Davies's death marked the end of an era. His brother Richard's son, Henry Rees Davies, who had been named as managing owner of the *Afon Alaw*, the *Anglesey* and the last of the ships, continued the family interest in the sea through his activities on behalf of the Anglesey Lifeboat Service and yachting in the Strait; a graduate of Trinity College, Cambridge, he became a leading figure in the public life of Anglesey as a county councillor, J.P., High Sheriff, and was a Vice-President and Chairman of the Council of the University College of North Wales, Bangor, whose library has been enriched by his gifts of rare books dealing with the history of the Menai Strait and its approaches. The history of the Conway and Menai Ferries, the result of many years of historical research by H. R. Davies himself, and by those whom he employed to transcribe documents for him, was published by the University of Wales Press not long after his death in 1940.[113] That he was able to be a generous patron and contribute to the study of maritime history was due in large measure to the hundreds of seamen, many of them from Anglesey, who had served in the Davies ships for the sixty years when British sailing ships had brought considerable wealth to their owners. The Davies family are a good example of those self-made men who were highly regarded in the Victorian age, the age of Victorian prosperity. Still known locally to very old people as 'teulu Davies baw adar', the 'Davies bird lime family', referring to the guano trade, they worked their ships, and the crews that sailed them, hard, and it is perhaps significant that they were known locally as 'one gull ships', for there was little food to spare on the Davies ships for following gulls. But typical of the Victorian age, with the thrift and careful management went much energy and enterprise, and Davies ships seldom, if ever, came home in ballast. There were many who had a financial interest in ships in nineteenth-century Anglesey, but no other family with Anglesey-based offices emerged as successfully from the nineteenth-century shipowning business as the sons of Richard Davies, the general store-keeper from Llangefni.

TO EMIGRANTS.

TO SAIL about the 15th November, from the Menai Straits for NEW ORLEANS, the following fine fast-sailing Ships :—

TAMARAC,

NEW SHIP—1,400 TONS BURDEN.

PELTOMA,

NEW SHIP—850 TONS BURDEN.

NORTHUMBERLAND,

700 TONS BURDEN.

To Persons emigrating to the United States, the above offers a most desirable opportunity, as Steamers proceed direct from New Orleans to Wisconsin, Missouri, Iowa, Indiana, Illinois, and Ohio, which makes the expense less than from any other port in the States.

The Commanders being well known Welshmen, is a guarantee to passengers that their comfots will be attended to.

New Orleans is as healthy as any town in the States from October to June ; this is mentioned to give Emigrants a true knowledge of the place.

For further information, apply to Messrs. Davies and Sons.

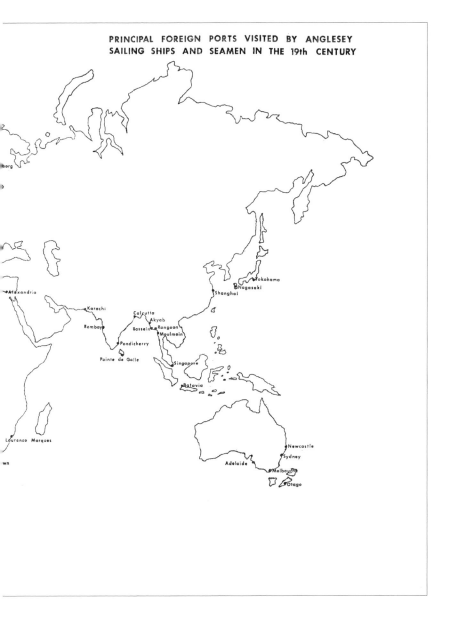

PRINCIPAL FOREIGN PORTS VISITED BY ANGLESEY
SAILING SHIPS AND SEAMEN IN THE 19th CENTURY

[1] 'The Puritan outlook stood at the cradle of modern economic man.' Max Weber, 'The Protestant Ethic and the Spirit of Capitalism', quoted in Judith Ryder and Harold Silver, *Modern English Society* (London, 1970), 18-20.

[2] R. Tudur Jones, 'Nonconformity' in *An Atlas of Anglesey* (Melville Richards, ed.) (Llangefni, 1972), 83-7.

[3] *NWC*, 5 Jan. 1906; *DWB*, 148-9, 151; *DNB*, Second Supplement, 475.

[4] There was an increase of 21% in the population of Anglesey in the intercensal period 1811-1821. By 1851 the population of the island had increased to 57,000. B. L. Davies, 'Population' in *An Atlas of Anglesey*, 121-9.

[5] Lord Bulkeley owned most of the property in the 'squares' at Llangefni and Menai Bridge, shrewdly recognizing the potential of the centres of these small villages. – E. A. Williams, *Hanes Môn yn y Bedwaredd Ganrif ar Bymtheg*, 10-11.

[6] *DWB*, 148; R. M. Williams, *Enwogion Môn* (Bangor, 1913), 8-9.

[7] *NWG*, 1823 quoted in E. A. Williams, *Hanes Môn*, 160. In 1823 Davies advertised salt for sale at Red Wharf at the Liverpool price, 12/- for 224 lbs., 2/- for the sack, and 1/- for the cost of transport from Liverpool. He charged a further 1/- a sack at Llangefni, to cover the cost of transport from Red Wharf to Llangefni.

[8] UCNW, Carter Vincent, Add MSS 3285. The indenture has a small diagram indicating that the land was situated between the area allotted for fairs, and faced Porth y Wrach.

[9] Cadwaladr Davies, *Hanes Dechreuad a Chynnydd y Methodistiaid Calfinaidd ym Mhorthaethwy* (Dolgellau, n.d.), 29.

[10] Davies, *Methodistiaid Porthaethwy*, 33.

[11] *ibid.*, 42. Among the 24 men and 18 women listed as members, John Edwards, Morris Williams, Richard Hughes, Ellen Humphreys and Margaret Williams all gave their address as 'Warehouse'.

[12] *ibid.*, 38. David Hughes was paid £20 by John Williams, Tyddyn tô, acting on behalf of the Methodists with John Davies, on 7 June 1838. John Davies had a pulpit built in the timber yard for John Elias to address an open air meeting there on one occasion. *ibid.*, 31-32.

[13] *BCR*, 1836, 1837. The Rev. John Elias had married, as his second wife, the widow of Sir John Bulkeley, of Presaddfed, Bodedern, in 1830, and they lived at Fron, Llangefni. *DWB* 203.

[14] *cf.* Basil Greenhill and Ann Gifford, *West countrymen in Prince Edward Island*, and Michael Bouquet, *Passengers from Torquay: Emigration to North America*, in which he describes the activities of the Crossman family, timber merchants.

[15] Helen I. Cowan, *British Emigration to British North America* (Toronto, 1961), 160. For emigration and timber ships generally, see Cowan; Wilbur S. Shepperson, *British Emigration to North America* (Oxford, 1957); Basil Greenhill, *The Great Migration* (London, 1968); Basil Greenhill and Ann Gifford, *West countrymen in Prince Edward Island* (Toronto, 1967); and

Alan Conway, *The Welsh in America* (Cardiff, 1961).

[16] R. S. Craig, 'British Shipping and British North American Shipbuilding in the early 19th Century, with special reference to Prince Edward Island', in *Exeter Papers in Economic History*, I, 1968, 25.

[17] *ibid.*, 26.

[18] Letter from Rev. Robert Williams to W. O. Pughe, 21 Jan. 1796, Bob Owen, 'Yr Ymfudo o Sir Gaernarfon i'r Unol Daleithiau', in *TCHS*, 1952, XIII, 53. A. H. Dodd in *The Character of Early Welsh Emigration to the U.S.* (Cardiff, 1957), discusses the nature of emigration from Wales 1791-1840, 20-31.

[19] Henry Hughes, *Immortal Sails* (London, n.d.), 50. Colonel Hughes estimated the *Gomer* to be a 90-ton wooden brig, 75' x 20' x 11.6'. According to the Beaumaris register she was rigged as a snow, 161 tons, 73.6' x 23'x 14', built at Traeth Bach in 1821. A contemporary advertisement read 'Brig Gomer (Rd. Pritchard Master) 158 tons now lying at Portmadoc ballasted with about 100 tons of slate is intended to convey to New York 54 adults, 16 under 14 and 24 under 7 years of age; Navigate with 9 men.' Bob Owen, 'Yr Ymfudo o Sir Gaernarfon', *TCHS*, 14, 43.

[20] *Y Cenhadwr Cymreig*, 1859, 79. Many Newborough seamen were said to have started their careers in sail in Owen Rhuddgaer's ships. O. Williamson, *Hanes Niwbwrch*, 44.

[21] Bob Owen, *TCHS*, XIII, 64, UCNW Bangor MSS 7312,6.

[22] Not all vessels were as well organized as the *Albion*; nearly forty years later evidence was still being given about the problem of sanitary conditions aboard emigrant ships: 'I confess we are at our wits' end on the subject of water closets.' *Parl. Papers*, XIII, 25.

[23] *Parl. Papers*, 1854, XIII, 88-9, 194. Greenhill, *The Great Migration*, 6.

[24] 'The average timber ship was little more than a shell; it had no compartments except the captain's quarters aft and the crew's quarters forward, so that on an eastward voyage the whole hull could be loaded with timber from keel to deck.' Cowan, *British Emigration*, 146.

[25] *ibid.*

[26] 'A four year old child died and everyone thought that the deep would be his grave. Some were falling from their beds, boxes were rolling, children crying, and the deck was shut down.' 'It is almost impossible to imagine the appearance of the people aboard, their clothes in rags, and their caps as if they had been a living room for bugs and fleas.' Extract from letters written by emigrants in Alan Conway, *The Welsh in America*, 14-51.

[27] UCNW Bangor MSS 5876, A. H. Dodd, 'History of Caernarvonshire' (Caernarvon, 1968), 301-10.

[28] ARO. H. R. Davies MSS Box 4, pencilled notes for a speech which H. R. Davies made at a St David's Day dinner in Menai Bridge.

[29] *CDH*, Dec. 7, 1842, 'There exists in fact a very imperfect knowledge amongst mariners generally as to the improved slate of the Channel ... natural change began to be evident less than 2 years ago in the South

Channel … we have now an excellent channel equal to the requirement of any vessel navigating the Port and the Menai and well buoyed so as to ensure perfect safety to the mariner. The arrival of the barque Hindoo is an instance in point. Her burthen is 500 tons and she draws full 15½ feet of water yet she came over the bar on Saturday last two hours before high water.'

[30] There had been considerable Parliamentary pressure to improve conditions aboard emigrant ships, although little improvement followed the 1835 Act. Cowan, 160. The quota of passengers was reduced from 3 to every 4 tons to 3 to every 5 tons burden, and the provision required was raised. The 1842 Act stipulated that emigrant ships must have permanent hold beams for the lower deck with six feet clear height above them. Cowan, 161.

[31] Basil Greenhill has drawn attention to 'the two different kinds of British emigration in the 19th century, one emphasised by historians and the other neglected. The bulk emigration was through the big ports where it was reported on, because, particularly for Liverpool (and in the early and middle decades of the century), the conditions were appalling: thus the statistics are available and much emphasis is put on this trade. This leads to the neglect of the smaller-scale emigration from the small ports of people who travelled in very different conditions. The shipowners gathered their passengers from a small area, often by personal recommendation, and unless they provided good conditions, they did not get passengers.' *Ports and Shipping in the South-West* (ed. H. S. Fisher), Exeter Papers in Economic History, 1970, 148.

[32] UCNW Bangor MS 3531. This document appears to have been hitherto neglected and therefore some extracts have been included in Appendix VII (ii) to indicate the nature of the material contained therein. The other details about the ships, their dimensions and builders, have been taken from the Lloyd's Registers, and the Mercantile Navy Lists.

[33] *NWC*, 21 April 1846; *CDH*, 12 Aug. 1846; 7 November 1846.

[34] *NWC*, 21 July 1846.

[35] *NWC*, 21 April 1846, UCNW Bangor MS 5876.

[36] *CDH*, 19 July 1845. It was stressed that the Oneco was '7½ feet high in 'tween Deck and presents one of the most favourable opportunities which has yet occurred to emigrants of proceeding to the United States of America.'

[37] *Y Cenhadwr Americanaidd*, Hydref, 1846, 317, 341. One correspondent writing from Philadelphia in October 1846 in the *Cenhadwr Americanaidd*, reported that Thomas Rawlings, editor of *The Old Countryman*, had held a meeting at Bethesda to encourage Caernarvonshire quarrymen to consider emigrating to Western Virginia, which had hitherto been unpopular with emigrants because of 'y felldith o gaethiwed', the 'curse of slavery'.

[38] *NWC*, July 1848.

[39] *CDH*, 14 March 1846.

[40] UCNW Bangor MS 4173.

[41] *ibid.,* 'A phan aeth yn ol digwyddodd fod llester
Yn harbwr llunlleifiad ai henw oedd Cortni
A Davies Pont Mena pan glywodd am dani
A brynodd y llong ond Hyn oedd beth Hynod
Yn gapten ar Hono gosodwyd fy mhriod
Rwi'n meddwl mae Deg-pynt fel cyflog penodol
Addawyd gan Davis i Robert yn fisol.'

[42] *ibid.,* 'Ond tywydd oer iawn a gafodd i lwytho
fel braidd a gallasant gael adeg i boeni
nad ydoedd cyn disgyn pob gronun yn rhewi.'

This is borne out by the *CDH* report: 'The weather had been colder and more frosty than for four years past . . . we had passed the Banks of Newfoundland when it came on to blow terrifically.'

[43] *ibid.,* 'Bum yno Dri mis ac wythnos o amser
A Robert a mina gadd lawer o bleser
Wrth fyned i Bartis ymhell ac yn agos
Am ddwywaith neu dair a hyny bob wythnos.'

[44] *ibid.,* ('to visit us and see the *Courtenay*'.) Captain Jones had left his wife at home in Holyhead while he went to superintend the discharging of the *Courtenay*'s cargo at Menai Bridge, and to take her to Caernarvon for a much-needed refit.

Ac felly hi aeth trwy gynol Pwll Ceris
cyrheuddodd Garnarfon yn ddigon llwyddiannus
a mina gychwynais yngherbyd John Edwards
cyrhaiddais y Dre bron gynted a Robert
ac yno bu y llong tan driniaeth y seiri
o ddiwedd Mehefin hyd ganol Mis Medi
roedd byw yngharnarfon mewn logins cyfforddus
tros gymaint o anser yn hynod o gostys
Ac eto mawr ydoedd Ein parch gerbron llawer
ar gyfrif fod Robert yn gapten fath lester
Ac eraill feddyliodd rhyw lawer o honom
Wrth weled Meister ffoli yn gymaint am danom

Pymthegfed o Awst os da rwyf yn cofio
nol Hir Faith ddisgwyliad fy mam a ddaeth yno
i edrych amdanom a gwel y Cortni
aeth adref ddydd Mawrth y cyntaf o fedi
a Medi deuddegfed aeth Cortni oddiyno
tros faran Caernarfon a stemar iw theuo.

[45] *ibid.,* fel gallem os byw i gyred mawr oedran
gael gweld pa fath oeddym yn chwe blwydd ar hugain.

[46] The years 1847-9 saw very many deaths through cholera aboard the emigrant ships, and although death knew no such distinctions, suggestions were made that certain notional groups were prone to carry the disease.

'There was a great deal of cholera in Germany last year … In all ships in which there was great mortality, except two, I find there were Germans on board.' *Parl. Papers*, 1854, XIII, 8-9.

[47] Margaret Jones stated that the *Tamarac* had been sighted in full sail off Holyhead after her quick passage from Quebec.

> Aeth heibio'n ddioed o tan ei llawn hwylia
> cyrhaeddodd Biwmaras mewn chydig o oria
> ac yno gadawodd fy Mhriod yn llester
> nes myned i'r Borth i siarad ai feister
> a mina mewn cerbyd a aethym iw weled
> cyrheuddais lle bron gynted a Robert
>
> ond pan gaed y llong at ochr Pont Mena
> yn aros iw threfnu rhyw gymaint o Ddyddia
> death Robert a Mina o ddeutu nos wener
> mewn car i Gaergybi tros chydig o Amser
> Ac felly pan ddaeth ac agor y tryngeia
> O bob-peth oedd ynddynt y beibl oedd hardda.

With her description of the *Tamarac*'s cargo at Menai Bridge, and the obvious impression the size of the new vessel had made there, Margaret Jones's narrative verse ends. Her father, William Thomas, stated that the remainder of the verses she wrote were in Captain Jones's possession aboard his ship, but from Thomas's own account it appears that Margaret Jones died on July 30th, 1852, at Holyhead. Captain Jones had resigned his command of the Davies's *Carleton* in which he had sailed to Australia, to bring his ailing wife home from London where she had gone to meet him. After years of service with the Davies ships, Captain Robert Jones returned to Holyhead as Lloyd's agent. Bangor MS 4173.

[48] UCNW Penrhyn MS 1800, 1371. Davies received another request in March to provide a vessel to take 'about 500 tons of slates for New Orleans' *ibid.*, 115.

[49] *ibid.*, 390 – There were demands for a vessel to take cargo to New Orleans in the same month, but neither the Davieses nor the Penrhyn agent could find a suitable one: the following is a typical entry in the Penrhyn letter book, addressed to the Davieses in June 1848, 'We have a freight for New Orleans not exceeding 526 tons burthen. Have you anything to offer?'

[50] *NWC*, October 1847.

[51] *ibid.*

[52] UCNW Bangor MS 3531.

[53] *Y Cenhadwr Americanaidd* 1849, Bangor MS 5876.

[54] *NWC*, April 1848.

[55] T. Charles Williams, *Y Drysorfa*, 1906, 101-107.

[56] *NWC*, Feb. 1901.

[57] *CDH*, 5 Jan.1850, contained an account of the arrival of the *Ancient Briton* at Swansea from Adelaide. 'She is a full rigged ship built at Pwllheli

and manned entirely by members of the principality.' The Welsh-American newspaper, *Y Cyfaill*, reported in 1850 that there were scores of Welsh emigrants arriving every week: The *Higginson*, owned by Humphrey Owen, Rhuddgaer, had brought 150 Welsh emigrants from Caernarvon, and the *Forest Queen* another 400 from Liverpool. Already class-consciousness had appeared; the Cyfaill reported that in both groups the emigrants were superior to the usual emigrant types, and there were three ministers of religion in their midst; 'yr oedd y rhan fwyaf . . . o radd uwch na'r cyffredin o ymfudwyr. Ymhlith yr ymfudwyr daeth tri o bregethwyr – Mr Griffiths, Anibynwr o Dowyn, Meirionydd, Mr Jones, Trefnydd Wesleiaid, a Mr Edward Evans, Trefnydd Calfinaidd.' Y Cyfaill, 1850, 183.

[58] Asa Briggs, *Victorian Cities* (London, 1971), 277-310.

[59] Asa Briggs, *The Age of Improvement* (London, 1960), 399.

[60] From 1850 to 1855 the *Infanta* sailed twice a year from Menai Bridge for Boston and Quebec. The *Peltoma* sailed twice from Caernarvon for New Orleans in 1847 and 1848, from Menai Bridge in 1849 and was sold in 1850 after another voyage to Quebec.

[61] From 1859, the *Highland Mary* was largely engaged in sailing from the Menai Strait for Quebec and from Cardiff and Antwerp for Buenos Aires and Montevideo. Like the other Davies vessels, her voyages to and from Quebec and North America took a little over three months, whilst those to Callao were usually of a little over a year's duration.

[62] The *Caroline* sailed on 7 December 1850 and arrived at Adelaide on 6 April 1851, whilst the *Carleton* left Liverpool on 24 January 1851, and was at Adelaide by 21 May. Three days later the *Caroline* sailed for Callao, arriving there 15 July, sailing again on 20 Oct., and arrived in London 14 February 1852. The *Carleton* left Adelaide on 5 July, arrived at Callao on 26 August, sailed again on 25 November and was back in London by 29 March 1852. The master of the *Caroline* was Captain T. Jones, whilst Captain Robert Jones, who had previously commanded the *Courtenay* and *Tamarac*, was master of the *Carleton*.

[63] By 1894 Callao had 6,815 length of quayage with 3 ballast cranes capable of loading 25 tons per hour. Iquique and Mollendo in Peru, and Taltal, Tocopilla, in Chile, were still used as anchorages where launches and lighters discharged cargoes; at Caldera and Coquimbo there were wharves for smaller vessels, whilst the larger vessels discharged and loaded by means of lighters. *Lloyd's Register, 1894*. Particulars of Wet Docks, Tidal Harbours, Quays, Ports, etc., 100.

[64] Alan Moorehead, *Darwin and the Beagle* (London, 1969), 185.

[65] Robert Thomas, a Caernarvon man, carpenter aboard the *British Princess*, has a good account of his time at the Macabi Islands in his log of her voyage in 1872, *infra*. For a later account of Lobos de Afuera, Captain H. H. Heligan in *SB* II (1946), 406-408, Sir James Bisset has a description of the *County of Pembroke* loading guano at Chincha Island in his memoirs, *Sail Ho* (1958), 188-203.

[66] John Roberts in *Llandudno Advertiser*, 17 April 1909.

[67] Dr. O. O. Roberts, the Radical leader, quoted in Dodd, *History of Caernarvonshire*, 360.

[68] *ibid.*, 360.

[69] UCNW PN MSS II, 411; E. G. Jones, 'Borough Politics and Electioneering 1826-52', TCHS, XVII, 75-85; Dodd, *History of Caernarvonshire*, 360.

[70] A. M. Davies, 'Life and Letters of Henry Rees' (Bangor, 1904), 201.

[71] Davies, *Henry Rees*, 214. The *Exodus* had sailed on 21 April 1855 from Liverpool, arrived Sydney 26 July, sailed again 27 September, arrived Callao 24 November, sailed on 21 January 1856 and arrived safely in Liverpool 12 May.

[72] *ibid.*, 227.

[73] *CDH*, 21 Nov. 1868.

[74] *Parl. Deb.*, 3rd Series, CCXXVIII, 638-86; Geoffrey Alderman, 'Samuel Plimsoll and the Shipping Interest', *Maritime History* I, 1, 73.

[75] E. A. Williams, *Hanes Môn yn y Bedwaredd Ganrif ar Bymtheg*, 224.

[76] *DWB* 149. In addition to his estates and farms, Richard Davies left personal property of the gross value of £294,446.11.0, *Byegones*, 30 Dec. 1896, 501.

[77] T. Charles Williams, *Y Drysorfa*, 1906, 101-107.

[78] UCNW Bangor MSS 5708. I am indebted to Dr. B. L. Davies for this reference.

[79] *Minutes of Evidence on Higher Education in Wales and Monmouthshire*, 1880, 135, evidence of R. Davies, Esq., M.P., 29 Oct. 1880. Davies added, 'Meetings were held throughout the island to consider his proposal, and everywhere it was unanimously accepted. Petitions were sent from each meeting to the Commissioners, urging them to give it their sanction. Much correspondence followed … I know, however, that no proposal of the Commissioners ever fully satisfied my brother.'

[80] *DWB*, 740. Parry was at different times a schoolmaster, a lawyer's clerk, a preacher, editor of *Y Wawr* in 1850-52, visited the United States, and wrote a long, rambling autobiographical introduction to his poetry in *Teithiau a Barddoniaeth Robyn Ddu Eryri*, 1857.

[81] *NWC*, Feb. 1901. Pierce contributed over £1,000 to the Prince's Road English Presbyterian Church when it was being built, £1,000 to the Calvinistic Methodist Forward Movement in South Wales, scholarships to the Bala Theological College, and £500 to the Minffordd Hospital. I am indebted to R. T. Pritchard for information regarding Pierce's connection with the City of Bangor.

[82] Appendix.

[83] E. J. Hobsbawm, *Industry and Empire* (1970), 178-9.

[84] Sir Ernest Royden, *Roydens, 1818-1893* (Liverpool, 1953). Thomas Royden, Senior, had, in the forty-four years before he retired in 1863, built over seventy ships; he left the firm when they started to build iron ships, but

his son, Thomas Bland Royden, built thirty-six iron ships in the three years 1867-69, and among these was the *Malleny*.

[85] The *Moel Eilian* and her two sister ships were built at Sunderland, the *Gwynedd* and the *Eivion* at Hylton, and the *Glandinorwig, Glan Padarn, Glan Peris* at Sunderland, the *Gwynedd* and the *Eivion* at *Hylton*, and the *Glandinorwig, Glan Padarn, Glan Peris* at Sunderland, all of them in the building boom 1877-84. For examples of the cost of building and the widespread investment by many sections of the community in north Wales in large sailing ships, *infra*.

[86] Appendix VII (i) gives some indication of the way in which Davies ships moved from the Atlantic trades to Rangoon, Singapore and San Francisco in the seventies and eighties.

[87] J. Glyn Davies, review of *Immortal Sails*, T. Cymm. 1948, 208.

[88] Basil Lubbock, *The Last of the Windjammers* (Glasgow, 1927), I, 203-4.

[89] Joseph Conrad's story *The Shadow Line* was based on experiences in the *Otago* during 1888 in the Eastern Seas he knew so well.

[90] Lubbock, *The Last of the Windjammers*, II, 141-2.

[91] The *Victory*, which had made ten voyages to India for Davies since 1867, had left South Shields on 12 April and was lost off Spurn Point two days later; the *Conway Castle*, which had been engaged in the South American trades apart from one voyage from Cardiff to Rangoon, was wrecked at Huanillos on 9 May, 1877. She had sailed from Antwerp for Callao in November 1876, arriving in March and leaving again for Huanillos three days later. She had been at Huanillos for a little less than a month when she was wrecked. The *British Empire* had sailed in the India and South American trades since 1863; she left South Shields in August 1882 and had not been seen since she had been sighted off Dartmouth at 12.30 p.m. on September 1st until she was reported lost through being 'burnt off Alleppy Jan 5, 1877', on the coast of Malabar, South-West India.

[92] Lubbock, *The Last of the Windjammers*, I, 34.

[93] Richard Larn and Clive Carter, *Cornish Shipwrecks* (1969), 217, state that wreckage from the *Afon Cefnui* (*sic*) 'was washed up at Scilly, Penzance, and Land's End; nothing was found of her crew and she was presumed to have foundered off Land's End during a heavy westerly gale a few days after she sailed.'

[94] D. T. Williams, *SB*, 1 (new series), 419.

[95] The *Lord Cairns*, for example, made seventeen annual voyages to San Francisco between 1882 and 1901, one to India, and another to Iquique. The *Montgomeryshire* made fourteen voyages to San Francisco, four others to Rangoon and Singapore, and two to Akyab, as well as her later passages to Yokohama and Newcastle, N.S.W.

[96] UCNW Bangor MS 3531.

[97] Lubbock, *The Last of the Windjammers*, II, 1938-9. The *Muskoka* was the sister ship of the *Oweenee*, Captain Robert Jones, Amlwch's last command.

[98] *NWC*, Oct. 1847, supra.

[99] *CDH*, 13 Dec. 1847.

[100] *SB* 10, 1950, 310. Evan Jones, in his letter, did not state the name of the vessel in which he first sailed, but from the dates and ports he mentions, confirms that it was the *Bacchus*, which sailed from Cardiff in September 1885, was at Rio on October 28, sailed thence on December 8, and arrived off Akyab March 20, 1886. The *Bacchus* arrived at Falmouth on September 25, 1886, and sailed again from Cardiff in December for Singapore. Evan Jones later served in William Thomas's *Colony* and *Kate Thomas*, as well as the Caernarvon-owned *Glan Padarn, Glan Peris, Glanivor* and *Glandinorwig*.

[101] UCNW Bangor MS 3531.

[102] G. N. Jones, *SB*, XXII, 23-31. Commodore Jones's description of the auction has a vivid authenticity: 'The remainder of Harry's kit lay in tidy heaps; the second mate took up the blue double-breasted shore suit, with its smart velvet collar and asked for a bid. This quickly came and soon the suit was sold for £2 and handed over to the bidder. Item after item was auctioned until at last all Harry's personal belongings had been sold and only a small heap of private papers and a Bible remained. These were carefully kept for sending home to his parents. I picked up the Welsh Bible and noted that it had been well-thumbed and on the inside page was written in Welsh: 'Search the Scriptures.' I had never thought of Harry as a religious man; he never spoke of religion, which was in any case a forbidden subject in a fo'c'sle of a sailing ship, the crew of which was usually mixed in nationality and religious belief, if any. But Harry's quiet, placid character, combined with a strong personality, placed him as a man who had an inner faith which was evident in his daily life.'

[103] CRO MS M/736/12.

[104] The *British Princess* sailed on her next voyage from Sunderland to Rangoon, and there then followed a series of voyages between 1874 and 1879 to the west coast of South America before she was sold in 1879.

[105] *Parl. Papers*, 1884, LXXI, 85-127.

[106] *Parl. Papers*, 1882, LXII.

[107] *DNB*, Second Supplement, 475.

[108] T. Charles Williams, *Y Drysorfa*, 1906, pp. 101-107.

[109] UCNW Bangor MSS 1001 (9). Letter from Robert Griffith to Robert Davies, 1 November 1900. Griffith addressed Davies as 'one of the most generous gentlemen in all Wales', and hoping to strike the right note, added, 'I happen to be a member of the Methodistiaid Calfinaidd and for 25 years I have been a member of the Rev. Dr William Jones' Welsh Chapel at Moss Side'. For good measure, he made an appeal to national pride and history: 'The English, the Irish, and the Scoch (*sic*) have ever so many large and good volumes on the Minstrelsy of their own country. But Wales has not one, although Welsh Minstrelsy is far more ancient and interesting than all the others ... I hope this letter will not give any offence to you sir. I only take advantage of one of the most ancient customs in Wales – that is the particular privilege of the poor followers of Bardism and literature always to

ask the gentry of their own country for almost anything they wanted.'

[110] UCNW Carter Vincent, Add MSS 3286.

[111] *ibid.*, '29 July 1904. Rev. T.C.W. (quite unsolicited) to go for a change of air, £40'. No doubt refers to his long friendship with his minister and friend at Menai Bridge, the Rev. T. Charles Williams, the distinguished Methodist preacher.

[112] *ibid.* The extract from his papers which follow are all from the bundle in UCNW Carter Vincent Add MSS 3286.

[113] H. R. Davies, *A Review of the Records of the Conway and Menai Ferries* (Cardiff, 1942). Davies also wrote Appendix XI, 'The Menai Ferries' in the Report of the Royal Commission on Ancient and Historical Mounments: *Anglesey* (1937).

An Anglesey Ship-Building Firm:
William Thomas and Sons, Amlwch

On the crest of the hill straddling either side of the winding road leading from Porth Amlwch to Llaneilian stand two large Victorian houses, both looking out to the sea where the vessels built and owned by the families of Bryn Eilian and Ponctaldrwst once sailed. As the Davies family of Menai Bridge have been taken as an example of a ship-owning family in Victorian Anglesey, so the vessels built by the Thomas family of Amlwch represent another aspect of the island's maritime history. Ship-owning and ship-building tended to go hand in hand in 19th century Britain, and the Thomases, like the Treweeks whose pioneering ship-building enterprise at Amlwch they extended, both owned and built ships, using the capital resources of the one to develop the other aspect of their activities. There were many who built ships around the coast of Anglesey during the first half of the 19th century, and found neighbours to venture with them in a fever which, in Anglesey, was something akin to the railway fever in other parts of the country. Often enough their hopes and hard-earned money were pinned on the small smack or sloop built on a strip of beach or open field near their homes. Typical of these small local builders was Ishmael Jones of Cemais who started his career as master of the *Mary*, a ten ton wherry, originally an open boat which had been raised and decked over at Cemais. Together with Robert Jones, timber merchant, and Owen Jones, a Llanfechell farmer, Ishmael Jones built three smacks, the *St Patrick, Selah* and *Hope*, and the schooner *Mona's Isle*, at Cemais in the 1830s. Soon after the accession of the young queen, Ishmael Jones built a 32-ton cutter, the *Queen Victoria*, launched in June 1838, and wrecked on the Scottish coast in 1839. The pace of building one vessel a year was increased in the next few years, and between 1839 and 1842 five vessels, including the 115-ton schooner *Margaret Ann*, were built. William Roose, an Amlwch merchant, Evan Owen Jones, vicar of Llanbadrig, Meshach Roberts, a Bangor druggist, two mail guards from Holyhead, and farmers from Llanfechell, Llanfair-yng-Nghornwy, Llangwyfan, Llanrhwydrys, and a druggist from Llannerch-y-medd were among the shareholders in these vessels built by Ishmael Jones.[1] It was the same story elsewhere on the island: Thomas Jones, who 'planned and built opposite to his dwelling house four of the Holyhead packets'[2] in the early years of the century at Holyhead, Thomas Gibbs, Henry McVeagh, Edward Meredith and Robert Carr, all at Holyhead, John Hughes who built the *Cambrian Cutter* at Dulas in 1833 for the Webster family of Amlwch, and on the Menai Strait there were builders at Beaumaris, Moel-y-don, Port Dinorwic, Caernarvon and Bangor. Edward Ellis, the Bangor builder, who had a patent slip at Garth Point, and built the *Mona*, one of the first vessels in which John Davies, the Menai Bridge shipowner, and Samuel Dew of Llangefni, had shares, launched the *Ellen* in 1842, a sloop in which the shares were held by Ellis himself, a Llangristiolus farmer, a spinster from Llanfair Mathafarn Eithaf, Margaret Parry, and John Phillips of Holywell, Flintshire, recorded in the register as 'preacher', but better-known as north Wales organiser for the British and Foreign Schools Society and as the fund-raiser for the Bangor Normal College. The building of the Britannia Bridge brought engineers who saw the possibilities of building their own vessels near the site of the bridge; the *Britannia*, a 35-ton flat, was built for and owned by Benjamin Powell, John Hemingway and Charles Pearson, all of Menai Bridge, and described as 'railway contractors'. The same group, together with Joseph Benjamin Hemingway of Manchester, also a railway contractor, owned the flat *Harriet*, built at Northwich in 1811; no doubt the two flats were gainfully employed in transporting materials for the bridge. The *Harriet* was eventually lost in the Bristol Channel, together with all her papers, in 1855.

The Treweek shipbuilding ventures at Amlwch were, therefore, far from unique, but the development of the copper industry and the steady call for ship-repairing services naturally gave them certain advantages. Moreover, as Captains R. Wynne and R. Jones, themselves brought up in Amlwch in the schooner trade and later to become successful captains in steam, recalled recently, it was soon found that the copper-stained water in the vicinity of Amlwch harbour was excellent for the treating of timber and had something of the properties of modern anti-fouling paint.[3] In the Amlwch area, in addition to the plentiful labour force drawn thither in the days of the copper mines boom, there were shop-keepers, farmers, and master mariners with the initiative to invest in coastal shipping which ever-expanding Merseyside and, to a lesser extent, the new and developing north Wales resorts demanded. Shipbuilding at Amlwch in the first half of the nineteenth-century was largely a Treweek monopoly; James Treweek's death in 1851 marked the end of an era. Despite the early death in 1832 of his brother Francis, and his own appointment at Liverpool as a broker and forwarding agent for Amlwch copper, Nicholas Treweek continued to build and repair sloops and schooners at Amlwch, and by the 1840s had also established a yard at Hirael, Bangor.[4] Living and working in the Liverpool of the pioneer ship-owners, Treweek was aware of the possibilities of the emigrant and timber trades, and the profit to be made out of buying and selling North American-built ships. Taken in conjunction with his holdings in Amlwch- and other British-built coastal craft, this led to Treweek having a financial interest during the years 1845-1855 in no less than three full-rigged ships, seven barques, six brigs, five brigantines, twelve schooners, three snows, nine sloops, three smacks and one galliot.[5] Thus, for example, in 1851 he bought a 632-ton barque from Thomas Morrison, a master mariner, described as 'formerly of Pictou, Nova Scotia, now of Liverpool,' at least the third ship he had acquired through Morrison in twelve months; she was registered at Beaumaris in April as the *Anglesey*, described as a barque 'rigged with standing bowsprit, square sterned, carvel built . . . one poop deck, three masts, 119.4' long, 27.2' broad, 21' depth'. Two years later Treweek sold the *Anglesey* to Edward Oliver of Liverpool, merchant, from whom he subsequently bought the 996-ton ship *Recruit* built in New Brunswick in 1852. The *Recruit* was soon sailing from Liverpool for Australia, one of the ever-increasing fleet of ships bound there in the post gold-rush boom.

No papers have survived to indicate how profitable this period in Treweek's life was, but in the ...fifties he was back in Amlwch having given up his office in Liverpool because of ill-health.[6] From the Beaumaris Transactions Register, it would appear that he sold or transferred a number of his shares to relatives in 1854 and 1855 – possibly because of ill-health – but the 1861 census return states that Nicholas Treweek was not only farming 80 acres and employing three labourers at Bodnyfa Fawr, but he was also listed as head of a ship-building firm employing 25 ship's carpenters and 4 boys, 5 smiths and 2 boys, 3 sailmakers and 2 boys and 4 riggers.[7] During the previous decade the Treweek monopoly at Amlwch Port had been increasingly challenged. The long-standing antipathy between the Treweeks,[8] who, despite their long residence in the area, were still regarded as 'pobl dwad', Cornish intruders who had benefited from the exploitation of the copper mines on the one hand and the local Welsh community on the other, may have had a bearing on the support given to William Morris, 'Mr. Nicholas Treweek's foreman at his sail-making department,' when he applied for permission to establish a rival sail loft 'in one of the warehouses at Amlwch Port'.[9] Evan Evans, chief clerk at the Mona Mine office, writing to Lord Anglesey's London agent, stated that Morris was a very steady young man 'considered a first rate hand at his craft' and was 'encouraged by many ship-owners to start a sail-making business on his own account'.[10]

One of the ship-owners who probably encouraged William Morris, and was later associated with him in the ownership of vessels, was Captain William Thomas, a near neighbour of Nicholas Treweek. Born in 1822, the son of Lewis Thomas, Cae Pant, a smallholding between Amlwch and Llaneilian, young William Thomas, finding work on the farm uncongenial, had gone to sea at the age of twelve.[11] Fifteen years later, in 1849, he had had sufficient success to be master and part-owner of the *Clyde*, a 123-ton brigantine, built in Nova Scotia in 1842 and registered at Beaumaris in 1849.[12] The owners of the *Clyde* were William Thomas himself, described as master mariner, his father, Lewis Thomas of Cae Pant, yeoman, and William Lewis of Ponctaldrwst, yeoman, who had married one of the Thomas family. In 1851 Captain Thomas relinquished command of the *Clyde* at Youghal to a Captain John Thomas (possibly his brother) and bought shares himself in Nicholas Treweek's *Kendal Castle*, an 85-ton coasting schooner sailing out of Liverpool. He remained master of the *Kendal Castle* until 1854 when he bought shares in a new schooner, the *Anglesea Lass*, built at Rhyl in that year. Captain Thomas was still listed as master and owner of the *Anglesea Lass* in Lloyd's Register of 1859, but there is evidence to suggest that he was already taking an active part in ship-building ventures in Amlwch by this time. In 1858 he formed a company to build the first iron schooner at Amlwch, the *Mary Catherine*; the owners, 'Jones and Company, Amlwch', and the builders, 'Hughes Thomas and Company', celebrated the event 'by partaking of a substantial dinner at Parry's Vaults', whilst the workmen were 'entertained to a dinner at the Britannia Inn'. The local press warmly congratulated the builders 'on the noble appearance of the ship on the water which looked a perfect yacht'.[13]

The *Mary Catherine*, to be commanded by Captain John German, an experienced master mariner at Amlwch Port, was probably built on or near the site of Treweek's original yard on the western side of the harbour. Nicholas Treweek had moved some years previously to the north-eastern side of the harbour, to seaward of and beyond the quays adjoining the copper hoppers, and had established his new yard, known to this day as '*yr iard newydd*'. Although this was a site much exposed to the elements, and far from the lake to the north of the Mona smelting works where timber was seasoned in the coppery water, there was more room here for expansion and it was Treweek land. The harbour itself still suffered from the overcrowding that had plagued James Treweek in earlier days. A new lighthouse had been built in 1853 on the 150 ft. pier, constructed in 1815 to protect shipping in the harbour. On-shore winds caused a swell in the harbour and according to the 1857 regulations the harbour master was empowered to call upon 'the master of every vessel that may be in the harbour to attend with at least two-thirds of his ship's crew to assist in putting down and taking up the balks at all times at the call of the harbour master or one of the hobblers.'[14]

Something of the atmosphere of the port itself in the early fifties is reflected in the autobiography of the wandering scholar, Robert Roberts, '*Y Sgolor Mawr*', who worked there as a schoolmaster about this time. He described vividly the rough toughness of this 'resort of sailors', with its 'black dust' and the 'sulphur fumes of the smelting works', where after an evening at 'old Mrs Roos's hostelry' near the harbour he had difficulty in piloting himself through the crowds watching 'no less than seven pugilistic encounters in the long street that led from the port to my lodging'.[15] The copper miners' thirst was shared by seamen, sawyers, caulkers, shipwrights, riggers, hobblers and labourers – for every shipwright there were several unskilled

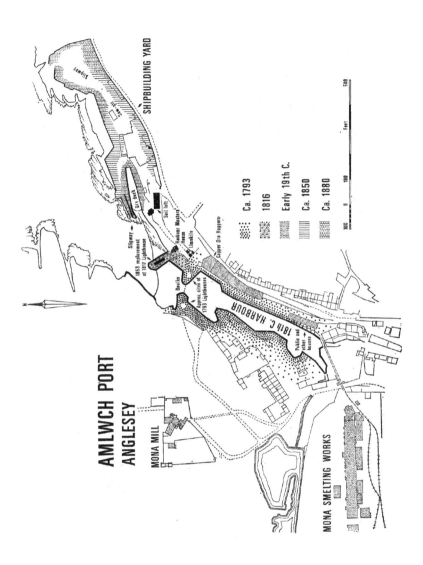

labourers. In the harbour area, the Beerhouse Act of 1830, which virtually permitted any householder who paid a small fee to sell beer on his premises,[16] was welcomed, so that almost every other little house supplied liquor, some of the ale coming from the Amlwch breweries nearby, although Greenalls, the St Helens brewers, had been supplying beer to Anglesey since 1786.[17] At the time of the 1851 census, apart from the mariners who were at sea, there were over a hundred seamen ashore in Amlwch and its neighbouring parishes on census night, 14 master mariners, 100 or so wives of absent seamen, 7 sail makers, 11 ship's carpenters, 6 shipwrights and a smattering of others whose occupations linked them very closely with the ships, hobblers, ship chandlers, and pilots. Ten years later the most marked increase was in ship-building crafts among the 30 or more shipwrights and ship's carpenters, and a dozen or so sail-makers and riggers who lived in Chapel Street and Quay Street.[18]

Anyone looking down from the road from which the eight great ore hoppers had been filled would have seen on census night, 7 April 1861, what was probably a fairly typical scene in Amlwch harbour in the early sixties, 10 small vessels described variously as schooners, smacks, sloops and a wherry, either alongside the quays or lying dry in the harbour.[19] As the tide went out that night and left the vessels on the mud, there would be many who viewed the ships and their rigging with interest, for in Amlwch there were a number of 'ship owners'. If there was a hedonistic attitude among those who frequented the quayside beer houses after toiling long hours at the Mona Smelting Works, or aboard the smacks and sloops, or in the shipyards, there were also those careful citizens, whose thrift, industriousness, and religion went hand-in-hand in Victorian Britain. Alongside those families who had benefited directly from the copper mines were local businessmen like Owen Owens, draper, David Edwards, the druggist, and John Lewis, London House, who, at the launching of the *Alliance* in 1858, rejoiced 'to see Welshmen becoming more active in the erection of vessels and other speculations that had a tendency to advance the nation.'[20] The Amlwch Literary and Scientific Institute, symbol of the 'progressive character of the times' which opened its doors in 1845 and had a library which proved useful to both Robert Roberts ('*Y Sgolor Mawr*') and Sir John Rhys when he was a schoolmaster at Rhosybol, was an indication of another side of life in Amlwch. With their avowed purpose the diffusion of useful knowledge, the members of the Institute were in the tradition of Brougham, Samuel Smiles, the Mechanics Institute and the Mutual Improvement classes, the middle class image of self-help; the Amlwch Institute's report of 1858 noted that 'it is felt that these are times of progress, that this Institution has its relation to the progressive character of the Times'.[21] In Amlwch, progress was inevitably linked with shipping. Captain William Thomas was to have much to do with that progress. The brief but highly profitable revival in the fortunes of the Parys Mountain Copper Mines between 1858 and 1870 under the energetic agent, Captain C. B. Dyer, and the increasing demand for the products of Hills, the chemical firm who had established themselves in Amlwch to manufacture artificial fertilizers,[22] meant that there was a considerable call of shipping, and Captain William Thomas was poised to take over from Nicholas Treweek.

In the year that the *Mary Catherine* was built, 1858, the reporter of the *North Wales Chronicle* registered his surprise at finding 'the new shipping yard of Messrs Treweek and Co. such a commodious place and so extensive works, in what is usually considered a rather obscure town'.[23] The vessel launched on the March morning that the reporter visited Treweek's yard was 'a beautifully modelled schooner', the *Alliance*, 'so named to show the union that exists between Amlwch and Holyhead', as Mr J. Lewis of London House, Amlwch, one of her owners, said at the launching dinner at the 'Dinorben Hotel'. The business interests of Holyhead and Amlwch were well represented with Captain C. B. Dyer, agent of the Parys Mine, as chairman, and when tributes were paid to the 'new building yard of Messrs Treweek, Sons and Company,' it was Captain William Thomas who rose to respond to the toast to the firm and it was his daughter who performed the naming ceremony at the launching earlier in the morning. After years of decline in the copper undertakings there was a new air of optimism at Amlwch by 1858; a new bank was opening, and a few weeks before the launching of the *Alliance* it had been reported that 'this thriving little port is full of bustle, being crowded with shipping, discharging and receiving cargoes, and the shipbuilding yard of Mr Treweek busily occupied with a fine schooner in wood nearly completed, and another in iron

– the first of that material ever constructed in north Wales'.[24] The *Grace Evans*, their first two-masted iron schooner, was launched from the Treweek yard in October 1859; Nicholas Treweek and Captain William Thomas each had a quarter share in her, and the remaining shares were held by Grace Evans, spinster, and Edward Morgan, tobacconist, both of Amlwch, a Llanbadrig farmer, and two Welshmen in business in Lancashire, William Hughes of Manchester, cotton merchant, and William Jones of Liverpool, flour dealer.[25]

In the absence of documentary evidence it is not easy to piece together the sequence of events in the next few years. According to a tradition firmly held in his family, Captain William Thomas is said to have taken part in the American Civil War during the years 1861-63, and to have been rewarded for some unspecified services by being given a plot of land which he subsequently sold in order to purchase the shipyard from the Treweek family in 1863. It is certainly evident that Captain Thomas was buying not only more shares in Treweek ships at this time but also buying several for himself and managing others for other Amlwch master mariners and businessmen. There is a brief note referring to the 'lease of Iron Foundry and premises from Mr Treweek in October 1860' among the family papers. But in 1861, as already stated, the census return indicates that Treweek was still head of a shipbuilding firm; notes prepared by one of Captain Thomas's grand-daughters in 1963 state that Captain Thomas 'bought the shipyard from Mr Nicholas Treweek in May 1863'.[26] A rival yard, that of William Cox Paynter, across the harbour, had completed the *Charles Edwin* in 1859, the year the *Alliance* had been built, and in 1865 the *Jane Gray*, a schooner which was to have a long association with the port, but in the sixties Captain Thomas seems to have been largely engaged in his ship-broker activities.[27]

By the mid sixties Captain Thomas was managing more than a dozen vessels and very well established in the Amlwch community; the mine agents Morcom, and a relative, Nicholas Morcom of St Agnes, Cornwall, described as a draper, and another draper, Owen Owens from Amlwch, and David Edwards, the druggist, and businessmen from further afield, like the Peakes, bonded store merchants of Cardiff, and many local farmers looked to him as a ship broker and ship manager whom they could trust. In 1866 he formed alliances with two men whose careers, though quite independent, were to be closely linked with his own for many years. He had already worked with Captain Robert Jones of Amlwch when the latter took command and the major share in the *Pride of Anglesea* in 1859, but in 1866 their alliance was strengthened by the purchase of the Prince Edward Island barquentine *Amanda*, in which again Captain Jones had by far the majority share, but in which Captain Thomas and William Thomas of Liverpool, 'ship broker', also had shares.[28] Captain Jones himself sailed in command of the *Amanda* to the Baltic and Mediterranean and both he and his son were to have close connections with Captain Thomas for many years.[29] It was in 1866 also that William Thomas, the Liverpool ship broker, took a minor share in another vessel which Captain Thomas bought, the Bideford brig *Clara Louise* and so started an association which was to bring considerable prosperity to them both.

Between 1850 and 1890 scores of young Welshmen, many of them from Anglesey, went to Liverpool to work. Among the most successful were those who built houses in the Everton, Bootle, Princes Road, Anfield, Waterloo and Crosby areas; Owen Elias, who had come to Liverpool on a small vessel from Amlwch when he was only nineteen with a few shillings in his pocket, eventually built a vast number of houses in the Everton district, and David Hughes, a native of Cemais, who had similarly come by sea from Amlwch as a young man, and had become one of the pioneers of the building industry on Merseyside, are two whose careers exemplified this trend.[30] The Liverpool Welsh community, closely knit and linked together by language and religion, invested much money in bricks and mortar, but some of them were also willing to speculate in the much riskier operations of sailing ships. William Thomas, eldest of the eight children of Robert and Catherine Thomas, was born at Hirgraig, Llanrhuddlad, on December 5th, 1837, shortly before his parents moved to Bont, a farm in the same parish.[31] After attending a small day school near his home, he went, at the age of eight, to the newly opened British school in the village of Llanrhuddlad. The master of the school, Robert Ll. Foulkes, trained briefly at Borough Road, London, was an exceptionally able man, and the school was singled out in the otherwise hostile report of 1847: 'the school is excellent and in consequence the attendance is very good. No school in north

Wales has made more progress.'[32] Here young William Thomas
proved to be such a promising pupil that his parents were persuaded
to let him remain as a pupil teacher from the age of 13½ until he was
17, no mean sacrifice for a family with seven younger children. In
1854 Thomas sailed from Porth Swtan (Church Bay) to Holyhead,
where he boarded a vessel for Liverpool, and found employment as a
clerk in a shipping office. Six years later, dissatisfied with his wages
and prospects, he set up in business on his own at the age of 23 as a
ship insurance broker and ship manager. Living with an aunt in St
Paul's Square, he moved easily in the Liverpool Welsh Calvinistic
Methodist community, and was still a young man in his twenties
when he was made a deacon of the Pall Mall Chapel. His
denominational and Anglesey connections soon brought him into
contact with Captain William Thomas of Amlwch.

A major financial success for the two Thomas Families was not
long delayed. In 1869 they acquired the *William Mellhuish*, a 680-ton
full-rigged ship built at Jersey ten years previously, and put another
William Thomas, a native of Newborough, in command of her. On
her first voyage the *William Mellhuish* not only paid for herself but
earned for the three Anglesey men called William Thomas five times
their original outlay according to the often repeated story.[33] The two
major shareholders, the Liverpool ship broker and the Amlwch
shipbuilder, ploughed back the profits into their respective
businesses and consequently expanded both concerns in the 1870
period. William Thomas, Liverpool, invested in the schooners
Captain Thomas built and in some of the best known schooners of
Ashburner, Fisher, and Postlethwaite,[34] but his main preoccupation
in future was to be the development of his own fleet of large sailing
ships and barques in the oceanic trades. Conversely, Captain
Thomas managed and part-owned several barques (some of them
with the Liverpool Thomas) in the South American and Far East
trades, but his main investment was in the development of his
Amlwch and newly-acquired Cumberland yards.

The seventies were busy years in Amlwch. The copper mines,
soon doomed to decline, and Hills Chemical Works were operating
at full stretch; Anglesey schooners and smacks and the great
schooner fleets of the north-west, of Fisher, Ashburner, and
Postlethwaite,[35] all busily distributing the industrial products of

Lancashire and Cumberland and north Wales slate, returning with china clay from the south-west for the potteries, besides the vast fleets of deep-sea sailing ships and barques of the seventies building boom – all these needed seamen, and Amlwch provided its share. Disraeli's 'Leap in the Dark', the extension of the franchise in 1867 had meant that instead of the 89 persons entitled to vote in Amlwch borough in 1860, there were 235 voters in 1870. Among them, in addition to those described as 'sail maker', 'rigger', 'chandler', there were 35 master mariners, and the lists often include the names of their ships to help identification in a port where they were so many Captains Hughes, Owen, Jones, Thomas, Lewis, Griffiths and Williams. In one street alone, in Chapel Street (where William Morris, the sail maker, lived), there were at least 16 master mariners entitled to vote as householders.[36] Some of them commanded ships owned by Captain William Thomas, now described as living in Ponctaldrwst, and the owner of a warehouse and yards at Amlwch Port. In July 1870, he had obtained permission from the trustees of Amlwch Harbour 'to lay and build a vessel at the upper end of the harbour to the extent of 100 feet for her keel'; he was allowed to occupy the area for eighteen months, 'to take every risk upon himself and not place any encumbrance or cause any obstruction to the harbour'.[37] In May 1871, Captain Thomas's application 'to place a strong gate near the mouth of the cave at the upper end of the harbour for the construction of a graving dock' was refused.[38] This application possibly refers to the dock which is still clearly identifiable at the eastern side of the harbour entrance, some little distance from the harbourmaster's house and the Treweek yard, for it is located at a spot which was once knows as 'Ogof Cwch y Brenin' (the cave of the king's boat), possibly the revenue cutters of the 18th century. Robert Algeo, who made a map of the harbour area in the late 1860s, shows a slipway on the site of the dry dock, and the area between it and the 1816 pier with its comparatively new lighthouse, boathouse and flagstaff is marked 'Pwll Cwch y Brenin'. On Algeo's map there are buildings covering a considerable area to the north-east, and projecting out parallel with the entrance is a short breakwater.[39] The 1888 edition of the Ordnance Survey 25in. map shows the present dry dock, the slipway relaid further to the north-west and the small projecting breakwater removed; it also shows the addition of the sail loft east of the main entrance to the shipyard. Another addition is a second larger slipway in a more exposed situation directly due north at the extreme north end of the yard; this presumably was constructed as the yard grew busier and larger vessels were being built.[40]

The refusal of Captain Thomas's request in 1871 may have been influenced by the fact that across the harbour William Cox Paynter had just completed the *Charles* for Captain Dyer, the Parys mine agent; the chairman of the Harbour Trustees who turned down Thomas's application was John Wynne Paynter, a prominent Amlwch merchant, and Dyer was a fellow trustee.[41] Despite the rivalry of the Paynter faction, Captain William Thomas appears to have forged ahead, and a little over a year after the refusal of his application he had a notice printed in May 1872 to inform 'his friends and the public generally, that he has lately purchased Mr Nicholas Treweek's extensive and commodious ship building yard and Dry Dock and that he is now in a position to execute any work entrusted to his care with the greatest promptitude and upon the most reasonable terms'.[42] By 1872 Captain Thomas had thriving ship chandlery business, a large store house for all kinds of building materials brought into Amlwch by his own coastal smacks, and he had a busy shipyard where the noise of the caulkers' mallets, the saws and the adzes, the smell of the stack of timber and the general air of brisk industry was to continue for over thirty years.

It is evident from this 1872 notice that Captain Thomas had already established his connection with Cumberland for he stated that he owned a large 'grid iron yard at Duddon'. An extensive shipbuilding programme for Cumberland shipowners now commenced in Amlwch and later at Millom. The first of these vessels was probably the one for William Postlethwaite for which the agreement survives in the County Record Office at Llangefni. In this document Captain Thomas agreed to build a new schooner of about 180 tons 'to be built to Class A1 for twelve years at Lloyd's' and to be completed ready for sea in six months from the date of the agreement in 1871. Postlethwaite, for his part, agreed to pay £12.10.0 per ton, paying by instalments, £200 when the keel, stern, stern-post and floors were laid down, a payment of £200 when the vessel in frame was complete, a further £400 when beamed and planked, and the remainder according to the builder's measurements when the vessel was ready for sea.[43] William Postlethwaite, of Holborn Hill, Cumberland, was rapidly expanding his fleet, and Thomas was only one of the builders whose fortunes were closely linked with him; Charnley built five schooners for Postlethwaite at Ulverston in the late sixties and seventies, and others were built at Chester and Conway.[44]

In 1872 Captain Thomas built, at Amlwch, the *Holy Wath* for William Morgan, described as 'of Hodbarrow in Co. Cumberland, Harbourmaster', an Amlwch man; in the following year Thomas built the *Nellie Bywater*, another two-masted topsail schooner, of almost identical dimensions, at Millom, for the Hadbarrow Mining Company. In 1874 Captain Thomas completed the *Cumberland Lassie* at Amlwch for William Postlethwaite; a three-masted schooner, she was later to become one of the best-known Kent colliers, carrying coal to Dover for many years.[45] The *Cumberland Lassie* was the largest schooner yet built at Amlwch, and she was followed two years later from his Amlwch yard by the slightly larger *Baron Hill*, again for the Postlethwaite fleet.[46] Captain Thomas and William Postlethwaite were listed as joint owners of the *Countess of Lonsdale*, another schooner built at Duddon by Captain Thomas in 1878, and the accounts of Thomas's Millom yard in 1880 indicate that he held a two-thirds share in the Millom business, whilst William Postlethwaite had a one-third share.[47]

One of the documents which have survived from the Amlwch yard of Captain Thomas is a little black notebook in which a conscientious clerk kept a list of prices of stores, nails, rivets, shackles, sheaves, blocks, oakum, warps, spunyarn, twine, oil and paints, different types of canvas and timber ranging from English, French, American and Italian oak to American red pine, pitch pine, teak and yellow pine.[48] At the back of this notebook there are some notes regarding the insurance values of Captain Thomas's vessels, insurance on their freight and protection in case of collision. The vessels mentioned include those that are recorded in the Lloyd's Registers of the late 70s and 80s as belonging to or being managed by Captain William Thomas of Amlwch, although it is clear from his own papers that William Thomas of Liverpool also had a financial interest in several of them. Space will not permit a detailed examination of the history of these vessels, but from the notebook it is possible to gain an impression where Captain Thomas's ships were, say, in the autumn of 1875.[49] The elderly *Albion*, Captain John Lewis, was already to sail from Rouen to Dublin, another schooner, the *Caroline*, Captain Hugh Owens, had arrived at Liverpool, the brigantine *Coila*, Captain W. R. Owen, had put into Falmouth from Boulogne bound for Ayr, the 43-ton flat *Dalton*, Captain John Thomas, had arrived from Liverpool at Cemlyn (where she was later wrecked). The *Edith Morgan*, Captain William Jones, had arrived at Santander, the *Euphemia*, Captain Isaac Jones, was at Amlwch repairing, whilst the *Jane Pringle*, Captain John Hughes, had just arrived at Amlwch from Cardiff with coal. The small sloop *John and Eliza* was at Ramsay bound for Duddon, whilst the barque *Linda*, Captain G. Morgan, had sailed from Monte Video for Queenstown. The elderly schooner, *Lord Mostyn*, Captain John Williams, had returned to Amlwch empty from Point of Ayr sands, the *Mary Ann*, Captain John Edwards, was at Runcorn, and the *Mary Elizabeth*, Captain John Thomas, had arrived at Amlwch with a cargo of timber and was due to enter dry dock for repairs. Captain William Owen, in the *Mountain Maid*, was loading oats at Red Wharf, Captain Robert Williams, in the *Thomas*, built 60 years previously at Ulverston, was at Dublin, whilst the *Toronto*, Captain Roberts, was newly-arrived at Huanillos from Callao, waiting her turn to load. The position of the *Velocipede* is not recorded, except for a brief note to say that she was eventually broken up at Bordd y Ffeiriad, but the lucky ship, *William Mellhuish*, Captain David Jones, was sailing home for London from Pondicherry. Another of Captain Thomas's larger vessels, the barque *Yuca*, Captain John James, was on passage from Cardiff to Iquique whence she sailed in ballast for Callao, and the schooner *Eleanor and Grace*, Captain John Owen, was loading in Cardiff for Troon.

From the correspondence between Captain Thomas and William Thomas, Liverpool, in the eighties, it is apparent that the Amlwch shipbuilder further extended his shipping fleet by buying and managing the *Barbara*, an iron barque built by Doxfords in 1877 at Sunderland during the feverish building boom of the late seventies. She was commanded by Captain Richard Hugh Roberts of Amlwch, who had previously been master of the *Toronto*. When Captain Roberts later had a dispute with the Liverpool ship broker, the latter made a note in his own hand that Roberts's money was ill invested 'in the ships *Toronto* and *Barbara* – the vessels he was master of under Captain William Thomas of Amlwch, who had kindly lent him money and became security for him to the Bank which with his wages enabled him to buy the shares'.[50] Captain Roberts had sailed the *Toronto* from Huanillos to Dunkirk with a cargo of guano in 1876, and in 1877 she sailed for Singapore and Bassein. The *Barbara* sailed in the oceanic trades from 1877 to 1882 when she was lost; in October 1880 William Thomas, Liverpool, wrote to Captain Thomas at Amlwch to inform him that he had heard from 'Captain Lloyd Dora Ann from West coast that Captain of Toronto died of small pox. The Mate of Dora Ann is appointed Master . . . It is a bad job I am afraid. Captain Lloyd says he will look after her the same as if it was his own'.[51] The *Dora Ann* was an iron barque owned by Richard James of Aberystwyth, and Captain Lloyd was a keen competitor, but when troubles came on the far West Coast of America, the Welsh drew close.

Over the years there were troubles enough. The *Anglesea Lass*, bought by Captain Thomas in 1871, was not a lucky ship; she lost a young apprentice from Sunderland at Rosario in the type of accident so common in ports all over the world. He had gone ashore to get an iron plate from the blacksmith's shop, slipped from a barque alongside the quay, and, despite the efforts of a ship's carpenter 'who dived three times but could not find him' and the steward of the *Anglesea Lass*, who had gone to meet him in the ship's boat, the apprentice disappeared, 'the current running very strong at the time'.[52] On her next voyage to South America the *Anglesea Lass* was wrecked, and three of her crew drowned.[53] In 1874 the *Lewis and Mary*, built by Captain Thomas at Amlwch three years previously, sailed from Antwerp for Greenock and was not heard of again; aboard her were Edward Pritchard, the master, who had a quarter share in her, Richard Rowland, the mate, Edward Pritchard, A.B., aged nineteen (possibly the master's son), all from Amlwch, and Hugh Jones of Manchester, who had joined the *Lewis and Mary* at Amlwch for his first, and last, voyage.[54] Others were lost nearer home: Thomas Jenkins, master of the *Elizabeth Martha*, was washed overboard, and his vessel subsequently wrecked 'near Duddon' in 1871.[55] The sea was not the only hazard. Captain William Lewis, a well-known Amlwch master mariner, was captured by natives in 1870 as he sailed his Ardrossan-built schooner, the *Loango*, up the Congo; he and the cabin boy were eventually rescued by H.M.S. *Growler*, but not before three townships had been set on fire and a native chief's son captured. The north Wales press reported in mild Victorian fashion 'much interest is taken in the occurrence at Amlwch and sympathy is extended to Mrs Lewis in her anxious trouble'.[56]

The late seventies and early eighties saw Captain Thomas busily engaged managing a few deep-sea ships, a considerable number of coastal vessels and maintaining a steady building programme of two vessels a year at Amlwch as well as the Duddon-built ships. Whilst some speculators and builders who had over-reached themselves in the boom of the seventies went to the wall – the Holyhead Shipbuilding and Trading Company went into voluntary liquidation in 1879, and their last vessel, the Norwegian barquentine *Try*, was sold to John Ellis, a Bangor sailmaker – Captain Thomas made steady progress. Among his papers are the specifications for the Queensland government agent in April 1875 for a new schooner of about 110 tons 'to draw about 10 feet of water, the length of keel to be 76 feet, main breadth 19 feet, depth 10 feet. To be classed 12 years at Lloyds. The whole of the frame to be of English oak, planking pitch pine. Copper and galvanized fastened, the buyer to pay Lloyd's expenses if required'.[57] In the same year as he built the *Baron Hill* for Postlethwaite, he also built at Amlwch the *Lady Neave*, which was to serve in the coasting trade until she was sunk in collision in July 1911 about 30 miles to the north of South Stack lighthouse.[58] The *Nantglyn* and the *Nesta*, both wooden schooners of almost identical dimensions, came from the Thomas's Amlwch slipways in 1877; the *Nantglyn*, built for Amlwch owners, was lost with all hands in October 1881, but the *Nesta*, built originally for S. R. Platt, the Oldham engineer whose family developed Llanfairfechan, had a longer life and was eventually sold to William Pritchard to join the well-known Portmadoc fleet in 1891. The owners of the next vessel to be built, the *Eilian Hill*, indicate the way in which the Thomas shipbuilding programme was linked with Amlwch's own industrial interests and with Merseyside, for they included Charles Hill, the manufacturing chemist, whose works at Amlwch were managed by

Lewis Hughes, Captain Thomas's son-in-law, W. S. Bennett of Great Crosby, and Griffith Jones of Bootle, both coal merchants. The *Eilian Hill* was destined to have a comparatively brief career, for in December 1882 she foundered off Penzance after being in collision with S.S. *Equist* of London. According to the account book of the *Glyndwr*, a smack built by Thomas in 1879 and lengthened in 1882, she plied locally with a variety of cargoes between Amlwch, Connah's Quay, Carlingford, Duddon, Liverpool, Dublin, and put in to a wide range of small havens on the Anglesey and Caernarvonshire coasts, Porth Golmon in Lleyn, Cemlyn, Moelfre, Dulas and Red Wharf in Anglesey. On the inside cover of her account book is a note 'Glyndwr went ashore half mile west of Point Lynas, May 9th, 1883.' And on the opposite page an even sadder man has written '*Glyndwr* ashore at Hilbre Island near Hoylake, 9th January 1886, likely to become a total wreck'. The *Glyndwr* was eventually sold to James Reney, a member of the Connah's Quay family of shipowners who were responsible for the survival of many sailing vessels at that port into the present century.[59] Another Thomas vessel to go to Flintshire was the *Pearl*, a two-masted schooner built in 1880 for Thomas Fanning Evans, a prominent Amlwch businessman, but sold ten years later to John Vickers of Connah's Quay. In keeping with his interest in American affairs, Captain Thomas named the next vessel *President Garfield* after the popular American President; she was rigged originally as a schooner, altered to ketch rig, and was eventually sold to Cornish owners in 1897.

It was in the 1880s that the firm base that had been provided by Captain Thomas was expanded and developed by his eldest son, William Thomas, who had formal training as a naval designer. The younger Thomas and his brother Lewis, a master mariner, took an increasingly important role, and it is likely that it was due to the younger William Thomas that they started to build small iron screw steamers at Amlwch. Although steamers had attracted investors and had been a common enough sight for half a century, it is evident that there was no great enthusiasm among Amlwch people to put their money into steam. The letters which Captain Thomas wrote to William Thomas, Liverpool, on behalf of Captain Richard Hugh Roberts, who had been compelled to leave the sea on grounds of ill-health, are discussed in a later chapter;[60] here it is sufficient to note that Captain Roberts, now employed by the Liverpool ship-broker to overlook the building of one of his ships at Sunderland, came home to Amlwch in 1879 and 1880 and called on many of the inhabitants to try to persuade them to join with him in investing in one of the steamers that the Liverpool firm intended to have built. In December 1879 Captain Roberts, writing from his home in Salem Terrace, Amlwch, had to admit his frustration to William Thomas, Liverpool: 'I find that people here seem to have less confidence in a steamer than a sailing ship – Just like them in a small place like this.'[61] Roberts's deprecatory comments were not likely to have made a favourable impression on the shrewd Liverpool ship broker, whose own roots were deep in rural Anglesey, and the unfortunate Roberts made a further mistake in trying to cause dissension between his former and present employers. Having given what is to the historian a fascinating account of the potential investors upon whom he called, the Paynters, Hughes Mynachdy, the Amlwch tobacco firms, and a solicitor – 'some say he is rich, others that he is not' – Roberts concluded his letter: 'Captain Thomas will take no shares. I did not think he would, but I called on him as a matter of course. I have an idea he is trying to Counter Move – Dont wonder – he will not beat us if he succeeds just now checking me. This is only my surmise.'[62] Captain Thomas was too shrewd a realist to consider the small steamers which his son William was now designing, a counter move to the 2,000-ton ship S.S. *Empire*, his Liverpool friend was having built by R. and J. Evans, Liverpool, and, in fact, when his own small steamers were built it was William Thomas, Liverpool, who advertised and later bought most of the shares in them.[63] Nevertheless, Captain Thomas thought it necessary to write to the Liverpool ship broker to inform him that Captain Roberts was going around Amlwch in 1880 stating 'that he was to be paid a percentage on the steamer according to the capital introduced by him'.[64] It was as well to keep the record straight.

It was at Duddon, not Amlwch, that Captain Thomas's first ventures into steam were built. The *Lady Kate* and the *Lady Louisa*, both small wooden screw steamers, were built in 1881 and 1882. The names of the first investors in the *Lady Kate* underline the Amlwch-Millom connection; Captain Thomas, together with his business associates, William Postethwaite, Millom, and William Thomas,

Liverpool, had the major holding, along with William Owen, Rhos-beirio, Rhosybol, David Hughes, of Wylfa, Cemais, the Liverpool Welsh builder, Edward Morgan Jones, the Amlwch tobacconist, and Richard Evans, a Millom chemist, whilst John Mathews, an Amlwch bank manager, three Millom men described as 'miners', John Jones, 'labourer', of Millom, Hugh and Micah Jones of Millom, 'carpenters', each had a £35 share. The *Lady Kate* was later managed by a Caernarvon firm, G. H. Fearn, and the *Lady Louisa* by Postlethwaite. In 1883 the first iron screw steamer to be built at Amlwch, the *W. S. Caine*, 180 tons, built for the contract price of £5,000, was launched. The engines for both the *Lady Kate* and the *W. S. Caine* were made by the Caernarvon engineering company, De Winton, better-known for their steam locomotives and machinery for the north Wales slate quarries. No doubt inspired by Jeffries de Winton, who had been apprenticed as a draughtsman to the Liverpool company of Fawcett and Preston, the Caernarvon firm started to build marine engines and boilers in the seventies. William Thomas had the hull of the *W. S. Caine* towed to Caernarvon where the engines and boilers were fitted. The contract price for the machinery was to be paid in five instalments: 'the sum of £332 when cylinders are cast and iron for boilers on ground, £332 when all heavy castings are made and boilers ready for rivetting, £332 when the machinery is ready for putting on board, and boiler tested, £332 when complete and after a satisfactory trial trip.' Other clauses in the agreement provided for arbitration in the case of disputes between Thomas and De Winton and an extension of time 'in case of a strike or lockout of workmen in the works of the said Engineers'. The trial trip was something of a social occasion. A number of Anglesey dignitaries were aboard when the *W. S. Caine* sailed from Caernarvon for Holyead, cruising for about two hours. From Holyhead at '3.0 p.m. a course for Amlwch was steered and the distance of twenty miles was covered in one hour and twenty minutes . . . the distance of 24 miles to Llandudno was run in 1 hr. and 44 minutes'.[65]

A year after launching the *W. S. Caine*, the Amlwch yard completed another new iron screw steamer, the *Exchange*, larger than the *W. S. Caine*; she was bought by William Thomas, Liverpool. Early in 1885 a small iron screw vessel, ketch rigged, was built and named the *Anglesey*; all of these small steamers had engines by De

Winton, Caernarvon. That same year, 1885, the younger William Thomas launched the vessel which may be regarded as the pioneer of his own iron sailing schooners, the *Elizabeth Peers*, built for William Postlethwaite and her first master, John Peers.[66] In Appendix IX (iii) the summary accounts of the steamer *Anglesey* and the schooner *Elizabeth Peers* have been reproduced from Captain Thomas's papers in order to indicate the comparative costs of building sailing vessels and small steamers in the closing decades of the century.

Mr Mathew Pritchard, one of the longest-serving employees of the Thomas yard, has a vivid recollection of the next launching, that of the *Gelert*, another iron schooner, with the appropriate figurehead of a dog to represent the legend.[67] Mr Pritchard was a very small boy clutching his mother's hand when he went down to the yard full of milling crowds to see the launching of the *Gelert* from the northernmost slip in 1887. When he was old enough he went to work in the yard and then went to sea in Amlwch and Barrow schooners such as the *Holy Wath* and the *Donald and Doris*, and later in large Cunard ships. He left the sea when he was 65, having been mate of the last of the Thomas ships, the *Eilian, Eilianus, Eleth, Dunleith* and the *Ardri*, and then continued to work in the yard until he was over seventy, when it was virtually deserted. Now approaching his nineties, the next vessel he remembers being built after the *Gelert* was the first *Eilian*, a wooden schooner launched in 1889. The masters of many of the vessels built in the Amlwch yard bought shares in their new ships: Captain Robert Griffiths, junior, of Chapel Street, Amlwch Port, bought 16/64 shares in the *Eilian* in October 1889 for £450, and Captain Thomas and his sons retained the remaining 48/64.[68] When the *Eilian* sank on 6th July 1899 after a collision with S.S. *Afrique* of Marseilles off St Catherine's Point, the rescued crew consisted of her master, Richard Griffith, aged 34, of 10 Chapel Street, Amlwch, Owen Jones of Caernarvon, the mate, Ebenezer Griffith, aged 19, Able Seaman, also of Amlwch, and Arthur Wood, the cook, a native of London, on his first trip to sea.[69]

The years 1890-1894 were particularly busy years for William Thomas, junior, and his brother Lewis, who served for some time as master of the *W. S. Caine* before becoming Lloyd's agent at Amlwch.[70] The policy of building steamers and sailing vessels side by side continued; in 1890-91 a steel screw three-masted steamer, the

Prince Ja-Ja, which was to become very well-known in the Menai Strait for many years,[71] and the iron steamer *Cygnus* were built, both with engines by De Winton, and the tiny *Enterprise*, first built on the Tyne in 1877, was altered, to enter a new phase as the familiar 'stemar fach' plying locally with miscellaneous goods.[72] Alongside them the iron barquentine *Detlef Wagner* was being built; she left Amlwch in 1891 to become a well-known vessel in European waters until she was sunk by a submarine in 1917. It was the custom among Welsh shipbuilders and owners to name vessels after merchants and agents with whom they had good business connections; Hans Detlef Jacob Wagner was a ship-owner and ship-broker at Hamburg, and was well-known to the Thomas family and the masters of their vessels.[73]

The actual building of the merchant schooners has been carefully described with a wealth of evocative detail by Basil Greenhill and Michael Bouquet; the techniques employed and life in an Appledore yard had much in common with those at Amlwch and Millom. The wages book at the Thomas yard when the *Detlef Wagner* was being built indicates that between sixty and seventy men were employed there. Compared with the wages paid elsewhere in Anglesey at the time, the workers in the Thomas yard considered themselves reasonably paid. The Royal Commission on Labour 1891-4 reported that the average rate of pay for agricultural labourers providing their own food was 14/10d a week in the eight Welsh districts surveyed; Lleufer Thomas, in his report, pointed out that a large number of farm labourers were paid partly by food, and the 'character and value of the food must vary considerably . . . Indoor servants' wages are said to be from £18 to £36 a year, in addition to board and lodging, the highest rate being in the district of Anglesey'. The Thomas wages book records the time spent by the workmen on each of the three ships being built in May 1889, for example, and also the wages paid in the various departments of the shipyard. Edward Jones was the highest paid worker at the sawmill, 4/2 a day, whilst of the six men working at the smithy, David Hughes was the highest paid at 3/6, and in the sailroom, where there were three men and a boy, William Owen was the senior man at 3/3. Hugh Thomas at the Block Shop was also paid 3/3, Thomas Roberts, 'the Engine', 3/-, and the three men in the Dry Dock at a rate of 2/9 a day. John Williams, a boy in the sail loft was paid 8d a day, whilst the highest paid worker in the yard was Elias Williams, receiving 6/- a day, at the head of the list in the employees wage sheet each week.[74] Elias Williams may have been the same man as the Elias Williams, Shipwright, native of Bangor, aged 29 at the time of the 1851 census, living at 17 Quay Street, Amlwch. If he was, then at the age of 70 he was still the highest paid worker, earning 7/- a day when the *Maggie Williams* was being built for William Postlethwaite in 1892. An iron three-masted schooner, the *Maggie Williams* was in the pattern of the fine vessels that the younger William Thomas was designing; she was of similar dimensions to the *Gelert*, built five years previously, and almost identical with the *Cymric* and *Celtic*, and the slightly larger *Gaelic* which followed her in 1893, 1894 ad 1898. It is generally recognised that these were all excellent vessels; in his definitive and authoritative history of the merchant schooners, Basil Greenhill, Director of the National Museum, has paid this tribute to the achievement of the younger William Thomas: 'though most of the few iron and steel schooners built seem to have been of very high standard of design and construction, William Thomas's vessels were considered in their time to be among the finest.'[75] Reuben Chappell's painting (Plate 16) suggests the impression made by the *Cymric* with her graceful curved stem, round counter stern and tall topmasts; with her white hull, she and her sister vessels had a yacht-like appearance. Appendix IX (ii) is a specification dated 3 May 1892 for an iron three-masted schooner 'to be built on the same model as the schooner *Maggie Williams*'; it may be taken as representative of the way in which the specifications for the *Cymric* and the vessels that followed the *Maggie Williams* were prepared in the William Thomas office overlooking Amlwch Port.

Captain William Thomas died in 1893, the year the *Cymric* was launched. He was then aged 71, and although he had suffered some ill-health in his later years, he had been going down to his beloved shipyard until a few days before his death. The *North Wales Chronicle* reminded its readers that Captain Thomas's contribution to the economy of the area had been all important: 'his extensive works have been the staple support of the place, even in the most depressed times.'[76] A successful sea-captain with an eye to business, he was known in Amlwch for his unobtrusive kindness to those in need; the

Tory *North Wales Chronicle* claimed: 'that he was a true Conservative, a member of the Calvinistic Methodists, but one who never supported or approved of an attack on the Church. His religious and political views were tolerant and expansive . . . his loss will be severely felt in the commercial world where he has held a stand for so long.' Among the chief mourners were his old friend and business ally, William Thomas, the ship-owner, now mayor of Bootle.[77] The letters which passed between them were all on a formal basis, but a footnote in one of the few that have survived sums up what had proved to be a very effective association. It was the time of the expansion of both their businesses in 1879, when William Thomas of Liverpool was having the '*County*' class built, and Captain Thomas added the footnote 'Dont forget sails for *County of Caernarvon*, that's a good boy'.[78] Captain Thomas was then aged fifty-seven, his Liverpool friend forty-two.

It must be remembered that in addition to their building programme, Captain Thomas's sons had the management of the vessels which remained from the fleet which he had owned or managed in the seventies and eighties. Apart from those which had been sold, several had been lost; the *Edith Morgan*, wrecked at Port Askaig in the Sound of Islay, *Linda* 'found waterlogged, bottom up and a derelict 50 miles off Queenstown, 6 Dec. 1880', *Barbara*, lost in 1881 off Milford Haven, *Welsh Girl*, wrecked at Cemlyn in 1882, and the comparatively new *Gelert*, wrecked on Catalinita Island in April 1890. A glance through the crew agreement lists for 1893 gives some indication of the activities of the vessels at the time of Captain Thomas's death. The *County of Cork*, for example, now forty years old, was plying between Lancaster, Bangor and Ireland, the *Mary Catherine*, with a crew of three Amlwch men, and a boy from Caernarvon on his first voyage as cook, sailed from Port Dinorwic for Weymouth, then to Fishguard, Newport, Pwllheli, Runcorn, Plymouth, Dublin, London, Ramsay, and then back to Port Dinorwic at the end of the year. They had tried three different cooks during the year, all on their first 'veoige' (*sic*), the other two being from Pwllheli and Amlwch. The *Pride of Anglesea*, the *Lady Neave*, the *Jane Pringle* and the *President Garfield*, all of them with predominantly Amlwch crews, were fully employed in the coastal trade; the most unusual crew was that of the elderly *Albion*. Her master was James Condren, aged 40, her mate was Robert Condren, aged 23, the Ordinary Seaman was Owen Condren, aged 20, and the cook was 18-year-old George Condren. They had all joined her at Wicklow and were possibly a father and three sons; they were all eventually discharged at Garston after the *Albion* had made three trips from Liverpool to Irish ports.[79]

The Thomas vessels were not the only ones to provide employment for Amlwch men, for across the harbour at the Paynter yard, 'iard'r ochr draw', a schooner that was to become very well known, the *Camborne*, was launched in 1885, to be followed by the *Ailsie*, and the *Donald and Doris*, built in 1897 for the Hodbarrow Mining Company and named after the children of Mr Barratt, the manager of the Cumberland company.[80] Reference is made in another chapter to their activities; in 1894 William Thomas was managing the *Hodbarrow Miner*, and at Duddon the *Happy Harry* was built. Hugh Jones, an Amlwch man who had gone to Millom to work in the Thomas yard, later took it over and in 1904 built for the Duddon Shipbuilding Company a three-masted barquentine which became a familiar sight in Amlwch harbour, the *Becca and Mary*.[81] She sailed from Duddon as a new vessel in October 1904 with a master and mate from Amlwch, for Ellesmere Port, Lymington, Portland, the Manchester Ship Canal, and Truro in her first few months. Her first master, Captain John Hughes, of Machine Street, Amlwch, was succeeded in 1907 by Captain Henry Thomas, also of Amlwch, who remained in command until 1913 when she was sold to Portuguese owners. Throughout this period when she put into small ports like Ayr, Buckie, Newlyn, Devoran, as well as the Thames and Mersey, with occasional visits to Hamburg, Antwerp, Dunkirk and Brest, she had a preponderance of Amlwch men in the crew and a fair number of foreign seamen, from Russia, Finland and the Scandinavian countries. Some of these schooner, such as the *Nellie Bywater*, over seventy years old, were still at sea in 1949 and are well remembered by Amlwch people today.[82]

The *Lady Neave* was a typical example of the hard-working schooner, built by Captain Thomas close on a hundred years ago; commanded for many years by Captain Isaac Jones of Amlwch, she was very much part of the life of Amlwch where the descendants of those who served in her are still called 'teulu Lady Neave'. Her accounts for 1888-1890 may be taken as an example of the work of one of the Thomas vessels engaged largely in the coastal trade;[83] during this time she earned £311.19.0 for William Thomas and Sons, her managing owners, who held 34/64 shares in her, and £73.8.0 for Captain Isaac Jones who owned 8/64, in accordance with the agreement that the master should remit to the owner half of all freight earned after deducting expenses.

Sturdy and hard-working though the earlier vessels were, the elite of all the schooners built at Amlwch were those designed by the younger William Thomas in the 1890s. It is not surprising that these fine vessels attracted outstanding Amlwch master mariners to take command of them. Captain Robert Jones, master of the *Cymric*, was the son of the other Captain Robert Jones who had had long association with Captain William Thomas; both father and son had

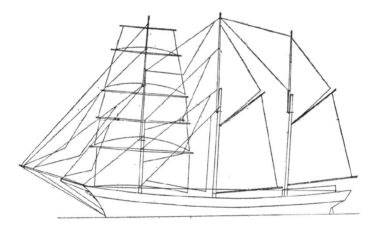

Reproduction of Blue-print of one of the younger William Thomas's Barquentine Schooners, c.1890.

commanded the Prince Edward Island brigantine *Amanda*, in which Captain Thomas and his namesake, the Liverpool ship-broker, had had shares. Captain Robert Jones, senior, had in his later years managed a number of vessels on his own account, and in 1884 had bought the three-masted *Lord Tredegar*, built by Westacott at Barnstaple in 1875. Among his papers are two cheques which had been paid, the one for £170, marked 'Deposit on *Lord Tredegar*', and

1888	Freight	From	To	½ owner's share	
13 July	160 tons Coal @ 4/6	Newcastle	Teignmouth	36. 0. 0	7.16. 1
15 Aug.	159 tons Clay @ 4/-	Teignmouth	Runcorn	31.16. 6	8. 7. 8
5 Sept.	155 $^{15}/_{20}$ tons Coal @ 10/-	Runcorn	Gibraltar	77.17. 6	23. 0. 1
19 Nov.	680 Qrs. Beans @ 4/6 Qr.	Rabat	Bristol	153. 0. 0	57. 5. 5
15 Dec.	155 tons Coal @ 7/-	Newport	Clonakilly	54. 5. 0	18.11. 4
					£115. 0. 7
1889					
2 Jan.	158 tons Coal @ 6/-	Newport	Charlestown	47. 8. 0	17. 3. 5
26 Feb.	157 tons Clay @ 5/3	Charlestown	Ellesmere	41. 6. 4	16.11. 6
27 March	158 tons Coal @ 9/-	Garston	Tralee	71. 2. 0	28.14. 9
26 April	Hay, lump sum	Tralee	Cardiff	18. 0. 0	3. 4. 2
14 May	161 tons Coal @ 4/6	Cardiff	Charlestown	36. 4. 6	12. 5.11
1 June	160 tons Clay @ 4/9	Charlestown	Runcorn	38. 0. 0	15. 4.11
19 June	164½ tons Coal @ 7/6	Runcorn	Fraserborough	61.12. 6	22.13. 6
11 July	153 tons Coal @ 5/6	Newcastle	Plymouth	41. 1. 6	12. 9.10
					£128. 8. 0
1889					
10 Aug.	163 tons Clay @ 4/9	Plymouth	Runcorn	38.16. 5	15.11.10
16 Sept.	159 tons Salt @ 7/-	Runcorn	Fisherrow	55.13. 0	23. 1. 4
2 Oct.	166½ tons Coal @ 5/-	Morrishaven	London	41.12. 6	16.15. 9½
24 Oct.	160 tons Cement @ 5/-	London	Plymouth	40. 0. 0	14.18. 1½
14 Nov.	160 tons Birches @ 4/-	Plymouth	London	32. 0. 0	9.13. 8
11 Dec.	160 tons Cement @ 6/9	London	Liverpool	54. 0. 0	21.11. 2
					£101.11.11

1890					
22 Feb.	155 tons Slates @ 9/-	Conway	London	69.15. 0	25.19. 5
11 Mar.	158 tons Cement @ 7/-	London	Bristol	55. 6. 0	20. 9. 8
27 Mar.	160 tons Burnt Oil @ 9/-	Bristol	Newcastle	72. 0. 0	23.19. 0
14 Apl.	157 tons Bricks @ 5/6	Newcastle	London	43. 3. 6	15.13. 5½
22 May	120 tons @ 8/-, 40 tons @ 7/-, Manure and Bricks	London	Conway and Saltney	62. 0. 0	22.11. 8½
21 June	165 tons Bricks & Tiles @ 5/6	Connah's Quay	Newry	45. 7. 6	12.10. 6
					£121. 3. 9
1890					
8 July	160 tons Stones @ 6/6	Newry	Limerick	52. 0. 0	18.18. 9
5 Aug.	160 tons Coal @ 4/-	Newport	Par	32. 8. 0	9. 3. 6
4 Sept.	158 tons China clay @ 5/6	Par	Ellesmere	43. 9. 0	18. 9. 9
27 Sept.	160 tons Oil cake @ 6/-	Liverpool	Bristol	48. 0. 0	16. 2. 9
24 Oct.	160 tons Coal @ 5/6	Newport	Mevagissey	44. 0. 0	15.16. 8
22 Nov.	156 tons Clay @ 7/-	Pentewan	Dieppe	54.12. 0	13. 6.10
24 Dec.	156 tons Flints @ 6/6	Dieppe	Runcorn	50.14. 0	19.10. 0
1891					
17 Jan.	160 tons Crushed bones @ 3/9	Liverpool	Amlwch	30. 0. 0	9.11. 6
					£120.19. 9

the other for £1,620, obviously the balance of the purchase money for the *Lord Tredegar*; both cheques were made payable to Alfred L. Jones of Liverpool. This connection with that 'most flamboyant and, in some respects, the most successful'[84] of all Liverpool nineteenth-century shipping men, the Carmarthen-born Alfred Lewis Jones who created the wealth of Elder Dempster and established a monopoly in the Liverpool-West Africa trade, is an intriguing aspect of the part played by Liverpool Welshmen in the development of the much smaller scale of Anglesey shipping. With Captain Robert Jones, Junior, as master, the *Lord Tredegar* sailed from Liverpool for Natal, thence to Pernambuco, Montevideo, Trinidad, returning to Greenock in the spring of 1885. In July she sailed again for Demerara and Jamaica, returning to Le Havre with a cargo of log wood in February 1886. Captain Jones, senior, indicated in his letters to the other shareholders the worries he had over the *Lord Tredegar*; in June 1886 he wrote that he was 'sorry that owing to the depression in shipping I have such a poor account to show'; he noted that she was 'expected shortly to arrive at Havre from the West Indies with a cargo of about 300 tons of Rum, the freight being only 23/9d per ton, this being so I am afraid she will hardly clear herself this voyage.'[85] The unfavourable situation continued, and so the inevitable economies had to be made; the insurance on freight and on the ship was drastically reduced and every item of expenditure was carefully considered.[86] On her fifth voyage, now commanded by a Captain Thomas, after taking a cargo of coal from Cardiff to Pernambuco, the *Lord Tredegar* was wrecked; her hull was sold, and although her owners received £1,400 in insurance payments, when all the accounts were paid they had less than half that amount to share out on an investment which had originally cost them a great deal more.

In 1890, the younger Captain Robert Jones was appointed to command the *Greyhound*, built by Thomas at Millom in 1886, and he was thus a highly experienced master mariner, aged 38, when he took command of the new and very handsome iron schooner, *Cymric*, in 1893. His mate was a man in whom he had implicit trust, for his brother, fourteen years younger than him, Richard Owen Jones, had served with him in the *Lord Tredegar* and possibly the *Greyhound*. The other members of the crew of the new vessel were

Griffith Jones of Caernarvon, aged 20, described as a second mate, Robert Jones, A.B., as cook, a native of Bangor, Owen Hughes, ordinary seaman, a nineteen-year-old Amlwch boy who had already seen service aboard the *Lady Neave*, Thomas Hughes, A.B., who came from Holyhead, and John Robert Jones, ordinary seaman, aged seventeen, also from Amlwch. This was the crew who took the *Cymric* to the Brazilian ports of Rio Grande do Sul and Porto Alegre and back to Runcorn, a round voyage of about a year.[87] An all-Amlwch crew, apart from Edward Ellis of Bangor, then took the *Cymric* from Runcorn to Cardiff.

The *Cymric*'s papers indicate a fairly regular pattern of employment in the Rio Grande trade;[88] a voyage of about a year, leaving Liverpool, for example, on 20 December 1895, arriving at the Rio Grande two months later in mid-February, remaining there about a month, then a Porto Alegre for another month, then back to Rio Grande by mid-June and arriving at Rio de Janeiro in mid July. Another month there and then she was on her way back to Europe, arriving at Hamburg on 24 November 1896. Here the crew of five, all from the Amlwch district, were paid off on 12 December, but the master and mate remained to sail her back to Bristol in January with a crew which consisted of a Russian, a Frenchman, two Norwegians, and a Finnish seaman.[89] She was then sailed from Bristol to Garston by a crew of two Welshmen, a Dane, a German and an Englishman; the three non-Welshman were paid off at Garston, and it was an all-Welsh crew who brought the *Cymric* to Amlwch in March 1897. On 1 June the *Cymric* was towed to Caernarvon (Captain Jones noted that he paid £8 for towage); here four men were paid £10.11.8 for loading 385 tons of slate, and the total charges for pilotage in and out of Caernarvon, harbour dues, brokers' and miscellaneous charges and the towage from Amlwch in all amounted to £32.9.11. On 23 June the *Cymric* sailed with a crew, including master and mate, of five Amlwch and two Caernarvon men;[90] they arrived at Harburg on 6 July. With the normal allowance for breakages it was in fact 406 tons of slate, 21 tons more than were officially noted at Caernarvon, which were unloaded at Harburg, and Captain Jones's faded little notebook records carefully all his payments to pilots, men unloading cargo, exchange rates, customs payments, and finally, the net profit, which was £121.16.1. Of this, half went to William Thomas and

Sons, the owners, and on 19 July Captain Jones sent them a cheque for £50 as part payment of the £60.18.0.

Among the many loose papers of jottings stuffed between the pages of Captain Robert Jones's notebooks is a note of a previous agreement between him and William Thomas in 1890 when he was master of the *Greyhound*. It illustrates clearly the relationship between the master and his owners: 'the said Robert Jones agrees to pay all *crew* wages, and *victualling*, also *half* of all port charges, whether in a foreign or British port and agrees to *remit half* of all *freight* earned, demurrage gratuities etc., after *deducting* port charges.'[91] Captain Jones had underlined what he considered to be the vital words in the agreement; he also agreed 'not to charge for discharging' cargo 'when it is done by the ship crew'. As a further safeguard, Captain Jones agreed to pay a deposit of £100 on taking command of the vessel as a guarantee that the agreement was kept in every detail, and undertook to give at least a month's notice before relinquishing command of the vessel, and 'to deliver the vessel in a safe port in England or Wales as instructed'. It would appear that the owners had a fairly tight control on their investment; equally, from the fact that captains like Robert Jones, Ishmael Williams, Robert Griffith and William Williams, experienced Amlwch captains who were masters of the *Cymric, Gaelic*, and *Meyric*, remained with them whilst they were owned by Thomas, the masters must have found this agreement satisfactory. Desertions were comparatively few in these ships and one gets the impression that, although the masters naturally kept expenses down to a minimum, and interpreted the 'sufficient without waste' clause regarding food carefully, the Amlwch crews were much happier in these schooners than in some of the large four-masted sailing ships which achieved notoriety in the closing decades of the century.[92]

From Harburg Captain Jones sailed with the same crew for Abo in Finland with a cargo of 'sulphate of alumina' and 810 barrels of Rosin, each barrel weighing on average 231 kilos; Captain Jones noted carefully how and where he stowed the cargo, the amounts paid at Abo with detailed calculation of Finnish and German exchange rates, payments to pilots, 'men attending ropes on shore', customs and all harbour dues. From Abo the *Cymric* was towed to Attu where a cargo of timber for Bridgewater was taken aboard, and

Captain Jones, who was always ready to learn and profit from his experiences, made detailed notes regarding the problems of stowing cargo. Mr Elias Jones, now aged ninety-six, who sailed with Captain Jones in the *Cymric* and the *John Lockett*, described recently the problems of a timber deck cargo when it was wet, accentuating the list of a sailing ship, and sure enough Captain Jones in his little notebook has recorded 'If loading light cargo again, especially carrying deck cargo, lift the boards and fill between the floors with gravel or stone or other ballast and trim the ship with the fore and after peak; the peaks could also be filled with ballast if the ship trim would allow'. Another note made by Captain Jones at this time underlines the financial implications for the master of every day; 'The crew were on board at Bridgewater at a cost per day of 15/- being £8.5.0, and half £4.4.0 paid to labourers (£2.2.0), Total £10.7.0 Only charged as above £8.17.4, half to owner £4.8.8. I thus pay £5.18.4 more than the owner which I could have saved by paying off when we first arrived as is customary.' William Thomas's share, as a result of this Baltic voyage, was £71.1.11.

The *Cymric* had arrived at Bridgewater from Finland on 19 October; by November she was at Cardiff ready for another voyage to the Rio Grande with a cargo of 355 tons of Welsh coal at 26/- per ton; she took forty-eight days on the voyage. Her crew for this voyage was a new one; the mate was now Rowland Francis, a Machynlleth man who had seen service aboard the *Beeswing*, a training ground for many Welsh seamen. The bosun was from Nefyn, the cook was a Dane, and the two young seamen came from Riga and Newport. On her return voyage, the *Cymric* was chartered to take a cargo of hides and horns from Pelotas, a little to the north of Rio Grande, to Uleaborg, Finland, deep in the Gulf of Bothnia. She put in to Falmouth en route and an entry in her crew list suggests that the second stage of his voyage from Falmouth through the Gulf of Bothnia must have been very pleasant for Captain Jones, for at Falmouth on 16 June 1897 two new names appeared: 'Elizabeth Jones, of Garden Cottage, Amlwch, aged 40, First ship, Captain's wife', and O. W. Ll. Jones, Amlwch, aged 10, First ship, Captain's son'.[93] This was a common practice and very many Anglesey wives and children went to sea with their husbands in the summer months; Captain Jones's son was to follow in his father's footsteps, serving with him at sea in the *Talus* and eventually becoming a master mariner in the Holyhead-Dublin service, at one time commanding the *Hibernia*. The *Cymric* brought a cargo of timber from Uleaborg to Conway on her return voyage, and the master's family left the ship at Conway when the remainder of the crew were paid off on 2 September 1898. The outward voyage with coal and the voyages to Uleaborg and back to Conway were profitable and the William Thomas share was well over £400. The *Cymric* made one further voyage, with coal from Liverpool to Gibraltar, then salt from Cadiz to Pelotas, and hides from Rio Grande to Le Havre, another highly profitable voyage, and then returned to Plymouth with 'plaster stones' in August 1899.

From Plymouth she sailed to Antwerp in September with 369 tons of clay; at Antwerp Captain Jones received a letter from William Thomas and Sons: 'What you think if we tried to secure an outward Freight by the time you arrive in the Mersey? We have not been quoted any freight lately, but think with an offer that we could get a cargo for Gib and thence Cadiz to Rio Grande.'[94] But when the Cymric arrived at Garston from Antwerp with 360 tons of 'Bog Ore' at 6/6 per ton, it was to be her last voyage for Captain Jones and William Thomas. She was sold to J. and S. Holt of Liverpool and, under their ownership, sailed from Le Havre to New York, Rotterdam to Lagos, and then in the European trades until she was bought by Arklow owners in 1906. For the next thirty years and more she sailed in Irish waters and to Spain and Portugal; it was on a voyage to Lisbon early in the 1939-45 war that she disappeared.[95]

William Thomas and Sons settled their account with Captain Robert Jones in March 1900; from their own statement of accounts, and Captain Jones's notebook, it is possible to summarize the amounts paid to them from 1894 to 1899 from the earnings of the *Cymric* in accordance with their contract with Captain Jones, i.e. 'half of all freight . . . after deducting port charges'.

1894	Sept.	Cardiff to Rio Grande	159.18. 3
	Dec.	Paranagua to Monte Video	65.19.10
1895	March	Montevideo to Pernambuco	212. 0.10
	May	Pernambuco to Rio Grande	109.10. 4

	Sept.	Rio Grande to Runcorn	119. 7. 0
1896	April	Liverpool to Port Alegro	216.19. 7
	May	Margem to Pelotas	13. 6. 8
	Dec.	Pelotas to Hamburg	120. 3. 2
1897	Jan.	Harburg to Bristol	50. 8.10
	Feb.	Bristol to Garston	24. 4. 5
	June	Carnarvon to Harburg	60.18. 0
	Aug.	Harburg to Abo	18.12. 0
	Oct.	Attu to Bridgwater	71. 1.11
1898	Feb.	Cardiff to Pelotas	177.18. 8
	July	Pelotas to Uleaborg	172. 7. 7
	Sept.	Uleaborg to Conway	94.16. 6
	Dec.	Liverpool to Gibraltar	47.17.10
1899	March	Cadiz to Pelotas	206. 5. 0
	Aug.	Rio Grande to Havre	222.13.10
	Sept.	Havre to Plymouth	14.16. 1
		Plymouth to Antwerp	33. 8. 6
	Oct.	Antwerp to Garston	40.14.10[96]

Since the days of her first voyage to the day she was sold by the Thomas family, Captain Robert Jones had had command of the *Cymric*. In those days shipowners rarely gave but the most brief and meagre references to their masters, but in the case of Captain Jones, William Thomas and Sons commanded him as 'very careful, steady and energetic, and a capable officer, and possessing abilities above the average to conduct commercial transactions. We can therefore with the greatest confidence recommend him'. Leafing through his notebook where every item is carefully notes, one cannot but agree. More significant still are the loose pieces of paper on which Captain Jones had made hurried notes. He must have been considering a charter to Guadeloupe when he jotted down in pencil on a scrap of paper, 'Sainte Marie, small but comparatively safe Harbour opposite Pointe a Pitre, vessel 13 to 14 feet', 'Baie du Canal good place'. 'Le Mante is small . . . bad place from Dec. to March wind in causing seas and difficulty to get out'. At Uleaborg he carefully noted how Dutch and Danish schooners towed their cargoes, and in other harbours recorded the names of merchants and agents who might be of service in future. Confidence in Captain Robert Jones was amply justified.[97]

The *Gaelic*, launched from the Thomas yard in 1898, was slightly longer but otherwise almost identical to the *Cymric*; William Thomas and Captain Lewis Thomas both had 32/64 shares in her when she was registered, but six days later they transferred four shares each by bill of sale to Captain Ishmael Williams, her new master. Like Captain Robert Jones, Captain Ishmael Williams was a well-known and highly respected Amlwch master mariner; to complicate matters for the historian, he, too, like William Thomas and Robert Jones, bore the same name as his father, who had also been an Amlwch master mariner, and young Ishmael had first gone to sea as an apprentice aboard his father's ship after attending Sellars school at Amlwch. Now aged 37, Captain Ishmael Williams had as his mate for the *Gaelic*'s first voyage a young Tudweiliog, Caernarvonshire, man, David Williams, aged 24, whose last ship had been the full-rigged *Carnedd Llywelyn*; the remainder of the crew came from Amlwch, Caernarvon and Llandudno. For the next ten years the *Gaelic* sailed regularly to South America, usually leaving Runcorn or Ellesmere Port for Gibraltar with a cargo of coal, then across from Cadiz with salt for Rio Grande do Sul and back to Hamburg and Runcorn with hides.[98] Occasionally she put into Welsh ports; she had some repair and maintenance work carried out at Degannwy in August 1900 and William Thomas sent one of their experienced sailmakers from Amlwch there to carry out the work.[99]

The success of the *Cymric* and her sister ships *Gaelic* and *Celtic* encouraged William Thomas to design three steel schooners somewhat smaller than their iron predecessors; the *Meyric*, the *Elizabeth Roberts*, and the *Cenric*. There were high hopes for the *Cenric*, built in 1905. Her master was Captain Maurice Parry of Borth-y-gest, an experienced Portmadoc master mariner who had at one time served in the pioneer *Frau Minna Petersen*. When Captain Parry left Portmadoc with a cargo of slate two days before Christmas 1905,[100] he had a young but experienced crew: he himself was aged 27, his mate, a Scotsman of the same age, had served in the *George Casson*, the two A.B.s, aged 23 and 20, had served in the *Elizabeth Llywelyn* and the *C. E. Spooner*, all three vessels being good examples of the beautiful Portmadoc ships, whilst the cook and ordinary seaman was a young man from Penrhynside, near Llandudno; the mate's wages were £4.5.0 per month, the A.B.s £3.5.0, and the

Cook/O.S. £1.17.0. This crew took the *Cenric* to Bremen by 8 January, and a month later they sailed for Belfast, and from Lough Larne they sailed for Cardiff arriving there on 12 March. Ten days later they sailed for Newfoundland; the Portmadoc men had been paid off at Cardiff and in their place Parry had signed a Gothenburg man as 'Bosn' (not as mate although the wages were the same), an A.B. named Dyer from Fowey, and A.B. called Hughes from Parry's home village of Borth-y-gest, and a young Cardiff Ordinary Seaman on his first voyage. It was also to be his last. The *Cenric* arrived safely enough in Newfoundland, but a melancholy note in the Customs Register states all that remains of her story, 'vessel missing, left Twillingate, Newfoundland, on 12 June 1906, and has not since been heard of.' Her papers were, of course, lost with her, but the Board of Trade Office Copy and the 'List C and D' of the crew were sent to William Thomas for confirmation, and the appropriate particulars of discharge were entered against the names of each member of the crew: 'Supposed Drowned. Vessel missing since 12/6/06.'

Captain Ishmael Williams had had ten years of successful running to South America when on 21 August 1909 the *Gaelic* was involved in a collision in the River Mersey and went aground on Egremont beach.[101] Hitherto the lack of incidents noted in the official logs of the *Gaelic* bore testimony to the quiet efficiency of Captain Williams; there are very few desertions from his crew throughout the period. It must have been a sad day for him and many of the older hands in his crew when he noted the death of Morris Roberts of Dyffryn, Merioneth, on 16 August 1904 at Hamburg, for Roberts had served with him on several voyages, sometimes as A.B., sometimes as cook. Captain Ishmael Williams had a number of African cooks, Amos Bovis and Amos Ashong were two of them; as the years went by, so the crew became more cosmopolitan, young German boys aged 17 and 15 from Hamburg on the 1905-6 voyage, Nicolau Mario Antonio from the Cape Verde Islands, who signed on at the age of 17 for the 1906-7 voyage, having previously served on the *Meyric* which he had joined at Rio Grande in 1906. When the *Gaelic* sank after the collision in the River Mersey, the crew included a German, a 21 years old A.B. from Finland, and fourteen years old Ernest Ellis from Egremont on his first ship as deck boy. The Amlwch-Millom connection was evident in the crew lists; in the

1903-4 voyage, for example, Alfred C. Walmsley of Pier Cottage, Millom, aged seventeen, was a member of the crew of the *Gaelic* sailing to the Rio Grande. Ishmael Williams's mate for several voyages was Thomas Thomas from Felin Fach, Llanarth, Cardiganshire; they were together in the 1903-4 voyage, at the time of the collision in 1909 and again in 1910-11 and 1911-12, by which time the master was aged 50 and the mate aged 62. Thomas Thomas served aboard other vessels belonging to the William Thomas firm – he was mate of the *Meyric*, the new steel schooner built at Amlwch in 1904 in her voyage from Grimsby to the Rio Grande in 1905-6, and with him were several of the crew who had served with him on the *Gaelic*, including Amos Ashong, the cook from the Cape Coast. This interchange of crews is again evident in the fact that Robert Griffith of Ael Eilian, Amlwch, master of the *Meyric* (who, like Ishmael Williams, had shares in his ship), also had among his crew both Anglesey and European lads who had served in other Thomas ships. On the death of Robert Griffith in 1908, the *Meyric* had a new master, David Thomas of Talsarnau, Merioneth. He brought with him a number of men from Portmadoc ships; the mate and the bosun were from Borth-y-gest and another A.B. had served on one of the well-known Portmadoc ships, the *George Casson*. The mate, Griffith Humphreys, had, in fact, served as mate with Ishmael Williams in the *Gaelic* in 1905-6 when Thomas Thomas had gone to the *Meyric*. In 1909, the new master of the *Meyric* was Captain William Williams, Ishmael Williams's brother; aged 50, he had been master of the *Ravenswood*, an iron barque of 1,123 tons, owned by J. B. Walmsley, the Liverpool shipowning company, which many Anglesey men served. He had been master of the *Ravenswood* for six years, and brought with him as bosun to the *Meyric* one of the crew who had served with him aboard the *Ravenswood*, Thomas Powell, Tŷ Capel, Pentraeth. His crews on the *Meyric* for the next three voyages were nearly all Amlwch men who had previously served aboard the *Happy Harry* and the *Mary Ashburner*, and among them was his son, eighteen-year-old Ishmael O. Williams.[102] The crew lists give a fascinating impression of the way in which these fine Amlwch vessels from the William Thomas yard were manned, and indicate the close ties between them.

Moreover, they were very much part of the life of Amlwch people ashore. Miss M. Williams, daughter of Captain Ishmael Williams of the *Gaelic*, described vividly the impact made upon the life of this small community by the departures and arrivals of the Thomas vessels:

'When a sailing ship was off on a long voyage, the harbour would be black with people from Amlwch and the vicinity. The families of the crew would be allowed to crowd round the 'watchhouse' to catch the last glimpse of their men-folk climbing down the ladder to the ship, never knowing whether they would see them again.
In those far-away days, every man in Amlwch Port knew every detail about the ships, as they were almost all built locally. So, when the ships were due back from a long voyage, there would be 'look out' men on what we call the 'Bonc'. They would sight the *Gaelic*, for instance, when it was miles away beyond Bull Bay, just a speck on the horizon. They would immediately rush round to tell my mother. There would then be a sort of 'bush telegraph' communication. In a very short time, people would be swarming all over the 'Bonc' to see the little ship proudly painted white and with the white sails gallantly helping it to sail past and on to Liverpool, but the pilot had to go aboard first.
My mother would have everything packed ready, and off we would go by train to Liverpool to meet my father. One of the greatest thrills would be to sail along the canal to Runcorn and Ellesmere Port. Even today, the smell of tarred rope gives me a feeling of nostalgia.'[103]

The era of the *Cymric, Gaelic,* and the *Meyric* was the high water mark in the history of William Thomas, Amlwch. The *Eilian*, built in 1908, a three-masted auxiliary schooner, marked the end of an era of ship-building at Amlwch. A small hospital ship, the *Morfudd*, was built during the 1914-18 war and moored for a time in the Menai Strait, naval torpedo boats were brought to the yard to be broken up for scrap after the war, and small steamers, the *Ardri*, built by Shearer, Glasgow, in 1892, and the *Dunleith*, built at Paisley in 1896, were added to the Thomas fleet, but the end was in sight. William Thomas, the designer of fine ships, died in 1930. In 1936 the *Ardri* foundered thirteen miles off Bardsey Island, the *Eilianus* and the

Eleth, both steam vessels engaged in the coasting trade, were wrecked, one off the Cornish coast, the other off Dunkirk, and the yard was finally closed in 1951.[104] The site is now a derelict wasteland, but on a bitingly cold day, standing on the slipways where so many beautiful ships slid into the sea, one can recapture something of the conditions that the craftsmen working there endured when the wind was from the north and the north-east. With a little imagination, one can people this derelict site with the excitement and clamour of a departure, arrival, or, more particularly, a launching day when the children had a day off from school, and everyone had flocked to the harbour. The graceful ships created by William Thomas and the adventurous energy of his father, Captain William Thomas, contributed much to the life of sailing ship communities, not only in Amlwch, but also in Lancashire, Cumberland, and far beyond this now sleepy Anglesey port.

[1]   Details relating to vessels built in Anglesey are based upon the entries in the Beaumaris Custom House Register, now housed at Custom House, Holyhead.

[2]   *NW Gazette*, Feb. 27, 1817. Over thirty schooners and smacks were built at Holyhead during the first half of the 19th century.

[3]   TR with Captains R. Wynne and R. Jones at Amlwch, June 1971.

[4]   In Slater's Directory of *Liverpool and its Environs*, 1844, Nicholas Treweek is listed as one of the four ship and boat builders at Bangor where there also were three 'Ship Bread Bakers', 2 Ship Brokers and 2 Shipsmiths – Ship Chandlers.

[5]   In 1855 Treweek is still named as managing owner of the *Arethusa*, 712 tons N.T., built at Quebec in 1845, the *Recruit*, 996 tons, *Helen*, 860 tons, again Quebec built, *Iris*, a brig of 277 tons built at Jersey in 1838, and a considerable number of smaller vessels, schooners and smacks in the costal trade.

[6]   UCNW MM MS 1796. He paid a brief visit to Cornwall 'in the hope that his native air will be of benefit to him'. Thomas Evans, brother of Evan Evans, the Chief Clerk, and uncle of Thomas Fanning Evans, was appointed to the Liverpool post.

[7]   E.A. Census Returns, 1861. Amlwch.

[8]   J. Rowlands, 'Cornishmen at the Anglesey Copper Mines', in *TAAS*

1963. 1-15.

[9] UCNW MM MS 3607. Morris suggested that one of the warehouses should be repaired and a floor added to it to make a sail loft.

[10] *ibid*. Evans did not wish his support for Morris to 'be construed by the Treweeks as arising from any pique which they might fancy as being entertained by me towards them'. Nevertheless he felt it 'would do away with a monopoly hitherto held by the party named above (i.e. Treweek) in this as well as the other branches of business connected with the shipping of this port'. May, 1853.

[11] R. Môn Williams, *Enwogion Môn, 1850-1912* (Bangor, 1913), 125; Y Genedl Gymreig, Ebrill 1893.

[12] BCR 5/1849. For details of the ships owned or built by Captain Thomas see Appendix compiled from BCR, *Lloyd's Registers*, and William Thomas Amlwch MSS in ARO.

[13] Undated cutting from local press report in Bryn Eilian MSS.

[14] ARO B/SH MSS Port of Amlwch, Byelaws, 28 Dec. 1857. A ball was hoisted 'on a pole on the Point called Llamycarw', on 'E.S.E. side of the Harbour's Mouth' as an indication to vessels intending to run for the harbour that the 'Breakwater Balks' were down 'across the entrance between the two Pier-Heads'. Captain W. Williams and other Amlwch master mariners recall that the pole at Llamycarw was acknowledged as a place of tryst, and many young seamen held the hand of their intended brides at the spot as an indication of an engagement which was binding on both parties.

[15] J. H. Davies (ed.), *The Life and Opinions of Robert Roberts, A wandering scholar, as told by himself* (Cardiff, 1923), 311, 321-322. Roberts also has lively descriptions of voyages he made with Captain Jack Evans in the *Vale of Clwyd* along the north Wales coast between Liverpool and Holyhead, and the great kindness shown to him by the rough old captain who was lost in the *Vale of Clwyd*, according to Roberts, 'with all on board on the night of the wreck of the Royal Charter.' 310. Robert Roberts wrote his autobiography whilst he was in Australia. For his career see also DWB 877, and T. O. Phillips, *Robert Roberts* (Cardiff, 1957).

[16] J. F. C. Harrison, *The Early Victorians*, 1832-1851 (London, 1971), 71.

[17] Michael Hughes, manager of the St Helens smelting works, who had a financial interest in the Amlwch breweries, introduced Sir Hugh Williams, of Friars, Beaumaris, to the Greenalls, and in 1786 they sent him a hogshead of strong beer, 'by the first sloop bound for the Port of Beaumaris'. T. C. Barker and J. R. Harris, *A Merseyside Town in the Industrial Revolution, St Helens, 1750-1900* (Liverpool, 1954), 100. In 1823 the Amlwch Brewery Company advertised their own 'very strong ale' at 64 shillings per barrel, *NWC*, 9 Jan. 1823.

[18] Enumeration Abstracts, Census Returns, Anglesey, 1851 and 1861.

[19] *ibid*. The *Confidence*, a 75-ton Lancaster vessel, was one of the vessels lying alongside the quay; she was commanded by Captain Ishmael Williams, who later served in the Fisher of Barrow ships, and was the father of

Captains Ishmael and William Williams, who commanded the *Gaelic* and *Meyric*, built by Thomas at the turn of the century. Master of the *Thomas*, in which Captain Thomas himself may have served at one time (note in Bryn Eilian MSS), was a young Whitehaven man, aged 23; his wife, Mary Ann, aged 21, was aboard with him.

[20] *NWC*, March 1858.

[21] I am indebted to Mr David Owen, Amlwch, for notes on the Amlwch Institute.

[22] E. A. Williams, Hanes Môn, 143-4; *NWC*, March 1858.

[23] *NWC*, March 1858.

[24] *NWC*, 13 March 1858. The new National and Provincial Bank, 'a substantial building' and the port 'which is about the snuggest in Britain' were regarded as portents of a prosperous future for Amlwch.

[25] BCR 1859. William Hughes, born in Amlwch in 1805, had a highly successful business career in Manchester and was a leader of the Welsh Calvinistic Methodists there. He returned in the 1870s and came to live at Bodednyfed, Amlwch. R. M. Williams, *Enwogion Môn*, 43.

[26] Bryn Eilian MSS. 'Treweek Sons and Co.' are still referred to in *Slaters Directory* for 1868 as shipbuilders and ship chandlers at Amlwch Port, and William Thomas is listed separately. Although Captain Thomas was identified with both concerns in the sixties, the Treweek name may not have been dispenses with until the seventies, when Captain Thomas in fact advertised that he had 'lately purchased Mr Nicholas Treweek's extensive and commodious shipbuilding yard and Dry Dock'. This was in 1872, *infra*. The latest information from Mr Robyn Williams of Holyhead, a descendant of Captain Thomas, indicates that the completion date for the purchase of the yard was 1874.

[27] A month after the *Grace Evans* was launched, Thomas bought shares in Treweek's brig *Resolution*, and bought the *Jane Pringle, Lord Willoughby, Albion, Lord Mostyn*, and *Cymro*, again from Treweek, during the 1860-1863 period. There was also a *Sarah Pringle*, she was commanded by Captain William Evans and Captain John Hughes, both of Chapel Street, Amlwch, according to the register of persons entitled to vote in 1870. For these and other vessels mentioned below, see Appendix IX (i) List of Captain William Thomas ships, based on BCR and Lloyd's Registers.

[28] The *Amanda* was purchased for the contract price of £920; Captain Thomas was paid £485.16.9½d 'for iron knees, calking ship round and sundrys', John Peters, shipbuilder, Holyhead, £37.4.6 for a new mast and sundries. The *Amanda* had this refit at Holyhead immediately after she had been purchased; Captain Thomas was paid his travelling expenses to Holyhead, whilst Elias Williams, his shipwright, was paid 6 days' wages at 4/6 a day at Holyhead, and an advance of 10/- cash for expenses. Together with payments to the blacksmith at Holyhead, the total cost of *Amanda* in 1867 was therefore £1,658.11.9½d. Among the payments recorded in the early years were £9,14.1 to 'Ahmed Halaway, Alexandria, calking decks', and

small amounts to 'Madam Laboy, Rouen', David Young, Ropemaker, Dublin, Thomas Rowland, Butcher, Amlwch, Wm. Jones, Tinman, and Isaiah Griffiths, for 5 cwts. of bread at £4.10.0. Captain Thomas was paid £115.11.0 between 1868 and 1870 for sailmaker's and carpenter's work, and Wm. Thomas, Liverpool, supplied a 'cabin grate' for £1.19.0 in Feb. 1868. Between 1867 and 1881 the *Amanda* paid a total of about £300 and £150 clear to Captain Thomas and William Thomas, Liverpool, for their 8/64 and 4/64 shares respectively. The *Amanda* was sold for £500 in 1881. ARO B/SH.2, *Amanda*'s account book.

29 ARO *Amanda*, 53682, Agreement lists and official log books. Captain Robert Jones sailed the *Amanda* to Riga and Alexandria in 1866-1868.

30 J. R. Jones, *The Welsh Builder on Merseyside* (Liverpool, 1946), 30-34, 43-45.

31 I am indebted to Mrs Ethel K. Williams, Liverpool, for much information regarding the career of her father, William Thomas, Llanrhuddlad and Liverpool. I am also grateful to her for allowing me to see the private papers still in her possession, which are referred to as WT Liverpool MSS.

32 H. Vaughan Johnson, appendix to *Reports of Commission of Inquiry into the State of Education in Wales (1848)*, 500; E. A. Williams, *Hanes Môn*, 258.

33 The story of the *William Melhuish*'s success is referred to in the obituaries published in the Welsh press at the time of the death of William Thomas, Liverpool, and the name 'Melhuish' has been perpetuated in the names of some of his descendants. The master mariner from Newborough who commanded the *William Mellhuish* on her first voyages for the Thomas families was probably Captain William Thomas, Cae Coch, Newborough. He is named as one of the successful 'second generation' master mariners in Owen Williamson's list. O. Williamson, *Hanes Niwbwrch*, 77.

34 There is a note in his papers in his own handwriting that he 'chartered and otherwise assisted more or less in the management' of the following vessels in which he had shares in 1873/4. *Ann Crewdson, Cumberland Lassie, Rossendale, Frank M. Fisher, Wm. Ashburner*. WT Liverpool MSS 2.7.1888.

35 *Lloyd's Register*, 1880, indicates that James Fisher and Sons of Barrow managed 41 vessels, William Postlethwaite 23, Captain Thomas 16, and Thomas Ashburner of Barrow 14 in 1880. Basil Greenhill, in *The Merchant Schooners*, Vol. II, 73-91, has described the schooner fleets of Lancashire and Cumberland in which many Welshmen first went to sea.

36 Captain William Evans, *Sarah Pringle*, Captains Griffiths and Solomon Ellis, Captains Thomas and Robert Griffiths, Captain William Jones, *Fanny*, Captain John Williams, *Mary Williams*, Captain Robert Jones, *Amanda*, Captain John Thomas, *Savent*, Captain Thomas Owen, *Alliance*, Captain Owen Owens, *Mona*, were among the master mariners living in Chapel Street and entitled to vote by virtue of having a house, or a house and garden in 1870.

37 UCNW Bangor MS 23851. Amlwch Harbour Trustees Meeting, Monday, 25th July 1870.

[38] *ibid.*, 1 May 1871.

[39] I am indebted to Mr W. H. Michael, Amlwch, for allowing me to photograph a section of Algeo's map which is now in his possession.

[40] I am grateful to Douglas B. Hague, RC on Ancient and Historical Monuments, for this information, and to him and Dylan Roberts, also of the RCAM, for walking over the site with me in June 1972. Map p. 295 was prepared by Douglas Hague and D. Roberts.

[41] John Wynne Paynter, of Maesllwyn, Amlwch, was a corn merchant, and also was one of the four Welshmen who took over the management of the Parys Mines under the leadership of Thomas Fanning Evans, son of Evan Evans who had been chief clerk of the Mona Mine and a critic of the Treweek faction. R. M. Williams, *Enwogion Môn*, 89.

[42] ARO B/SH MS 16. The notice added, 'He employs a most efficient staff of workmen, including Carpenters, Joiners, Smiths, Sailmakers, Block-makers, and others. He also begs to intimate that he keeps all sorts of SHIP CHANDLERY STORES and has constantly on hand a large stock of BUILDING MATERIALS; such as Boards, Bricks, Chimney Tops, Lathes, Nails (in great variety), Ridge and other Tiles, Slabs, Slates, Timber, etc.'

[43] ARO B/SH MS 11. Memorandum of Agreement, Holborn Hill, Cumberland, 24 Jan. 1871.

[44] The *Anne Crewdson, Maggie Brocklebank*, commanded in 1875 by a Captain Ellis (from Amlwch?), built by Charnley, the *Margaret Hobley*, built at Pembroke Dock, the *Millom Castle*, built at Ulverston by White.

[45] Basil Greenhill, *The Merchant Schooners*, II, 47, 77.

[46] Twenty-five years later, the *Baron Hill* was showing a dividend of £2 per 1/64 share on the year ending 31 Dec. 1890. During the course of the year, Wm. Postlethwaite, her managing owner, reported that she had sailed from Grimsby to 'Santa Fe', Santa Elma to Antwerp, Antwerp to Newport, Cardiff to Huelva, and Huelva to Amlwch, and Amlwch to Galway. Audited Account, 31 Jan. 1891. Millom, Cumberland, ARO B/SH MSS.

[47] ARO B/SH 1, Box II, MS 18. According to the report of the accountants, R. J. Miller and Co., Barrow-in-Furness, after various adjustments, Captain Thomas's holding was £2,002.3.6 and that of William Postlethwaite £964.7.2.

[48] I am grateful to Mr E. Cockshutt, Amlwch, for allowing me to examine this note book, which is now in his possession.

[49] Some of the smaller vessels were already out of the *Lloyd's Register* 1875. Most of the vessels in the note book were insured for varying amounts with the Amlwch Mutual Ship Insurance Company, Bangor Mutual Ship Insurance Society, Bangor and North Wales Mutual Marine Protection Association, Nevin Provincial M.M. Ins. Soc., and their freights with the Bangor Freight and Outfit Insurance Co., the Nevin Cambrian Freight and Outfit M.M. Insurance Co., Liverpool Mutual Marine Insurance Association, and the Bristol Avon Freight Club. Protection in case of collision was with the Bangor and North Wales M.M. Protection

Association, City of Bangor M.M. Protection Association, and the Bristol Protection Club. There were about thirty different Mutual Marine Insurance Companies formed in north Wales by shipowners, and they were an essential part of the development of shipping in the second half of the 19th century. David Thomas listed 5 of these clubs at Portmadoc, 11 at Nevin, 1 at Caernarvon, 5 at Bangor; that at Amlwch was the only one in Anglesey. It was formed in 1882, and, inevitably, Captains William Thomas, Robert Jones, and John German were among the first directors, together with Thomas Fanning Evans, Thomas Morgan, Owen Owen and Lewis Hughes, Captain Thomas's son-in-law. UCNW Bangor MS 23854.

[50] WT Liverpool MS 2/7/88. Most of the correspondence consists of letters copied by a clerk, but this memorandum was obviously prepared and written by William Thomas himself and gives a detailed account of his business transactions with Captain Roberts. The Account Book of the *Barbara* for a voyage from Cardiff to Zanzibar, thence in ballast to Rangoon where she loaded a cargo of rice for the Channel for orders, is in ARO B/SH MS 13. On arrival at Queenstown she was ordered to proceed to Liverpool, but was wrecked in Freshwater Bay, 22 November 1881. The *Barbara* had left Doxford's yards in 1877, another of the building-boom vessels. The *Toronto* was a smaller, older vessel, built at Quebec in 1872. When she was lost, the Nevin, Bristol, Avon and Bangor and Provincial Mutual Marine Insurance Societies paid out £5,300; this, together with the £652.5.7½ 'other amounts for advances on Freight', was distributed to the owners, £1,476.16.9½ being 'paid in or settled from Amlwch.' The balance of £4,235.5.9½ was then paid to the shareholders, according to their shares, e.g. William Jones of Egremont, who held 16/64, received £1,058.16.4½, William Thomas, Amlwch, Thomas Williams, Liverpool, R. H. Roberts, Amlwch and E. Morgan Jones, Amlwch, who each held 8/64, received £529.8.2¾, William Thomas, Liverpool, William Hughes, Amlwch, James Clarke, Mold, each received £264.14.1½ as their 4/64 shares, and William Williams, London, and William Owens, Gadlys, £132.7.0¾ each as their 2/64 share. ARO B/SH MS 2/7.

[51] WT Liverpool MS, 11 Oct. 1880.

[52] ARO *Anglesea Lass*, agreement and crew list signed by David Jones, master, November 1871, and Official Log Book of *Anglesea Lass*, delivered to shipping master at Berwick-on-Tweed, 24 June 1872. The melancholy list of the young apprentice's effects gives an indication what a young first voyager possessed in 1871: 'Eight shirts, five trousers, four Drawers, four vests, three mufflers, four pairs of stocking, one pair of shoes, one singlet, three jackets, one rug, two ties, one cap, one oilskin pants, seven books, one small box with letters and sundries.'

[53] ARO Agreement and account of crew of *Anglesea Lass*, Feb. 1873. David Jones, the master, was a native of Aberaeron. The master and the mate, Owen Jones of Amlwch, were among those saved.

[54] ARO *Lewis and Mary*, July 1874. Her register was closed in BCR on 8

May 1875.

[55] The crew saved were Owen Jones, mate, of Amlwch, Henry Campbell, A.B., of Londonderry, and Richard Owen, ship's boy, from Cemais. ARO, *Elizabeth Martha*, List D, 1871.

[56] *Caernarvon and Denbigh Herald*, May 7, 1870.

[57] ARO B/SH MSS, 11 April 1875. The full specification of this vessel and a copy of a letter from the 'Port Office', regarding 'a pilot vessel for this port as proposed by Mr Thomas', dated 5 Jan. 1876, give a detailed indication of the type of vessels Captain Thomas was building in the mid-seventies. In 1875 Captain Thomas built the *Mersey*, a wooden schooner of 79 tons, which became Mersey Pilot Boat No. 11. She was sunk near the Bar Light Vessel in 1885.

[58] ARO. The crew agreement lists, official logs, and the account books of the *Lady Neave* from 1888-1901, and her Freight Account book 1895-1901, are at Llangefni.

[59] Basil Greenhill, *The Merchant Schooners*, II, 70.

[60] *Infra*.

[61] WT Liverpool MS. Captain Roberts to W. Thomas, 9 Dec. 1879.

[62] *ibid*.

[63] ARO B/SH MSS, 14, 15. The printed particulars of the steamers 'Hull built by Messrs. Thomas and Sons, Amlwch, and the Machinery by Messrs. De Winton & Co., Caernarvon' were distributed by Wm. Thomas & Co., 30 Brunswick Street, Liverpool. Shares were sold at £20 each. William Thomas, Liverpool, eventually had the major holding in the W.S. *Caine* and the *Exchange*, and shares with Postlethwaite in the *Lady Louisa*.

[64] WT Liverpool MS 2/7 1888.

[65] *NWC*, May 1883. There is a brief note on De Wintons in R. Abbott, 'Chronicles of a Caernarvon Ironworks', *TCHS*, 17, 86-94, but there is no reference by Abbott to the link with the Amlwch-built vessels of Captain Wm. Thomas, although five out of the first six ships he names were built by Thomas.

[66] Basil Greenhill, *The Merchant Schooners*, II, 67.

[67] TR interview with Mr M. Pritchard, Amlwch Port, July 1972.

[68] ARO Eng. 6, agreement and crew lists of *Eilian*. The Griffiths family are referred to again in the chapter 'The end of an age' (p. 457) in connection with their vessel, the *Irish Minstrel*.

[69] ARO. Official Log book of *Eilian*, half-year beginning January 1899.

[70] ARO B/SH MS II, 17. A letter dated 8 June 1887 authorised Captain Lewis Thomas as Lloyd's Agent to salvage dead cattle from the wreck of S.S. *Athlumey*.

[71] The *Prince Ja-Ja* carried miscellaneous goods for north Wales shopkeepers, and the jetty which preceded Bangor Pier was known as the Ja-Ja Jetty. It used to be said that a favourite refrain of Anglesey and Caernarvonshire shopkeepers to customers was 'Sorry, we haven't any in stock – waiting any day now for the Prince Ja-Ja!' The late Professor J. Glyn

Davies recalled her later years: 'The *Prince Ja-Ja* of hilarious memory was another of the Trafalgar Dock Welsh fleet, but she was owned by Admiral Parry of Warrington. Her masters were Captain Griffith Williams, a dear old shellback, and Captain Anderson, a Welsh-speaking Swede who came over to Wales when he was 21, settled down in Caernarvon, and married a Welsh wife, and was as devoted to Welsh preaching as he was to non-teatotal drinks. The dual command of the *Prince Ja-Ja* is an amusing story in itself.' *T. Cym.*, 1948, 213.

[72] The *Enterprise* was owned by Captain Jones, Fagwyr, Llaneilian.

[73] I am grateful to Dr. Jürgen Meyer of the Altonaer Museum in Hamburg for this and other information on German merchants with whom Welsh shipowners had business connections. Detlef Wagner is mentioned in Dr. Meyer's *150 Jahre Blankeneser Schiffart 1785-1935* and *Hamburgs Segelschiffe 1795-1945*.

[74] ARO B/SH MSS. William Thomas Wages Book, 1891.

[75] Basil Greenhill, *The Merchant Schooners*, II, 67.

[76] *North Wales Chronicle*, 29 March 1893.

[77] *Y Genedl Gymreig*, Ebrill 1893. The account of his funeral in 'Y Genedl' also referred to the very large number of mourners who followed the hearse, draped in the Union Jack, to the cemetery at Llaneilian, and to Captain Thomas's extensive holdings of lands and cottages in Anglesey.

[78] WT Liverpool MS. Letter addressed to Wm. Thomas at 25 Water Street, Liverpool, from Amlwch Port, 5 Oct. 1879. Captain Thomas told Wm. Thomas to arrange a charter for his vessel *Linda* at Connah's Quay, for Bermuda, 'get all you can for her with dispatch'. The other reference in Captain Thomas's letter, 'Get me Countess Account', probably refers to the *Countess of Kintore*, a wooden ship of 738 tons, which is listed in *Lloyd's Register* 1880 as being managed by Captain Thomas. It could, however, be the *Countess of Lonsdale*, the wooden schooner which he owned jointly with Postlethwaite; from his own papers the Liverpool Thomas does not appear to have had any large share in either vessel.

[79] Details in this paragraph are taken from the half-yearly agreement lists of the vessels mentioned, and from the block notebook of the Thomas yard now in the possession of E. Cockshutt, Supra. The *Pride of Anglesea*, over thirty years old, earned £498.10 between 1888 and 1893, but the bills for repairs were heavy, and Thomas informed Captain Robert Jones, Garden Cottage, who held a 16/64 share in her, that a meeting was to be held in April 1894 'at our office . . . to decide what to do with the vessel, which requires repairing'. I am indebted to Mr Hugh Farrell for allowing me to see the *Pride of Anglesea*'s papers for her last years, now in his possession.

[80] Basil Greenhill, *The Merchant Schooners*, II, 68. The Reuben Chappell portrait of the *Donald and Doris* is one of two in the 'fair weather and foul weather' tradition.

[81] She was named after Hugh Jones's children. The *Happy Harry* was another three-masted schooner built by the Duddon Shipbuilding

Company in 1894.

[82] When John Anderson wrote *Coastwise Sail* in 1934 he described some of the storms the *Happy Harry* had survived in 1932 and 1933.

[83] ARO B/SH MSS. Account Book of *Lady Neave*.

[84] F. E. Hyde, *Liverpool and the Mersey* (Newton Abbot, 1971), 46. Sir Alfred Lewis Jones (1845-1909) started his career in Liverpool, like William Thomas, Llanrhuddlad, as a clerk in a shipping office. By 1884, when Captain Robert Jones made out the cheques to him, Alfred Jones had just become the controlling partner in the Elder and Dempster firm. By 1890 Alfred Jones was controlling Liverpool's trade with West Africa.

[85] ARO. Captain Robert Jones MSS. In January 1887, Captain Jones, Senior, wrote to one of the shareholders: 'I am very sorry the vessel is not paying. It is really difficult to know what to do with shipping.'

[86] *ibid.* Captain Jones reported that he had reduced the insurance on the vessel £900, 'that is £600 on the vessel and £300 on freight and outfit'. He added, 'the Bangor club is winding up, I may insure the freight at London the premium is not so high'. Captain Jones had previously written to one of the shareholders on the need to reduce the insurance payments; 'The first year the vessel was insured for £2,000, but now it is £1,900 and £300 upon her freight and outfit. As the insurance runs so very high I intend next year to reduce it to about £1,400 and if you have any objections I shall be glad to hear from you'. Letter from Captain Jones, Amlwch, 22 June 1886.

[87] ARO Eng. I, papers for the *Cymric* crew agreement for voyages 13.4.93 to 17.4.94. The mate's pay was £5.10.0 a month, the cook £3.5.0, the 2nd mate £3.0.0, the A.B. £2.15.0, and the O. Seamen £2.10.0 and £1.15.0.

[88] ARO *Cymric* Eng. I, 20.12.95 to 14.1.97. The details of the *Cymric's* subsequent voyages are taken from Captain Jones's MSS and the crew agreement lists.

[89] For this voyage from Liverpool in December 1895 the mate was Robert Owen, aged 37, of 27 Llaneilian Road, Amlwch, the bosun and carpenter, William Jones, aged 24, of Dulas, the cook and seaman was Rowland Owen of the Britannia, Amlwch, and the three A.B.s were D. Hughes, aged 24, of 19 Upper Quay Street, Amlwch, Samuel Roberts, aged 27, of 16 Bryngwynt Street, Amlwch, and David Davies, aged 26, of Penrhoslligwy. Their replacements the 'runners' from Hamburg to Bristol, were all young men between the ages of 25 and 19, 2 from Trondheim, 1 from Bordeaux, 1 from Altona, 1 from Finland, and 1 from 'Petersburg'.

[90] The mate, a Caernarvon man, was paid £4 a month for this voyage and the following voyage to the Baltic; he had previously served aboard the *Welsh Girl*, built by Captain Thomas in 1869. Hugh Thomas, aged 19, of Chapel Street, Amlwch, served as bosun at a rate of £3.5.0, whilst two others, one from Amlwch and the other from Moelfre, both of whom who had just left the *British Queen*, were signed as A.B.s at £3.0.0.

[91] ARO. Captain R. Jones MSS, dated 29 Dec. 1890, Amlwch.

[92] Basil Greenhill has written that 'The parochialism of the schooner crews

was of a type unusual at sea in modern times. A Welsh or Cornish schooner would leave her home port, carry mixed cargo to Spain, load salt for the Labrador coast, take in fish there for the West Indies or Brazil, take up a fixture for hides to the Mediterranean, cross again with salt to some small port on the north tail of New-foundland . . . when she arrived (at her home port) still have the same crew she set out with more a year before'. Greenhill, *The Merchant Schooners*, II, 11. The Amlwch and Portmadoc schooners were in this tradition: it was from the large barques and sailing ships that the crews deserted at ports like San Francisco, Seattle and Newcastle N.S.W., cf. *infra*.

[93] ARO. Eng. I, *Cymric*, 13.11.1897 to 2.9.98.

[94] ARO. Captain R. Jones MSS. Letter to Captain Jones, Barquentine *Cymric*, c/o Mr Hartley, Antwerp, dated 26 Sept. 1899, Amlwch Port.

[95] Basil Greenhill, *The Merchant Schooners*, II, 67. For her activities 1914-18 *infra*.

[96] ARO. Captain R. Jones MSS. Statement of accounts 25 May 1896, 25 May 1897, 15 March 1900.

[97] Captain Robert Jones's subsequent career, as master of the large four-masters sailing out of Liverpool and Cardiff in the Edwardian era, is described in the chapter 'The end of an age' (p. 457).

[98] ARO. *Gaelic* papers, Eng. I, voyages 24.12.98 to 19.12.99 and subsequently to 1909.

[99] ARO. B/SH 3. William Thomas, Sailmaking Ledgers. William Owen, the sailmaker's expenses at Deganwy, 20 Aug. to 8 Sept. 1900, amounts to 17/6, and the *Gaelic*'s account was also charged £2.12.0 for 'Wm. Owen's time working on board at Deganwy'. In the following year June 1901, William Owen was working aboard the *Gaelic* at Runcorn; there are charges on 17 June 1901 'To Wm. Owen's expenses to Runcorn 20/-; Wm. Owen's time at Runcorn, 9 days at 6/-, £2.14.0; Miss Owen, Calico for Boat Sails, 4/8'.

[100] Captain Parry had a 16/64 share in the *Cenric* and the Thomas family held 48/64. The details which follow are from the *Cenric*'s crew agreement lists, now housed at Llangefni.

[101] The *Gaelic* appears in the photograph on the top of p. 58

[102] ARO. *Meyric* papers. Eng. I, 4.12.05 to 17.11.06.

[103] Extract from a letter from Miss M. Williams, daughter of Captain Ishmael Williams. Miss Williams generously spent many hours contacting survivors of the age of sail and searching for material for this book.

[104] I am indebted to Miss Gertrude Thomas, Bryn Eilian, daughter of William Thomas, the designer, for her kindness in allowing me to photograph some of her father's vessels at Bryneilian, and to the family for making available the papers which remain concerning the shipyard.

Anglesey Wrecks and Rescues

When there was talk of Charles I sailing to Ireland in 1642, the merchants of Chester were quick to draw attention to the perils of the sea: 'Winde and waters making no difference betwixt the greatest king and the meanest subject.'[1] They had good reason to recognize this, for they, like the Beaumaris merchants, had lost many vessels, not only in the normal way of trade, but also on extraordinary occasions such as that in April 1625 when five ships, transports bound from Chester for Carrickfergus, were lost, together with three hundred men.[2] An appeal was made to clothe and feed the survivors at Beaumaris, whilst thirty years later, on the eve of the Restoration, a naval captain reported the extremely bad weather which 'has caused more shipwrecks in these seas than has been known for many ages'.[3] The dwellers on the coasts of Anglesey knew as well as the merchants of Chester that the restless, hungry sea was no respecter of persons, nor was it a respecter of ships. Two hundred years later the same truth applied; the *Royal Charter* was a fine, well-found iron ship only four years old, the small wooden paddle-steamer *Monk* carrying livestock to Liverpool market was elderly. Both are among the hundreds of vessels that foundered on the coasts of Anglesey.

Lewis Morris in 1745 drew the attention of his readers to the 'melancholy accounts of shipwrecks and losses, so frequent on the coast of Wales', and suggested that a major cause was the inaccuracy of the charts of the coasts of Wales, and the particular need for detailed 'Sea Draughts of Harbours, Bays and Roads'. To enable him to 'search carefully for those dangers, which all others endeavour as carefully to avoid, 'Lewis Morris claimed that he had frequently 'been overtaken by violent storms, sometimes upon a lee shore, and at other times among banks and rocks'.[4] His son, William Morris, in his revised edition of 'Plans of Harbours', claimed that: 'It is notorious that ten vessels are lost upon the coast of Wales for one that is lost on the opposite coast of Ireland.'[5] The Morrises were echoing the warnings of earlier cartographers, from the makers of portulan charts and the Armada pilot, to Robert Dudley who, in his *Arcano del Mare*, 1645, warned: 'the Strait of St George between England and Ireland are considered dangerous seas, and wrecks are often heard of.'[6] Captain Greenville Collins' general statement in 1693 that 'It sometimes happens, and that too frequently, that when ships have made long and dangerous voyages, and are come home richly laden, have been shipwrecked on their native coast whereby merchant owners and mariners have been impoverished',[7] had a special relevance for Liverpool's rapidly increasing shipping fleet, many of which came to grief on Anglesey's shores. Whereas wrecks were accepted, gratefully, by the inhabitants in the seventeenth and eighteenth centuries, the fact that more of their own kith and kin were sailing in these ships, to say nothing of an increasing economic involvement, led to the changed attitude of the nineteenth-century. Inevitably, the interests of Liverpool shipowners also added a powerful spur to the improvement in the provision of navigational aids on this island directly in the path of their richly laden, but still vulnerable, ships.

Until the nineteenth-century, however, there was little ashore to aid mariners; Monson, in the sixteenth-century, had recognized that one of the first requirements of the coasting master was that he should 'know the land as soon as he shall descry it',[8] and Greenville Collins, in his seven-year survey of the coasts in the yacht provided by Charles II, tried to furnish the stranger with a quick means of establishing his position by identifying landmarks ashore. He noted the 'ruined chappell with a steeple' on Priestholme as one approached the Menai Strait from the east; for the westerly approach, over Caernarvon Bar, 'the mark of the Bar is Tuttle Hill, a Tower on the North end of Caernarvon Town, and a little house on the larboard side going in, which standeth on a low sandy point; bring these three in one or any two of them, and this will carry you into the ferry, and afterwards anchor as you please'.[9] His comments on the remaining ports of Anglesey indicate their limitations: at Holyhead 'the wind at the North makes a sea in the harbour . . . the harbour is dry at low water where ships lye on the sand': Fearon and Eyes in their early eighteenth-century survey reckoned 'Amlock harbour . . . no place for a stranger to deal with in a vessel of burthen', and Moelfre 'a small inconsiderable place, and only fit for boats and small vessels . . . can scarce by of any use but to these who are well acquainted'.[10]

There were other navigational hazards, prominent among them

the off-shore Skerries which were to have the first light on the coast, in 1724, when a certain William Trench was granted a patent to establish a coal fire light there.[11] The Skerries had already claimed many victims when the *Mary*, originally Charles II's yacht presented by the Dutch at his Restoration, struck 'about two o'clock in the morning' in foggy weather on the 25th March 1675. According to reports from some who were aboard her, she 'touched upon a rock of the N.W. of the Skerrys that lye to the Eastward of the bay of Holyhead': at the time most of the crew and passengers, including the Earl of Meath and his son, 'were for the most part under Decks'. At her first striking the rock, the seamen cried 'all was well but immediately the ship struck uppon another rock and there sank'.[12] Some of the passengers and crew got ashore on to the rocks at the Skerries, but the Earl of Meath and more than thirty were drowned. Nearly two hundred years later, in 1971, the *Mary* was found, her guns brought up, and the site investigated for what may prove to be one of the most rewarding nautical archaeological discoveries made on the Anglesey coast.

Throughout the eighteenth-century the toll of the sea mounted; William Morris writes to his brother of ships lost at the Skerries, Holyhead, Friars and Caernarvon Bar, and tells his brother Richard living in smokey London, that he little knows what it is like to live on a rocky coast by snarling seas.[13] The Custom House and the Morris letters have frequent references to retrieving cargoes from wrecks, and in the late eighteenth-century the papers of Poole, the Beaumaris solicitor who acted on behalf of the Vice-Admiral, Hugh Owen, living in far-off Pembrokeshire, indicate the problems of keeping track of all that was washed ashore. In 1779 at Red Wharf there was a dispute whether 'several pieces of masts and yards', which had come on shore, were the rightful possession of the Vice-Admiral or the Bishops of Bangor.[14] Light cannons, 'lying on Mr Meyrick's land near the harbour of Holyhead', and cannon and anchors lying on Sir John Stanley's land, also near the harbour, were also in dispute – though not with the Bishop – whilst it was alleged that Thomas Williams of Llanidan had claimed he 'held a patent under the Prince of Wales' to timber from a wreck that 'was cast away near Penrhos Villew', where all the crew perished in October 1779.[15] Thomas Williams had not yet reached his controlling position in the copper trade, but he showed in the 1770s that he had an eye to the main chance; the Vice-Admiral's deputies claimed repeatedly that Mr Thomas Williams of Llanidan's men were seizing timber and goods for his use.

In February 1776 *Les Deux Frères*, a sloop said to be bound from 'Rockford to Brest', 'came on shore under Ynys Wyddel', and a record was sent to Poole at Beaumaris of the Cod-fish, cable, anchors, sails, three compasses, an' Iron Kettle', and with true Protestant disdain, 'a case of images'.[16] These were the wrecks and cargoes recorded: there were many which disappeared as the deputies wrote piously 'no wrecks' or 'a hogshead of brandy intirely concealed from me', as the Cefnamwlch agent recorded in nearby Caernarvonshire.[17] Much was conveniently written off: 'a pipe of nasty wine not worth meddling with.'[18] There were problems enough with irate owners, as one writer from Penrhos near Holyhead noted, 'the owner of the wreck is come hear, and is going to hang half a dozen of the Thieves who rob'd the wreck'.[19]

Some undated late eighteenth-century documents in the Penrhos papers of an incident which eventually ended up before the justices at Llanerch-y-medd, give a full account of the type of dispute that arose in connection with wrecked goods.[20] The *Providence* of Hastings, bound from Dublin for London with wine, linen cloth, skin and 'feathers', was driven ashore at Rhoscolyn. The crew were rescued due to the efforts of Thomas Roberts of Bodior, who organized the carrying of a boat 'over men's shoulders . . . for a quarter of a mile' to the nearest point to the wrecked vessel. As they were afraid 'of ye contagion in France', Roberts and his neighbours questioned the shipwrecked crew carefully. Lloyd, the Customs collector from Holyhead, arrived the next day and asked Roberts to collect the casks of wine in his carts as otherwise 'all ye wine would be carryed off and drunk by the countrey people before the next morning'. But a dispute soon arose between Lloyd and Roberts as Lloyd 'in a huffing manner' claimed that he could traverse 'any man's ground in ye king's name', to collect wrecked goods; Roberts, for his part, called Lloyd an ungrateful 'rascall, vilain and a scoundrel' and took up a stick. An ugly scene developed, but eventually Roberts and his neighbours went home. It was far from the end of the matter, as claim and counter-claim were made; it is little wonder that a powerful individual such as Thomas Williams of Llanidan took the law into his own hands.

Thomas Williams' family, however, had a different role in the nineteenth-century, for it was largely due to his nephew, James Williams, and his wife Frances, that Anglesey became one of the most active areas in Britain in the saving of life from shipwreck. James Williams, in his work for the Anglesey Association for the Preservation of Life from Shipwreck, showed the same flair for organization, the drive, energy and determination that his uncle had shown in amassing a vast fortune in the copper trade. The son of John Williams of Treffos, Llansadwrn, rector of Llanddeusant, Llangaffo and Llanfair-yng-Nghornwy (and a brother of Thomas Williams, Llanidan), James Williams went up to Jesus College, Oxford, in 1807, graduated in 1810, and was a Fellow of the College from 1813 to 1822.[21] Curate of Llanfair P.G. and Penmynydd from 1814 to 1821, he succeeded his father to the three livings in the north-west of Anglesey in 1821, and it was in this area that he first became prominent in lifeboat work. James Williams' young wife Frances, daughter of Thomas Lloyd of Glan Gwna in Caernarvonshire, was a very gifted and determined woman: her talent as an artist has been inherited by her direct descendant, Kyffin Williams.[22]

Owen Lloyd Williams, son of James and Frances Williams, has recorded the events which led to the foundation of a lifeboat service in Anglesey.[23] On the day that they arrived in their new home in Llanfair-yng-Nghornwy, March 20, 1823, James Williams and his young wife went out riding, and were helpless witnesses of a tragedy when the sailing packet *Alert*, on passage from Howth to Parkgate, was becalmed and drawn on to the rock known as the West Mouse by the tide which runs strongly between the Skerries and the mainland of Anglesey. The holed *Alert* sank almost immediately, and although the weather was calm, one hundred and forty people were drowned, the few survivors getting ashore in the one small boat available and according to one account, clinging to floating hen-coops. The lesson was not lost on the Williamses. Had boats been available, the loss of life would have been much less. Frances Williams determined to raise funds to provide means of avoiding a similar tragedy. A woman of considerable resource, she lithographed a sketch she had made of the scene at Holyhead when George IV had visited the port in 1821. Copies of her work were sold, and from the proceeds a fund known as the 'King's Landing Fund' was started, with the object of rewarding those 'who exerted themselves in saving lives of property in cases of wreck, whether on the coast of Anglesey or Caernarvonshire'.[24]

The dramatic increase in the shipping in Liverpool Bay had motivated another man, a few hours' sailing from Anglesey, to draw attention to the 'disaster by sea, shipwrecks and peril of human life': Sir William Hillary, whose courage and tenacity had been responsible for saving many lives in Douglas Bay, published his 'appeal to the British Nation' in 1823, about the time Frances Williams started her work in Anglesey.[25] Hillary saw that individual efforts were not enough. What was needed was a national organisation which would have as its object the preservation of life from shipwreck, and would serve the 'people and vessels of every nation, whether in peace or war'. In 1824 the National Institution was formed, largely due to Hillary's pioneering work. James and Frances Williams were soon to become closely associated with this work, although for the first twenty-five years or so Anglesey's lifeboats and organisation were solely the responsibility of local people like James Williams. And Anglesey had need of lifeboats.

In 1825 at least fourteen vessels were wrecked on the Anglesey coast, in 1826 another twenty-five, and in 1827 another twenty-one: the statistics make little impact, but the bare sentences in the record of Lloyds give some impression. On the 25 November 1826 the *Marquis of Wellington*, Liverpool to Bahia, parted her chain-cable at the entrance to Holyhead harbour, 'during a tremendous gale from NW, and drove upon the rocks at S.E. part of the Bay, where in a few minutes she went to pieces, and all on board, including a pilot belonging to this place, drowned' – and next day at Holyhead were washed ashore 'a great quantity of goods . . . plain and printed cottons, umbrellas, sail canvas', bales, and butter, of which about 150 firkins were saved. Often enough the reports record the helplessness of the watchers ashore: 'a large ship is driven among the rocks, and no boat can venture to her assistance'; others are lost within sight of harbour: 'this day at noone, a Brig with yellow sides, no head, main boom painted green, of about 140 tons, and appeared rather deeply laden, was observed between the North and South Stack, close under the Head, when a heavy squall laid her down on her beam ends. She remained in that position about 20 minutes, and then disappeared with all on board.'[26] The number of vessels run down at night was increasing: the *Margaretta* of Waterford run down off Point Lynas by the *Brothers*, inward bound for Liverpool from Lima early in 1828, was but one example of many. The *Cambrian Cutter*, owned by Amlwch merchants, and plying regularly between Liverpool and Amlwch, run down in the Mersey by a steamer, the *Antelope*, a few years later, was a similar case.[27]

It was a clear, starlit night, crisp with cold, a few days before Christmas 1836, when the *Cambrian Cutter* dropped down the Mersey a little after midnight with a cargo of general goods, coal and flour for Amlwch, Captain John Williams was at the helm, Owen Williams, the mate, who stated in evidence that he had spent the last thirteen years sailing between Liverpool and north Wales, was up for'ard keeping a look out, with William Crow, the ship's boy. When Owen Williams called out that he could see a steamer half a mile ahead, the boy was ordered to display the ship's lantern; he had it by his side, ready lit by 'one of the female passengers', and immediately hoisted it, making it fast to the forestay with a piece of rope. Crew and passengers of the *Cambrian Cutter* later swore that the steamer kept coming towards them although they had seen her over half a mile away, and one after another stated they were 'certain no man could have been on the look out in the steamer', or they would have seen the *Cambrian Cutter*'s light and heard their shouts. The steamer, the *Antelope*, was stemming the tide, coming up slowly, and all aboard the Amlwch vessel thought she was bound to alter course. On passage aboard the *Antelope*, a seaman, William Dixon, survivor of a Lancaster vessel lost near Wexford, was sitting 'on the Paddle Box with his back towards the vessel's head' near the 'plank which is fixed between the paddle boxes to enable the crew to pass from one side to another over the cattle'. Dixon testified that there was no one for'ard of where he sat, and alleged that even when the *Cambrian Cutter* had been seen, there was a fatal delay whilst the *Antelope*'s engineers, who had both rushed on deck when they heard shouts, went down below again to stop the engines. The smack was struck 'a little abaft the main rigging on the starboard quarter', and started sinking immediately the steamer's engines went astern; the master of the *Cambrian Cutter* swung himself aboard the steamer by grabbing the cable chains, whilst the mate, boy, and two passengers clambered aboard by the stern rigging. Owen Williams, the mate, went back aboard the smack to rescue a female passenger who had remained rooted in the cabin, and succeeded in getting her into the ship's boat just before the *Cambrian Cutter* sank. Williams and the young woman drifted helplessly seawards for about an hour before they were rescued by the *Antelope*'s crew. No lives were lost in this incident, but it may be taken as an example of an increasingly common occurrence with claim and counter-claim between the Websters of Amlwch, owners of the *Cambrian Cutter*, and the Glasgow and Belfast Steamship Company, owners of the *Antelope*. Captain Williams stated in evidence that he had been at the helm all the time since leaving Salthouse Dock, apart 'from five minutes when he put on his Great Coat abreast of George's Dock', whilst a passenger aboard the *Antelope* testified that her master was down below in his cabin and was not seen until after the collision had already taken place. For his part, the master of the *Antelope* swore the *Cambrian Cutter* had no business to be in that position and should have altered course to starboard, even though it was the 'practice for a steamer to give way to a small vessel'. Those aboard the *Cambrian Cutter* were fortunate it was a fine night. Throughout the century collisions feature in the lists of wrecks, often with the dismal comment 'run down and sunk by an unknown steamer'.

In view of the increasing number of casualties on the Anglesey coast in the 1820s, Frances Williams persuaded her husband to write to George Palmer, the Essex designer of lifeboats who had been a Commander in the service of the East India Company. Palmer's first lifeboat was adopted by the National Institution in 1828, and it speaks much for the Williamses that they immediately saw its relevance to the Anglesey situation. James Williams' letter must have been a good one. His letter was received on 12 April, on 30 May a boat was ordered, and on 3 November 1828 James Williams reported her safe arrival at Cemlyn, the first Anglesey lifeboat.[28] But this was not enough for Frances Williams and her husband. In the words of James Sparrow of Holyhead, who became first secretary of the Anglesey Association: 'it now became evident to Mrs Williams that the services of a lifeboat could not be availed of at any great distance from the point where stationed, and as all parts of the coast of Anglesey, except the Menai Strait, are exposed and dangerous, it was clearly manifest to her that much more had to be done.'[29] Thus in December 1828, a meeting was held in the Grand Jury Room at Beaumaris and the Anglesey Association for the Preservation of Life from Shipwreck came into existence. At a further meeting at Mona in January 1829 a committee was elected with James Williams as treasurer and James Sparrow, of H.M. Customs at Holyhead, as secretary; the other members came from prominent Anglesey families, Williams Bulkeley, Meyrick, Colonel James Hughes, of Llysdulas, veteran of the Peninsular War, who in 1824 had erected a tower 'as a beacon – or place of refuge – to the shipwrecked' on the rocky islet at the entrance to Dulas Bay; experienced mariners like Captain Skinner, R.N., and Captain Goddard, Post Office Packet agent at Holyhead and owner or part-owner of a number of coastal vessels, together with members of the Beaumaris Book Society who had strong maritime and naval interests.[30] To place the Anglesey lifeboat movement of the 1820s and 1830s in its right perspective, it is necessary to recognize that many of those involved were people described in the other chapters dealing with the nineteenth-century – there were shipbuilders like McVeagh of Holyhead, investors in coastal shipping, and men who had family links with the growing naval interest in the county. The activities of the lifeboats and their supporters were reported in much detail in the local press, which, in turn, reflected the interests of the local gentry. In true early Victorian style, they were great believers in improvement and progress, and much attracted by scientific gadgetry.[31]

It was James and Frances Williams who acted as catalysts in the case of the lifeboat movement. The boat which James Williams had received from the National Institution as the result of his personal representations was a six-oared lifeboat, 26¼' x 6' x 2½', slightly smaller than the standard Palmer Boat. In common with the others designed by George Palmer, she had two lugsails, could be steered with a scull or rudder as the occasion required, and was 'built as a whale boat, sharp at both ends, fuller at the bow than at the stern, light in weight for easy transport, with specially designed buoyancy cases, sufficient to bear the weight of up to thirty persons'.[32] Once the Anglesey Association was formed, they took over the responsibility for the Cemlyn boat from James Williams, and ordered two further lifeboats, the contract for them going to Henry McVeagh, the Holyhead shipbuilder. The two Holyhead boats were

(1.)—MR. PALMER'S LIFE-BOAT.

A PLAN for fitting all Boats, so that they may be made secure as Life-boats, at the shortest notice : *George Palmer*, Esq. late Commander in the service of the Honourable East India Company.

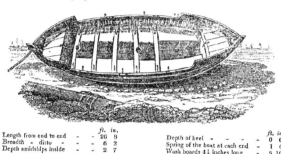

	ft. in.				ft. in.
Length from end to end -	- 26 8	Depth of keel - - -	-	-	0 6
Breadth - ditto -	- 6 2	Spring of the boat at each end	-	1 6
Depth amidships inside -	- 2 7	Wash boards 4½ inches long	-	5 10

built to the Palmer design, but one of them was a bigger boat, 32'6" x 6'6" x 2'7". James Williams, James Sparrow and Captain Goddard supervised the building of these Holyhead boats, and in October 1829 the larger boat 'gave every satisfaction under oars and sail' in a NNE gale, supporting 31 people when filled to her thwarts at her trials, which were critically watched by 'a full muster of the Committee'.[33] By 1830 the Anglesey Association had three lifeboats on station, at Cemlyn, Holyhead and Rhoscolyn; Captain Manby's rocket apparatus, originally designed in 1808, was provided at Amlwch, Cemlyn and Holyhead to rescue crews from the rigging of stranded vessels close to the shore.[34] Another Palmer designed boat was placed on the Penmon station in January 1831.

The next few years were busy for James Williams. In 1833 he took over as secretary of the local Association, since James Sparrow, the Customs officer, had been appointed to a post away from the Island. These years had proved to be disastrously stormy years for coastal shipping, over fifty vessels being lost or in distress off Anglesey in 1833 alone. Many of them were coasters, such as the *Jane and Ann*, from Mostyn to Caernarvon, lost with all hands on the

Lavan Sands, the *Flora*, from Liverpool to Wexford, 'struck on Dulas Rock', the *Swift*, from Strangford to Liverpool, lost with all hands on the Dutchman's Bank; others were bound for or from Liverpool for New York, Newfoundland, Montreal.[35] After repairs, some were able to continue their voyages. James Williams, in his 1834 report, sensibly pointed out that not only were the lifeboats rescuing lives, but were also the means of putting pilots aboard ships seeking shelter in treacherous and sometimes unfamiliar waters; in just two days, he said, in the Menai Strait area, the Penmon boat was instrumental in bringing 1,716 tons of shipping and 120 crew members 'into safety, which could not otherwise have been obtained'.[36] The Anglesey lifeboats, now familiar and welcome sights to mariners, with their lugsails and painted black and white bands on the outside and red inside, were each fitted with James Williams' invention, the 'Messenger Lifebuoy', 'strongly recommended by that veteran unrivalled in saving life from shipwreck, Sir William Hillary, and by Captain Denham, R.N., Marine Surveyor and superintendent of lifeboats at Liverpool'.[37]

James Williams was no back-room academic, no 'boffin'. His part in actual rescue operations was quite outstanding. Two examples must suffice. On 7 March 1835 the smack *Active* of Belfast, driven from her anchors in Ramsey Bay, attempted to enter Cemais, but 'grounded a long way from shore, every wave making a complete breach over her'. All attempts at launching boats to go to her assistance failed, but James Williams, who had ridden over from Llanfair-yng-Nghornwy as soon as he had news of the *Active*, took charge of the rescue operations, and swam his horse out to a position where he could throw a grapnel into the bowsprit shrouds of the stranded vessel. With a line secured to the *Active*, a boat was then hauled out to her, and the crew of five were found huddled in the cabin, exhausted and too weak to move without assistance. Williams' own account is typically modest.[38] Later in the year when the ship *Sarah* from Liverpool to Demerara was driven into Caernarvon Bay and on to the rocks near Trecastell, two miles west of Aberffraw, Williams' report simply states that he 'happened to be in the neighbourhood'. It was fortunate for the crew of the *Sarah* that he was, for he took charge of the rescue work, and under his directions 'a line was got from the masthead to the cliffs, whereby fourteen men were safely landed, the vessel going to pieces a few minutes after the last man had reached the shore'. Frances Williams may have been an eye-witness of the wreck of the *Sarah*; she had made many sketches and paintings of vessels in fair weather and foul, but this was her first attempt[39] at recording visually an actual rescue and no doubt, its painting gave rise to much discussion regarding the accuracy of details in the Williams rectory at Llanfair-yng-Nghornwy.

The evening before the *Sarah* rescue, at dusk on 10 September 1835, in the same gale, the American ship *Plutarch*, from New Orleans to Liverpool, under bare poles, had come to an anchor about half a mile from Holyhead Pier. It was apparent to the watchers ashore that in such a gale she would soon be driven to her destruction, but the sea was running so high that it was very doubtful whether a boat could reach the *Plutarch*. After two attempts, and three hours of toiling in the violent gale, Captain William Owen of the brig *Stanley* of Holyhead, with a crew of volunteers, reached the *Plutarch* and rescued all eleven survivors of her crew.[40] James Williams, as secretary of the Association, communicated the details of the *Plutarch* rescue in his report, stating that the Anglesey Committee felt justified in stating that seldom had 'a more gallant act' been achieved, and Captain William Owen was awarded the Gold Medal of the National Institution. At the same Awards Sub-committee in London, it was decided to award the Gold Medal to James Williams for his part in the *Active* and *Sarah* rescues, so that the first Gold Medals that came to Anglesey were both awarded on the same day. As James Williams' medal was for his role in the *Active* rescue in the previous March, as well as for the September rescues, it can be truthfully said that he was the first Anglesey Gold Medallist.[41]

Between 1829 and 1856, when the Anglesey Association became part of the Royal National Lifeboat Institution, over four hundred lives were saved by the Anglesey lifeboats,[42] their full story has been told elsewhere.[43] Frances Williams died in the last year of the Association which she had done so much to support, on 25 October 1856. Apart from her efforts in raising funds for the Association, she had shown considerable bravery herself, and despite ill-health in her later years, it was her courage which her contemporaries remembered. They recalled incidents such as that when a signal was made at the Skerries that one of the light-keepers was ill and medical assistance was required. A northerly gale made it difficult for a boat from Holyhead to attempt the passage, but 'although a very heavy broken sea was running at the time, as the lifeboat from Cemlyn could fetch the Skerries on a tack', Frances Williams immediately went out with her husband in the lifeboat, 'taking with her her medicine chest, and afforded the poor man the aid he required'.[44] Her son, Owen Lloyd Williams, who had graduated at Jesus College, Oxford, in 1851 and was ordained in 1852, a young curate at Rhoscolyn, went out in the Rhoscolyn lifeboat soon after he arrived there, and in 1854 it was Owen Lloyd Williams who commanded the Cemlyn lifeboat when the iron screw steamer, *Olinda*, bound from Liverpool to Brazil, ran ashore in darkness during a north-west gale, inside the Harry Furlong rocks. The previous year he had taken the Cemlyn boat to rescue five of the crew of a Salcombe schooner in Holyhead Bay, and when he moved to a living in South Caernarvonshire a few years later he became one of that county's leading lifeboatmen.[45]

James Williams himself remained very active in the work of the lifeboat service throughout the years that he served as secretary of the Anglesey Association. He rode his horses many miles visiting the lifeboats at their remote stations on the island. A fifth lifeboat had been obtained and a station established at Llanddwyn in 1840, no doubt in consequence of the very large number of wrecks and loss of life in Caernarvon Bay in 1833-34. Between 1825 and 1840 the reports to Lloyd's indicate that there were eighty-six casualties in the Caernarvon Bay area, over sixty of them of a serious nature, and thirty-five resulting in total loss. There were ninety-six losses north and east of Holyhead during the same period, but the impression one gets from reading these reports is that, in addition to bad weather, many of the casualties were due to defective equipment and gear, the general unseaworthiness of many vessels, overloading and bad storage, and possibly cases of negligence.[46] At Llanddwyn (where a light was placed in 1845 to supplement the two whitewashed towers) the pilots who lived in the houses belonging to the Caernarvon Harbour Trust were paid an extra £5 per annum for manning the lifeboat when necessary, and four men from Newborough were added to make up the complement of the new boat in 1840. In the pilot's log-book, in addition to details of weather conditions, and entries relating to vessels like the *Hindoo*, and later the Davies North American ships, which were piloted across the Bar, there are James Williams' reports on his visits to Llanddwyn. In July 1843 his report reads: 'visited the station, and found that the Lifeboat required painting inside and out, and the tin cases to be recoated with India Rubber composition. Pilots all at their stations and everything in good order.'[47] On another occasion he was not so pleased, 'found boat house lumbered with Tar Barrel and other things, Laniards . . . Pins all out of order, . . . grommets gone . . . no bridle for Boat carriage, pilots all absent'.[48] The pilots themselves found their lot a thankless one; in a November storm they put out in search of a schooner off Malltraeth with all her sails carried away, and their feelings are eloquently summed up in their report: 'we poole back and fored till after 3 o'clock in the morning, cant find the ship on count the ship wont anser our lights.'[49] Early in January 1845 James Williams received a letter from Mr Jackson, the Caernarvon Harbour Trust surveyor, who was in charge of the Llanddwyn lifeboat, reporting the sad loss of the *William Turner*, which had struck in the hours of darkness, and had not been seen by the pilots at Llanddwyn or anyone else until daybreak: 'as there is no one left to tell the tale, the particulars cannot be ascertained.'[50]

In 1848 it was decided to establish a sixth lifeboat station in Anglesey, and Lady Vivian offered to help the Association to purchase a lifeboat for Red Wharf. James Williams, after taking the advice of 'Pilots and other seafaring men', decided that this was not a suitable site for a station and 'the proferred aid was consequently withdrawn'. Nothing daunted, Williams continued to stress the need for a lifeboat between Cemais and Red Wharf, and urged that a boat should be placed at Moelfre, where he recognized 'an unlimited supply of first rate boatmen offered great facilities'. When a new boat was obtained for Penmon in 1858, therefore, the older boat was transferred to Moelfre, where, Williams was pleased to report, 'an excellent Boathouse was built by the late Lord Dinorben'.[51] In 1854, a new boat built at Holyhead was sent to the Moelfre Station, and this is the boat illustrated at the head of Williams' 1846-54 report, and probably the work of Frances Williams not long before her death. James Williams' faith in the 'first rate boatmen' of Moelfre has been amply justified in the last hundred and twenty-four years.

The provision of lifeboats was one way of saving lives; navigational aids, strategically placed, were fundamental. Beacons placed by Trinity House on West Mouse in 1810, Rhoscolyn in 1820, the lighthouse at Penmon in 1834, with a light, 'stationary and of red colour' in 1838, and the Llanddwyn light in 1846, went some way to meet the needs of mariners, supplementing the lights at Point Lynas, the Skerries, Amlwch and South Stack. In 1842 a beacon was placed on the 'Harry Furlong' rock, on which twenty-six vessels were said to have been lost in the previous eighteen years. It was James Williams who had persuaded Trinity House of the need for the beacon, which was built in the shape of a tower, twenty-two feet above the rock, 'and twelve feet above high water spring tides', and on top there was 'a cage or Crow's Nest capable of affording temporary refuge to 8 or 10 persons'.[52] There were other ways in which James Williams encouraged people ashore to help seamen; here, again, one example must suffice. In January 1846 the *Alhambra*, bound from Dublin to Cadiz, was driven by gales into Caernarvon Bay and was standing in dangerously to the Anglesey shore. A twenty-year-old farmer's son, Owen Jones of Cerrig yr Adar, Rhoscolyn, seeing the danger, ran to a nearby promontory and attempted to signal to those on board to warn them of the dangers from off-shore rocks. Failing to attract their attention, and realising there was no time to launch a boat, even if it were possible in the high seas then running, he plunged into the water fully clothed and swam to a small islet off-shore. Scrambling up the west rocks, he waved his jacket to attract the attention of the crew of the *Alhambra*. According to the local press account: 'Here his presence of mind was a remarkable as his intrepidity . . . The people on board having acknowledged that they saw him, he instantly dropped both arms in a manner that was intelligible to them, when the ship instantly rounded to and dropped her anchor, and was in comparative safety.' When the weather moderated, the *Alhambra* was beached with the assistance of the Rhoscolyn lifeboat, and then taken to Holyhead for repairs. James Williams, enthusiastic about Owen Jones' 'extraordinary act of gallantry', was quick to point out that the *North Wales Chronicle*'s account was mistaken when it stated that Jones had swum 60 to 80 yards to the islet; 'The Ordnance Survey Map makes it 110 yards. In such a sea as must have been running . . . it exhibited most extraordinary nerve and promptitude, and there can be no doubt that he was the means of saving ship and crew.' Williams warmly associated himself with the newspaper's project to open an award fund for Owen Jones, and added, quite typically, 'I am planning the means of effecting a communication with the island in similar cases of emergency. You will find it in the Ordnance Map under the name of Ynys Traws.'[53]

When the Mona Mine Company's *Marchioness of Anglesey* drove ashore at Llysdulas on a dark Friday night in April 1818, Captain Evan Hughes of Amlwch, most of his crew and passengers, and a considerable quantity of miscellaneous goods for Amlwch were lost.[54] It was alleged that there had been much plunder of goods before James Treweek, manager of the Mona Mine, arrived on the scene, and it is likely that Anglesey people throughout the century occasionally found salvage from wrecks highly profitable. Despite the earlier notoriety of 'lladron creigia Crigyll', there is little or no evidence of deliberate wrecking; on the contrary, there were signs of a growing awareness of the responsibility of those ashore towards the victims of shipwreck. In December 1847, the same page of the *North Wales Chronicle*, reporting violent storms along the coast, contained two contrasting accounts.[55] When the *Archduke Paladino*, laden with Indian corn, from Constantinople to Dublin, 'struck upon the sands in the bight of the day, close under the village of Llandudno', the local inhabitants were accused of doing little to save the lives of the crew, but a great deal of plundering, 'all work seems to be at a standstill, men, women and children have been fully engaged in robbing the vessel'. The Liverpool ship *Frankfield*, outward bound for Cape Horn, was wrecked on the Anglesey shore in the same storm; in contrast to their Caernarvonshire neighbours, 'scores of the good people of Cemaes were immediately on the beach . . . the survivors were immediately conducted to Ty'n-y-Llan where they continued to receive every attention and kindness from Mr Morris Owen and family'. No doubt attitudes were influenced by the nature of the shipwrecked cargoes; a few years earlier, when the *Adelaide* was wrecked on Ynys Wellt, Cymyran Bay, the 'two hundred puncheons of brandy' washed ashore soon disappeared, and many good Anglesey folk were 'conveyed back to their dwellings in an insensible state in carts and on planks'. The advocates of temperance had eagerly bought a pamphlet published at Llannerch-y-medd in the 1830s following the loss of the brig *Brown* of Whitehaven in Llanrhuddlad Bay. On 8 August 1829, about 3 o'clock on a fine afternoon, the *Brown* had sailed from Dublin bound for Liverpool with a cargo of 50 cows, 39 sheep, 50 pigs, a crew of six, the wife of the Mate, and ten passengers. With much shaking of heads, Anglesey people read the story of the voyage: 'Alas, instead of being thankful to God for fine weather, the seamen gave sacrifice to Satan in their favourite drink, Whisky,' and with only an inexperienced youth on watch had found themselves in thick fog off the Anglesey coast with only a vague idea of their position. Shortly after two o'clock in the morning they struck a rock in Llanrhuddlad Bay. To add to the scandalised pamphleteer's horror, local people had flocked to the scene of the wreck at daybreak, some to help but many more to steal everything in sight, encouraging their children to do likewise, and this on the Sabbath morning. Alas for the church and chapel services that morning.[56]

It was in this same month that the Anglesey Association for the Preservation of Life from Shipwreck published its first report with accounts of rescue services to the brigs *Harlequin* and *Fame* off Holyhead, the rescue by two Crigyll boatmen of the master of the *Daly and Ann* near Trecastell, and the crew of the sloop *Alexander* on the Lavan Sands rescued by Beaumaris pilots. As early as the 1840s there were professional attempts at salvage; the 'Brothers Jones, divers, of Hirael', were reported to have successfully raised a number of vessels in 1845, 1846 and 1848, including the *Cymro* and the *Cymraes*, smacks which had been carrying stone from Moelfre to the Britannia Tubular Bridge and had been wrecked off Penmon.[57] Another Bangor diver named Edwards was employed on the *William Turner* wreck, and was reported to have raised anchors, chain, copper bolts and a gun.[58]

Following the death of his wife and the transfer of responsibility for the lifeboat to the Royal National Lifeboat Institution, James Williams continued his work for lifeboats until his own death in 1872. It is important to remember that lifeboats were far from being his only interests. Professor R. T. Jenkins described him aptly as 'a squarson of the old school, a justice of the peace, very well off and highly respected'.[59] A stern but very fair magistrate, he was deeply involved in many aspects of the life of the island; a keen member of the Anglesey Agricultural Society, he is said to have been the first to introduce iron ploughs to Anglesey.[60] An enthusiastic supporter of the National Eisteddfod, which he rarely failed to attend, Williams was anxious to improve standards of education in Anglesey in his capacity as Diocesan Inspector of Schools; at Amlwch, for example, he commented in 1853 on the methods of a teacher who belonged to 'bye-gone days before the introduction of modern aids and improvements in the art of teaching'.[61] He himself was regarded as a very successful lecturer both in English and Welsh; in 1854 a correspondent in the *North Wales Chronicle* described Williams' lectures: 'I have myself heard the Rev. Gentleman lecture on Geology in Welsh, and if it is praise to a Lecturer to be familiar and perspicuous, without a tinge of vulgarity, – to give utterance to language pure and classical, without a shadow of pedantry – in the opinion of all who heard him, he had earned that praise.'[62] It was the time of the Crimean War, and not surprisingly, in view of his own interests and connections, Williams had been angered by the violent opposition to the war in the Welsh radical newspaper, *Yr Amserau*. Williams' reaction was typically vigorous; he held a series of meetings in National Schools in the villages of Anglesey where he lectured in Welsh to explain the 'actual facts, incidents and operations of the present war'. Whatever one may have thought of the content of his lectures, it was apparent that they attracted attention, not least for his methods of presentation. At Llanfechell National School, for example, his 'lucid and forcible lecture' dealt with many aspects of the war, the battles of Alma and Inkerman, and the Siege of Sebastopol, 'illustrated by various plans and drawings, exhibiting much artistic skill, and called forth the greatest admiration'. For good measure, for the benefit of this Welsh audience in a village schoolroom so far removed from the real horror of the Crimean campaigns: 'A model of a mortar, throwing a ball at an elevation of 45 degrees, gave infinite delight to the juvenile part of the audience; while a red shell and fuse, and the mode of propelling and exploding it at various distances, seemed greatly to interest the adults. But what seemed to be the most successful part of all was sections of redoubts and trenches, and shewing on the blackboard how the parallels were advanced by zig-zag approaches up to the walls of the citadel.'[63] There is little doubt that James Williams used the same lecturing techniques and visual aids, some no doubt provided and drawn by Frances Williams, to popularise and raise funds for the lifeboat movement.

A notable contribution to Welsh life was James Williams' encouragement of a young teacher at the British school in Rhosybol, John Rhys. It was James Williams who paved the way for Rhys to go to Oxford and thus embark upon his distinguished career as Celtic scholar, philologist, Principal of Jesus College, Oxford, 1895 to 1915, and a leading member in many educational commissions relating to Wales.[64] Another who benefited from the friendship of the Williams family was that prolific Welsh writer of the nineteenth-century, R. J. Pryse (Gweirydd ap Rhys), the self-educated weaver of Llanrhuddlad. In 1830 Frances Williams discovered Pryse's talent as a weaver of herringbone patterns, and ordered gowns, shawls, aprons, waistcoats from him, making his work fashionable on the Island, particularly after the Princess Victoria was presented with a specially woven mantle by Pryse at the time of the Beaumaris Eisteddfod in 1832.[65] Unorthodox in his own religious beliefs, Pryse agreed in his early years to assist in the formation of a musical society based at the Llanfair-yng-Nghornwy Church out of respect for the Williams family.[66] Inevitably, Williams himself shared many of the views and attitudes of the landed class to which he belonged, but both he and his wife had respect for talented individuals, however much their background and their religious and political views differed from their own. Although only one of a rich variety of interests, the Williamses' work for the lifeboats was part of a genuine desire to improve the conditions of life in mid nineteenth-century Anglesey.

Owen Lloyd Williams, their son, eventually returned to Anglesey in 1889 after thirty years as Rector of Bodfean in South Caernarvonshire. His gallantry on many occasions in the Lleyn lifeboats had been acknowledged by the Royal National Lifeboat Institution's silver medal and clasp together with silver mounted binoculars, and a gold watch presented by Welsh mariners, inscribed 'anrheg gan forwyr Cymreig fel mynegiad o'n hedmygedd ohono am ei ymdrech a'i ddewrder mewn achub bywydau'.[67] It was largely due to his efforts that lifeboat stations were established at Portin-llaen in

1864 and at Abersoch in 1869.[68] He continued to give active support to the Anglesey lifeboats on his return to the island as rector of Llanrhuddlad, and in 1907, when there was talk of not replacing the old lifeboat at Cemlyn, vigorous representations were made, 'more particularly by that veteran in lifeboat service, the Rev. Chancellor O. W. Williams, with the result that another lifeboat has been placed upon the station'.[69] One of his letters of that time has survived; it was to Charles Dibdin, Secretary of the Royal National Lifeboat Institution. Reluctantly acknowledging that he could not deny that the coxswain of the Cemlyn lifeboat was getting older, Williams declares that he himself thought 'he is good for many years,', adding that the coxswain was younger than he, Williams, was. At eighty years of age the old Chancellor wrote, 'I cannot help feeling I should like much to go out on service if there was a chance of rescuing anyone'.[70] The family of Frances Williams of Llanfair-yng-Nghornwy served the lifeboats of Anglesey well.

Three years after Frances Williams' death, the disastrous wreck of the *Royal Charter* provided a powerful illustration of the might of the sea on the coast of Anglesey. The story of the *Royal Charter* has been told many times:[71] as this book is being written, yet another group of divers are groping their way in the dark waters, seeking, and finding, what remains of the best known wreck of the century. The 'Royal Charter gale' was unusual in its ferocity; the loss of life in one ship of over four hundred and fifty men, women and children, and its golden cargo, all drew attention to the little village of Moelfre. But as some seamen were quick to point out, the isolated incidents of the wreck of the *Pomona*, earlier in the year on the Irish coast, with a loss of nearly four hundred lives, and that of the *Royal Charter*, distorted the pattern and diverted attention from one of the gravest features of shipping losses in mid nineteenth-century Britain. The wreck of one large passenger ship caused greater loss of life than a hundred casualties in colliers and small ships, but the increasing number of small vessels wrecked indicated that there was need for an investigation into the reasons for so many losses. The 1843 report on shipwrecks had heard evidence regarding the neglect and incompetence of masters, 'not attending sufficiently to the position of the ship, to heaving the lead, to taking all those precautions, in short, which ought to be taken by a good seaman anxious for the safety of his ship and knowing how to take care of her'.[72] They had also heard of the losses from the want of harbours of refuge to which vessels could run in adverse weather. But in the year 1859, of 1,645 lives lost, 926 had been lost in three fine ships: the '*Royal Charter* was lost just after passing Holyhead, the *Pomona* near Wexford, and the *Blervie Castle* in the English Channel, all of them under circumstances in which no Harbour of Refuge which has ever been suggested could have been of the slightest use'.[73] In a memorandum prepared by the Board of Trade in 1861 it was emphasised that in 1860, a 'year almost unprecedented for constant bad weather', only a third of the number of lives lost in the previous year perished; there were actually many more casualties, over 300 more than the average for the previous years. In 1860, unlike 1859, they were lost in ones and twos in small ships.

In normal weather conditions, well-found, properly loaded and well-manned ships naturally preferred to seek safety by standing out to sea, but there were many vessels which merited the scathing condemnation of Captain Bedford in his evidence to the Harbour of Refuge Commissions of 1858-9: 'many owners cannot afford to repair their vessels properly, and they are thus kept running too long, though unseaworthy . . . they are mostly undermanned.'[74] Captain Bedford was thinking particularly of the East Coast colliers, but his comments were also applicable to the West Coasts: 'An "old basket" is a common expression for their vessels, and a very significant one too, for pumping seems to be their chief employment.'[75] To such vessels certainly the new harbour of refuge at Holyhead was a great mercy, but it was being increasingly used by a wide range of vessels large and small, sound and unsound, new and old; in 1861 3,518 vessels found shelter in the harbour and roadstead of Holyhead, in 1862, 3,595, and in 1863 3,813 vessels.[76] There were still energetic and vociferous supporters of the development of Portin-llaen as an alternative harbour and point of departure for Ireland in the 1860s,[77] and in 1865 a list was prepared to show how many casualties in Caernarvon Bay might have been avoided had there been a harbour of refuge at Portin-llaen.[78] Between 1829 and 1863 it was estimated that ninety-five vessels which became total losses, and a further one hundred and thirteen vessels which were stranded but subsequently got off, might have been saved. The question was an academic one, as too much money had already been invested in the Holyhead Harbour development for Portin-llaen to replace Holyhead, but the number of vessels involved gives some indication of the casualties in the Caernarvon Bay area, many of them on the west coast of Anglesey.

Since 1847 Holyhead had seen the building of the massive break-water designed by J. M. Rendel, one of those engineers whom, as Asa Briggs has suggested, the mid-Victorians chose as their folk heroes.[79] The work, which was to take until 1873 to complete and was to cost well over a million pounds (in addition to the lives of many workmen), was as much a source of pride in the wonders of mid nineteenth-century progress as Brunel's *Great Eastern* which visited and rode out the '*Royal Charter* gale' at Holyhead. In such conditions all the stone from Moelfre quarries and from Holyhead mountain which had gone into making the breakwater seemed puny when battered by the might of the sea, and even in the lee of Anglesey the 19,000-ton *Great Eastern* was hard put to survive.[80] There had been much criticism of Rendel's original design and in the event, the plans for the east breakwater were abandoned whilst the north breakwater had to be extended considerably until it was eventually one and a half miles long, affording shelter to over six hundred acres of water. Captain Norris Goddard, James Williams' friend in the lifeboat cause, was quoted by an opponent of Rendel's scheme as having said that the length of the breakwater 'in an east and west direction would afford much opportunity for strong winds from W.S.W. to N.W. to raise a short yet sharp sea at its entrance; a deep laden or crippled merchant vessel, under those winds, would experience great difficulty when seeking to enter'.[81] Captain John Askew, harbour master at Liverpool, was said to have serious disquiet at the possible consequence of a hundred or more vessels dragging in N.W. or N.E. winds, particularly as there were doubts regarding the sufficiency of the holding ground within the harbour of refuge. Rendel himself was accused of accepting too readily hearsay evidence from one or two captains, rather than investigating the nature of the foul rocky bottom within the harbour for himself. Rendel was much occupied with other schemes: the Birkenhead, Grimsby and Garston docks, another harbour of refuge at Portland, work in Genoa, Rio de Janeiro, and Hamburg, to name but a few, yet despite many criticisms, his harbours of refuge at Portland and Holyhead have been hailed as his greatest achievements.[82] Seven years after his death in 1857 and ten years before the breakwater was finally completed, in December 1863, a violent storm went some way to proving that there was some substance in the criticism of Rendel's original plans, but alongside this isolated incident should be placed the records of the many thousands of ships that sheltered securely in Rendel's harbour of refuge at Holyhead. The events of December 3rd, 1863, however, may be taken to illustrate the use the harbour was being put to in mid-century by vessels of many nations and may also serve to represent those agonizingly long hours of anxious anchor watches and checking bearings by hosts of masters concerned lest their vessels should be dragging their anchors whilst sheltering off Holyhead.[83]

André Tittevin, master of the 79-ton *Esperance* of Bayonne, had sailed from Liverpool with a cargo of sugar and earthenware for Nantes on the 30 November 1863, on a pleasant autumn day in a fine south-easterly breeze. The following day the wind, increasing all the time, had veered to the south-west, and a heavy sea was running, so Tittevin put into Holyhead, anchoring in the 'Refuge Harbour' with sixty fathoms of chain out on each of his two anchors. The weather deteriorated, and at seven o'clock in the morning of 3 December, Tittevin realised that the *Esperance* was dragging her anchors. In the darkness, with squalls of hurricane W.N.W. winds, he and his crew did all they could, 'bended the stream-hawser to each anchor, and the warp to the kedge', but still she dragged until she went aground at Penrhos Point. It was now past midday, and Tittevin and his four crew members took refuge in the mainmast rigging. The wind and cold was too much for the cabin boy and within the hour, he had fallen into the sea and was drowned. Another member of the crew was swept away three hours later, another died from exposure. At six o'clock the following morning the Holyhead lifeboat came alongside and rescued Tittevin and the other survivor.

They were fortunate. The *Elizabeth*, a North American-built wooden barque, had been bound for Halifax, Nova Scotia, with a cargo of general goods from Liverpool when she put into Holyhead and anchored in the new harbour because of the rapidly deteriorating weather on the 1st of December. At almost the same moment as Tittevin realised he was dragging at 7 a.m. on 3 December, the master of the *Elizabeth*, with 75 fathoms of cable on his starboard and 60 fathoms on his port anchor, realised that he too was dragging. He attempted to put sail on his vessel to try to make the old harbour, 'but the sails were split in setting'. At nine a.m. the *Elizabeth* struck a reef 'about two miles from land, on the east side of Holyhead Bay'; the master ordered that the fore and main rigging should be cut to allow the masts to go overboard, and was just congratulating himself that the vessel was making little or no water when the *Catherine of Cork*, a schooner, drove across the stern of the *Elizabeth*, lifting it, at which the *Elizabeth* began to fill with water. Their boats were smashed; some of the crews of both vessels got ashore on an improvised raft and floating wreckage, but five were drowned. The brig *Westbourne* dragged her anchors and drove on to Penrhos rocks where her crew of nine took to the boats, which capsized and all were drowned.

As it became lighter that stormy December morning, more vessels were seen to be dragging their anchors; by 10 a.m. 'the wind in the N.W. blowing a hurricane' the 162 vessels which had been in the harbour, and the 57 in the roadstead the previous night, were nearly all in difficulties, but the majority avoided disaster. One of the hazards was being run foul by another vessel. This is what happened to the *Industrie*, 130 tons, bound for Ostend with a cargo of rock-salt from Liverpool; her anchors had held firm all day until she was run foul by a barque in the early evening. Compelled to slip his anchors, the Belgian master put sail on his vessel, but she drove on to the rocks at the South Pierhead, where the crew managed to scramble ashore. The *Climax* of Fowey, bound with coal from Runcorn to Plymouth, the *Rifleman*, bound for Antwerp with rock-salt from Runcorn, also collided; the *Pearl* of Fowey, with a cargo of rock-salt from Runcorn to Ipswich, run down by a Maltese barque, parted her chains and eventually struck on Penrhos rocks. Her master testified to the bravery of men ashore: 'five men (names unknown) came off in their boat . . . at great personal risk, saved the lives of himself and crew.' The brig *Hibernia* of Workington ran aground on a sandbank at Penrhos Point; the schooner *Aerial* of Caernarvon, the barque *Elizabeth Morrow* of Glasgow, bound for Old Calabar, West Africa, with a cargo of rum, general goods and tobacco (her crew were rescued the following day by the Holyhead lifeboat), the schooner *R.T.K.* of Fowey, the *Diamond* of Belfast, the *Palermo* of Workington (whose crew were rescued from the rigging by the boats of the *Diamond*) were other vessels that found themselves aground at Penrhos or Peniel.[84]

People ashore assisted the crew of the barque *Helen Campbell* of Nova Scotia to safety from the rocks near Trefadog; the crew of the *Confiance* of Liverpool having spent the night aground at Penrhos Point, were rescued by the Holyhead lifeboat on the 4th when the weather had moderated a little, whilst the crew of the *Harmony* of Drogheda scrambled ashore, all except one boy who was 'taken off about three o'clock a.m. upon the 4th December by the police'. The *Scottish Lass* of Belfast, a brigantine bound for Dublin with coal, ran aground at Peniel; her crew took to the rigging where one of them died from exposure, but the others were taken off by a boat from the shore, which must have been an act of great heroism and skill in the conditions that prevailed on the night of 3 December. The barque *Abbots Reading*, 421 tons, bound for Valparaiso from Liverpool with a cargo of salt and coal, had been running on bare poles but was leaking so badly that she 'squared away again' for Holyhead, where she ran foul of an Italian barque; enable her to ride out the gale, an expedient also employed by the master of the *Ernest Second* of Rostock. Other vessels were towed to safety by tugs,[85] but of the 219 ships in the harbour and roadstead another Italian, the barque *Regina Maria* of Genoa, had four anchors down but began to drag and her master cut her masts away to ? [*sic*] of Holyhead, and the additional 24 that arrived during the day of 3 December, four vessels were lost through dragging their anchors, with a loss of sixteen lives, four were compelled to cut away their masts, but lost no lives, three were lost and three damaged attempting to enter Holyhead harbour, with a loss of two lives. The Holyhead lifeboat had saved at least forty-four lives, and boats from ashore another dozen. Twenty-four hours in Holyhead Bay: twenty-four hours which not only demonstrated the willingness of those ashore to risk their lives in saving others from the sea, but also indicate the way in which Holyhead had now become a haven or refuge for ships of different nations, different rigs, different cargoes. So it remained throughout the century.

The Board of Trade Wreck Chart for 1863 gives an impression of

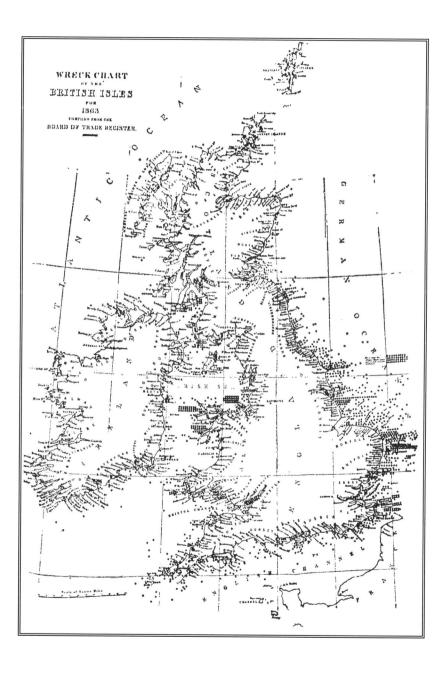

the toll of the sea; the distribution of wrecks reflects the busy traffic of certain sea areas, as well as the navigational hazards involved. It also indicates that wreck statistics were being more carefully compiled and that public concern was mounting 'that 1,000 ships and their cargoes are wrecked annually within the narrow limits of the United Kingdom . . . still more when we are told that not less than 1,000 lives are lost annually in these shipwrecks'.[86] Again, although the chart and the incidents at Holyhead described above are confined to only one year, 1863, they may be studied in the context of the other chapters in this book; vessels were wrecked on the Anglesey coast and Anglesey vessels were lost in many of the 'black spots' on the chart over the course of the years, as indicated incidentally on other pages. The Irish Sea claimed more than its share in the loss of life in the years 1859-1863, and even if one omits the large number involved in the *Royal Charter* wreck, the number of lives lost on the coast are high; in 1861, 234 out of a total of 721 lost on the British coast were lost between St David's Head and the Skerries and the Mull of Kintyre, and in 1863, 100 out of 330.[87] The wreck report for 1863 suggests that more than half the casualties happened when the wind was at force 8 or under 'when a ship, if properly found, manned, and navigated, would keep the sea and make her voyage in safety'.[88] This was not, however, the case with the wrecks on the Anglesey coast in 1863: the *Pamela Flood*, a barque with a cargo of cotton, oilcake and hides, foundered in January 12 miles ESE of Holyhead in what was described as 'a force 12 NNW hurricane', and the vessels lost on 3 December foundered in a force 12 NW and WNW hurricane. But there were cases of elderly vessels getting into difficulties: the schooner *Cambria*, well over fifty years old, lost her sails and one of her crew in a SW force 9 wind off the Skerries in 1860, and the *Sarah*, a 42-year-old sloop, foundered off Cemais on 17 December in the same year, and with her went the two members of her crew.

A glance through the careful records J. M. Stubbs and Emrys Jones of Amlwch have compiled to complement their underwater investigation of wreck sites on the Anglesey and Caernarvonshire coasts indicates the wide range of vessels involved. Stubbs has extracted records of about three hundred incidents between 1808 and 1863 from the files of the local newspapers, and another two hundred and fifty between 1863 and 1914. The wrecks occur, as one would expect, with monotonous regularity on certain sections of the Anglesey coast; Emrys Jones has notes of close on a hundred wrecks located in the Holyhead area, over forty near Amlwch and Point Lynas, a score or more in each of the Skerries, Menai Strait and Moelfre areas, with Cemlyn, Cemais, Rhoscolyn and Aberffraw not far behind. Gales were not the only hazard. The *Niagara*, a ship of New York, descried as 'one of the largest sailing vessels', with a cargo of cotton and 200 sewing machines, was wrecked on the rocks at Penrhosfeilw in dense fog in June 1875, and a month later, the *Abbotsford*, 'a steamer of the American line, 2554 tons' was wrecked at Wylfa Head again in a 'heavy fog'. The Gwynedd branch of the British Sub-Aqua Club, systematically investigating wreck sites, have found the remains of the S.S. *Missouri* wrecked on Craig Llwyd rocks near Porth Dafarch in 1886; recently they were engaged in a detailed survey of a vessel which might prove to be the *Tenby Castle*, wrecked off Porth Ruffydd on 17 December 1889, when the crew of a small boat put out in very heavy seas to rescue three survivors. What Stubbs, Jones, and many serious nautical archaeologists fear is the indiscriminate looting of these sites by clumsy 'treasure seekers', without a disciplined attitude towards methodical recording, men without a sense of history.

To see the appalling loss of life at sea in the nineteenth-century in its true perspective one must remember the high casualty rate of industry ashore, in factories and mines, and the harshness of the life of dockside workers and agricultural labourers; the grimness of conditions ashore for a large section of the working class goes some way to explain why men were willing to risk a life at sea. By the beginning of the twentieth-century, apart from isolated incidents, most of the Anglesey men who lost their lives at sea did so in the deep-sea trades, in the Atlantic, off Cape Horn, or in the Indian Ocean. The casualties for that same stretch of coast, from St David's Head and Carnsore Point to the Skerries, and from the Skerries to Fair Head and the Mull of Kintyre, which in 1863 had claimed a hundred lives, in the year ending June 1905 claimed thirty-seven, although over fifty vessels were lost there during the year.[89] Between 1895 and 1905, thirty-six vessels were reported stranded on the Lavan Sands, nineteen on the Platters Rocks in Holyhead Harbour, seven on the Skerries, two on the West Mouse rocks, two on the Middle Mouse, off Cemais, one on Maen Piscar off Rhoscolyn, and one on the Cippera Rock to the east of Holyhead.[90]

When the Lord Bishop of Bangor rose to make his maiden speech in the House of Lords in November 1906 in the debate on the Merchant Shipping Acts Amendment Bill, he began by stating that 'no-one could fill the office which I hold without taking the liveliest interest in these matters. In my diocese there is probably the largest amount of sea coast in any diocese in the United Kingdom, and at one time – thank God that time is now past – there were more wrecks on that coast than in any part of the kingdom'.[91] The Bishop attributed this welcome improvement in part to better training facilities for seamen, and paid tribute to the work carried out aboard the *Clio*, 'just in front of the windows of my house'.[92] Although he did not say so, the Bishop must have known that to generations of local boys, the *Clio* was a threat which irate parents hurled at them in cases of misbehaviour, the ultimate sanction for undisciplined boys. Later in his speech the Bishop alluded to changing attitudes towards seafaring in his diocese where fewer men were going to sea: 'Thirty years ago nearly every small farmer around the coast was also a good boatman. That is no longer the case, and we find that we have not the same multitude of people to draw from as we had before to man our lifeboats.' Whilst the seamen themselves might have been somewhat cynical about the way in which he expressed himself about life at sea, 'There is a certain poetry about their life which we all admire', the Bishop received support in the House for his plea that conditions aboard all types of ships should be improved so as to 'attract fresh recruits to the profession upon which, after all, depends not only the wealth but the very food and nourishment of our country'.

The stiffer requirements of the Merchant Shipping Acts and improved navigational aids made the sea a safer place in normal weather conditions. There were still wrecks which attracted much attention because they were well-known ships like the former China tea clipper, *Norman Court*, which had been wrecked in Cymyran Bay in 1883 when great gallantry was displayed by the crews of the Rhosneigr and Holyhead lifeboats, and many people ashore.[93] Another wreck whose story has been told so often that it has almost become part of folk-lore was that of the *Primrose Hill* off South

Stack;[94] at the time it attracted attention largely because of the allegations that, of the crew of thirty-four 'twelve were apprentices and six had not previously been to sea'.[95] The father of one of the lost apprentices succeeded in having questions raised in the House of Commons, but the Board of Trade, the owners, and everyone else seemed intent on stonewalling silence; having once got into the position she was in, it is hard to see what even the most experienced crew could have done in a fierce south-westerly gale off the South Stack and that bay known as Abraham's Bosom. Ashore in Holyhead shipwrecked mariners had been well looked after at the Stanley Sailors' Home which was opened in 1873; the annual report for 1905 stated that the 'Superintendent is always on the alert in times of storms and has fires, restoratives for every emergency'.[96] Mr Seal, the Superintendent, entered many familiar names of schooners in the Wreck Book; occasionally men brought to the Home for shelter after being taken from vessels dragging in strong gales were happily able to return aboard when the weather moderated.[97] For others, however, survivors of total wrecks, there were clothes and food before they were sent to their homes. Such a crew were the survivors of the *Mignone*, from Bayonne to Swansea, who had been overtaken by fog and subsequent gales, 'and saw nothing after leaving the Longships' in March 1899. There is a curiously evocative air about the entry in the Wreck Book: 'The French sailors expressed themselves very grateful and contented and begged the Englishmen present in the Reading Room of the Sailors Home to sing 'God Save the Queen' to them. The captain's body was washed ashore at noon on Wednesday and buried on Good Friday, 31 March, at Llanfaelog Churchyard.'[98]

The lifeboats which James and Frances Williams had done so much to establish saved 253 lives between 1828 and 1856, whilst 156 more were rescued by other means such as the rescue for which James Williams himself was awarded the Gold Medal. The Williamses' work is brought into perspective when one realizes that in 1849, out of a total of nineteen lifeboats stationed on the entire coasts of the United Kingdom, six were in Anglesey. By 1863 it was a very different picture, with 178 lifeboats on the coasts, but Anglesey still had twice as many boats as any other Welsh county. Henry Parry, himself a Portin-llaen lifeboatman who knew the coast well, has written a detailed account of the subsequent history of these lifeboats; how, for example, the Holyhead boats alone have saved over eleven hundred lives. The modest heroism of their crews spans the years from James Williams' days to our own; in that tradition was the gallant, skilful service of the Moelfre lifeboat in October 1927 under Second Coxswain William Roberts when they rescued the crew of the *Excel*, a tragic story told graphically by Captain Hugh Shaw, who, as master of the *Camborne*, was off the Skerries himself in that October hurricane.[99] A generation later, under Coxswain Richard Evans, the Moelfre lifeboat again gave magnificent service in the rescue of the crew of the *Hindlea* in October 1959, in much the same spot as the *Royal Charter* almost a hundred years to the day, and, in company with the Holyhead lifeboat, to the Greek motor vessel the *Nafsiporos* in December 1966.[100] Ashore, too, there were those who were willing to venture into raging seas, as James Williams had done at Cemais in 1835. One example must suffice. On a stormy morning in August 1941,[101] a strong S.W. gale, an aircraft crashed some way off the shore of Rhosneigr, and unhesitatingly, there went into the sea to rescue the Polish airman ordinary people running from their everyday tasks, young boys, the coastguard, the local policeman, soldiers, airmen, a merchant seaman home on leave, in a tragic but vain attempt in which eleven of the would-be rescuers lost their lives. The spirit of service to those in peril on the sea, which started with Frances Williams of Llanfair-yng-Nghornwy so long ago, is one of which Anglesey has reason to be proud.

Frances Williams's sketch of vessels sailing off Beaumaris, April 26, 1821.

[1]   The Humble Petition of 85 Gentlemen and Freeholders . . . of Chester,'
printed in Chetham Society's *Civil War Tracts*, 1909, 65.

[2]   *CSPD 1625-26*, 5-6.

[3]   *CSPD 1660-61*, 309.

[4]   Lewis Morris, *Plans of Harbours*, 1748, iv.

[5]   William Morris, *Plans of Harbours*, 1801.

[6]   Robert Dudley, *L'Arcano del Mare* (Florence, 1647), vi. 13.

[7]   Greenville Collins, *Great Britain's Coasting Pilot* (London, 1693).
Preface to the Reader.

[8]   M. Oppenheim (ed.), *The Naval Tracts of Sir William Monson*, iv, 31.

[9]   Collins noted that 'there are some ships that have lain wind bound at
Beaumaris bound for Virginia, and not daring to come out at Priestholme
have gone through the Swilly and so over Carnarvon Bar: but the rocks at
Swilly are dangerous, the passage narrow, and the Tydes very strong'.
Collins, *Coasting Pilot*, 15.

[10]   Fearon and Eyes, *Description of the Sea Coast of England*, 1736.

[11]   H. R. Davies, 'An Account of the Private Lighthouse of the Skerries',
TAAS, 1924; 1928. The light was probably erected in 1716, but the patent
was granted later: in the patent it is described as 'a Light House or Beacon,
with a Light or Lights therein continually burning in the night time, in or
upon the Island or Rock call'd Skerries lying in the Sea near Holyhead'. In
1748 Lewis Morris recommended that a light should be placed on
Priestholme: 'It would be of great service to the Northern Trade to direct
them in the Night into a safe Road if the Tower on Priestholme Island (the
Ruins of Seiriol Chapel) was converted into a Light-House'. Lewis Morris,
Plans of Harbours, Buoys and Roads in St George's and the Bristol Channels,
1748, 2.

[12]   PRO, SP, Chas. II, 369, 109, 11. Mathew Anderton to J. Williamson,
Chester, 31 March 1675. The writer added: 'A Wicklow vessel from
Beaumaris went as near the Isle as she durst and took in the 15 passengers
and 24 seamen and landed them on Sunday last at Beaumaris.' Dr P. N.
Davies, of the Department of Economic History, University of Liverpool,
kindly drew my attention to this document; Dr Davies is actively engaged in
an archaeological survey on the site of the wreck of the *Mary*.

[13]   *ML*, II, 158.

[14]   CRO. Poole Papers. 6500, 5212. September 1779.

[15]   CRO. Poole Papers. 6849, 6795. 3 September 1770.

[16]   CRO. Poole Papers. 6794. 99 boxes of oil were taken 'to the house of
Owen Morris of Ynys Wyddel'.

[17]   *ibid.*, 6288. Rowland Eames of Cefnamwlch to Richard Poole, 2 August
1776.

[18]   *ibid.*

[19]   *ibid.*, 6155. James Bradley to Poole, 21 December 1778.

[20]   UCNW Penrhos MSS, 1296, 1298.

[21]   *DWB* 1044.

[22] I am much indebted to Mr Kyffin Williams for allowing me to quote material from family papers in his possession in the account which follows.

[23] Kyffin Williams MSS, *Anglesey Branch of the RNLI 1906 Report*, 9-10.

[24] James Sparrow, *The Lifeboat*, 1857, quoted in *Anglesey Branch RNLI Report*, 1907.

[25] William Hillary, *Appeal to the British Nation* (London, 1825); an account of the formation and history of the Anglesey branch is given in H. R. Davies' articles in the Anglesey Branch Reports 1906-1913, and a brief summary in A. Eames, 'Frances Williams and the Anglesey Association for the Preservation of Life from Shipwreck', 1828-1857, *TAAS*, 1957, 20-25.

[26] UCNW Bangor MSS 3535. This list was compiled from the records of Lloyds from 20 January 1825 to 22 December 1840 for H. R. Davies when he was Hon. Sec. and Treasurer of the Anglesey Branch of the R.N.L.I. There are letters from and to H. R. Davies from the Secretary of Lloyds and the Marine Department of the Board of Trade 1909-1911; this is yet another illustration of the way in which Davies' wealth from the shipping industry was used to stimulate research into Anglesey's maritime history. Davies had the wealth to employ researchers to transcribe materials and to purchase rare books which he had handsomely bound, many of them are now housed in UCNW Library, Bangor.

[27] NLW Rumsey Williams MSS. Bundle of papers for counsel's advice re *Cambrian Cutter*.

[28] H. R. Davies. An Account of the History of the Anglesey Branch, *Anglesey Branch Report*, RNLI, 1907, 19.

[29] James Sparrow, *The Lifeboat*, 1857: *NWC*, December 15, 1856. Of the 17 Mayors of Beaumaris between 1814 and 1831, 9 were members of the Sparrow family. UCNW B + A MSS, iv, 319a.

[30] Captain Goddard was related by marriage to the Williams family: another master of the Holyhead packets, Captain Davies, was also a member of the Committee, as were the Rev. Hugh Wynne Jones, father of the naval Lieutenant Wynne Jones, another clergyman who was very active in the lifeboat service, and Thomas Williams, Beaumaris, a prominent member of the Beaumaris Book Society.

[31] James Williams himself was very interested in the technical development of lifeboats and rescue equipment, hence the 'Messenger Lifebuoy', *infra*.

[32] Appendix 16 to *Parl. Papers. First Report from the Selected Committee on Shipwreck*, August 1843.

[33] Davies, *Anglesey Branch Report*, RNLI, 1907, 20.

[34] Captain G. W. Manby first proposed his rocket apparatus in 1808; he published an account of his ideas in '*Practical Observations on the Preservation of Mariners from Stranded Vessels and the Prevention of Shipwreck*'. (Yarmouth, 1827.)

[35] UCNW Bangor MS 3535.

[36] James Williams, *Anglesey Association Report*, 1834.

[37] *ibid.* Denham's evidence to the 1843 Select Committee on Shipwreck

indicates how seriously he was concerned regarding the causes of shipwreck, *First Report on Shipwreck*, 1843, 82-95.

[38] James Williams, *Anglesey Branch RNLI Report, 1835.*

[39] Now in the possession of Kyffin Williams, Esq.

[40] James Williams, *Anglesey Branch RNLI Report, 1835.*

[41] Grahame Farr, who has made transcripts of the brief numbered case histories of rescue which appeared in the pre-1850 Reports of the RNLI, has kindly provided me with the following information: 'The *Active* rescue of 7.3.35 has been considered at an Awards Sub-Committee meeting on 29.7.35 and awards made to five men involved (case no. 481). At the next meeting, on 7.10.35, they considered the case of the *Plutarch* on 10.9.35 and awarded Captain Owen the Gold Medal (case no. 487). They also considered the case of the *Sarah* on 11.9.35, and rewarded the men involved (case no. 488). They then considered afresh both the *Active* and the *Sarah* and awarded the Rev. Williams the Gold Medal (case no. 490).' I am grateful to Mr Farr, who is Honorary Archivist to the Lifeboat Enthusiasts' Society, for his kindness, interest and encouragement.

[42] H. R. Davies, *Anglesey Branch RNLI Report 1908*, 47. Davies has a detailed list of services rendered by the Anglesey lifeboats, and also the rewards paid.

[43] H. R. Davies' accounts already referred to and Henry Parry, *Wreck and Rescue on the Coast of Wales*, I. *The Lifeboats of Cardigan Bay and Anglesey* (Truro, 1969).

[44] James Sparrow, first Secretary of the Anglesey Association in *The Lifeboat*, January 1857.

[45] Henry Parry, *Wreck and Rescue on the Coast of Wales*, 1, 84.

[46] H. R. Davies, *Anglesey RNLI Report 1910*, 19.

[47] Caernarvon Harbour Trust MSS, 2, Thursday, 27 July 1843.

[48] *ibid.*, 17 July 1844.

[49] *ibid.*, 19 November 1843. The pilots had first noted the schooner 'aper to be a stranger' at 4 p.m.; it must have been getting dark by the time they launched their boat, and in the N.W. to N.N.W. winds, searching for her for eleven hours or more must have been far from pleasant. The last they saw of the vessel was about five o'clock in the afternoon when she was obviously in distress.

[50] *ibid.*, 139, 99. On this occasion the *William Turner* had a cargo of guano aboard. The senior pilot at Llanddwyn had informed Mr Jackson that 'he was on the look out until dark and nothing was in sight – she must have struch early in the evening as the wreck was on shore at High water mark at daylight on Saturday morning'. Jackson reported to Williams that the *William Turner* 'was 488 tons register and must have had 16 or 18 hands on Board'. He was fairly certain that the lifeboat could have done little even if the *William Turner* had been seen. 'The destruction of the vessel must have been almost instantaneous as I perceived the Long Boats (one inside the other) capsized on the Beach, had they time they would certainly have taken

to them.'

[51] James Williams, *Anglesey Association Report 1846-1854*. Lord Dinorben was a member of the Hughes, Llys Dulas, family who had acquired their wealth from the Parys Mine, and would, therefore, be very well known to James Williams.

[52] H. R. Davies, *Anglesey Branch RNLI 1907 Report*. Davies discusses the origin of 'Harry Furlong' and notes that both Lewis Morris in the 1740s and Lieutenant Robinson in 1835 record it as 'Harry's Furlong' on their charts.

[53] CDH, January 24, 1846. James Williams' letter is dated 'Llanfairynghornwy January 22, 1846'.

[54] B. L. Jones, 'Llongddrylliad y Marchioness of Anglesey', *TAAS*, 1965, 42-43; UCNW, MM MSS 1342; *N.W. Gazette*, 16, 23 April 1818.

[55] *NWC*, 14 December 1847.

[56] *NWC*, 11 Feb. 1841; J. M. Stubbs, 'The Wreck of the *Stewart* revisited', Caernarvonshire Record Office *Bulletin*, 5, 34-5; UCNW Bangor MSS 19062.

[57] *NWC*, August 1848. Vessels were raised by them at Fishguard, 12 Jan. 1845, Ramsay July 1845, and off Puffin Island and Red Wharf in 1846. The *Cymro* and the *Cymraes*, which had foundered in August 1847, were raised in June and July 1848.

[58] I am indebted to J. M. Stubbs for this reference. Mr Stubbs and other members of the Gwynedd Sub-Aqua Club have located a number of wrecks on the north Wales coast, and both he and Mr Emrys Jones of Amlwch have generously discussed their findings with me. Mr Stubbs has traced references in the files of the local press to over 550 wrecks in the Gwynedd area between 1808 and 1914. He has written a brief account of the work of the Gwynedd branch of the British Sub-Aqua Club in *Bulletin 3, 1970*, of the Caernarvonshire Record Office, 21-3.

[59] *DWB*, 1044.

[60] E. A. Williams, *Hanes Môn yn y Bedwaredd Ganrif ar Bymtheg*, 125.

[61] UCNW MM MS 3388.

[62] *NWC*, 16 December 1854.

[63] *ibid.*, 9 December 1854.

[64] Sir John Rhys (1840-1915), a member of the Aberdare committee on education in Wales, 1881, and commissions relating to University education in Wales and Ireland, was a pioneer research worker in the field of Celtic and Welsh philology; according to Sir Ifor Williams in *DWB*, 'he rendered priceless service to learning, education, and culture, particularly in Wales'.

[65] UCNW Bangor MSS 1682, 726, *DWB*, 809 for article by Enid Pierce Roberts on Pryse, and also '*Detholion o Hunangofiant Gweirydd ap Rhys*' (Llandysul, 1949), 133-5.

[66] UCNW Bangor MSS 1683, 788.

[67] *Y Clorianydd*, October 1918. 'A gift from Welsh seamen as an expression of our admiration of his efforts and courage in saving lives.'

[68] *ibid.*

[69] *Anglesey RNLI Report*, 1912, 4.

[70] Undated letter in the possession of Kyffin Williams, Esq.

[71] Alexander McKee, *'The Golden Wreck'* (London, 1961) is the most recent and has a bibliography. R. R. Williams, 'Anglesey and the Loss of the Royal Charter', in *TAAS*, 1959, is a detailed study which has formed the basis for much that has been written subsequently. For 4 synoptic charts indicating barometric pressures at different hours during the *Royal Charter* Storm; *Parl. Papers*, 1864, LV, 190-197.

[72] *Parl. Papers, Minutes of evidence before the Select Committee on Shipwrecks*, 1843, 1-2. Evidence of Captain R. Fitzroy, R.N. He added, 'my opinion is decidedly that ships which are not struck by lightning, nor disabled by fire, nor any casualty which it is not within man's power to control, are lost upon known coasts by the mis-management of those in command of them'. Captain Fitzroy argued strongly that 'if barometers were put in charge of the coast guard at the principal stations round the coast, so placed as to allow anyone passing by to look at them . . . because no bad weather ever comes on our coasts without timely warning being given by the barometer'.

[73] *Parl. Papers*, LV, 1864, 454.

[74] *Parl. Papers*. Harbours of Refuge Commission, 1858-59, 1, 244. Evidence of Capt. Bedford, R.N. *Parl. Papers*, LV, 1864, 452.

[75] *ibid.*

[76] *Parl. Papers*, LV, 1864, 671. Return of vessels that have taken shelter in the Harbour and Roadstead of Holyhead, 1861, 1862, 1863.

[77] Dodd, *History of Caernarvonshire*, 266-268.

[78] *On the Desirability of an Harbour of Refuge being made on the West Coast of Wales at Porthdynllaen* (1865).

[79] Asa Briggs, *The Age of Improvement* (London, 1960), 395.

[80] McKee, *The Golden Wreck*, 43, 52-53.

[81] Charles W. Williams, *Remarks on the Proposed Asylum Harbour at Holyhead* (Liverpool, 1847), 37, 41.

[82] *DNB*, 896-897.

[83] The details of the events of 3 December 1863 which follow are taken from the depositions made before the Collector of Customs at Holyhead by the survivors, in accordance with Section 432 of the Merchant Shipping Act, 1854, and recorded in *Parl. Papers*, LV, 1864, 643.

[84] The *Hibernia*, 178 tons, bound for Dublin, had a crew of 5, the *Aerial*, 79 tons, owned by a Mr Hughes of Portmadoc, was bound there in ballast from Belfast with a crew of three; the *Elizabeth Morrow*, 394 tons, had a crew of eighteen 'and one stowaway', and had had a very bad time since she had first taken in sail on 3 December, at 4 a.m. 'then under close-reefed topsails, fore topmast staysail and mizen staysail, at 6 a.m. wind shifted to N.W. by W. blowing a complete hurricane, all sails blown away: vessel on her beam ends for three hours: vessel then 18 miles from Holyhead, S.E. by S. Threw a portion of cargo overboard; wind changed to N.N.W.: bore up for Holyhead at 9 a.m.'. The Cornish schooner, *R.T.K.*, 85 tons, bound from Rouen with a

cargo of sand for Runcorn, had five men aboard, the brig *Diamond*, 211 tons, with a crew of nine, was bound from Belfast for Swansea, in ballast, and the *Palermo*, 138 tons, and six crew, with coal from Workington for Dublin.
[85] Among them was the *Margaret* of Liverpool, 97 tons, bound for 'Kinsembo in Africa' with a cargo of general goods and a crew of eleven, which had collided with the brig *Duke of Saxe Coburg and Gotha* in Holyhead Roads.
[86] *Parl. Papers*, LV, 1864, 441. Board of Trade Memorandum on Harbours of Refuge, 1861, 3.
[87] *Parl. Papers*, LV, 1864. These figures are extracted from the various wreck returns of the years 1859-1863.
[88] *ibid.*, 1045.
[89] *Parl. Papers*. Abstracts of Shipping Casualties, Board of Trade, July 1904 – June 1905.
[90] *ibid.*, Appendix A.
[91] *Parl. Debates* (Lords), 27 Nov. 1906, 1378-1380.
[92] HMS *Clio* was launched at Sheerness 28 August 1858; became training ship in Thames 1876, transferred to Menai Strait 1877. Sold to breakers 3 October 1919, and broken up at Bangor 1920.
[93] Henry Parry, *Wreck and Rescue on the Coast of Wales*, I, 102-103. The *Norman Court*, reduced to barque rig, bound for Greenock from Java, struck the rocks in Cymyran Bay on 30 March 1883. The Rhosneigr men took their lifeboat, the *Thomas Lingham*, out twice in very heavy seas through rocks and shoals to get a line to the *Norman Court*. When they returned exhausted to the beach, their places in the *Thomas Lingham* were taken by men from the Holyhead lifeboat crew who had come by train to Rhosneigr to assist; twenty of the crew of the *Norman Court* were rescued. The Holyhead lifeboat had already made an attempt to get to the *Norman Court* some hours previously.
[94] Henry Parry, *Wreck and Rescue on the Coast of Wales*, I, 127; D. Lloyd Hughes, Holyhead, *The Story of a Port* (Holyhead, 1967), 218-220.
[95] UCNW Bangor Penrhos MSS 1536. The correspondence between J.W. Huggins, father of the 15-year-old apprentice, Herbert Huggins, and the Board of Trade, 11 June–13 July 1901, reflects the former's anger at the 'persistent silence' and 'casual manner' of the Board of Trade. A recent reconstruction, 'The loss of the Primrose Hill', by Richard M. Cookson, is in SB 47, 329 (May, 1973), 315-320.
[96] *Stanley Sailors Home and Reading Room, Holyhead*, Report, 1905.
[97] Among the schooners and ketches mentioned were *Gauntlet* and *Ann James* 1899, *Margaret Garton* and *Mary Ann* 1905, *Millom Castle* 1906. In July 1911 the survivors of the *Lady Neave*, the Amlwch schooner, were brought to the Home. *Stanley Sailors Home MSS.* I am indebted to Mr Frank Bell, Holyhead, for allowing me to examine the Wreck Book of the Stanley Sailors Home, *infra*.
[98] *ibid.*

[99] *SB* 21, 1956, 239. One of the Moelfre lifeboatmen lost his life in the 1927 rescue. Second Coxswain William Roberts was brother to Captain Henry Roberts of *Sara* and *Earl of Lathom*. Norah Ayland (ed.), *Schooner Captain, The Story of Captain Hugh Shaw* (Truro, 1972), 124-126.

[100] Henry Parry, *Wreck and Rescue*, I, 136-7. Coxswain Richard Evans of Moelfre was awarded a bar to his gold medal on this occasion, and the crews of both lifeboats received silver and bronze medals, some of them bars to medals already awarded for previous rescues.

[100] *ibid.*, 103-104.

The Sea for Work

The sea, which had for centuries provided work for some of the inhabitants of Anglesey, became, in the second half of the 19th century, the source of employment for a substantial portion of the male population of working age. The sea dominated the life of the island; in the Register of Births, in the minister's notebook of just one chapel, the Independent Chapel at Amlwch Port, from January 1833 to September 1848, there are 27 master mariners to whom children were born,[1] whilst in the last days of sail Captain Henry Roberts has named over 40 master mariners whom he remembers living in Moelfre.[2] At Holyhead, Amlwch, Beaumaris, Moelfre, Newborough and across the Menai Strait in Hirael, Bangor, at Portdinorwic and Caernarvon, there were streets which had seamen living in almost every house. The census for 1851 and 1861 recorded about 100 seamen's wives living in the Amlwch district, whilst on census night in 1851 there were 108 seamen ashore in Amlwch, 215 in the Holyhead area, 56 in the Menai Strait area.[3] In 1861 there were fewer seamen actually ashore on the night of the census: 68 in Amlwch, 136 at Holyhead and 75 in the Menai Strait area, but the total number of Anglesey merchant seamen by this time was well over 600, by far the largest occupational group apart from those engaged in agriculture. The maritime interest in the county was on the increase; in 1851 there were 18 described as shipwrights or ship's carpenters at Amlwch, 25 in the Holyhead area and 7 in the Strait area, but by 1861 there were 31 at Amlwch, 48 at Holyhead and 8 in the Menai Strait area. Together with the names of pilots, sail makers, riggers, ship chandlers, ship's bakers, lighthouse keepers, coastguards, hobblers and boatmen, shipping clerks, customs officers, fishermen, harbour officials and engineers, Greenwich pensioners and a few officers and men of the Royal Navy, the census returns present a community in Anglesey for whom the sea was very much part of its way of life. Chapel Street, Well Street, Upper Quay Street, Bricks Street in Amlwch, Bath Street, Stanley Row, Forge Hill, Cross Street, Well Street, Cybi Place and Newry Street in Holyhead, Church Lane, New Street and Rosemary Lane in Beaumaris were some of the streets which housed mariners and

shipyard workers and their wives in 1861. At the entrances to the
Menai Strait at Llanddwyn and Penmon, there were pilots' cottages,
whilst at Newborough, Brynsiencyn, Llanfairpwll, Llandegfan,
Moelfre, Llaneilian, Cemais, Rhoscolyn and Aberffraw men went to
sea in increasing numbers.

Newborough boys had long looked wistfully across the Strait to
the smacks and schooners plying to and from Caernarvon; the
considerable development of the slate industry and the consequent
demand for shipping gave many of them the opportunity to go to sea.
Owen Williamson (1840-1910), village schoolmaster, who himself
taught many future seamen, recorded the considerable development
in the maritime interest since the days at the beginning of the century
when two Newborough seamen, Owen Williams and Thomas
Hughes, had been captured by the French. He noted the scores of
Newborough boys who had first gone to sea as galley boys aboard
the coasting ships of Captain John Jones, Bodiorwerth, and the larger
vessels of Mr Humphrey Owen, Rhuddgaer, the *Royal William*,
Hindoo and *Higginson* engaged in the Atlantic trade in the forties.[4]
Williamson stressed that most of the older generation of
Newborough seamen, with few opportunities for education, had
served all their years before the mast, but many of them so valued
education that they made every effort to keep their sons at school as
long as they could before they too went to sea. It was this second
generation of seamen whom he and other schoolmasters had first set
on the road to becoming master mariners. In one of this notebooks,
a school exercise book, Williamson had a list of the names and
addresses of thirty-nine Newborough seamen who gained a Board of
Trade Master's Certificate in accordance with the 1854 Merchant
Shipping Act, five others who were licensed because of their
experience and known competence, six who had a coasting master's
certificate, and sixteen who had passed their mate's examination. He
also named four Newborough men who were pilots at Liverpool, and
three master mariners living in Australia.[5] One of these, Captain
Owen Hughes, so prospered that when he died in New South Wales,
he was able to leave £500 in his will to the 'Methodist Chapel in
Newborough, Anglesey', an ambiguity which led to a dispute
between the Wesleyan and Calvinistic Methodists and a High Court
action.[6] Many of these second generation seamen served aboard the

ships of Davies, Menai Bridge, the brothers who themselves gave much support to the Nonconformist British schools on the island, and it is not surprising to find the names of at least two sea captains among the first governors of the British school in Newborough in 1868.[7]

Most of the active seamen in the Newborough district were away from home on census night 1861; some miles away, at Llanidan, Captain Hugh Pugh and his seaman son, David Pugh, were at home. Captain Pugh was now aged 65, and the flat, *Ann*, which inspired the late Professor Glyn Davies' song, had been lost three years previously in 1858.[8] On census night 1861 there were seventeen vessels in the Strait, ranging from the 250-ton Dublin vessel *Birmingham* to the 24-ton smack *Jane Margaret* of Conway. Two examples must suffice: on the night of April 7th, 1861, the 30-ton sloop *Sampson* of Amlwch was at anchor off Beaumaris, and aboard her were Richard Hughes, aged 52, master, a native of Llanbadrig; Owen Jones, aged 52, the mate, also of Llanbadrig; William Jones, aged 14, seaman, of Amlwch; Ellen Jones, aged 22, 'domestic at present out of situation, passenger', a native of Liverpool; and William Hughes, aged 45, able seaman, also of Llanbadrig, but listed as 'passenger'. At anchor nearby was the *Sarah*, a 67-ton Runcorn schooner, and aboard her were John Thomas, aged 37, her master, a native of Amlwch; David Rowlands, aged 26, the mate, also of Amlwch; two young seamen from Amlwch, and a cabin boy, John Thomas, aged 12, possibly the master's son, and Margaret Thomas, aged 34, the master's wife, who was a native of Moelfre. The sea was a family affair.

Life ashore was hard for the majority of Anglesey people in mid nineteenth-century and it was not much different at sea. On the 10th December 1849 John Williams, master of the brig *Abel*, 94 tons, owned by John Parry, a Hirael shipbuilder, recorded in his log book an uneventful departure from the Menai Strait: 'unmored ship, got underway at 12 midday light winds and variable: 12 midnight abreast of Point Leinas.'[9] It was a routine voyage to John Williams from the Strait to London with slates, a voyage undertaken by hundreds of Anglesey and Caernarvonshire seamen who preferred the sea as a place of work to the farm or the quarry. The *Abel*'s crew lists indicate that they were for the most part men whose homes were on the Menai Strait, Bangor, Llandegfan, Caernarvon, with occasionally an

Amlwch or Llaneilian man, and for single voyages, natives of Stornoway, Dublin and Fishguard. For most of the voyages for which her papers have survived, the mate's wages were £2.15.0 a month, the able seamen £2.5.0 or £2.2.0, the ordinary seamen between £1.10.0 and £1.2.0, and the boy between 16/- and 12/-.[10] Between November 1839 and November 1844 the *Abel* made fifteen voyages to ports ranging from London, Harwich, Plymouth, Liverpool, Newhaven, Charleston and Limerick, but her main trade was slate for London. John Williams, her master in 1849, may have been the John Williams who had served in her from 1840 for a number of voyages, first as a boy and then as ordinary seaman. He recorded in his log of December 1849 that they had taken three days to get to Milford, where they anchored: 'took in the fore and main top galan sails Double reef the fore and main topsail, at this time blowing strongly, at 2 p.m. Bore up for Milford Haven at 5 came to an Anchor at this time a strong gale wind about S.E.'[11]

The *Abel* remained windbound at Milford for five days, and then sailed for Falmouth, coming to anchor there in a 'Stif Brees E.N.E.' two days later. They had snow and strong winds as they lay at anchor at Falmouth over Christmas, but on Boxing Day they sailed again in fine, clear weather. This soon passed, and snow and the freezing conditions made the next two days unpleasant, as Captain Williams recorded in his log:

'Thursday, the 27th these 24 houars comenced with strong Brees from N.N.W., at 5 a.m. took in both top galan sails and Double Reef both topsails, Start bearing W. by N 4 or 5 miles, at 2 p.m. Portland N.N.W. 1 mile, at 10 p.m. St Cathereine Light N.W. 4 miles Strong Breeses from the Northward with snow showers. Friday 28th: these 24 houars Comenced with Strong Brees from N.N.W. with heavy snow showers and verry wild appeariance, at 4 p.m. toock our Jib and mainsail in, at 6 a.m. so thick with snow and freeshing verry hard, a Dreadful squall took us till she was all underwater we lowerd Both topsales and Trysail down to lighten her and owing to so much snow and that frozen we could not clew the fore topsail up so therefore topsail Bet to peeces at the seame time while in the act of try to tack the sails off her she shipet a very heavy sea over her Quarter and filed the Trysail which we thought she would not rise. So we thought it Necessary to cut the Trysail of her for the Security of our Ship and Cargo and lives what was done as soon as Possible at day break Blowing a Whole Gale about N by W close Reefed the Main Top Sail and set it to keep her too the Sea was Making a Compleat Breack over her, at 9 a.m. set the forsail and Mainstay sail seen that the vessal would soon be on the french shore, at 12 wind veered to NNW with heavy squall and Snow, Beachy Bore NE by N about 2 miles so it was Nessasarity to cut off the for top sail which was split and all the Gear Blonging to it and PM close under fairleegh, wind from N. to N.N.W. with Snow Showers and freeshing evrrything on Deck and all the Rigin so we got our Anchor Ready to come too, Blowing a gale at the time took in Main topsails Main stay sail and in trying to tak the fforsail off her evry thing sail and all was so much frosen that we could not get her off her and vessel drifting out fast so we let go the Anchor and beied out 60 fathom chaine, vessel still Driving so we had to cut the forsail and the topmast stay sail Clear off her, then the Anchor held, at 12 middnight Blowing Strong and freeshing very hard.'[12]

Two days the like of which could be repeated in countless logs had they survived, two days of routine in a life spent at sea in cold, wet ships, far removed from the popular Christmas card concept of beautiful sailing barques spanking along with all sails set in balmy breezes and sunlit sparkling seas. Eventually the *Abel* made Dover in another snow storm, 'at 3 a.m. came to with Great Many in Company, at 4 a.m. got both our top galan yards down and secyar the windlass as wel as possible, at 7 a.m. wind veered Round to Eastward Blowing Strong with snow several of the vessels slipping their Anchors But we held on.' Anyone who has experienced a gale with vessels dragging in a crowded anchorage in darkness, even without snow blowing into their faces, will know how Captain Williams and his crew must have felt. And they will also recognize the mixed feelings which Captain Williams must have had when he entered into his log the next day: 'still laying at Dover. Capn went up to London by train for new sails and ropes which was cut away. Men employd in repering damages.'

The 1830s and 1840s were the years when the more prosperous

sections of society began to have their attention drawn to the condition of the mass of their fellow men, when Select Committees and Royal Commissions were set up to investigate working conditions, when, as Carlyle said, 'a feeling very generally exists that the condition and disposition of the Working Class is a rather ominous matter at present; that something ought to be said, something ought to be done in regard to it'.[13] One of the Select Committees was that appointed 'to inquire into the Shipwreck of British Vessels' whose first report was published in 1843. In his evidence to the Committee a Scottish merchant, John Mitchell, drew attention to the conditions in which seamen lived:

'In British ships the men are not treated as they ought to be. I have taken particular notice of their place of abode, which is in almost every ship of small size, a small dark cave, without light or warmth, or not such a kind of place wherein they may rest and repose themselves; and in point of size it is sometimes six or seven feet square for six or seven men, stowed half full of ropes and dails, damp and wet . . . The very small accommodation the poor men have in bad weather completely enervates them; they are thus rendered unable to perform their duty, and shipwrecks follow from the inability of the men. I went into the forecastle of ten different ships and measured them, and I have the measure here. There was no proper accommodation where they could stretch themselves out. There was room for hammocks, but in several of them there was no skylight, and if they shut the hatches of the forecastle there was no air and no light. I also consider that the want of accommodation in the forecastle of the ship may be one of the causes of intemperance because if the men have no place to repose themselves in a seaport after arriving at the port, the men are compelled to go to a public house, and thus become intemperate.'[14]

What the good Mr Mitchell did not say was the conditions ashore for the majority of the population, living in small, overcrowded cottages, frequently near famine at poverty level, were little better than the dark, damp forecastle, which would possibly have proved a wetter place if provided with the skylight he wanted. In this same year, 1843,

Captain Evan Lloyd of Holyhead, known afterwards as 'the Seamen's Missionary', wrote a letter to the Welsh Calvinistic Methodist magazine, *Y Drysorfa*, appealing for funds to support the work of the 'British and Foreign Sailors Society'.[15]

Nonconformist and temperance movements were already well established in north Wales; in Anglesey, men like the Davieses of Menai Bridge were to plough back a certain amount of the capital earned from shipping into the building of chapels and schools. The Methodist movement went some way to enabling the working classes to suffer the tribulations and the conditions of their everyday life in the contemplation of a better fate in the New Jerusalem, and Welsh seamen throughout this period found comfort and consolation in their new-found religious beliefs.[16] It was in 1843 that a Captain John Roberts, master of the *Emily Jane*, writing from Dartmouth and Falmouth in February and March, gave accounts of preaching meetings held aboard ships from north Wales;[17] on 8 February 1843 he recorded that there must have been fifty Welsh ships lying at anchor at Falmouth, and as evening approached, from one after another of them the small ship's boats were pulled alongside the *Surprize*, where Captain Hugh Hughes, master of the *Eagle* of Portmadoc, preached a sermon on the eleventh chapter of Paul's epistle to the Hebrews to over three hundred seamen. The 'Bethel Flag' was the signal that a service was to be held aboard, and the strength of the movement was such that some masters would only sign on crew members who shared their religious zeal.[18] Captain Evan Lloyd of Holyhead worked tirelessly to obtain good facilities ashore for seamen, and his efforts were not in vain; Mrs Elizabeth Jones, who sailed with her father in the *Gauntlet* from Amlwch, still remembers how much the Sailors' Home, the Sailors' Institutes and the canteens were valued in the ports she visited. And the tradition of chapel membership persisted; Captain R. Wynn and Captain R. Jones of Amlwch recall how when they were very young members of the crew of the *Donald and Doris* they had to go to the Welsh chapel in Duddon, sit in the same pew as their captain, Captain Ellis of Aelybryn, and each say a verse if the occasion demanded it.[19]

Captain John Washington, R.N., giving evidence to the 1843 Select Committee on Shipwrecks, stated in May 1843 that he believed the chief cause of shipwrecks to be 'the incompetency of the commanders: often times not only incompetent to the duty of navigating a ship, but incompetent as practical seamen; they are men not brought up to the sea'; or, as is commonly said, 'they are men that come in at the cabin-window instead of working their way aft through the hawse-holes'.[20] The vast majority of Anglesey seamen 'worked their way aft through the hawse-holes'; going to sea as 'boys' and as 'cooks', they learned their seamanship the hard way. But if their practical seamanship was assured, there were many doubts expressed as to their education in navigation. In this, they were not unusual, for witness after witness before the 1843 Commission testified to the need for an improvement in the facilities and educational opportunities available for masters and mates, in which Britain compared unfavourably with many European countries, particularly Prussia.[21] The Merchant Shipping Act of 1854, which resulted from this, and other, enquiries, improved all aspects of service at sea, not least the stipulations regarding the proofs of competence of masters and mates. The very magnitude of British merchant shipping made the examining of officers a much more complex matter than in the smaller fleets of other European countries. Ultimately, however, standards were raised by the need to satisfy examination by their fellow master mariners at their home ports, so that they could obtain command of a vessel insured by their own local marine insurance societies. 'Pasio'r clwb', passing the examination of the marine insurance societies, became an essential part of the training of Anglesey masters and mates, particularly during the second half of the century.[22]

The importance of education in navigation had, however, been the subject of considerable discussion in Wales in the 1840s. The intense indignation felt throughout Wales at the Report of the Commissioners appointed to enquire into the State of Education in Wales, published in 1847,[23] 'Brâd y Llyfrau Gleision', as it came to be known, led to violent protests from both Anglicans and Nonconformists at the way in which the able but somewhat unwise young Commissioners had interpreted their task and presented their findings. The implications, political, religious, linguistic, and educational of the Report and the reactions of the Welsh people to it have been discussed ever since. Some of the evidence and the implied criticism of the Report can be attributed to the

Commissioners' assumption 'that ignorance of the English language was, in all respects, synonymous with illiteracy';[24] many of the logs of Anglesey vessels, like that of the *Abel*, already quoted, indicate that the masters would have been much happier expressing themselves in Welsh. In the nineteenth-century, however, this was unthinkable: Welsh was the language of everyday life and the chapel, English the language of officialdom and work. Lack of facility in English was not an insuperable bar to success. One witness had to confess, much to his obvious surprise and regret, 'many have become very rich by their trade, without any knowledge of reading or writing English'. More significant was the allegation that 'many of our captains know nothing of navigation. They can just go to London, Hamburgh, the French coast, and different ports by the help of certain clues which they have'.[25] The master of the National School at Caernarvon confirmed this: 'There has been no education whatever for the sailors of this port. They know nothing of navigation except a sort of knack which they have acquired by practice and by tradition. All the navigation which has been learned here as a science has been taught by an old woman of Caernarvon.'[26] Much the same could have been said about the coasting trade in many parts of Britain, but 'Master of a Coaster', writing in the *Caernarvon and Denbigh Herald*, was not willing to allow this to go unchallenged, pointing out that 'the old woman of Caernarvon' was none other than the 'daughter of that respectable old master mariner, Mr William Francis, who, in zeal for his country, left the sea and established a school in Amlwch to teach navigation: I suppose because he had not a son he taught the art to his daughter, who has a talent to impart the same with great dexterity'. This old coasting master was an early champion of feminine rights – 'If I am not misinformed, the best navigators in London are taught by a Sailor's wife, on Tower Hill. What can women not do if they like?'[27]

Whilst sympathising with his understandable indignation, the tendency hitherto has been to accept the general picture presented by the Commissioners regarding the lack of navigational instruction, and their statement 'navigation has been as much neglected as every other branch of industrial knowledge, and the same ignorance characterizes the adult sailors at Holyhead, Amlwch, Bangor, Barmouth, Portmadoc and Conway' has been accepted without challenge. Recently, evidence has come to light which suggests that 'Coasting Master' had firm grounds for his condemnation of the misleading nature of the 1847 Report. By a fortunate chance, an exercise book belonging to a young seaman who attended William Francis' school at Amlwch has survived.[28] On 28 February 1842 John Hughes of Simdda Wen, Penrhoslligwy, bought the book in Amlwch; he was the son of Thomas Hughes, master mariner, and part-owner of the *Marianne*, a two-masted schooner built by Nicholas Treweek at Amlwch in August 1839 as a sloop, and altered to schooner rig three years later. Indeed, it may have been whilst the *Marianne* was being altered, refitted and given her additional mast that Thomas Hughes, her master, had urged his son to attend Mr Francis' school. John Hughes was by this time aged 19, and had obviously served some time at sea, no doubt with his father aboard the *Marianne* and possibly the *Cymraes*, the 22-ton sloop of which Thomas Hughes had been the master and part-owner with Nicholas Treweek, who had built her in 1836.[29]

The school which young Hughes attended had been established by William Francis in 1814, not exclusively 'out of zeal for his country' as 'Master of a Coaster' averred, but for more mundane and natural reasons, as he indicated in a letter some years later. 'I was the latter end of 1813 loading a general cargo at Liverpool for Gibraltar in the *Dublin* of Amlwch of which vessel Mr Joseph Jones and myself were part owners and of which I then resigned the command, on account of the solicitations of my wife on account of the risk of capture.'[30] At his school, Francis offered instruction not only in 'Spelling, reading and writing English' but also 'mensurations universally, land surveying, geography and astronomy, the use of maps, charts, terrestial and celestial globes', and at higher fees, £1.5.0 per quarter, 'The elements of geometry, plain and spherical trigonometry, algebra, theoretical navigation', whilst for £2 a quarter the student was offered 'practical navigation with the use and construction of sea charts, keeping a journal at sea, etc.' and for the highest fee, £3 per quarter, 'Theoretical and practical navigation, the use of globes, quadrants and sextants, double altitudes and lunar observations'. From the outset this enterprising master mariner envisaged his school as providing not only for children of both sexes but also for adults: 'Seamen and others may be accommodated with

Board and Lodging on very moderate terms in the neighbourhood.'[31]

Francis had his problems in his first years a a schoolmaster largely because of the success of his school and the number of pupils it attracted: in 1821 he attempted to obtain alternative accommodation because of his suffering each summer 'from the smallness of my schoolroom (being the loft of a very low built house), the proximity of which to the slate roof renders it intolerable hot; and the air thereof, from the want of free circulation, and the crowded state of the room,must become highly unwholesome and dangerous'.[32] Francis was annoyed that his attempt to find alternative accommodation was being baulked by Mr Morgan at the Mines, for the old Assay Office near Parys Lodge would have suited his purpose because of its situation, 'Having a fine view of the Horizon, where I had often occasion to resort with many of my Pupils to explain the adjustments and use of Hadleys Quadrant and other Nautical and astronomical instruments for which purposes and Apparent Horizon is highly serviceable'.[33] But in 1824, through the good offices of Colonel Hughes, M.P., of Llys Dulas, who erected the Tower 'as a beacon or a place of refuge to this shipwrecked' in the same year on Dulas Rocks, Francis obtained his new schoolroom, 'Mount Pleasant School contiguous to Parys Lodge Garden' – Francis advertised his school in the local press with considerable enthusiasm:

> 'The situation is one of the most delightful imaginable: a few yards distant from the centre of the town of Amlwch, commanding a fine view thereof, and of the surrounding country from Linas Point, round Llaneilian and Parys Mountains to the Garnynghornwy, westward: with the towering tops of Snowdon, etc. in the distant background, southward. To the northward it takes in a part of St George's Channel with a fine north horizon (so necessary to the adjustments of nautical and Mathematical Instruments). And on a clear day, the mountain of Mourne in Ireland, the Isle of Man, the Black Comb, in Cumberland, may be seen with a naked eye – Also the various American, East and West Indian Fleets, together with the numerous Steam Packets and other Traders that flock to Liverpool, pass in view, and within a short distance of the schoolroom.'[34]

Francis also emphasised his experience as a master mariner, having had 'the command of different vessels in the foreign and coasting trades' for his last ten years at sea, and in his school he claimed to have 'for the use of his pupils divers sea charts, Quadrants, Sextant and Globes, with original foreign and channel journals, containing his own drawings of the appearance and bearings of headlands'.

In view of the 1847 Report's blanket condemnation of all attempts at teaching navigation in Amlwch and everywhere else in north Wales it might be tempting to dismiss Francis' advertisement as unsubstantial froth of the type often found in the Victorian press, but in John Hughes' exercise book there is evidence of the work done at the school four years before the Commissioners' visit. Starting with the first problem set, 'At sea observed the Linas Light bear by Compass S.W. thence sailed W.N.W. 6 miles and the same Light bears S. by E. Required the ship's Distance from Light at the Last Station, Variation 2½ points westerly', John Hughes worked through a considerable number of graduated exercises relating to 'Chart Navigation', finding a ship's position on the chart, the depth of water and the quality of the soundings in given positions on the charts, the setting of the tide, tidal observations at springs and neaps, and then there followed examples of how to keep a journal at sea. It is evident that Francis had taught himself much of his navigation with the aid of a practical textbook on navigation written by J. W. Norie who had a 'naval academy' at 'Heather's Navigation Warehouse', 157 Leadenhall Street, London, in the early decades of the nineteenth-century. The format and theoretical rules follow Norie's textbook closely, but Francis always uses exercises which relate to his students' local knowledge of Liverpool Bay and the St George's Channel. Moreover, although he follows Norie's precedent of furnishing his students with an imaginary journal of a log at sea, it is not a slavish copy of Norie's *Journal of the Voyage of the Britannia from England to Madeira in June 1809*, but rather a simulated exercise suited to the needs of his individual students in Amlwch in 1842. John Hughes recorded in his exercise book the details of an imaginary voyage 'from Londonderry to Lisbon with a cargo of provisions', and then from Lisbon to St Michael's to load a cargo of fruits for Liverpool. The vessel is the *Mary Ann*, the name of his father's schooner, and the commander named for the voyage is William Francis, his teacher, whilst he himself, John Hughes, is the mate. Courses and times are carefully noted, distances recorded, as well as Latitude and Longitude and bearing and distance from St Michael's, and in the 'Remarks' column are appropriate entries: 'Strong breeze take in our top gallan sail and reef in our main sail'; 'saw a Brig before the wind'; 'at 2 p.m saw a ship on the larboard bow going to the southward'. Obviously Francis wanted his students to envisage different conditions and situations; the entries in the journal for Friday, 18 March 1842, for example are entered in Hughes' exercise book for three different types of day: the first, 'These 24 hours fine breeze and clear weather', envisaged the *Marianne* sailing W.N.W. three to five knots and making good a distance of 103 miles, the second 'strong gale from North-ward Lay to these 24 hours drift 2 miles per hour, very heavy sea' resulted in the *Marianne*'s position being 48 miles S by W¾W, at the end of the day, whilst the third version was 'strong gale from NNE with heavy snow, lay to these 24 hours under close reef mainsail' and here the course made good was SW by S¼W, again a distance of 48 miles. In each case Hughes' journal notes the ship's position and the bearing and distance from St Michael's. The following week Hughes embarked upon another simulated exercise, the journal of a voyage from St Michael's to Liverpool with a cargo of fruits, and this time his father, Thomas Hughes, is named as Master, and he, John Hughes, again goes as mate; in this exercise these are more detailed observations, but the pattern is much the same, and one suspects from the attempt at copperplate handwriting that the journals were copies from Francis' originals.

There is no way of ascertaining how much actual chart work was carried out by the student himself in conjunction with the exercises. The handwriting is much freer and less formal in the journal which records a voyage of the *Marianne* from Youghal to London in April 1843, which may have been an actual voyage, and the format is so different to the schoolroom exercises that it may not be the work of John Hughes – the imaginary journeys are all dated March 1842, soon after he had bought the exercise book. The remainder of the book contains exercises, problems and rules of Plane Trigonometry and Plane Sailing which have obviously been copied out painstakingly, not without errors; this theoretical work is firmly based on Norie's text, sometimes word for word, and as the handwriting had again changed, may have been the work of another member of the Hughes family. The saddest irony is this battered exercise book of one hundred and thirty years ago, which contains many scribbled notes by various hands, addresses, and half-finished words written by younger children, is a little note inserted in the last of the imaginary journeys of March 1842, the voyage from Liverpool to Shetland, for in the middle of the remarks column, between 'at 2 Tacked to the Northward' and 'Variation 2½ points westerly', someone, probably John Hughes himself, has written 'Pan byddwn Farw' (when we are dead). In the nearby churchyard at Penrhoslligwy there is a gravestone marked 'John Hughes, o Simdde Wen, Tach. 21, 1844, yn 21 mlwydd oed'.[35] The ironic premonition in Francis' classroom was fulfilled in a little over two years.

Towards the end of the eighteenth and the beginning of the nineteenth-century, the older grammar school tradition with its undue emphasis upon the classics came under attack from educational innovators, among the most interesting of whom was David Williams, who, in his school at Chelsea, abandoned so much of the then current classical curriculum in favour of the teaching of science and economics.[36] David Williams was at one time on the pay-roll of Thomas Williams, the Copper King, for whom he wrote a political pamphlet attacking the Bishop of Bangor and the Governors of Friars School, Bangor, in a dispute which had its roots in Amlwch.[37] What is more intriguing in this present context is to ask whether William Francis was aware of David Williams' ideas regarding observing children and contriving situations in which they could learn from their own experience, the teacher's role being, in Williams' own telling phrase, 'the management of curiosity'. Williams was a radical thinker, a follower of Rousseau, the friend of Benjamin Franklin, and Joseph Priestley, and his ideas were influential in Revolutionary France.[38] When William Francis died in Amlwch in 1853, in addition to the tributes paid to him as a teacher of navigation – 'he had a peculiar and successful way of imparting instruction to every capacity, and as a teacher of mathematics he was unrivalled' – the writer of his obituary did not forget to mention Francis' radical and liberal ideas in his early years, when liberalism was equated with sedition, 'so far as his individual opinions went, he was the zealous advocate throughout life of civil and religious liberty, and lived to see all the measures carried out of which (at one time of life, in a circle of some extent) he was almost the only supporter. To his inflexible advocacy much of the spirit actuating the town of Amlwch for liberal principles may be attributed'.[39] In fairness to the Commissioner of 1846 it must be stated that his comments inferred that a school such as Francis' was beyond the means of the majority: 'great numbers of the inhabitants of Amlwch are engaged in connexion with shipping and the poor have no means of procuring instruction upon this subject (navigation) except at private schools, which are far too expensive.' Nevertheless it is strange that the Commissioner saw fit to ignore the work of such a man as William Francis. According to the Census of 1851 he was still listed as a teacher of navigation, aged sixty-nine, living in New Street, Amlwch, and from the evidence of John Hughes' exercise book a few years previously his methods were certainly worthy of notice. It has been wisely said that the good teacher is both interested and interesting. John Hughes' exercise book suggests that Francis certainly was interesting, with his imaginary voyages ranging from South Stack, Point Lynas, and the Great Orme's Head, to Lisbon and the Shetlands, and both his own record, and that of his daughter, Mrs Ann Edwards, in Caernarvon, indicate that he was very interested in Anglesey and north Wales seamen. It is dangerous to generalise from the evidence of one student's notebook, but if one remembers that the Francis family were teaching mariners navigation over several decades at a time when there was a dramatic increase in shipping at both Amlwch and Caernarvon, and a consequent need for navigational training, it would seem that the Francises made an important contribution to the development of both the copper industry of Amlwch and the slate industry of Caernarvonshire.

In 1859, William Roos,[40] a member of a family well-known in the Amlwch shipping community, completed a portrait 'of Mrs Ann Edwards who has taught Navigation in Caernarvon upwards of 29 years, and long may she live to follow the branch of Education in which she is said to excel. This portrait is painted by William Roos, one of her father's late pupils'. Roos had attended William Francis' school; Mrs Ann Edwards was the 'old woman' of the 1847 Report, who is said to have taught Captain T. Barlow Pritchard, later master of the *Mauretania*, his early navigation.

Francis' work at Amlwch was carried on by John Sellars at his 'Academy'; another successful schoolmaster, Sellars had among his pupils many Amlwch captains and their parents, among them Captain Ishmael Williams of the *Gaelic*. 'Ysgol Sellars' was part and parcel of the development of the maritime interests of Amlwch in the era of Captain William Thomas, and many of his leading shipyard employees had benefited from John Sellars' instruction.[41] At Holyhead there had long been a tradition of instruction for mariners; as early as 1816 Robert Roberts informed prospective clients that at 'Mill Street school, Holyhead' which he had established nine years previously, he and his brother offered instruction in 'navigation including the mode of ascertaining longitude by Lunar observations'.[42] Another Holyhead school, that of H. W. Owen, taught navigation, whilst later in the century future seamen were being taught at schools in Bodedern, Rhoscolyn and Newborough.[43] Owen Williamson recalls that at Newborough in the forties there was an evening school where young seamen regularly attended classes in navigation and seamanship. The Newborough schoolmaster noted that many of his contemporaries in mid-century were motivated by the smart appearance of seamen home on leave, with their yellow buttons and Panama hats with long ribbons. The smart appearance of one of the newly-qualified young master mariners, Captain Richard Davies, who had himself attended the evening school in earlier days, was said to have inspired many young Newborough boys to emulate him.[44]

An intelligent mariner or shipbuilder or sailmaker in mid nineteenth-century Anglesey very often shared the enthusiasm for self-improvement which was such a marked feature of the attitudes both of the followers of Samuel Smiles and the leaders of Welsh religious and educational movements. Thomas Ellis of Cross Street, Holyhead, aged 48 at the time, was one of the fourteen sailmakers registered as such in the 1851 census; among the book which he had in a tin chest when he moved to Bangor later in the century were a wide variety of religious tracts, *Diagrams illustrating the Science of Astronomy and Geography, Elements of Practice of Mensuration and Land Surveying* and several historical works.[45] By the 1870s young Anglesey seamen may have shared the experience of John Lloyd Jones of the barque *Assel* of Ayr who was presented with R. H. Dana's

Seaman's Manual (not so well-known as his *Two Years before the Mast*). Young Jones recorded his name on its fly-leaf when he was at Port Adelaide, but it had been bought in Caernarvon and given to him 'on his departure from home on his first voyage to sea by his attached Auntie Mary Ann Williams'. For the really serious-minded student there was Steel's *Ship-Master's Assistant, and Owners Manual*, 1832, a 1,128 page volume; there is a copy in the University Library at Bangor in which someone has written on the fly-leaf 'Wreck and Salvage Act passed 9+10 Vict. c. 99' – perhaps it had a particular significance for him.

Among the more serious-minded masters there were instances of them competing in Eisteddfodau, and the Eisteddfod in its turn showed its concern for them, for in 1866 the Rev. David Griffith of Portdinorwic won a prize at the National Eisteddfod at Caerleon for an essay on Welsh seamen.[46] In his essay Griffith described the life of contemporary seamen sailing from Holyhead, Portdinorwic, Port Penrhyn, Liverpool and London, and the efforts made by various religious societies on their behalf. According to Griffith, the representative of the British and Foreign Sailors Society made 1,143 visits to ships in Holyhead Harbour during 1865, and over 12,000 seamen had attended religious services held either aboard ships in the harbour or ashore in Holyhead itself during the year. Griffith urged that a Sailors Institute should be established at Holyhead and Bangor, such as that which opened its doors to seamen in Caernarvon in 1860, and the very pleasant though small Reading Room which had been in existence at Portdinorwic for a number of years. The 'British and Foreign Sailors Society' had a representative, P. W. Jones, working among the Welsh seamen at Barrow-in-Furness; Griffith reported that over four thousand Welsh seamen visited Barrow each year. It was significant that the Eisteddfod prize had been the gift of Welshmen living in Runcorn, a port much frequented by seamen from north Wales,[47] and among the advertisements accompanying the published version of the essay were invitations to Welsh seamen to obtain English and Welsh books, account books, books on seamanship and navigation, and specially reduced rates for seamen of the publication *Y Pregethwr*, which contained a collection of sermons by John Jones, Talysarn, John Pritchard, Amlwch, and others, with an introductory essay on the art of preaching by Henry Rees of Liverpool. Highly regarded in mid-Victorian Wales for their oratorical prowess, the preachers themselves were probably more in touch than their successors with Welsh shipping and seamen: Henry Rees, father-in-law of Richard Davies, the Menai Bridge shipowner, held special preaching meetings for Welsh seamen in Liverpool and on the Clyde; John Jones, Talysarn, had regularly sent money by the masters of the Davies, Menai Bridge, ships to his son, John Lloyd Jones, in Cambria, Winsconsin, whilst John Pritchard, Methodist minister at Amlwch Port in the sixties, had at the age of nineteen, in 1840, left his work as a labourer in the Parys Mines to attend the school of William Francis, teacher of navigation, and must have been a near contemporary there of the young seamen John Hughes whose exercise book has already been discussed.[48] One of the main themes in Griffith's essay is the need to extend the opportunities for seamen to educate themselves, and his publishers did not miss the opportunity to accept advertisements designed to interest the intelligent mariner. Humphreys and Parry of London Place, High Street, Bangor, had special stocks of charts, navigation and seamanship manuals, 'Log books, Scales, Parallel Rulers, Dividers and Mathematical Instruments', whilst the Nelson Emporium, Caernarvon, informed Welsh seamen that here were stocked the cheapest and best materials for seagoing folk in the whole of Wales. And at the top of the page are details relating to the Sunday services at the Welsh chapel in Runcorn. It was the age of religion and self improvement.

The 'Coast and Sailing Directions' for Anglesey compiled by Lieutenant Charles G. Robinson, R.N., and published in 1837 by Captain John Corden, R.N., drew the attention of mariners to the problems of navigation in the Menai Strait, particularly the Swellies, 'no vessel is justified in attempting it without a pilot: who are a distinct class from either those at Penmon or Caernarvon: consequently a vessel going through the Strait is subject to three distinct Pilots.' The pilots were an essential part both of the life of Anglesey and of visiting seamen, and the log-book of a Menai Strait pilot in the sixties and seventies of the nineteenth-century presents another view of the everyday world of work. Books of all kinds, school exercise books, notebooks, log-books have long borne jottings and scribbled notes by writers who have had time to spare and have idly thought that their book might some day pass into other hands. In the case of Henry Edwards, his pious hope has been fulfilled. In January 1867, Edwards, Swellies Pilot, No. 8, began his log-book with a firm indication that he was recording its details for posterity; on the fly-leaf, Edwards wrote in a flowery hand the jingle 'When I am dead and in my grave/and all my bones are rotten/Here's the book you'll see my name/When I am quite forgotten'.[49] For the next eleven years Henry Edwards carefully noted in his log the names of the vessels he piloted through the Menai Strait, the pilotage fees he received and for the first few years at least, the state of the weather on each occasion. Apart from the intrinsic interest of this record of shipping in the Strait, there are the comments which Edwards interspersed among detailed entries of vessels, fees, and weather; on Christmas Day 1869 he whiled away the hours copying out some satirical doggerel in Welsh: 'Rhai od ydyn Nhw.' He has noted the deaths of colleagues and neighbours, loans which he made from time to time to the masters of vessels passing through the Strait, 'Lent £2 to Hugh Jones, Schooner *Glan Menai*', occasional accidents, 'A man nearly kilt in a timber ship, by the Bridge, done accidentally by the winch handle' and happier events such as the birth of children or the Oddfellow Procession. On 20 June 1871, Henry Edwards was married at Bangor Baptist Chapel to Elizabeth Williams, and his log-book records his eleven-day honeymoon voyage from Holyhead to Dublin and Liverpool, together with congratulatory verses composed especially for the occasion by a friend, S. J. Griffith, Morswyn, Holyhead. A staunch Baptist, Edwards noted matters relating to his denomination in the middle of the entries relating to shipping: on 3 September 1872, 'Cyfarfod Agoriadol Capel y Bedyddwyr, Beaumaris' (no ships were piloted that day); in October 1869, '14th, Tea party and concert at Sion Chapel, 15th W.N.W. Moderate Gale and Showers'; 17 April 1871 'N. Moderate. Darlith yn Capel Sion y Bedyddwyr Llandegfan'. His Sabbatarian instincts are clearly reflected in the melancholy entry for 11 April 1868: 'Calm, fine and clear, Colonel Williams, Graig y Don, Vallat drowned by Bathing on a Sunday.'[50] But the most frequent entries, apart from the vessels piloted and the state of the weather, are the wrecks and those who lost their lives in course of normal work. Here are some taken at random: 20 July 1873, 'American ship towed on beam ends to Penmon'; 25 March 1872, 'Man lost from the Schooner *Madryn* off Portdinorwig'; and 20 February 1869, 'Northerly gale which Gale 21 vessels went ashore at Red Wharf, Anglesey, and the *Catherine* of Pwllhely swamp with all hands'. There are several references to the hazards of piloting vessels in the Swellies area and the problem of boarding vessels' on 24 July 1869 Edwards records a near tragedy to one of his fellow pilots, 'Jack Pierce's boat with his two lads when boarding the *Walter Dean* under the Britannia bridge capsized, Jack being near drowned'. And there are the inevitable tragedies for well-known local people: on 24 June 1873 'The Garth boat capsized on Beaumaris Bank, Dick Hussar's daughter drowned', and two months later, on 6 August, 'Jack Crow and Johnny White Lion Beaumaris drowned, the yacht *Dare* lost on Taylors Bank Liverpool, one saved'.

Many of the vessels Edwards piloted were obviously in the coastal trade, with Caernarvon or Port Penrhyn and Beaumaris as regular ports of call, vessels like the F*lying Dutchman*, the *Britannia, Louis Napoleon, Walter Dean, Brothers, Miss Maddocks, Olive Branch, Bagatelle, Vine, Scotia, Viper, Monarch, Geneva, Rhuddlan Trader, Taliesin, Abbey, Emily, Alice, Boaz, Alice Williams, Surprise, Pearl, Success* and *King William the Fourth*, all passing through the Strait frequently. But Edwards also piloted more exciting visitors: an easterly gale was blowing when he took H.M.S. *Royal Charlotte* through on 13 May 1864; on 20 May 1874 he piloted a French schooner, and sometimes quite lucrative fees were paid to him by the owners of yachts, such as the *Caroline* and the steam yacht *Star*. At the back of his log-book Edwards has noted that he piloted the Queen's yacht *Vice Versa* on 5 September 1879, and there is a copy of the note certifying that he had piloted *H.M.S. Tay* from Beaumaris to Caernarvon, 'where he left her in safety on the 3rd day of August 1881'. But for much of his time he piloted vessels which had a close connection with Anglesey and its inhabitants, and were regarded as familiar friends, the schooner *Heir Apparent*, the *Gomer*, the *Menai Packet* and the *Amlwch Packet*.

Henry Edwards spent much of his working life sailing the Strait he knew so well, but other Anglesey seamen were venturing to more distant seas. One of them recorded his memories in his old age.[51]

Born in Upper Bangor, Caernarvonshire, in September 1852, John Parry went to Bangor, Pennsylvania, with his parents as a baby; his father worked there in a slate quarry, but returned to Anglesey on his wife's death, twelve months later. Parry attended the British School, Llangefni, until the death of his father when he was twelve years old, and then worked as farm labourer for sixpence a day, but in May 1868 he gathered together a few belongings and walked to Portdinorwic where he joined the *Catherine Williams*.[52] Captain Hudson, her master, was the grandfather of the late Professor Hudson Williams, her mate was Owen Hughes, and there were three crew members. Parry's pay was eight shillings a month. They sailed for Hamburg with a cargo of slates, a voyage of fourteen days, then for Cork with salt, and back to Caernarvon. Parry recalled that on this voyage one of the crew, John Williams, from Pwllheli, who had been kind to him and had taught him to box the compass, was taken very ill, so that they were shorthanded, as another member of the crew had jumped ship at Cork. Captain Hudson paid Parry 10/-, a bonus of two shillings, to persuade him to return, but after a week at home in Anglesey he joined the *Margaret Ann*,[53] her master, Captain Griffiths, agreeing to pay him £1.8.0 a month.

On her passage for London, the *Margaret Ann* ran into contrary winds and they were forced to shelter first in the Scillies and then to beach her at Falmouth to discover where she was leaking. By September 1868 she was in the Thames, a month after leaving Bangor, and the young Anglesey boy recorded his astonishment at seeing so many sailing-ships of all nations in the river. A fortnight later, with the countryside white with frost on both banks of the river, they sailed for Ipswich with a cargo of 'Indian corn', narrowly avoiding being run down in the night by a large collier. As the pilot brought them safely into Ipswich, young Parry in the rigging of the *Margaret Ann*, viewed with much pleasure the red tiled roofs, a striking contrast to the slate of north Wales houses, and never had he heard such a tune as the church bells made on that cold, frosty morning. But there were many Welsh sailing-ships there, and the convivial activities of the master of the *Belt*, another Bangor schooner, and his own captain caused young Parry some concern. The revels of the captains had to come to an end, and three weeks after entering Ipswich the *Margaret Ann* sailed down the river in company with the *Belt*, the former for Dumfries and the latter for Belfast. By the end of October they were off Holyhead in bad weather, and had to seek refuge for about a fortnight. It was the time of the famous Parliamentary election of 1868 and young Parry recorded the excitement in Holyhead at the victory of William Owen Stanley. More immediately relevant to Parry, however, was the fact that the master of the *Margaret Ann* had gone ashore and had broken his arm ('through drink', Parry alleged) and had to be replaced by another master who took the schooner out on a wild-looking morning, in a strong south-easterly wind. Their progress towards St Bees Head was much too rapid for comfort, and the master bore away for Ramsay, but they eventually found that it was better to make for Belfast Lough. Here a squall carried away the *Margaret Ann*'s top-mast, but their two anchors held, much to their relief, for they were afraid of dragging, with seas washing over the schooner. After a stay of over three weeks in order to get a replacement mast and new sails, they eventually reached Dumfries, where they were rejoined by their own master again. His broken arm had done nothing to improve his temper, and he immediately quarrelled with the mate and another member of the crew, so that Parry was left as sole member of the crew. Matters were made worse when a high wind and spring tide took the *Margaret Ann* high up on to the beach. Parry recalled how 'the top man' from Bangor Insurance Club had to come to inspect her, and how they had to dig a channel to refloat the *Margaret Ann*. This accomplished, they loaded timber for Liverpool, but again had bad weather and had to run for shelter in the Menai Strait. When they eventually reached the Mersey, even the master's habitual bad temper could not spoil the morning for young Parry as he gazed in wonderment at the vessels of all nations entering and leaving the Liverpool Docks. He longed to serve aboard one of these fine barques but the master would not pay him the wages due to him, and when he went to a seamen's lodging house populated by men of all nationalities, the master followed him and persuaded him to return to his ship for the voyage back to the Menai Strait with a cargo of coal.

When they arrived at Hirael, Bangor, the master could not, or would not, pay more than £1 out of the eight pounds owing to Parry, but promised to pay the balance within a few days. His experience in coastal vessels for the next months was more fortunate; he sailed from Bangor to Dublin in the *Hope*, which, on the return journey, brought a cargo of 'Dublin Porter' to Menai Bridge (no difficulty in getting help to unload this – three captains assisted), then had a spell in the *Jane and Ann*, again sailing for Ireland; this time Parry has a very good word for the master, Captain Jones, 'a kind man'. A week after leaving the *Jane and Ann*, he joined the *Jane Hunter*, a dandy rigged vessel which features frequently in Henry Edwards' log-book; she was owned by John Lloyd of Bangor.[54] Her master was Captain Parry, the mate John Jones, and the other crew member William Lewis; on passage for Bristol she showed herself to be an excellent sailing vessel. Voyages to Britton Ferry with pig iron, coal to Bangor, slates for Bristol, Cardiff and Liverpool are then described by Parry, and he remembered that whilst at Cardiff there had been 'a great fuss' about the new Board of Trade ruling regarding navigation lights 'which cost us £10'. His vivid descriptions in colloquial Welsh are not easy to translate effectively, but they indicate evocatively the life of an ordinary seaman in the coasting trade in the sixties and seventies of the last century: the *Jane Hunter* driving deep into high seas with a following wind, and having to take in sail off Bardsey as 'she was drowning herself'; taking refuge at Holyhead in company with many other small vessels 'much more battered than ourselves', Parry caught sleeping on watch by the Dock Police in Liverpool, and how glad he was to leave because of the necessity to keep a 'tide watch'; his experiences as cook aboard the *Liza Catherine*, then in the *Charlotte*[55] in the Pentland Firth bound for Berwick, thence to Poole which he found 'a most interesting place'; sailing short-handed from Poole to Runcorn, where the master's wife joined them, 'a nice enough woman but more work for me'. Before sailing for Wick with a cargo of salt, Parry bought himself a new pair of sea-boots, and was pleased that Wil Pengroeslon, a native of Benllech, had joined the crew. It was not an easy voyage, for although Captain Jones was a kindly man, the mate was a very surly fellow and Parry was in his watch; because of the light winds, progress was slow and even the master became increasingly ill-tempered, for every day meant additional costs in food and wages for him. Moreover, when they arrived in Thurso Bay they had to ride at anchor in company with many other sailing-vessels to wait for a favourable tide to take them through the Pentland Firth, but at last they arrived at Wick where Parry noted the large number of herrings brought in every morning by the fishing-boats. The *Charlotte*'s cargo of salt was welcome for the fishing industry, and after four days unloading, her crew took another seven days to load casks of herrings for Rotterdam. After a rough passage, Parry noted the many vessels of all types at Rotterdam, ships of all nations, but he was particularly interested in German vessels which had escaped the clutches of the French, 'remember there was fighting between the French and the Prussians . . . it was August 1870 and after ten days the news came that Napoleon and four thousand men had laid down their arms . . . there was a very wild place here'.

Parry was glad to get back to Garston from Rotterdam for the weather was breaking, and the vessel small, so he decided to look for a larger ship in Liverpool. Parry's subsequent experiences cannot be followed here – his voyages in the Whitehaven brigantine *Margaret and Elizabeth*, with coal for Portugal, and copper ore on the return passage, voyages in larger vessels to India and Burma, the West Indies, a spell serving aboard a Canadian vessel on the Great Lakes, and a fast passage cross the Atlantic in a handy little Brixham schooner, the *Stena*. His story ends abruptly when he takes the old Brixham master, for whom he had great admiration and affection, ashore at Penarth Roads, after a passage from Brixham when the *Stena* had sailed 'like a yacht'. The crew rowed the master the four miles to the shore, and he gave them two shillings to get a lunch of beer and cheese whilst he himself went for orders. What is striking about this document is the lively interest which Parry took in every new port he visited, his awareness of contemporary affairs, whether noting a Parliamentary election or the Franco-Prussian war, his quickness to seize upon evocative detail which brings such a lively quality to all his descriptions, whether they be of seamen, boarding-house keepers or ships. His impressions and feelings are related simply but with vivid authenticity – what a relief it was to sink into a corner with a bowl of coffee in one hand and a hard biscuit in the other after a long and weary Christmas Day in the Bay of Biscay, the fields of grapes and figs in Portugal which hungry seamen dared not approach because of the armed guards, elephants in Burma carrying timber, and his own discomfort at mosquito bites, the insistence of a

North American master mariner that Parry and all the crew should have an orange before they turned to, even before they had their coffee, a different lodging-house every night in Brooklyn, and his delight at seeing men and girls working in the hay in the field near 'the little ancient city of Exeter' after long, grey days at sea on a diet of salt beef and duff. His writing has a refreshingly direct quality, and although his Welsh is far from orthodox, this is only to be expected for he would not have been allowed a formal lesson in the Welsh language in school at Llangefni, or anywhere else in Wales for that matter. In his simple, modest, factual way, Parry gives an authentic impression of what must have been a fairly typical life of a seaman from Anglesey during the sixties and seventies.

Reading through the thousands of crew agreement lists, the 'Articles' as seamen called them, and the official logs of Anglesey and Caernarvonshire ships from the 1860s, literally tons of documents, one gradually comes to get an instinctive recognition of the type of ship the papers belonged to – the happy ships are those where the pages for unusual occurrences, offences, punishments, illnesses, deaths are, for the most part, blank, where the master has to record few crew changes and desertions, where the crews are discharged with 'very good' against their conduct, where the log is a mere factual record of the beginning and the termination of the voyage. Even in the worst years, most of the Anglesey ships were like that. But there are those where an ill-tempered master has recorded complaint after complaint about a recalcitrant crew, where desertions are frequent, accidents and illnesses common, and even the elements seem to have conspired against what may not even have been a well-found ship in the first place. Occasionally before the passing of the 1854 Merchant Shipping Act, stories of atrocities at sea had come to the ears of Anglesey people: the *North Wales Chronicle* reported fully a case heard at the Anglesey Assizes in March 1847 when the master and mate of the brig *Athelstone* were accused of the 'wilful murder of John Martin, a youth, on the high seas'.[56] The *Athelstone*, bound from Quebec with a cargo of timber for Swansea, had put in to Holyhead after a very rough passage; the crew, who had been 'pumping her day and night' for most of the passage, were discharged at Holyhead and alleged that the Captain offered them a free passage to Liverpool or Dublin if they would leave Holyhead 'that night'. Most of them were glad enough to go, and he might have got away with murder, as many brutal masters undoubtedly did. But one of the crew went to Captain N. M. Goddard, a Holyhead magistrate and former master and agent for the Packet Boats, and told him of the way in which John Martin, aged thirteen, a 'rather delicate' boy, had been so flogged with a knotted rope and beaten with a boat hook by the captain that he died, 'lying on the chain cables . . . with his shirt on only and exposed to the weather'. The wretched lad, described by one witness as 'a small boy, of delicate constitution' had been a little late coming on deck 'at five o'clock in the morning, when all hands were called up to make sail'. The mate had had him hauled on deck 'and ducked him for five or ten minutes in the sea water which was coming over the lee side'; then followed the brutal beating by Captain William Peck. The jury who heard the case included James Treweek, Stephen Roose, Hugh Beaver, W. W. Sparrow, W. B. Panton and William Bulkeley Hughes, M.P., and they heard the defence counsel argue that they should remember 'the responsibility which devolved on the captain embarrased with an ill-conditioned vessel beset by gales of wind', and that 'the punishment administered to the deceased was the usual and ordinary mode of treating skulkers on ships, however rough it might appear to landsmen'. After a twenty minute consultation, the jury rejected the charge of wilful murder, and returned a verdict of manslaughter against the master, Peck, who received two years imprisonment, and acquitted the mate on all charges. Compared with such a brutal case, the action resulting from a drunken brawl between the master and the mate of Treweek's *Amlwch Packet*, heard at the same Assizes, seemed very tame. After the passing of the Merchant Shipping Act of 1854, masters of all British merchant ships were bound to keep an official log (which should not be confused with the ordinary ship's log in which the officers kept a day-to-day record of wind, weather, courses and distances). The official logs had to be handed in at the end of the voyage in the case of foreign-going ships and at the end of each half-year, in June and December, in the case of home-trade ships. The crew agreement lists contain the signatures (or marks) of the crews, when they agreed to sail within certain 'limits', usually 75 degrees N and 65 degrees S in the case of foreign trade, 'for a voyage not to exceed three years', the scale of provisions allowed, and the regulations for maintaining discipline in accordance with the Merchant Shipping Act.[57]

One of the Anglesey-owned vessels which emerges as an unhappy ship from her official logs and papers was the *N.E.V.A.*, built at Newport in 1855. Her name did not commemorate the river of which today's inhabitants of Leningrad are so proud, but was the abbreviated title for Napoleon Eugenie Victoria Albert. Four years after her launching, now Plymouth registered, she was sailing home in May 1859 with a cargo of bone dust and horns from Montevideo for Liverpool when she was wrecked near Wylfa, Cemais. Her cargo was saved, and what remained of the wreck was bought at the subsequent auction by Nicholas Treweek, who rebuilt her. In 1861 she was re-registered at Beaumaris as a 3-masted brigantine with, curiously enough in view of her pretentious name, an Indian chief as her figurehead. Under Treweek's management, and commanded by Thomas Hughes of Amlwch, and then by Lewis Walters of Red Wharf, she sailed uneventfully from 1861 to 1867, mainly to Rio Grande do Sul, Brazil, with predominantly Welsh crews. In 1867, on a voyage from London to Nassau, Walters had trouble with John Richards, a young Aberystwyth man who had signed on as mate in place of William Griffith of Pembroke who had been very unwell on the previous voyage to Rio Grande. Walters had been at a loss what to do with Griffith 'complaining of a shortness of breath . . . the medecine he ask for was an opium pill the which he took and a dose of castor oil the following morning'. Two days later Griffith was still sick and complaining of the same symptoms 'shortness of breath the Medecine which he is now taking now Cod Liver Oil 3 times a day'. Walters, a kindly man, was much concerned and noted in his log "still he is very unwell by all appearance'. It was probably with much relief that he wrote six days later 'William Griffiths all well'.[58] It was a different matter with his new mate: at Nassau 'John Richards mate refused to do his duty by saying that he would not do any more work on board of the damn'd ship so I told him several times to go to his duty but he refused several times'. Two days later, Richards was discharged 'by mutual consent'. Walters' next voyages in the *Neva* to the Bahamas and the Mediterranean were uneventful, but in 1870, when Edwin Phillips, a native of Penzance, took command, the *Neva*'s troubles began in earnest. On the voyage to the Rio Grande, with Owen Jones of Anglesey as mate, Phillips recorded that he had

had trouble with Richard Ellis, a Bangor man, who was eventually discharged at San Jose de Noste. In the light of the subsequent history of the *Neva*, Phillips' account in the log is probably a masterly understatement, 'at 7.30 a.m. Richard Ellis, A.B. causing great disturbance and at 8.30 a.m. I the master called him aft to enquire into the matter, his complaint was he had no coffee this morning previous to going to work. I at once tendered him his discharge which his reply was that was all he wanted'. The desertions increased each voyage under Phillips' command, three at Hamburg, three at Rio Grande, two at Cadiz, three more at Rio Grande the next voyage and another at Lisbon; Phillips refused permission to a West Indian seaman suffering from veneral disease to go ashore to see a doctor at Penarth, and logged him for refusing to take the medicine he prescribed. Four days later Phillips smugly recorded: 'I called him into the cabin where he begged my pardon for the insolence he gave me and would take any medicine offered and hoped I would forgive him for the crew had persuaded him to act as he did.' On his next voyage from Hartlepool to Rio Grande, Phillips took with him his son, Edwin H. Phillips, aged eleven, 'First ship', and at the South American port signed on Catherine Reynolds as 'stewardess' with her husband who signed as an ordinary seaman: she replaced the cook/steward who had deserted at Rio Grande, taking 'the boat from the Davits unknown to anyone'. Phillips was not the only master to have troubles aboard the *Neva*. David Lloyd, her next master, recorded that he had reduced the wages of one of the crew who had signed on as A.B., but had since 'proved himself not only unqualified to discharge his duties as an able seaman but as an ordinary seaman not being able to make the usual splices and bents or pass an earing which Duty is required daily on board a ship'.[59] The seaman in question was reported as a constant source of disturbance. He and another member of the crew fought aboard the ship in the South Atlantic: 'at 7 a.m. Danny Supple came aft with his head scalded and said that Thos. H. Llewellin Through some Hot water when he was asleep on his head To which Thos. H. Llewellin confess and as the cause of it he said that David Supple through a match on his face at 4 o'clock the same morning and called a son of a bitch.'

Apart from the ships that foundered and therefore left no logs or seamen to tell the tale, there are details of nightmare voyages which emerge from the bare bones of the ships' papers. Such is the story of the *John Arthur Pritchard*[60] of Caernarvon in which Ralph Williams, an Amlwch man, shipped for a voyage which began on the 13 March 1861. Sorely battered by Atlantic storms for three months, the *John Arthur Pritchard*, a ten-year-old 198-ton snow built at Pwllheli, reached Rio de Janeiro urgently requiring repairs. No sooner had she come to an anchor than the whole crew went aft to ask for their discharge. Three days later they refused duty and went ashore to see the British Consul at Rio. The result was that the master, John Jones, had to appear before the Consul to face the crew's charges 'that spirits have been too freely used in the cabin'. He may well have had good reason for taking to the bottle, but he had to sign a statement to bind himself 'to have all spirituous liquors removed from the Cabin and placed below hatches and promise that the same shall not be touched during the voyage from this port to Guatemala'. A boisterous passage round Cape Horn was followed by increased troubles off the west coast of South America; at Guayaquil, Ecuador, the Governor was most reluctant to allow the battered *John Arthur Pritchard* to enter lest the fever aboard should spread to other ships in harbour, but eventually two doctors came aboard and two of her crew were put ashore. When they finally reached San Francisco there were more cases of intoxication and insubordination, and on the return journey the master and crew went ashore on the coast of Guatemala but were unable to return to the *John Arthur Pritchard* because of the heavy surf running. That night ashore further complicated matters, for several of the crew drank large quantities of native liquor, the master himself reporting that he had been too ill of the fever to stop them. When they left Guatemala he noted somewhat cryptically in his log 'all in good health, except myself, at least, no one complaining'. A week later, matters were very different. They were in a position 12°16'N 88°33'W when the master recorded 'all that had been on shore, first having lost their appetite, not able to swallow anything but water which they drank much'. Despite his ministrations 'Gave them the Vomit, Purge', one by one the crew got weaker, including Ralph Williams, the Amlwch man, who was one of the first to be taken ill. A few days later a Whitehaven man died; the master had recorded the symptoms of his illness in more detail than was usual, but an hour after reading the burial service, he wrote, almost as though to console himself, and the others, that the death was nothing to do with the night ashore at Guatemala, 'his health had been rather on the decline about two months previous to his death'. In his heart he must have been very uneasy, for now all the crew appeared to be getting worse, even though the master 'treated them as prescribed in the medical guide book' which he no doubt thumbed through as he had never done before. A second man died, a native of Aberdeen, but somehow the severely depleted, sickly crew managed to get the vessel to the Falkland Islands where the sick, including Ralph Williams, were discharged. They were lucky. The *John Arthur Pritchard* was wrecked in March 1863.

The log-books and crew agreement lists of other ships make happier reading. The *Amanda*, Captain Robert Jones, Senior, of Amlwch, sailed from Llanelli to Alexandria and back in 1868: in addition to her master, the boatswain, cook and an ordinary seaman came from Amlwch, and the mate from Caernarvon, in a crew who remained together for both the outward and inward passages. She traded to the Mediterranean for a number of years, and her official logs have few incidents recorded, and no desertions apart from one troubled passage under a relief captain and a largely Irish crew recruited in Glasgow. But even in such a well-ordered vessel as the *Amanda* accidents happened. On her second voyage to Alexandria, Robert Jones had to record in his log that on January 10th, 1870, as they sailed homeward off the coast of Britanny, 'Griffith Jones a native of Portmadoc was washed off the Jib boom while make the Jib fast and disapered in a few minutes'. The melancholy list of the effects of the deceased were recorded: 'one pair of boots, 2 caps, 4 pairs trousers, 2 vests, 1 Flanell shirt, 1 Jacket, 2 Jumpers, 1 Rug, 1 Blanket, 2 Drors, 1 Pillow, 1 Bag, all in bad order.' According to the 'Articles' Griffith Jones was twenty-two years of age; when he first went to sea he probably had more kit in better condition. About the same time, another young boy from Portmadoc, who fell overboard at Stettin from the *Mary* of Caernarvon in his eagerness to get into the ship's boat to fetch some of his older shipmates hailing him from the shore, left a rather fuller list. Perhaps it was his first voyage and his mother had seen to it that he was fitted out well, for he left '2 pairs of Molskin Trousers, 2 Blue shirts, 3 Check Shirts, 2 singlets, 3 pair of Drawers, 4 pair of Stokins, 1 pair of shoes, 3 westcoats, 2 Chacked, bed and pilow, 1 Blanked, small box with little Welsh Bible and 3 other Boks'.

Robert Jones' own son, Robert, the future master of the *Cymric*, *Talus* and *Oweenee*, was aged fifteen when he sailed on the *Amanda*'s next voyage to the Mediterranean later in 1870 with Owen Jones, her master, and seven of the crew of eight from Amlwch. Six months later Owen Jones was taken ill soon after his ship left Glasgow bound for Berbice, British Guiana; he was put ashore sick at Holyhead and was replaced by Captain Evan Williams who, unlike the other masters of the *Amanda*, made fairly frequent use of the official log. Some of the Irishmen signed for this voyage at Glasgow were accused of losing the ship's boat at Holyhead 'through their neglect got on the spreey' whilst a young Dubliner who had signed as an ordinary seaman 'after been at sea for a short time found out that he was no more than a boy first passage on sea could not steer nor stowed the smalest sail when Requir to taked in nor even reeved the Royal haliers now i will Reduce his wages to one pound per month according to his competency.'[61]

Evan Williams did not remain master of the *Amanda* for long; James Williams, who succeeded him, had little trouble in a period of busy coastal trading, with many cargoes for Rouen. By 1875 Robert Jones, Junior, was serving as her mate in this trade, and in 1878 he obtained his first command, as master of the *Amanda*, when he was aged 23, and his mate, William Jones from Cemais, aged 29. Apart from a brief period when she was 'unemployed at Amlwch from 1st January until February 12th' 1879, they sailed the *Amanda* hard in the coastal trade, transforming her losses into profits, and they were still together as master and mate when she was sold. Salt from Weston Point and Runcorn to Newcastle and coal from Newcastle to the south-western ports of Ireland were her main cargoes. During these three years, out of the ninety-seven names in the six-monthly crew agreement of the *Amanda* (many of them the same men signing on again and again), over sixty came from Amlwch and its neighbourhood. Seven of the Amlwch group and nine of the others were unable to write their names and marked the agreement with a cross against their names. It is an indication of educational changes ashore that as the years go by there is a marked decrease in the number of seamen who were unable to write their names in the crew agreements.

The *Amanda* is an example of a British North American vessel owned by Captain Robert Jones and the two William Thomases which sailed first in the Mediterranean and Atlantic trades and then in her later years was confined to coastal and near European waters in the general coasting trade. Small British-built vessels often had a reverse role: starting in the home trade in the years before the railways had made their full impact, as time went on they were compelled to seek cargoes in the more remote areas where the railways had not yet penetrated to the same extent, and then to the European trades, particularly the slate trade with the German and Scandinavian ports.

The dramatic expansion of London in the 1850-1880 period, the development of its suburbs, and those of Liverpool, Manchester, Newcastle, and the rapid growth of new towns like Middlesborough,[62] meant that there was much demand for building materials, and although by 1867 the railways were for the first time carrying more coal to London than came by sea,[63] the main seaports had ample work for coastal shipping. This was in turn reflected in the boom in the building of both sailing ships and steamers for the home and deep-sea trades in the 1870s and 1880s. Until the disastrous strike at the Penrhyn quarry at the end of the century, there was ample work for the slate schooners of the Menai Strait and Portmadoc despite the competition from the railways. The great fire which destroyed over two thousand homes in Hamburg in 1842 had brought a new demand for slates, and sales had been further stimulated by the Great Exhibition of 1851.[64] Whilst the demand from the Australian and American markets expanded in the second half of the century, it would be true to say that the exceptional growth in the export of slate after 1868 was largely due to the great increase in the demand in the German market for Welsh slate. The chief entrepot for this trade was Hamburg, from which Welsh slate was forwarded by rivers and canals to all parts of Germany and beyond; the fashion for roofing railway stations and municipal buildings in Germany with Welsh slate, and the demands from other European countries such as Hungary, led to a call for shipping which effectively gave sailing ships a new lease of life at a time when the development of the railways in Britain seemed bound to destroy their coastal trade. Whilst Welsh slate was effectively kept out of the

French market, and the disruption of the American Civil War and the development there of slate quarrying with the help of many Welsh immigrants led to a dwindling of slate exports to the U.S.A. in the seventies, the exports to Europe through the ports of the Elbe increased dramatically. By 1876 72% of the total value of slate exports went to the German market.[65] Dr Jürgen Meyer of the Altonaer Museum in Hamburg confirms that there was a striking similarity between the development of the North German schooner trade and that of the north Wales ports during this period. A cursory glance through the account books and crew agreement lists of the north Wales slate schooners, and also, of course of the ocean-going sailing ships and barques whose voyages so often began and ended at Hamburg, is sufficient to lead one to a recognition of this close link between Welsh shipping and the Elbe. Some German merchants had mutually beneficial business relationships with Welsh shipowners and Welsh master mariners, and it was not surprising that new Welsh schooners were called *Frau Minna Petersen, Konsul Kastner* and *Detlef Wagner* in honour of particularly good German customers. At Hamburg the ship stores of the Marquard family were much patronised by Welsh seamen, who eventually made the Marquard warehouse their central meeting place. Caesar Marquard went out regularly to meet Welsh ships and learnt Welsh so well that the overlooker of the Liverpool 'Cambrian' ships claimed that Marquard 'could speak Welsh like a native with a good Caernarvonshire accent'. The firm of Caesar Marquard is still in existence, but unfortunately their records were all lost in the bombing of Hamburg during the 1939-45 war, so that it has not been possible to get accurate information regarding the Marquard-north Wales connection.[66] It is fairly certain, however, that many Anglesey seamen of the last century knew Caesar Marquard and had their letters from home addressed to them care of Marquard's warehouses, like the young Lleyn boy, new to the sea, who wrote to his grandparents begging them to write to him 'on board briganteen *Rebecca* at Marquarte at Hamburgh' in 1872.[67]

So many Anglesey seamen served in the merchant schooners of the second half of the century that it is impossible to do justice to the extent of their work during this period, but in order to illustrate the nature of this 'sailing for a living', the fortunes of just one Anglesey family will be traced through the account books and crew agreement lists of their schooners, the *Heir Apparent* and the *Fomalhaut*.[68]

The *Heir Apparent* was built at Runcorn in 1842, and first registered at Liverpool in that year. In 1853 she was bought by Owen Williams of Red Wharf Bay, master mariner, who had a 32/64 share in her, the remaining shares being taken by William Jones, John Jones and Ebenezer Edwards, all of them Liverpool pilots, but by virtue of their names (there were many Welshmen employed as Liverpool pilots) quite possibly countrymen and even kinsmen of Owen Williams, her new master.[69] Owen Williams kept a careful half-yearly account of the *Heir Apparent*'s earnings, and these, together with the list of expenses incurred, must have been typical of the smaller Anglesey schooners of the time. This account book opens on January 1855 with a payment of a subscription of £6.15.0 to the Bangor Mutual Insurance Society, 9/9d to Mr Reynolds for Twine, etc., £7.1.5 to Mr Richardson for warps, 4/6 for a gallon of lamp oil, 5/- for Hogs Lard, 13/- for canvas, and a variety of small items such as varnish, shovels, 3/- for a deck light, cork fenders and paint. Against these expenses, there was offset the moiety of freights, to London for £50 in February, to Dublin in March for £28.6.8, £45 for a freight to Hull in May, and £5.6.9 to Newcastle in June. The profit on the half-year's sailing amounted to £95.4.1 and Owen Williams and his fellow shareholders must have been reasonably satisfied.

In the second half of the year 1855 there are more detailed entries relating to the nature of the cargoes carried: on 17 July, 156 tons of coal from Newcastle to Dublin; on 3 August, 160 tons of iron ore from Barrow to Neath at the rate of 6/- per ton; on 13 August, 160 tons of coal from Neath to Liverpool at 6/6 per ton; and on 11 September, 158 tons of coal from Liverpool to Youghal at 6/6 per ton. The *Heir Apparent* then sailed in ballast for Pembrey, and on 25 September she sailed from there to Amlwch with 166 tons of coal at 6/- per ton. From Amlwch she sailed in ballast to Barrow where she picked up a cargo of 159 tons of iron ore for Britton Ferry, and her final trip of the year was from Britton Ferry to Cork with 167 tons at 7/6 per ton. Although this half-year, superficially at least, appeared to be profitable, with earnings of over £300, the expenses incurred offset almost half this: there were charges for ballast to be paid, payment to pilots, harbour dues, buoyage and anchorage charges, payments to 'hobblers', owners of small boats which tended upon vessels entering or leaving harbour, or men who actually assisted in loading or discharging cargoes or ballast at a daily wage. Turning the yellowing pages of Owen Williams' account book, one can trace the fortunes of the *Heir Apparent* year by year; in January 1856 carrying coal from Llanelli to Londonderry, in May slates from Bangor to London, in June chalk from London to Runcorn, and iron ore at the end of the month to Cardiff, whence she sailed on 4 July for Waterford, then back in ballast to pick up a cargo of coal from Llanelli for Cork, and in September another cargo of coal from Llanelli to Amlwch, then an unspecified cargo from Amlwch to London, bricks from London to Plymouth, and coal from Pembrey in November to Amlwch, where she presumably spent a welcome few weeks refitting over Christmas.

The refit was carried out at the yard of Nicholas Treweek, some years before it was finally taken over by Captain Thomas, and the major repairs amounted to £62.10.0, in addition to £20.15.11 to William Morris, Treweek's rival sailmaker, for new sails, and other payments such as 'John Richards, a piece of Chaine 9/6', 'Mary Lewis, a Coil of Rope, £2.12.3', and for new blocks, nails, paints, adjusting the compass, postage, stationery and carpenter's wages. After a hard half-year the balance amounted only to £14.4.7, so that Owen Williams had £7.3.3½ as his share after many, many weary hours of sailing. Some years were better than others: his half-yearly share in 1857 was £40.12.2½, in 1858 £20.1.8 for the first half-year, and £23.15.6½ for the second half of 1858.[70] As the years go by, Owen Williams had to seek new ports and new cargoes; in 1861 the *Heir Apparent* carried a cargo of slates to Hull, salt to Newcastle, coal to Dublin, slates to Leith, pig iron from Middlesborough to Poole, clay from Poole to Runcorn, salt from Runcorn to Peterhead, herrings from Wick to Rotterdam, pig iron from Middlesborough to Cardiff and coal from Cardiff to Newry. In the following year, 1862, the *Heir Apparent* took a cargo of slates from the Menai Strait to London in May, then in July a cargo of pig iron from Middlesborough to 'St Valary', flints to Runcorn in August, and a week later coal to Bangor. There followed a period of refitting; there are bills for £6.13.5½ for caulking the deck, 8/- for scraping the pitch off the deck, small sundry renewals such as brooms, a cabin mop, and a major expenditure of £47.3.4 for a new anchor and 45 fathoms of chain, then in October she was away from the Menai again bound for London with slates, and in November carried coal to Dublin.

This pattern of coastal trade continued for some years, but cargoes were harder to come by. The pilots who had been Owen Williams' original partners sold their shares in 1865, but Owen Williams continued to remain her master and major shareholder. There are no early crew lists for the *Heir Apparent*, but in 1863 the crew who sailed her from Bangor to Newcastle, thence to Dublin and back to Bangor, were all Anglesey men; so, too, apart from the mate, who came from Bangor, were the crew who took her to Hamburg, Middlesborough, Aberdovey, back to Bangor and thence to Leith later in the same year. For this voyage she had, in addition to the master and mate, two A.B.s, one ordinary seaman, and a boy, William Owens, aged thirteen. One of the A.B.s, William Williams, took over as mate at Bangor before she sailed for Leith, and two years later, when he was aged twenty-four, he is entered as master of the *Heir Apparent*. He was not left entirely on his own with his new responsibility as he might have wished; the crew list bears the name of Owen Williams, her previous master, now managing owner, as mate for the next voyages.[71] William Williams was Owen Williams' son, both then living at 'Bryn Gola', Tynygongl, the house which Owen Williams had built near his smallholding "R. Hows";[72] the father had obviously decided that before he settled down to his farming he would make certain that his son William would have someone to turn to on his first voyage as master.

The papers of the *Heir Apparent* suggest that Owen Williams saw to it that, whether by accident or design, he was with his son whilst he sailed most of the coastal waters and into harbours with tricky approaches which he would later sail by himself. These voyages brought together all the previous knowledge that William had learned the hard way sailing with his father as ordinary and able seaman – from Bangor they now sailed west through the North Channel, past Malin Head and the coast of Donegal for Sligo in February and March 1866, then north about for Hartlepool in April, then down the east coast, no doubt emphasising carefully the treacherous Goodwin Sands, passing through the Strait of Dover and down-Channel for Poole, all the time indicating the intricacies of the tides, noting landmarks and potential sources of refuge to run for in foul weather. From Poole they sailed west and then north through the Irish Sea and made for Runcorn, having thus circumnavigated the coast in the first six months of 1866. But this was not enough. The 'old man' sailed again as mate as they went north about again, this time bound for one of the many Scottish ports the *Heir Apparent* was to know well, Peterhead, then south for Newcastle, then Poole and back to Runcorn, thence to Dublin and home to Bangor by the end of the year. The crew lists for the next few years are missing, so it is not possible to say positively whether Owen Williams made any further passages in the *Heir Apparent* or whether his two round trips had been sufficient to convince him that William could now be trusted to take her anywhere in any weather. There must have been many master mariners in Anglesey who, like Owen Williams, their sea-going days over, turned to farming. And Anglesey in the second half of the century was not unlike the Lleyn peninsula, for here too the ways of the sea had invaded the land. The late Professor J. Glyn Davies' evocative description of Lleyn might equally be applied to Anglesey: 'The whole of Lleyn was permeated with sea life. Even the hay carts were redolent of it; with eyesplice, bowline, clove hitch and timber hitch, and every rope-end properly finished off in sea fashion. The solid paintwork about the farms could be recognized at half a glance as sea-taught.'[73] When Owen Williams returned to Tynygongl he found neighbours who had similar interests in the sea; John Williams, draper, of Tynygongl, for example, had shares in the schooner *Idwal*, built at Bangor in 1857 and commanded by Thomas Jones, Ysgubor Fawr, Llaneugrad. In the sixties the Ysgubor Fawr family had shares, with the farming families of Tŷ'n lôn and Tŷ'n llan, a few fields away, in the schooners *Gazelle* built at Berwick-on-Tweed and the *Isabella* built at Fraserburgh; they sold the *Gazelle* in 1863 to a Bangor master mariner and Robert Hughes of Gaerwen and Owen Thomas of Islington, 'both ministers of the Gospel', and similarly sold a quarter share in the *Isabella* in 1864 to William Thomas, the Liverpool ship-broker. As he looked out to sea at the schooners sheltering in Moelfre Bay, and the smacks dried out at Traeth Bychan or Traeth Dinas, and thought of his own vessel entering Fraserburgh or Peterhead, Captain Owen Williams, master mariner turned farmer, settled easily into a community as 'permeated with sea life' as Professor Glyn Davies' Lleyn.

In the spring of 1867, the *Heir Apparent* left Bangor with a cargo of slate for Leith, and then Captain William Williams took a cargo of pig-iron from Burnt Island to Middlesborough, and a similar cargo from Middlesborough to Newport, and rails from Newport to Liverpool. Despite these freights, however, the *Heir Apparent's* account book had an unhealthy look, with debts amounting to over £129 by the time she reached Liverpool. But there was now the considerable demand at Hamburg for Welsh slate, so Captain Williams' next voyage was with a cargo of slates for the German port, then with wheat to Aberdeen, and in ballast to Newcastle where she took in coal for Dublin. Better prices due to the continued demand for slate at Hamburg in April, a cargo of wheat from Hamburg to Barmouth, then three voyages with coal from Swansea to Le Havre, and flour from Rouen to Londonderry improved the financial position in 1868. Early in 1869 she sailed from Bangor to Limerick, Limerick to Bristol, then to the following ports: Cardiff, Fécamp, Runcorn, Bangor, Galway, Glasgow, Bristol, Cardiff, Dublin, Bangor, Galway, a very busy year in which her debts were considerably reduced, and in 1870 she at last began to make a profit again. In that year she sailed further afield, carrying cargoes of coal from Swansea to Dieppe and by visiting Runcorn, Bangor, Limerick, Ardrossan, St Malo, Par, Runcorn, Rotterdam, Newcastle, Poole, Runcorn and Belfast within the course of the year she finally cleared her debts. She was now nearly thirty years old and repairs became increasingly expensive, although in 1871 she took cargoes from Bangor to Sligo, then from Sligo to Gloucester, Gloucester to Antwerp, Poole to Runcorn, Runcorn to Lossiemouth, Newcastle to Poole, Poole to Runcorn, Runcorn to Beaumaris and Bangor to Shoreham, and made about the same profit on the year's working as she had in her early years.[74]

The account book for the *Heir Apparent* closes in the year 1872; in that year she took cargoes from Shoreham to Runcorn, Bangor to Aberdeen, Clackmannan to Plymouth, Bangor again to Sligo, Sligo to Liverpool, Liverpool to Peterhead, Peterhead to Hamburg, and Hamburg to Cardiff. This last year shown in the account books seems to have been a much more profitable year for she earned

£221.18.9¼, and the charges against her were £56.8.2½, so that her owners had their best profits for many years. It was this and the undoubted age of the *Heir Apparent* that probably prompted Owen Williams to sell her and buy the schooner *Fomalhaut*. The bare record presented in these pages of the distances sailed in all weathers by the *Heir Apparent* cannot in any way recapture in full measure what this amount of sailing meant in wear and tear both on the ship and her small crew; it is but a typical record of the activities of the small Anglesey schooners which plied both in the coastal and the North European trade during the middle of the nineteenth-century.

On the 11 November 1873 Owen Williams sold the *Heir Apparent* to Robert Evans, of Highfield Street, Liverpool, described as a carpenter. She was then sailed, with John Prichard, 'of Bardsey Island', as master in the coastal trade for some years, and then, in 1878, Humphrey Jones, born in Barmouth, but living in the slate port, Port Dinorwic, took shares in her and sailed as master. He was not to have the good fortune of Owen Williams with the old vessel, for she was now nearly forty years old. On 1 July 1880, she sailed from Runcorn to Lossiemouth where she arrived twelve days later; she sailed from Lossiemouth on the 25th for Blyth, and on 29 July she left Blyth for Brest. Eleven days out from Blyth the *Heir Apparent* was wrecked, abandoned in a sinking condition ten miles off Start Point, but all hands were saved 'by our own boat and landed at Dartmouth on August 9th'. A letter from the Custom House, Plymouth, 12 August 1880, contains the last words about the *Heir Apparent*: 'The undermentioned portion of a wreck has this day been delivered into my charge; a piece of bulwark about 8 feet long marked (in yellow letters on a black background) HEIR APPARENT, picked up about 6 miles S.S.W. of the Start Point on the 9th instant, by the *Concorde*, John P. Bisson, master, of Jersey.' So ended the story of the *Heir Apparent* off the Devon coast at four o'clock in the darkness of a rough August morning.

In December 1873, a month after Owen Williams had sold the *Heir Apparent* and his son William had come home from Liverpool where he had left her, they contracted with Samuel Roberts of Plas Llwyd, Bangor, shipbuilder, 'on the purchase of the new vessel now on the stocks at the yard of Mr T. T. Parry at Garth for the sum of £1680'. By the terms of the contract, the Williamses were to pay

£200 at the signing of the contract, £400 on launching day, and the balance of £1,080 before the vessel left the port. In practice, Captain Williams made three payments, £180 on signing the contract, £750 in January 1874, and a further £750 in February. So the *Fomalhaut* was launched into the Menai Strait in 1874; she was a two-masted schooner with a round stern, carvel built, her tonnage, after deductions for crew space, etc., was 72 tons, she was 74.4' long, with a beam of 20' and a depth of hold of 9½', a little longer and broader in the beam than the *Heir Apparent*. Her accounts are contained in the same notebook as Owen Williams' for the *Heir Apparent*: they commence in 1874 when, much to the consternation of her owners, she sustained some damage on her maiden voyage from Bangor to Galway: 'April 17th, Received for damage done at Queenstown £8,' and she had to have minor repairs as well as a main gaff, £2.10.0. Returning in ballast to Bangor from Galway, she had to have the remainder of the damage attended to by Parry, the shipbuilder, a new jib-boom provided, and some iron work carried out by Hughes, the blacksmith.

The expenses and earnings of the *Fomalhaut* from April 1874 to 21 December 1888, when the entries come to an end, give a comprehensive picture of the typical working schooner of the period in much the same way as those of the *Heir Apparent* had done for the earlier years of the nineteenth-century. She visited a wide range of ports including Liverpool, Peterhead, Hamburgh, Middlesborough, Swansea, Newry, Silloth, Dundalk, Glasgow, Kingstown, Lossiemouth, Thurso, Warrenpoint, Annan, Fraserburgh, Limerick, Nairn, Leith, Dieppe, Weston Point, Birkenhead, Greenock, Porthcawl, Waterford, Poole and Newcastle. In the first few months of 1876 when she sailed from Bangor to Silloth, then across from the Solway Firth to Dundalk, thence to Glasgow and Dublin, her crew consisted of William Williams, her master, his brother, Lewis Williams, two years younger, John Roberts, the A.B., all from Anglesey, and a young ordinary seamen from Bangor. The last two were replaced by an Anglesey A.B. and an ordinary seaman aged seventeen from Beaumaris for the next voyage to Hamburg in May; the mate's wages were £4 per calendar month, the A.B. £3.10.0, and the Ordinary Seaman and cook £2.10.0. In 1880 the *Fomalhaut* plied in the beautiful yet sometimes treacherous waters of the north of

Scotland, the Hebrides, the Shetlands and the Pentland Firth, for in July she took a cargo from Bangor to Thurso, then in early August sailed from Stornoway to Wick, then from Buckie to Lerwick. From the Shetlands she sailed in October for 'Danzic', thence to Hartlepool, and from Hartlepool to Treport. The account book does not indicate the nature of the cargoes which she carried in this year, but Owen Williams' share for the year 1880, after all this sailing, is noted as £8.10.0 for the first half of the year and £17.0.11¼ for the second half, a total to December of £25.10.11¼.

William Williams had by this time moved from Bangor to live in his wife's home, The Finger, Llansadwrn, and took over the management of the *Fomalhaut* from Owen Williams in 1880. The Finger (now called Erwyn), and Gorffwysfa, were two houses built alongside the village shop by the shopkeeper and blacksmith at the Llansadwrn crossroads; William Williams used to call at this shop, a convenient stopping-place on his long walk from his father's home in Tynygongl to their schooner at Beaumaris, a distance of several miles. William Williams married the shopkeeper's daughter, Margaret, then aged 18. They had nine children, four of whom died in infancy; three sons and one daughter were sent as boarders to Beaumaris school, and the eldest daughter for a brief period to a school for young ladies at Bangor until she was withdrawn, possibly because money was not available for fees and she was required to help with the younger children. Margaret Williams appears to have been a woman of considerable resource; she was the untrained nurse and midwife who was called upon by the whole district, and used to walk along the footpaths to Garth Ferry, across the Strait in the ferry to Bangor and back to buy lengths of cloth to make clothes for her husband and sons. Nothing was ever wasted. Old suits were made into 'mat racs' when they could no longer be mended, and the *Fomalhaut* bore ample evidence of Margaret Williams' skill as a needlewoman and housekeeper. There was need for care; in the articles of 1881 William Williams' wages are noted as £6 per calendar month, whilst his new mate, Owen Jones, another Anglesey man, received £3.10.0, the A.B. £3, and the Ordinary Seaman £2.10.0.

In 1881 the *Fomalhaut* sailed to Treport, Weston Point, Dingwall, Thurso, Greenock, Gourock, Liverpool, Porthleven, Runcorn,

Anstruther, Caen, Sunderland, Poole, Runcorn, Londonderry, Warren-point, returning only once to Bangor and the Menai Strait. From January to March 1882 she remained there being refitted; caulking ship's bottom, wedging mast, etc., at a cost of £16.19.0½, repairing her mainsail at a cost of £3.14.4, and having various iron work carried out at 'the Foundry' (probably at Port Penrhyn, although this is not stated). She then set sail for Newcastle, and although the ports were different, the pattern of work was much the same; from Newcastle she sailed for Belfast, then back to Bangor for a cargo to Lossiemouth, then down the east coast and through the English Channel to Totnes, then from Teignmouth to Runcorn, Runcorn north about for Fraserburgh, and from there north again for Lerwick, then a short haul cargo to another port in the Shetlands, Scalloway, and back to Lerwick for a cargo to Hamburg and from Hamburg to Irvine in the Firth of Clyde, all in ten months.[75] Her voyages are recorded quite simply in a single line, 'moiety of freight Runcorn to Frazerburgh', but if one stops to think for a moment what each line meant in terms of a sailing-ship voyage and then, often enough, the back-breaking unloading of heavy cargoes in remote, windswept harbours, one begins to realise what was involved.

The account book comes to an end in 1888, but the *Fomalhaut* had another fourteen years of sailing ahead of her. In Appendix X the accounts for 1885 and 1886 are reproduced, and give an indication of the income and expenditure of an Anglesey schooner in the slate trade; the payments made illustrate the connections with well-known British firms, and with the Marquard family in Hamburg, as well as the costs of refitting in the Menai Strait. The accounts of the Williamses' earlier vessel, the *Heir Apparent*, similarly contain many payments to some of the firms that have been mentioned in the chapters dealing with both the merchant schooners and the deep-sea sailing ships. William Ashburner carried out work when she was at Barrow, as did the Paynters, Captain Thomas and William Morris, the sail-maker at Amlwch, and in the Strait, Rees Jones, the Portdinorwic builder and father of W. E. Jones, who designed and managed large barques and ships in the late 70s. One of the last generation of Cape Horners, Captain W. H. Hughes, remembers being in his father's Portmadoc schooner at Preston at the same time as a vessel with an unusual name, the *Fomalhaut*, and her tall, quietly spoken master, Captain William Williams. The seafaring community of the north-west was close-knit.

In 1886 Lewis Williams, William Williams' brother, made a number of voyages in her as master, with Richard Williams of Moelfre as mate, and two other Moelfre men as crew, sailing for the most part between Londonderry, Thurso and Newcastle, and making at least one voyage from Thurso to Duddon, and another from London to Whitehaven.[76] But Captain William Williams was soon back in command of his ship: in 1897, with Joseph Williams of Moelfre as mate, and another Moelfre man, Hugh Williams, as ordinary seaman, and a Bangor A.B., he took slate from Portmadoc to Southampton, then sailed in ballast for Redbridge where he took aboard a cargo for Belfast, then again in ballast for Portmadoc and another cargo of slate for Sunderland. In July 1902, writing from London to his family in Llansadwrn, Captain Williams described their 'longish passage' down the east coast of England, 'head wind as usual, and on Saturday it came so heavy that we were obliged to put into the River Humber and remained there till Sunday morning'. Cargoes were not easy to obtain, 'I find that business is very dull here again, several vessels here can't get anything and freights very low'.[77] The *Fomalhaut* took a week on passage from North Fleet to Portland in very changeable weather, but on their arrival there they had had a 'a fine sight, eighteen Navy ships coming in together', and Captain Williams added, 'hope we shall soon have a change in the weather that we may be able to keep to sea again'.

In the first week in September, the *Fomalhaut* was on the west coast of Ireland, in the Shannon at Foynes, and Captain Williams happily reported in his letter to his wife 'that the cargo turned out better than I expected for there were only ten bags too bad . . . and fortunately we had ten bags over the bill of lading, consequently he (i.e. merchant) had nothing to say as we had turned out our Quantity in good order and I got my freight in full'. But the narrow financial margins operated and the prevarious nature of the very hazardous life of the master of a coasting schooner come out clearly in his next sentence. 'As I am obliged to leave in ballast I must keep enough money to clear the ship from the next port and can only send you this ten pounds you see it's the merchant's cheque which I believe is quite safe.' Captain Williams decided to return to Caernarvon 'as freights are so low everywhere that I could not do anything out of them', and a week later he wrote a short note to say that they had arrived safely in the Strait, and had got into the harbour at Caernarvon 'just before dark' on 14 September. Some years earlier at Caernarvon Captain Williams had had his photograph taken, standing on the shiningly polished deck, at the *Fomalhaut*'s tiller, with its carefully carved dog's head; in the background the walls of the castle hard by the quay may be dimly seen. Known to his family and contemporaries as a gentle and very kind man, Captain Williams had the reputation of being a fine seaman; the *Fomalhaut* was always kept at a high level of efficiency. On the walls of his home the locally painted picture of the *Fomalhaut* had an honoured place.

The *Fomalhaut*'s next voyage as her last. On 14 October 1902 she left Caernarvon during a heavy gale, in company with the *Lady Louisa Pennant*, both being bound for the Clyde with a cargo of slate. Neither of them arrived. Two days later, the Llansadwrn postman, dumb with grief, took Williams' young daughter into his arms as he silently handed the dreaded telegram to her mother. Handed in at Silloth, it read, 'Boat, mast and other wreckage also papers belonging *Fomalhaut* come ashore must fear worst for crew'. Captain Williams knew all about the extensive sandbanks of the Solway Firth; the Silloth Bank which the Sailing Directions for that very year described as 'a long sandy tongue between North Bank and Silloth, dry in places about half tide' . . . 'There is a heavy sea on Workington Bank in bad weather.'[78] What happened will never be known. From the position in which the wreck was found, Hugh Williams, his eldest son, who had himself sailed in the *Fomalhaut* as a seaman,[79] firmly believed that Captain William Williams must have been washed overboard early in the storm. Ironically, shortly before her last voyage, Captain Williams had stopped paying the insurance of the *Fomalhaut*, saying that there was no need for it, that he was always so careful. All hands were lost when the *Fomalhaut* foundered, among them Captain Williams and his youngest son, Wil. The years of hard sailing and the search for freights had come to an end on a wintry night on the inhospitable, treacherous coast of Cumberland.

[1] Mr Norman Sheldrake kindly made a transcript of the minister's notebook entering the names of the master mariners and the ships in which they were serving at the time of the birth of their children.

[2] Captain H. Roberts, Moelfre, TR June 1972.

[3] Mr Emrys Hughes, Llangefni, gave much assistance with the Census Returns for Anglesey in 1851 and 1861, carefully extracting the names, ages and addresses of all those connected with the sea.

[4] Owen Williamson, *Hanes Niwbwrch* (Lerpwl, 1895), 41-46.

[5] UCNW Bangor MSS 7395, 7398.

[6] H. Owen, *Hanes Plwyf Niwbwrch* (Caernarfon, 1952), 169-70. Richard Davies, M.P., Treborth, was the chief negotiator for the Calvinistic Methodists.

[7] *ibid.*, 194.

8 J. Glyn Davies, *Cerddi Huw Puw* (Liverpool, 1923), XIX.

[9] UCNW Bangor MS 491.

[10] UCNW Bangor MS 490.

[11] UCNW Bangor MS 491.

[12] *ibid.*

[13] J. F. C. Harrison, *The Early Victorians*, 1832-1851 (London, 1971), 55.

[14] *First Report from the Select Committee on Shipwrecks, together with Minutes of Evidence* (London, 1843), 20-21.

[15] Captain Lloyd claimed that the Welsh chapels had not been as active as the English in this context, yet despite the poor support from Wales, the Society had a paid missionary who spoke Welsh working among the Welsh seamen whose vessels visited the Thames. *Y Drysorfa* (1843), 301; D. Thomas, *Hen Longau Sir Gaernarfon*, 164-6.

[16] It was not until 1874 that the North Wales Quarrymen's Union was formed, and despite the articles by John Owen Jones (Ap Ffarmwr) in *Y Werin* on the grievances of agricultural labourers in Anglesey in the 1890s, no trade union was formed, C. Parry, *The Radical Tradition in Welsh Politics* (Hull, 1970), 1-14. In August 1872 the seamen in harbour at Caernarvon made representations for better wages. *Baner ac Amserau Cymru*, 28 August 1872.

[17] *Y Drysorfa* (1843), 114. For a discussion of earlier Methodism's 'function as a carrier of work-discipline', E. P. Thompson, *The Making of the English Working Class* (London, 1970), and his essay, 'Time, Work-Discipline and Industrial Capitalism', in *Past and Present*, December 1967.

[18] At a meeting aboard Captain Watkin Williams' brig in Caernarvon harbour in July 1822, it had been unanimously decided to form a 'Caernarvon Seamen's Friends Society and Bethel Union', or 'Unol Gymdeithas Cyfeillion y Morwyr'; 'that the Society should buy a Flag to be hoisted up, where and when a Meeting is intended to be kept, also to buy Four numbers of the "Sailors' magazine" for the use of members'; 'that the object of the Society shall be the promotion of Religious Knowledge among seamen that may be in the Port, by preaching or explaining the Word of God

and keeping prayer meetings without partiality as regards to sect or party; Christians of different denominations shall be invited to unite their efforts to promoting its designs'. *North Wales Gazette*, 18 July 1822. For Captain Watkin Williams, who had 'worked his ship as a supply ship to the British army during the Napoleonic Wars', see Sir Ben Bowen Thomas, 'The Schooner Mary Watkins', in *TCHS*, 1942-3, 86.

[19] TR of conversations with Mrs Elizabeth Jones, Gauntlet, Captains R. Wynn and R. Jones at Amlwch, June 1971.

[20] *Parl. Papers, Report on Shipwrecks*, 1843, 95.

[21] *ibid.*, 16. 'In Prussia a mate before he is licensed must be 20 years of age, and have been five years at sea . . . The Captain has three grades: the first class certificate qualifies him to navigate everywhere . . . the second class qualifies him for the Seas of Europe, the Mediterranean, and the Black Sea and the Atlantic; the third class is qualified, like the mate of the second class, to Navigate the Baltic in ships of any size, the Cattegat and Skaggerak but with ships of not above 40 lasts, that is, about 80 tons, as far as the Naze of Norway. It is also requisite that before a licence can be obtained as captain of first class, he must be not less than 28 years of age, he must have sailed on distant voyages as captain of the second class not less than two years.'

[22] Rule 43 of the Portmadoc Mutual Ship Insurance Society, formed in 1841, stated that 'The master of every vessel insured in the Society who shall not have previously commanded a ship or vessel for 12 months, shall appear before the committee to be examined as to his competency'. – H. Hughes, *Immortal Sails*, 55; Greenhill, *The Merchant Schooners*, I, 206, II, 241-246. The first Newborough master mariner to gain a certificate under the 1854 Act was Captain Robert Hughes, Erw Wen, father of the Rev. Robert Hughes, Valley. – E. A. Williams, *Hanes Môn*, 267. By 1872 there were 309 vessels insured with the Bangor Mutual Ship Insurance Society, and 202 with the Bangor and North Wales Mutual Marine Protection Association. The late David Thomas calculated that in 1871 the capital of the Caernarvonshire Mutual Marine Societies amounted to £805,690; in 1881 it was £1,592,753, and in 1885 £997,295. UCNW Bangor MSS 19078.

[23] *Report of the Commissioners of Inquiry into the State of Education in Wales, 1847* (London, 1848).

[24] David Williams, *History of Modern Wales* (London, 1951), 255.

[25] *Report on Education in Wales*, 1847, 525.

[26] *ibid.*

[27] *CDH*, 1 January 1848. William Francis did in fact have a son, but he had been physically handicapped from birth. In March 1821 Francis had written to Sanderson, the Plas Newydd agent, requesting permission to rent accommodation in the old Assay Office near Parys Lodge office, as he was 'lately very much pressed to admit more into my school' and 'particularly as my Son (who was unfortunately rendered hump-backed by a fall in his infancy) is now become fully competent to act as my assistant'. UCNW PN MSS II, 1163.

[28] I am indebted to Captain R. K. Jones of Moelfre and his brother, Mr H. Jones of Penrhoslligwy, for allowing me to see the exercise book which has been in the possession of their family since the days of John Hughes. I am also grateful to Mr B. Royston Jones of the Department of Education, UCNW, for his comments on the mathematics in the exercise book.

[29] BCR, 1836, 1842.

[30] UCNW PN II, 1168.

[31] *NW Gazette*, 17 February 1814.

[32] UCNW PN II, 1163.

[33] *ibid.*, 1168.

[34] *NW Gazette*, 22 April 1824. 'Mount Pleasant' was probably the area known locally as 'Pen-bonc-llan'.

[35] His father, Captain Thomas Hughes, who died in 1845 aged 51, and his brother, Captain Henry Hughes, also of Simdda Wen, died 1897, are also buried at Penrhoslligwy. Captain R. K. Jones, Moelfre, kindly took me to see these and other mariners' graves in the churchyard.

[36] W. A. C. Stewart and W. P. McCann, *The Educational Innovators, 1750-1880* (London, 1967), 35-42.

[37] '*Letter to the Right Reverend Dr Warren, on his conduct as Bishop of Bangor*' (1796) – O. Llew Owain, 'Pwy ydoedd "Shôn Gwialen"?' 'Pwy ydoedd Shôn Gwialen', in *Y Traethodydd*, 1947, TCHS, 1940, 77, *DWB*, 969-970.

[38] David Williams, 'The missions of David Williams and James Tilly Mathews to France (1793)', *English Historical Review*, 1938.

[39] *Caernarvon and Denbigh Herald*, 5, 19 November 1853.

[40] Bedwyr Lewis Jones, 'William Roos Yr Artist', *TAAS*, 1963, 109-119. The portrait was then (1963) in the possession of Mr R. Williams, Marbryn, Caernarvon. Both Roos and 'Master of a Coaster' in the *CDH* letter positively identify Mrs Edwards as the daughter of William Francis, teaching navigation at Caernarvon, and the latter confirmed that she was 'the old woman of Caernarvon' of the 1847 Report. She was 79 when she died in 1889, and as Roos indicates, had been teaching navigation in Caernarvon since about 1830. As a woman in her mid-thirties when the Commissioner visited Caernarvon, she would have hardly been described by him as 'an old woman', but it must be remembered that the description is that given by a witness, the Headmaster of the National School, Caernarvon, who would have been hostile to her father, William Francis, and herself, on political and religious grounds.

[41] *CDH*, 12 April 1889. When George Owens, an Amlwch seaman, was lost overboard in the North Sea, his widow was determined that her son, Owen, aged fifteen, should be apprenticed for seven years as a carpenter at Captain Thomas' yard. The indenture was signed in 1874, a few weeks after her husband's death, and 'Owen did serve his time with distinction and was later acknowledged as a craftsman of high degree in the shipyard'. T. G. Walker, 'Nain, a brief History', *TAAS*, 1967, 66.

[42] *NW Gazette*, 4 Jan. 1816.

[43] At Bodedern John Hughes and William Lewis were schoolmasters who taught a number of future masters and mates. Hughes also taught at the Llanddeusant school which was largely financed by the Rev. James Williams of Llanfair-yng-Nghornwy out of his own pocket. The Newborough boys were taught by Williamson at the Llangeinwen school as the British School at Newborough itself did not open until 1868. The Rhoscolyn school, established in 1846, was much indebted to the financial encouragement of J. Hampton Lewis, Bodior, who wished the school to be a free, non-sectarian school. – E. A. Williams, *Hanes Môn*, 267.

[44] O. Williamson, *Hanes Niwbwrch*, 46.

[45] These included a *Naval Biography or the History and Lives of Distinguished characters of the British Navy*, published in the year of Nelson's death at Trafalgar, and a *Grammar of the Several Kingdoms of the World, by William Guthrie* (all 1,019 pages of it). The books were found by Miss F. Cale when the last sail-loft in Hirael, that of Mr D. W. Cale, closed in 1972. In Slater's Directory of 1844 there were four shipbuilding firms, 3 ship Bread Bakers, and 2 sail-makers firms listed at Hirael; Nicholas Treweek, Hirael, is one of the shipbuilders mentioned. By 1868 there were five ship chandlery firms listed at Amlwch Port, and in 1883 three sailmaking firms. William Evans (1833-1897), later a prominent Anglesey Wesleyan Methodist minister, was one of the sailmaker's apprentices at Amlwch in the 1850s. – R. Môn Williams, *Enwogion Môn*, 18.

[46] David Griffith, *Morwyr Cymru* (Caernarfon, 1866). The booklet contains an introduction by Dr Lewis Edwards, Principal of the Theological College at Bala, in which he contrasted the interest taken in the fate of seamen in wartime with the apparent lack of concern for their welfare in peacetime.

[47] Griffith stated that according to the Customs officials at Runcorn, half of the 4,418 vessels which visited the port in 1865 were Welsh ships. He quoted from a friend's letter which described the way in which the 'elders of the sea' took a prominent role in the Welsh chapel at Runcorn when they were in port just as though they were in their home chapels in Nefyn, Caernarvon or Aberaeron: 'Daw blaenoriaid y mor . . . ar eu hunion i'r set fawr yma fel y gwnaent yn eu cartrefi yn Nefyn'. *ibid.*, 78. Griffith outspokenly criticised the lack of support for Sailors' Institutes from the wealthy; for example, it was all very well for the Pennants to build Penrhyn Castle and the Penrhyn Hall, but there was need for a building for seamen near the port, and it was strange that the sailors had to collect funds for themselves for a reading room. *ibid.*, 80. In 1856 Wyatt had written on behalf of Colonel Pennant to Captain J. Jones to express an interest in the proposal to 'establish a school of navigation in connection with the Museum' at Bangor. – UCNW Penrhyn MSS 1800, 824.

[48] *supra*. For John Jones' connection with the Davies family, UCNW Bangor MSS 18952, 135; for John Pritchard, R.M. Williams, *Enwogion Môn*, 96.

[49] The log-book is now housed in the Anglesey County Library and I am indebted to the Librarian, Mr Dewi O. Jones, for drawing my attention to it. Some years earlier, James Wyatt, writing on behalf of the slate quarrying interests, had drawn attention to the need for an increased number of pilots for the Menai Strait: 'Since the death of John Hughes, Junr., and the withdrawal of Hugh Jones, we have only two Swelly Pilots stationed at Bangor, the rest being at Cadnant and Portdinorwic, and there being a considerable number of vessels trading from this place, much inconvenience is felt for want of another Pilot at Bangor'. UCNW Penrhyn MSS 1800, 773.

[50] The unfortunate valet is not the only one whose death whilst bathing (though not on a Sunday) is recorded, for Edwards noted on 24 August 1869, 'Mrs McIvor drowned by Bathing near Garth, Anglesey'.

[51] I am indebted to Mr Emrys Hughes, Llangefni, for allowing me to see his transcript of the original documents now in the possession of Mrs Moreland. Mr Emrys Hughes intends to edit and publish the original Welsh version in full in a future volume of *TAAS*.

[52] The *Catherine Williams* was a 107-ton schooner, built at Caernarvon in 1856, 79.2 x 21.4 x 10.9. The late Professor J. Glyn Davies has recorded that his uncle, Richard Davies of Edern, served as mate to Captain Hudson when his crew were accused of dumping some Irishmen in the sea after a fracas on board at Cork. – J. Glyn Davies, *Cerddi Huw Puw* (Liverpool, 1923), xviii.

[53] Probably the schooner built at Beaumaris in 1840 and later owned by Burlace and Company, Brixham, according to the Lloyd's Register of 1871-72. This vessel was an 84-ton schooner, 67.1 x 17.8 x 10.1.

[54] The *Jane Hunter* had been built at Bridport in 1858; 73.7 x 17.3 x 9.2, 63 tons, cf. Greenhill, *The Merchant Schooners*, II, 26.

[55] There are ten '*Charlottes*' in the *Lloyd's Register* for 1871. The vessel in which Parry served was probably the schooner of that name built at Portmadoc in 1852, commanded in 1871 by a Captain Humphreys. She was a 62-ton vessel, 77.5 x 16.5 x 9.3.

[56] *NWC*, 30 March 1847. There is a Sunderland-built *Athelstan* in the 1846 Lloyd's Register.

[57] The official logs for the Anglesey ships upon which the details which follow are based have recently been acquired by the Anglesey Record Office from the Public Record Office; Mr Dewi O. Jones kindly allowed me to consult them before they were catalogued and therefore they have not yet been given a reference number in the Anglesey MSS.

[58] Walters and Griffiths would have read '*The Seaman's Medical Guide*'. In the 1856 edition instructions were given regarding the administration of opium pills. 'An opium pill is a proper remedy when there is much pain . . . opium is a valuable medecine, but requires great discretion in its use. There is reason to believe that it is sometimes used needlessly and too often.' I am grateful to W. Jones, Llannerch-y-medd, for lending me his copy of *The Seaman's Medical Guide* which on 1 Dec. 1856 belonged to Captain Brown of the ship *Conquest* (not in Lloyd's Register).

[59] Earings were 'small ropes employed to fasten the upper corners of sails to the yards'. – Norie's *Navigation*, 276. The *Neva* was sold in 1877 to R. H. Roberts, 70 Farnsworth Street, Everton, who also owned the barquentine *Gaerwen* in 1880. The *Neva* does not appear in the *Lloyd's Registers*; her official number was 5720 and she is registered in BCR 9/1861. Her dimensions were 107.2' x 21.5' x 11.9'.

[60] Mr R. Bryn Parry, County Archivist, kindly drew my attention to this case as the papers of the *John Arthur Pritchard* are in the Caernarvon Record Office.

[61] At Berbice Captain Williams had further trouble with the Irishmen. After three weeks at sea, Williams recorded in the log that a young Donegal boy who had shipped as cook and seaman at £2.10.0 a month was 'neither cook nor seaman, and I have to reduce his wages to £1 a month according to his ability'. After a fracas at Berbice, Williams recorded that another of the Irishmen 'call me out to fight for pount of tobacco and then he call me son of bitch son of hore and then turn his backside to me and tould me to kick it for a Irishman that he was one of OConor boys and tould the Mate he would make his wife a widow before leaving here'. – Official Log Book of *Amanda*, 53682, voyage commenced 6 October 1870, incident recorded 30 December 1870, Berbice.

[62] Asa Briggs, *Victorian Cities*, 312-360; 241-276.

[63] Harold Perkins, *The Age of the Railway* (London, 1970), 102.

[64] Dylan Pritchard, 'The Slate Industry of North Wales, a study of changes in Economic Organization from 1780 to the present day' (Unpublished M.A. Wales thesis, 1935), 83. Following the great fire of 1842 at Hamburg, Mathews, the enterprising quarryowner of the Rhiwbrifdir Quarry, had gone over to Germany and succeeded in persuading the Hamburg city authorities that Ffestiniog slate was particularly well suited for roofing municipal buildings.

[65] *ibid.*, 86-87.

[66] Dr Jürgen Meyer has generously given of his time to answer my enquiries regarding Hamburg and North German shipping. Jürgen Meyer, *150 Jahre Blankeneser Schiffahrt, 1785-1935* (Hamburg, 1968); *Hamburgs Segelschiffe 1795-1945* (Nordestadt, 1971).

[67] D. Thomas, *Hen Longau Sir Gaernarfon*, 154.

[68] I am indebted to Mrs Dilys Humphreys, Bryn Golau, Tynygongl, for granting me access to the papers and account books of her grandfather, Captain William Williams. The pages which follow are based upon these personal papers and information provided by Mrs Humphreys.

[69] According to the Customs Register the *Heir Apparent* was a 2-masted wooden schooner, 69.6 x 18.6 x 10.5, 89.4 tons. Square sterned, carvel built and schooner rigged, with a boy's head as figurehead.

[70] Appendix X is a summary of the *Heir Apparent*'s accounts for the second half-year of 1858 and for 1859.

[71] In addition to having his father as mate, William Williams had two

experienced local able seamen in his crew for his first voyage as master, William Jones, aged 30, whose birthplace is noted as Tynygongl, and Owen Thomas, aged 31, born at Llanfair, whence the young ordinary seaman, Robert Lewis, also hailed.

[72] ''R Hows' (The House Willow), a small farm, had been bought by Owen Williams from the Marquis of Anglesey, and Bryn Golau was for some years the home of his widowed daughter.

[73] J. Glyn Davies, *Cerddi Huw Puw*, X. The details relating to the vessels owned by the Llaneugrad farmers are in BCR 10/1857, 18/1862, 6/1864. Owen Jones of Tŷ'n lôn and Thomas Jones of Ysgubor Fawr may have been the Llaneugrad mariners of that name who owned the *Brothers*, a 16-ton smack built at Traeth Bychan by Henry Williams in 1846. BCR 2/1846.

[74] Her earnings amounted to £197.1.7 in 1871, but expenses for equipment, repairs and insurance calls on the Bangor Club amounted to £139.19.11½.

[75] The most lucrative of these freights was for the voyage from Bangor to Lossiemouth; the total earnings for all this sailing amounted to £203.13.9. Out of the £143.6.5 expenses for the year 1882, £95.12.6 were insurance call payments.

[76] When all the bills were paid for this year's sailing, 1886, the balance left for the owners of the *Fomalhaut* was only £6.18.11.

[77] Captain Williams' mind was very much with his family at home as he asked them to write to him: c/o Hugh Edwards, Ship Broker, Great Tower Street; he hoped his son Owen was better again, and in his next letter, on August 18th, from Portland, he gives a clue to the nature of Owen's injury, 'hope that you are all well and that Now bach's eye has come to its natural colour'.

[78] *Sailing Directions for the West Coast of England*, 1902 (London, 1902), 429. The Workington Bank, the Three-fathoms bank, Two-feet bank, Robin Rigg and North banks, all subject to change 'on account of the shifting nature of these sands' presented serious problems to the mariner even in moderate weather.

[79] He was a member of the crew in the 1897 voyages, and was then described as ordinary seamen, aged 16.

The Sea for Leisure

William Bulkeley sailed from Holyhead one dark October evening in 1735 in the *Wyndham* packet boat for Dublin, he undertook a voyage which he, and countless others before and after him, took for granted. The sea was there to be sailed across; if it was fine and sunny, well and good, if it was cold and stormy, they could do nothing about it, but hope that the voyage would soon be over. On this occasion he sailed at five o'clock in the evening, and at six o'clock next morning, a cold, raw day, they came to an anchor in Dublin Bay,[1] a much better voyage than he had experienced on his return journey to Holyhead a few months previously. Then they had battled against easterly winds for two days and nights: 'the old crazy ship stretching the 6 hours ebb to the north and the 6 hours flood to the south to gain 2 leagues in a tide. Before night we got within 4 or 5 leagues of the Head, but about sunset a great storm arose and blew easterly all the night, and by morning we were drove back again in sight of the Irish shore.'[2] Two days later the *Prince Frederick* was still at Dublin, and Bulkeley ashore in lodgings where he 'drank some hot punch and went to bed, having got a severe cold on board that leaky crazy vessel'. For the most part, Bulkeley regarded his visits to Dublin as business trips, but there were opportunities for pleasure, a visit to 'Smock-Alley playhouse to see the Recruiting Officer acted' in December 1735, as well as 'Don John', 'Harry IV' and 'The Pilgrim'.[3] Dublin had become an agreeable playground for Anglesey gentlemen, and when Bulkeley sailed home a couple of days after Christmas in 1735 in the *Carteret*, with Thomas Hughes, a Holyhead man, as master, he paid his half-guinea for his passage and accepted the discomforts with resigned equanimity.[4] Half a century before Bulkeley, Clarendon, the Stuart statesman, had found the Holyhead crossing tempestuous: 'The sea is, they say, always very rough; I am sure it was so now, everybody was sick and I was worse than even in my former voyage.'[5] His feelings and those of many like him throughout the centuries must have been something akin to that early seventeenth-century Welshman, James Howell, who summed up the experience of all landlubbers after a rough passage when he wrote 'I was pitifully sick all the voyage, for the weather was rough and the wind untowards . . . Having been so rocked and shaken at sea, when I came ashore I began to incline to Copernicus his opinion, which hath got such sway lately in the world, viz. that the Earth as well as the rest of her Fellow Elements is in perpetual motion, for she seemed so to me a good while after I had landed.'[6]

There were fairer days at sea, and by the nineteenth-century the new steamboats were being used in the Irish Sea and Liverpool Bay not only for the transport of cargo, but also as early forerunners of the 'pleasure steamers', taking the newly affluent shopkeepers of Liverpool to north Wales. The steam packets already established at Holyhead set the fashion, and soon there were others plying between Liverpool and Beaumaris, Menai Bridge and Caernarvon. In 1822 a press report claimed somewhat breathlessly that 'The *Albion* steam packet performed a passage on Monday which has never been accomplished before by any vessel. The *Albion* left Liverpool at 7.00 a.m. with a large party and arrived opposite Bangor Ferry before 1.00 p.m. where she remained nearly two hours so that the party on board might inspect the stupendous work now in progress for the new chain bridge':[7] Telford's Suspension Bridge, which was completed four years later. The *Albion* returned to Liverpool that evening; she was the first of many vessels which brought passengers in their leisure hours to this new place of pilgrimage for those who wished to marvel at one of the wonders of early nineteenth-century Britain. The 'spirited proprietors' of the new steam vessels were quick to see the possibilities of their vessels. The St George Steam Packet Company, the registered owners of the *Prince Llewelyn*, built at Liverpool in 1822, a 96-ton steam vessel, not only included a number of drapers, wine merchants, druggists and grocers from Liverpool, but also prominent Beaumaris people such as Edward Rice, tanner; Richard Lloyd, grocer; James Harris, timber merchant; John Boggie, gent.; Thomas Parry, druggist; Eleanor Redding, inn-keeper; John Jones and Thomas Williams, solicitors; William Morgan of Amlwch, gent.; Samuel Dew, Llangefni; William Owen, also of Llangefni, a grocer; and Ann Hughes of Mynydd y Gof, spinster.[8] John Jones, Edward Rice and Thomas Williams were the Beaumaris representatives, along with William Fawcett and other prominent Liverpool and Manchester trustees, of the 'Liverpool and North Wales Steam Packet Company', in whose name the *St David*, a 100

CONVEYANCE OF GOODS
BETWEEN
LIVERPOOL, BEAUMARIS, BANGOR, AND CARNARVON.

THE Public are respectfully informed, that on FRIDAY, MAY 6th, 1830, the ABBEY Steam Boat will commence running between the above places, for the conveyance of Goods, and will continue to sail regularly every FRIDAY from *Liverpool*, and every MONDAY from *Carnarvon*, &c.

In soliciting the support of the Public to this arrangement, the Proprietors beg to state, that Agents and Store-houses will be established at Liverpool and Carnarvon, for the receipt and forwarding of Goods by this conveyance, from any part of Great Britain throughout the year.

Time of Sailing, Eight o'Clock in the Morning, from George's Pier Head.

Agent at Liverpool, Mr. George Daney, 5, Strand street.

Agent at Carnarvon, James Galt, Baths.

The above Boat will also sail every Tuesday morning from George's Pierhead at eight o'clock, with Goods and Passengers to Amlwch.

G.  R.

FOR LIVERPOOL.

THE Public are respectfully informed, that the War Office Steam Packets the PRINCE LLEWELYN, of 200 Tons burthen, and 70 horses power engines, JOSEPH WRIGHT, R. N. Commander; and the ORMROD, of 150 Tons burthen, and 50 horses power, JAMES GALT, Commander, commenced plying between Menai Bridge, Bangor, Beaumaris, and Liverpool, on TUESDAY, the 4th of MAY inst.—The PRINCE LLEWELYN sailing every Monday, Wednesday, and Friday; and the ORMROD every Tuesday, Thursday, and Saturday, at eight o'clock in the morning from the Bridge, and at nine o'clock from Beaumaris; returning from Liverpool every morning at ten o'clock, and will continue to do so every day (Sundays excepted) throughout the season.

Cabin Fare.......... 10s. 6d.
Steerage............ 5s. 0d.
JOHN WATSON, Agent.

Water Street, Liverpool, April 27th, 1830.

ton schooner-rigged vessel, was built by Humble and Hurry, the Liverpool shipbuilders, in 1824.[9] The *Prince Llewelyn* and the *St David*, both with 75 h.p. engines, sailed regularly from Liverpool for Beaumaris and Bangor, and made excursions to the Isle of Man – in 1831, for example, the *Prince Llewelyn* sailed from Menai Bridge on Saturday evening at seven o'clock, and Beaumaris at eight, 'for Douglas where she will remain the whole of Sunday, and leave that evening at Ten o'clock precisely for the Menai Bridge'.[10] The return cabin fare was 12 shillings and the deck fare to Douglas and back six shillings.

The commanders of these early steam packets were often naval men: J. Wright, R.N., was commander of the *Prince Llewelyn*, Lieutenant John Tudor, R.N., commander of the *Air*, described in the 1830s as a 'fine war office steam packet', sailing from Caernarvon for Dublin every Tuesday, Thursday and Saturday and from Dublin to Caernarvon every Monday, Wednesday and Friday. The most colourful and the best known in Anglesey of all the masters of steam packets was Commander J. M. Skinner, R.N., who had commanded post office packets from Holyhead for over thirty years when he was washed overboard from the *Escape* off Holyhead in 1832. An eccentric and romantic figure, with a pet raven frequently perched on his shoulder, and owing something to the Nelsonian legend, for Skinner too had lost an eye and an arm, he had gained much popular attention following the voyage of George IV in the packet *Lightning* on his visit to Holyhead in 1821. John Skinner, born in North America but serving in the Royal Navy in the American War of Independence, had become very much an Anglesey man; he was a prominent member of the Anglesey Hunt, an energetic collaborator with the Rev. James Williams in the Anglesey Lifeboat Association, and a generous friend to all sections of the community in Holyhead. The monument erected to his memory overlooking the harbour, a landmark for mariners, was the outward expression of a genuine sense of loss at his tragic death, itself a telling vindication of his scathing criticism of the post office packets. In his forthright evidence to the various commissions of enquiry regarding the Holyhead station and its vessels, Skinner comes to life, as he does in a letter from Margaret Owen of Penrhos, Holyhead, writing to her grandson at St John's College, Cambridge, in 1800, soon after

Skinner's appointment. The old lady, after congratulating her grandson on his graduation, and commenting on the scarcity of corn, and the sickness among the poor of Holyhead, waxed enthusiastic about her new tenant, 'in Captain Goddard's house . . . theirs a Gentleman Captain Skinner who has but one arm appointed to one of the Pacquets a very pleasant agreeable Gentleman he lost his arm in the American War when a boy but eleven years old, he can shuffle and deal the cards with his left hand much better than I can, and is most agreeable affable he is very sheerful and is always the same in company'.[11]

In his early days on the station, Skinner confided to Margaret Owen how time consuming the work of the commanders of the packets was, and she wrote to her grandson that Skinner 'does not like the employ as they Captains are obligd themselves by the order of Government not to miss going every trip wch. makes it very slaveist Pece of Business'.[12] Following the Act of Union, 1801, the need for quick and reliable transport between Dublin and Holyhead was emphasised by Select Committees and Commissions of Inquiry. Some notoriously long passages by the sailing packets, as long as 51 hours on one occasion in 1818, had led to the adoption of steam packets. By 1826 some 12,000 cabin and 2,300 deck passengers crossed the Irish Sea during the year, and the average time of crossing was cut by half.[13] Philip Bagwell's careful examination of the history of the Post Office Steam Packets has shown how the Holyhead Station suffered a reversal of fortunes in the 1827-35 period when packet boat repairs from all stations were concentrated there, thus increasing expenditures enormously, just at the time when the Post Office packets were facing increased competition from private operators, including the St George's Steamship Company, and the City of Dublin Steam Packet Company. This competition with private companies, and the alternative routes from Liverpool, caused Skinner and his fellow-commanders of the Post Office packets much concern, but for passengers it meant that fares had to be kept down, and more and more people made use of the services offered by the increased number of steamboats.

It was not only to Ireland that there were more steam packets available: the *Cambria*, which had extended its services from the Liverpool-Bagillt run to Beaumaris, Bangor and Caernarvon, the

REDUCTION OF FARES.

CABIN, 4s.; DECK, 2s.

Liverpool and Menai Bridge.

THE POWERFUL AND FAST SAILING STEAMER

CAMBRIA,

Captain JOHN HUNTER,

Will leave the MENAI BRIDGE on TUES-DAYS, THURSDAYS, and SATURDAYS, at 9 Morning, and will leave LIVERPOOL on MONDAYS, WEDNESDAYS, & FRIDAYS, at 11 Morning.
☞ At the Menai Bridge apply to Mr. Robert Humphreys, Jun., at Liverpool to
PRICE & CASE.
16, Exchange Buildings, Liverpool.

On SATURDAY the 12th instant, the CAMBRIA will sail from LIVERPOOL, at a Quarter to Four, Afternoon, for MENAI BRIDGE, and will leave there on MONDAY MORNING, the 14th instant, at a Quarter to Six o'clock, and will continue every alternate Saturday from Liverpool, and every alternate Monday from the Menai Bridge, till further notice.

Conveyances will leave the Menai Bridge for Carnarvon and Holyhead on arrival of the Cambria.
Liverpool, 20th June, 1848.

REDUCED FARES.

CABIN.... 4s.; FORE CABIN.... 2s.
Children under 12 years old, Half-fare.

DIRECT STEAM COMMUNICATION
BETWEEN

Menai Bridge, Bangor, Beaumaris, and Liverpool.

THE CITY OF DUBLIN COMPANY'S Splendid and Powerful NEW IRON STEAMER the

PRINCE OF WALES,

(Of 400 Tons Burthen, and 200 Horse power,

W. H. WARREN, R. N., Commander,

(Built expressly for the Station,)

COMMENCED her SUMMER SAILINGS, on Monday, 3d of May, and will continue to leave MENAI BRIDGE, on *MONDAYS, WEDNESDAYS,* & *FRIDAYS,* at Ten o'clock in the Morning; returning from GEORGE'S PIER HEAD, LIVERPOOL, on *TUESDAYS, THURSDAYS,* and *SATURDAYS,* at Eleven o'clock in the Morning.

Coaches for Holyhead, Carnarvon, & Amlwch, wait the arrival of the Prince of Wales, to convey Passengers forward, and return in the Morning in time to proceed to Liverpool.

The MEDINA now plies between the Menai Bridge and Carnarvon, to forward Passengers and Goods.

Further particulars may be had on application to Mr. E. W. Timothy, or Messrs. R. & H. phreys, Menai Bridge; Mr. Robt. Pritchard, Post-master, Bangor; Mr. T. Byrne, Post-master, Beaumaris; Mr. J. Jones, Ship-agent, Carnarvon; or to Mr. J. K. Rounthwaite, at the Company's Office, 24 Water Street, Liverpool.

Vale of Clwyd and the *Eclipse*, which sailed between Caernarvon and Aberystwyth, as well as Beaumaris and Conway, the *Ormrod*, the *Air* and the *Rothesay Castle* had joined the *Prince Llewelyn* as regular visitors to the Menai Strait. By the 1840s the City of Dublin Steam Packet Company had the *Erin-Go-Bragh*, and the *Prince of Wales*, both paddle-steamers, which plied regularly to north Wales.[14]

It has already been noted that Anglesey people had financial interests in the St George's Steam Packet Company; by 1843 it was apparent that they were not content to allow the merchants of Liverpool and Dublin a monopoly of the new steamboat business. A public meeting was held at Llangefni in October 1843, with Thomas Peers Williams, M.P. of Craigydon, grandson of Thomas Williams, the 'Copper King', in the chair; it was decided at this meeting that 'it would be for the advantage of Anglesey and Caernarvonshire that a Company be formed to purchase a safe and commodious steamer to ply between these counties and Liverpool . . . for the safe transportation of Pigs, Farming Produce Merchandize, Passengers, etc. during the winter as well as summer months'.[15] Whatever the Liverpool companies may have thought of the pleasure steamer traffic, this Llangefni meeting seemed to have placed passengers somewhat lower on their list of priorities; their interest was mainly in exporting goods and animals to the Liverpool markets, and they were firmly of the opinion that 'the company to be formed should consist exclusively of persons resident in or connected by property with the counties of Caernarvon and Anglesey'. What came of this particular venture is uncertain, but steam vessels increasingly carried goods to and from Caernarvonshire and Anglesey, and the 'stemar fach' became a common sight in many small harbours. But the 1840s were also the age of 'railway mania', and by 1849 the railway to Holyhead was complete; the steamboat had a rival. Both railway and steamer had the advantage over sail by being able to give regular times of arrival and departure, and by mid-century so much progress had been made in extending communications that the old days were quite forgotten when: 'a winter journey from Caernarvonshire to Liverpool was an era in a man's life, and the Cambrian who was necessitated to make it set his house in order and made his will.'[16]

The steamboat provided for the needs of passive passengers whose flight to the sea in their leisure hours was one aspect of life in early nineteenth-century Britain.[17] But there were others who were more positive in their approach; yachtsmen found relaxation in the skilful use of wind and tide, although here too the novelty of the steam-engine inspired the building of some very curious craft for the gentry to amuse themselves, particularly in sheltered waters like the Menai Strait. Yachting as a sport had been introduced to Britain when the City of Amsterdam had presented Charles II with the yacht *Mary*, which was later to founder on the Skerries in 1675.[18] English shipwrights had quickly seized the opportunity presented by the royal interest to design improved yachts for English waters, giving them deeper keels instead of the leeboards which had been found suitable for the shallow waters of Holland, yachts of the type in which Captain Greenville Collins made his survey of the coasts in the 1680s. Any vessels designed with sharp lines were suspect as smuggling vessels in the eighteenth-century, and there were few yachts north of the English Channel until after the ending of the French Wars in 1815.

One of the first to sail his own yacht for sheer pleasure in the Menai Strait was Henry William Paget, later to become the first Marquess of Anglesey, whose bronze statue on its stone column dominates the Strait. In the admirable biography of his distinguished ancestor, 'One Leg', the present Marquess records Paget's love of the sea, dating from his early days at Westminster School when he sailed from Roberts' boat-building yard on the South Bank of the Thames, and later in the Menai Strait where 'there was built for him his own yacht, and much of the high summer was spent in gratifying his ruling passion'.[19] Two vessels were registered in the name of his father, the Earl of Uxbridge, in 1787 at Beaumaris; the ship-rigged three-masted 168-ton *Mona*, built at Rotherhithe in 1786, and the cutter *Druid*, 37 tons, also built at Rotherhithe in 1787.[20] Colin Jones is named as master of both vessels in the Beaumaris Register; it is probable that he was the Captain Jones who gave evidence before the Committee on Holyhead Roads and Harbour in 1810 with reference to the navigational hazards that might follow from the building of a bridge across the Menai. By that time Captain Jones was master 'of the *Uxbridge* packet in Government service on the Holyhead station to Dublin', but he stated that previous to his fifteen years in the Post Office service, he had served thirty years in the Navy, and knew the

Menai Strait well as he had 'been through every part of it very often, commanding a vessel belonging to the Earl of Uxbridge for seven years while in the Navy'.[21] No doubt Henry William Paget learned some of his seamanship from Colin Jones; in later years, as Marquess of Anglesey, he owned the *Pearl*, the beautiful yacht in which he sailed to Cronstadt on his visit to the Czar, and in which he sailed to Cowes in a gale when he was aged eighty-three.[22] The Marquess was regarded as an expert whose advice was sought in alterations to the Emperor Nicholas of Russia's yacht at Cowes in 1851;[23] Lord Clarence Paget, his son, who had a distinguished career in the Royal Navy, was appointed to command the *Pearl* corvette in 1837, 'a particular compliment to Anglesey, for it was he who proposed to Sainty, the ship designer, that a corvette should be built upon the lines of his yacht *Pearl*, which was the clipper of those days'.[24] This was not the first time that the Marquess and Sainty had been consulted regarding ship design. In 1819, when the Select Committee heard evidence from the Holyhead packet boat commanders, Captains Weston, Skinner and Rogers, regarding the ideal design for a packet boat for the Holyhead-Dublin service, they also called in both the Marquess and Philip Sainty, the Colchester shipbuilder, who had built two vessels for him. In his evidence in support of Sainty's ability as a builder and designer, the Marquess stated that the smaller of these two vessels, a forty-two tonner, 'has the reputation of being as fast for her tonnage as any in England'. He had had little opportunity of sailing one against the other, but his larger vessel, 80 tons, promised to be an even better performer. When asked by the Committee if he had paid 'much attention to the object of constructing and managing vessels for the purpose of fast sailing' the Marquess' answer was: 'It has been for many years my principal amusement'.[25]

It is likely that there were others who sailed the Strait for pleasure in the early nineteenth-century; among the prized possessions of the Royal Anglesey Yacht Club are two small leather-bound minute-books which record the activities of the Beaumaris Book Society from January 1802 to the day eighty-three years later when its name was changed overnight to the Anglesey Yacht Club.[26] Captain Robert Lloyd, R.N., had come ashore in 1802 on relinquishing command of the *Mars*: the Treaty of Amiens in that year was hailed by statesmen as a peace that was to be lasting, 'a reconciliation between the two first nations of the world', was the way one British statesman put it.[27] The British Navy was drastically reduced, and Lloyd, already made wealthy by his prize-money, was glad to return to Anglesey to attend to the development of the Tregayan estate and the new farm buildings. But he also had time to devote to the affairs of the Island, and in December 1802 Captain Lloyd was one of the company who met at the Bull's Head Inn, Beaumaris, to decide upon the twenty-six rules of the Beaumaris Book Society.[28] From the outset the members of the Society appeared to have had maritime interests and connections; in addition to Lloyd himself, there was J. B. Sparrow, the Collector of Customs, and members of his family, Rice and Harris, merchants who had interests in the steam packets, and representatives of other prominent Anglesey families, the Lewises, Hamptons, Whites, Pantons and a number of clergymen. Among the original signatures following the Bull's Head meeting in 1802 was that of Miss Hester Meyrick, the only lady member; she resigned in 1804. Captain Lloyd was Chairman at many meetings and it was he who selected to propose the vote of thanks to Lord Bulkeley, in December 1804: 'for the very handsome manner he has supplied us with the room and filled it up'.[29] The news of Napoleon's flat-bottomed boats assembled on the coast of the Channel he knew so well, and Nelson's Trafalgar in the following year must have made Lloyd anxious to serve at sea again, but it is not until April 1807 that there is a minute recording, 'Capn. Lloyd, the Chairman of the Committee having left, Mr White is proposed to succeed him'.[30] It will be recalled that a few weeks earlier Captain Lloyd had written from Beaumaris acknowledging receipt of his new appointment to the command of the *Hussar*,[31] and before long he was off Copenhagen taking part in the bombardment, a far cry from Beaumaris Book Room meetings on a Monday night between six and seven o'clock. The year 1811 saw Lloyd back in Anglesey, and in 1812 he was again elected Chairman, but a month later he was appointed to the *Plantagenet*, so once again the Sparrow, Lewis and White groups had to provide leadership for the society until 1815, when Lloyd came home for good and his name was restored to the top of the list of members present.

The members of the Beaumaris Book Society did not have yachts to compare with those owned by the family of Thomas Williams, the copper tycoon. His eldest son, Owen Williams, who died in 1832, was a banker, partner of Pascoe Grenfell; his brother-in-law, Colonel Hughes, later Lord Dinorben, 'son of the poor curate who had made his fortune on Parys Mountain'; Thomas Peers Williams, Owen Williams' son, was a very wealthy man, and this may have some bearing on the fact that three of his daughters were married to members of the House of Lords, two others to sons of Lords, whilst his son Hwfa Williams and his wife were prominent figures at the Court of Edward VII.[32] In 1824, Owen Williams registered at Beaumaris the *Gazelle*, an 87-ton cutter built at Colchester in 1820, possibly by Sainty, the Marquess' shipbuilder, and Thomas Peers Williams, the *Hussar*, a 119-ton schooner, an ex-slaver, which in 1820 had been 'condemned by a Commission Court at Sierra Leone for a violation of the laws for the prevention of the slave trade.[33] Frances Williams had made a sketch of the *Gazelle* soon after she had been built; her work is dated November 1820.[34] It would seem likely that James and Frances Williams, both of whom were so interested in the sea, would have been much taken with James' uncle's new boat, and may have sailed in her at the time of Frances' sketch. Many years later, the Caernarvon yachtsman, Sir Llewelyn Turner, recalled that he had sailed in the *Hussar*, 'a very handsome vessel', both when she was schooner-rigged and afterwards as a brig: although she looked better in the latter rig she did not sail as well, as Williams found out to his cost when sailing off the Isle of Wight.[35] According to Turner, Williams had 'a fine establishment of yachts' which were 'wintered in a little bay amongst the rocks of Craigydon', his estate on the Menai Strait.[36]

The Beaumaris Book Society, now known as the Beaumaris News Room, with another room 'upon the Green' from 1826,[37] took a prominent part in the Regatta which was arranged for 1830, and one of their members, Wiliam Boggie, was secretary of the Regatta. Four events were rowing races, and four for sailing vessels, one for yachts not exceeding 50 tons, one for those not exceeding 25 tons, one for boats not exceeding 12 tons, and another for those 'not exceeding 17 feet on the keel'. The steam packets *Prince Llewelyn* and *Ormrod* changed their hours of sailing for Liverpool, 'so as to afford every accommodation to those who may wish to enjoy the pleasure of the

Gazelle — Nov 1820.

Regatta and Ball at Beaumaris'.[38] So successful was the 1830 Regatta that it was decided to have a more ambitious event in August 1831. This Regatta was to be under the stewardship of J. H. Hampton Lewis, a member of the Beaumaris News Room and supporter of James Williams in the Lifeboat Association, and Thomas Assheton Smith, owner of the slate quarries, soon to be a member of Parliament for Caernarvonshire but known to early nineteenth-century society as the outstanding sporting landowner, cricketer, pugilist, 'the best and hardest rides England ever saw', whom Wellington described as 'the Field Marshall of Fox-Hunting'. The races were again to be for the same classes of yachts and rowing-boats, and the steam packets *Prince Llewelyn*, *Air* and *Eclipse* were to be diverted from their usual voyages so as to be 'in attendance for the accommodation of passengers, and will accompany the yachts in their respective races'.[39]

It was not to be. A week before the Regatta, on the night of 17 August 1831, the *Rothesay Castle*, another steam packet, bound for the Menai Strait from Liverpool, after a long day of labouring in heavy seas off the Welsh coast, went to pieces on the Dutchman Bank with the loss of some 130 lives.[40] In the darkness people ashore knew nothing of the disaster until early the next morning when it was too late for most of the passengers. A few were rescued by boats which went out hurriedly from Beaumaris once the news of the wreck reached there, and the yacht *Campeodore*, belonging to Ralph Williamson, one of the subscribers to the Regatta funds, gave such distinguished service that Williamson was later awarded the silver medal of the Lifeboat Institution.[41] The scandal of the *Rothesay Castle*'s wreck, the allegations of drunkenness and incompetence on the part of the master, and negligence on the part of the owners, caused such a stir that Beaumaris attracted almost as much interest as Moelfre at the time of the *Royal Charter* wreck. In view of the tragedy and the involvement of men like Sir Richard Bulkeley in the inquest into the disaster, the Regatta of 1831 was cancelled.

This was a bitter blow; as early as mid-July the local press had reported 'This delightful watering place fills apace with company'. To the gentry the Assizes and the Regatta were both social occasions, and the press linked them together as forthcoming attractions, 'so that Beaumaris during the incoming month will be full of bustle and gaiety'. The first stone of the Bulkeley Arms Hotel had been laid in 1830, and by summer 1831 many more had been laid (the bulk of them, it was whispered, from the old town wall); the *North Wales Chronicle* reported: 'The New Hotel a most splendid edifice, is nearly finished, and will be opened in a few days, whereby great additional accommodation will be afforded to the numerous fashionables whom the Regatta is certain to attract.' The day before the tragedy the same newspaper had excitedly forecast that 'in addition to the other numerous attractions of this gay scene, we understand it is intended to have a steam race betwixt the *Rothesay Castle* and *Prince Llewelyn* Packets. The competition betwixt these leviathans of the deep will form a grand and interesting spectacle'. The 'leviathan of the deep' took on a cruelly ironic context a day later.[42]

The visit of the Princess Victoria and the Duchess of Kent, and the National Eisteddfod, made 1832's regatta at Beaumaris a much publiced affair; despite the cholera outbreak, yachting in the Strait had truly become fashionable. The 1833 regatta attracted attention for its own sake, with even larger attendances than in the year of the Eisteddfod and Victoria's visit. The reporters of the *North Wales Chronicle* found it difficult to curb their exuberance: 'the Green was covered by eleven o'clock with a splendid assemblage of the fair and the fashionable . . . In the bay the rowing boats were seen shooting with arrow-like swiftness from point to point, and a numerous fleet of fairy frigates fluttered their white canvas and gay variegated ensigns in the breeze.' It was not only the sea that attracted the reporter's eye: 'the fair assemblage found ample shelter in the elegant houses on the Green, the windows of which when filled by our Welsh belles presented an appearance equal in splendour and gaiety to the box rows of the Opera House.' Most of the rowing-boat races were won by Sir Richard Bulkeley's *Diable Boiteux*, closely followed by *Jack's Alive*, belonging to John Jones: J. Grindrod, probably the first commodore of the Royal Mersey Yacht Club (or a relative bearing the same name), won the race round Puffin Island for yachts under 15 tons in *Tickler*, whilst the *Emerald* cutter won the race for vessels under 30 tons. The first race was described by the *North Wales Chronicle*'s reporter: 'At 12 o'clock, the preparatory gun was fired, as a signal for the vessels entered for a cup to be contested by Yachts under 15 tons burden to make ready for a start. Six yachts of this description were at the rendezvous, and after an interval of three minutes, the second gun being fired, all in an instant displayed their snow-white sails. In three minutes more, the moment the smoke was seen to issue from the mouth of the third gun, moorings were slipt and a most beautiful Start took place, the *Emily* leading and the other five following all abreast and close up to her. The course was round Puffin Island and back to the spot whence the start took place; and in running down to the Island the Yachts kept together very close, but after turning in, in beating up against a very fresh gale, they seperated, and the *Tickler* came in first in beautiful style, close reefed, and pretty closely followed by the *Royal Eagle*, *Ivanzoe* and *Emily*. Two others which started were not placed.'[43]

The regatta was not all gaiety. On the third day, in the race for sailing-boats not exceeding 18 feet in keel, J. P. Wright, editor of the *Caernarvon and Denbigh Herald*, was drowned when his boat *Recreation*, carrying too much sail in an attempt to catch up with the other competitors, sank instantly 'almost abreast of the Watch House on the Green'. The *George* of Garth, the *Antelope* and *Resolute* of Beaumaris, the *Queen Bess* of Bangor, had all gained on the *Recreation*; the press reports suggested that Wright had been unwise in his rash tactics, carrying 'too heavy a press of sail' and standing too far out, the 'wind was blowing fresh, about W. by N. and any person acquainted with sailing will perceive that a boat tacking under Friars, and standing out on the starboard tack until abreast of the Watch House, would be a very considerable distance from shore, and thus lose all shelter from the land'. A fund was immediately opened for Wright's widow and six children; the list of subscribers contains the names of most of the Caernarvonshire and Anglesey gentry, the members of the Beaumaris News Room, as well as 'the servants at Baron Hill', the 'Young ladies at Miss Sambrook's', and the 'compositors at the office of the Caernarvon Herald'.[44] Meanwhile the races continued, the Regatta Ball was a great success, and it was decided to make the Beaumaris Regatta an annual affair to be held at a date which would 'not interfere with any other, and thereby secure the attendance of yachts belonging to the different clubs in Ireland, the Isle of Man, the Clyde, etc.' Yacht racing had come to stay in the Menai Strait.

The bleak contrast which Howitt in mid-century discovered in

BEAUMARIS REGATTA.

SIR JOHN HILTON, ₎ Stewards.
W. P. LHOYD, ESQ. ₎

THIS REGATTA will take place on the 20th and 21st Days of August, 1833, when the following Prizes
will be contended for:—

1.—A CUP, value 40 SOVEREIGNS, to be sailed for by Yachts not exceeding 50 Tons.   Entrance, 30s.
2.—A CUP, value 20 SOVEREIGNS, to be sailed for by Yachts not exceeding 30 Tons.   Entrance, 20s.
3.—A CUP, value 10 SOVEREIGNS, to be sailed for by Yachts not exceeding 15 Tons.   Entrance, 10s.
4.—The following Prizes for Sailing Boats not exceeding 18 Feet on the Keel.   No Entrance :—
      To the 1st Boat .... 5 SOVEREIGNS.
            2d Ditto...................... 2   Ditto.
5.—The following Prizes for Six Oar Boats of every description.   No Entrance :—
      To the 1st Boat......................15 SOVEREIGNS.
            2d Ditto...................... 7   Ditto.
      Three Boats to start, or the 7 Sovereigns to the 2d Boat will not be allowed.
6.—A CUP, to be called *The Bulkeley Cup*, in honour of the birth of an Heir to Baron Hill, for Six Oar
Boats, to be rowed and steered by Gentlemen Amateurs.   Entrance, 10s. per Oar.
7.—The following Prizes for Four Oar Boats of every description, on the same conditions as Prize No. 5.
      To the 1st Boat......................10 SOVEREIGNS.
            2d Ditto...................... 5   Ditto.
8.—The LADIES' CUP, value 20 SOVEREIGNS, for Six Oar Boats, to be rowed and steered by Gentlemen
Amateurs.   Entrance, 10s. per Oar.
9.—The following Prizes for Six Oar Boats, belonging to any Ports in, and to be rowed and steered by
Residents of, Anglesey or Carnarvonshire.   To be run in Heats.   No Entrance.
      To the 1st Boat ....10 SOVEREIGNS.
            2d Ditto...................... 5   Ditto.
10.—The following Prizes for Four Oar Boats belonging to any Ports in, and to be rowed and steered by
Residents of, Anglesey or Carnarvonshire.   To be run in Heats.   No Entrance.
      To the 1st Boat .... 5 SOVEREIGNS.
            2d Ditto...................... 3   Ditto.
      The Competitors must enter their Vessels and Boats with the Secretary on or before the 17th day of August
next.   Those who may be unable to attend personally are requested to communicate in writing, the name,
rig, and tonnage per register, or keel's length of their Vessels, according to the sailing class to which they
belong, or if Rowing Boats, to specify the number of Oars.   It will also be proper to state distinctly the
Prize or Prizes for which they intend to compete, and the distinguishing Flag which they propose to carry.
      All letters should be addressed (postage free) to the Secretary.   Subscriptions will be received by the
Secretary, at Beaumaris, and at the Bank in Carnarvon.
      On the 20th of August there will be an Ordinary for Gentlemen, at 5 o'Clock, and a Ball in the evening.
            On the 21st, a Public Breakfast, for Ladies and Gentlemen.
                  Signed, by order of the Committee,

Beaumaris, 2d August, 1833.   WILLIAM BOGGIE, Secretary:

rural England 'between the mansion of the private gentleman and the hut of the labourer on his estate',[45] the gulf between Disraeli's 'two nations' was apparent to anyone who sailed the Menai Strait in August 1846. Earlier in the month, two hundred emigrants had boarded Davies' *Chieftain* at Menai Bridge, bound for Quebec, with earnest hopes of a better future than they could expect in Anglesey or Caernarvonshire, others had found space for themselves between the slates and straw for a cheap fare to Boston, others took passage to Liverpool to look for work in the rapidly expanding seaport, whilst offshore the starving Irish, fleeing from famine, huddled together on the sea-swept decks of the cattle boats, en route for Liverpool and Quebec. The battered slate ships and the small sailing coasters with their much-repaired sails presented a stark contrast to the beautiful yachts of the gentry, bedecked with flags; Mr and Mrs Assheton Smith's *Fire Queen* 'with a party of fashionables' aboard, and 'Lord Newborough's natty little steamboat, which is worthy to be called General Tom Thumb' were evidence of that prosperity in which mid-Victorian Britain took great pride.[46] So too were the other yachts participating in the Beaumaris and Caernarvon Regattas of August 1846: the *Vision*, a 44-tonner built at Poole, owned by Colonel Birchall of Preston, which won the race round Puffin Island, the *Leander*, a 30-tonner owned by Dr Grindrod, Commodore of the Royal Mersey Yacht Club, the *Zoe* owned by H. Beaver, probably a relative of the Anglesey privateer captain, the *Diamond* owned by Colonel Douglas Pennant, the Penrhyn slate quarry owner and M.P. for Caernarvonshire, and the *Mervinia*, R. A. Poole's yacht built at Caernarvon, where, according to his neighbour, Llewelyn Turner, 'the building of yachts was not of sufficient frequency to make them likely to meet successfully those turned out by Wanhill of Poole, Fife of Clyde, White of Cowes or other well known builders'. The *Mervinia* often sailed, but did not win, at the Regattas; in August 1846 at the Caernarvon Regatta she was placed as a marker off Caernarvon, flying 'flags of all nations'. These yachts had their paid crews, but the races which were the most fully reported were still the rowing races, particularly the race for four-oared boats between the '*Snowdon Ranger*, by quarrymen working at Mr Assheton Smith's slate quarry at Llanberis, and the *Fanny* manned by men resident in Beaumaris'. At the Beaumaris Regatta the *Fanny* won, rowing a distance of two miles in eleven minutes; two days later she repeated her success in the 'Llanciau Eryri Purse', her closest adversary at Caernarvon being the *Snowdon Ranger*, in a race which 'was productive of great rivalry and repeated foulings'. The enthusiastic reporter of the *North Wales Chronicle* underlined the social stratification of society: 'A handsome marquee raised its snowy surface on the high ground adjacent to the Green, for the refreshment of the Baron Hill party: and some dingy looking tents were put up on the low ground for the refection of low people.' On the Strait, the newly affluent came by the steam-boats, *Cambria* and *William Stanley*, to gawk at the Duke of Marlborough's yacht, the *Wyvern*, 'arrayed in full colours', whilst on the Green, 'The Rechabite band, and some strolling German musicians, performed, to the best of their ability, marches, waltzes and other footstirring airs during the day'. At night the Rev. James Williams of Llanfair-yng-Nghornwy took his daughters to 'the elegant ball and supper at the Bulkeley Arms Hotel', attended by the Bulkeleys, the Stanleys, Meyricks and the leading members of the Regatta committees.

The undoubted popularity of the Beaumaris and Caernarvon Regattas and his own successes in the Harwich and Yarmouth Regattas in the *Ranger*, stimulated Llewelyn Turner, youngest son of William Turner, Assheton Smith's erstwhile partner in the Caernarvonshire quarries, to bring together those interested in yachting in the Menai Strait to form the club which emerged in 1847 as the Royal Welsh Yacht Club at Caernarvon.[47] Llewelyn Turner, a wealthy young lawyer, had considerable gifts as an organiser, and as a result the new club had an impressive list of officers: the Commodore was the first Marquess of Anglesey, Robert Stephenson, the engineer who built the Britannia railway bridge across the Strait, was Vice-Commodore, with Turner himself Rear-Commodore. Turner was then aged twenty-two, but had already had much sailing experience both in his school days and immediately afterwards, when his father had bought the *Nautilus*, built at Bangor by one of the Strait pilots, John Hughes. The *Nautilus* was a fast open sailing-boat, but Turner graduated to larger yachts, including the yawl *Gleam* and a cutter, *Circe*, a very good sea-boat, in which he cruised for many years in the Irish Sea. In his old age, Sir Llewelyn Turner recalled some of his experiences sailing off Llanddwyn, or

Point Lynas – the thick weather on one occasion when he sailed the *Circe* inside the half-tide rock off Aberffraw, and his lively memories of some of the men who sailed with him, including the Vicar of Caernarvon, James Crawley Vincent, whose courage and self-sacrifice during the cholera epidemic in 1867 in Caernarvon impressed him as much as his fearless behaviour aboard Turner's yacht in a fierce gale off St David's Head.[48]

By 1855 the Royal Welsh Yacht Club had a beautifully situated clubhouse at Porth-yr-Aur, the town gate to the sea, in the centre of the town walls, overlooking the Menai Strait. The work of designing and supervising the building of a clubhouse which would blend with the surrounding town walls was undertaken by Longueville Jones, founder of the Cambrian Archaeological Association, scientist and inspector of schools, who had come to live in Anglesey, at Llandegfan, in 1846.[49] The popularity of yachting is indicated by the membership of the Royal Welsh Yacht Club in its early years: in 1856 it could claim over a hundred members and twenty-seven yachts; by 1895 there were 191 members with seventy-eight yachts; as early as 1858, regattas were organized in the sequence Dublin, the Isle of Man, Morecambe, Caernarvon, Holyhead and Criccieth, and it is evident from Turner's 'Memories' that some yachtsmen were regular visitors to the Strait, men like Charles Trevor Roper of Plas Teg, Flintshire, in the *Wyvern*, Sir David Gamble, sometime Commodore of the Royal Mersey Yacht Club, whose *Chanticlere*, a yawl of 123 tons, was one of the largest yachts to race in the Strait, David McIver, M.P., in the *Cecilia*, and an Irishman called Leader who lived at Talgarnedd in Anglesey. Yachting had become a symbol of Victorian prosperity, and only occasionally were there the jarring reminders of unpleasant far-off events like the Crimean War which may have given some a taste for the sea following their voyages through the Mediterranean. Young Hampton Lewis found himself at Balaclava, Inkerman and Sebastopol when he was twenty-one;[50] he returned to Anglesey to become Mayor of Beaumaris, High Sheriff, a prominent supporter of the lifeboats and the Beaumaris Club, and later the Royal Anglesey Yacht Club. Charles H. Evans, son of Henblas, Llangristiolus, was another who sailed for the Crimea; in a letter to his family he described how they had sailed from Cork in the *Great Britain*, 'with a beautiful wind at the rate of thirteen knots an hour, so that we soon got on to the Bay of Biscay, where we were tossed about in fine style'.[51] His letters from the camp before Sebastopol have survived, but he himself was killed there in August 1855.[52] Most of the gentry, however, were content to make a brave show at home sporting the uniform of the Anglesey Militia under Colonel T. Peers Williams of Craigydon, whilst in later years Llewelyn Turner made great efforts to enlist local seamen in the Royal Naval Reserve, introduced by Lord Clarence Paget, Secretary of the Admiralty. Admiral Lord Paget, who came to live at Plas Llanfair, constructed a large statue of Nelson on the Anglesey shore of the Menai Strait, close to the Britannia Bridge, in 1873, 'to show to the thousands of sailors that passed through these Strait that there lived in all their hearts the memory of an immortal hero'.[53] The vast majority of these sailors still regarded the sea as a place of work, but the numbers of the privileged and leisured classes who sailed past the Nelson statue were increasing every year.

Linked together by marriages, mutual friendships and common interests in the Anglesey Hunt, the Royal Welsh Yacht Club, the Royal National Lifeboat Institution, as well as their political and religious affiliations, the gentry of Anglesey continued to support the Beaumaris News Room.[54] Most of the minutes of the Committee over the years are concerned with routine matters: subscriptions, membership, newspapers to be taken, with an occasional touch of light relief such as that meeting in 1861 when the Committee considered 'what was to be done in consequence of the continual state of insobriety of the marker'.[55] In 1868, the year when Gladstone and the new Liberal government embarked upon their policy of reform, when Bismark was preparing for the unification of Germany and clearing the ground for the Franco-Prussian War, when nearer home the wealthy Nonconformist shipowner, Richard Davies, was elected to represent Anglesey, the members of the Beaumaris News Room bought a new carpet for their room, agreed that 'the Wood work in the News Room be ground in Oak, and the Curtains be cleaned' and unanimously decided: 'That the members of the Phoenix Club be requested to avail themselves of the use of the News and Billard Room during their approaching Cricket in Beaumaris.' By 1875 the title of Beaumaris News and Billard Room was changed to the 'Beaumaris Club'.[56] By this time the new generation of members included Professor A. C. Ramsay, the geologist who first gave the name 'Cambrian' to one of the earth's strata, and who in the summer of 1850 had been invited to stay with the Rev. James Williams at Llanfair-yng-Nghornwy and had married one of his daughters two years later.[57] Other members during these years were Admiral Ogle; Dr Brisco Owen who had been one of Lord Clarence Paget's supporters when the alternative candidate, Richard Davies, won such overwhelming support at the 1868 election;[58] R. Wynne Jones whose family had been closely associated with the lifeboat movement in Anglesey since its inception; Colonel Hampton Lewis; Captain Pritchard Rayner who fought the 1885 election against Richard Davies; Colonel W. H. Thomas, H. B. Mitchell, W. Massey, Harry Clegg and W. M. Preston, who was secretary of the Anglesey branch of the Royal National Lifeboat Institution for over thirty years. At the annual meeting of the members of the Beaumaris Club in January 1885, Sir R. H. Williams Bulkeley and Colonel Hampton Lewis proposed 'that the Beaumaris Club be converted into a yacht club to be called the Royal Anglesey Yacht Club'.[59] Within a few months the Anglesey Yacht Club was formed from the existing members of the Beaumaris Club and twenty-three other gentlemen with Sir R. H. Williams Bulkeley as Commodore, the Marquess of Anglesey as Vice-Commodore, Colonel Hampton Lewis as Rear-Commodore, and Captain Johnston as Honorary Secretary.[60] The Marquess, grandson of the first Marquess, shared the family love of the sea, and when he came to reside at Plas Newydd had 'brought with him a fine steam yacht called *Santa Cecilia*, and a smaller one besides'.[61] In June 1885, a few months after the original proposal to change the name, approval was officially given for the club to 'be styled the Royal Anglesey Yacht Club'.[62] Life membership of the Club was conferred upon Captain R. I. Johnson, R.E., at a meeting in 1889 in recognition of the 'able, energetic and cordial manner in which he has so kindly carried out the duties appertaining to the Secretaryshire of this Club, during the five years that have elapsed since its conversion into a Yacht Club'. In 1890, 'a cap badge designed by the Marquess of Anglesey' was adopted by the Club and it was decided to print lists of yachts belonging to the Royal Anglesey Yacht Club, now firmly established.

The minute books of the club for the years 1885-1914 reflect the energetic support of many who already had an interest in working vessels at sea: Bulkeley, Chadwick, Preston, Platt and Mitchell had shares in the slate schooners, and the steam vessels bought in the 1890s: Fanning Evans was a member of the Amlwch family that had long had interests in the shipping of that port; H. R. Davies, who was taking over responsibility from Charles Pierce for the Davies ocean-going fleet, was elected a member in 1888, and the Davies family subsequently played an important part in the development of the club. The naval interest, first represented long ago by Robert Lloyd, was continued for many years in the membership of Admiral Thomas Ogle, who was for a time Lloyd's representative in the area.[63] It was still evident later in the century in the person of Captain E. H. Verney, R.N. Educated at Harrow, Verney had served in the Crimean and Indian Mutiny campaigns, had had command of vessels in the Pacific, West African and Mediterranean stations; in 1875 he had commanded the Liverpool division of the coastguard service, but from 1877 had taken an increasingly active interest in Anglesey affairs.[64] Chairman of the Anglesey Quarter Sessions from 1877 to 1890, Captain Verney was one of the members of the Beaumaris Club who had been co-opted to serve on the special committee 'to consider the desirability of converting the Club into a yacht club', in the spring of 1885. Prosperity on Merseyside and in Lancashire brought many wealthy yachtsmen to establish homes in Anglesey; by the 1890s both Royal Anglesey and Royal Welsh were flourishing yacht clubs.

The years before the First World War were the halcyon days of the privileged classes; large yachts with paid crews were familiar sights. In 1894 the Royal Anglesey Yacht Club decided to invite neighbouring yacht clubs to bring their yachts to Beaumaris, asking owners 'to place their yachts in two lines and to decorate and to illuminate in the evening', on the occasion of the visit of the Prince of Wales, should he decide 'to take a cruize down the Menai Strait'. In the same year protests were recorded against the *Psyche* in the race from Beaumaris to Caernarvon 'on the ground that she was steered by a paid hand before the Bridges were reached and after they were passed'. Two years later, a protest that some yachts were 'carrying more hands than the class rate or Y.R.A. allow', was not upheld and it was agreed that 'after taking into consideration the intricate and dangerous nature of the navigation through the Swillies Channel . . . Pilots should be allowed for the race from Beaumaris to Caernarvon'. There were already indications, however, that some enthusiastic yachtsmen were turning to yachts they could handle for themselves, smaller yachts of the same design which obviated complicated handicapping: the one-raters of the Royal Anglesey Yacht Club sailed by J. H. Burton, Chadwick, Schwabe, Livingston, J. R. and H. R. Davies, and the *Seabird* class – sixteen foot on the water line – became familiar sights on the Menai Strait.[65] At Holyhead there was a certain amount of sailing for pleasure during the nineteenth-century; the harbour of refuge was a great boon for cruising yachts, but it was so crowded with working schooners that the large yachts tended to confine their visits to the regatta period. A sailing club was formed in 1905 at Holyhead (although as early as 1858 there had been talk of a 'Royal Holyhead Yacht Club', and races had been held between yachts of over 15 tons); the club formed in 1905 was the Porth-y-Felin Sailing Club which catered for small local craft, and after the 1914-18 war the Holyhead Sailing Club established themselves in a small hut at the end of Newry Beach.[66] Elsewhere there was little yachting; very much a minority sport before the 1914-18 war in Anglesey, the sea was a place for work.

Leisure hours were limited for the great majority; fishing was traditionally a part of the working life of the community, hardly regarded as a leisure activity. Yet the sea was there for adventurous youth on public holidays: on Whit Monday 1870, the *Caernarvon and Denbigh Herald* reported the exploits of six young men who had set off from the Caernarvon entrance to the Menai Strait in a gig, the *Volunteer*, to row round Anglesey. By two o'clock in the afternoon, nine hours after their early morning start, they landed at Amlwch for a meal, and then continued their row, past Moelfre and Beaumaris, arriving at Caernarvon shortly after ten o'clock at night; 'the distance rowed was upwards of seventy miles'.[67] For the less energetic, if they could afford the money, there were the steamers; the second *St Tudno* replaced her namesake in 1891.[68] The *Hercules* and the *Columbus*, the *Snowdon*, *St Elvies* and the best known of them all, *La Marguerite*, which came to north Wales in 1904, all provided opportunities for pleasant sea voyages for communities for whom trips to Liverpool or the Isle of Man were still regarded as great events.[69] The railways had widened horizons considerably, but some Welsh shopkeepers from Anglesey, Caernarvonshire and Cardiganshire still went by sea for their holidays to visit relatives, sailing between Aber-porth in Cardiganshire to Portmadoc or Connah's Quay, Amlwch to Liverpool, Holyhead to Barmouth or Milford in the small working schooners belonging to their relatives or friends.[70] It was customary for these small sailing-vessels to carry parcels and passengers, for with their limited cargo space they did not dally long in harbour but made a speedy turn round, which naturally suited people ashore who wanted transport for themselves or their parcels. This was certainly common in the early nineteenth-century, and later in areas where sea transport could compete with the railways. Michael Bouquet's 'No Gallant Ship' evocatively recalls the days when the cargoes of smacks and ketches were made up of 'very small parcels of goods – groceries, ironmongery, fruit, books or drugs – the day to day needs of local shopkeepers', and David Thomas described the 'bwndalins', the small parcels carried for Lleyn people, clothes, socks and honey, to and from relatives in Liverpool.[71] By the nineteenth-century the sea had become very much part of the normal life of coastal communities; Thomas has recorded that it was the practice for South Caernarvonshire people to go by sea from Portin-llaen to Caernarvon for denominational and fraternal gatherings. If they encountered contrary winds, they were late for the sermon.[72] The involvement in religious activities in pre-1914 Wales is perhaps hard for present-day generations to envisage, but, as sociological studies of Welsh rural communities have amply demonstrated, in many a coastal village there were two fairly distinct cultures. The differences in group values and codes of behaviour which reflected linguistic, social class and religious background, were as apparent in Anglesey as in Caernarvonshire or Cardiganshire villages of the nineteenth and early twentieth centuries. Sabbatarianism and temperance were firmly held tenets of Welsh Nonconformity and between English yachtsmen and the pleasure-steamer urban trippers on the one hand, and the masters of Welsh working schooners on the other, many of whom would take great pains to avoid leaving harbour, wherever they were, on a Sunday – there was a considerable gulf. Generalisations are notoriously misleading, but the economic factors and the pre-1914 attitude to leisure in Nonconformist Wales may go some way to explain why, for the most part, yachting was regarded as a pastime for an alien, albeit respected, elite.

The coming of the motor-car changed patterns of leisure in twentieth-century Britain, and transformed north Wales from being the quiet preserve of a few dedicated families with a passion for yachting and mountaineering into an area where thousands flock each weekend to climb and sail. Paradoxically, it was the pioneers of yachting who introduced the motor-car to Anglesey. The first motor-cars licensed in Anglesey in 1903[73] belonged to Sir Richard Bulkeley, H. R. Davies, Treborth, J. R. Davies, Ceris, J. H. Burton and S. T. Chadwick, all leading members of the Royal Anglesey Yacht Club; in the Lloyd's Register of Yachts for 1911 the same names occur among the owners of the twenty-five yachts based at Beaumaris, for example, J. R. Davies' Cowes-built *Kootenay*, a twin-screw vessel said to be capable of sixteen knots, and J. H. Burton's *Dwynwen*, an auxiliary schooner about 50 tons and over 90 feet long.[74] Burton, unable to follow a naval career because of a physical disability, was one of the few owners listed in *Lloyd's* who had obtained the Board of Trade's certificate of competency as a Master Mariner; his services to yachting and the lifeboat service in Anglesey were very considerable, and he is remembered as one of the pioneers in the post-1918 period in developing the beautiful Fifes, which still grace the Menai Strait.

The years immediately before the 1914-18 war saw the disappearance of many features of earlier regattas; the races for wherries and sailing-boats no longer existed, nor did the rowing-boat races. In the 1830s and 1840s the Strait Regattas occupied many columns in the local newspapers which at that time catered primarily for the affluent elite, with detailed reporting of the interminable Regatta dinners and their endless toasts and speeches. By the twentieth-century the local newspapers reflect their extended clientele and their much greater interest in cricket and golf, which take up many columns, whilst the Regattas were fortunate to get a bare half-column. The entries in the Regattas themselves had declined in the first decade of this twentieth-century; it was the lull between the large yachts of the mid-Victorian period and the democratisation of the sport following two World Wars. In August

1913 the local newspapers briefly reported the Strait Regattas, and summed up the Regatta held at Caernarvon thus: 'Owing to the fact that no rowing races took place, the public took very little interest in the events.'[75] The following August saw the outbreak of the 1914 war. There were no regattas.

[1]   Hugh Owen (ed), 'The Diary of William Bulkeley', TAAS, 1931, October 10-12, 1735.

[2]   *ibid.*, April 4, 1735.

[3]   *ibid.*, Dec. 22, 1735. According to Gilbert, *History of Dublin*, 2, 74, the Smock Alley Theatre had been taken down and rebuilt in 1735, reopening on December 11, 1735. Bulkeley, in his diary, notes that he went there to see Henry IV on December 15, 1735, 'cost me 2/6 Irish – This was the first play that was ever acted at the New Play House in Smock Alley'.

[4]   *ibid.*, December 28, 29, 1735. In 1816 the fare was £1.1.0 'Full Cabin', 10/6 each for children and men servants, £1.1.0 for each horse. UCNW PYA MSS 31519, 31524.

[5]   Quoted R. T. Pritchard, 'Travellers in Anglesey in the Seventeenth and Eighteenth Centuries', *TAAS*, 1961, 28. H. R. Davies, 'The Conway and Menai Ferries', 107, quotes PRO SP Chas. II, 281, 9, to correct the error in Watson's '*Royal Mail to Ireland*', which states that 122 passengers were lost in December 1670 when the packet boat from Holyhead was lost. 'Ye loss of ye packet boate called ye Guifte in her passage from Holyhead . . . and 22 passengers in her drowned amongst whom Capt. Bulkeley a brother of ye Ld. Bulkeley's is said to be one.'

[6]   James Howell to his brother, Dr Howell, 1 April 1617, in James Howell, '*Epistolae Hoeliance*', *The Familiar Letters of James Howell*, ed. J. Jacobs (London, 1892), 25.

[7]   F. C. Thornley, *Steamers of North Wales* (Prescot, 1952), 4.

[8]   BCR 23/1822.

[9]   BCR 35/1834.

[10] *NWC*, August 1831.

[11] Bangor, Penrhos, 1619.

[12] *ibid.*

[13] Philip Bagwell, 'The Post Office Steam Packets, 1821-36, and the Development of Shipping in the Irish Sea', *Maritime History*, April 1971, I, I, 4-27.

[14] Thornley, *Steamers of North Wales*, 14-16.

[15] *Caernarvon and Denbigh Herald*, November 4, 1843.

[16] A. H. Dodd, *Industrial Revolution in North Wales* (Cardiff, 1933), 129.

[17] In the 1840s there were weekend trips from Liverpool for north Wales; the *Albert*, Captain Geary, another of the City of Dublin's steamers, was billed to leave St George's, Pierhead, Liverpool, at 4 p.m. on Saturday, 22nd August 1846, for Beaumaris, Bangor and Menai Bridge. She was then to sail from Menai Bridge at 9 p.m. for Dublin, but north Wales passengers could 'have the advantage of returning by the *Prince of Wales* on Monday morning at Ten o'clock. Fare for the round, 7s. 6d. Deck, 4s. 6d'. *NWC*, August 18, 1846.

[18] *supra.*

[19] Marquess of Anglesey, '*One-Leg, The Life and Letters of Henry William Paget, First Marquess of Anglesey, K.G., 1768-1854*' (London, 1961), 23, 38.

[20] BCR 79/1787; 80/1787.

[21] *Second Report from Committee on Holyhead Roads and Harbour*, 1810, 25 May 1810, 39. Capt. Colin Jones was an enthusiastic supporter of the project to export coal from Penrhyn Mawr via Red Wharf for Ireland in 1812. T. M. Bassett and Geraint James, 'Coalmining in Anglesey', *TAAS*, 1969-70, 144. Captain Colin Jones is one of the figures represented in a lithograph of Captain Skinner's House, described by James Sparrow, and reproduced in D. Lloyd Hughes, *Holyhead, the Story of a Port*, Plate 7, 201-6.

[22] Marquess of Anglesey, *One-Leg*, 302, 328.

[23] *ibid.*, 329.

[24] *ibid.*, 384.

[25] Fifth Report, Select Committee on Road from London to Holyhead (Mails and Packets), 1819, 371-374. Sainty, in his evidence, stated: 'I have generally been employed for vessels of fast sailing,' and advocates building a vessel 'of 105 or 110 tons . . . with a pretty good breadth of beam, flat in the floor, and rather finer aft than vessels are generally built', for the Irish Seas.

[26] I am deeply indebted to the officers of the Royal Anglesey Yacht Club for allowing me to consult their records; the extracts from the minute books will be referred to below as RAYC MSS.

[27] Addington to the French representative, General Lauriston, *Moniteur*, 16 Oct. 1801, quoted H. Richmond, '*Statesmen and Sea Power*', 214.

[28] RAYC MSS. Meeting held 8th December 1802. The 'Rules originally entered into by the Society on 1st January 1802' were 'entirely cancelled': a room was to 'be procured in Beaumaris in which the Books shall be deposited', to be open from 9 a.m. to 10 p.m.

[29] RAYC MSS, December 7, 1804. Among the members present on this occasion, in addition to Lloyd, were Sir Robert Williams, Captain William Sparrow, Rev. Morris Lewis, Mr Rowland Williams, Mr John Jones, and the Secretary, Dr Griffith Roberts.

[30] RAYC MSS, 20 April 1807.

[31] *supra.*

[32] *DWB*, 1072.

[33] BCR 44/1824; 52/1824.

[34] This sketch, as all of Frances Williams' work, is now in the possession of Kyffin Williams, Esq.

[35] J. E. Vincent (ed.), *The Memories of Sir Llewelyn Turner* (London, 1903), 373.

[36] *ibid.*, 377.

[37] RAYC MSS, 23 May 1826. At a general meeting of the Society it was decided that 'Books, Pamphlets, Maps and Furniture be presented to the Corporation of Beaumaris to be placed for public use in the new Room upon the Green, under the management of the Committee for the time being . . . That this Society henceforward hold their meetings at the new Room upon the Green'.

[38] *NWC*, August 1830.

[39] *NWC*, August 1831.

[40] The best account of the wreck of the *Rothesay Castle* is in G. A. Usher, 'An Anglesey Disaster', *TAAS*, 1955, 2-11; there are a number of contemporary accounts all of which are noted in the above article.

[41] *Anglesey Branch RNLI Annual Report*, 1908, 18.

[42] *NWC*, 16 August 1831.

[43] *NWC*, August 1833.

[44] Headed 'A Case of Deep Distress', the *North Wales Chronicle* had a long list of subscribers to the Appeal Fund, among them the Duchess of Kent, Members of Parliament, W. H. Whitbread, Anthony Lelfroy, as well as many clergymen including not only the local men like James Williams, but also Archdeacon Samuel Butler of Shrewsbury, whose cutter *Petrel*, built at Liverpool in 1829, had David Jones as Master, and was registered at Beaumaris. BCR, 19/1833.

[45] William Howitt, *The Rural Life of England* (London, 1833), II, 126-9, quoted J. F. C. Harrison, *The Early Victorians, 1832-51* (London, 1971), 87-88.

[46] *NWC*, 1 September 1846.

[47] G. W. Taylor Morgan, *The Origins and Records of the Royal Welsh Yacht Club* (London, 1933), 11.

[48] Turner, *Memories*, 343-386.

[49] Taylor Morgan, *Royal Welsh Yacht Club*, 12-15; *DWB* 465.

[50] E. A. Williams, *Hanes Môn yn y Bedwaredd Ganrif ar Bymtheg*, 87.

[51] UCNW Henblas MS 1699.

[52] On July 1st, 1855, he wrote from a camp before Sebastopol, 'my duty in the trenches comes every third night, we are for twenty four hours at a time, our most advanced trench is within two hundred and forty yards of the Russians, no one dare show his head over the parapet for if he does he is sure to be knocked over, as the Russians are capital shots . . . My first night in the trenches was easily the worst'. UCNW, Henblas, 1706.

[53] Turner, *Memories*, 255-67. The quotation is from Paget's speech at the unveiling of the Statue, Turner, 263.

[54] A glance through the list of High Sheriffs of Anglesey in the nineteenth-

century indicates the influential position in the county of its members.

[55] RAYC MSS, 12 November 1861. It was resolved 'That the young man from Chester now a marker at Woods Billiard Room be taken as Marker and News Room Keeper here at a salary of 15/- a week subject to his producing a good character from his present Master backed by the Gentlemen who frequent the Chester Billiard Room'.

[56] RAYC MSS, 25 January 1875.

[57] *DNB; DWB*, 1044.

[58] E. A. Williams, *Hanes Môn yn y Bedwaredd Ganrif ar Bymtheg*, 90. The meeting in 1869 to adopt a Liberal candidate was held significantly at Llangefni rather than Beaumaris which had been for centuries the administrative centre for the county.

[59] The meeting in January 1885 appointed the Managing Committee and Captain Verney, R. N., Captain R. ap Hugh Williams, Griffith Williams and J. Bodychen Sparrow to consider the matter and report back. In April the Marquess of Anglesey, Colonel Hampton Lewis, Captain Robert Williams, William Massey, George MacCorquadale, W. M. Preston, Harry Clegg and L. O. Williams were appointed to draw up rules for the new club, and in May these rules were adopted.

[60] In addition to the existing members of the Beaumaris Club, the following were among those invited to become members: Lord Boston, H. A. Duff, T. Fanning Evans, Captain C. Hunter, George Lambert, George Meyrick, Glynn Massey, Douglas Pennant, R. R. Rathbone, Fred Schwabe, W. Turner, Colonel D. Gamble, Major Longman, S. R. Platt, Sir James Ramsden, Peter Stubbs, Sir Andrew Walker.

[61] Turner, *Memories*, 360.

[62] RAYC MSS, letter from Home Office, Whitehall, dated 18 June 1885.

[63] Ogle had achieved captain's rank by 1838; he had entered the Navy as a First Class Volunteer aboard the *Saturn* in 1809.

[64] Verney, born in 1838, educated at Harrow, entered the Royal Navy in 1851, and among his commands had been the *Grappler* in the Pacific, 1862-1865, the *Oberon* on the West Coast of Africa, 1866, and the *Growler* in the Mediterranean, 1870-73. He had two homes in Anglesey, Rhianva on the Menai Strait and Plas Rhoscolyn, as well as an estate in Buckinghamshire; he was one of the first County Councillors in Anglesey as well as being a member of the London County Council, and was M.P. for North Bucks., 1885-86, and 1889-91.

[65] Taylor Morgan, *Royal Welsh Yacht Club, 1847-1933*, 56. Others who sailed the one-raters, which lasted until 1926, were Messrs. Heap, Heywood, Trevor and Sir R. Dent; many of these 'were designed by Mr Charles Livingston, Vice Commodore of the Royal Mersey, and a member of the Royal Welsh'. The Seabird class were said to be very good sea boats, 'many of them invariably sail on their own bottoms from the Mersey to the Strait regattas'.

[66] *Holyhead Sailing Club Official Handbook* (n.d.), 6-7. In the 1923 Regatta

there were handicap races for yachts above 15 tons, T.M., for Halfraters, Pilot Hobblers or Fishermen's Boats, dinghies, and Lug Sail Sailing boats.

[67] *CDH*, June 11, 1870.

[68] The first *St Tudno*, originally the *Cobra* built in 1889, arrived in north Wales in 1890; she was sold in the next year, and replaced by another *St Tudno*, also built by Fairfields. Thornley, *Steamers of North Wales*, 24-25.

[69] *ibid.*, 27-53, for a detailed account of these vessels.

[70] D. Jenkins, 'Aberporth', in *Welsh Rural Communities* ed. Elwyn Davies and Alwyn D. Rees (Cardiff, 1960), 4.

[71] Michael Bouquet, *No Gallant Ship*, 24; D. Thomas, *Hen Longau Sir Gaernarfon*, 139.

[72] Thomas, *op. cit.*, 182.

[73] E. A. Williams, *Hanes Môn yn y Bedwaredd Ganrif ar Bymtheg*, 319.

[74] *Lloyd's Register of Yachts, 1911*. TR. Miss Burton, Beaumaris, 1971. W. H. Rowland, Garth, Bangor, 'yacht-builder', built a number of Lloyd's registered yachts, including the *Iëre*, a cutter owned by Sir W. L. Lewis of Bryn Llwyd, Menai Bridge, and the *Ikinoo*, owned by Sydney Smith of Liverpool: Professor J. O. Arnold, Professor of Metallurgy at the University of Sheffield, had an elderly cutter built in 1870 at Barrow, *Redwing*, which remained in the Beaumaris Register until 1923, when she was broken up.

[75] *NWC*, August 1913.

The End of an Age

Boys scurrying out to play and bursting from schoolrooms in Anglesey villages in the closing decades of the last century talked and dreamed of the days when they would be sailing to 'Frisco, Callao, Bombay, Rangoon or Sydney. The days of sail may have been numbered, but to boys with few alternative sources of employment there was much in the lure of the big square-rigged ships and barques which they saw sailing to and from Liverpool. At the turn of the century they would have seen on the walls of many Anglesey houses the carefully-posed photographs of crews taken at San Francisco, or paintings by William Godfrey, a marine artist who was also a photographer at Newcastle, New South Wales, where many Anglesey seamen spent long days waiting for freights. Boys at school in Holyhead went down to the harbour and gazed in wonder when 'the barque *Caernarvon Bay* sailed into the harbour, the master, a man from Pwllheli, handling her in superb manner, and throwing her up into the wind as though she were a small boat. It was blowing a gale at the time, too'.[1] From South Stack, Carmel Head, Llanbadrig, Cemais, Point Lynas, Amlwch and Moelfre boys on their way home from school, or working in the fields, looked out to sea and saw the tall ships pass and no amount of harsh realism on the part of their parents could dull their romanticism. Later generations from Anglesey and Lleyn were to find outlets for their abilities as teachers and doctors, scientists and preachers, but in the eighties and nineties many boys of considerable intellectual ability, courage and resource decided that the sea was the career for them. Some of them followed the long-established practice of going to sea as boys aboard coastal ships belonging to their fathers, or with masters who were family friends, and then graduated to larger vessels; others, when their families saw their minds set upon the sea, were apprenticed to one of the Liverpool shipping companies and thus found themselves aloft in a large four-masted square-rigger bound for Australia on their very first voyage. Many of them, whether as apprentices, seamen, or master mariners, sailed in ships belonging to or managed by the Welsh ship-brokers of Liverpool.

By the seventies William Thomas, the former Llanrhuddlad pupil teacher, was well established as a ship broker. In addition to his links with the expansion of the fleet of Captain Thomas, Amlwch, and the Lancashire and Cumberland schooner owners, William Thomas had 'bought the following ships for myself and other friends as Co-owners and have had the sole control and management of them since, viz. in the year 1872, *North Star, Lady Young,* 1873 *Sappho,* 1874 *Malabar, Julia,* 1875 *Buckhorn and Havelock'*.[2] To command these ships he appointed Anglesey or Caernarvonshire men who were known to him; for example, Captain David Evans, Nefyn, commanded the *North Star* and *Malabar,* the *Havelock* was commanded by Captain Owen Jones of Criccieth,[3] and then by Captain John Jones of Barron Hill, Newborough, who subsequently commanded a number of other Thomas vessels. Whether as a direct result of the financial success of the *William Mellhuish* or as part of a more general boom in the launching of sailing ships,[4] William Thomas saw the possibilities of having vessels specially built for him, which he would manage as single ship companies in which he would invite his fellow Welshmen in Liverpool and north Wales to invest their capital. Although still a young man, Thomas was a respected Elder of the Welsh Calvinistic Methodist community in Liverpool, many of whom were amongst the most prosperous builders on Merseyside, and he was not without friends who were willing to put their trust in his business acumen.[5] Recognizing the importance of carefully designing a sailing ship which was not excessively large, but could be used profitably and economically in the long distance carrying trade, Thomas commissioned W. E. Jones, a Port Dinorwic ship-builder, to make a model for him in line with the specifications which he, Thomas and W. E. Jones thought most efficient.[6] It was with this model that William Thomas then went to R. and J. Evans, the Liverpool shipbuilders, and Doxfords of Sunderland, and contracted to have a fleet of iron sailing ships of almost identical dimensions built. In the light of the subsequent high reputation and sailing qualities of some of these vessels, it is appropriate to record that they were the outcome of William Thomas' discussions with the highly professional W. E. Jones, who was at this time completing, at Port Dinorwic, the largest vessel to be built on the banks of the Menai Strait, the *Ordovic.* Jones himself, recognizing the possibilities of the boom, was having vessels built, the *Moel Eilian, Moel y Don,*

Moel Rhiwan, Moel Tryfan, all iron sailing vessels of over a thousand tons constructed for the *Gwynedd Shipping Company,* and all on the stocks in the Doxford yards at the same time as William Thomas' new ships.[7] Few of Thomas' personal papers have survived, but one interesting document is a memorandum written in his own hand in 1888[8] as the result of a dispute with an Amlwch master mariner whom he had employed to act as one of his overlookers when these ships were being built some ten years previously. In the memorandum, Thomas stated: 'I contracted to have the following iron ships built for myself and other friends as Co-owners, and have been the sole manager ever since.'

Name of Vessel	Design of Model and Specifications	Overlookers
County of Flint	W. E. Jones and Self	Wm. Hughes
County of Carnarvon	R. & J. Evans and Self	Capt. R. Roberts, Pwllheli
County of Anglesea	do., Capt. Parry and Self	Capt. S. Parry
County of Denbigh	W. E. Jones, Self and D. Jones	Capt. R. Jones
County of Cardigan	R. & J. Evans and Self	Capt. O. Hughes
County of Merioneth	W. E. Jones and Self	Capt. R. H. Roberts
County of Pembroke	W. E. Jones and Self	Capt. Thos. Williams and small portion by R. H. Roberts
Kate Thomas	W. E. Jones and Self	Capt. Thos. Williams
Principality	W. E. Jones and Self	Capt. Thos. Williams and Capt. J. Jones
Colony	W. E. Jones and Self	Capt. R. Roberts, Pwllheli and Capt. T. Owen
Province	W. E. Jones and Self	Capt. R. H. Jones
Metropolis	R. & J. Evans, Capt. H. Williams and Self	Capt. Thos. Williams

These vessels were built in a comparatively short period: the *County* class between 1877 and 1881. Three years later Thomas was managing seventeen vessels, including the *Menai* and the *Ogwen* which he had taken over from the *Arvon* shipping company, 'the majority of the shareholders remaining shareholders with me and those that did not (I) bought their shares'. In 1885 Doxfords built the *Kate Thomas* and the *Principality* and in the following year the *Colony* and the *Province*, almost identical four-masted barques, and in 1887, R. and J. Evans completed the slightly larger *Metropolis*.[9] Experienced mariners looking back over the years remember the excellent design and fittings of these vessels; a Devon man remembered one of them at Melbourne in 1903 making fast astern of the three-masted barque in which he was serving and described her, the *Principality*, thus: 'to me she was a thing of beauty; everything about her seemed so proportionate,'[10] whilst a Somerset seaman who was at Melbourne some years later wrote: 'I consider the *Metropolis* to have been one of the most handsome of all vessels; her deck fittings especially were particularly well finished and attractive.'[11]

William Thomas' dispute in 1888 had been with Capt. R. H. Roberts of Salem Terrace, Amlwch, who had previously commanded and part-owned the *Toronto* and the *Barbara* managed by Captain William Thomas, Amlwch. Owing to ill-health, Captain Roberts had had to come ashore in 1879, and Captain William Thomas, when on a visit to Liverpool in that year, asked his namesake if he could employ Roberts in any capacity. William Thomas was at the time negotiating a cargo for Captain Thomas' *Linda* from Connah's Quay to Bermuda, and as a favour to his Amlwch friend, agreed to appoint Captain Roberts as overlooker at Sunderland where Doxfords were building the *County of Merioneth* for him.[12] It is clear from the correspondence that the two Thomas firms were quite distinct although they co-operated in a friendly way; William Thomas, Liverpool, pointed out that he could not give Roberts a permanent post, 'if he was between us, of course he cannot serve both if the vessels were home the same time, as they no doubt would be very often'.[13] Moreover, the Liverpool broker already had Captain David Evans, the Nefyn master mariner, who had commanded a number of vessels for him, as 'outdoor superintendent of sailing ships . . . for the purpose of looking after and assisting in discharging, loading and dispatching, reporting on the condition of the ships and their outfit and seeing to the painting and the necessary repairs, etc., being effective'.[14] From time to time he employed other master mariners, Captain Thomas Williams, Treborth, Captain Robert Roberts,

Pwllheli and Captain William Jones of Caernarvon, 'to assist when Captain Evans would be otherwise engaged'. Whilst he was willing, therefore, to do his best for one of Captain William Thomas' men, the Liverpool ship manager had his own captains to consider; 'I throw as much responsibility as possible on the captains, and being all good men they . . . might object having any superintendence' and 'of course it is best to carry the men with you as much as possible'.[15]

Captain Richard Roberts' lengthy correspondence from Sunderland in 1879-80 whilst the *County of Merioneth* was being built is full of information of the type that William Thomas must have been receiving from several sources; frustration and delay when the busy Doxford's yard was held up for iron deliveries, 'iron is only coming in very small quantities . . . it is nearly the same in several other yards. The rolling mills cannot supply the demand'; specifications and descriptions of vessels being built for rival companies which Roberts gleaned as he made 'a Cruise of Stock taking' through Palmers, Osborne's, Thompsons and Laing's yards, going 'on board some new steamers seeing what was to be seen'.[16] William Thomas had decided to go into steam, and in December 1879 Captain Roberts was in Amlwch approaching prosperous citizens to interest them in shares in the proposed ventures, hoping thereby to advance his own position and assuring them that William Thomas, Liverpool, did 'not purpose to have any more sailing vessels, as experience shows that steam proportionately must pay better than sailing'.[17] Thomas clearly had not come to such a decision, and built and bought a number of sailing ships after this date. His letters are brief in contrast with the garrulous Roberts, but together they provide a fascinating impression of the building of both sailing and steam vessels in the closing decades of the century.[18] William Thomas was annoyed that Roberts had allowed Doxfords to deviate from the contract and insisted that the contractors should keep to the letter of their agreement, 'I wish sufficient time to be taken to complete her properly'.[19] Thomas was personally involved and interested in every detail from the masts, spars, sails, ventilators, to the name; 'Call her the *County of Merioneth*. Have the name cut into the iron on the bow and stern, and everything about the bow made the same as Liverpool ships are made, and the same as the *Denbigh*.'[20] Awaiting Thomas' arrival in Sunderland to inspect his new vessel, Captain Roberts reported in an embarrassed fashion that the new *County of Merioneth*'s white paint 'is now covered with coal dust, it is blowing quite a gale of wind . . . and you can imagine its effect on white paint'. A few days later Thomas wrote: 'I have appointed a captain, William Griffith, late master of the *Bianca* and a friend of Captain Jones, Menai Strait, to the command of the *Merioneth*,' and 'a young man from New Quay as mate. He seemed a decent man but rather quiet. He has passed Master but has never been an officer with large iron ships. He has been with large ships before the mast of course'.[21] When the *County of Merioneth* sailed on her first voyage for Batavia,[22] Captain Roberts went to London to supervise some work for Captain Thomas, Amlwch, and was then rewarded for his enthusiasm for steam by being appointed by William Thomas, Liverpool, to overlook the building of the steamers *Empire* and *Kingdom* at Evans' and Doxford's yards respectively. He afterwards superintended their loading and discharge at various ports, particularly at London and Antwerp, in their early years.[23]

The correspondence between Thomas and Roberts in the eighties reflect something of the excitement of the intense competition, not only between rival shipbuilding yards, but also between rival Welsh ship managers. Complaining of delays at Doxfords, Captain Roberts reported in 1882 to his employer that one of his future rivals in Liverpool, 'Mr Thomas of Criccieth was in the yard yesterday . . . his vessel will be laid down after Mr W. E. Jones' is launched'.[24] Sailing ships certainly attracted Welsh investors; William Thomas, writing in April 1882, informed Captain Roberts that he would do his best to allocate shares to one of the latter's friends in one of the ships he had recently bought, '*Portia* is all and more than taken. Mr Williams, who would have taken a ¼ has only a little over ⅛th . . . Captain Evans says she is a splendid vessel'.[25] Thomas always keenly compared the cargoes carried by his ships. When the *County of Cardigan* came out of dry dock at South Shields in October 1880, he wrote to Captain Roberts hoping that she would take on 'close on 2,000 tons cargo, *County of Caernarvon* had 1,940 tons besides stove coal and was light. *Cardigan* carries about 50 tons more than her. She delivered about 70 tons more rice. I want as much cargo as you can put in her without being too deep. She was much too light from here last time'. And on the next day he wrote again: 'If not too deep I should like to have 2,000 tons in her; in proportion to *Merioneth* she ought to have this.' The building of steamers led to negotiations by Thomas with south Wales coal companies, such as David Davies', and there are letters advising his captains to keep Nant y Glo and Ferndale coal separate, 'to enable us to ascertain which will answer best. I have had a good name for Nantyglo and it is cheaper'.[26] He arranged for masters of sailing ships to transfer to steamers; Captain Roberts, late master of the *County of Flint*, went for experience as mate with Captain Davies in the *Empire* to Port Said 'for fear he may be sometime without getting a chance'.[27]

Constantly assessing the profitability of Bombay, Java, American and Black Sea freights, Thomas sought information from his captains regarding conditions at ports ranging from Chittagong to San Francisco. As his fleet of ships expanded, so his captains gained in experience. Captain John Jones of Baronhill, Newborough, may be taken as one example of the many Anglesey mariners who served in Thomas' ships. Appointed to command the *Havelock* in November 1880, he made two voyages in her.[28] From Cardiff he sailed her to Callao, Antofagasta and back to Antwerp, whence he sailed with a general cargo for Shanghai, then to Victoria and Puget Sound, thence to Iquique, Lobos de Afuerra, putting into Valparaiso for repairs, and back to Liverpool where he left her on 21 January 1884.[29] William Thomas appointed him on the next day to the command of the *Menai* in which he sailed to San Francisco, where he arrived on 17 July 1884.[30] The Menai was at Queenstown for orders in January 1885 and discharged her cargo at Limerick; Captain Jones left her at the end of February, and after a three-month spell ashore was appointed by Thomas to superintend the building of his new vessel, the *Principality*, at Doxford's Sunderland yard. Here he relieved Captain Thomas Williams of Treborth, near Bangor, another of Thomas' long-serving captains, who had previously supervised the building, and now took command, of the *Kate Thomas*. It had obviously been decided that Captain John Jones was to be the first master of the *Principality*, and when in October 1885 she was ready for sea, Captain Jones had every reason to be proud of her, for she was a fine vessel. According to William Thomas' own notes, the *Kate Thomas*, *Principality*, *Colony*, *Province* and *Metropolis* were all 'duplicates' and the 'model was made by W. E. Jones, Portdinorwic'.[31]

When these vessels were being built, William Thomas had leaflets printed and distributed in Liverpool and north Wales inviting investors to purchase shares in them. Thus the *Kate Thomas* was due to be completed by May 1885, so in November 1884 handbills with 'Particulars of New First Class Four Masted Iron Sailing Vessel to be built under contract by Messrs. William Doxford and Sons, the Builders of *County of Flint, County of Merioneth, County of Pembroke* and s.s. *Kingdom*' were published.[32] The contract price of '£9.15.0 per ton nett register, equal to £16,477.10.0', was to be raised by the sale of shares of £100 each payable in six instalments.[33] The seventy-nine investors, who between them had the 165 shares in the *Kate Thomas*, reflect the wide interest in William Thomas' ships in north Wales and among the Welsh community in Merseyside. Recorded in Thomas' little black notebook,[34] in which he kept the names and addresses of the shareholders of the *Kate Thomas* and the *Principality*, are the names of more than a dozen master mariners from Anglesey and Caernarvonshire, a fitting comment on the soundness of the ships themselves, and several Welsh businessmen from Liverpool and Bootle, including David Hughes, from Cemais, who had sailed from Amlwch to Liverpool in a small sailing vessel earlier in the century and had become a wealthy builder of houses in the Anfield, Bootle and Everton areas, as well as of warehouses in the dock area. This link with Anglesey-born Calvinistic Methodist builders on Merseyside was not new; there is a note in William Thomas' papers that he built the *County of Pembroke* 'in conjunction with Mr Morris Owen', who had progressed from his native Anglesey via an apprenticeship as a joiner, and then time at sea as ship's carpenter, to become a large-scale builder in the Edgehill and Smithdown Road districts and director of the Chatham Building Society in Liverpool. North Wales interests are reflected in addresses like 'Medical Hall, Holyhead', 'Apothecaries Hall, Menai Bridge' and 'Clock House, Holyhead'. Alongside innkeepers from the Union Inn, Trefriw, the Liverpool Arms Hotel, Bangor, and the Min-y-don Hotel, Red Wharf, post office-shopkeepers from Llanrug, Rachub and Brynsiencyn, are the names of ministers of religion who were well known in Victorian Wales, Evan Jones of Segontium Terrace, Caernarvon, Owen Owens of Anfield Road, Liverpool, Evan Davies of Trefriw and D. Williams of Northumberland Terrace, Liverpool, farmers like Owen Jones, Tŷ'n Lôn, Marianglas, whose family had long been associated with shipping, Robert Roberts of Tŷ Golchi Farm, near Bangor, drapers like William Bayne of Upper Bangor, Robert Algeo of Menai Bridge, whose map of the Amlwch harbour area has already been mentioned, and Edward Morgan Jones, tobacco manufacturer, of Amlwch. Many of the investors shared William Thomas' own Calvinistic Methodist background and they were drawn not only from Merseyside and Anglesey, but also from Merioneth, Caernarvonshire and Denbighshire; one of those who had a share in the *Kate Thomas* was John Wheldon, Llwyn Celyn, Llanberis, whose son, T. J. Wheldon, was a prominent and influential Calvinistic Methodist minister at Blaenau Ffestiniog and Bangor.[35]

It will be recalled that Thomas had bought two of the *Arvon Shipping Company*'s vessels, the *Menai* and the *Ogwen*, and had stated that the majority of the shareholders had remained 'shareholders with me'. A comparison of Thomas' note book and the Register of members of the *Arvon Shipping Company* in 1878 confirms this; many of those who had shares in the *Kate Thomas* and *Principality* had also held shares in the *Arvon Shipping Company*, which numbered several Anglesey merchants and farmers among its members, as well as schoolmasters, drapers, ministers of religion and quarrymen from Caernarvonshire. There had been earlier investors from the slate quarrying districts of Caernarvonshire in Thomas' ships; when the *County* class were being built, *Y Genedl Gymreig* reported a meeting at the Douglas Arms, Bethesda, in 1877, when quarrymen were encouraged to invest their savings in the *Bethesda Shipping Company* which had taken shares in the *County of Flint*, bound for Singapore, and the *County of Denbigh* soon to make her maiden voyage.[36]

The 'Welsh connection' of William Thomas, Liverpool, went beyond his own personal involvement in the design and building of his ships and his Welsh investors for he almost invariably had Welsh master mariners in command of his ships and a Welsh 'afterguard'. A cursory glance through the crew agreement lists for one year, 1888,[37] illustrates this tendency. The *Principality* had sailed from Bremerhaven via Cardiff for Bombay 'and for any other Port or Ports within the limits of 75° North and 60° South', on a voyage not to exceed three years, with Captain John Jones, aged 48, of

Newborough, in command, Thomas Evans, aged 32, from Cardigan, as mate, and Robert Evans, aged 25, from Portmadoc, as second mate. The crew consisted of an Irishman, one Englishman, eight Swedes, one Russian, three Germans and five Norwegians; the three apprentices, whose birthplaces are not recorded, were called Jones, Edwards and Williams. In the same year, the *County of Flint* was commanded by David Edwards, an Aberystwyth man, with Hugh Owen from Trefriw as his mate, and the remainder of the crew consisted of Americans, Swedes, Germans and Scotsmen. The *County of Merioneth*'s master was William Meredith of Caernarvon who had previously commanded the *Havelock*, with Ellis Thomas of Nefyn as mate, and a William Thomas, aged twenty-two, 'of Anglesey', who had served in the *Principality* on her maiden voyage, as second mate. On arrival in Astoria with a cargo of steel rails for Portland, Oregon, from Maryport, Captain Meredith recorded that they had had 'boisterous weather and heavy seas', and on their return voyage one of the Americans in the crew was 'drowned at sea'.[38] Master of the *County of Caernarvon* was Captain Robert Roberts of Nefyn, with W. S. Richards of Bangor as mate, and John Evans, a young Anglesey man who had already served aboard another of the Thomas ships, the *Colony*, as second mate. When the *County of Cardigan*, commanded by Captain William Williams 'of Anglesey', arrived in Liverpool in September 1888, at the end of a voyage from Penarth to 'Kurrachee' and back, among the crew discharged were David Evans, the mate from Aberaeron, Robert Parry of Amlwch, the carpenter, and Thomas Jones of Caernarvon, the sailmaker, who had both previously served together in William Thomas' *Portia*, and of the ten A.B.s four were Welshmen from Holyhead, Amlwch, Portmadoc and 'Anglesey', whilst the ship's boy was a Holyhead youth on his first voyage. The mate's wages were £6 a month, the carpenter £4.5.0, the A.B.s £2.10.0 and the boy 16/- a month. The *County of Anglesea* had returned in April 1888 to Liverpool after a voyage which had taken her from Antwerp in December 1886 to Sydney under the command of Robert Wynne, a 40-year-old Conway man, with Ellis Jones of Pwllheli as mate, Owen Williams, aged 24, of Moelfre, as second mate, Evan Roberts of Pwllheli as steward and cook, and John Wynne, possibly the master's son, and William Ellis, aged sixteen, of Nefyn among the remainder of the crew who came from Finland, Germany, Holland and Sweden. Four of the overseas men deserted at Sydney and were replaced by a number of other Europeans, some of whom again deserted at Wilmington, California.

Bare statements of voyages hardly convey what they meant in human terms, and the seamen of the eighties had little time to record their feelings. Captain John Jones, Newborough, had made his voyage to San Francisco and home again in the *Menai* in 1884 in the better months of the year, but the *Enterprise*, another of the *Arvon Shipping Company*'s full-rigged ships (which, incidentally, Thomas had refused to buy), did not leave Cardiff until May and experienced typical weather in a winter passage round Cape Horn. Aboard the *Enterprise*, commanded by Captain George Lewis, with David Parry as first mate, and W. James as second mate, and a crew of twenty-five hands, was a young first-voyager – acting as under-steward and, for a time, as cook – John D. Jones, who kept a diary.[39] Written in indelible pencil, in handwriting that fluctuated considerably according to the weather conditions, young Jones' diary expresses something of the loneliness of homesickness mingled with excitement and wonder which many of his less articulate young contemporaries must have felt on their own first voyages aboard these large sailing ships. Far from his Welsh rural background and religious upbringing, the young steward found time, between scuttling around preparing and serving meals in the cabin, to record his day-to-day life aboard the *Enterprise* as she battled her way round Cape Horn in the winter of 1884.

64 days out. Sunday July 27/84.
Read in Psalms. A showery morning ... 4 bells, it's dark soon after 5 o'clock and I wonder when it gets dark at home, I should like to be going to chapel tonight ... I wonder how poor mother is and all the rest. I think a deal about them whether they do me. Read in Luke, Proverbs.

65 days out. Monday July 28/84. 1 a.m.
All hands called out, a tremendous gale hardly a rag on the old ship sea like mountains . . . 2 a.m. whole gale two men at the wheel, great excitement getting worse . . . had a narrow escape

Eng. 1.

G., C. & H. O.
RECEIVED.

Executed in Twelve Pages.

Any Fraud, Entertainment, or Alteration in this Agreement will be void unless attested by some Superintendent of a Mercantile Marine Office, Officer of Customs, Consul, or Vice-Consul, to be made with the consent of the persons interested.

AGREEMENT AND ACCOUNT OF CREW.
FOREIGN-GOING SHIP.

The term "Foreign-going Ship," means every Ship employed in trading or going between some place or places in the United Kingdom and some place or places situate beyond the Coasts of the United Kingdom, the Islands of Guernsey, Jersey, Sark, Alderney, and Man, and the Continent of Europe between the River Elbe and Brest, inclusive.

Name of Ship.	Official No.	Port of Registry.	Port No; and Date of Register.	Registered Tonnage.		Nominal Horse power of Engines (if any).
				Gross.	Net.	
Coronula Chrysanthemum No. 606 Liverpool			140 1877	1103	1066	

REGISTERED MANAGING OWNER.

Name.
(State No. of House, Street, and Town.)

No. of Seamen for whom accommodation is certified. (30 & 31 Vict. c. 124.)

Distance in feet and inches between centre of the Disc showing the Maximum load line in salt water and upper edge of lines indicating the position of the Ship's decks above that centre.

First Deck above it.

Second Deck above it.

ft. in.
ft. in.

The several Persons whose names are hereto subscribed, and whose descriptions are contained on the other side or sides, and of whom .... are engaged as Sailors, hereby agree to serve on board the said Ship, in the several capacities expressed against their respective Names, on a Voyage from ...

Scale of Provisions to be allowed and served out to the Crew during the Voyage, in addition to the daily issue of Lime and Lemon Juice and Sugar, or other antiscorbutics in any case required by 30th & 31st Vict. c. 124. s. 4.

SUBSTITUTES.

Note.—In any case an equal quantity of Fresh Meat, or Fresh Vegetables may, at the option of the Master, be served out in lieu of the Salted or Tinned Meats or Preserved or Compressed Vegetables named in the above Scale.

And the Crew agree to conduct themselves in an orderly, faithful, honest, and sober manner, and to be at all times diligent in their respective duties, and to be obedient to the lawful commands of the said Master, or of any Person who shall lawfully succeed him, and of their Superior Officers, in everything relating to the said Ship and the Stores and Cargo thereof, whether on board, in boats, or on shore: in consideration of which Services to be duly performed, the said Master hereby agrees to pay to the said Crew as Wages the Sums against their Names respectively expressed, and to supply them with Provisions according to the above Scale. And it is hereby agreed, That any Embezzlement or wilful or neglectful Destruction of any part of the Ship's Cargo or Stores shall be made good to the Owner out of the Wages of the Person guilty of the same: And if any Person enters himself as qualified for a duty which he proves incompetent to perform, his Wages shall be reduced in proportion to his incompetency: And it is also agreed, That the Regulations authorized by the Board of Trade, which are printed herein and numbered

And it is hereby stipulated that any of the Clauses printed herein, and numbered ____ are adopted by the parties hereto, and shall be considered as embodied in this Agreement: And it is also agreed, That if any Member of the Crew considers himself to be aggrieved by any breach of the Agreement or otherwise, he shall represent the same to the Master or Officer in charge of the Ship in a quiet and orderly manner, who shall thereupon take such steps as the case may require: And it is also agreed, That

[handwritten portion of agreement]

In Witness whereof the said parties have subscribed their Names on the other Side or Sides hereof on the days against their respective Signatures mentioned.

Signed by ____ *Robert Dyhane* ____ Master,

on the ____ 10 ____ day of ____ *December* 188 6

These Columns to be filled up at the end of the Voyage.

I hereby declare to the truth of the Entries in this Agreement and Account of Crew, &c.—

[signature] Master.

Date of Commencement of Voyage.	Port at which Voyage commenced.	Date of Termination of Voyage.		
15 Dec/ 1886	Antwerp	7/4/88		

The authority of the Owner or Agent for the allotments mentioned within is in my possession.

{ Superintendent, Officer of Customs, or Consular Officer.

This is to be signed if such an authority has been produced, and to be scored across in ink if it has not.

Port at which Voyage terminated.	Date of Delivery of Lists to Superintendent.
Liverpool	7/4/88

Twelve Pages.

with a wave just caught a rope or would have rolled over ship. 8 p.m. all hands called out f Top Sail carried away . . . if the ones at home saw this terrible storm at sea one would hardly believe that a large vessel like this is but a feather, she is quite on her side the deck full of water, poor sailors up to their waists clinging for life to rope. I shall never forget this day . . . poor sailors oblige to go to top of ship in all Darkness, first mate got very excited very near bewildered, Capt. Lewis is quite cool, had a fine lot of water under my bed 12 mid all hands out again. She rides a little easier. Fowls taken forward almost drowned . . . Read part of Psalm. Bitterly cold. Should like to see J. W. and Gron here.

89 days out. Thursday, Aug. 21/84.
A heavy fall of snow during the night. 8 bells still snowing . . . More icebergs in sight; man continuously on the look out . . . 11 a.m. 6 bells Immense icebergs coming towards us obliged to turn the ship on another tack to keep clear, they look like if you were looking towards Carn'shire mountains. Its wonderful and worth coming if only to see such scenery.

90 days out. Friday, Aug. 22/84.
Read in Psalms . . . 3 p.m. 6B. wind changed Top G+f Sail taken in, rather heavy sea at times. I read 3 Psalms. Barrel of Pork broached. 18.45. Blowing a stiff gale, all hands out (Grog served out tonight) refused it 2 men knocked down in the heavy sea, hope Mother is well.

91 days out. Saturday, Aug. 23/84.
Read in Psalms. A strong Breeze with fair wind. We are today going East and the clock is put fast instead of slow. We have not much sail on Foresails upper main. In the Pacific Ocean 3.45 a homeward bound passed us, supposed to be a Swansea barque, seemed to be rolling heavy. 8.5 p.m. Blowing hard and a very heavy sea rolling; sails reefed and all snug, shipping a deal of big seas, so endeth 14th Sat. on Sea. In Pacific Ocean. Doing 9 knotts tonight.

92 days out. Sunday, Aug. 24/84.

Has blown a terrible gale all night. Tremendous sea, two men at the wheel, 2nd mate knocked down on the Poop with the heavy sea. Its a grand sight to see the water, slept well: old ship going like a yacht, doing 9 to 10 knots ... immense waves washing over us ... I hope it does not carry our houses off their foundation. How well off are those in chapel now, instead of being tossing on the billows. Hope poor mother is well.

101 days out. Tuesday, Sept. 2/84.

Read 4 Psalms. 4 p.m. Finished reading Book of Revelation. The old ship looks beautiful tonight she has had her Top S.S. on and every stitch of canvass; moonlight and blowing a good breeze and we are travelling along A1.

Old seamen of other nationalities sometimes alleged that Welsh ship managers and captains deliberately signed on as many of their countrymen as possible so that they could have 'spies' in the fo'csle and information passed to them in the Welsh language, which no one else could understand. Once the storms off the Horn were over and the *Enterprise* was moving almost imperceptibly forward in calm weather, trouble broke out between the English and the German and Scandinavian members of the crew, and young Jones was sent for by Captain Lewis; all the other entries in his diary are in English, but most of this day's events were recorded in Welsh, in case it fell into anyone else's hands.

111 days out. Thursday, September 11/84.

A calm morning very light breeze just keeps us moving. Heddyw boreu bu twrw ymladd rhwng y Saeson ar bobl or wlad bell, Saeson yn llwyddianus, bu twrw hefyd yn y caban rhwng amryw galwyd fi o flaen y Cabden, ac rhoddodd orders i mi beidio gwneud dim byd ond cerdded o gwmpas a cadw fy llygaid yn agored a bod yn detective, peidio a chymryd dim tafod gan neb neu i'r heurns y rhoir pawb, ofni mutiny ydwyf ond mi gadwaf fy llygad yn agored; 8 Bell 4 p.m. dead calm sea like a sheet of glass. Read in Llyfr Pregethwyr I hope Mother is well.[40]

Captain Lewis had no more trouble, but when they arrived at Panama City, several of the crew deserted, two died, and three others, including J. D. Jones, the under-steward, were discharged, 'paid off sick'. After ninety-seven days in harbour, Jones was not sorry to leave the *Enterprise*; on 3 January 1885 he had seen something of the revolution in Panama City, and noted in his diary 'Heavy fighting, Captain and myself took to our heels, all business places closed up'. The next day was his last aboard the *Enterprise*: 'finished my work on board, only waited at table today, did not turn to.'

Inevitably, there were casualties. William Thomas recorded the loss of the *Buckhorn, Lady Young* and the *County of Denbigh* in 1880; one of the five *County* vessels built for him in 1877, the *County of Denbigh* was thus a comparatively new ship, commanded by Captain Robert Roberts of Nefyn, when she was lost with all hands on passage from Astoria to Queenstown in 1880. The *British Commerce*, bought by Thomas in 1883, was lost in collision with the *County of Aberdeen* off the Isle of Wight on her next voyage. The *Ogwen*, taken over from the *Arvon Shipping Company*, was lost in March 1886; 'I replaced her with the *Colony*.' Two years later the Malabar, one of the earlier Quebec-built ships, commanded at one time by Captain David Evans of Nefyn, Thomas' senior Captain and superintendent, was lost. The *County of Carnarvon*, commanded by another Nefyn man, Captain Robert Roberts, Bryn Noddfa, was lost with all hands in 1889 on passage with a cargo of coal from Newcastle, N.S.W., for the West Coast of South America; much of the wreckage of the *County of Carnarvon* was washed ashore on the coast of New Zealand. The *Nation*, a large steel 4-masted barque, built at Doxford in 1891 and commanded by Captain Robert Wynne, previously master of the *County of Anglesey*, left Rangoon in March 1892 for Falmouth, and was never heard of again. The loss of one of William Thomas' ships made a deep impression in Anglesey; years later Holyhead people remembered the loss of the *Cape Wrath* with many Holyhead men aboard, and the *Menai* with Captain John Farrell of Amlwch in command and a Holyhead man named Roberts as first mate. The *Menai* had left Newcastle, N.S.W., on 23 February 1895 for Tocopilla; she disappeared without trace, possibly another victim of the careless coal trimmers of Newcastle.[41] Shifting cargoes killed many ships.

Some of the captains were known as great carriers of sail. Captain William Meredith, who had commanded the *Havelock* and the *County of Merioneth*, was one; he had been employed by William Thomas for eleven years when appointed to the command of the last of the sailing ships to be built for him by Doxfords, the steel four-masted barque, *Dominion*, in 1891. A vessel of 2,539 tons, she was larger than the earlier Thomas vessels, and on her maiden voyage Captain Meredith, who wished to make as fast a passage as possible, had trouble with the crew, who alleged that she was over-sparred and undermanned.[42] Captain Meredith was not a man to be easily deterred; one who sailed in her wrote: 'I sailed in the British ship *Dominion* once from Barry to San Francisco, and I never did see such sail carrying. As for the main deck, you could not put your foot on it in bad weather without fear of going overboard.'[43] After eight years of hard sailing, on 19 January 1899, the *Dominion* left Honolulu for Vancouver in ballast; she never arrived. Basil Lubbock, in *The Last of the Windjammers*, stated that the contemporary explanation was that she had been insufficiently ballasted and had capsized in a squall, but he was mistaken in his assumption that Captain Meredith was still in command of the *Dominion*. Her master on her last voyage was Captain T. Jones who had replaced Meredith when the latter was appointed in 1898 to command the *Annie Thomas*, 1,764 tons, the last of the big sailing ships to be built for William Thomas, completed at Mackie and Thomson's Glasgow yards in 1896. Ironically, nine months after the loss of the *Dominion*, Captain Meredith too was lost, for the *Annie Thomas*, bound from Cardiff to Acapulco with a cargo of coal, and her crew of 27 men were never heard of again after being spoken to on 19 October 1899 in a position given as 57°25'S, 70°30'W. Had Captain Meredith of Ropewalk, Nefyn, carried too much sail once too often in Cape Horn seas, or had the coal cargo gone on fire – only the wind and the sea knew the answer.

Apart from the sadness in Anglesey when disasters occurred from time to time, there was also considerable interest in the achievements of the Thomas ships. At the turn of the century, the *Principality*, commanded by Captain Evan Jones since 1891, and the *Metropolis*, commanded by Captain Richards since 1892, were regarded as the fastest sailers in the Thomas fleet, and made some of the speediest passages of the sailing ship era. The late Basil Lubbock, in his classic *The Last of the Windjammers*, claimed that 'when Captain Jones commanded the *Principality* and Captain Richards had the *Metropolis* there were very few ships that could get past either of them'. According to Lubbock, the *Principality*'s fastest voyage was from Astoria to Queenstown in ninety-six days in 1895 and Cardiff to Valparaiso in seventy-four days. Two years later the *Principality* and the *Metropolis* made the round voyage together of Barry to Rio, Rio to the west coast of South America and back home again in eight months, the *Principality* being a few days faster on each leg of the voyage.[44] On the *Principality*'s record passage from Portland, Oregon, to Queenstown in 1895, Ellis Roberts of Caernarvon (later to become a master of ocean liners) was the second mate, and he recalled how Captain Evan Jones of Pencaenewydd, her master, turned to him as they ran before a gale off Cape Horn carrying as much canvas as they dared, saying, 'Mr Roberts, you will take the masts out of her'. They did not, and apparently 'The only complaint Mr William Thomas, the owner, made about the *Principality*'s record voyage was that a heavy sea took our port and starboard light screens, sidelights and all, to the bottom somewhere off the Old Head of Kinsale when she was diving bows under'.[45]

William Thomas, who had moved from his original office at 25 Water Street to 30 Brunswick Street, Liverpool, about 1880, moved again in the 1890s to 14 Water Street, the offices of T. Williams and Company, owners of the *Cambrian* ships. As his fleet increased and more and more Welsh seamen entered his employment, so William Thomas' office employed more young Welshmen as clerks. William Lewis and Richard Farrell were two young clerks who started work on the same day in 1891 in Thomas' office. Lewis was the nephew of one of the most experienced of Thomas' master mariners, Captain Thomas Davies of Bangor, whilst young Farrell had come as a boy to Liverpool when Captain John Hughes Farrell had moved his family, 'lock stock and barrel' to Liverpool in the *Cumberland Lassie* from Amlwch, following his decision to forsake deep-sea sailing to command the *Hercules*, a little steamer plying between Liverpool and Holyhead. In later years Lewis was to become a successful and wealthy rival ship-manager, whilst Farrell remained and became secretary and a director of the company established in the post 1914-

18 war era by Thomas' son, Sir Robert J. Thomas. In the 1890s
Thomas continued to acquire ships; the Lloyd's Register of 1901
indicated that in addition to his own ships, he was managing, as
single-ship companies, a number of the Williams vessels, the
Cambrian Chieftain, Captain M. Jones, the *Cambrian Hills*, Captain
A. Evans who had been her master since 1892, the *Cambrian Prince*,
Captain T. Owen, the *Cambrian Warrior*, Captain J. Jones, and the
Cambrian Princess, Captain W. Roberts.[46] The problem often
enough at this distance in time is to identify these Welsh master
mariners whose names are inevitably so much alike. Commander
Alan Villiers, in his excellent book, *The War with Cape Horn*, writing
of this period, amusingly noted, 'Take all the Lloyds, Llewellyns,
Lewises, Hugheses, Davieses, Williamses, Owenses, Jenkinses – or
only the Joneses – from the British merchant service and more than
the half of it would come to a full stop. Considerably more than half
the Cape Horn ships would not have sailed'.[47] Sometimes they were
members of the same family – the Jones brothers of Pwllffannog on
the Anglesey shore of the Menai Strait are but one example of seven
brothers who all went to sea. William Jones served aboard the
Cambrian Chieftain and later as sailmaker aboard the *Metropolis*
when his brother Peter Jones commanded her, and his son served as
ship's boy; Peter Jones had served as A.B. aboard the *Cambrian Hills*
before becoming mate of the *Principality*, and later master of the
Boadicea, the *County of Cardigan* and the *Metropolis*. All the
Pwllffannog Jones brothers had started their careers in coastal sail,
Peter and his brother Ishmael later commanding the *Pride of the Dee*
of Runcorn, a topsail schooner.[48] Captain Thomas Owen, who
commanded the *Cambrian Prince*, and Captain William Owen,
sometime master of the *Cambrian Princess*, were brothers, members
of the Tŷ'n Pwll family, Moelfre, whilst another Moelfre man who
commanded one of Thomas' ships was Captain David Lewis, master
of the *County of Anglesea*.[49] Commander Villiers, describing his
meetings with some outstanding German and Scandinavian masters,
noted that many of them graduated to the large four- and five-masted
sailing ships by way of hard but effective training in small coastal
vessels in the comparatively local waters of the Baltic and the North
Sea.[50] This was true of many Anglesey seamen, and not only of the
future master mariners. Their first experience was often in small

sloops, smacks or schooners, plying from Holyhead, Amlwch, or the Menai Strait to Liverpool, or even in smaller vessels which dried out on the Anglesey beaches with general cargoes to be carried inshore by horse and cart. Mr Elias Jones, now 96 years of age, and known affectionately to everyone in Amlwch as 'Lei Bach', was working as an errand boy when he met an erstwhile schoolmate walking up from the harbour, having just left a schooner which was ready to sail. Lei ran down to the harbour, persuaded the master to take him as he stood, and was half-way to Liverpool in the little schooner before his mother was told by the 'hobblers' that he had sailed. After a spell in the coastal trade running from Runcorn to Falmouth, the nimble Lei moved to serve aboard the *Gaelic*, under Captain Ishmael Williams in the South America trade, then in the *John Lockett* with Captain Robert Jones, and after some years ashore in Australia, served as an able seaman for many years on the Australian-Cape Horn routes. Lightly built, Lei was well suited for scrambling up the highest rigging, leaving his heavier-built companions way behind as he swung upwards and outwards on the yards; his problem was that he was so short that he had difficulty in jumping to the life-lines when heavy seas were shipped and threatened to sweep the crew away. Recently Mr Jones gave me an apt description of the big four-masted iron barques: 'when you were on her deck it was like being on a football field, but when you were up aloft, her deck looked like a pocket handkerchief.'[51]

A more conventional, if less dramatic, way of going to sea was the practice, particularly among the sons of coastal masters, of going to sea with their fathers during the school holidays.[52] Among the many who did this is Captain W. H. Hughes, D.S.C., of Holyhead. A Portmadoc boy, his father took him with him in the summer holidays of 1898 in the schooner *Arfon* when she sailed north about from Caernarvon to South Shields; he well remembers putting in to Stornoway for repairs, waiting for the tide in the Pentland Firth, unloading slates at South Shields, and the subsequent passage to pretty Sibboreen with a cargo of coal. He then went back to school until the following summer when he joined the *Arfon* as a regular member of the crew, sailing from Portmadoc to Hamburg, Scotland and Norway. It was on passage from Norway with a cargo of timber that they ran into very heavy weather, and young Hughes found himself being hauled ashore half-drowned, in a lifebuoy, the youngest, and therefore, the first to be rescued from the wreck of the *Arfon* as she lay pounded by heavy seas, after being driven ashore near Lowestoft.[53] Whilst his father then made a trip in the well-known *Frau Minna Petersen* before buying an elderly wooden schooner, the *Miss Pritchard*, built at Portin-llaen in 1870, young Hughes sailed in the *Faith*, a small schooner plying from Lancaster,[54] and then rejoined his father in the *Miss Pritchard*. Slates for Papenburg and for Copenhagen, timber for Pwllheli from Norway, salt from Cadiz for Newfoundland, then the usual run, avoiding icebergs off Newfoundland, back to Europe, this was the pattern of trade of the little *Miss Pritchard* like so many of the Portmadoc schooners. Soon another brother was ready to join his father in the *Miss Pritchard*, so W. H. Hughes moved to one of the larger Portmadoc schooners, the *Nesta*, sailing to Bremen and then back to Dublin with a cargo of asphalt. After three more years in Portmadoc vessels,[55] Hughes served again in the *Miss Pritchard* (with his father and brother aboard, so that out of the crew of five, three were from one family). He was mate of the *Miss Pritchard* when she sank off Cape Wrath shortly after leaving Stornoway in 1904; all the crew were saved, getting ashore in their own ship's boat, and then rowing a further fifteen miles or so to Loch Inver when the weather moderated.[56] W. H. Hughes had thus had six years' experience in schooners before he went to Rotterdam and signed as an able seaman in the crew of twenty-four who manned the Portmadoc Pritchard brothers' barque *Beeswing*, bound for Australia in August 1904.

Having served his time as an able seaman aboard the *Beeswing*, Hughes obtained a second mate's berth aboard the full-rigged ship *Deccan*, commanded by Captain Llewelyn Rees, whose father was minister of the Baptist Chapel, Holyhead. The Rees family had come from south Wales and Llewelyn Rees had served in his early days in that 'hardest of all deep-water trades', in the small copper ore ships between Swansea and the Chilean coast, aptly described by Joseph Conrad as 'coal out and ore in, deep-loaded both ways as if in wanton defiance of the great Cape Horn seas'.[57] After this spell in the copper-ore trade and service as second mate in William Thomas' *Portia*, Rees had eventually taken command of the *Morven*, managed by

William Lewis, another of the Liverpool Welsh ship managers. Misfortunes had already come Captain Rees' way: a few months previously, off the Shannon, without a pilot, he had tried to wear ship, but the *Morven* had driven ashore on Loop Head in December 1906. In a photograph a group of Irishmen look disconsolately down from the headland at the stricken barque, with her sails backed indicating the last desperate efforts to keep her off the rocks. Earlier that year Captain Rees and his young wife, a New Zealander, had stumbled through tons of debris from their shattered hotel in San Francisco at the time of the great earthquake and fire, to reach safety aboard the *Morven*. The crew of the *Morven*, whose second mate was Rees' younger brother, Inglis, had reason to respect their captain for he had earned their loyalty and a formidable reputation among seamen for his tough, uncompromising refusal to be bullied by the 'crimps' of Portland, Oregon. Captain Llewelyn Rees was a powerful figure in a world of hard men, and young Hughes aboard the *Deccan* soon had reason to admire his qualities as a seaman. When Captain Rees later moved to the *Marion Fraser*, again managed by William Lewis,[58] Hughes went with him as his second mate, a sure sign of their mutual respect and trust.

After two years in the *Marion Fraser*, Hughes was back as mate of the first of the large square-riggers in which he had served, the *Beeswing*, and soon had to put into practice not only his seamanship but also his knowledge of first aid, when the second mate suffered a broken shoulder blade in the storms off the Horn as they drove on with their cargo of Cardiff coal for Antofagasta. After loading nitrates at Mejillones, the *Beeswing* made a slow, hard passage of 150 days back to Dunkirk and Hughes came ashore to take his master's ticket in Liverpool in May 1911. A short spell in steamers and the lure of sailing vessels proved too great; he went back for another trip in the *Beeswing* as chief officer to Captain John Roberts, a Criccieth man. After a comparatively fast passage to Callao and back to Rotterdam, Hughes was then offered command of the *Beeswing* or another vessel belonging to Walmsleys which was soon due home. He was aged twenty-four and spent a sleepless night debating with himself whether he should accept. The *Beeswing*, with a heavy cargo of copper ore from Huelva, and now over twenty years old, might well run into some disaster at that time of the year off the Horn, not the best fate for any man's first command. In the morning he reluctantly declined the offer and went into steamers with Lamport and Holt running from Liverpool to New York.

In contrast to this gradual introduction to deep-sea sailing after extensive experience in smaller vessels, the apprenticeship scheme, a form of cheap labour, threw considerable burdens on raw recruits. Captain T. P. Marshall, who was later to become British Principal Examiner of Masters and Mates, has described how he was interviewed as a boy of fifteen by William Thomas in 1899 and started his career in the full-rigged ship *Cambrian Hills* as an apprentice to 'the Liverpool firm of sailing ship owners, William Thomas and Company, which at that time operated some thirty to forty fine sailers'. Captain G. C. Archer, in his reminiscences of his apprenticeship aboard the *James Kerr*, another four-masted barque managed by William Thomas, describes vividly a number of voyages in the hard years of 1905-1909, recalling passages made under Captain Evan Jones' command and the activities of the apprentices, of whom there were twenty-three belonging to William Thomas' ships alone at one time at Iquique.[59] The fullest account by one of William Thomas' apprentices is that by Sir James Bisset, Commodore of the Cunard Line and Captain of the *Queen Mary* and *Queen Elizabeth* during the 1939-45 war. His book, *Sail-Ho*, is exclusively concerned with his life at sea in Thomas' service from the day he attended for interview with William Thomas at 14 Water Street, Liverpool, in October 1898 and sailed as an apprentice in the *County of Pembroke*, commanded by Captain John Williams of Pwllheli, to a foggy day over six years later when he left Captain William Roberts of the *County of Cardigan* at North Shields in December 1904 after passages to Australia and the west coast of South America as his young but now very experienced Second Mate. Bisset's account of his experiences as an apprentice, able seaman and Second Mate aboard the *County of Pembroke* and the *County of Cardigan* reflects vividly the harsh reality of life aboard sailing ships at the turn of the century, and provides much detailed information about the *County* ships themselves and the way in which they were sailed by the vastly experienced Welsh master mariners who commanded them. Despite his bitterness at the meanness of a master like Captain 'Wingy' Hughes of the *County of Pembroke*,

Bisset had unbounded admiration for the seamanship of the Welsh masters, mates, tradesmen and seamen who formed the hard core of the Thomas ships.[60]

Although his apprenticeship was served with another Liverpool firm, the De Wolfe's, the experiences of Commodore Gerald N. Jones, C.B.E., D.S.O., may be taken to illustrate the life of Anglesey boys who went to sea as apprentices at this time. Fourth son of the headmaster of the British School in Holyhead, 'Gerald Bach yr Ysgol', as he was known to his contemporaries, joined his first ship, the full-rigged *Glenesslin*, built by Roydens, in March 1902.[61] Her master was Captain Thomas Barlow Pritchard of Caernarvon, already one of the outstanding master mariners of his time, and in the crew were several other Welshmen, at least three of whom were from Caernarvon, including Bob Jones, the sailmaker, who was to teach the new apprentice much of his early seamanship, and Mr Hughes, the third mate, who taught the apprentices navigation for an hour each day in the dog watches when conditions allowed. Commodore Jones wrote a vivid account of his first voyage some years ago, recalling the setting of sails off the Skerries when the towing tug cast off, and two young stowaways, discovered in the forepeak, had been put off in the pilot's boat at Point Lynas. In a fresh N.N.W. wind, every sail full and drawing, the *Glenesslin*, low in the water with a general cargo for Melbourne, making twelve knots or so, filled young Jones with both awe and admiration; he was thrilled when Captain Pritchard one day waited for and then raced past the *Loch Katrine*, one of the Glasgow 'Loch' barques on her way to Adelaide. Seventy-seven days after leaving Liverpool they came to anchor off Williamstown, Melbourne, one of the best passages by a sailing ship from the Mersey to Melbourne. Gerald Jones served two years as an apprentice with Captain T. Barlow Pritchard in the *Glenesslin*, and the incidental references in his memoirs indicate many of the Anglesey links with the sea in the first decade of this century. Captain Pritchard himself was the son of Robert Barlow Pritchard, a well-known Caernarvon seaman, owner of the three-masted schooner *Elizabeth Llewelyn*, a familiar sight in the Menai Strait. Robert Pritchard trained his four sons for the sea; Thomas Barlow Pritchard, master of the *Glenesslin* and later of the *Mauretania*, Owen Barlow Pritchard, master of the de Wolf's barque

Haddon Hall, and later of the *Blythswood* in which he died 'of acute rheumatism' at the age of forty-three at Haiphong on the Gulf of Tonkin,[62] as Commander Villiers has recently discovered, and two younger brothers (one a second mate in the four-masted barque, the *Forest King*), both of whom were lost at sea at an early age. Captain Thomas Barlow Pritchard received his early navigation lessons from Ann Edwards, of 13 Tithebarn Street, Caernarvon, 'the old woman of Carnarvon' of the 1847 report, whose grave in Llanbeblig Churchyard bears witness to the fact that until her death in 1889 she had been 'for nearly 60 years a teacher of navigation in this town'. And Ann Edwards was none other than the daughter of William Francis, the teacher of navigation at Amlwch.[63]

The mate of the *Glenesslin* for much of the time that Gerald Jones was an apprentice aboard her was a Newborough man, Hugh Jones, who had already been at sea for twenty years in small schooners, and then in deep-sea ships, although he was only thirty-nine years of age when he joined the *Glenesslin* at Portland, Oregon, where he served a spell ashore as head rigger. Hugh Jones, an outstanding seaman and skilful navigator, was later to command steamships in the Indian Ocean; at this time he was remembered not only for his excellence as a mate in sail, but also as middleweight boxing champion at Portland, Oregon. When the *Glenesslin* was at East London shortly after the end of the Boer War, they signed two new able seamen from among the many discharged soldiers from the rough-riding regiments; one of them, an American, a particularly unpleasant and aggressive character, was out to cause trouble from the moment he came aboard. Hugh Jones of Newborough knocked him out after a long and bitter bare-knuckle fight on the deck of *Glenesslin*. There was no more trouble.

In the tough world of the sailing ships, at sea or in harbour, there was little room for weaklings. No sooner had the *Glenesslin* reached Portland than the boardinghouse runners were swarming over the side and most of the crew disappeared. The west coast ports of the North American seaboard were notorious for the activities of boardinghouse keepers like Larry Sullivan at Portland, Oregon, who tricked seamen of their hard-earned money and took 'blood money' from masters who needed to complete their ship's company to make good the many desertions caused by these very same boardinghouse keepers. The vicious system persisted for several years, certainly until 1906, when Lloyd George, during a debate on the Merchant Shipping Bill, stated that 'in the course of a single year the desertions from the British mercantile marine amount to 28,000'.[64] Commodore Gerald Jones stated that reform at Portland, Oregon, 'was largely due to the action of a Welsh ship master, Captain Llywelyn Rees of Holyhead, of the four-masted barque *Morven*, whose crew refused to listen to the boardinghouse runners and were attacked by these ruffians in an attempt to force them to leave the ship. Captain Rees brought an action against Sullivan, the head of the boardinghouse men, for illegally boarding his ship and causing a riot on board in which several men were injured'.[65] Sullivan had powerful friends and Captain Rees lost his case, but the publicity given to the incident led eventually to intervention by the American authorities to put an end to the racket.[66] Gerald Jones' delight at being aboard the *Glenesslin* when she made a record voyage from Portland and the Columbia River to Portuguese East Africa was marred by two tragedies, both examples of an all too frequent occurrence aboard these ships. A young 18-year-old German, Fritz Rheinhart, who had joined the *Glenesslin* at Portland, had become very friendly with Jones and they were both aloft on the topsail yard in a gale when the young German tumbled off the footrope and crashed to his death on the deck below. At Laurenco Marques, Mozambique, where the *Glenesslin* lay discharging part of her general cargo, Mrs Pritchard, the Captain's wife, who was often to be seen walking the poop with him, at sea as well as in harbour, was taken ashore and there, 'to the great grief of her husband and of us all, she died, and was buried in the little cemetery above the town'.[67] Having served his two years aboard the *Glenesslin*, Gerald Jones joined the *Silberhorn*, again as an apprentice, then the full-rigged ship, the *Ladye Doris*, as an A.B., and in 1906 became second mate of Robert Thomas' *Conway Castle*. One of his apprenctice friends in San Francisco in 1904 had been another Holyhead boy, named Edwards, from the *Glenburn*, a Glasgow ship which was lost on passage to Liverpool soon afterwards, early in 1905. She had almost completed her voyage when she was last seen approaching the entrance to the St George's Channel.

The year 1905, and indeed, 1906 and 1907, were notoriously bad years for vessels rounding Cape Horn, especially those bound westward for the Chilean and Californian coasts.[68] Many were lost and many more had to turn away from the Horn, giving up the attempt at least until they were repaired in the Falkland Islands or at Montevideo. William Thomas' *Principality* left Junin with a cargo of nitrates bound for Rotterdam and disappeared with all hands, one of the fifty-five British vessels which were lost in 1905.[69] The *Cambrian Hills*, bound for Havre from Iquique, foundered nearer home approaching the English Channel in March 1905. Another ship managed by William Thomas, the *Pengwern*, on passage from Rotterdam to Coquimbo in Chile, had to put back to Montevideo, whilst the *Kate Thomas* had a hard battle in the same year. Her boatswain, Mike Flaherty, was swept from the foc's'le head off the Horn, and her young captain, Charles Hughes, a Holyhead man, died of 'debility' and possibly exhaustion at the early age of 32 within sight of Leith, having brought her safely to port after a nightmare passage from Iquique.[70] Ironically, the girl that Charles Hughes was coming home to marry, a young woman who lived at Penybonc, near South Stack, died on the day that the *Kate Thomas* reached Leith. Charles Hughes' body was brought down to Holyhead and he and his intended bride were buried in the same grave.[71] The *Kate Thomas* appears to have been an unlucky ship, judging by the number of accidents aboard her over the years, and she was lost off Land's End in the darkness of an April morning in 1910 following a collision with the steamer *India*. The *Kate Thomas* was being towed from Antwerp to Port Talbot with a crew of 17; both the captain and the mate had their wives aboard for what should have been a routine voyage. The only survivor was an apprentice called Jack Nelson.[72]

For those who weathered all the storms of the first decade of this century, life was hard aboard these cold sailing ships. Although in some respects the master's life was regarded as infinitely preferable to their own lot by apprentices and seamen, the burden of responsibility for the master of a large four-masted ship was great. No papers belonging to masters of the William Thomas ships are available, but those of another Anglesey master mariner, Captain Robert Jones of Amlwch, who served with similar Liverpool companies, may be taken to illustrate some of the problems confronting the deep-sea master mariner in sail in the Edwardian age.

Captain Robert Jones of Amlwch had served William Thomas, Amlwch, well as master of the *Cymric*, and he had similar success in the *John Lockett*, an iron barque of some eight hundred and forty tons, built in 1884 by R. & J. Evans of Liverpool for the firm of W. and J. Lockett, but later purchased by J. B. Walmsley and Company of Liverpool. During the boom conditions of the Boer War, Captain Jones took the *John Lockett* to Capetown with a cargo of 1,215 tons of coal at the high freight of 24/- per ton. He then sailed for Newcastle, N.S.W., but the 1,202 tons of coal that he took from there to Valparaiso and Tocopilla was at a much reduced rate compared to the Boer War boom, 11/3 a ton. In January 1904 Captain Jones secured a cargo of 1,219 tons of nitrate of soda at 23/3 per ton from Taltal to the Adriatic port of Fiume, where the *John Lockett* arrived in June.[73] The crew were finally paid off at Dunkirk, and Captain Jones was paid the balance of his wages, £12 a month, when he arrived in Liverpool in November 1904. 'Lei Bach' was only one of the several Anglesey men who sailed with Captain Jones in the *John Lockett* during the two years and ten months he commanded her; in the photograph of Captain Jones and the crew of the *John Lockett* at Cape Town there are two Amlwch men who had also served together under Captain Ishmael Williams in the *Gaelic*, 'Lei Bach' and John Newham. The Walmsleys spoke of their entire satisfaction with Captain Jones' work when he left their service in December 1904 to take command of the *Talus*, a much larger ship managed by William Lewis and Company, another Liverpool ship-owning and ship-broker firm, who also managed the *Marion Frazer* and the *Morven*. The *Talus*, described by Lubbock as 'a magnificent ship', had made some fine passages in the nineties from Liverpool to Melbourne, Newcastle, N.S.W., and San Francisco;[74] to be appointed her commander must have given Captain Jones much satisfaction. Among Captain Jones' papers is the letter from the William Lewis Company appointing him to the command of the *Talus*;[75] it is brutally uncompromising in its statement of the master's responsibilities to the owners. Bearing in mind the nature of the Cape Horn and deep-sea trade generally in the first decade of the twentieth-century, the phrases have an ominous yet hollow ring about them:

'Whilst we do not wish, at any time, that you should run any risk, it is imperative that no effort be spared to make smart passages and complete your voyage in the shortest possible time ... we are convinced that much time is unnecessarily lost by vessels both at sea and in port, and we look to you to do all in your power to push on as much as possible, and not to lose an hour. Remember that every day saved means money to the Owners and we would like the *Talus* to do better than any of our ships in this respect.'

The refrain is the same throughout the letter, 'whether at home or abroad use the most rigid economy ... examine all accounts yourself, checking the amounts, calculations and additions, and taking off all discounts'. As towages and pilotages were expensive, the master was urged to dispense with them whenever possible, 'consistent with safety and efficiency'; to save money unloading and discharging cargoes, 'whenever and wherever possible you will dispense with Stevedores, and load and discharge your cargoes and ballast with your own men'.[76] The master was to set a good example regarding discipline, to see that his officers treated the crew firmly yet 'to be careful not to be unnecessarily harsh', for 'when men are treated properly, good work may be expected from them in return'. Lewis promised 'to endeavour to supply you with good wholesome provisions', but the master was to ensure that it was:

'dispensed properly in accordance with Board of Trade regulations. Do not leave this to the Steward and Cook, but allow the matter to have your own careful supervision. So far as fresh provisions in port are concerned, you will of course see that no more than is absolutely necessary is bought, but should the crew be working cargo or ballast, we are not averse to a little extra allowance being given then, but this must be in moderation.'

After this almost self-conscious and grudging generosity, reality is underlined again in the sentence 'Advance as little cash to the crew, and provide them with as little tobacco and slops as possible so that in the event of desertion the ship may not suffer'.[77] Page follows page of instructions to Captain Jones regarding bills of lading, charter parties, communications with the owners whose telegraphic address was 'Gwalia, Liverpool', insurance claims, care of logs, work to be carried out on both outward and homeward passages,[78] care of cargo (particularly that the temperature of coal cargoes should be taken daily), stowage and ventilation, 'buy nothing abroad unless absolutely necessary', 'time always means money', and ending with the all-embracing: 'Do everything at all times that a good ship Master is expected to do in the interests of his Employers.'

Thus Captain Jones took command of the fine looking *Talus* at Port Talbot in mid-December 1904.[79] On 15 December he noted his expenses 'going to Swansea and back signing crew, 4/-'. For his first voyage in the *Talus*, Captain Jones had a crew which included a number of Welsh names;[80] the second mate was Richard Ivor Jones, a Holyhead man, the boatswain was Richard Owen and Richard Edwards, carpenter; most of the A.B.s were Scandinavians, but among them were William Owen and G. Williams, whilst the master's son, O. Llewelyn Jones, who had gone as a ten-year-old boy on that trip to the Baltic with his mother in the *Cymric*, and was later destined to become a master of the Holyhead-Dublin steamers, was listed as one of the ordinary seamen along with another Welshman, Gwilym Roberts, who also became a master mariner and later, marine superintendent for William Thomas at Antwerp. The *Talus* took on a cargo of 3,277 tons of coal at a freight charge of 10/3d. per ton at Port Talbot; in the following April she was at Caleta Buena, Chile, where Captain Jones noted that he bought potatoes from another British ship, discharged some of his coal and then proceeded to Iquique to discharge the remainder in May 1905. At Iquique they took on stiffening ballast, but as they had to remain there for six months before sailing for Australia on 16 December 1905, they thus missed the worst of that fearful winter of 1905 when, as Alan Villiers in *The War with Cape Horn* has described, the *Deudraeth Castle*, owned by Robert Thomas of Criccieth, had had her battle with thick snow and heavy south-west gales blowing across a high north-west sea, when William Thomas' ship *Pengwern* and the *Penrhyn Castle* had had to run back to Montevideo. The *Talus* reached Sydney on 26 February 1906, and was towed to Newcastle, New South Wales, for the usual cargo of coal. Newcastle was notorious for its labour disputes (Captain W. H. Hughes remembered that there always seemed to be a strike when he was there), but on this occasion, despite the troubles and the queues of ships waiting for cargoes, the *Talus* had a comparatively brief stay and was sailing again for Valparaiso within a month of her arrival with a freight of 3,273 tons of coal at 15/9d per ton. A passage of fifty days and they were in Valparaiso on 24 May 1906. There they remained until 1 August, and Captain Jones had to arrange with W. J. Griffiths, an 'engineer' ashore, to supply two labourers to work coal in place of two seamen who had deserted. The *Talus* then sailed north for Port Townsend and Seattle, arriving there in fifty-seven days. Here a cargo of wheat, 3,312 tons at 25/10½d per ton gross weight, was embarked and Captain Jones noted, among his other payments, 275 dollars 'blood money', 55 dollars a head, to replace five seamen who had been spirited away by 'crimps'. On 23 November 1906 the *Talus* sailed for Falmouth, arriving there in early April, finally discharging the wheat and paying off at Liverpool in May 1907, some two years and five months since she had left Port Talbot. This, briefly stated, is a fairly typical voyage of a large sailing ship of the period; coal out to the fuelless coast of western South America, a trans-Pacific voyage to Newcastle, New South Wales, for another cargo of coal, again for Valparaiso, then north to Puget Sound for a grain cargo back to Europe. The *Talus* had rounded the Horn twice in the more favourable months for weather, and she had come home safely during the years when so many similar ships had been lost; a Government White Paper indicated that 'between 1904 and 1908 twenty-six of the larger British sailing ships alone – the Cape Horn type – had to be written off with all hands because they 'went missing'.[81] Captain Robert Jones' notebook, of course, contains every little item relating to the accounts of the voyage, and at Liverpool, after making his final payments '10/- to carpenter, unbending sails and stowing same away, clearing hold and awnings under cargo and gratuities', he agreed with William Lewis the summary accounts which can be seen on page 478. Overleaf he noted that the accounts did not include the £4,285.12.3 for the cargo of wheat from Seattle, nor the 'light dues, pilotage, Towage, £35 from Lynas, Tonnage dues', and the costs of discharging the cargo at Birkenhead in April.

Captain Robert Jones did not stay long at home in Amlwch. His salary was increased to £18 a month, and by November 1907 the

Talus had again rounded Cape Horn, this time with a general cargo, 3,283 tons at 26/3d a ton from Liverpool for San Francisco, which a year previously had suffered the violent earthquake and fire. The subsequent energetic rebuilding of San Francisco had led to temporary boom conditions for shipping, and the *Talus* was one of the sailing vessels which benefited thereby. After a stay of sixty-six days in the new city now emerging from the ruins of old San Francisco, the *Talus* sailed north for Tacoma, Washington, in February for a homeward grain cargo of 3,353 tons at 31/3d per ton. This was Captain Jones' last voyage in the *Talus*, for in August 1908 he took command of the *Oweenee*, a steel four-masted barque of 2,432 tons, very highly regarded by seamen and managed for the Thames and Merseyside Shipping Company by Lewis, Heron and Company, an amalgamation of the Wm. Lewis, Liverpool, company with that of John Heron and Company, London.[82] Captain Jones and the mate, Mr Collins, joined the *Oweenee* in August, and the main body of the crew were signed on in September at Middlesborough. They were the usual international mixture, a German boatswain, several Scandinavians, a number of British apprentices, and some Welshmen including Hugh Ellis, boatswain, John Roberts, carpenter, Richard Hughes, A.B., William Hughes, A.B., and John Owen, ordinary seaman. The wages of the first mate were £9 per month, the second mate £5 per month, the boatswain's £3.15.0, the A.B.'s £3.5.0, and of the ordinary seamen £3.0.0d. Captain Jones must have protested that his vessel was undermanned, and as a result Lewis and Heron sent their marine superintendent, armed with the crew lists of their other ships, 'the *Altair, Arracan* and *Marion Frazer*, which are practically the same sized ships as the *Oweenee*'. Couched in the jargon of 'office' English, the letter to Captain Jones arranging the meeting so long ago aboard the *Oweenee* as she lay in the Tees might well pass unheeded on the Company's files, but it may be taken as yet another illustration of the common cultural background that this close-knit Welsh seafaring community shared. When Captain Jones greeted the marine superintendent as he stepped on to the decks of the *Oweenee*, he had to recognize that here was a man who knew what he was about, for Captain Thomas Davies of Bangor had been one of the most experienced captains commanding the ships of William Thomas, Liverpool, and was

Messrs. The "*Talus*" *Ship Company Limited.*   Messrs. *William Lewis & Co., Managers.*

In Account with Robert Jones Master Ship Talus.

Dr.

	£ s. d.	£ s. d.
To personal Expenses at Belfast, Port Talbot and Liverpool		3. 1.11
Cash deposited by apprentice McKhan's Father		1.10. 0
Disbursements at Caleta Buena		106.18. 8
" at Iquique		719.17.10
Remittance from Iquique		408. 0. 0
" " Newcastle N.S.W.		5. 5. 5
Disbursements Sydney & Newcastle		701. 9. 1
do. at Valparaiso		567.13. 8
Remittance from Valparaiso		2000. 0. 0
Disbursements Puget Sound		980. 0. 7
Supplies to Crew at Falmouth		33.17. 9
Balance wages to Crew & Sundries Liverpool		1029.10. 7
Supplies to Crew during voyage		163. 9.10
Wages as Master from Dec. 8th 1904 to May 7th 1907, 29 months @ £16 per Month		464. 0. 0
		£7176.15. 4

Cr.

	£ s. d.	£ s. d.
By freight received @ Iquique		1116.14. 3
Sale of Butter		1. 8. 1
Credit received for Carpenter work @ Iquique		3. 0. 0
A. E. Sartorie draft from Iquique		116.19. 7
Cable remittance to Newcastle NSW		750. 0. 0
Freight on Coal Newcastle NSW to Valparaiso 3,273 tons @ 15/9		2577. 9. 9
Gratuities received @ Valparaiso		10. 0. 0
Amount due Kenrick & Co. £14.19.6 & 17/3		15.16. 9
Cable remittance to Seattle		960. 0. 0
Sale of old Shakings @ Puget Sound		10. 4. 8
Draft on Owner from Puget Sound		42.12. 9
Cash @ Liverpool £1017.2.1 & £100		1117. 2. 1
Sale of old Shakings Liverpool		8. 9. 0
Allotments paid to Mrs. Jones		216. 0. 0
Insurance on Effects for voyage		8.12. 1
		£6954. 9. 0
		222. 6. 4
		£7176.15. 4

Received from William Lewis & Co. Managers of the Talus Ship Co. Ltd. the Sum of Two hundred and twenty two pounds six shillings and four pence in full settlement & discharge of all claims against and monies due to me from the Said Company.

London E.C.
May 17th 1907

Sgd. Robert Jones
17.5.07

indeed the master mariner whom the latter had appointed to command his first steamer, the *Empire*, when she made her voyages to New York and through the Suez Canal way back in 1881-2. Captain Davies had been one of the original shareholders in the *Principality*, and there are many references to him in the William Thomas correspondence. He had, moreover, brought up his sister's children, and had been instrumental in starting one of them, William Lewis, on his career as a shipping clerk in William Thomas' office. Captain Davies had left the service of William Thomas to become marine superintendent for his young relative, soon to become a serious rival of William Thomas' company. Thus when they met aboard the *Oweenee*, Captain Thomas Davies of Bangor and Captain Robert Jones of Amlwch had a healthy respect for each other, knowing each other's background and well aware of their many mutual contacts, ranging from the Liverpool Welsh chapel community to mariners like Captain Rees and W. H. Hughes of the *Marion Frazer*, one of the vessels to be compared with the *Oweenee*. Captain Davies came to support Lewis and Heron's letter which informed Captain Jones, 'As you know we have no desire for our vessels to be other than well and efficiently manned, but if the Captains of the other vessels are quite satisfied with the crews that they have, we fail to see that the *Oweenee* could not likewise be efficiently handled'.[83] Captain Jones had made a pencilled note in the margin of this letter that the *Altair* had a crew of 29, 5 of whom were apprentices, and the same was true of the *Arracan*, whilst the *Marion Frazer* had a crew of 30. The crews had therefore already been reduced to meet the needs of economy, for Captain W. H. Hughes remembers that when he sailed with Captain Rees in the *Marion Frazer* they had a crew of 36. One can almost hear Captain Robert Jones putting this argument in forceful Welsh to Captain Davies, for they both knew Captain Rees well. Lewis and Heron had instructed Captain Davies 'to go thoroughly into the matter with you, and you are to decide the point together'; in the event, Captain Jones had his way, for according to his wage sheets he had a crew of 25 and 5 apprentices.

The *Oweenee* sailed from Adelaide for Middlesborough on 23 September with a cargo of two thousand tons of pig iron and 1,638 tons of steel rails, arriving there in the first week of January 1909.

Captain Robert Jones' views on his new command's sea-going qualities are not recorded, but among his papers is a letter he received just before he sailed from a certain John Jones who wrote from aboard the *Talus*, then in Barry Dock. After a discussion regarding the need to have the *Oweenee*'s compasses checked, and deviation cards prepared in view of her present cargo, John Jones reported that the *Talus* had had to put back 'with loss of most of her sails and some damage about her decks'. John Jones' next sentence suggests that he had seen service previously in the *Oweenee* and illustrates the mutual cultural background that both he and Robert Jones shared. 'Well, I have had an opportunity now to see the *Talus* for the first time, and can only say, the same as an old Anglesey Preacher said once in Sasiwn Menai Bridge, Mae yn dda gen i bobl Sir Gaernarfon, ond mae yn well gen i bobl Sir Fôn, ac felly finna'r Oweenee.'[84]

From Adelaide the *Oweenee* sailed for Newcastle, N.S.W., arriving ten days later on 6 June 1909; she had already paid off half of the crew and was taken there by the remainder and a crew of 'runners' who were paid £6 per man for the passage. At Newcastle Captain Jones paid £6 to 'J. J. Dalton Runner Blood Money', 12 men at 10/- each, and advance notes to 12 seamen, 1 at £5, 10 at £4.10, and 1 at £3. The *Oweenee* sailed for Chile on 14 July, arriving at Mejillones on 3 September. She sailed again for Chile on 14 July, arriving at Mejillones on 3 September. Here Captain Jones had a thoroughly bad-tempered letter from Lewis, Heron and Co.;[85] 'these awful expenses in Adelaide have made a hole in this vessel's earnings which it will be very difficult to fill up . . . expenses in Australian ports have grown to such an extent that we are disposed to avoid the place altogether in future'. They complained that although the actual loading time at Newcastle was three days, the vessel was there for thirty-nine days; the cargo of 3,606 tons of coal was disappointingly small,[86] 'another of the scandals attaching to the port of Newcastle'. Grudgingly they admitted that Captain Jones had done his best, 'although the total is disastrous you appear to have kept things down as reasonably as possible'. Forwarding copies of the *Marion Frazer*'s and the *Englehorn*'s disbursements they piously hoped Captain Jones would do better 'with your usual care you will be able to improve on both of these'. They had a few days previously written to say that stores would be awaiting the *Oweenee* at Valparaiso, and typically added, 'It appears to us we have given you really rather more than was necessary, but of course we look to you to exercise all economy with regard to the use of them'. The *Oweenee* remained at Mejillones for a period of ninety-two days and then sailed, on 4 December 1909, for Hamburg with a cargo of nitrates. Twenty months after they had left Middlesborough in 1908, the crew of the *Oweenee* were paid off, in April 1910, at Hamburg. The owners were patently surprised to hear from Captain Jones that he did not wish 'to undertake another long voyage' owing to the state of his health, and accepted his resignation 'with much regret as our relations have always been pleasant and we have always looked upon you as a thoroughly reliable and trustworthy shipmaster'.[87] The gracious tone of this last letter was in stark contrast to the hectoring of earlier letters, but it was to no avail. Captain Robert Jones had had enough of sail and returned to a well-earned retirement at Amlwch.

He had come a long way since his days as a boy of fifteen aboard his father's *Amanda*. The pencilled notes on scraps of paper reflect not only his care for detail regarding his ships and their cargoes, but also events and people in many parts of the world; a note on the last sighting of the *Caernarvon Bay* after she sailed from Melbourne in January 1909,[88] and on the same page the address of the Reverend Mona Jones in Newcastle, New South Wales, for relatives at Fedw Uchaf, near Dulas; the names of other master mariners he had met, such as Captain Walter of the *Herzogin Cecile* at Mejillones in November 1909, and Captain Hughes, a native of Llandudno, master of S.S. *Mendoza*, whom he met at Valparaiso; a note on the draft, forward and aft, of the *Muskoka*, sister-ship of the *Oweenee*, as she left Seattle; the addresses of efficient firms ashore, Alfred Munte, Stevedore, and W. Delfs, Schifstakler-rigger, of Hamburg, and one or two kindly postcards to Mrs Jones and himself from men who had sailed under his command and were themselves now sailing in steamships in South Africa, New Zealand and Australia. To have successfully commanded such fine vessels as the *Cymric, Talus* and *Oweenee* is in itself a measure of the skill and seamanship of the quiet, modest master mariner who returned to Garden Cottage, Amlwch. His sons and their contemporaries went into steam, as Captain W. H. Hughes had done. As for the *Oweenee*, the owners contemplated sending Humphreys, their ship-keeper, 'or another man from Newborough', to keep a watchful eye on her until they decided whether to lay her up or not.

William Thomas, Liverpool, still owned or managed a considerable fleet according to the Lloyds Register in 1910-11, despite losses like the *Principality* and the *Kate Thomas,* and the sale of some of the older vessels, the *County of Anglesea* and the *County of Merioneth.*[89] Among his larger ships were the second *Cambrian Princess, James Kerr, Rowena, Boadicea* and *Crocodile,* a steel four-masted barque built at Southampton in 1892 and commanded since 1907 by Captain H. Roberts of Benllech, who had joined William Thomas' ships as a boy. The Menai Bridge ship-owner, H. R. Davies, had sold the *Afon Alaw* at San Francisco in November 1903; in the following year she was sailing for William Thomas, who put Captain J. Davies, and then, from 1907 Captain Evan Jones, in command of her. As might be expected from Captain Evan Jones, there followed some of her fastest passages: 77 days each way out to Mejillones from Barry and back to Falmouth in 1907-8. The *Metropolis,* Captain Jones' old rival, was still sailing under William Thomas' management, as were the *Colony, County of Flint,* and the *Wynnstay,*[90] built at Glasgow in 1884. But Thomas was too shrewd a businessman not to have realised that the future lay with steam vessels; back in 1888 he had noted that more clerical work was necessary with steam ships, 'as they do so much work, I consider it is at least as much as doing the work of half a dozen sailing ships'.[91] He had progressed a great deal since the days of the little Amlwch *W. S. Caine,* and by 1910 he owned and managed ten steel screw steamers of between three and four thousand tons apiece. These were all comparatively new tramp steamers, and like their sailing predecessors, almost invariably had Welshmen in command, several of them younger men in Thomas' employment who had moved over from sail to steam.[92] By 1914 William Thomas had thirteen steamships under his management, but the larger sailing vessels had decreased to five.[93] A few months after the outbreak of war, he lost his first vessel, the steamer *Hemisphere,* captured and scuttled by the *Kronprinz Willhelm* 400 miles NE by E from Pernambuco.[94] Shortly before his death early in March 1915, Thomas bought the *Schlesian,* a prize vessel which had previously been owned by North German Lloyd.

It was over sixty years since the fair-haired young pupil teacher had left Llanrhuddlad school and sailed for Liverpool to work as a clerk in a shipping office. A man of great energy and enterprise, William Thomas had worked very hard himself to create a shipping empire which had brought him wealth and had provided careers for many Welshmen, particularly from Anglesey and Caernarvonshire. He was tough, single-minded and shrewd. There are conflicting memories about the conditions aboard his ships. By 1906 concern regarding the poor food aboard sailing ships in particular had been expressed in many quarters, and Lloyd George, as President of the Board of Trade, introducing the Bill to amend the Merchant Shipping Acts, linked desertions from British ships with the harsh conditions of service for seamen: 'When we are so anxious to reduce the number of foreigners on British ships and to increase the number of British sailors, one thing to do is to make the Merchant Service as attractive as we can and the first condition undoubtedly is to provide fairly good food.' Whilst admitting that some shipowners did provide reasonable food, there were others who hardly reached the minimum standards of the Board of Trade, and were 'not much better, if at all, than this meagre, monotonous, miserable scale of salt beef, biscuits, tea and sugar'. Moreover, Lloyd George argued, even when the food itself was of good quality, the Board of Trade had independent evidence that 'the cooking on sailing ships is, as a rule, wholly uncharacterized by skill'.[95] Lloyd George had found it politically expedient to be interested in matters relating to the sea, which affected the lives of so many of his constituents and their relatives, since his early days at Portmadoc; one of his sisters was married to a master mariner, and although he had many friends among the shipowners, he was also something of a hero to many Welsh seamen. Just as Lloyd George had found that there was much conflicting evidence regarding conditions in general, so there are conflicting memories about William Thomas' ships. Once a vessel sailed, much depended on the master's interpretation of Board of Trade regulations. Sir James Bisset remembered vividly the criminal meanness of Captain Hughes aboard the *County of Pembroke*,[96] but recalled that William Thomas himself had indignantly blamed the Captain for neglecting to provision the ship adequately. Bisset and the crew of the *County of Pembroke* had reason to believe that

Captain Hughes had been involved in a racket with a rascally ship chandler at Callao who had provided foul stores. Incidents such as that of the *County of Pembroke* led to much notoriety for a company among seamen regarding 'hungry' ships. In contrast, Captain Ellis Roberts of Caernarvon, who had served as second mate aboard the *Principality*, had much happier memories – 'all I can say about William Thomas' ships (14 Water Street, Liverpool) is that they were well found ships in sails, tackle, and very good grub'.[97] To make sense of such conflicting reports we must accept that experiences aboard the different ships with different masters varied as much as the personalities of those who made the comments, and possibly, the impact of time on the memories of such experiences.

Ironically, William Thomas was a poor sailor. He would arrange for relatives or friends to make passages in his ships, but he himself avoided the sea. It was sufficient for him that his beloved office, where he spent most of his life, was a centre from which he directed his ships to ports where cargoes could be obtained quickly, and at good freight rates, even in the worst years for sailing ships. His contemporaries recognized that he had an uncanny gift for arranging profitable voyages, a nose for smelling opportunities, so that his ships were in the right ports to bring back grain cargoes to Europe when freights were high, or nitrates to areas where wars brought increased demands. Inevitably he had his moments of anxiety. 1905 was a bad year, with the loss of his much-admired *Principality*, and a near-disaster to the *County of Anglesea* bound from Rouen for Liverpool with silver sand ballast such as had recently destroyed the *Moel Tryfan*.[98] Dismasted and aground in Portland Bay (Plate 10), the *County of Anglesea* was later repaired, and sold to Russian owners. Thomas was not a man to discuss his affairs, and kept his own counsel in moments of crisis. The most telling tribute to his ability was the mutual respect, loyalty and friendship over the years of many seamen and mates, sailmakers and carpenters, and many fine master mariners whom he employed in various capacities, men like Captain David Evans of Nefyn, Captain John Jones of Newborough, Captain Thomas Williams of Treborth, Captain Evan Jones of Pencaenewydd, the Captains Owen and Lewis of Moelfre, and many others. That so many officers and men from his own background served in his ships year after year suggests that they accepted him as a forthright, careful, but very fair and able shipping manager. Although his base was Merseyside, Thomas' career touched on many facets of Welsh history. His master mariners and many of his crews came from north Wales, but his ships were essentially part of the economic history of south Wales, for William Thomas readily recognised the importance of shipping Rhondda coal from the expanding south Wales coal ports. As Dr E. D. Lewis, in his study of the Rhondda valleys, has indicated, British shipping between 1870 and 1914 was much indebted to the coal industry, for both sailing and steam ships were provided with bulk cargoes outwards 'to balance the incoming timbers, ores, grains and other bulky raw materials and foodstuffs. Coal exports saved British ships from having to sail half-filled or in ballast, and so kept down transport costs'.[99] Thomas had much in common with self-made men like Davies the Ocean, whose energy and enterprise had provided his ships with so many cargoes at Barry and other south Wales docks.

On a fine, clear day in March 1915, William Thomas' coffin was borne on the shoulders of four of his former captains to the cemetery at Llanrhuddlad.[100] Although he had at one time been prominent as mayor, alderman and chairman of the Finance Committee of the Bootle Borough Council, his main interests outside his office had been related to his membership of the Calvinistic Methodist chapels in Liverpool and Bootle. The library of the Theological College, Bala, benefited considerably from his practical interest, as did his own chapels at Llanrhuddlad and on Merseyside. Occasionally, a minister of religion went on a long sea trip for his health's sake, but William Thomas always meticulously paid the company for his passage out of his own pocket so that shareholders would not be contributing in any way. With his roots deep in Victorian Wales, it was not surprising that he should have written to his overlooker when the *County of Cardigan* was being hurriedly made ready for sea at South Shields in October 1880. 'They should not have painted the ship on Sunday. I trust they are giving good paint.'[101] At the turn of the century he bought the old school in Llanrhuddlad village and built a new one about a quarter of a mile away as a token of his gratitude to the school where he had himself been a pupil and a pupil teacher. Typically, he planned and designed the school himself.[102] He bought about forty farms in Anglesey; the farmhouses and farm buildings were repaired, stone walls replaced broken hedges, good gates were provided, the farm made shipshape and tenants encouraged to practice good husbandry. His youngest daughter remembers that he took a deep personal interest in each farm and took her with him on his frequent visits.[103] Everything he did, he did thoroughly.

William Thomas' ships were sold and his company wound up in 1916, a year after his death. His eldest son, Robert J. Thomas, retained his father's name in a company which was established after the war, 'the William Thomas Shipping Company Limited'.[104] An assiduous attempt was made to win Welsh investors and prospectuses were printed in both Welsh and English, but there were hard times ahead for shipping. The immediate post-war boom, the scarcity of ships and high freight rates, which encouraged the purchasing of old ships at grossly inflated prices and the building of new ships, was short-lived. There was massive speculation in 1919-20 in many undertakings, from cotton mills to shipping, which had been successful in the past because of the initiative and skill of individual owners.[105] By 1921 the bubble had burst. In common with many shipping concerns, Sir Robert Thomas and his fellow directors found post-war conditions much more difficult than those years in which his father had succeeded. Theirs was an ill-starred venture. Many Anglesey investors who had had great confidence in William Thomas himself, suffered grievous financial blows in the depression years between the wars. The later misfortunes of the company under Sir Robert Thomas in the cruel twenties and early thirties have led to an under-estimation of the achievement of his father, whose skill and drive had created the wealth of the original company. In many ways, the death of William Thomas of Llanrhuddlad and Liverpool marked the end of an age for Anglesey's seafaring community.

The merchant schooners of the closing decades of the nineteenth-century, belonging to an older tradition, more closely tied to the small ports which had been the main sources of supply in the days before the railways, maintained more intimate links with Anglesey than the large four-masted ships and barques with their international crews sailing from the major ports, but even for the merchant schooners the end was in sight. Anglesey shipping since Elizabethan times had been affected by the fortunes of the Caernarvonshire slate quarries: the numbers of ships and seamen of Anglesey had grown in response to the demands of the carrying trade in Caernarvonshire slate. The nineteenth-century had seen a mid-century boom in the export of slates, and as part of this industrial complex, Anglesey's shipping had expanded both in the range of activity and in the percentage of the population directly engaged in maritime occupations. The period between 1870 and 1914 has been described as the era of the merchant schooner, and in the years up to 1914 Holyhead, Amlwch, and the Menai Strait saw them often, taking temporary refuge as well as, particularly up to 1900, taking slate to the German ports. In addition to the three-masted Portmadoc schooners which, with their similar dimensions, rigging plan and quality, were recognized as an élite,[106] there were scores of other schooners not only from north Wales but from the south-west, from the Irish and Scottish ports, and particularly from Cumberland, all busily plying off the coast of Anglesey before the 1914-18 war overtook them. Here it is only possible to indicate a few examples of vessels which were in a very real sense part of the way of life of Anglesey in the 1890-1914 period.

The *Camborne*, a three-masted double topsail schooner, was built by the yard of W. Cox Paynter and Company at Amlwch and was managed there by Captain Thomas Morgan's Company in the years before the war of 1914-18.[107] Her crew agreement lists from 1886 to 1898 indicate that she was manned throughout these years by Amlwch seamen; of the 150 signatures (or marks), 120 are of Amlwch men. Her master from 1886 to 1893 was Captain Owen Owens, and from 1893 to 1898 Captain Owen Thomas, both of them from Amlwch; under their command she sailed largely in the home trade, visiting for the most part Newcastle, London, the south-west china-clay ports, Hamburg and the west coast of Scotland, with occasional visits to the Shetlands, Limerick, Aberdeen and Treport. In the spring of 1888 Captain Owen, with an all-Amlwch crew, took her from Hamburg to Morocco and in the following year she sailed from Lerwick to Bilbao. For the voyage to Bilbao a new master, Captain Owen Rowlands, also of Amlwch, was engaged, but Captain Owen Owen sailed in her as 'purser' and William Jones, her usual mate, signed as 'Bos'n', all presumably to keep within the regulations of a foreign-going voyage, for which Captain Owen did not possess an appropriate certificate under the Merchant Shipping Act. Captain Owen resumed command when she returned to the coastal trade in the following year, with William Jones back in his accustomed role of mate.[108] The *Jane Grey*, later sunk by enemy action in 1915, and the *Donald and Doris*, both built by Paynter's yard at Amlwch, were other well-known vessels in the coastal ports. The *Donald and Doris*, in which Captains Wynn and Jones served their apprenticeship during the early years of the 1914-18 war, sailed for many years for the Cumberland Hodbarrow Mining Company: Captain Ellis of Amlwch, her master and part-owner in her later years, had a reputation for careful sailing, and Captain Jones well remembers how, as young boys, they used to get impatient with him when he shortened sail for they wanted to get in to Millom, say, to receive their pay and to go ashore.[109] Captain Ellis' comment was always: 'you'll be glad about midnight tonight that we've taken in sail now, and you haven't got to go aloft in the middle of the night.' Despite his caution, Captain Ellis was occasionally stung into a race with the Duddon ships, much to the delight of the younger members of the crew, who still remember with amusement and affection their old captain having reluctantly taken up one such challenge, obstinately muttering to himself, 'I Duddon 'rydan ni'n rhwym, ac i Duddon 'rydan ni'n mynd' ('To Duddon we are bound and to Duddon we will go'), keeping to his course as other schooners in company made for Belfast Lough for shelter. Captain Ellis was a steady, religious master mariner of the type common to many of these schooners, but he too had his superstitions. If he had dreamt of old ladies with tall silk hats, then he firmly believed that this was an augury of bad weather, and again his crew remember that whether it was due to his uncanny ability to sense changes in the weather or to his somewhat curious dream fantasies, Captain Ellis was seldom caught out by the elements.

The painting reproduced on the dust jacket of [the 1976] volume is of the *Donald and Doris*, one of a pair in the 'fine weather and foul' tradition, by Reuben Chappell, who spent a lifetime painting portraits of ships. Chappell's work has been recognised in recent years as an unique record of the vessels which he painted when they visited the china-clay quays of Fowey, Par and Charlestown where he worked for thirty years after leaving his native Goole. In the 1890s

Chappell used to sell his watercolours of 5 shillings each (and 30 shillings for oils), and as his customers were the men who sailed the ships he naturally had to produce paintings which were technically accurate.[110] One painting by this soberly-dressed hard-working artist, well known to many Anglesey seamen, has been reproduced in this book (see page 59), but there are many more examples on the walls of houses in Anglesey, a permanent reminder to their inhabitants of their family's link with this busy era in the Island's maritime history.

The *Gauntlet* is one of them. Mrs Elizabeth Jones, now a sprightly little lady in her eighties, remembers very clearly the days at the turn of the century when she first went with her mother in the *Gauntlet*, a 120-ton wooden schooner built at Glasson Dock, a creek of the port of Lancaster, in 1857.[111] By the time Elizabeth Jones went aboard her, the *Gauntlet* was already forty years old, but to a child she was a source of great delight. She recalled that her mother used to try to break the 'ship's biscuit/sea pie' routine menu by taking red cabbage, fresh butter, 'menyn pot', and other delicacies for her husband, Captain Bob Jones, 'Hurricane Bob' as he was known in Amlwch, who followed up his years as a quartermaster of one of the China tea-clippers by serving as master of the *Gauntlet* for many years, retiring after he had spent fifty-three years at sea. Elizabeth Jones went home to school in Amlwch after her early voyages, and did not go to sea with her father during the difficult years of the 1914-18 war, but after the Armistice she became a regular member of the crew of the *Gauntlet*. Although her main duties were as cook, in times of stress, either because of weather or shortage of crew members, she kept watch with the mate, James, an Irishman who served with Captain Jones for twenty-two years. Her proudest memory is that of sailing the *Gauntlet* up the Solent when her father was ill in his bunk with a severe bout of influenza. The pilot had come aboard, the mate and the other seaman were required to attend to the sails, and so 'Lizzie' put on her oilskins and steered the ship, under the paternal eye of the pilot, much to the surprise of another Amlwch crew sailing out of Southampton water who did not recognize the new young 'master'. Nor was she idle in harbour: up the mast in a bos'n's chair, scraping it ready for varnishing, wearing black protective glasses following up the work of the caulkers in Runcorn Dock, looking after a dog for another Amlwch master who could not take it with him 'foreign' because of quarantine regulations (she swears the same dog saved them from being run down in dense fog by barking and giving both vessels on collision courses a last-minute warning), going with her father to court to give evidence in another collision case, this time when she herself had been steering in thick mist and drizzle, having a rare treat of strawberries and cream in a French harbour, singing 'Cwm Rhondda' in a Falmouth seaman's mission – these are but glimpses of a life full of incident. Small wonder then that Elizabeth Jones looks at Chappell's portrait of the *Gauntlet* with affection and recalls her father's wish, 'Cofia di, tra byddi di fyw, paid byth a gollwng d'afael ar lun y *Gauntlet*; mae hi wedi ennill ambell i damaid i'r tŷ yma'.[112]

Chappell's water-colour of the *Irish Minstrel* was painted about 1905 and was one of the examples of his work chosen for the exhibition at the National Maritime Museum and the Bristol City Art Gallery in 1970. Built at Dundalk in 1879, this wooden schooner was bought by Ebenezer Griffiths, Efail Fawr, Amlwch, in 1899 and sailed in the coastal and European trades until the war of 1914-18. Richard Griffiths, of Chapel Street, Amlwch (and later of Bull Bay), was her master for most of these years, although he had to be relieved for one or two passages, because of rheumatic fever, by a Portmadoc captain and also a Swedish captain. Captain Ebenezer Griffiths, also of Bull Bay, remembers his first voyage as a boy of fourteen aboard the *Irish Minstrel*, bound for Hamburg a few years before the war.[113] His father, Richard, was against his making the sea a career. Already one brother, Thomas, had served a hard apprenticeship aboard the *Minstrel*, another, Robert, had made his first voyage about two years previously, so that from the moment Ebenezer went aboard the *Minstrel* his father did his best to disenchant him. This took the fairly obvious course; as they approached the German coast, young Griffiths were ordered aloft to look out for the Weser Light Vessel. It was midwinter and freezingly cold, and as the minutes turned to hours, the youngster was obviously in difficulties, and the mate, another Amlwch man, very angry with the 'old man', went up to help the boy down, and then told his father what he thought of him. The mate also told Mrs Griffiths when they got home to Amlwch, and Richard Griffiths, despite his understandable motives, no doubt rued the day he had allowed Ebenezer aboard. But the new recruit was not to be discouraged; he continued to sail in her until he went into steam vessels and eventually became a master mariner himself. In light airs, Captain Griffiths admits the Portmadoc schooners would easily sail past the *Irish Minstrel*, but in heavy weather she gave them a run for their money: Captain Griffiths, remembers her as a 'stiff' vessel, sailing out of Hamburg and keeping up with the *Cariad*, which was considered to have made the fastest crossing by a Portmadoc vessel from Newfoundland to Oporto. He also recalls another occasion, a day or two before Christmas, when, despite contrary winds and stormy conditions, his father refused to reduce sail and made Caernarvon from Dublin in well under ten hours. When tacking up the English Channel, Richard Griffiths would turn to the mate: 'I'm turning in now, you'll see Start Point two points on the bow there in ten minutes or so', and sure enough, thick drizzly weather as it was, he was always right; he had the uncanny instinct of many of these sailing masters of knowing where he was whatever the conditions. The *Irish Minstrel* ended her days as a hulk in the Mersey, destroyed eventually by being set on fire deliberately, and Captain Ebenezer Griffiths, then master of a steam vessel, saw her burn.

On the wall of his home in Moelfre, Captain Henry Roberts has another of Chappell's paintings, the *Earl of Lathom*, well known in the Menai Strait and at Connah's Quay. Captain Roberts had already seen much service when he took command of the *Earl of Lathom*; the village of Moelfre was steeped in maritime traditions by Henry Roberts' time and his career may be taken as typical of the Moelfre mariners who remained in the coastal trade.[114] In the 1890s Henry Roberts was aged nine when his father, captain and owner of the *Mary Stewart*, died aboard his ship at Bowling in the Clyde. Young Roberts' eldest brother, then aged sixteen, went to the *Mary Stewart*, nominally in command, but with a sailing master, Captain Thomas Parry of Moelfre, taking charge of the vessel until the young man had gained sufficient experience. Henry Roberts, when he was fifteen years of age, went to sea first as a galley boy aboard the *Dinas*, a smack carrying stone from Traeth Bychan to Port Dinorwic where the new dock was being built. Visitors to Traeth Bychan today will be familiar with the disused quarries near the beach and the disused dock; in the days of the *Dinas* scores of men were working for half-a-crown a day, from six till six, quarrying stone which was taken away at the top of the tide by small vessels like the *Dinas*. The *Dinas* was used purely in the immediate local trade, carrying building materials; she collected slate from Port Dinorwic or Port Penrhyn where there was also a general store for cement and sundry building materials which made up the remainder of the cargo. Thus having taken a full cargo aboard in the Strait, the *Dinas* sailed for Benllech, Traeth Bychan or Moelfre, or any of the open beaches, where she dried out and her cargo was unloaded by horses and carts for the local builders' merchants. After two years in the Dinas, Henry Roberts went as mate to the *Sara*, of which his brother was now master, and when his brother gained the command of the ketch *James*, Henry Roberts became master of the *Sara* at the age of eighteen. His mate was another Moelfre man, aged 21, and a boy of 14 made up the crew; the *Sara*'s main trade was carrying coal and general cargo from the Mersey to the beaches and small ports of north Wales. There were certain beaches where the freight was higher because of their position; Porth Swtan (Church Bay) was one. Captain Roberts left the *Sara* after some years and went to lodge in Liverpool so that he could attend the Nautical School run by Captains Thornborough and Frith in Lord Street, Liverpool. He felt he could not afford to stay there more than a month, but he successfully took his mate's examination and his next ship was the *Skelwith Force* in which he served as mate. But life aboard a steamer did not appeal to Captain Roberts, so he became master of the *Elizabeth Hyam*, a Connah's Quay schooner owned by Hancock's Brickworks. He remained with this company until the outbreak of the First World War, being promoted first to the *Catherine Lathom* and then to the *Earl of Lathom* about 1910. The latter was a Lloyd's registered vessel, so Captain Roberts had to pass an examination held by five other Connah's Quay captains before he was given command, but once 'pasio'r clwb' was over, he was very happy for she was a good vessel which responded to his coaxing. Captain Roberts sailed the *Earl of Lathom* to many ports around the coasts of Britain, to Germany and the Baltic, carrying bricks from Connah's Quay and slate from the Menai Strait. Comparing his life in sailing ships with his later commands in steam, Captain Roberts felt there was much more time to do everything in sail, he preferred 'sailing by the share' to his later experiences working for a wage for slave-driving steamship companies.

In 1914 Captain Roberts married a Moelfre girl, daughter and sister of master mariners, and appropriately their honeymoon was in the *Earl of Lathom*, carrying slate from Caernarvon to Hamburg, then sailing to Boulogne, Ipswich, Newcastle, Pentewan and eventually back to Moelfre, where Mrs Roberts went ashore a few weeks before the outbreak of the war. Her father was master of the *Margaret Jane* which had been sunk after a collision with a German liner, a brother was mate of the *Jane Gray*, a Paynter-built Amlwch vessel destined to be sunk by a U-boat in 1915, another brother served with Captain Jabez Rowlands of Moelfre (first master of William Thomas' *County of Flint*, and father of Dr Helen Rowlands, the Welsh missionary in India),[115] when his four-masted barque *Serina* lost four men, washed overboard soon after leaving Melbourne, whilst her fourth brother became a master mariner in steamers in the White Star Line. Moelfre was such a village; Captain Roberts named over forty master mariners living there, besides the scores of men sailing as crew, both in the foreign and coastal trades.

These were still busy days for sailing ships. Captain Roberts remembers anchoring in Holyhead harbour, one of nearly two hundred vessels windbound there in 1909. When the weather improved there was the unforgettable sight of ships of all types, schooners, ketches, barquentines, barques, the occasional full-rigged ship, all weighing anchor, setting their sails and shaping their different courses, a fleet putting to sea, but all going their separate ways, for Ireland, the Mersey, Milford, the Clyde or more distant ports in Europe or America. Another memory of Captain Roberts' is one common to many Anglesey seamen of this period – sailing up the Thames to a wharf near London Bridge where Roberts, the slate merchant, had cargoes discharged, the crew, including the master, working all day with the shore labourers to unload the slate by hand.

A frequent visitor to this wharf was the *Ailsie*, a three-masted wooden schooner built by Paynters at Amlwch just across the harbour from where the *Cymric* was beginning to take on the very fine lines designed by William Thomas. The *Ailsie* was launched at Amlwch in 1892 and owned by the Platts of Oldham, she was managed by their accountant and agent at Gorddinog,

Llanfairfechan, J. M. Baker; her master was John Hughes, who lived at Richmond House, Llanfairfechan. An Anglesey-built ship, owned in Caernarvonshire, her crews over the years were drawn from both counties and her career is typical of the slate schooners of the Menai Strait during this period.[116] In June 1892 Captain Hughes commenced his entries in the *Ailsie*'s cargo book in which he recorded the names and addresses of ship-brokers and agents at Great Yarmouth, London, Runcorn, Bridport, Fowey, Plymouth, Galway, Portmadoc, Port Dinorwic and Caernarvon with whom he obviously had considerable contacts, the details of all cargoes carried, the shippers and the consignees. On her first voyage the *Ailsie*, whose registered tonnage was 98 tons, took a cargo of 220 tons of slates from Port Dinorwic to Newcastle, then 198 tons of 'Gas coals' from Newcastle to Portland, and early in July 187 tons of Portland stone to London. From London she carried 210 tons of 'whiting' in 1,728 bags from Grays Chalk Quarry Company for the Dacca Twist Company of Preston and Manchester. At the end of August, 1892, she left Port Dinorwic again with a cargo of 220 tons of slates for Altona, near Hamburg, arriving there some six weeks later. The *Ailsie* then took 178 tons of 'Pitt chocks' from Hamburg to Sunderland, arriving there on Guy Fawkes Day and leaving a week later, appropriately, with 200 tons of firebricks for a London merchant. Three days after arriving in the Thames she embarked 210 tons of 'whiting' for Runcorn, and a month later she was loading a further cargo of 'house coal' at Runcorn for Londonderry. Arriving there on 4 February, she came home in ballast; it was often a problem to get return cargoes from Ireland, particularly the west, and the Penrhyn Letter books of the late nineteenth-century reflect the reluctance on the part of masters to go to the west of Ireland. The ballast deposited by scores of schooners on the foreshore at Hirael, explains the considerable amount of Irish and other 'foreign' stone in the walls of Bangor houses and gardens. In mid-March the *Ailsie* shipped a further two hundred and seventeen tons of slate for Harburg, taking just a month to deliver her cargo. Four days later she left Harburg with 213 tons of oilcakes for Great Yarmouth, arriving on 5 April, and taking 118 tons of starch in cases for the shippers, Colmans, for Belfast, where she arrived on 6 June. Thus in her first twelve months she had spent a minimum time in harbour, and after a brief refit, she left Portmadoc in August with a further cargo of slate for London. Her crew, which consisted of master, mate, two A.B.s and an ordinary seaman/cook, included in this first year two Caernarvonshire able seamen who had previously served in the highly regarded Cape Horners of William Thomas, the *Principality* and the *Metropolis*, whilst the youngest member of the crew came from Talwrn, Anglesey.[117]

For the next ten years, the *Ailsie's* cargo book indicates that she carried a wide range of cargoes, slate from Port Penrhyn, Port Dinorwic and Portmadoc, usually for the Elbe ports and the Thames, cement and general cargoes for the Irish ports from London, coal from Garston or Runcorn for Cornwall, Ireland and north Wales, china-clay from Fowey to Runcorn and from Plymouth to Harburg, whiting from London for Lancaster, for the linoleum works, manure for north Wales and Ireland, firebricks from Newcastle to London, herrings from Lowestoft for Dublin, and cement for Menai Bridge and Bangor from London. Among those to whom she delivered cargoes were 'Mr Waggner, Slate Merchants, Harburg', 'Krogman Becker, and Alkan and Co., Slate Merchants, Harburg'.

The entries in the cargo book of the *Ailsie* indicate the nature of her trade in 1899 (see page 507).

The slate schooners were not solely confined to vessels owned locally: the *Elizabeth Bennett*, owned in Aberdeen, was a regular visitor to the Menai Strait, carrying slates largely from Port Dinorwic, and although an Aberdeen ship, her master for many years was Captain Moses Owen of Benllech. One of the best known of the slate schooners was the *Mary B. Mitchell*. A three-masted topsail steel schooner, she was built at Carrickfergus by Paul Rodgers, 'one of the great figures in merchant schooner building and one of the very few builders who turned over their production capacity to the building of steel schooners'.[118] Rodgers' vessels were already well known in Anglesey: Captain Ishmael Williams, Senior, father of the master of the *Gaelic*, had served aboard one of Rodgers' earlier ships, the *Annie Park*, belonging to the Fisher fleet of Barrow, and many others were to serve in Rodgers' ships, the *Mary Miller*, the *Pool Fisher*, the *Shoal Fisher* and the *Creek Fisher*. The *Mary B. Mitchell* was the second Rodgers'-built vessel to be bought by two Anglesey business men, William Henry Preston of Lleiniog Castle, and Samuel Taylor

Date of shipment	Cargo	Shipped by	From	To	To whom consigned	Arrived
1899						
17.2.99	197 tons of Clay (China)	J. Lovering & Co. St. Austell	Fowey	Runcorn	to Order	3.3.99
10.3.99	85 ton 7 cwt of Coals	T. Crossley Esq. Altrincham	Runcorn	Pt. Dinorwic	The Honble W. W. Vivian Pt. Dinorwic	16.3.99
28.3.99	213 ton 7½ cwt Slates	The Honble W. W. Vivian	Pt. Dinorwic	Harburg	Krogman Becker Elkan & Co. Slate Merchants, Harburg	6.6.99
25.5.99	207 ton 17 cwt 1 Q 25 lbs Oilcake	Mr. H. Tharl	Harburg	King's Lynn	J. & C. H. Finch, Merchants, King's Lynn	
8.6.99	200 tons Burnt Ore	Colchester & Ball	King's Lynn	Newcastle Tyne	Scott Brothrs, 46, Sand Hill, Newcastle Tyne	
28.6.99	209 tons of Bricks & Fire clay	H. Foster & Co. Newcastle-on-Tyne	Newcastle Tyne	Woolwich	Superintendent, Brick Shed, Building Works, Woolwich Canal. D—— bad place.	15.7.99
18.7.99	210 tons Whiting	Grays Chalk Quarry Co.	Grays (Essex)	Lancaster	J. Williamson & Son.	12.8.99
15.8.99	Ballast		Lancaster	Newquay		
30.8.99	203 tons 18 cwt Slates	Penmachno Slate Co.	Deganwy	Conway Folkestone	Mr. H. Toffutt & Son, Merchants, Folkestone	21.10.99
25.10.99	Ballast 40 tons	Pike Brothrs. & Co. Ltd.	Folkestone	Poole		27.10.99
15.11.99	200 Blue Clay	T. K. Wilson	Poole	Runcorn	Anderton & Co, Runcorn	22.11.99
—.12.99	198 Coal			Amlwch	Mona & Parry's Mines Ltd. Amlwch	4.12.99
30.12.99	204 tons Slates	The Honble W. W. Vivian	Port Dinorwic	Aberdeen	Messrs. Bonaccord & Co. Ltd. Aberdeen.	

507

Chadwick of Haulfre, both of Beaumaris, in the early 1890s; the *Anglesey*, a new screw steamer, made of steel and schooner rigged, was built at Carrickfergus in 1891, and the *Mary B. Mitchell* in the following year.[119] In Penmon Churchyard a gravestone commemorates Mary Brasier Mitchell of Lleiniog Castle, Penmon, who died 6 December 1895, aged 79; the stone was erected by 'her sincere and sorrowing friend W. M. Preston', who had a few years previously named his new schooner after her, a notable tribute to a septaugenarian lady.

According to oral tradition, the *Mary B. Mitchell* was originally intended to be a yacht for Lord Penrhyn and his friends, but it would appear that soon after her arrival in the Menai Strait she was sailing in the slate trade; E. A. Young's arrival as agent for Lord Penrhyn coincided with a much tougher line with schooners at Port Penrhyn, the old friendly arrangement with the merchant schooner owners whereby Penrhyn slate was transported by independent schooners was drastically changed, and Penrhyn began to acquire steamships to transport his slate from his own quays, excluding all other vessels. The acquisition of the *Mary B. Mitchell* must be seen in the context of the arrival of the *Bangor*, a new screw steamship, again schooner rigged, built at Bowling, Dumbartonshire, which was built and came to the Strait in 1894, owned originally by a group who included Sir R. H. Williams-Bulkeley of Baron Hill, Preston, Chadwick, S. J. Millar, a London stockbroker, and O. T. Jones, the ship manager, who sold her in the same year as he bought the *Mary B. Mitchell* to E. A. Young, in 1898. Young also acquired the *Pennant*, a steam screw schooner built at Bowling in 1897, from Jones in 1898; all the vessels passed into Lord Penrhyn's hands on Young's death in 1911. To the local community, unaware of bills of sale and changes in the legal registered owners, the *Mary B. Mitchell* and the steam vessels were all 'llongau Penrhyn', and the *Mary B. Mitchell* became a familiar sight not only in the Menai Strait, but also at Hamburg and in the Thames where the bulk of her cargoes were discharged.

The crew agreement lists record the ports the *Mary B. Mitchell* visited for the twenty years before the First World War, and also the crews that manned her. In 1896, a week after leaving Port Dinorwic, she was stranded on Texel, off the Dutch coast, on Boxing Day, and her crew had to abandon ship.[120] She was eventually successfully refloated, repaired, and David Davies, of New Quay, Cardiganshire, then aged forty-three, went out to Amsterdam to take command of her. 'Davies Bach', as he was known to contemporary seamen, remained master of the *Mary B. Mitchell* until the 1914 war, apart from a brief spell of illness; his mate for the early years was Thomas Davies, some years older than himself, also from New Quay, and then, in later years, William Williams of Port Dinorwic took over as mate. The 'Articles' indicate that whilst there were exceptions like Charles Peco, a native of San Francisco, Wilhelm Hess, a boy of 15 from Saxony on his first voyage, and seamen from Harbour Grace, Newfoundland, Norway, Finland, Sweden, Australia, Oregon (nearly all for just one or two voyages), and an A.B. from London who had the somewhat exotic name R. Alfred de Relton à Abrabelton, the crews were from the Menai Strait ports and their environs. If one examines the names of the ships in which they had previously served one gets an interesting glimpse of the close ties which linked this north Wales maritime community – the Amlwch, Connah's Quay, Holyhead, Caernarvon and Portmadoc ships are mentioned time and time again.[121] Captain Davies himself was highly regarded as a seaman by his contemporaries, something of a 'driver', but it was not his skill alone that kept the *Mary B. Mitchell* sailing in the Penrhyn trade when so many others had left. The clash between the obstinate and determined Lord Penrhyn and his equally determined employees at Bethesda had disastrous consequences not only for the quarries themselves, but also for the slate schooners.

Although there had been lean years for the slate quarries, the demand for slate in the nineteenth-century had meant that there were always many schooners either alongside or ready to come in to load at Port Penrhyn. Captain Henry Roberts of Moelfre and others remember that, when they were young, it was not uncommon to see the slate schooners three abreast alongside the quay, with the port full, and others at anchor in Bangor Pool or Friars Road. The two wharves with a tidal basin between them about four hundred yards in length were the scene of considerable activity, but the Penrhyn strike, or 'lock out', changed all that. R. T. Pritchard, a Bangor local historian,[122] recalls a fine sunny Sunday morning when, as a small boy walking to chapel holding his father's hand, his father pointed out the port, full of ships, their tall masts like a forest. It was the first

Sunday after the fatal breakdown in relations between Penrhyn and his employees. The schooners left, one after another, to search for new freights. They never returned.

The *Mary B. Mitchell*, like the other vessels owned by Lord Penrhyn, continued in the monopolistic trade from Port Penrhyn throughout the pre-war years. It is over sixty years since William Roberts, now sexton at Llandegfan, went aboard the *Mary B. Mitchell* for his first voyage, but he remembers it as though it were yesterday.[123] There was the excitement of going from Llandegfan to Port Penrhyn to sign on, his impatience as he waited for the loading to finish, and then, when she lay that night off Lleiniog, in view of her original owner's mansion, he remembers his delight at keeping an anchor watch just before dawn; he had been trusted, everyone else was asleep, and so stealthily he climbed the rigging and up to the topsail yard to get the feel of what is was like to be aloft. But deflation and misery soon overcame him once they had passed Point Lynas as he asked a kindly Norwegian seaman how long his sea-sickness would last; there was little wind and the *Mary B. Mitchell* was wallowing uneasily, longing for a stiff breeze to drive her along. It was a much chastened young Roberts who arrived at the Penrhyn Slate Wharf in the Thames a fortnight later. At Port Penrhyn there were workmen to load the slates, but in London it was the crew's responsibility to unload them, and Roberts well remembers the three hundred and more tons handled from 6.30 a.m. to 5.30 p.m., heavy work for the 3/6d a day allowed by the slate merchant. Eight days later they sailed for Swanscombe, Kent, for a cargo of cement, half of it for Pembroke Dock and, half for Caernarvon, where there was an air of excitement concerning the investiture of Prince Edward of Wales. William Roberts sailed many times in the *Mary B. Mitchell* after that first voyage; he remembers the occasional bad passage when the foremast broke and they had a frantic struggle to cut it adrift, when they were towed into the Mumbles after hours of frustration with snapping towropes and wires, but most of all his memories being to life the names recorded in the crew lists: Captain Davies himself, and his mate, William Williams, both superb seamen, John Baptist, the Mauritian cook, who looked after the captain very well, but was also a fine seaman, and so many others now long since dead. Above all, he remembers the elegance of the *Mary B. Mitchell*, a heavy old ship on the arms of her crew, but also, with her graceful lines, an object of beauty, a ship to be proud of serving in her, despite the cramped, damp forecastle with its eight berths, and the mate's unchanging cry as they went below 'keep yourself handy'. The *Mary B. Mitchell* continued in the coastal trade until she was requisitioned by the Admiralty and entered upon her career as one of the most famous of the Q-ships of the 1914-18 war. That part of her story belongs to the next chapter. But, as in the case of the deep-sea ships, for many Anglesey seamen in the coastal trade, the 1914-18 war was to mark the end of an age.

[1] *SB* 6, 258 (1948), Letter from B. Thomas to Commodore Gerald N. Jones, C.B.E., D.S.O.

[2] WT Liverpool MSS. Memo. 2.7.1888.

[3] Captain Jones' wife used to sail aboard the *Havelock* with him; two of her sons were born whilst the *Havelock* was on the South America nitrate coast, one at Callao and the other at Pisco. Three of Captain Owen Jones' sons began their service at sea in Portmadoc schooners. *SB* 27, Jan. 1959, 374-6. Captain Owen Jones was one of the seven sons of Captain Richard Jones whose schooner, *Edward*, was lost off Anglesey on February 19th, 1868. Captain Owen Jones' sister married Captain R. Cadwaladr Jones, who commanded the Portmadoc schooner *Cadwalader Jones* for many years, whilst his son, Captain W. Ellis Jones, commanded another Portmadoc vessel, the *Elizabeth*, in which he sailed from Maracaibo, Venezuela, to Liverpool in 23 days.

[4] In the seventies very many iron sailing ships were built, cf. Michael Bouquet, *South Eastern Sail* (1972), 74, in which he describes the *Alaston* launched at Sunderland in 1875: 'The year 1875 was a peak for sailing ship launchings, and the crest of a minor boom for sail. These were large new iron sailing vessels, not so heavily rigged in proportion to size as some of the earlier wooden ships of the sixties, but with much greater carrying capacity.'

[5] J. R. Jones in *The Welsh Builder on Merseyside* (Liverpool, 1946) indicates that in the early years 'the proportion of Anglesey people among the members (of the Pall Mall Calvinistic Methodist Chapel) was as two or even

three to one from all the other Welsh counties'. Most of the builders listed in Jones' work had come to Liverpool by sea from Holyhead, Amlwch or Beaumaris, as William Thomas himself had done, and by the time he became an elder in the Pall Mall Chapel at the age of 27, among his fellow elders were many who had already acquired wealth through their building operations. William Thomas moved to live to Bootle in 1879, another area where Anglesey Welshmen were actively engaged in much building work. Daniel Jones of Bodwrog, a builder, Thomas Owen Hughes, of Aberffraw, an accountant, were to become prominent members of the Bootle Borough Council at the same time as William Thomas. William Thomas' work as Chairman of the Finance Committee of Bootle Borough Council was regarded highly by his contemporaries who recognized his thoroughness, care for detail, and his ability to overcome complex difficulties. He was Mayor of Bootle in 1892-3, and again in 1899.

[6]   W. E. Jones, and his father, Rees Jones, built a number of ships at Port Dinorwic, including the *Ordovic*, 825 tons, which was completed in 1877. Both father and son played an important part in the activities of the many north Wales Ship Insurance Clubs. According to the late David Thomas' records they built twenty-eight ships on the banks of the Menai Strait, most of them schooners. The *Ordovic* was lost in 1894 off Cape Horn. D. Thomas, *Hen Longau Sir Gaernarfon* 144-6, 198-9.

[7]   Although nominally owned by the *Gwynedd Shipping Company*, W. E. Jones was undoubtedly the real driving force, and by 1890 he is named in Lloyd's Register as the owner of the *Moel Eilian* and the *Moel Tryfan* and manager for the Gwynedd Company of the *Moel y Don*. The *Moel Eilian* and *Moel y Don* were both iron barques of about 1,100 tons, built by Doxfords in 1877 and 1882, the *Moel Tryfan*, an iron 4-masted ship of 1,691 tons built in 1884. The *Moel Rhiwan* built in 1878 was out of the Register by 1884.

[8]   W. T. Liverpool MSS, 2.7.88.

[9]   Appendix XI for details of these vessels from *Lloyd's Register*. When Basil Lubbock wrote his *The Last of the Windjammers*, the sails and sail areas of which he gave details in Appendix 1, were all of ships owned by William Thomas, viz., *Principality, Metropolis, Pengwern, Cambrian Prince, County of Cardigan* and *Colony*. Lubbock, *The Last of the Windjammers* (Glasgow, 1927), I, 5/2.

[10]   *SB* 18, 65 (1954). Letter from L. Glanville of Kingswear, Devon.

[11]   *SB* 19, 384 (1955). Letter from 'Binnacle', Shepton Mallet.

[12]   WT Liverpool MSS. Letters between Captain Thomas and William Thomas, October 1899. On 7 October, William Thomas had written to tell Captain Thomas that he believed the latter had 'delayed too long in making up your mind to offer' for a freight from Connah's Quay to Bermuda, but he had hopes that there might be an alternative cargo for Demerara, and a very good prospect of a cargo home from Pensacola.

[13]   *ibid.*

[14]   WT Liverpool MSS 2.7.88.

[15] *ibid.*, 7.10.1879. William Thomas had no doubt that Captain R. H. Roberts was the Amlwch firm's man; 'He has been your Captain all his lifetime and if you can employ him ashore the best plan is for you to do so and everything I can put in his way I shall be glad to do so.' But Captain Thomas could not find him suitable employment in Amlwch: 'he seems to think he would not do in this yard as I do . . . I believe him to be a very valuable man where there is plenty for him to do'. William Thomas later visited Amlwch 'on my way home and saw Captain Roberts and there agreed with him to superintend and see that the specifications of the new ship were carried out by Messrs. William Doxford'.

[16] *ibid.*, 24.11.1879; 28.11.1879. Thomas had told Captain Roberts to collect information regarding steamers being built in various yards in the north-east.

[17] *ibid.*, 2.12.1879. William Thomas' caution contrasted markedly with the effusive enthusiasm of Captain Roberts, and he was not impressed with the latter's easy shedding of his ties with Captain Thomas. Roberts wrote: 'I gave it out that I was now quite free of Captain Thomas except owning a little of some of the ships that he manages and that for the future I was to be identified with you'.

[18] In his own memorandum in 1888 Thomas recalled that he had mentioned to Captain Roberts whilst the *County of Merioneth* was being built that 'as a large portion of the trade was being done by steamers, increasingly so, I thought I would build a steamer next, provided I could get my friends that had hitherto joined in the sailing ships to join in the steamer, but as they knew nothing about steamers I said I was afraid I would have some difficulty in inducing them to join and subscribe to such a large capital as would be required to float a steamer'. It was in the context of this conversation that Roberts visited Amlwch hoping to bring in financial support and so strengthen his own position with Thomas. In 1880 William Thomas contracted with R. & J. Evans and Company to build the steamer *Empire*, 'the capital of which is £31,000', and of this, eventually, 'the capital brought by R. H. Roberts and through him was £4,400'.

[19] WT Liverpool MSS, 4.3.1880. Thomas asked, 'What is the cause of Doxford not putting the diagonal ties throughout in the tween deck where it is in the agreement. I find they are only in way of masts. Don't you think it would have been better to have them the whole length, the same as in the main deck?' He did not wish to see the job rushed: 'Likely they will be in a hurry to launch her so as to get their instalment. As you know, good painting is of great importance'. In March 1880 Thomas asked Roberts to check very carefully the rigging and sail plan of the new vessel as he had found discrepancies in the 'masts, yards, Bowsprit and Jibboom' of the *County of Flint* and *County of Denbigh*, and now the *County of Merioneth*, although they were supposed to be 'duplicates'.

[20] WT Liverpool MSS, 17.2.1880. The *County of Denbigh* had been built by Doxfords in 1877.

[21] *ibid.*, 27.4.1880. The 'Captain Jones, Menai Strait' referred to was probably Captain John Jones of Baronhill, Newborough, one of William Thomas' favourite master mariners, who commanded the *Havelock, Menai* and *Principality*. Captain Roberts had hoped that both the mate and carpenter would have been Amlwch men, but he had to report to Thomas that he had had a 'reply from Amlwch stating that the Mate we thought of has sailed from Liverpool on Saturday last. I have heard nothing further from Carpenter'. *ibid.*, 3.5.1880. On the next day, Thomas wrote to say that he 'had sent to a man from Portmadoc now at Newcastle' to report to Roberts for the carpenter's berth: 'If he comes make best bargain wages, not to exceed £5'.

[22] The *County of Merioneth* sailed from Sunderland on the morning's tide, May 15, 1880 and according to Captain Roberts' letter she had 'as cargo 1660 tons' of coal with 15 tons 'in addition for ship's use'. WT Liverpool MSS, 13, 14, 15.5.1880.

[23] The relations between Thomas and Roberts deteriorated in the eighties; Thomas refused Roberts' request for a share in the *Kate Thomas* 'and gave him as my reason that his ideas and ways were different to mine, and besides that I already agreed with Captain Thomas Williams to superintend the building and command the ship'. Following further disputes over several vessels, including the *Alliance* built by Roberts with the help of Thomas and six of his captains, matters came to a head in 1888 and Thomas' memoranda are related to this final break.

[24] WT Liverpool MSS, 23.5.1882.

[25] *ibid.*, 17.4.1882. The *Portia*, an iron ship built by Palmers at Newcastle in 1868 was previously owned by S. R. Graves of London. Captain Thomas Jones of Nefyn commanded the *Portia* for some years, with Llewelyn Rees of Holyhead as second mate.

[26] WT Liverpool MSS, 27.2.1882. 'Nantyglo Co. have to supply 450 tons bunker coal and the shippers of the cargo, the Ferndale Co., the remainder.'

[27] *ibid.*, 6.3.1882.

[28] WT Liverpool MSS, undated notes in William Thomas' hand relating to the building of the *Principality*.

[29] *ibid.*, Disbursement of the *Havelock*. She was at Shanghai from 24 July to 28 August 1882, at Victoria and Puget Sound from 11 October to 22 December, at Valparaiso and Iquique 9 March to 24 May 1883, at Lobos de Afuerra 4 June to 23 July, and called at Valparaiso for repairs 28 August to 30 September 1883.

[30] *ibid.*, Captain Jones' accounts at San Francisco include payments to 'water police guarding crew' and to 'shipping master procuring crew', evidence no doubt of the activities of 'crimps'.

[31] *ibid.*, undated notes in W. Thomas' hand regarding building of *Kate Thomas, Principality, Colony, Province* and *Metropolis*.

[32] According to the handbill, the dimensions of the new vessel were 258' x 39'6" x 23', about 1,690 tons net register, 2,620 tons carrying capacity. 'Class

100 A1, the highest class of Lloyd's; Special Survey with the following extras to Lloyd's requirement: 1-16th of an inch extra thickness of iron in Bilge Plates and Sheer Strake, 50 per cent additional width in Diagonal Ties throughout main and 'tween decks, Bilge Stanchions, 'Tween Deck laid Complete, and extra size of Rigging.'

[33] £10 per share was payable in the following instalments, when (1) the keel was laid, (2) framed, (3) plated, (4) decked, (5) launched, and £50 when the vessel was completed.

[34] WT Liverpool MSS. Address Book 1st New Ship, *Kate Thomas*, and 2nd New Ship *Principality*.

[35] Father of the late Sir Wynn P. Wheldon, sometime Registrar of UCNW, Bangor and Permanent Secretary, Welsh Dept., Board of Education, 1933-45, and grandfather of Huw Wheldon of the BBC. There is a brief account of John Wheldon in D. D. Williams, *Cofiant Thomas Jones Wheldon* (Caernarfon, 1925), 17, 19-22.

[36] *Y Genedl Gymreig*, Tachwedd 1, 1877. In the following year the same newspaper satirically suggested that the quarrymen now they had become 'shipowners' were studying geography as avidly as the pupils of the Board School, and that Bombay, Valparaiso and Singapore came as easily to their lips as Cwm y Glo and Brynrefail. *Y Genedl Gymreig*, Ionawr 24, 1878; D. Thomas, *Hen Longau Sir Gaernarfon*, 147. The Register of members of the is in CRO M/543. There is a fine painting of the *County of Flint* off Sydney in Mrs E. K. Williams' possession; Captain Jabez Rowlands of Moelfre, father of Dr Helen Rowlands, the Welsh missionary in India, and Canon Rowlands of Llandudno, was at one time master of the *County of Flint*.

[37] ARO Crew Agreement Lists of vessels named.

[38] ARO Crew Agreement List for *County of Merioneth*, voyage ending 15.10.1888. Captain Meredith was known as a great sail-carrier, and life aboard his ships must have been arduous. Thirteen of the crew deserted at either Astoria or Portland, and two young Welsh boys on their first voyage, John Hughes Griffiths of Montgomeryshire, aged fourteen, and Hugh Williams, of Anglesey, aged seventeen, deserted at Portland. Captain Meredith was listed as aged fifty at the time, so he must have been in his sixties when he was lost in the *Annie Thomas*.

[39] UCNW Bangor MSS, 4877. Jones' notebook contains recipes, notes on slop payments, and a list of the crew; the Steward died during the voyage. There are notes regarding the *Enterprise*'s accounts at Panama in the *Arvon Shipping Company*'s ledgers in CRO Plas Brereton MSS, 220.

[40] 'This morning there was fighting between the English and the foreigners, the English won, there was also trouble between some of them in the cabin. I was called before the Captain, and he gave me orders not to do anything but to walk about keeping my eyes open as a detective, and not to take any argument from anyone or they will all be put in irons. I am afraid of a mutiny but I will keep my eyes open . . . Read in Book of Ecclesiastes.' UCNW Bangor MSS, 4877. In his list of the crew, Jones had indicated the mixed

nationalities of the seamen: Jim Conway, Bill (Darkey), Black Sam, Oscar, Big John, Old Dick, Hans, German John, Welsh Ned, Charlie, Little Johnson, Richard Cowling (Long Dick), Curly Bristol and Edward Rawney. Whatever their nationalities, a number of them later deserted, and Jones noted 'run away' against the names of German John, Welsh Ned, Big John and Long Dick.

[41] According to his own notes, William Thomas sent Captain David Evans to 'sight the bottom of *Menai* at Antwerp', and Captain R. H. Roberts to similarly inspect the *Ogwen* at Dublin before he took them over from the *Arvon Shipping Company*. The company had invited him 'to buy or take over all their ships. I declined to have anything to do with them except *Ogwen* and *Menai*'. The details of these losses are based on William Thomas' own notes, the Henry Parry papers in CRO and *SB* 6, 211 (1948), for the Holyhead memories. Captain John Farrell's youngest brother, Hugh Farrell, was lost from the yardarm of another ship a few months later in approximately the same area. Information from Hugh Farrell, Llaneilian, descendant of Captain Robert Jones, Amlwch.

[42] B. Lubbock, *The Last of the Windjammers*, II (1966), 173.

[43] Quoted from Stevenson's *By Way of Cape Horn* in Lubbock, II, 173-4. The details of the losses of the *Dominion* and the *Annie Thomas* are in *Parl. Papers* 1900, LXXVII and 1901, LXVIII, Appendices C. The *Annie Thomas* was named after William Thomas' second wife, Annie Hughes, whom he married in 1885 following the death of his first wife, Catherine, after whom the *Kate Thomas* had been named.

[44] According to Lubbock the *Principality* sailed from Barry to Rio in 38 days, arriving on August 4, 1900, whilst the *Metropolis*, which had arrived five days earlier, had taken 41 days; from Rio to Caleta Buena, the *Principality* took 35 days, the *Metropolis* taking 40 days from Rio to Taltal. 'On the homeward run the ships were separated, and there was no test of sailing. After this date both captains went into steam, and the ships are not supposed to have been so hard sailed.' Lubbock, I, 325.

[45] Captain Ellis Roberts, described as 'first master of the *Reina del Pacifico*' in 1946, went to sea first in a Caernarvon schooner in the coastal trade at the age of 13. He had served aboard the *Merioneth*, the Menai Bridge Hughes company's full-rigged ship on her record passage from San Francisco to Portland, as well as on the *Principality*'s record passage. *SB* 2, 1946, 284. He was master of the *Orduna* on the first of the cruises by Urdd Gobaith Cymru in 1933, and published his memoirs, *Ar Frig y Don* (Liverpool, 1934).

[46] *Lloyd's Register*, and information in WT Liverpool MSS.

[47] Alan Villiers, *The War with Cape Horn* (London, 1971), 204.

[48] *SB* 25, 378 (1958). The eldest brother Thomas was lost off Cape Wrath, 1890. John was disabled by an accident at sea, Owen was lost in 1909 at sea, whilst Robert Jones, the fifth brother, served in McIver ships. Details in letter from H. Conway Jones, Southall, Middlesex. Captain W. H. Hughes, D.S.C., recalled that Captain Peter Jones later became one of the Belfast

pilots. For Captain Peter Jones' last voyage in the *Metropolis* in 1913-14, Lubbock, *The Last of the Windjammers*, I, 326-7.

[49] Information provided by Captain Henry Roberts, Moelfre, 1971.

[50] Villiers, *The War with Cape Horn*, 211-12.

[51] 'Pan oeddech chi ar ei dec hi, roedd hi fel cae pel droed, ond pan oeddech chi fyny'r rigin, roedd hi fel hancas-boced.' TR with Mr Elias Jones, Amlwch, 1971.

[52] There are frequent references to absences from school in the school log-books, e.g., the log-book of the Edern, Caernarvonshire, school, 'Aug. 12th, 1864, Thomas Roberts, 2nd class, has been absent this last fortnight, having had leave to go with his father for a sea-voyage', quoted D. Thomas, *Hen Longau Sir Gaernarfon*, 155.

[53] TR interviews with Captain W. H. Hughes, D.S.C., at Holyhead, 1971. They had landed close to the mansion of one of the Colman family, and were well looked after, for Mrs Colman was the niece for whom Robert Davies had had the English Methodist Church built, so that she could be married at Menai Bridge.

[54] The details of this voyage, which had elements of bizarre comedy as well as danger, in the *Faith*, manned only by the master and young Hughes, still a boy, are recalled in David Lloyd Hughes, *Holyhead, the Story of a Port* (1967), 144.

[55] In the brigantine, *George Casson*, the brig *Excelsior*, and the three-masted schooner David Morris. The *Beeswing*, a steel barque, was built by Russells at Glasgow in 1893 and registered at Birkenhead: 1,462 tons, 236.5 x 36.0 x 21.7.

[56] She was bound for Copenhagen with slates; the Board of Trade return gives the position of foundering as 'about ten miles N. of Stoer Head, Sutherlandshire'. *Parl. Papers*, Abstracts of Shipping Casualties, 1904-5, 108.

[57] Quoted Lubbock, *Last of the Windjammers*, I, 385, The *Deccan*, a steel ship, 1,985 tons, was built by R. Duncan and Co. in 1897. She was lost on the 'Breaker Coast' having weathered Cape Horn in December 1909, bound from Port Talbot to Tocopilla with a cargo of coal, but Captain Rowlands and her crew got ashore on Desolation Island, Tierra del Fuego and were subsequently saved. Lubbock, I, 98, 99.

[58] The *Marion Frazer*, 2,396 tons, 295 x 43 x 24.1, was a steel 4-masted barque built by Connell at Glasgow in 1892. Plate 38 is a photograph taken of her in Dry Dock, Quarter Master Harbour, Tacoma, Washington. 14 December 1905.

[59] *SB* 14, 158 (1952). Captain Marshall describes the voyage round Cape Horn to San Francisco, where they loaded grain for Cape Town at the time of the Boer War, and the kindness of Captain Evans and his wife to him as a young apprentice. He recalled that one of William Thomas' brothers was aboard the *Cambrian Hills* as a passenger for this voyage. The *James Kerr*, built by Royden in 1892 was commanded by Captain Evan Jones when

Archer joined her. The other Thomas ships at Iquique in 1907 when Archer found so many other apprentices from the same company to compete with in boat races, etc., were the *Crocodile, Rowena* and *Colony*. Captain Harry Fuller, who left the *James Kerr* at Rotterdam in 1905, remembered her well, 'The *James Kerr* was commanded by Captain Evan Jones – a good seaman – and manned by nine A.B.s and sixteen boys . . . on that voyage the only time we spent ashore was one day in ten months, at Taltal, Chile'. Captain Archer stated that on the 1908/9 voyage only two of the original A.B.s remained at Seattle where they loaded Oregon pine 'destined to be used in the making of the new dock at Newport, Mon.' *SB* 13, 162 (1952).

⁶⁰ Sir James Bisset, *Sail Ho, My Early Years at Sea* (1958). Bisset's portrait of William Thomas and some of his captains is not a flattering one. It lays stress on the strict economies and the penny-pinching which led to some near disasters. In fairness, Bisset pointed out that basically the problem was not the efficiency of the ships or the men at sea, or even the fault of the owners, but rather the lack of port facilities and suitable cargoes which led to some sailing ships spending eight months a year incurring expenses in port. One suspects, however, that Bisset's 'ghost writer', P. R. Stephensen, has added somewhat to the text in order to create atmosphere; each time a Welshman speaks – and they are in the majority in the book – they preface what they have to say with 'Indeed to goodness'. This might belong to burlesque 'stage Welshmen', but would hardly have been uttered by an Anglesey Welshman like William Thomas himself.

⁶¹ Commodore Gerald N. Jones, C.B.E., D.S.O., spent 46 years at sea; he was staff captain in the *Georgia, Aquitania, Queen Elizabeth* and *Queen Mary*, and commanded the *Ascania* and *Franconia*, all Cunard White Star Line. During the First World War he served in destroyers and was awarded the D.S.O. when in command of H.M.S. *Sprightly*, whilst in the Second World War he was awarded the C.B.E. in 1941 for his services as commodore of convoys. His father, Humphrey Bradley Jones, 'Garmonydd', was appointed Headmaster of the British School at Holyhead in 1886; among Gerald Jones' brothers were Alderman Cyril O. Jones of Wrexham, who did much service for radical causes in Wales, and Fred Llewelyn Jones, M.P. for Flintshire. I am indebted to Mr Frank Price Jones, UCNW, Bangor, for the details of Commodore Jones' family background. Commodore Jones' reminiscences were published in *SB* 19, 318; 20, 87, 238.

⁶² A. Villiers, *The War with Cape Horn*, 98.

⁶³ *SB* 20, 89. Gerald Jones, the apprentice, recalled Captain Pritchard's own willingness to teach apprentices (in itself a comparatively rare quality among the sailing masters of the day); as the *Glenesslin* sailed close to one of the Marquesas islands in the Pacific, 'Captain Pritchard, always ready to give information to the apprentices, brought out the heavy volume of the 'Pacific Pilot' and told us the name of the island the ship was passing'.

⁶⁴ *Parl. Debates*, 4th Series, 154, March 1906, 247. For a discussion of the reasons for desertions, Villiers, *The War with Cape Horn*, 165-178.

[65] *SB* 20, 239.

[66] There are several versions of this story: one is that two of the dockside 'crimps' were shot dead by the boatswain of the *Morven* in a scuffle aboard one of the boats bearing away the 'shanghaied' crew. It appears that both Sullivan and the authorities were content to have the matter 'hushed up', but seamen who sailed with Captain Rees were in no doubt that it was Rees himself who had shot the 'crimps' to prevent his crew from falling into their hands.

[67] *SB* 20, 239.

[68] Villiers, *The War with Cape Horn*, xii-xiv. Captain W. H. Hughes remembers these years when he was serving in the *Beeswing* and *Deccan* as years when they saw many icebergs.

[69] *ibid.*, 65-84. The *Cambrian Hills*, commanded by Captain W. Williams, foundered 50°42'N., 7°17'W., but her crew were saved. *Abstracts of Shipping Casualties*, 1904-5, 112.

[70] *ibid.*, 124, 100.

[71] *SB* 6, 262 (1948). 'Charlie Hughes, the Shop, Laingoch . . . went to sea when still a boy and by the time he was 21 had obtained his master's certificate.'

[72] Lubbock, *The Last of the Windjammers*, I, 328. Villiers, *The War with Cape Horn*, 124. The *Kate Thomas*, named after William Thomas' first wife, did not make as fast passages as her sister ships, but she was regarded as a fine looking vessel by those who knew her.

[73] ARO Captain Robert Jones MSS. This collection consists of miscellaneous notebooks and papers belonging to Captain Jones and have recently been deposited at the Record Office, Llangefni.

[74] Lubbock, *The Last of the Windjammers*, II, 125. The *Talus* was a steel full-rigged ship, 274.6' x 41.3' x 24.0', 2,090 tons, built by Barclay, Curle and Company, the Glasgow shipbuilders. She could load 3,359 tons of wheat or 3,381 tons of coal.

[75] ARO Captain Robert Jones MSS. Letter from William Lewis and Co. to Captain Jones, dated December 13, 1904.

[76] Lewis', like all shipowners, were mightily concerned regarding the 'large number of vessels that have, from time to time, been lost whilst proceeding from port in ballast'. Captain Jones was, therefore, to exercise 'the greatest caution in taking sufficient ballast to make the vessel perfectly safe, and to enable her to make a good passage to wherever she may be bound'. The orders were clear-cut: 'Decide first of all on the draft of water that you require the ship immersed to, to make her perfectly safe and then (having carefully studied your Displacement Scale, which should show you exactly what the vessel would have on board on that draft) make the best arrangement you can as regards price, with whosoever supplied the ballast, to put the vessel down to the agreed-upon draft to your safisfaction. By making such an arrangement beforehand there can be no misunderstanding afterwards as regards weights.'

77   Owners varied in their attitude towards the sale of 'slops' (clothing) and tobacco by the masters of their vessels; some regarded it as reasonable that their masters should handle this themselves and make a profit as one of their 'perks', but others insisted that the profits should be paid to the company. Captain Robert Jones always kept detailed notes of his sales to his crew. In a photograph of him and the crew of the *John Lockett* 'Lei Bach' can be clearly seen to be wearing a kind of tam-o-shanter which he had made for himself rather than pay the price for the 'slop' headgear provided by Captain Jones. Masters were allowed cargo space by some companies and most captains took consignments of small goods where and when they could to sell on their own account. A Captain Henry Thomas was said to have bought harmoniums from Van Crusens of Liverpool and sold them at Singapore at 300% profit. UCNW Bangor MSS 18952.

78   'We would like you during the present voyage if possible to remove the wedges of the masts on the Main Deck and clean and paint the Masts on the wake of the same and fit with new mast coats. Also we would like the Chain and Cable Lockers thoroughly cleaned on the homeward passage and the Cables blacked.' The Lewis Company had arranged for 'a considerable quantity of new canvas to be sent aboard for the making of an upper top gallant sail, sails, two royals and also for customary repairs and renewals'.

79   After all this, it was perhaps hardly necessary for them to remind Captain Jones that 'You will find that, provided you give us every satisfaction, we shall treat you well and give you every encouragment; but, on the other hand, unless your utmost is, at all times, done we shall be obliged in the interests of the Ship and Owners to deal with you harshly'.

80   As one would expect from his previous experience in the *Cymric*, Captain Jones kept notebooks and papers in which he jotted down all his transactions at every port, his dealing with agents, payments to crew, etc. The account which follows is based upon these jottings made in many different parts of the world, no doubt often in trying circumstances. His son, O. Llewelyn Jones, was at one time relief master of the *Hibernia* with Captain W. H. Hughes; he died in 1941.

81   Villiers, *The War with Cape Horn*, 68. The total tonnage of these twenty-six ships was 31,490 registered tons.

82   The *Oweenee*, built at Stockton in 1891 and previously managed by F. C. Mahon of Windsor, Nova Scotia, had been commanded until she was bought by Lewis, Heron and Co. by Captain C. M. Burchell, who had built up a formidable reputation for her with many fast passages which are recorded in Lubbock, II. 137.

83   Letter from Lewis, Heron and Company, dated 14 September 1908, to Captain Robert Jones, at Middlesborough. Captain W. H. Hughes supplied the information about Captain Thomas Davies, Bangor, Lewis' marine superintendent.

84   Letter to Captain Robert Jones, Ship *Oweenee*, Middlesborough, from John Jones from the ship *Talus*, Barry Dock, 5 September 1908. 'I like

Caernarvonshire people, but I prefer those from Anglesey and thus it is that I prefer the *Oweenee*.' A. J. Jones was listed as master of the *Oweenee* in Lloyd's Register in 1908; this could have been before Robert Jones took command. In his letter John Jones reported that he had discussed the need for deviation cards with Captain Burchall (her former commander), who stated that there was 'little or no error in the standard compass, consequently had no deviation cards for it. Nevertheless, the ship should be swung, loaded with the present cargo, he said'.

[85] Letter to Captain Robert Jones at Mejillones from Lewis, Heron and Company, 27 August 1909. The opening paragraph indicates the tone of the letter, 'we have received your letters of 11th and 13th July, but these carbon copies you send us are almost unreadable. Why do you not send us the original letter and keep the carbon copies for your own reference?' In all, sixty-two names are recorded by Captain Jones in his portage bill as having signed on for varying periods during these twenty months. Thirteen are recorded as 'deserters', others served for only limited stages of the voyage. The only ones who completed the whole voyage were the mate, second mate, John Roberts, the carpenter, Hugh Ellis and Harry Wuherfenning, the two bos'ns, William Hughes and Erik Nielsen, A.B.s, Richard Hughes and John Owen, ordinary seamen. This was typical, the stable element being provided by the 'afterguard' and a handful of foc'sle hands who were from the same background as the master himself, who possibly knew their families.

[86] The *Oweenee* was able to take a cargo of 3,713 tons of coal on a draught of 22½ feet. Lubbock, *The Last of the Windjammers*, II, 136.

[87] Lewis, Heron and Company to Captain Jones, 29 April 1910.

[88] The *Caernarvon Bay*, a steel ship built by A. Rodger and Co., Port Glasgow, in 1894, which had been commanded for many years by Captain W. Griffith, went missing about this time. The *Herzogin Cecile* was the famous German training ship which Lubbock states sailed from Mejillones to the Scilly Islands in 63 days. The *Muskoka*, the *Oweenee*'s sister ship, was claimed by Lubbock to have been 'the fastest sailing vessel afloat' when commanded by the Nova Scotian, Captain Albert Crowe. Lubbock, *The Last of the Windjammers*, II, 138.

[89] The *County of Anglesea* and the *County of Merioneth* were owned in 1910 by the Pettersons of Mariehamn, Finland, but were registered as sailing under the Russian flag.

[90] Originally the *Manydown*, built by Oswald, Mordant and Company at Southampton in 1884.

[91] WT Liverpool MSS, 2.7.88.

[92] For detail of these vessels see Appendix XI.

[93] Villiers, *The War with Cape Horn*, 8.

[94] *Parl Papers*, xlii, 14 (1919), *Merchant Shipping Losses*.

[95] *Parl Debates*, Fourth Series, 154, March 1906, 238-294. Lloyd George maintained that 'The Board of Trade scale is a sort of traditional scale; it is

very little beyond salt meat, biscuits, tea and sugar'. *ibid.*, 247.

Attention had been drawn to the large numbers of foreign seamen in the British Merchant Service, and uneasiness was felt regarding the implications of this for the country in the event of a war. Lloyd George pointed out that the growth of the British mercantile marine had been so rapid since 1870 that it was not possible to provide the manpower to keep pace with it and at the same time to man the Royal Navy. 'The Navy has taken the cream of our men engaged in seafaring life . . . I do not despair of being able to do something with the assistance of the shipowners, who seem to me just as anxious as anybody to get British seamen into British ships, and we are considering all sorts of schemes at the present time.' Lloyd George had already contacted the Liverpool-Welsh shipowner, Sir Alfred Jones, who 'has been down to Swansea, and he has suggested that in each port you should set up some arrangement for the purpose of training British sailors. I think that is an admirable idea . . . '. *ibid.*, 243.

[96] The worst part of this voyage, which started on 23 November 1901 and ended 30 March 1903, was the homeward passage with a cargo of guano from Chincha Islands. Captain John Hughes had neglected to take in provisions at Newcastle, N.S.W., Callao and Pisco and the *County of Pembroke*'s crew were in a starving condition when S.S. *Lowlands* answered their distress signal and stopped to give them supplies in mid-Atlantic. When S.S. *Lowlands* reached New York, the plight of the *County of Pembroke* was reported and newspapers in America and Britain gave prominence to the story. This case, and other similar incidents of near starvation in sailing ships, were cited in the political agitation which eventually led to Lloyd George's attempts at reform through Board of Trade regulations. Sir James Bisset, *Sail Ho*, 164-230.

[97] *SB* II, 1946, 284.

[98] *Parl Debates*, Fourth Series, 149, 10-21 July 1905, 1503. Lord Muskerry drew attention to the dangers of ships taking insufficient or unsuitable ballast, and quoting the loss of the *Moel Tryfan* and the near loss of the *County of Anglesea* as examples, made a general attack on the owners of sailing ships. The *County of Anglesea* was dismasted and abandoned and later drove ashore at Portland Bay. After repairs, she was sold. *Supra*, note 89.

[99] E. D. Lewis, *The Rhondda Valleys* (London, 1963), 139. The Barry Docks and the railway to connect the Rhondda coalfields with them, were largely due to the energy and initiative of David Davies (1819-1890), who had realised the potential of Rhondda steam coal. By 1914 Cardiff and Barry were the greatest coal-exporting ports in the world; Dr Lewis shows that the increase in coal exported from Cardiff, including Penarth and Barry; was from 3,770,169 in 1874 to 7,974,935 in 1884 and 20,379,794 in 1904. For David Davies' career, see Ivor Thomas, *Top Sawyer, A biography of David Davies* (London, 1938). It was his grandson, then David Davies, M.P. for Montgomeryshire (1880-1944), whom William Thomas supported in the

campaign against tuberculosis.

[100] *Y Brython*, Mawrth 1, 1915; *Y Goleuad*, Mawrth 19, 1915.

[101] WT Liverpool MSS, 19.10.80.

[102] The school is still in use today as the County Primary School, Llanrhuddlad.

[103] The information regarding the farms was kindly provided by Mrs Ethel K. Williams, William Thomas' youngest daughter.

[104] The directors of the Company were Sir Robert Thomas, who claimed that he had twenty-five years' experience in his father's company, and 'all the other Directors of the Managing Company were in the service of the old Managing Company for over twenty years, viz., Mr Hughes as the Marine Superintendent, Mr Farrell as Secretary and Chief Accountant and Mr Cookson as Insurance Manager'. W. O. Hughes, M.I.N.A., M.I.M.E., whose address was given as Bodfa, Beaumaris, had been with William Thomas for over thirty years.

[105] Charles Mowat, *Britain Between the Wars*, 25-26.

[106] Basil Greenhill, *The Merchant Schooners*, I, 58. The historian of the merchant schooners has described Portmadoc ships in unforgettable terms: 'They were lovely ships. The grace of their hulls and the balance of their tall spars gave them a beauty, both under way and lying to an anchor, not exceeded in all the history of sailing vessels.'

[107] The *Camborne* was owned after the 1914-18 war by W. A. Jenkins of Swansea, the Hook Colliery Company of Haverfordwest, and then by Captain Hugh Shaw, whose record of sailing in her is in the National Maritime Museum, Greenwich, as well as photographs taken by Captain Shaw's sons. Some examples of these, taken aboard the *Camborne*, are included in Basil Greenhill's *The Merchant Schooners*, I, 20, 188-9, and II, 68, 17, 35. Captain Shaw's story has been edited and published by Norah Ayland, *Schooner Captain* (Truro, 1972).

[108] The details relating to the crew of the *Camborne* are based on the half-yearly crew agreement lists, Eng. 6, 1886-1898.

[109] TR interview with Captain R. Wynn and Captain R. Jones at Amlwch, August 1971.

[110] Arnold Wilson, Director of the City Art Gallery, Bristol, has observed penetratingly that Chappell's pictures 'are *reportage* from a way of life followed by men who were proud of the vessels in which they risked their lives for very little pay, a way of life now replaced by safer and more efficient forms of transport, less elemental and less capable of inspiring affection. It was not only photography that put a term to the ship portrait painting that faded out with Chappell's death, it was also the contraction of the mariner's pride in his craft, occasioned by technological change. Needing to risk less, to invest less effort, he derived less satisfaction from achievement and consequently generated less regard for his ship . . . Reuben Chappell . . . was a pop Artist (in today's parlance) who truly and unselfconsciously brought art into the homes of every-day working people, faithfully recording for

them the appearance of objects for which they had deep affection'.

[111] Plates 43-4. TR interview with Mrs Elizabeth Jones at her home, Gauntlet, Amlwch, August 1971.

[112] 'Remember, whilst you live, never part with the picture of the *Gauntlet*, she has earned many a meal for this house.'

[113] TR interview with Captain E. Griffiths, Bull Bay, September 1971. The *Irish Minstrel* was 99.1 x 25.0 x 11.4, 154 tons, built by Connick at Dundalk in 1879.

[114] TR interviews with Captain Henry Roberts, Moelfre, January-August 1972.

[115] There are brief references to Captain Jabez Rowlands in the biography of Dr Helen Rowlands by G. Wynne Griffith, *Cofiant Cenhades, Miss Helen Rowlands* (Caernarfon, 1961).

[116] I am indebted to Mr I. Jones for allowing me to consult the papers of the *Ailsie*. The details of her crew are from the half-yearly crew agreement lists now at the ARO, Llangefni.

[117] ARO *Ailsie* Crew Agreement lists. Captain Hughes remained master throughout and the *Ailsie*'s crews were largely drawn from Caernarvonshire and Anglesey. In 1899, when she sailed for Harburg, apart from the master, who was aged sixty, they were all young local men: James Jones, aged 24, mate, William Cale, aged 21, A.B., both of Bangor, Griffith Jones, aged 20, of Port Dinorwic and Elias Jones, aged 21, of Amlwch, ordinary seaman. This Elias Jones, who also signed on for the next voyage as 'Cook and Seaman' was probably the Elias Jones, 'Lei Bach', who later served on the *John Lockett* with Captain Robert Jones.

[118] B. Greenhill, *The Merchant Schooners*, II, 74-75.

[119] BCR 3/1892. *The Mary B. Mitchell* is described in the Registers as 129.7 x 24.45 x 10.85, three-masted, schooner rigged, elliptical stern, clencher built, with a female bust as figurehead. Preston and Chadwick had 32/64 shares each in her; from 1892 Owen T. Jones, of Erw Fair, Bangor, is named as ship's husband and manager. She was transferred by bill of sale 5 April 1898 to Emilius Alexander Young of Tanybryn, Bangor, agent.

[120] The original log book and articles were lost when the vessel sank, but O. T. Jones recorded her crew list in duplicate, signed at Bangor in 1897. When she sank, her master was G. H. Preston, aged 33; his wages per calendar month were recorded as £8, those of the mate, Robert Jones, aged 24, were £4, the cook, W. Jones, aged 45, was paid at the rate of £3.15.0 per month, the two A.B.s, Thomas Parry and Robert Howells, both in their early twenties, £3, and the Ordinary Seamen, William Cale, aged 19 and John D. Jones, aged 18, were paid at the rate of £2.10.0 and £2.5.0 respectively. They were all saved and discharged at Texel where the vessel had been stranded.

[121] Among the vessels in which her crews had served from time to time were the *Eilian, Fomalhaut, Olive Branch,* S.S. *Pennant,* S.S. *Bangor,* S.S. *Vaynol, Ailsie, Fleetwing, Miss Morris, W. D. Potts, Elizabeth Llewelyn, British Queen.* Some of her crew members were to become well-known boatmen on the

north Wales coast in their later years. Trefor Davies of Llandudno, who signed on as a 'boy, first ship' at Bangor in October 1910 and remained a regular member of her crew for the next few years, was later coxswain of the Llandudno lifeboat and a very well-known boatman in his native town.

[122] I am indebted to Mr R. T. Pritchard for allowing me to include some of the photographs from his valuable collection relating to the history of Bangor, and for his interest in this present work.

[123] TR interview with Mr William Roberts, Llandegfan, July 1971. According to the crew agreement lists, he actually signed on for the first time on July 24, 1911.

War at Sea Again
1914–18

The heady idealism of the 'war to end wars' which swept through the land-bound communities of Britain in 1914 was far removed from the everyday life of Anglesey seamen, who found it an unwelcome complication in their already busy lives. Captain Henry Roberts of Moelfre, sailing out of Limerick, was much surprised when the *Earl of Lathom* was hailed by a destroyer at the mouth of the Shannon and ordered to the nearest port. He interpreted this in a liberal fashion – he made for Moelfre where he came to an anchor a couple of weeks after the outbreak of war. Others were not so fortunate: the crew of the steamer *Saxon*, commanded by Captain R. Humphreys, a Porth Amlwch man with at least six other Amlwch men aboard, were interned at Hamburg, and remained prisoners of war in Germany for four long years.[1] Young W. H. Michael, whose father was Chief Engineer aboard the *Saxon*, as the eldest of a family of four, felt it his duty to support the family, so he went to sea aboard the *Mary Miller*, a wooden schooner built in the same yard as the *Mary B. Mitchell*, by the very able Paul Rodgers and the fine shipwrights who lived in Unity Street, Carrickfergus. Michael graduated from the *Mary Miller* to the Fisher fleet and to the steam vessels carrying coal from the south-west ports to St Malo, and then to the Mediterranean. He was but one of many Anglesey boys who went to sea at an early age during the 1914-18 war. The coastal trade wanted men for both steam and sailing vessels, for freights were good and men were in short supply. There had not been a naval war to disturb the coastal trade for nearly a hundred years.

The pre-war naval planners in both Germany and Britain had envisaged war in terms of battles between big ships and fleets, and the British had for the most part thought little of the dangers of newer weapons such as mines and submarines.[2] Some six months before the outbreak of war, Lord Fisher, who had retired in 1909 from the office of First Sea Lord, but was still acting as Winston Churchill's unofficial adviser, prepared a memorandum of which there is a copy among the manuscripts of Lord Jellicoe. Fisher warned that Britain's traditional naval strategy was likely to be completely shattered by 'the advent of the long-range ocean-going submarine'; he argued that there was 'little to prevent the Germans from stationing submarines off our principal commercial ports and, indeed, on the great trade routes ... it is not invasion we have to fear but starvation.' One of Fisher's recommendations was that 'full consideration should be promptly given to the question of diverting our commerce to our far western ports in war-time, and of developing the port and railway facilities of such harbours as Plymouth, Falmouth, the Bristol Channel ports, Fishguard, Holyhead. There is no doubt that if commerce can be diverted in this way, the difficulties in the way of German infesting the close approaches to our commercial ports will be enormously increased.'[3] In the event, Holyhead did not become an alternative port in the Fisher sense, but in 1915 it did become a naval base, and the submarines which had so haunted Fisher did sink a large number of ships plying to and from Liverpool off the coast of Anglesey.

For the first months of the war, however, in 1914, the merchant ships lost were the victims of either surface vessels or mines. The Portmadoc vessel, the *Frau Minna Petersen*, was one of the first, captured by a torpedo boat and taken into Emden a few days after the outbreak of war,[4] the steamer *North Wales* captured and sunk by the *Dresden* in November, and at the end of December,[5] William Thomas, Liverpool, lost their steamer *Hemisphere*, captured and scuttled by the armed vessel *Kronprinz Willhelm* four hundred miles North-East by East from Pernambuco.[6] An Amlwch man, R. Gussey, was one of the crew of the *Colby*, also sunk by the *Kronprinz Willhelm*; after an unpleasant spell of captivity in the hold of the *Kronprinz Willhelm*, Gussey and his companions were put ashore at Newport News, Virginia.[7] But these were far-away events. It was a different matter one Saturday afternoon in late February 1915 when the bedraggled survivors from the three thousand ton steamer *Cambank* were brought ashore by the Bull Bay lifeboat at Amlwch. Two small boys gathering snowdrops remember it well; they heard a muffled explosion and ran to the cliffs to see the death of a ship. It was the first glimpse of war for the future Captain William Williams, and for Cecil Thomas, later to serve at sea aboard the ships of his father, William Thomas, the Amlwch ship-builder. Bound for Garston from Huelva with a cargo of Spanish ore, the *Cambank* had been torpedoed about four miles East North East of Point Lynas; she had just taken the pilot aboard off Amlwch and was proceeding at eight knots towards Mersey when the crew spotted a periscope at a distance that they afterwards estimated at two hundred yards.[8] Amlwch readers of the Welsh newspaper *Y Genedl Gymreig*, which reported the sinking of the *Cambank* with the loss of four of her crew, must have found it somewhat ironic that on another page of the same edition Winston Churchill was reported to have told the Commons that every German ship had been swept from the sea by the British Navy, which remained ruler of the waves. Significantly he did not refer to beneath the waves. A fortnight earlier the same newspaper had reported the sinking, some eighteen miles from the Liverpool Bar Light-Vessel, by the *U-21* of the *Linda Blanche*, Lord Penrhyn's new steamer, just six months old.[9] She was bound for Belfast with a general cargo when the U-boat surfaced, gave the crew ten minutes to get into the boats, and then sank the *Linda Blanche*. This was the earlier, 'gentlemanly' phase of the war; the Germans, according to the local press, gave cigars to the *Linda Blanche*'s crew, and treated them in a very kindly fashion. Captain Ellis, a Bangor man, who was master of the *Linda Blanche*, later reported that the U-boat commander had apologised profusely and expressed his great regret at having to sink such a new vessel.

This somewhat unreal chivalry could not last long, for by their very nature submarines were best suited to sinking enemy vessels on sight, without warning, and in May 1915 the sinking of the *Lusitania*, with the loss of nearly twelve hundred lives, aroused outraged indignation, not least in the United States. Some miles from the position where the *Lusitania* was torpedoed, two days previously, the *Earl of Lathom*, which Captain Henry Roberts of Moelfre had just left, was captured and sunk by the gunfire of a German U-boat.[10] The pressure was beginning to tell; Captains Wynn and Robert Jones of Amlwch recalled that the mate of the vessel in which they had sailed as fifteen-year-old boys from Garston to New Ross about this time deserted in Ireland as he had heard that the U-boats were active off the Tuskar Rock, and they well remembered how the master, a fine-looking red-bearded old man (not so old, but he appeared so to them), had brought his ship back to Garston with just young Wynn and Jones, allowing them a 'trick' at the helm, but doing most of the work aloft himself as he was unwilling to put his young crew at risk.[11] The adverse effect on neutral opinion of the sinking of the *Lusitania* influenced the Germans to halt their activities, and schooners like the *Camborne* and the *Donald and Doris*, in which Wynn and Jones served, were allowed to proceed in comparative peace in the Irish Sea and Liverpool Bay in 1915 and 1916.

In more distant waters, however, there were actions which cast a gloom over the people of Anglesey in 1915. The Holyhead passenger steamer *Hibernia* had been requisitioned by the Admiralty in 1914, and, renamed H.M.S. *Tara*, had served on patrol duties in the North Channel, based on Larne and Campbelltown, until 1915 when she was sent to the Mediterranean.[12] A few minutes after ten o'clock on the fine sunny morning of 5th November 1915, H.M.S. *Tara* was approaching the port of Sollum, some three hundred and fifty miles west of Alexandria, when her look-out spotted a torpedo approaching on the starboard bow. The officer of the watch immediately gave the order to put the helm to hard aport, but the *Tara* was hit amidships, her engineroom destroyed, and within minutes she had sunk stern first. The *U-35*, the German submarine which had fired the torpedo, surfaced, and the survivors, some towed in the *Tara*'s boats, others huddled on the wet, slippery deck of the *U-35*, were taken to Port Sulieman (afterward Bardia) and handed over as prisoners to the Turkish authorities ashore. The *Tara*'s paymaster, Sub-Lieutenant Alfred Dutton, R.N.V.R., kept a pencilled diary of the subsequent events, and it is from this diary, and that kept by Captain Gwatkin Williams, R.N., appointed to the command of the *Tara* at the outbreak of the war, that the story has been reconstructed.[13] Dutton noted that ninety-three out of the ship's company of one hundred and four were handed over to the Turks, and both diaries record the death of W. Jackson, the ship's cook, on their first day ashore, the Captain 'saying as much of the burial service as we could remember, and marking his grave with a cairn of stones and two broken oars to form a cross.'[14]

This was the first of one hundred and thirty-five days of captivity for a crew, most of whom came from Anglesey, men of all ages who two years previously had been plying peacefully between Dublin and Holyhead but now suddenly found themselves 'absolutely cold and practically naked,' taking what shelter they could from two tattered tents, in the hands of a group of fierce-looking Senussi tribesmen commanded by a Turkish officer, Nouri Pasha. Their food ration for their first day in captivity was one biscuit and a piece of roast goat; on the second day Dutton noted that they moved camp further east, and 'had one biscuit and water, and a little boiled rice.'[15] The next day they marched through mountainous country along five miles of rocky roads, 'most of the crew with bare feet,' carrying William Thomas, quartermaster, who had a shattered leg, on an improvised stretcher made from a boat's sail and oars. That night they slept, the luckier ones, in the shelter of two small caves and the ruins of what Captain Williams believed to be 'an ancient Roman farm.' The less fortunate suffered the intense cold of the night in the open, but in the morning some Arab clothing, some Turkish shoes and Arab blankets arrived for about half the men, and for the next few days they remained in the shelter of the caves.[16] By the Saturday of their first week in captivity, William Thomas's condition had so deteriorated that his foot had to be amputated 'with a pair of scissors without anaesthetics,' and at 11.30 p.m. he died, 'brave and patient to the last.'[17] He was buried at 8.30 the next morning, and Dutton noted in his diary, 'very touching service was held by Captain Tanner, nearly everyone crying, most pathetic scene.'[18] Clad in tattered Arab clothing, seamen out of their element ashore, they sang in Welsh and English as darkness fell upon a desert full of strange noises; Dutton noted, 'Hymns sung in evening by whole crew. Everyone feeling very lonely and quiet.'

The next weeks were spent marching, sometimes up to ten hours on only a drink of water, and sleeping in the open desert; Thomas Owen, coal trimmer, was reported missing, having escaped on the sixteenth day of their captivity, and on the next day Dutton himself fainted on the march and was put on the back of a camel for some hours.[19] Day after day they marched until, on 26 November, they reached two old Roman walls which were to serve as their prison encampment. Here they remained; Dutton notes the monotony of the diet, boiled rice and water, with, very occasionally, roast goat, but also it becomes apparent that as the days went by they became acclimatised to their lot, they found sleep easier, and 'sheer hunger made us eat drowned camel.' Apparently a four-month-old camel had fallen down a well and 'Captain Williams was lowered down and tied it up. Was cut up by W. Rowlands (QM.) and shared amongst us.' In December the thick fog which they encountered made their life even more difficult, but Dutton found opportunities to discover a new talent for cooking: 'Having had a little more Flour issued to us in lieu of shortness of rice, I managed to knead some flour and boiled rice together and wrapped some in the leg of a Mahomad trousers, boiled it in a bucket. This proved a great success.' Not everyone shared these delicacies; the next day, Dutton recorded, 'Thos. Owen, Coal Trimmer, was brought back to camp by 2 Arabs after an absence of 1 month exactly.'

By Christmas the conditions of living were somewhat improved, for they had built stone walls which gave them some shelter, and Dutton noted in his diary that on Christmas morning 'Mr Richardson got up at 3 a.m. to boil our Xmas pudding which we enjoyed fine for dinner. 11/45 soup made of goat bones, little rice . . . very enjoyable under circumstances.' They had carefully put aside some food for the day: 'at 3.30 p.m. we all gathered round for our wack of duff which we had been anxiously waiting for all day, and a glass or two of Green tea, which had been saved for some days.' The day ended with the captives singing carols around the fire to the accompaniment of much wailing from distracted Arab women who had just heard of the death of relatives at a battle at 'Marsa Matruha, Egypt, fighting going on there.'[20] Whether it was the result of eating the carefully husbanded food on Christmas Day or not, there followed a period of considerable ill-health throughout the camp; Dutton himself was too ill to write anything except to note the days of the week and to write cryptically against four days that he felt 'absolutely rotten and bad with no medicine at all in the camp.' His throat was very sore, but by the second week in January he was well enough to record sadly the death and burial of John Hodgson, seaman. Dutton himself had been too ill to record the death five days previously of George M. Cox boilermaker, but Captain Williams noted that Cox had been buried to the south of the camp, and added, 'at all of our funerals as much of the Burial Service as can be remembered is repeated, and the hymns 'Abide with me' and 'A day's march nearer home' sung. The ship's company being mostly Welsh, this is then followed by Welsh hymns and prayers in that language. No one is any longer ashamed of their tears, which flow freely.'[21] The heavy rain, cold nights, and scanty diet, which was now virtually confined to rice and a little salt, was taking its toll, and they had to walk further each day to collect firewood to keep themselves warm. On the seventy-fourth day of their captivity they received a tablet of 'Green made soap' and a few days later their hopes were raised by a rumour that the Senussi might make a separate peace with England, so ensuring their early release. But nothing came of this, the rains continued, their rations were reduced still more, and Dutton noted in his diary on 26 January: 'Chief Engineer was very bad, removed to a corner billet.' Two days later, Engineer Lieutenant Robert Williams, the Chief Engineer, died of dysentery, and Captain Williams noted in his own diary: 'Nothing could exceed the devotion with which he had been attended by Mr Hughes and Mr Davies, who never left him, day or night, and washed, tended and carried him.' Dutton's diary has a little sketch indicating the graves of Hodgson, Cox, and Williams, and notes quite simply: 'Chief Engineer Williams was buried alongside Cox and Hodgson.' Death had become familiar.

Captain Williams made a strong plea at the end of January to the commandant of the camp for increased rations for his men, but to no avail, and his letters to the Turkish, Senussi and British authorities brought no response. Both diaries reflect the increasing doubts regarding any release and the monotony of the meagre diet, but their resolve to survive despite everything remained, and Dutton wrote on the one hundred and first day of their captivity: 'nothing exciting, meals just same, practically starving; I think it is Sunday, having such meals makes one more determined than ever.' Snails were gathered and made into soup, but Dutton admitted towards the end of the same week: 'we are in a terrible state of hunger, also cold and miserable.' On the 19th February, Owen H. Roberts (fireman) died of dysentery, accentuated by lack of food, and was buried the same day. The next day, Dutton notes (in shorthand, lest it should be seen by his captors) the departure of Captain Williams, and two days later he wrote: 'Captain Williams was missed . . . terrible scenes in camp. We complained he must have gone astray through insufficient feeding.' Captain Williams's escape was, in fact, carefully planned; he had been given food from his fellow-prisoners' meagre rations, and wore his tattered naval uniform under his Arab clothes in case he needed to identify himself in an emergency. His hopes of reaching Sollum and the British lines were doomed, however, for within two days he was captured by Bedouin tribesmen who eventually handed him over to the Turks, and ten days later he was back in captivity with the crew of the *Tara*.[22]

Despite repeated promises of increased rations, the food situation worsened, and on Monday, 13 March 1916, Dutton wrote in his diary: 'We are on our last legs and feeling that weak that it is hardly possible to walk.' Four days later he noted: 'myself I don't feel like walking four yards but struggle on. Managed to gather some wood and green vegetables and garlic. Feeling done up, must go for a good sleep. All officers and men are breaking down, some fainting in heat.'[23] This was to be the last entry in his faint, indelible pencil. On that day, St Patrick's Day, 1917, the British prisoners could not believe their eyes when they saw some khaki-coloured motor cars driving up to their camp. It was an armoured car force commanded by the Duke of Westminster who had apparently heard of the fate of the crew of the *Tara* from one of Captain Williams's letters which had accidentally been discovered in an Arab house. Within ten hours they were all safely encamped at an outpost of the Australian Camel Corps; the next day they arrived at Sollum whence they were put aboard a hospital ship for Alexandria.[24] In the desert, the bodies of their Arab guards lay some distance from the piles of stones which marked the grave of the four members of the crew of the Tara who had died at El Hakkim, their prison camp.

Although his diary thus ends abruptly on 17 March, the day of their rescue, Paymaster Dutton's battered briefcase contains much detail regarding their subsequent movements; the long-awaited telegrams to relatives indicating their safety, the travelling arrangements for the crew back to Holyhead, the returned letters to relatives with the ominous stamp 'Ship Lost', and a careful list of those members of the crew who had pay due to them.[25] A glance through this list is sufficient to indicate how many of them had home addresses in Holyhead; out of the 75 names in Dutton's list, 59 were from Holyhead, one came from nearby Valley, one from Cemais, another from Llanfair P.G., one from Caergeiliog, one from Bangor, two from Campbelltown, four from Ireland, and five from England (although one of these, Dutton himself, who gave his home address as Chester, was associated with Holyhead for the remainder of his life). Other letters and cuttings refer to a visit which over sixty of the survivors made to the Chester home of the Duke of Westminster on 16 August 1919, when a presentation silver casket was given to him on behalf of the *Tara*'s crew. The gracious Saighton Grange, where they were received by the Duke and his daughter, Lady Mary Grosvenor, the grounds of Eaton Park and the motor launch trip on the River Dee must have seemed to the men of Holyhead a very far cry from the days when they had wandered, dressed like Biblical characters, in the Libyan desert.

The *Tara* was not the only casualty among the Holyhead ferry ships: eight days after her sinking, her sister ship, the *Anglia*, which had been converted into a hospital ship transporting the wounded across the English Channel, struck a mine about a mile off Folkestone.[26] Within minutes the *Anglia* sank, but most of the wounded soldiers and nursing staff aboard were saved, and thirty-one of the fifty-six crew, most of whom came from Holyhead.[27] A further loss to the London and North Western Railway Company's fleet followed in 1916 when the *Connemara*, a twin-screw steamer on the Greenore-Holyhead service, collided in a gale in Carlingford Lough with a collier, the *Retriever*, on 3 November.[28] Only one survived out of the ninety-four people aboard the two vessels that dark and very stormy night; at least twenty-five of those who perished had their homes in Holyhead.[29] Three month later, the City of Dublin Steam Packet Company's *Connaught* was torpedoed in the English Channel, and a month before the end of the war this company's *Leinster* was torpedoed seven miles east-south-east of the Kish Light vessel when bound for Holyhead, with very heavy loss of life, including twenty-four crew members who came from Holyhead.[30]

The sinking of the *Leinster* was but one incident out of many during the closing stages of the war, but in the earlier years there was something of a lull after the sinking of the *Lusitania*. The naval base at Holyhead, which had been established in 1915, had responsibility for an area extending from the Mull of Galloway to Bardsey on the west, and from Secker Point to the Great Orme's Head on the east, and through this area may hundreds of vessels sailed each year. Among them were some of the merchant schooners mentioned in previous chapters. The *Mary B. Mitchell* continued to carry slate cargoes to London in 1915 and 1916, returning with cement for Bangor or Douglas, and the occasional cargo of china clay for Garston or whiting for Lancaster.[31] She was thus engaged in trade which took her through the Irish Sea and the English Channel where there were dangers from both U-boats and mines; more important, as far as the Admiralty was concerned, she was considered to be suitable for conversion into a decoy ship, the first sailing ship to be used for this purpose in the English Channel and the Western Approaches.[32]

The *Mary B. Mitchell* had sailed on 7 April 1916 from Liverpool with a cargo of oilcake nuts for Plymouth and was due to embark a cargo of china clay for the return voyage, both at the highly profitable freight rates being paid owing to war-time risks.[33] In order to maintain absolute secrecy, her own crew were paid off on the pretext that it was necessary to carry out extensive repairs as a result of damage sustained on the passage from Liverpool, and a specially trained crew were put aboard under the command of Lieutenant M, Armstrong, R.N.R. She was now armed with three guns, one 12 pounder and two 6 pounders, all concealed, the former in a collapsible structure on the poop, the others under two hatches, mounted on swinging pedestals. Carefully camouflaged, the *Mary B. Mitchell* (or the *Mary Y. Jose* of Vigo, or the *Jeanette* of La Houle, or the *Neptun* of Riga, as she was now called as circumstances demanded) cruised in the Western Approaches and the Bay of Biscay in all weathers, avoiding putting into harbour or running for shelter lest her identity should be revealed.[34] On 20 June and 3 August 1917 she engaged enemy submarines to such good effect that they were severely damaged, possibly sunk: one of her officers, Lieutenant T. Hughes, R.N.R., who was awarded the D.S.C. and bar for service in her, was a native of Pwllheli and married to the daughter of a Llangefni hotelier. He later reported how in case, soon after they had been attacked, they had sent off some of the crew of the *Mary B.* in a boat, the 'panic party' pretending that the ship had been completely abandoned, and, when the U-boat surfaced and came within range to inspect the schooner, the crew remaining hidden aboard had opened fire with their cleverly concealed guns, hitting the U-boat at close range.[35] The *Mary B. Mitchell* remained in

Admiralty service until September 1919, Lord Penrhyn receiving £60 per month for her hire on time-charter.[36]

The successful conversion of the *Mary B. Mitchell* encouraged the Admiralty to requisition more sailing ships as decoy or Q-ships for they had certain advantages: they could remain at sea for much longer periods than the steam tramps or trawlers, their roomy decks were suitable for the erection of dummy deckhouses to conceal their guns, and it was hoped that, as they rarely used engines, they might silently come across a U-boat on the surface charging her batteries during the hours of darkness. In November 1916 the Amlwch Thomas's vessel *Gaelic* was requisitioned, armed with two 12 pounder guns and the usual additional Lewis guns and small arms. In April 1917, under the command of Lieutenant G. Irvine, R.N.R., she was off the Old Head of Kinsale on a quiet Sunday evening when she was attacked by a U-boat which shelled her and killed two of her crew. When the submarine came within range, the *Gaelic* returned the fire, inflicting such damage that the U-boat submerged again and broke off the action. After a number of similar engagements, the *Gaelic* was refitted and sent to the Mediterranean,[37] whilst her sister ship, the *Cymric*, was converted into a Q-ship early in 1918, and even more heavily armed. The *Cymric* fulfilled a double role, carrying cargoes of coal to Cherbourg and at the same time hoping to engage enemy submarines which might be tempted to attack her.[38] The most famous of the Q-ship commanders was Gordon Campbell, a young Lieutenant Commander R.N., whose tramp steamer *Farnborough* sank the *U-68* in March 1916. Campbell followed this with a number of actions in different vessels which earned for him the Victoria Cross, the D.S.O. and two bars, and promotion to the rank of Captain. Once the enemy had realised the dangers of the Q-boats they naturally became much more wary, and Campbell deliberately allowed his vessels to be torpedoed and shelled, remaining on board with his hidden gunners until the U-boat, having seen the crew abandoning the ship, came within close range.[39] One of the crew who served with him in all his actions was William Williams, an Amlwch seaman, who had grown up in sight of the schooners which came from William Thomas and Paynter's yards. As a boy he had spent many hours watching vessels being made ready for sea, and both he and his brother John went to sea as soon as they were old enough. Whilst John went to the elderly *Gauntlet*, William went to the *Meyric*, and when war broke out joined the Royal Navy.

On 17 February 1917 the *Farnborough* was torpedoed off the south-west coast of Ireland. Campbell had made no attempt to avoid the torpedo, which had been fired at long range, and the 'panic party' of two lifeboats and a dinghy with 'all' the crew rowed away from the ship. For nearly half an hour those left aboard lay hidden, not daring to move, as the U-boat circled around the striken vessel, which was slowly sinking by the stern. When the *U-83* was almost alongside, Campbell gave the order to fire, the *Farnborough*'s wheelhouse, her hen coops, and other deck fittings all collapsed, revealing the 12 pounder guns and other armament, which so shattered the U-boat at point blank range that she sank with her conning-tower open within minutes.[40] Seamen William Williams was one of the guns' crews, and along with several others he was awarded the D.S.M. A few months later he was one of the crew of the *Pargust*, disguised as a merchant vessel with a dummy gun aft, when she was torpedoed at close range. Again the 'panic party' abandoned ship and, when the submarine surfaced, the lifeboat pulled towards the starboard side of the *Pargust* so that her disguised 4-inch gun could be brought into action. Slowly the U-boat followed the lifeboat until she herself was only about fifty yards away from the supposedly stricken ship, and it was then, and only then, thirty-six minutes after she had been torpedoed, that Campbell gave the order to fire. The *U.C. 29* sank four minutes later.[41] Campbell, in his account of these actions, pointed out that any false move by any one man under the considerable tension would have destroyed the element of surprise, and it was this quality of courage, remaining completely still and passive until the appropriate moment, that was essential. But there was also on this occasion a positive act which saved the day. Campbell's own description indicates what happened: 'When the explosion of the torpedo took place, the releasing weight of the starboard gun-ports was freed by the force of the explosion, and but for the great presence of mind of Williams in taking the whole weight on the port on himself and so preventing it falling down and prematurely exposing the gun, the action might never have taken place.'[42] When it was announced that the Victoria Cross was to be awarded to one officer and one rating from the *Pargust*, a ballot was arranged, and Lieutenant Stuart, D.S.O., the first lieutenant, and Seaman William Williams, D.S.M., were awarded the Victoria Cross.[43]

This was not the end of the story of Campbell or Williams. On the morning of 8 August 1917, off the coast of Brittany, the *Dunraven*, a 3,000-ton Cardiff vessel, was attacked by a U-boat. As the submarine commanders were now well aware of decoy ship tactics, Campbell this time pretended to try to escape, returning the fire of the U-boat with the 2½ pounder gun which, as an ordinary merchant vessel, the *Dunraven* might have been expected to carry. The gun's crew were ordered to fire short so that the U-boat would be encouraged to come closer; Campbell's men acted their part with some flair: 'They also had frequent misfires and delays – in fact, their firing was . . . a prefect disgrace to any naval gunner. As a matter of fact, the crew consisted of three very fine men – Leading Seaman Cooper, Seaman Williams, V.C., and Wireless Operator Statham. They had a difficult job and were fully exposed to the enemy shell-fire, without any cover, and not only did they carry out their job to perfection, but appeared to enjoy the humour of it.'[44] Eventually, Campbell ordered his 'panic party' to abandon ship, but the U-boat continued to shell the *Dunraven*. Campbell and the remaining crew had to lie motionless, knowing that the ship was on fire and that each second this fire was spreading closer and closer to the magazine directly under the hidden 4 inch gun and its crew. The inevitable explosion aboard, which blew the gun and its crew into the air, warned the U-boat commander so that he quickly submerged, correctly guessing that the *Dunraven* was not the comparatively harmless merchant ship she appeared to be, and a little later a torpedo hit the *Dunraven* abaft the engine room. Again some of the crew left the *Dunraven* on rafts, a second 'panic party', and again the U-boat surfaced and shelled the vessel, which must now have appeared to have been completely abandoned. But there were, in fact, still some hidden members aboard, who suffered further shelling until Campbell, unable to use his guns, attempted to torpedo the U-boat. Although this failed and the U-boat finally left the scene, this action, which had taken several hours, was generally regarded as one of the most courageous of the war; the American Admiral Sims who was working with Admiral Lewis Bayly at Queenstown summed up his feelings in a letter to

Campbell: 'I know nothing finer in naval history than the conduct of the aft gun crew or, indeed, of the entire crew, of the *Dunraven*.'[45] Two further Victoria Crosses were awarded, and Seaman William Williams, V.C., received another bar to his D.S.M. and the Médaille Militaire. Little wonder, then, that Williams received a hero's welcome on his return to his native Amlwch; known affectionately as 'Wil V.C.' in Holyhead, where he lived in later years, William Williams brought distinction to, and typified, a generation of Anglesey seamen who had learned their seamanship the hard way.

Despite their successes, the Q-ships were only touching the fringes of a vast problem, particularly since the German High Command had decided to introduce unrestricted submarine warfare from 1 February 1917. Henceforth, all shipping proceeding to and from British ports were to be sunk at sight without warning, a logical enough step to take. Anglesey people had become accustomed to news of appalling losses in the land campaigns and also to the gloomy tidings regarding the loss of ships in far-off seas, but the unrestricted submarine warfare from February 1917 brought evidence of violence to their very beaches. Six vessels were sunk in the vicinity of Bardsey Island in five days in the second week of February; the crew of the steamer *Sellagh* (325 tons) reported that they had been attacked off Bardsey by gunfire from a German submarine, killing the Chief Engineer and wounding others of the crew, who had taken to the boats; the *Sellagh* was then blown up by bombs placed aboard by the Germans. The *Sellagh*'s survivors were picked up and landed at Holyhead by the steamer *Greenland* (1,763 tons), but thirteen of the *Greenland*'s crew were back in Holyhead four days later after their vessel was blown up south-west of Bardsey; the German U-boat had a good haul, for the *Ferga* (791 tons), *Margarita* (375 tons), *Olivia* (242 tons), and the *Kyanite* (564 tons) were also captured and sunk during the week, all in the same area. Mr Murch, the Shipwrecked Mariners Society Agent, and Mr Seal, Superintendent of the Stanley Sailors' Home at Holyhead, had a busy time, for the survivors of *Sellagh*, *Ferga* and *Greenland* were landed in the port and fed and clothed before being sent home by rail. Survivors of actions in more distant waters were also now arriving at Holyhead: in March, the survivors of the steamers *Trevose* and *Alnwick Castle*, sunk some three hundred miles west of the

Scillies, landed in Holyhead and told tales of other sinkings they had themselves witnessed. The war at sea was getting very near. In four days towards the end of March, eight vessels were sunk, five of them east of the Arklow Light Vessel, which was itself boarded and destroyed by the crew of a German U-boat on 28 March, whilst the *Fairearn* (592 tons) was sunk sixteen miles W.N.W. of South Stack, and the *Snowdon Ranger* (4,662 tons) torpedoed without warning twenty-five miles west of Bardsey. The survivors of the *Snowdon Ranger* reported that four men had been killed when the torpedo struck, and that 'the enemy carried off all the provisions they could get hold of and finally sank her with bombs. After being in their boat about 9 or 10 hours they were picked up by the S.S. *Somerset Court* off the South Stack and landed in Holyhead.' The *Snowdon Ranger* had been bound from Philadelphia to Liverpool; Mr Seal, Superintendent of the Stanley Sailors' Home, added in his report, 'I have since heard that of 6 Big Vessels which left Queenstown about the same time, only 2 got through and are now lying in the Roads.' Further gruesome stories were told to Mr Seal a couple of days later when thirteen survivors of the crew of over a hundred men of S.S. *Crispin*, bound from Newport News, Virginia, for Avonmouth with a cargo which included seven hundred horses, landed at Holyhead after thirteen hours 'in an open boat in a nasty sea.'[46]

Over two hundred British merchant ships were sunk in February and March, and early in April Admiral Jellicoe gloomily admitted to the American Admiral Sims that he could not see a solution to the problem.[47] In April one ship out of every four that left a British port never returned; during the month nearly a million tons of shipping were sunk, two-thirds of the total being British.[48] There were many large steamers among them, but also several sailing vessels like the *Miss Morris*, the Portmadoc schooner built by David Jones in 1896 and sunk by *U-35* twenty miles off the Spanish coast on 11 April 1917. In the same month, the *Ellen James*, another Portmadoc schooner, was sunk by a submarine in the Bay of Biscay while on passage with a cargo of copper ore from Huelva, with the loss of all hands. A month earlier the *Elizabeth Eleanor*, built by David Williams at Portmadoc in 1905, had been sunk in the Bristol Channel.[49] Lloyd George who had spent his early years in a solicitor's office in Portmadoc when that port was the home of many fine merchant schooners, had a lively appreciation of the agony of British merchant seamen; as Prime Minister he realised that the U-boats were winning the war for Germany.

There are conflicting opinions regarding the belated introduction of the convoy system in May 1917; the view of Jellicoe and the Admiralty was that they gradually came to their own decision to introduce convoys, and Rear-Admiral Duff had produced a paper to that effect on April 27th; Lloyd George himself, Churchill, Beaverbrook, younger naval officers like Captain (afterwards Sir) Herbert Richmond, Commanders Henderson and Kenworthy, who had been introduced to Lloyd George by Sir Herbert Lewis, were in no doubt that it was Lloyd George's pressure, culminating in his visit to the Admiralty on April 30th, that finally decided the issue.[50] A. J. P. Taylor states roundly: 'Convoys were due to Lloyd George alone, his most decisive achievement of the war.'[51] It is likely that the combination of the large losses in shipping, and the pressure group of young naval officers whom Lloyd George had consulted, influenced Jellicoe and his senior colleagues, despite their many hesitations regarding the ability of merchant ships to keep station.[52] Lloyd George, certainly in retrospect, had little sympathy with this attitude, for he recognised the ability of merchant seamen of the type he must have known well in Portmadoc: 'The seamanship of experienced mariners, who steered the tramp through all weathers across the wild and foggy seas that surround and lead to these islands was completely underestimated.'[53] And, of course, he was right; the merchant ships in convoy did keep station, and the convoys dramatically reduced the shipping losses. It is curious that they should have been introduced so late; the seamen of Blake's navy in the seventeenth-century had recognised the need for convoys to protect trade from pirates more rapidly than the Admiralty had in their war against the U-boats nearly three hundred years later.

Paradoxically enough, although the introduction of ocean convoys reduced shipping losses in the Atlantic and the Western Approaches by 90% in the second six months of 1917, the effects upon the inshore routes were very different. The U-boats, compelled to look for alternative targets because of the difficulties of attacking the ocean convoys, turned their attention to the inshore routes, where vessels for the most part still continued to sail independently along patrolled lanes.[54] This, therefore, had repercussions in the seas off Anglesey, for U-boats which had hitherto been more active further afield now operated with such effect in the sea lanes leading to and from Liverpool and in the Irish Sea that many vessels were sunk off Anglesey during the last eighteen months of the war. Among them were the *Eskmere*, 2,293 tons, sunk 15 miles W.N.W. of South Stack in September 1917, the *Apapa*, 7,832 tons, three miles N. by E. from Point Lynas, with a loss of seventy-seven lives in November, and a few days later, the *Earl of Elgin*, 4,448 tons, ten miles W. of the Caernarvon Bay Light Vessel, and a number of smaller sailing vessels. Sixty-four survivors of the *Apapa* were landed at Holyhead, some of the injured being taken on stretchers to the Stanley Hospital; the *Apapa* had been homeward bound from Lagos for Liverpool when she was torpedoed a little after four o'clock in the morning off Point Lynas. The Stanley Sailors' Home log-book somewhat curiously singles out for mention among those on board the 'son of the Station Master at Henley, who took charge of a child in one of the ship's boats who had had her arm blown away by the explosion.' Two days after the *Apapa* sinking, the *Derbent*, an oil tanker, bound from Liverpool to Queenstown, was sunk off Point Lynas, again in the early hours of the morning. There were more British losses in December, among them nine vessels sunk off Anglesey; the survivors of the *Abgeri* (4,821 tons), who were landed at Holyhead, included a number of naval personnel, who told the Superintendent at the Stanley Sailors' Home that the ship, bound from Dacca to Liverpool, had been sailing in convoy when she had been torpedoed on Christmas Day off Bardsey. They had been rescued by the escorting vessels, one of which, *P.56*, 'which, I believe, they call a Decoy Ship, destroyed the submarine and crew, none of whom were saved.'[55] In the first three months of 1918 a further twenty vessels were sunk off Anglesey.

To meet this alarming situation, steps were taken to strengthen the naval base at Holyhead. Lieutenant-Commander R. de Saumarez, R.N., was appointed with special responsibility for the reorganisation of the trawlers and drifters into a more effective anti-submarine force in March 1918, and in the same month the Irish Sea Hunting Flotilla, under the command of Captain Gordon Campbell, V.C., D.S.O., in H.M.S. *Patrol*, arrived at Holyhead.[56] Campbell's flotilla consisted of six destroyers and sixteen motor launches, which were later augmented by a number of American Navy motor launches. Saumarez's yachts, trawlers and drifters spent five days at sea and two in harbour, whilst 'the Hunting Flotilla, with smaller coal and fuel capacity, did 48 hours out and 48 hours in harbour'; the vessels attached to the Holyhead base remained for the most part within a limited patrol area, whilst the Hunting Flotilla ranged more widely in the Irish Sea. After the sinking of the *Dunraven*, Campbell had been told by Admiral Lewis Bayly that he had to leave the decoy ships and take command of all anti-submarine operations in the Irish Sea, and it was in this role, and as Bayly's Flag Captain, that he steamed into Holyhead in March 1918.

It was not before time. In the previous month the *Mexico City*, 5,078 tons, had been sunk fifteen miles W. by S. of South Stack, her survivors being landed at Holyhead by the *Leinster*, two weeks later two oil tankers, the *British Viscount* (3,287 tons), bound from Liverpool for Queenstown, and the *Birchleaf*, from Devonport for Liverpool, were sunk, the former twelve miles N. by W. from the Skerries, the latter off South Stack. According to the survivors of the *Birchleaf*, she had been torpedoed aft, and the U-boat had surfaced to sink her by gun-fire, taking the master, 'who was a native of Beaumaris, a prisoner on board' the submarine.[57] It was claimed by the survivors that the U-boat may have been later sunk by one of the Holyhead flotilla, *P.42*. What became of the Beaumaris master mariner? The first week in March brought more bad news to the watchers ashore in Anglesey; the yacht *Vanessa* landed the survivors of the *Penvearne* (3,710 tons), torpedoed and sunk fifteen miles off South Stack with a loss of twenty-two men, and on the same day the *Carmelite* (2,583 tons) and the *Kenmarc* (1,330 tons) were torpedoed, the one in a position given as twenty miles S.W. by W. of the Calf of Man, and the other twenty-five miles N.W. of the Skerries. Twenty-nine men, including the master, were lost in the *Kenmarc*. Two days later there was only one survivor of the crew of thirty-five of the *Romeo*, torpedoed in the same area; towards the end of the week a U-boat was operating further south, and the *Tarbetness* (3,018 tons) and the sailing vessel *Erica*, whose survivors landed in their own boat on the Anglesey coast, were both torpedoed nearer Bardsey. A few days later the Spanish vessel, *Arno Merndi*, outward bound from Ayr, was torpedoed just before midnight, and local reporters claimed to have seen the U-boat a quarter of a mile off South Stack; nine of the twenty-five crew of the Spanish vessel got ashore on life-rafts. The *Cressida* (157 tons), bound for Dublin with coal, was torpedoed a few hours later, in the early morning, sixteen miles off the Skerries, and on the same day the *Sea Gull* (976 tons) was sunk seven miles N.E. from Point Lynas with the loss of twenty men including the master. To add to the melancholy of Anglesey people came the news of the end of the well-known Amlwch schooner, *Jane Gray*, captured and sunk by gunfire by a U-boat about 14 miles N.W. by W. from the Smalls, off the Pembrokeshire coast. The *Anteros* (4,241 tons) was torpedoed and sank sixteen miles W. by N. from South Stack in the third week in March, and at the end of the month, survivors of the cargo steamer *Conago*, a German prize taken at Melbourne in the early days of the war, landed at Holyhead. Among the yachts attached to the naval base at Holyhead was the *Vanessa II*, commanded by Lord Newborough, who had obtained his master mariner's ticket after years of service as a young man in sail and steam in the Far East. When Lord Newborough and one of his crew boarded the *Conago*, which had remained afloat after the torpedoing, all they found were dead bodies on the deck, a live South African ram and the ship's cat, which they took back to *Vanessa II*.[58] The attempt to tow the *Conago* failed when she was again torpedoed and sank off Holyhead.

Despite the presence of Campbell's flotilla and de Saumarez's reorganisation, April was not much better; at least nine vessels were sunk with a considerable loss of life, all of them in an area well S. of the Calf of Man, W. of South Stack and N.W. of Bardsey. All these vessels were torpedoed, it was unusual for the U-boats to surface since the days of the Q-ships, but torpedoes were an expensive way of sinking small ships, and it was with gunfire from a surfaced U-boat that the *Kempock* was attacked towards the end of the month. She was further N. than the other vessels, and, as she steamed from Belfast for Garston, probably a very tempting target for the commander of a new U-boat just arrived in the area, for the *Kempock* was only a small vessel of 255 tons. Commanded by Captain John Roberts of Moelfre, she had just left Belfast, where she had had a gun mounted, when she encountered the U-boat, some six and a half

miles S.E. by S. of the Copeland Island Light Vessel, at the entrance
to Belfast Lough. For two hours the *Kempock* returned the U-boat's
fire, but, eventually, heavily outgunned, Captain Roberts had to
order his men to abandon ship, and they landed in their own boat at
the little port of Donaghadee, where a sad and a very weary Captain
Roberts reported the loss of his ship to the naval authorities. This
was not the end of the story, however, for shortly afterwards the U-
boat itself was sunk when she met a naval patrol vessel: the U-boat
commander was rescued and stated that they had suffered so much
damage in their encounter with the *Kempock* that they would not
offer any resistance. As a result of the U-boat commander's evidence.
Captain Roberts was awarded the Distinguished Service Cross, and
he and his crew received the usual monetary reward and high praise
for their courage and skill in destroying a new U-boat.[59]

The summer months of 1918 saw a considerable decrease in the
number of vessels torpedoed, although there were still instances of
isolated sinkings; in May, eleven fishing smacks were captured and
sunk by U-boat actions some twenty miles off the Calf of Man.[60]
Nearer home, Holyhead people heard gunfire close inshore on the
evening of 5 May. The schooner *Pandora*, owned and registered at
Fraserburgh, was bound for Garston from Dublin with a
miscellaneous cargo including pit props when she was attacked off
South Stack; five of the crew later told their story at the Stanley
Sailors' Home to Mr Seal, the Superintendent. Their attacker was 'a
big submarine mounting 2 guns,' which had fired at the schooner,
but although her crew had abandoned ship, the *Pandora* was later
towed in to Holyhead by one of the trawlers of the patrol flotilla,
which had found her hull sound enough, although her masts and
rigging had been much damaged. Seal and the crew of the *Pandora*
were surprised that she had not been sunk, and Seal concluded his
report: 'the fact that her hull was practically untouched doesn't say
very much for their shooting. This occurred very close, for the sound
of guns could be heard all over Holyhead and for my own part I really
thought that a submarine had attacked a convoy, every vessel of the
convoy replying, the firing was so rapid.'[61] The war against the U-
boats was taking its toll of the more experienced German naval
crews, and it is possible that the *Pandora*'s attackers were
comparatively new and inexperienced submariners. During the first

seven months of 1918 eight submarines were destroyed in the approaches to the Irish Sea and to the N.W. of the North Channel, and by August Lloyd George was claiming in the House of Commons that 'at least 150' German U-boats had been sunk, and lists of German U-boat crews, dead and captured, were widely published in order to damage German morale.[62] On 4 June 1918 the local press reporter at Holyhead noted that the 'Motor Schooner *Eilian* brought 5 survivors of enemy submarine into Holyhead. Submarine sunk by decoy schooner in Caernarvon Bay during the day.'[63] One of the most recent lists of U-boats sunk in 1918, compiled from both German and British sources, does not include any U-boats sunk on this date, the nearest (as far as date and position are concerned) being the *U-B.119*, commanded by Kobel, which had sailed from Germany on 27 April for the Irish Sea area, and sank after a depth charge attack in 52° 42'N, 05° 03'W on 19 May.[64] It was not until September 1918 that the naval authorities at last introduced convoys for inshore routes, vessels assembling in Holyhead Outer Harbour and then being escorted by the trawlers to join the main ocean convoys at Milford. In August the *Boscawen*, 1,936 tons, was sunk between Bardsey and Holyhead, and a few days earlier the *Snowdon*, on passage from Holyhead to Dublin, was torpedoed but managed to survive the attack. On this occasion the changing balance of forces was apparent. Within minutes of the attack, destroyers and patrol boats were on the scene, and the *Snowdon* had an airship escort for her passage. The airship station at Llangefni was transferred, along with other Royal Naval Air Service Stations, to the Royal Air Force in April 1918, but there was now close liaison with the escorting naval forces, and Captain Gordon Campbell, writing from H.M.S. *Patrol*, reported to Admiral Lewis Bayly in September 1918 that he had had a confidence with the Commanding Officers of the Air Stations in Llangefni and Aber in Caernarvonshire regarding the types of aircraft most suitable for convoy work.[65] An additional base in the Menai Strait for motor launches in Campbell's command was formed in September 1918, as these small craft had found it difficult to refuel at Holyhead in north-easterly gales. But the end was now in sight, and the sinking of the *Leinster*, and the *Dundalk*, 794 tons, some five miles N.W. of the Skerries in October, were the final blows in the U-boat campaigns.[66] Two days after the signing of the

Armisticle in November 1918, all available naval personnel from the Hunting Flotilla and the Holyhead Naval Base came ashore for the parade and service on Turkey Shore, Holyhead. Among those present were survivors from merchant ships, from the *Tara*, the *Anglia*, and the other Ferry ships, men from the merchant schooners as well as the crews of the destroyers, trawlers, and motor launches. The senior naval officer present was Captain Gordon Campbell, V.C., D.S.O. This, too, was the end of an age.

In the post-1918 world, Anglesey seamen who had been brought up in the age of sail proved themselves time and again in the difficult years for world shipping and the gloom of the depression of the twenties and thirties. That story is beyond the scope of this present work. But, by way of postscript, one example must be given. The men of the *Scotia* in 1940, like the men of the *Tara* in that earlier European war, were for the most part Anglesey men, whose peacetime occupation was sailing out of Holyhead for Ireland. Master of the *Scotia* was Captain W. H. Hughes, some of whose experiences in sailing ships have been mentioned in an earlier chapter.[67] After service in the Portmadoc schooners and the large sailing ships of Liverpool, Captain Hughes had long since settled in Holyhead, where both he and his brother, Captain J. Hughes, commanded cross-channel ferry steamers.[68]

On 26 May 1940, the *Scotia* was at Southampton under two hours notice to sail. The previous night the British Army had begun to withdraw towards Dunkirk. Hitler was confident; the Germans had driven down the Somme Valley towards the Channel coast, and the only port left open to evacuate the British and French armies was Dunkirk.[69] Even Churchill feared that within a week he would be compelled 'to announce the greatest military disaster in our long history,'[70] Whilst the Admiralty mustered every craft it could to take part in the evacuation, Churchill and many of his advisers feared that at most about 30,000 men would be re-embarked; in the event, thanks to the heroism of the seamen and ships of all types, more than ten times that number were snatched from the beaches and harbour of Dunkirk by 4 June, and Churchill was able to state that 'the nucleus and structure upon which alone Britain could build her armies of the future' had been saved.[71] Despite his victory, Hitler had, in ten days from 25 May to 4 June, failed to gain the full advantage of his triumph, and the seeds of his final defeat were being sown effectively on the beaches of Dunkirk. With the hindsight of the historian we can see that it was here that Germany's defeat and Europe's liberation began; in those dark days, however, there was little cause for celebration, and the crews of the ships that sailed for Dunkirk to embark the defeated British and French armies must have felt that theirs was a near hopeless task.

The *Scotia* was ordered to sail for Dover on the evening of 27 May, but did not receive her orders to leave the Downs until 17.00 hrs. on the following day.[72] She arrived off the Eastern Channel entrance to Dunkirk at 21.45 hrs., passing a number of British destroyers who were shelling enemy positions, and proceeded cautiously, without a pilot, in the dark towards the now blazing Dunkirk. About an hour after midnight, Captain Hughes, in his report, stated that the *Scotia* 'was struck abaft the engine room on the port side. It was sounded all round, but was found not to be making any water, and all compartments were dry. This proved afterwards to have been a torpedo which had struck the bilge keel and failed to explode.'[73] The master of a small sloop which they met told them to approach Dunkirk very cautiously, but added 'you are very badly needed.' The *Scotia* berthed close to the lighthouse on the East Pier at about 01.30 hrs. and left two and a half hours later with about 3,000 exhausted troops on board, weaving her way in the early light of dawn past a sunken destroyer and a grounded troopship. Captain Hughes noted: 'vessels of every description – large and small, some proceeding towards Dunkirk and others returning, carrying as many troops as their craft would hold. It was quite inspiring to see these vessels doing their best to render help.'[74]

By ten o'clock the next morning the *Scotia* was disembarking the troops at Dover: 'Berthing was rather difficult as the ship had a heavy list owing to the troops crowding to the shore side. However, disembarkation went smoothly.' The *Scotia* coaled in Margate Roads, not an easy operation, as there were no facilities, and members of the crew from all departments helped in bagging, heaving up and bunkering the coal from the coaster *Jolly Days*. Ordered to proceed to Dunkirk again, the *Scotia* left Margate Roads about 07.40 hrs. on Saturday, 1 June. As they approached No. 6 buoy at the western entrance, Dunkirk Channel, they saw ten German bombers approaching them, but although bombs were dropped all around them, the *Scotia* was not hit. Captain Hughes manoeuvred with helm at full speed, avoiding bombs, wrecks and buoys in an intricate approach, and came alongside the West Mole of Dunkirk where 2,200 French troops were quickly embarked.

Waves of German aircraft had been attacking the assembled troops on the beaches and in the harbour area since dawn, and German heavy guns had been brought to bear on the harbour and shipping off shore, yet during this long first day of June over sixty thousand men were safely landed in England.[75] But there were many casualties, including the destroyer *Keith*, *Basilisk* and *Havant*, the minesweeper *Skipjack*, and the *Brighton Queen* with French and Moroccan troops aboard. The *Scotia* had embarked her troops within twenty-five minutes. Captain Hughes kept close to the buoys as he left harbour to avoid wrecks and small incoming craft, but as he passed No. 6 buoy he was twelve enemy bombers coming from astern. 'They came in formations of four . . . in each case they swooped low, the two outside planes machine-gunned and the two inner each dropping four bombs.'[76] The first formation did not score a direct hit, although the spurts of water ahead and the hail of gunfire which hit the bridge and funnels showed the *Scotia*'s crew how near they were; the second formation, flying very low, were more successful. 'One bomb struck the ship abaft the engine room on the starboard side and another on the poop deck starboard side. Immediately the third four swooped over again and one of their bombs dropped down the after funnel, while the others dropped on the stern.'[77] Captain Hughes who, until the *Scotia* had been hit, had been manoeuvering with the helm and steaming full speed, saw that his ship was about to sink and ordered that the seven remaining lifeboats (three had been shattered by the bombs) should be lowered. The French troops, weary to death of war, tended to rush the boats, and the Chief Officer of the *Scotia* had to threaten to shoot if they disobeyed his orders and refused to allow the crew to man the falls and lower the boats away.

In the meantime, the destroyer *Esk*, H.15, commanded by Commander Couch, R.N., had sailed at full speed out of Dunkirk, and come alongside the *Scotia*, which was now heeling over. Captain

Hughes, in his report, paid tribute to the seamanship of Commander Couch. 'He very skilfully put the bow of his ship close to the forecastle head, taking off a large number of troops and picking up hundreds from the sea. Backing his ship out again, he came amidships on the starboard side, his stem being now against the boat-deck, and continued to pick up survivors.'[78] By this time the *Scotia* had heeled over to such an extent that her forward funnel and mast were in the water; the German bombers, despite heavy gunfire from the *Esk*, continued to drop their bombs and machine-gunned those swimming and clinging to the wreckage. The *Scotia*'s port bilge-keel was now out of the water, and Couch handled the *Esk* with great skill around to the port side where hundreds of troops huddled together: many who could swim now made for the nets slung from the *Esk*, and the troops who had climbed the bilge were 'comparatively easily rescued.' All who were able to help themselves thus found themselves aboard the *Esk*; on the *Scotia* there remained the dead, three seriously wounded men, and Captain Hughes. The latter would not leave them; first he caught a rope thrown from the destroyer's decks, and tied this around a badly wounded steward of the *Scotia*. Using this rope, and a boat fall lying across the side of the *Scotia*, Captain Hughes was able, 'by holding on to it, to ease the jerk into the water and against the side of the destroyer. He was very badly injured, but he was very patient and never grumbled. I learn that he has since had one leg amputated.'[79] Captain Hughes then made certain that the remaining two French soldiers were rescued in the same way, and, 'having assured myself that everyone who was still alive had been taken off, a boat spar was swung from the *Esk* on to the *Scotia* by which I climbed aboard the *Esk*.'

In his report, Captain Hughes pays tribute to the skilful seamanship of Commander Couch of the *Esk*, who was responsible for saving many hundreds of lives, to the Chief Officer of the *Scotia*, who, in his handling of the troops, prevented panic from developing, and, indeed, to all the officers and men of the *Scotia*. Thirty of the crew of the *Scotia* and about two hundred French troops died. The purser of the *Scotia* later commented: 'The sinking itself was not very spectacular – I could not swim at all, but I propose to learn to swim now.'[80] The modest, matter-of-fact report by Captain Hughes is supplemented by two letters written a few days after the sinking of the *Scotia*. The Dover pilot who was aboard wrote to the L.M.S. Railway Company reporting the conduct of Captain W. H. Hughes: 'He upheld the highest traditions of our Merchant Navy when the persuasive calling of *Esk*'s commander went unheeded until he saw that every man had left the ship and had a fair chance of survival . . . I feel honoured to have served such a man.' Aboard H.M.S. *Esk* Lt. Cdr. Richard Couch wrote to the Marine Superintendent of the L.M.S. Railway Company on 12 June 1950: 'I have made a special report on the magnificent work done by Captain W. H. Hughes on this occasion. With the ship on fire and sinking, in fact, beyond all hope, his only thought was the rescuing of the wounded, which he carried out with great energy and no regard for his own safety. It was with some difficulty that I persuaded him to leave his ship after all rescue work was completed.'[81] The boatswain of the *Scotia*, W. Williams, and three seamen were awarded the Distinguished Service Medal and Captain W. H. Hughes was himself awarded the Distinguished Service Cross. His career is symbolic of the generations of Welsh seamen, a fraction of whose history has been recounted in this book. The lessons in seamanship gained from those hard, strenuous years in the beautiful schooners of Portmadoc, and the long hours on watch in the *Beeswing* and the *Deccan*, bore fruit in full measure in the dark days of 1940 at Dunkirk.

[1]   TRs with Captain Henry Roberts, Moelfre, and Mr W. H. Michael, Amlwch, June 1972. The *Mary Miller* was one of the schooners in which many Anglesey seamen served; she sailed for many years to and from Burrow, Runcorn, and the china clay ports of Cornwall and Ireland. David Jones, *Cewri fy Ardal* (Amlwch, 1919), gives some indication of the impact the war made upon the seafaring community of Amlwch, and the losses sustained in both the Merchant and Royal Navies.

[2]   A. J. P. Taylor, *The First World War, an Illustrated History* (London, 1963), 34-35.

[3]   A Temple Patterson, *The Jellicoe Papers, NRS,* cviii. (London, 1966), I, 34.

[4]   *Parl Papers* xlii, *Merchant Shipping Losses,* 1 August 1919. The *Frau Minna Petersen* was later renamed the *Jane Banks*, and owned by the West Country schooner owners, the Stephens family of Fowey.

[5]   *ibid.*, 3. On February 27, 1915, the sailing vessel *Conway Castle* was captured and scuttled by the *Dresden* about five hundred and sixty miles S.W. by W. from Valparaiso.

[6]   *ibid.*, 4.

[7]   David Jones, *Cewri fy Ardal.*

[8]   *Parl Papers* xlii, 1919, 4, gives the position of the *Cambank* as ten miles east of Point Lynas, but Mr Emrys Jones of Amlwch, who has dived on the wreck, locates it much nearer inshore.

[9]   *Y Genedl Gymreig,* 9 Chwefror 1915. Mr W. Roberts of Llandegfan, member of the crew of the *Mary Mitchell*, and Mr R. T. Pritchard, a near neighbour of Captain Ellis in Bangor, remember clearly the impression the conduct of the Germans U-boat commander made locally.

[10]   *Parl Papers,* xlii, 1919, 6.

[11]   TR interview with Captains Wynn and Jones at Amlwch, 1971.

[12]   The S.S. *Hibernia,* 21 knot ship running passenger services for London and North-Western Railway Co. from Holyhead to Dublin.

[13]   Paymaster Dutton's diary consists of a loose-leaf notebook written in indelible pencil, the first entry written on Friday, November 5th, 1915, the last on Friday, 17th March 1916, their 134th day of captivity. It will hereafter be referred to as *Dutton MSS.* Captain R. Gwatkin Williams's diary was published in 1916 by Mrs Gwatkin Williams, entitled *In the hands of the Senoussi.* Another version was also published in 1916, with the title *The Black Hole of the Desert, being the Diary of a Yeoman-Signaller, one of the survivors of H.M.S. Tara.'* This is a more popular account written by an imaginative writer, H. R. S., who based his narrative on an account which he claimed to have been given to him by one of the crew of the *Tara* when he was lying in hospital in Alexandria slowly recovering his health.

[14]   *Gwatkin Williams,* op cit., 20.

[15]   Dutton MSS, 6.11.15.

[16]   *ibid.,* 8.11.15 – 14.11.15.

[17]   *Gwatkin Williams,* 27.

[18]   Dutton MSS, 14.11.15. Captain Tanner was the original master of the

Hibernia; when she became H.M.S. *Tara* he was retained as master responsible for navigation 'and the internal organization of the ship.' *Gwatkin Williams*, 7.

[19] *ibid.*, 20.11.15; 21.11.15.

[20] Dutton MSS, 25.12.15, 51st day in captivity.

[21] *Gwatkin Williams*, 52.

[22] *Gwatkin Williams*, 95. Dutton recorded that the Captain 'was flogged . . . he was placed in a Sheep Pen, no one allowed to go near him.' When darkness fell and the other prisoners could not see what was happening, Captain Williams was surprised to receive the Arab Commandant's own supper, whilst the sentry gave him a cigarette and lit a large fire to keep him warm. Williams added a cryptic note, 'Such is the Arab character.'

[23] Dutton MSS, 17.3.16.

[24] *Gwatkin Williams*, 101-110.

[25] The story of the *Tara* and her survivors' ordeal in the desert retains a special place in the minds of Holyhead's older citizens, but this is the first time that the late Paymaster Dutton's diary had been used to reconstruct their story, and I am much indebted to Mrs M. Burke for her kindness in granting me access to her father's private papers. Mr Dutton was for many years hon. secretary of the Holyhead Sailing Club and Regatta Committee and his services to sailing in the area were recognized by public presentations made to him by Sir Richard Williams Bulkeley in 1934 and by Col. the Hon. H. O. Stanley in 1948 on behalf of the Sailing Club.

[26] *Parl. Papers*, xlii, 1919, 12.

[27] Captain L. J. Manning, master of the *Anglia*, had served his apprenticeship at sea in the vessels of the British Shipowners Company, and later, commanded the *Cambria* and the *Scotia*.

[28] R. E. Roberts, *Holyhead and the Great War* (Holyhead, 1920), 37.

[29] *ibid.*, 39.

[30] *Parl. Papers*, xlii, 98, give the number of casualties as 176, including the master, but according to Roberts, *Holyhead and the Great War*, 501 lives were lost.

[31] CRO PQ 92/62. From 17 April 1915 to 20 March 1916, the *Mary B. Mitchell* made five voyages to London with slate cargoes.

[32] E. Keble Chatterton, *Q-Ships and their Story* (London, 1922), 67-76. The logs of a number of Q-ships are in ADM/53 in the PRO, but unfortunately none of those belonging to the vessels mentioned in this chapter are housed there.

[33] CRO PQ 92/62.

[34] E. Keble Chatterton, *Q-Ships and their Story*, 67-68.

[35] *ibid.*, 71-76, and local press interviews with Lieutenant T. Hughes, R.N.R.

[36] CRO PW 92/62.

[37] E. Keble Chatterton, *Q-Ships*, 65-6, 178-9, 183-4. The *Gaelic* was known as *Brig II, Gobo* and *Q-22*.

[38] *ibid.*, 189-190.

[39] Gordon Campbell, Vice-Admiral, R.N. (1886-1953). For Campbell's own account, *My Mystery Ships* (London, 1928); Lewis Bayly, *Pull Together, The Memories of Admiral Sir Lewis Bayly* (London, 1939), Chapters VIII, IX, and XI.

[40] E. Keble Chatterton, 38-51. Gordon Campbell, 170-194.

[41] E. Keble Chatterton, 199-204, Gordon Campbell, 213-231.

[42] Gordon Campbell, 229.

[43] Campbell himself had already been awarded the V.C. for the action in February against *U-83*.

[44] Gordon Campbell, 253.

[45] *ibid.*, 283. William Williams received an enthusiastic reception from the crowds who gathered to see him presented with a gold watch at Amlwch, and a £150 war bond and an illuminated address in the market place at Llangefni by the Lord Lieutenant, Commodore Sir Richard Williams Bulkeley; at the Council School in Amlwch a tablet was placed 'in honour of Seaman W. Williams, V.C., D.S.M. and Bar, Médaille Militaire, a former scholar of this school.

[46] *Parl Papers*, xlii, 32-40. I am much indebted to Mr Frank Bell, of Holyhead, himself the friend of seamen for many years, for allowing me to consult the log-book kept by the Superintendent of the Stanley Sailors' Home, Holyhead, where many survivors were given temporary shelter, and also the annual reports of the Sailor's Home and Reading Room, Holyhead.

[47] D. Lloyd George, *War Memoirs of David Lloyd George* (London, 1934), III, 1159-60.

[48] A. J. P. Taylor, *English History, 1914-45* (Oxford, 1965), 84.

[49] Basil Greenhill, *The Merchant Schooner*, II, 214-5.

[50] For a discussion of the controversy regarding the introduction of the convoy system, see Marder, *From Dreadnought to Scapa Flow*, 4, 115-67; Lloyd George, *War Memoirs*, III, 1120-1268; Thomas Jones, *Lloyd George* (London, 1951), 98-102; A Temple Patterson, *Jellicoe Papers*, II, 113-162; A. J. P. Taylor, *English History, 1914-45*, 83-85, and *The First World War*, 138; Admiral Sir Herbert Richmond, *Statesmen and Sea Power* (Oxford, 1946), 284-287.

[51] Taylor, *English History, 1914-45*, 85. This was also the view of the merchant seamen of Anglesey, most of whom were firm admirers of Lloyd George.

[52] The ten masters of merchant ships whom Jellicoe invited to a meeting at the Admiralty on 23 February 1917 shared these doubts, *Jellicoe Papers*, II, 113, 149-51.

[53] Lloyd George, *War Memoirs*, III, 1145. Lloyd George felt that the merchant service masters whom Jellicoe had consulted were over-cautious, and clearly underestimated the ability of their fellow master mariners in small ships. 'It surprised me to find that the Captains of the liners who were first consulted by the Admiralty shared Sir John Jellicoe's doubts as to the

capacity of the small tramp to keep station. It is simply the arrogant sense of superiority which induces the uniform chauffeur of a Rolls Royce to look down on the driver of what is contemptuously stigmatised as a "tin Lizzie".'

[54] 'It must remain a curious and indeed painful reflection that ocean convoy having been found to be the efficient antidote to U-boats operating in the Atlantic and Western Approaches against our ocean-going ships, and to U-boats operating against the cross-channel trade and the Scandinavian trade, the same antidote was not promptly applied to the U-boat inshore activities which immediately ensued. But instead of observing the principle of concentration of force implicit in convoy, the principle of dispersion of A/S force was adhered to for inshore operations.' Lieut. Commander D. W. Waters and Commander F. Barley, Paper No. 49, *U-boat and Anti-Submarine Warfare, First World War, 1914-18*. Marder, *From Dreadnought to Scapa Flow*, 4, 282.

[55] *Parl Papers*, xlii, 69-85, and Stanley Sailors' Home Log-book are the sources for the sinkings and survivors records.

[56] Lieutenant Commander R. de Saumarez's own account of the naval activities at Holyhead is included in Roberts, *Holyhead and the Great War*, 44-53. H.M.S. *Patrol*'s logs for this period are in the PRO ADM 53/54659-54667.

[57] Stanley Sailor's Home Log Book.

[58] *SB*, 1954, 17, 94-5.

[59] Information provided by Captain Henry Roberts, Moelfre, brother of the late Captain John Roberts, D.S.C. The U-boat was probably the *U-B-85*, which had left Germany on 16 April: her commander, Krech, explained to his captors that his surrender was due 'to the low morale of his crew, many of whom were suffering from *Grippe*,' R. W. Grant, *U-boats Destroyed* (London, 1964), 113. Captain Henry Roberts's own vessel, the *Lynburn*, struck a mine in August 1917, seven miles east of Wicklow Head, and after several hours, Captain Roberts and two out of his crew of fourteen were rescued by the Wicklow lifeboat. Some of those lost were young men from Moelfre.

[60] In May 1918, eleven fishing smacks were captured and sunk by U-boats some twenty miles off the Calf of Man. *Parl Papers*, xlii, May 30, 1918.

[61] Stanley Sailor's Home Log Book, May 1918.

[62] R. M. Grant, *U-boats Destroyed*, 134.

[63] R. E. Roberts, *Holyhead and the Great War*, 63.

[64] R. M. Grant, *U-boat Intelligence, 1914-18* (London, 1969), 182-190.

[65] Captain S. W. Roskill, R.N., (ed.), *Documents Relating to the Naval Air Service* (NRS, London, 1969), 1, 723-4, 748.

[66] *Parl Papers*, xlii, 98. The Amlwch-built *Camborne* sailed throughout the war, and her master, Captain William Williams of Amlwch Port, was commended 'for his good services' by the Lords Commissioners of the Admiralty in August 1918.

[67] *Supra*.

[68] I am much indebted to Captain W. H. Hughes, D.S.C., not only for allowing me to consult his private papers, but also for spending many hours discussing his experiences aboard sailing ships. His report on the Dunkirk action and the loss of the *Scotia* is referred to as Hughes MSS.

[69] Chester Wilmot, *The Struggle for Europe* (London, 1954), 18-21; L. F. Ellis, *The War in France and Flanders, 1939-1940* (London, 1953), 153, 248.

[70] Wilmot. *The Struggle for Europe*, 19.

[71] *ibid.*, 21. According to the official history, 17,804 men were evacuated by the Navy on the 28th, 47,310 on the 29th, 53,823 on the 30th, by the 31st, when Lord Gort and his staff left for England, 194,620 troops had been evacuated. Ellis, *The War in France and Flanders, 1939-1940*, 213-238.

[72] Hughes MSS. This was Captain Hughes's official report of the *Scotia*'s actions.

[73] *ibid.*

[74] *ibid.*

[75] Ellis, *The War in France and Flanders, 1939-1940*, 244, 64,429 men were evacuated from Dunkirk during the day, 47,081 from the harbour, 17,348 from the shore. The numbers who waited to be embarked cannot be accounted for so accurately, for, as Ellis had stated, 'There could be no roll of the men who had been crowded on board from the long queues on the harbour mole or the beaches and it is not possible to know the number of those who were lost.'

[76] Hughes MSS.

[77] *ibid.*

[78] *ibid.* Ellis, 244, describes the sinking of the *Scotia*, the rescue of the *Esk*, and states that some of the survivors were rescued by the *Worcester* and small craft.

[79] Hughes MSS.

[80] George C. Nash, *The L.M.S. at War* (London, 1946), 59.

[81] Lieut. Cdr. Richard Couch, R.N., *H.M.S. Esk*, to Captain Harris, Marine Superintendent, L.M.S., 12.6.1940.

Appendix I

Beaumaris Port Book, 1595-6. Source: Lewis, E. A., *Welsh Port Books, 1550-1603* (London, 1927), 274-280.

Port Book. K.R. 1327/11

Book of the Customers' and the Controllers' entries in the town of Beaumaris, a creek of Chester, of all goods to be carried betwixt port and port and for certificates from Michaelmas, 1595, to Michaelmas, 1596.

Date	Name of Ship	Master	–	Merchant
8 June	The Cuthbert of Chester (12)	George Comes	OUTWARDS Chester	Richard Johnson of Beaumaris, the elder.
14 July	The Harrye of Heswall (20)	John Gryffith		Richard Bavand of Chester, alderman, by J.G. his factor
28 April	The Bartholomew of Chester (16)	John How	INWARDS Chester	Gabriell Roberts of Beaumaris
30 May	The Cutbard of Chester (12)	George Comes	Chester	Gabriell Roberts of Beaumaris
10 June	The Katherine of Neston (20)	John Launcelott		Docter Vaughan of Bangor
14 June	The Suzan of Shoram (30)	Thomas Cheeseman		John Grawick
30 June	The Elizabeth of Beaumaris (3)	William Griffith	Chester	John Wine Owen of Llanvethley
8 July	The Bartholomew of Chester (16)	John How	Chester	William Dobb of Beaumaris
9 July	The Harry of Heswall (20)	John Gryffith		Gabriell Roberts of Beaumaris

Cargo

4 dikers tanned leather.

7 t. English iron.

2 t. iron, 5 t. salt, 4 cwt. madder, 4 cwt. alum, 5 cwt. castle soap, 2 cwt. brasell, 2 cwt. sugar, 1 cwt. pepper, 800 yds. canvas, 60 yds. broadcloth, 1 cwt. starch, 3 pieces raisins, 3 cwt. currants, 1 cwt. prunes, 5 bags steel, 4 bags nails, 5 brls. wool cards, 5 cwt. hops, 2 trunks apparell, 1 basket cups, 6 halberts, 4 fkns soap, 2 bundles frying pans, 1 pair cart wheels, 1 joynted bed, 7 cwt. pewter, 4 cwt. brass pots, 8 cwt. brass pans.

3 t. Gascony, 1 butt seck, 1 butt canary, 4 t. salt, 3 cwt. madder, 2 cwt. soap, 3 cwt. alum, 500 yds. linen cloth, 3 cwt. hops, 10 loaves white sugar, 5 doz. hemp, 5 balls flax, 4 bags steel, 2 pieces great raisins, 1 cwt. currants, ½ t. iron.

14 bushels malt, 6 do. wheat, 20 t. coal, 6 empty casks.

30 t. English iron.

8 brls. salt, 1 cwt. brass pans, 1 grate of iron, 1 comb, 3 doz. crocks, 2 doz. saddle trees, sadler's wares, 3 doz. scythes, 3 doz. sickles, 3 chairs, 2 wheels.

5 hhd. Gascony wine, 7 t. white salt, 4 brls. wool cards, 2 cwt. hops, 4 brass pans, 4 doz. crocks, 6 doz. saddle trees, 2 saddles, 1 basell skins, 4 doz. trene warre combes and stones, 4 pair cart wheels, 200 yards linen cloth, 1 fardel of reparell, 11 cwt. wet lead.

10 t. salt, 1 t. Gascony, 700 yds. linen cloth, 2 cwt. madder, 2 cwt. castle soap, 2 cwt. alum, 10 bags nails, 10 doz wool cards, 2 bags steel, 12 brls. iron ware, 5 brls. wool cards, 10 fkns. soap, 2 fkns. currants, 1 hamper fells, 2 baskets trenchers, 1 basket tassells, 2 fkns. gunpowder, 4 combs, 2 doz. chairs, 4 doz. crocks, 4,000 laths, 4 cwt. pan brass, 4 cwt. pot brass.

Date	Name of Ship	Master	–	Merchant
11 July	The Elizabeth of Beaumaris (16)	Richard Dobbe	Chester	Peires Gryffith of Penthrin, Esquire
12 July	The Cuthbert of Chester (12)	George Combes		Richard Dobbe of Beaumaris
18 Aug.	The Harrye of Heswall (20)	John Gryffith		Gabriel Roberts of Beaumaris

Cargo

9 t. 3 hhd. beer, 24 cwt. bisket bread, 4 brls. hardware, 5 cwt. iron, 2 half barrels salt.

6 t. salt, 2 brls. hardware, 1 chest surgery wares, 3 packs trene wares, 1 bedstead, 1 cubbert, 2 pair wheels, 2 bags madder, 3 bags fardinand buck, 1 bag alum, 17 chairs, 7 tubs, 2 iron grates, 2 bundles wool-cards, 7 wheels, 4 churns, 1 brl. pitch, 2 bags hops, 1 brl. candles, 6 coil ropes, 9 joyned stools.

5 t. salt, 20 balls flax (3 cwt.), 2 bundles flax, 5 cwt. madder, 4 cwt. alum, 3 pieces raisins, ½ cwt. green copperas, 1 cwt. sugar, divers apparel and household stuff, 2 cwt. pan brass, 2 cwt. pot brass, 1 cwt. pewter, 1 calliver, 3 hhd. wine.

Appendix II

Bangor MS 484, probably a copy of the Port Books, for the several ports under the jurisdiction of Beaumaris, retained locally for their own records by the local Custom House officials, contains a detailed record of all vessels that sailed to and from the north Wales ports from June 1729 to December 1730. The monthly arrivals and departures at Conway, Beaumaris, Holyhead, Caernarvon and Pwllheli are recorded, together with the names of masters of the vessels, their tonnage and cargoes. The late David Thomas, in *Hen Longau Sir Gaernarfon*, pp. 40-43, has statistical tables based on the inward and outward cargoes extracted from Bangor MS 484 and has compared these figures with the slate cargoes recorded in another MS at UCNW, Penrhyn MS 1642. According to Bangor MS 484 the following vessels entered and/or left Beaumaris and Holyhead during the period June 1729 to May 1730; the names and crew members are as they are recorded in the MS. Not all the changes of masters have been included, and although obvious discrepancies in the recording of the tonnage of the same vessel have been eliminated, it may be that the same vessel has been entered more than once under a different description, although most would have been well known to the officials as local vessels engaged in the coastwise trade.

Name of Ship	Of	Master	Tons	Men
Alice	Liverpool	Henry Backhouse	5	3
Anglesey	Liverpool	William Jones	7	2
Anglesey	Holyhead	John Bowser	25	4
Ann	Holyhead	John Jones	20	3
Bonny Venture	Mostyn	Edward Griffith	12	2
Betty	Chester	Robert Jackson	16	3
Bull	Beaumaris	John Williams	6	1
Bull's Head	Beaumaris	John Williams	6	2
Blessing	Beaumaris	John Williams	12	2
		Robert Pritchard		
Boadicea	Dublin	Robert Morris	40	4
Blessing	Caernarvon	Robert Evans	25	3
Blessing	Holyhead	Rice Jones	15	3
		Rowland Michael		
Batchelor	Caernarvon	William Thomas	26	3
Bodowen	Milford	John Warlow	40	4
Bideford	Bideford	John Bird	40	6
Betty	Cemaes	Hugh Lloyd	15	2
Coytmore	Beaumaris	William Williams	16	2
		William Henry		

Name of Ship	Of	Master	Tons	Men
Cotton	Conway	Hugh Owen	10	1
Catherine	Caernarvon	Robert Foulkes	4	2
Carteret	Dublin	Thomas Griffiths	70	8
Crane	Holyhead	John Bowser	30	3
Catherine and				
John	Mostyn	Peter Jones	7	2
Charming Molly	Liverpool	Richard Rimmer	12	2
Dolphin	Red Wharf	Henry Thomas	9	2
Dolphin	Caernarvon	William Roberts	8	2
Dolphin	Holyhead	William Pritchard	6	2
Darling	Conway	William Davies	6	2
Defiance	Aberdovey	Henry Morris	6	2
Eagle	Conway	Richard Davies	12	2
Eagle	Caernarvon	Rice Thomas	4	2
Experiment	Beaumaris	H. Witton	2	2
Expedition	Workington	Henry Carley	50	6
Fancy	Liverpool	John Coppock	40	2
Friendship	Dumfries	Thomas Sutherland	20	3
Fox	Dulas	John Morris	12	2
		Edward Williams		
Foresight	Dublin	William Lawson	40	6
Grace	Beaumaris	Peter Williams	20	1
		William Henry		
		Charles Norton		
Golden Apple	Red Wharf	Owen Davies	14	2
George	Holyhead	William Pritchard	6	2
George	Caernarvon	David Jones	15	2
Grafton	Dublin	Thomas Hughes	70	10
George	Warrington	John Cartwright	30	3
Gwen Vainol	Caernarvon	David John Griffith	6	2
Hopewell	Amlwch	William Peters	16	2
Hopewell	Dumfries	Jonathan Nicholson	15	2
Hopewell	Conway	Daniel Williams	8	2
Hopewell	Beaumaris	John Lloyd	8	2
Hopewell	Holyhead	John Hemkey	16	2
Happy Escape	Caernarvon	John Pritchard	24	3
Hopewell	Barmouth	Griffith Roberts	4	3
John and Sarah	Liverpool	Henry Tyrer	30	3
Jane	Liverpool	John Bootle	30	6
Kent	Ramsgate	Henry Darling	60	7
Mermaid	Caernarvon	John Williams	24	3
Mayflower	Beaumaris	Hugh Williams	14	2
Morning Star	Caernarvon	Jacob Jones	8	1
Mackerill	Burlington	Thomas Robson	35	4

Name of Ship	Of	Master	Tons	Men
Marigold	Caernarvon	John Hughes	20	2
Mary	Beaumaris	Michael Leech	15	3
Marlborough	Caernarvon	Robert Jones	6	2
Mayflower	Dulas	Hugh Lloyd	15	2
Morning Star	Pwllheli	John Roberts	8	2
Mary Pomey	Holyhead	John Michael	2	2
Marygold	Caernarvon	William Jones	20	3
		John Jones		
Mary and John	Caernarvon	Rice Jones	28	3
Martha and Jane	Caernarvon	William Thomas	16	3
Mary	Holyhead	William Vickers	20	4
Open Boate	Beaumaris	Richard Parry	3	2
Providence	Beaumaris	John Roberts	20	3
Providence	Pwllheli	Thomas Samuel	15	2
Prince	Dublin	James Queltra	60	9
Prince of Wales	Chester	Edward Griffith	8	2
Pretty Betty	Dublin	James Fitzpatrick	50	8
Phoenix	Cardigan	Jenkin Jenkins	20	3
Prince Frederick	Dublin	Lewis Jones	60	11
Queen	Pwllheli	Morris Humphreys	40	4
Robert	Newry	James Morris	5	2
Richard and Jane	Beaumaris	Hugh Hughes	20	3
Success	Barmouth	Griffith Roberts	4	2
Stout John	Red Wharf	Edward Parry	8	2
Susannah	Fishguard	Thomas Langhan	10	3
Sinah and Jones	Caernarvon	Evan Jones	16	3
Submission	Caernarvon	Rowland Owen	10	2
Sharke	Caernarvon	Owen Jones	7	2
Squeril	Beaumaris	Owen Davies	15	2
		Robert Hughes		
		Richard Hughes		
		Rice Williams		
St Michael	Dumfries	John Perys	15	2
Speedwell	Amlwch	William Jones	8	2
Swan	Caernarvon	George Roberts	5	2
Speedwell	Caernarvon	Roger Edwards	4	2
		John Williams		
Tryal	Byrne	Milford Orde	40	4
Thomas and John	Bangor	Thomas Hughes	12	1
Three Brothers	Whitehaven	Isaac Milner	85	8
Unicorn	Woodbridge	Edward Waugh	50	7
Willing Mind	Whitehaven	Henry Thompson	35	3

Appendix III

As indicated in the chapter 'Legal and Illegal Shipping, (p. 119), Professor
R. Davis and Mr R. C. Jarvis have warned that eighteenth-century shipping
statistics may often be misleading, but the returns compiled by Customs
officials, known as 'Dalley's Tables', BM Add MSS 11255-6, and the
Liverpool Papers BM Add MSS 38429-32 have been used by them to
illustrate the general trends in the development of shipping. In 1751 the
Board of Customs called upon all ports of registry to provide returns of the
shipping of the ports in respect of each year from 1751, and retrospectively
for each seventh year from 1709 (the first complete year after the Act of
Union). The table that follows is taken from BM Add MSS 11,255,
extracting the returns for Beaumaris (i.e., which included almost all the
north Wales ports) from the 'Tables shewing Tonnage of all the ships of the
several ports of England that have traded to and from foreign ports, or
coastwise, or have been employed as fishing vessels, 1709-1782 . . .
accounting each vessel but once.'

Beaumaris		Tonnage		
1709	44 foreign	292 coastwise	171 fishing	507 total
1716	122	534	160	816
1723	99	552	166	817
1730	68	651	162	881
1737	12	656	158	826
1744	60	796	163	1019
1751	12	858	159	1029
1752	30	976	159	1165
1753	–	1169	155	1324
1754	56	1037	151	1244
1755	–	1169	155	1324
1756	–	1275	125	1400
1757	–	1288	125	1413
1758	26	194	200	420
1759	24	194	235	453
1760	24	194	–	218
1761	660	4190	269	5119
1762	132	2118	242	2492
1763	146	765	202	1113
1764	286	1385	192	1863
1765	565	183	195	943
1766	589	4560	185	5334
1767	699	3950	92	4741
1768	573	4241	92	4906

Beaumaris		Tonnage		
1769	719	5956	92	6767
1770	674	4445	92	5211
1771	731	5051	92	5874
1772	770	5674	92	6536
1773	717	5678	92	6487
1774	662	5886	–	6548
1775	1060	5273	92	6425
1776	1026	5730	87	6843
1777	977	5824	–	6881
1778	1187	6199	94	7480
1779	691	5659	89	6439
1780	488	5549	80	6117
1781	892	5379	80	6351
1782	982	5114	76	6172

Appendix IV

Beaumaris Registry of Merchant Ships

The significance of the Act of 1786 (26 Geo. III, cap. 60), which required owners to register and obtain a certificate of registry for all sea-going ships, has been described in detail by Robert Craig and Rupert Jarvis in the introduction to their *Liverpool Registry of Merchant Ships* (Manchester, 1967), and also by Graham Farr in his *Records of Bristol Ships, 1800-1838* (Bristol Record Society, XV, 1949), and his *Chepstow Ships* (Chepstow, 1954). The Beaumaris Register Books from 1786 are now housed at Custom House, Holyhead, and my original intention was to include here the details of all vessels registered in the port for the first two years, 1786 and 1787 (as owners of ships belonging to ports in Great Britain had 12 months following the Act to re-register under the new Act) and for 1836 when there was a general renewal of registers following the adoption of 'New Tonnage' (5, 6, William IV, cap. 56). Limitations of space have made this impossible, and the extracts which follow are, therefore, a few random examples of the hundreds of vessels recorded in the early Registers to indicate briefly the information available from this source.

As the entries in the original Registers are spread across double pages of the quite large volumes, I have rearranged the particulars, and not included all the details, e.g., descriptive matter relating to sterns, figureheads, type of build – clench (clinker) or carvel – and details relating to changes of masters, in the interest of making the extracts more concise. Preceding the ship's name is the number in the Beaumaris Register for the particular year, then her measured tonnage, length, breadth, and depth in feet and inches, the number of decks and masts, her rig or general type, where and when built, the names of her owners, and her master's name. From 1786 to 1824 owners were named, but not the amount of their holding; from 1824 the Registers indicate how the vessels were owned in 64ths shares. For simplification, all tonnages are shown to the nearest whole figure, although in the Registers they are shown as calculated in the 'Old Measurement', i.e., in fractions of a ton in 94ths from 1786 to 1836, then in 3500ths up to 1855, when the decimal system was adopted for tonnages as well as for dimensions. Only examples of vessels with obvious Anglesey connections have been included, although it must be remembered that up to 1840 the Beaumaris Registers contain the names of all vessels registered in north Wales from the Clwyd to Towyn in Merioneth. (In June 1840 Caernarfon was given a separate register, and for a short time there was also a Pwllheli register.)

Craig and Jarvis, in their work on the Liverpool Registers, drew attention to the regional differences in the economic and social pattern of ships-ownership by analysing the occupations of owners in the Registers: whereas at Liverpool in 1786 and 1804-5 about 80% of all owners were merchants, only about 12% were from a maritime background (mainly mariners); at Whitehaven for the same period about 40% of all owners came from a wide spread of maritime interests, 30% were widely spread in business and trade, and a further 30% were professional men, yeomen, widows and spinsters (Craig and Jarvis, *Liverpool Registry of Merchant Ships,* xxxix, and Tables 26). C. H. Ward-Jackson, in his study of the port of Fowey at the turn of the eighteenth-century , has analysed a random sample of 220 owners in the Fowey Registers and concludes that about 'one-third were mariners, one-third were people whose income was derived from the sea, and one-third a general assortment.' The approximate %s for two representative years, 1786 and 1836, of owners of vessels with definite Anglesey associations in the Beaumaris Registers are:

1786		1836	
merchants	58%	merchants	14%
mariners	30%	mariners	22%
farmers	5%	farmers	20%
business and tradesmen	5%	business and tradesmen	18%
		'gentlemen'	18%
professional,		widows, spinsters	5%
widows, spinsters	2%	professional	5%

As one might expect in an agricultural community, in Anglesey the proportion of farmers who had shares in ships is much higher than in the ports analysed by Craig, Jarvis and Ward-Jackson. The percentages above, based on the Beaumaris Registers, should, however, be treated with caution, for the term 'merchant' seems to have been used widely in the 1786 Register, and many of those described as 'merchant' were involved directly as agents or officials of the Mines Companies at Amlwch. By 1836 members of these same families are more often described in the Register as 'gentlemen'. The owners from Lancashire, Flintshire and south Wales whose business interest linked them with the copper industry and the Amlwch Shipping Company in the 1786 Register, were replaced in later years by successful businessmen, drapers, grocers, house builders, who had emigrated to England, and invested financially in the ventures of their relations who were mariners in their native Anglesey, as well as by shopkeepers and tradespeople resident on the Island itself. The general impression is, moreover, that by the 1830s the local Welsh community were much more involved in shipowning than in the years immediately following

1786 when the initiative seems to have been taken by 'pobl dwad' ('outsiders'), e.g. Cornish mine agents and English engineers and contractors employed in building the Holyhead Road, Harbour Works and the Menai Bridges.

The late David Thomas, in his article 'Anglesey Shipbuilding down to 1840' in *TAAS*, 1932, 107-118, compiled from the Registers' lists of vessels built at Beaumaris (15), Red Wharf (8), the North-East Coast of Anglesey (7), Amlwch (13), Cemais (9), Holyhead and its vicinity (32), the South-West Coast (3) and the Menai Strait (8). (Some of these vessels had been built before 1786 and several of these were either vessels brought to Anglesey to be rebuilt or open boats decked over, so that the numbers are somewhat misleading.) At Amlwch the Treweeks built 6 vessels described as sloops, 3 smacks and one brigantine between 1825 and 1840, Robert and Ishmael Jones built 3 smacks, 2 schooners, and one cutter at Cemais during the same period, and Henry McVeigh, Edward and Robert Meredith and T. Gibbs built vessels at Holyhead, but again it is important to remember that the registered builder was not always the man who had carried out the work but may have been the owner for whom the vessel was built. It must be emphasised that the examples which follow are merely random examples: it is hoped to publish the complete Registers for selected years in future issues of the Transactions of the Anglesey Antiquarian Society. I am indebted to the Commissioners of H.M. Customs for permission to publish these extracts from the Registers.

1/1786 *Edward and Mary*, 34t, 39 x 14.4 x 6.6, 1d, 1m, Sloop,
    built Barmouth 1777.
    John Parry, maltser, Beaumaris. John Harrison, ma.
    Margaret Evans, victualler, Beaumaris. Wm. Pritchard ma.
    Dec. 1786.

23/1786 *Molly*, 28t, 35.5 x 14 x 6.4, 1d, 1m, Sloop,
    built Pwllheli 1771.
    William Morgan, Mariner, Llandegfan. Richard Williams ma.
    Owen Hughes, farmer, Llandegfan. Robt. Williams, ma. 1787.
    Richard Parry, farmer, Penmon.

36/1786 *Eleanor*, 81t, 53 x 19.2 x 10.6, 1d, 2m, Brig,
    built Red Wharf 1786.
    John Price, merchant, Amlwch. William Williams ma.
    Stephen Roose, merchant, Amlwch. Ed Owen ma. Dec. 1789.
    Jonathan Roose, merchant, Amlwch.
    Amlwch Shipping Company.
    Lost and Register not saved 1794.

88/1786   *Pennant*, 30t, 36.6 x 14.3 x 6.4, 1d, 1m, Sloop,
built Conway 1775.
Owen Williams, mariner, Llanallgo. Owen Williams ma.
Shadrach Williams, farmer, Llanrhwydrys. Hugh Jones, ma. 1791.
Wm. Morgan, farmer, Llandysilio.
Owen Williams, farmer, Llechynfarwy.

196/1786   *Jane*, 102t, 64 x 19.10 x 12, 1d, 2m, Brigantine,
built Chester, 1785.
Robert Roberts, James Roose, both mariners, Amlwch, Wm.
Williams, merchant, Beaumaris, John Price, Stephen Roose,
William Hughes, Jonathan Roose, Snr., Jonathan Roose, Jnr., Wm.
Hughes, Thomas Turner, John Jones, Richard Jones, Owen Owen,
Samuel Howson, John Byrne, Thomas Roose, all merchants,
Amlwch, John Jackson, James Percival, David Jones, all merchants,
Liverpool, Michael Hughes, Ravenhead, Samuel Williamson,
Richard Jones, David Donbaven, Wm. Jones, all merchants of
Holywell, David Richards of Swanzey, merchant.
Taken by the French, reg. delivered up and cancelled
Joseph Rathbone, ma.

64/87   *Earl of Uxbridge*, 120t, 64.10 x 22.1 x 11.10, 1d, 2m, Brig,
built Moelydon, Anglesea, 1783.
James Bradley, merchant, Holyhead. Richard Sullivan, ma.
Margaret Williams, grocer, Holyhead.
Richard Sullivan, mariner, Bridgwater.

106/87   *Lord Bulkeley*, 52t, 48 x 16 x 19, 1d, 1m, Sloop,
built Beaumaris 1787.
Robert Williams, mariner, Beaumaris. Robert Williams, ma.
John Hampton Jones, Esq., Beaumaris.
Benjamin Wyatt, merchant, Llandegai.
William Williams, merchant, Llandegai.
John Jones, Esq., Beaumaris.
Wm. Williams, grocer, Beaumaris.
Edward Edwards, victualler, Beaumaris.
Ann Crow, Spinster, Beaumaris.
Lost and register not saved, 1795.

25/1801   *Welfare*, 52t, 48 x 16 x 4.9, 1d, 1m, Sloop,
Was a prize taken from the Dutch by the *Royal George*,
Excise yatch. Letter of Marque of Leith and condemned as a good
and lawful prize in H.M. High Court of Admiralty of Scotland,
1797.

John Price, merchant, Amlwch. William Pritchard, ma.
William Hughes, merchant, Amlwch.
Evan Richards, merchant, Amlwch.
Theopilus James, merchant, Amlwch.
Lost and Register not saved.

41/1801   *Sisters*, 27t, 39 x 14 x 6.8, 1d, 1m, Sloop,
           built Nefyn 1788.
           Wm. Price, gentleman, Llandegfan.
           John Hughes, mariner, Llandegfan. John Hughes, ma.
           Henry Morgan, shopkeeper, Llandisilio.
           Richard Jones, farmer, Penmynydd.
           Owen Williams, mariner, Llanallgo.
           Lost and register 1805.

39/1802   *Nelly*, 29t, 38.9 x 12 x 6.1, 1d, 1m, Sloop,
           built Aberdovey 1767.
           Rowland Owen, mariner, Holyhead.
           Owen Williams, shoemaker, Holyhead. Rowland Owen, ma.
           Owen Humphreys, farmer, Llanfaelog.

22/1819   *Auckland*, 90t, 61 x 19.1 x 9.7, 1d, 1m, Cutter,
           built Topsham, 1801.
           John Jones, mariner, Criccieth.
           Richard Sailsbury, farmer, Llanfairynghenedl.
           William Rowland, farmer, Llanfaethlu. John Jones, ma.
           Owen Parry, labourer, Llanfaethlu.

25/1819   *Fanny*, 42t, 45 x 15 x 6, 1d, 1m, Sloop,
           built Bangor 1770.
           John Rowlands, mariner, Cadnant.
           Erasmus Griffith, merchant, Beaumaris. John Rowlands, ma.
           Elizabeth Richards, dressmaker, Beaumaris.
           Hugh Rowlands, shopkeeper, Cadnant.

25/1821   *Holyhead Trader*, 78t, 64.5 x 16.8 x 8, 1d, 2m, Schooner,
           built Frodsham 1821.
           John Jones, mariner, Holyhead, Owen Owens, att. at law,
           Llwydiarth Escobion, Llandyfrydog, Wm. Bulkeley Jones, Druggist,
           Edmund Roberts, farmer, John Pritchard, merchant, John Hughes,
           tallow chandler, Richard Rowlands, book-keeper, Wm. Roberts,
           gentlemam, John Williams, yeoman, all of Holyhead, Griffith Jones
           and Richard Sailsbury, merchants, both of Llanynghenedl, George
           Bradley Roose, Attorney at law, Amlwch, J. Rimmer, Wm. Rimmer,

Robert Rimmer, John Spencer, Richard Jones and Joseph Thompson, all merchants, of Liverpool. John Jones, ma.

7/1822   *Lady Robert Williams*, 168t, 77.2 x 23 x 13, 1d, 2m, Snow, built Red Wharf 1821.
Erasmus Griffith, merchant, Beaumaris. Harry Evans, ma.
Thomas Hughes, merchant, Caernarvon.
Griffith Jones, gentleman, Llandwrog.
John Owen, farmer, Llanallgo. Lost and register (no date).
Owen Jones, shopkeeper, Pentraeth.
Elizabeth Williams, widow, Llanbedrgoch.

53/1824   *Eliza Goddard*, 57t, 51.7 x 16.8 x 5.5, 1d, 1m, Smack, built Bangor 1824.
Thomas Philips, mariner, Holyhead. 32.
Lewis Jones, mariner, Holyhead. 16. Thomas Philips, ma.
Hugh Jones, mariner, Beaumaris. 2.
Samuel Howson, merchant, Holyhead. 4.
William Roberts, mariner, Holyhead. 4.
Nicholas Treweek, merchant, Amlwch. 4.
William Hughes, mariner, Amlwch. 2.

24/1825   *Unity*, 68t, 54.10 x 17.4 x 9.1, 1d, 1m, Sloop, built Amlwch 1825
Certif. under the hand of Nicholas Treweek, the builder, 2 June 1825.
William Morgan, gentleman, Amlwch. 8.
Robert Jones, mariner, Amlwch. 4.
Nicholas Treweek, Amlwch. 2.
William Hughes, gentleman, Madyndysw, Amlwch. 4.
Robert Jones, ma.
James Treweek, gentleman, Mona Lodge, Amlwch. 4.
John Paynter, gentleman, Maesllwyn, Amlwch. 4.
James Roose, Surgeon, Amlwch. 4.
William Roberts, mariner, Amlwch. 4.
William Hughes, mariner, Amlwch. 4.
John Hughes, mariner, Amlwch. 2.
Thomas Gaunt, gentleman, Pembry. 8.
John Edwards, gentleman, Pembrey. 4.
Thomas Eyton, gentleman, Flint. 8.
William Astbury, gentleman, Buckley Mountain. 4.

120/1826 *Marquis of Anglesey*, 64t, 53 x 17.3 x 9.5, 1d, 1m, Sloop, built Amlwch 1826. Certif. under the hand of Nicholas Treweek,

the builder, 29 June 1826.
William Morgan, gentleman, Amlwch. 16.
Stephen Roose, gentleman, Amlwch. 8.
William Hughes, gentleman, Amlwch. 8.
George Bradley Roose, solicitor, Amlwch. 8. Hugh Thomas ma.
James Treweek, gentleman, Amlwch. 4.
James Roose, surgeon, Amlwch. 4.
Jane Jones, widow, Amlwch. 8.
Thomas Eyton, gentleman, Flint. 8.

39/1827   *Admiral Nelson*, 65t, 64.6 x 15.2 x 6.8, 1d, 1m, Flat,
built Northwich 1798.
Rev. Wm. John Lewis, Trosymarian, Llangoed, clerk. 64.
John Hughes, ma.

14/1828   *Henry*, 75t, 63.6 x 16.6 x 6.6, 1d, 1m, Flat,
built Northwich 1803.
Rev. William John Lewis, Trosymarian, Llangoed, clerk. 64.
William Lewis, ma.

37/1830   *Deborah*, 19t, 31.6 x 12.4 x 6.3, 1d, 1m, Smack,
built Holyhead 1830. Certificate under the hand of Edward
Meredith, the builder, 18 October 1830.
William Jones, farmer, Llanfwrog. 16.
Richard Jones, shopkeeper, Llanfaethlu. 32.
Elias Roberts, farmer, Llanfaethlu. 16. Owen Griffith, ma.

4/1831   *James and Jane*, 130t, 68.4 x 21.10 x 11.7, 1d, 1m, Brigantine,
built Amlwch, and launched 4 Oct. 1830.
Certificate under the hand of Treweek Brothers, the builder, Feb.
1831.
James Treweek, gentleman, Mona Lodge. 64. John Hughes, ma.
Vessel foundered in Bay of Biscay 1840.

14/1832   *Amlwch Packet*, 37t, 42 x 15.1 x 8, 1d, 1m, Smack,
built Amlwch and launched 3 May 1832, Treweek Bros., builders.
James Treweek, gentleman, Mona Lodge, Amlwch. 64.

7/1833   *Eagle*, 20t, 34.5 x 12.11 x 5.11, 1d, 1m, Smack,
built Holyhead and launched 23 March 1833. Owen Jones, the
builder.
Owen Williams, mariner, Llanfachraeth. 22.
Elinor Williams, spinster, Llanfachraeth. 21. Owen Williams, ma.
Ann Williams, spinster, Llanfachraeth. 21.

11/1834 *Wakefield*, 125t, 70.9 x 20.4 x 12.6, 1d, 2m, Brig,
built Liverpool 1815.
Wm. Owen, mariner, Holyhead. 16.
Wm. Roberts, steward of one of His Majesty's Packets, Holyhead.
16.
John Johnson, Engineer, Holyhead. 16. John Roberts, ma.
Isaciah Gill, Road Contractor, Holyhead. 16.

29/1835 *Stanley*, 152t, 80.10 x 20.11 x 12.11, 1 and poop d. Brig (?),
built Holyhead this present year 1835. Certificate under hand of
Robert Meredith, the builder.
William Owen, mariner, Holyhead. 64. William Jones, ma.

34/1835 *Arion*, 246t, 86.6 x 26.7 x 16.7, 1d 2m + try sail. Snow,
built Sunderland 1829.
William Roberts, merchant, Holyhead. 22. John Roberts, ma.
Robert Spencer, merchant, Holyhead. 21.
Wm. Bulkeley Jones, merchant, Holyhead. 21.
Vessel wrecked and register cancelled at Cape Town, Cape of Good
Hope, 13 August 1842.

29/1836 *Cymraes*, 21t, 36.3 x 11.6 x 21, 1d, 1m, Sloop,
built Amlwch 1836. Certif. Treweek Bros., the builders.
Thomas Hughes, mariner, Penrhoslligwy. 16. Thomas Hughes ma.
Nicholas Treweek, merchant, Amlwch. 48.

199/1836 *Cornist*, 46t, 54.7 x 13.7 x 6.8, 1d, 1m, Galliot,
built Chester 1811.
Thomas Williams, Esquire, Red Wharf. 16.
Wm. Pritchard, formerly mariner but now farmer,
Llanfair-mathafarneithaf. 4.
Grace Williams, widow, Beaumaris. 9.
John Owen, Esquire, Hendregadog. 17. Owen Pritchard, ma.
Robert Roberts, farmer, Llaneugrad. 4.
Ellen Hughes, widow, Feram. 5.
Richard Griffith, merchant, Liverpool. 9.

201/1836 *Endeavour*, 35t, 48 x 13.5 x 8, 1d, 1m, Sloop,
built Chester 1817.
John Price, mariner, Holyhead. 16.
Richard Jones, Shoemaker, Holyhead. 8.
Hughes Jones, Hatter, Holyhead. 8.
William Owen, Coal Merchant, Holyhead. 4. John Price, ma.
Richard Griffith, Farmer, Penycledog. 8.

Owen Griffith, Farmer, Hendy. 8.
Thomas Elias, Corn Merchant, Llanfwrog. 4.
Richard Williams, Corn Merchant, Rhoscolyn. 4.
Thomas Lloyd, Corn Merchant, Trearddur. 4.

15/1840   *Margaret Ann*, 116t, 67.1 x 16.8 x 10.7, 1d, 2m, Schooner,
           built at Cemaes & launched 21 Jan. 1840, certificate of Ishmael
           Jones, the builder, 22 April 1840.
           Owen Price, farmer, Cafnan, Llanfaethlu. 4.
           Hugh Roberts, farmer, Penbol(?), Amlwch. 4.
           John Hughes, farmer, Penrorsedd, Llanrhwydrus. 4.
           Richard Price, farmer, Cafnan. 8.
           Ann Price, spinster, Cafnant. 4. Wm. Griffith, ma.
           John Parry, farmer, Bwlch, Llanfechell. 4.
           Jane Parry, spinster, Bwlch, Llanfechell. 4.
           Jane Hughes, spinster, Cefncoch, Llanfechell. 4.
           John Hughes, merchant, Madyn, Amlwch. 4.
           Owen Hughes, farmer, Mynachdy, Llanfairynghornwy. 4.
           John Jones, farmer, Llangwyfan. 4.
           William Lewis, farmer, Trecastell, Llangwyfan. 4.
           Griffith Williams, druggist, Llanerchymedd. 4.
           Owen Owens, solicitor, Holyhead. 8.
           Lost, Brixham (?), 23 Jan. 1866.

5/1842   *Prince of Wales*, 129t, 73.5 x 18.7 x 11.2, 1d, 2m, Schooner,
           built at Cemaes & launched 28 Feb. 1842, certificate of Ishmael
           Jones, the builder, 28 March 1842.
           Robert Spencer, gentleman, Llanynghenedl. 32.
           Frances Maria Spencer, spinster, Llanynghenedl. 4.
           Margaret Jones, spinster, Llanynghenedl. 4.
           John Hodgson, mail guard, Holyhead. 8. Hugh Roberts, ma.
           David Roberts, labourer, Holyhead. 8.
           James Wallace, mail guard, Holyhead. 4.
           Evan Owen Hughes, vicar, Llanbadrig. 4.

4/1844   *Cymro*, 21t, 34.5 x 12.6 x 6.2, 1d, 1m, Smack,
           built at Amlwch and launched 20 March 1844, certificate of
           Nicholas Treweek, builder, 20 April 1844.
           Nicholas Treweek, merchant, Amlwch. 56. William Jones, ma.
           Samuel Treweek, Greathead, Book-keeper, Amlwch. 4.
           Evan Jones, book-keeper. 4.
           Vessel sunk + certif. of registry destroyed by salt water.

2/1846   *Brothers*, 16t, 32 x 10.5 x 6.2, 1d, 1m, Smack,
built at Traethbychan, Anglesey, and launched 13 Jan. 1846, certif.
of Henry Williams, the builder, 22 Feb. 1846.
Owen Jones, mariner, Llaneugrad. 40.
Thomas Jones, mariner, Llaneugrad. 16.
John Jones, mariner, Llaneugrad. 8. Owen Jones, ma.

Appendix V

Among the Porth yr Aur MSS at UCNW, Bangor, are a bundle of 47 certificates signed by the Commissioners appointed for the Port of Beaumaris under the 'act for procuring a supply of men, from the several ports of this Kingdom, for the service of His Majesty's Navy.' The 47 men whose names are contained in the following list were the first to be recruited for the Navy under the 'Quota' system; the Caernarvon Commissioners alleged on 19 May 1795 that 'the Commrs. at Beaumaris have acted very irregularly by certifying the amount of the Bounty settled by them to be given able seamen was £31.5.0, to Ordinary Seamen £23.10.0, and to Landmen £17.10.0 which exceed the Bounty approved of by the Lords Commissioners of the Admiralty.' PYA MSS 33075.

No.	Name of man enrolled	Age	Calling	Place of birth or settlement
1	John Tyrer	38	Seaman	Beaumaris
2	Robert Roberts	30	Ship's Carpenter & Seafaring man	Denio, Caerns.
3	John Owen	44	Seaman	Amlwch
4	Thomas Kitto	22	Seaman	Redruth, Cornwall
5	John Owen	33	Shoemaker	Ceidio, Anglesey
6	William Jones	24	Seaman	Tregwalchmai, Anglesey
7	Robert Dooding	27	Miner	Penrhyn du, Co. Carnarvon
8	William Williams	23	Labourer	Llanfaes, Anglesey
9	John Parry	17	Labourer	Llandyfrydog, Anglesey
10	William Pritchard	19	Labourer	Llanwenllwyfo, Anglesey
11	Richard Roberts	19	Miner	Llandyfrydog, Anglesey
12	David Williams	19	Labourer	Llangefni
13	Rowland Jones	18	Labourer	Heneglwys
14	William Roberts	19	Labourer	Llangefni
15	Thomas Roberts	21	Labourer	Nevin, Caerns.
16	Jeffrey Boyd	24	Gardener	Waterford, Ireland
17	Henry Parry	25	Seafaring man	Caernarvon
18	John Williams	19	Seafaring man	Llanbeblig, Caerns.
19	John Williams	37	Able Seaman	Holyhead
20	William Parry	25	Landman	Bangor
21	William Lewis	21	Labourer	Llangaffo
22	Jno. Williams	38	Tailor and Seafaring man	Ceirchiog, Anglesey
23	Robert Hughes	41	Labourer	Denio, Caerns.
24	Owen Roberts	22½	Labourer	Llanllechid
25	Humphrey Jones	24	Labourer	Llantrisant, Anglesey
26	Maurice Jones	18	Labourer	Llangwyfan, Llangweinwen, Anglesey
27	Robert Roberts	38	Labourer	Llandrillo, Denbs.
28	Evan Jeffreys	24	Seaman	Clynyn, Merioneth
29	Richard Hughes	19	Ordinary Seaman	Liverpool
30	Thomas Morris	29	Landman	Llangian, Caerns.
31	John Owen	18	Landman	Llanddeusant
32	John Williams	18	Landman	Amlwch
33	John Humphreys	42	Seaman	Llanaber, Barmouth
34	William Lister	32	Shoemaker	Blackburn
35	Hugh Jones	20	Labourer	Ynys, Caernarvon
36	Robert Francis	36	Miller	Llannor, Caernarvon
37	Evan Evans	19	Seafaring man	Llanbeblig, Caernarvon
38	John Thomas	19	Labourer	Llanddeiniolen, Caernarvon

Capacity, whether seaman or landman	Bounty	Advance at time of enrolment	Date
Able Seaman	£31. 5. 0	£8.15. 0	25 April 1795
Ordinary Seaman	£21. 0. 0	£7. 0. 0	27 April 1795
Able Seaman	£31. 5. 0	£8.15. 0	28 April 1795
Able Seaman	£31. 5. 0	£8.15. 0	28 April 1795
Landman	£23.10. 0	£7. 0. 0	28 April 1795
Seaman	£31. 5. 0	£8.15. 0	28 April 1795
Landman	£17.10. 0	£5. 5. 0	28 April 1795
Landman	£17.10. 0	£5. 5. 0	28 April 1795
Landman	£17.10. 0	£5. 5. 0	28 April 1795
Landman	£17.10. 0	£5. 5. 0	28 April 1795
Landman	£17.10. 0	£5. 5. 0	28 April 1795
Landman	£17.10. 0	£5. 5. 0	28 April 1795
Landman	£17.10. 0	£5. 5. 0	28 April 1795
Landman	£17.10. 0	£5. 5. 0	28 April 1795
Landman	£17.10. 0	£5. 5. 0	28 April 1795
Landman	£17.10. 0	£5. 5. 0	1 May 1795
Ordinary Seaman	£21. 0. 0	£7. 0. 0	4 May 1795
Ordinary Seaman	£21. 0. 0	£7. 0. 0	4 May 1795
Seaman	£31. 5. 0	£8.15. 0	5 May 1795
Landman	£15.15. 0	£5. 5. 0	7 May 1795
Landman	£15.15. 0	£5. 5. 0	9 May 1795
Ordinary Seaman	£23.10. 0	£7. 0. 0	11 May 1795
Landman	£15.15. 0	£5. 5. 0	11 May 1795
Landman	£15.15. 0	£5. 5. 0	11 May 1795
Landman	£15.15. 0	£5. 5. 0	14 May 1795
Landman	£15.15. 0	£5. 5. 0	14 May 1795
Landman	£15.15. 0	£5. 5. 0	16 May 1795
Able Seaman	£26. 5. 0	£8.15. 0	15 May 1795
Ordinary Seaman	£21. 0. 0	£7. 0. 0	28 May 1795
Landman	£15.15. 0	£5. 5. 0	28 May 1795
Landman	£15.15. 0	£5. 5. 0	28 May 1795
Landman	£15.15. 0	£5. 5. 0	28 May 1795
Able Seaman	£26. 5. 0	£8.15. 0	28 May 1795
Landman	£15.15. 0	£5. 5. 0	3 June 1795
Landman	£15.15. 0	£5. 5. 0	5 June 1795
Landman	£15.15. 0	£5. 5. 0	5 June 1795
Landman	£15.15. 0	£5. 5. 0	6 June 1795
Landman	£15.15. 0	£5. 5. 0	8 June 1795

No.	Name of man enrolled	Age	Calling	Place of birth or settlement
39	John Pritchard	21	Labourer	Llanddeiniolen
40	William Griffiths	19	Seaman	Denio, Caerns.
41	William Jones	23	Seaman	Llanbeblig, Caernarvon
42	Robert Jones	29	Labourer	Amlwch
43	William Dodd Stephens	26	Miner	Llanllyfni, Caernarvon
44	Robert Miller	21	Miner	Holywell, Flints.
45	William Hoskins	27	Miner	Cornwall
46	William Gray	17	Miner	Llanbadrick, Anglesey
47	Richard Jacobs	25	Seaman	London

Capacity, whether seaman or landman	Bounty	Advance at time of enrolment	Date
Landman	£15.15. 0	£5. 5. 0	8 June 1795
Ordinary Seaman	£21. 0. 0	£7. 0. 0	10 June 1795
Ordinary Seaman	£21. 0. 0	£7. 0. 0	11 June 1795
Landman	£15.15. 0	£5. 5. 0	13 June 1795
Landman	£15.15. 0	£5. 5. 0	13 June 1795
Landman	£15.15. 0	£5. 5. 0	11 June 1795
Landman	£15.15. 0	£5. 5. 0	11 June 1795
Landman	£15.15. 0	£5. 5. 0	10 June 1795
Able Seaman	£26. 5. 0	£8.15. 0	18 June 1795

Appendix VI

Captain Robert Lloyd's letter to Sir John Warren, the Admiral in command of the British naval forces on the American Station, was released by the Admiralty Office in March 1814 and published in the London *Gazette*, 1814, p. 512.

> His Majesty's ship Plantagenet,
> off Bermuda, Dec. 29, 1813.

I beg leave to enclose you a list of vessels taken and destroyed by His Majesty's ship under my command between the 8th Day of September and the 17th instant.

Sloop Jolly Robin of 4 men and 50 tons from Boston bound to Charleston, captured September 8th, 1813.

Schooner Torpedo of 40 tons from New York bound to New Orleans, captured September 11, 1813.

Sloop Olive Branch of 50 tons captured same date.

Schooner Delight of 50 tons captured September 15, 1813.

Schooner, name unknown, of 50 tons, captured same date.

Schooner, Jack's Delight, of 1 gun from New Orleans, bound to New York, captured October 12, 1813.

Schooner, Sparrow, of 1 gun and 100 tons from New Orleans, bound to New York, captured November 3, 1813.

Sloop, Elizabeth of 30 tons captured November 5, 1813.

Sloop James Madison of 1 gun and 25 tons from Charleston bound to New York, captured November 7, 1813.

Sloop Active of 5 men and 57 tons, from New York bound to Savannah, captured November 12, 1813.

Sloop Lady Washington of 15 men and 70 tons from Savannah bound to New York, captured November 15, 1813.

Schooner Betsey of 5 men and 60 tons from Savannah bound to New York, captured November 21, 1813.

Schooner Margaret and Mary of 5 men and 37 tons, from Philadelphia bound to New York, captured November 27, 1813.

Sloop Anna Maria, of 7 men and 60 tons from Philadelphia bound to New York, captured same date.

Schooner John and Mary of 60 tons from New Orleans, bound to New York, captured November 29, 1813.

Sloop Five Sisters of 5 men and 60 tons from New York bound to Philadelphia, captured December 2nd, 1813.

Sloop New Jersey of 42 tons from Barnygate bound to New York, captured same date.

Sloop Two Peters of 3 men and 38 tons, from Little Egg bound to New York, captured same date.

Schooner Batsh, of 3 men and 61 tons from New York bound to Little Egg, captured December 4, 1813.

Schooner Unicorn of 6 men and 30 tons from Savannah bound to New York, captured December 5, 1813.

Schooner Margaret of 2 men and 36 tons from New York bound to Barnygate, captured December 8, 1813.

Sloop Victory of 60 tons from Savannah bound to New York, captured December 10, 1813.

Schooner Little Mary, of 3 men and 26½ tons, from New York bound to Charleston, captured December 12, 1813.

Schooner Rapid of 21 men and 1 gun and 115½ tons, from Havannah bound to New York, captured December 16th 1813.

Schooner Mary, of 4 men and 34 tons, from Philadelphia bound to Salen, captured December 17, 1813.

R. Lloyd (signed)

Appendix VII (i)

The Davies, Menai Bridge, fleet, R. Hughes & Company, Menai Bridge, 1843-1905

Year	Name	Rig	Tonnage	When	Built by	at
1843	Chieftain	W.S.	795	1842	–	St John's N.B.
1844	Enterprise					
1845	Agnes	S.	651	1844	–	Miramichi N.B.
1845	Courtenay	W.S.	609	1837	–	St John's N.B.
1845	Cape Fraser	–	–	–	–	–
1846	Argo	Snow	211	1845	–	Nova Scotia
1846	Ann Davies	Bg.	203	1845	–	Petite Nova Scotia
1847	Oregon	S.	1004	1847	–	Quebec
1847	Peltoma	Bk.	470	1846	–	Magaquadarie N.B.

| Reg. dimensions | | | | Main Ports visited and |
Length	Breadth	Depth	Masters	ultimate fate
137.2	29.1	22	Williams 1846	Menai Bridge, Quebec, New Orleans, Mobile. Sold 1848.
				Liv., Quebec, New Orleans, Caernarvon.
123.1	29.3	21.3	E. Bell 1846	Menai Bridge, Quebec, New Orleans. Wrecked on Pillar Rocks near Quebec 1846.
128	29.1	20	R. Jones 1846	Menai Bridge, Liv., Quebec, St John's, New York. Sold 1847.
–	–	–	–	–
–	–	–	R. Davies	Cardiff, Malta, Richibucto. Wrecked off Cape Verde Is. 11.12.1847.
90	22.6	13.2	R. Hughes 1846 Humphreys 1851	Menai Bridge, Richibucto, Baltimore, Quebec, Boston, Dalhousie. Sold 1848.
150	32	22	David Evans 1847 R. Jones 1852 – Williams 1853	Liv., Quebec, Menai Bridge, Baltimore, New Orleans, New York, Coquimbo, Callao, San Francisco. Sold 1855.
195	25	17	E. Bell 1847 R. Hughes 1851	Liv., New York, New Orleans, Menai Bridge, Quebec. Sold 1850

Year	Name	Rig	Tonnage	When	Built by	at
1847	*Tamarac*	S.	802	1846	–	Monkton N.B.
1847	*Eliza Caroline*	Bk.	832	1846	–	Cromvet N.B.
1848	*Northumberland*	Bk.	499	1848	–	N. Brunswick
1848	*Infanta*	Bk.	522	1847	–	Pasborough Nova Scotia
1850	*Lord Stanley*	Bk.	749	1849	–	Quebec
1850	*Highland Mary*	Bk.	502	1849	–	Sheet Harbour Nova Scotia
1851	*Carleton*	S.	758	1850	–	St John's N.B.
1851	*Caroline*	S.	732	1850	–	St John's N.B.
1851	*Mersey*	S.	828	1850	–	N.B.

| Reg. dimensions | | | | Main Ports visited and |
Length	Breadth	Depth	Masters	ultimate fate
135.8	29.5	21.4	R. Jones 1847-9?	Liv., Menai Bridge, Quebec, Savannah, New Orleans. Sold 1849.
143.5	30.1	22.1	E. Bell J. Rowlands 1851 W. Morgan 1854	Liv., Quebec, St John's, New Orleans, Port Phillip, Chinchas, Callao, Sydney, San Francisco. Sold 1865.
499	–	–	Roberts	Menai Bridge, Caernarvon, Liv., Quebec, New Orleans. Sold 1849.
116	25	16.5	J. Rowlands 1848 W. Griffith 1851 W. Evans 1852	Menai Bridge, Liv., St John's, Quebec, Port Phillip, New York, Boston. Sold 1855.
140	29.4	21.4	E. James 1851-4 W. Thomas 1854	Plymouth, Cardiff, Antwerp, Sydney, Bombay, New York, Callao, Pensacola, Genoa, Kingston. Sold 1868.
125.4	26.3	19.7	P. Griffith 1851	Liv., Callao, Montevideo, Caldoa, Savannah, Pensacola, Buenes Aires. Wrecked 14 Oct. 1844 off Portness, St Lawrence.
144.3	28.6	20.4	R. Jones 1851-2 W. Williams 1852-5	Liv., Adelaide, Callao, Heradura. Wrecked on Cape Craysfort, Falkland Is. 1855.
138.2	28.5	21.2	T. Jones 1851 W. Pritchard 1852	Liv., Adelaide, Callao, S. Francisco. Sold 1853 (?).
			O. Evans 1851-3	Liv., New York, Menai Bridge, New Orleans, Callao. Sold 1853. Bennet & Co., London.

Year	Name	Rig	Tonnage	When	Built by	at
1851	*Lord Ashley*	S.	531	1850	–	Nova Scotia
1851	*Amidas*	W.	807	1850	–	New Brunswick
1851	*Olivia*	W.S.	799	1850	–	Quebec
1851	*Lady Louisa*	W.S.	948	1851	–	Quebec
1851	*John Davies*	W.S.	924	1851	–	New Brunswick
1852	*Avon*					
1854	*Exodus*	W.S.	1138	1854	–	Quebec
1856	*De Salabery*	W.S.	854	1855	–	Quebec
1857	*William Wright*	W.S.	758	1856	–	New Brunswick
1857	*Minnehaha*	W.S.	845	1857	–	New Brunswick

| Reg. dimensions | | | | Main Ports visited and |
Length	Breadth	Depth	Masters	ultimate fate
			J. Roberts 1851	Liv., New York, New Orleans, Quebec. Wrecked in towing a derelict on Havana Bar, 1852.
			J. Hughes 1851-3	Liv., New York, New Orleans. Lost on fire 38.30 S, 53.30 W., 1853.
			T. Williams 1855-9	Liv., New York, Melbourne, Callao, Quebec, Montivideo. Sold 1868.
153	31.8	22.6	J. Thomas 1852 Griffiths 1853-5 S. Parry 1859	Liv., New Orleans, San Francisco, Melbourne, Menai Bridge, Quebec, Callao, Pensacola, Bombay. Sold 1870.
			R. Hughes 1851-5	Liv., New Orleans, Callao, Quebec, Rio. Sold 1869.
				Menai Bridge, Quebec.
			R. Jones 1855 Evans 1859-60	Liv., Sydney, Melbourne, Callao, Akyab, Montivideo. Sold 1867.
			G. Elsh 1859	Liv., Melbourne, Callao. Savannah, Rio. Sold 1868.
157	33.5	21.8	W. Williams 1857-8 H. Thomas 1875	Liv., Melbourne, Callao, Valparaiso, Gunape, Coquimbo. Sold 1877.
158	33.7	22.4	W. Morgan 1859 H. Roberts 1871	Liv., Melbourne, Caldua, Bombay, Callao. Wrecked Pennines Head, Scilly Is., 18 Jan. 1874.

Year	Name	Rig	Tonnage	When	Built by	at
1858	Caspian	W.S.	1018	1857	–	New Brunswick
1858	Glen Monarch	W.S.	974	1857	–	
1859	Ebba Brahe	W.S.	1437	1852	–	Quebec
1861	Royal Visitor	W.S.	1220	1860	Oliver	Quebec
1863	Edward Allison	W.S.	1323	1862	Rowan	New Brunswick
1863	Cilminar	W.S.	799	1862		New Brunswick
1863	Pekin	W.Bk.	539	1857	–	Quebec
1863	Magnificent	W.S.	1283	1863	Valin	Quebec
1863	British Empire	W.S.	1414	1863		Quebec
1864	Etta	W.S.	1154	1863	Dinning	Quebec

| Reg. dimensions | | | | Main Ports visited and |
Length	Breadth	Depth	Masters	ultimate fate
170	36.2	22.7	T. Hughes 1859 H. Curwen 1875	Liv., Melbourne, Callao, Gunape, Pensacola, Macabi. Sold 1876.
			T. Williams W. Jones 1875	Liv., Bombay, Melbourne, Calcutta, Akyab, Callao, Macabi, Rangoon. Sold 1876.
			D. Owen 1859	London, Cardiff, Bombay, Mauritius. Became leaky & sold, Mauritius 1861.
192.6	37.5	23	T. Jones J. Llewellyn 1871 J. Roberts 1875	Rangoon, Mollendo, Macabi, Lobos, Callao. Sold 1879. Liv., Calcutta, Bombay, Melbourne,
179.1	38.5	24.8	Morgan	Liv., Calcutta, Callao, Bahia, Rio. Lost 1868.
159.7	34.0	21.7	Roberts	Liv., Calcutta, Karachi, Bombay, Rangoon, Manila. Lost 1870.
147.8	28.7	19	T. Williams	Antwerp, Canterbury, Callao, Hamburg. Sold 1864.
189.9	37.1	24.8	Thomas Griffiths 1871 Richards 1875	Liv., Calcutta, Melbourne, Callao, Aden, Pensacola. Sold 1875. Abandoned in N. Atlantic 1893.
198.4	39.3	24.5	R. Jones 1865-6 W. Lewis 1871 Rickers 1875-80	Liv., Bombay, Callao, San Francisco, Macabi, Lobos, Moulmein. Wrecked, burnt off Alleppy, Jan. 5, 1883.
181	36.4	24	W. Pritchard 1871-80	Liv., Philadelphia, Callao, Gunape, Mollendo, Rangoon, Coquimbo, Amherst, Capetown. Sold 1887. Wrecked 1888.

Year	Name	Rig	Tonnage	When	Built by	at
1864	*Glensannox*	W.S.	1004	1864	Potts	New Brunswick
1865	*Disraeli*	W.S.				
1865	*Superior*	W.S.	1375	1864	Valin	Quebec
1865	*True Briton*	W.S.	1390	1865	Dinning	Quebec
1865	*Glentils*	W.S.	297?	1854?	–	Pictou
1866	*British Princess*	W.S.	1402	1864	Nevins	St John's New Brunswick
1866	*Dolbadarn Castle*	I.S.	989	1863	T.R. Oswald	Sunderland
1866	*Ajmeer*	W.S.	1163	1861	Gass	St John's
1866	*Conway Castle*	W.S.	1299	1866	Gass	St John's

Reg. dimensions				Main Ports visited and
Length	Breadth	Depth	Masters	ultimate fate
168.3	35.7	23.2	O. Thomas	Liv. Wrecked off Bombay 12.3.1865.
				Liv., Calcutta, Callao, Bombay, Teneriffe, Akyab. Lost. Sailed from Akyab 15 April 1868.
201.7	38.4	25	W. Williams 1870 D. E. Jones 1875	Liv., Coquimbo, New York, Cardiff, Callao, Melbourne, Lobos, Singapore, Moulmein. Sold 1880.
204	38	24.2	D. Jones 1870-5	Liv., Melbourne, Callao, Lobos, Ballista, Singapore, Moulmein. Sold 1881.
				Liv., Melbourne, Calcutta, Rangoon, Bombay, Callao, Pensacola. Sold 1876.
199.7	38.8	23.9	G. Stewart 1871 – Pike 1875	Liv., Bombay, Calcutta, Valparaiso, Rangoon, Cardiff, Callao, Macabi, Lobos, Mollendo, Huanillos. Sold 1879.
198.9	34.1	20.9	W. Hughes Williams 1880-84 T. Morgan 1871-5 G. Stewart 1878 J. Le Maistre 89-92	Liv., Calcutta, Rangoon, Callao, Melbourne, Singapore, Cardiff, Bassein, Yokohoma, San Francisco, Akyab, Sydney, Rio. Sold 1893.
189.2	37.9	23.0	R. Pugh 1875	Liv., Callao, Mollendo, Cardiff, Payta, Lobos, Antwerp. Sold 1875.
188.6	38.3	24.0	H. Roberts 1871-75	Liv., Calcutta, Rio, Akyab, Rangoon, Lost at Huanillos, 9 May 1877.

Year	Name	Rig	Tonnage	When	Built by	at
1867	*Victory*	I.S.	1199	1863	Hill	Port Glasgow
1868	*Curlew*	W.S.	1224	1867	Gilmour	Quebec
1869	*Canute*	W.S.	1215	1869	McKay	Quebec
1869	*Arizona*	W.S.	1302	1869		New Brunswick
1870	*Bacchus*	I.S.	1250	1867	G. R. Glover	Birkenhead
1870	*England*	W.S.	1812	1870	Samson	Quebec
1871	*Malleny*	I.S.	1025	1868	T. Royden	Liverpool
1873	*Edinburgh*	W.S.	1572	1872	Gingras	Quebec

| Reg. dimensions | | | | Main Ports visited and |
Length	Breadth	Depth	Masters	ultimate fate
205	36	22.9	W. Davies 1871 – Jones 1875	London, Calcutta, Bombay, Rangoon, Singapore. Lost off Spur Point 14 April 1876.
188.5	36.8	23.9	Humphreys 1871 Griffiths 1875 W. Jones 1878 J. Jones 1880	Liv., Cardiff, Bombay, Callao, Mollendo, Huanillos, Rangoon, Singapore. Sold 1885. Broken up 1896.
197.5	38.4	23.4	D. Elias 1871 W. Lewis 1875	Liv., Bombay, Callao, Macabi, San Francisco, Antwerp. Sold 1876.
189.5	37.7	24.1		Liv., Cardiff, Calcutta, Callao, Singapore, Montivideo. Sold 1885.
216	36.2	23.7	W. Jermain 1871 J. Davies 1880 – Thomas 1875	Liv., Calcutta, Rangoon, Akyab, Singapore, San Francisco, C'Town. Sold 1896. Russia. B.U. 1903.
231	42	25	– Thomas 1871	Liv., Calcutta. Wrecked 19 miles south of Bombay 6 July 1872.
204.7	34.8	20.9	H. Curwen 1875-84	Liv., Calcutta, Singapore, Bassein, Rangoon, Cardiff, San Francisco. Wrecked 1 mile from Ogmore Point and Tuskar Rock, 7.30 p.m. 15 October 1886.
212	40	25	Roberts 1875 Taylor 1880-4	Cardiff, Singapore, Calcutta, Lobos, Callao, Bombay, New York, Iquique, Hamburg. Sold 1887, Germany. Lost 1899. Norway.

Year	Name	Rig	Tonnage	When	Built by	at
1873	Houri	W.Bk.	966	1867	Gibbs	Bathurst
1875	Anglesey	I.S.	1297	1875	T. Royden & Sons	Liverpool
1875	Merioneth	I.S.	1408	1875	T. Royden & Sons	Liverpool
1876	Denbighshire	I.S.	1367	1876	T. Royden & Sons	Liverpool
1876	Flintshire	I.S.	1273	1876	T. Royden & Sons	Liverpool
1876	Carnarvonshire	I.S.	1227	1876	T. Royden & Sons	Liverpool
1877	Cardiganshire	I.S.	1400	1877	T. Royden & Sons	Liverpool

| Reg. dimensions | | | | Main Ports visited and |
Length	Breadth	Depth	Masters	ultimate fate
175	34.5	21.4	R. Barrow 1875	London, Callao, Macabi, Browershaven. Previously owned by Thomas & Roberts, Nefyn. Sold 1875.
219	38.3	23	Roberts 1878 Richards 1880 H. Lewis 1891-02	Liv., Cardiff, Swansea, Rangoon, Singapore, Akyab, San Francisco, Capetown, Newcastle NSW. Sold 1905, Norway.
231.4	38.9	23.6	J. Perrin 1878-80 R. Thomas 1880-91 J. T. Rowlands 1891-1902	Liv., Cardiff, Swansea, Rangoon, Bombay, Singapore, Akyab, San Francisco, Nagasaki. Sold 1905, Italy.
231.4	38.9	23.6	Murdoch 1878-80 Lewis 1884	Liv., Cardiff, Hamburg, San Francisco, Calcutta, Singapore. Rangoon, Coquimbo, Bassein. Sunk after collision off Dover 19 Jan. 1889.
224.1	36.8	21.9	W. Lewis 1880-82 O. Pierce 1882-91 J. Williamson 91-5 H. O. Jones 96-02	Liv., Cardiff, Swansea, Singapore, Rangoon, San Francisco, Capetown, Sydney, Iquique, Newcastle NSW. Sold 1903, Norway.
224	36.8	21.8	W. Roberts 1876-91	Liv., Cardiff, Swansea, Rangoon, Singapore, Akyab. Wrecked on Yohane Point, W. Ireland, 12.30 a.m., 11 April 1896.
235.4	38.1	23.0	G. Agar 1878-81 M. Kechnie 84 J. Taylor 87-98 D. R. Stephens 99-02	Liv., Cardiff, Swansea, Calcutta, Singapore, San Francisco, Rangoon. Iquique, Sydney, Newcastle NSW. Sold 1904, Italy.

Year	Name	Rig	Tonnage	When	Built by	at
1877	*Montgomeryshire*	I.S.	1452	1877	T. Royden & Sons	Liverpool
1877	*Sarah & Emma*	I.Bk.	1097	1860	T. Vernon & Son	Liverpool
1882	*Lord Cairns*	I.S.	1473	1877	Harland & Woolf	Belfast
1884	*Dunnerdale*	I.Bk.	1066	1867	G. R. Glover	Birkenhead
1884	*Chinsura*	I.S.	1266	1868	G. R. Glover	Birkenhead
1891	*Afon Alaw*	Steel 4 mstd. Bk.	2052	1891	A. Stephen & Sons	Glasgow
1892	*Afon Cefni*	Steel 4 mst. Bk.	2066	1892	A. Stephen & Sons	Glasgow

| Reg. dimensions | | | | Main Ports visited and |
Length	Breadth	Depth	Masters	ultimate fate
235.4	38.1	23.0	Nelson 1878 J. Hughes 83-91 R. Edwards 93-02	Liv., Cardiff, Swansea, Singapore, Rangoon, San Francisco, Akyab, Iquique, Yokohama, Tacoma, Newcastle NSW. Sold 1904, Norway. Lost Tonga 1907.
199.6	33.8	22.9	J. S. Pike 1878 Lewis 1880-4 G. Patterson 1890-5	Liv., Cardiff, Swansea, Rangoon, Singapore, Akyab, Bombay, San Francisco, Yokohama, Coquimbo, Hamburgh. Sold 1903, Italy, B.U. 1905 (out of register 1897-8).
230.8	36	22	J. Davies 82-02	Liv., Cardiff, Swansea, San Francisco, Inquique, Sydney, Newcastle NSW, Capetown. Sold 1903, Italy. B.U. 1922.
210.2	35.1	21.6	Edwards 1884 J. Williamson 1884-91 W. James 1891-5	Liv., Cardiff, Rio, Bassein, San Francisco, Coquimbo, Hamburg. Sold 1895. Originally owned by Brocklebank.
215.5	37.1	22.8	J. Williams 1883-91	London, Cardiff, Swansea, San Francisco, Sydney, Coquimbo. Sold 1895, Italy.
284.4	41	23.7	R. Thomas 1891-02	Cardiff, Swansea, Rangoon, San Francisco, Singapore, Bassein, Hamburg. Sold 1903 at San Francisco. Owned by Wm. Thomas, L'pool, 1909-15.
285.4	41	23.7	J. Hughes 1893	Cardiff, Rio, Rangoon, Hamburg, Swansea. Lost. Left Swansea 5 Jan. 1894.

Appendix VII (ii)

Specimen pages for Bangor MS 3531, the Sailings Book of Davies, Menai Bridge.

Ships

Ships	sailed	From	arrived	at	sailed	arrived	at	sailed	arrival
Chieftain	17 May (1843)	Liverpool	14 July (1843)	Quebec	11 Aug (1843)	1 Oct (1843)	M. Bridge		
Do	9 Nov (1843)	M. Bridge	12 Jany (1844)	N. Orleans	March (1844)	5 June (1844)	Liverpool		
Enterprise	3 July	Liverpool	19 Aug	Quebec	7 Sept	12 Oct	M. Bridge		
Chieftain	22 Do	- do -	1 Sept (tho)	Do	28 "	29 "	Liverpool		
Enterprise	30 Nov	Carnarvon	18 Jany	N. Orleans	17 Fdy (1845)	27 Fby (1845)	Wrecked on the		
Chieftain	7 Decr (1845)	Liverpool	28 do	Do	1 Mar	11 May	Liverpool		
Agnes	12 Apr	- Do -	18 May	Quebec	18 June	23 July	Do		
Chieftain	23 May	- Do -	25 June	Do	1 Aug	29 Aug	M. Bridge		
Courtenay	18 June	- Do -	6 Aug	Do	3 Sept	2 Oct	Do		
C. Fraser	15 July	Greenock	15 Sept	Malta		27 Nov	Liverpool		
Agnes	12 Aug	Liverpool	17 do	Quebec	12 Oct	11 Nov	M. Bridge		
Chieftain	11 Sept	M. Bridge	20 Oct	Do	14 Nov (1846)	19 Dec (1846)	Do		
Courtenay	22 Oct	- Do -	2 Decr	St John	24 Jany	17 June	Do		
Agnes	17 Decr (1846)	- Do -	27 Jany	N. Orleans	2 Mar	30 April	Liverpool		
Argo	25 Fby	Cardiff	27 Mar	Malta	23 Mar	30 June	Do		
Northumberland	11 Apr	M. Bridge	20 May	Quebec	24 June	20 July	Carnarvon		
Chieftain	15 do	- Do -	20 do	- Do -	24 June	29 July	M. Bridge		
C. Fraser	26 do	Liverpool	2 June	Windsor. N.S.	28 June	25 July	Carnarvon		
Agnes	13 May	- Do -	11 - do -	Dalhousie	8 July	4 Aug	M. Bridge		
A. Davies	28 Do	M. Bridge	3 July	Parsboro	3 Aug	1 Sept	Do		
Argo	23 July	Liverpool	9 Sept	Richibucto	24 Sept	29 Oct	Liverpool		
Oregon	28 July	- Do -	12 Sept	Quebec	19 Oct	24 Nov	M. Bridge		
Chieftain	12 Aug	M. Bridge	28 Sept	- do -	26 Oct	26 Nov	- do -		
Northumberland	12 do	Carnarvon	1 Oct	- do -	26 Oct	26 Nov	- do -		

Voyages.

at	sailed	arrived	at	sailed	arrived	at	Length of Voyage	
							Mᵒ. hᵒ	
.	.	. .	. .	.	. .	.	4 14	
.	,,	. .	.	. .	. .	. .	6 . 27	
.	.	. .	. .	. .	. .	.	3 . 9	
.	.	. .	. .	. .	. .	,,	3 . 7	
	Bahama Islands						*Wrecked*	
.	.	. .	.	.	. .	.	5 . 4	
.	,,	. .	.	. .	. .	.	3 . 11	
.	,,	. .	.	. .	. .	.	3 . 7	
.	.	. .	.	. .	.	.	3 . 14	
.	.	. .	.	. .	,	.	4 . 12	
.	.	. .	.	. .	.	.	2 . 30	
.	,,	. .	.	. .	.	.	3 . 8	
Waterlogged & got to Killybegs thence by Steamer						.	7 . 26	
.	.	. .	. .	.	.	.	4 . 6	
.	.	. ,,	.	. .	.	.	4 . 5	
.	.	. .	,,	.	. .	.	3 . 14	
.	.	. .	.	.	.	.	3 . 14	
.	.	. .	.	.	.	.	2 . 27	
.	.	. .	.	. .	.	.	2 . 22	
.	,,	. .	.	. .	.	.	3 . 8	
.	.	. .	.	. .	.	.	3 . 6	
.	,,	. .	.	.	.	.	3 . 26	
.	,,	. .	.	. .	.	.	3 . 14	
,,	.	,, .	. .	.	. .	.	3 . 14	

Ships

Ships	sailed 1846	From	arrived 1846	at	sailed	Arrived	at	sailed	Arrived
C. Fraser	12 Aug	Carnarvon	5 Octr	Montreal		25 Nov.	M. Bridge	.	..
Agnes	4 Sept	M. Bridge	9 Octr	Wrecked on the Pillar Rocks				near	
A. Davies	10 Sept.	—Do—	30 Octr	Richibucto	6 Nov.	31 Decr	M. Bridge	.	.
Courtenay	18 Sept.	Carnarvon	2 Nov 1847	St John	1 Decr	31 Decr 1847	Liverpool	.	.
Chieftain	3 Feby	M. Bridge	10 March	Mobile	7 May	21 June	—Do—	.	.
Oregon	24 .	Liverpool	11 April	Baltimore	1 June	26 June	—Do—	.	.
Courtenay	7 March	—do—	17 April	New York	19 June	23 July	M. Bridge	.	.
Argo	9 March	Velin-heli		London	6 April	12 Aug	Liverpool	.	.
C. Fraser	24 Mar	Carnarvon	21 May	Baltimore	25 June	1 Aug	Londonderry	. 1847	.. 1847
A. Davies	29 Mar	—Do—	22 May	—Do—			St John NB	15 July	10 Aug
Peltoma	28 Mar	Liverpool	11 May	New York		18 Sept.	M. Bridge	.	.
Tamarac	26 May	—Do—		Quebec	13 Aug	17 Sept.	—Do—	.	.
Northumberland	13 May	Carnarvon	23 June	—do—	17 July	28 Aug	Conway	.	.
C. Caroline	3 May	Liverpool	12 June	—do—	22 .	1 Sept	M. Bridge	.	.
Chieftain	3 July	—Do—	23 Aug	—Do—	20 Sept.	24 Oct	—Do—	.	.
Courtenay	11 Aug	M. Bridge	24 Sept.	—Do—	19 Oct	16 Nov.	—Do—	.	.
Oregon	16 July	Liverpool	29 Aug	—Do—	25 Sept.	29 Oct	Hull	.	.
Anne Davies	26 Aug	M. Bridge	2 Oct	Dalhousie	13 Oct	16 Nov.	M. Bridge	.	.
C. Caroline	28 Sept.	—Do—	26 Oct	St Johns	27 Nov.	25 Decr	—Do—	.	.
Argo	17 Oct	Liverpool	11 Decr 1848	Wrecked off the Island of Mayo	1848	1848		.	Cape
Peltoma	21 Decr	Carnarvon	15 Feby	N. Orleans	18 Mar	16 May	Cork	.	.
Northumberland	21 Decr	M. Bridge	17 Feby	—Do—	17 Apr	2 June	Liverpool	.	.
Oregon	27 Decr	Hull	8 Feby	Mobile	23 May	7 May	—Do—	.	.
Tamarac	30 Decr	M. Bridge	22 Feby	Savanah	12 Apr	22 May	—Do—	.	.

Voyages

at	Sailed	Arrived	at	Sailed	arrived	at	Length of Voyage mᵒ . dys	
							3 . 13	
Quebec							Lost	
							3 . 21	
							3 . 13	
							4 . 18	
							4 . 6	
							4 . 17	
							5 . 3	
							4 . 7	
M. Bridge							4 . 12	
							5 . 20	
							3 . 21	
							3 . 15	
							3 . 29	
							3 . 22	
							3 . 5	Sold
							3 . 13	
							2 . 21	
							2 . 27	
de verd.	on a sunken rock.						Lost	
							4 . 26	
							5 . 12	
							4 . 10	
							4 . 23	

Ships	sailed	From	arrived	at	sailed	arrived	at	sailed	arrived 1855
Carlton	28 Apr	London	6 May	Cardiff	26 May	29 Aug	Callao	18 Dec	24 Mar
Infanta	30 Apr	M. Bridge	11 June	Boston	26 June 1853	13 July	Quebec	7 Aug	3 Sept
Mersey	4 May	Liverpool	9 Dec	Callao	9 Feby	9 June	Queenstown	9 June	17 June
Amidas	7 May	– Do –	24 July 1853	Went on Fire	in Lat 35.30 S	Long	63 . 30 1854		
L. Louisa	25 June	– Do –	12 Jany 1854	San Francisco	24 Mar 1852	18 May	Callao	29 Sept	2 Feby
J. Davies	22 July	– Do –	9 Nov	Portland Bay	22 Nov	13 Jany	– Do –	28 Apr	1 Oct
Avon	17 Aug	– Do –	28 Sept	Quebec	27 Oct	3 Dec	M. Bridge	"	"
Infanta	10 Sept 1853	M. Bridge	19 Octr	– Do –	6 Nov 1854	11 Dec 1852	– Do –	"	"
Oregon	7 Jany	Liverpool	2 Mar	New Orleans	13 Mar	29 May	Liverpool	"	"
High. Mary	19 Jany	London	12 – • –	Mobile	12 Apr	31 May	– Do –	"	"
E. Caroline	24 Jany	Antwerp	19 – • –	New Orleans	18 Apr	7 June	– Do –	" 1853	"
Infanta	3 Mar	M. Bridge	9 – • –	Cardiff	27 Mar	12 May	New York	3 June	29 June
Avon	5 Apr	Do –	23 May	Quebec	19 June	7 July	Holyhead	" 1854	" 1854
Carlton	25 May	London	16 Sept	Aradena	13 Oct	20 Oct	Callao	4 Jany	31 Mar 1854
Olivia	5 July	London	10 July	Plymouth	30 July	12 Nov	Adelaide	1 Dec	26 Jany
H. Mary	11 July	Liverpool	14 – • –	Cardiff	16 Aug	21 Aug	Queenstown	30 Aug	9 Nov
L. Stanley	31 May	– Do –	5 Aug	New York	8 Sept	29 Sept	Quebec	29 Oct	24 Nov
Avon	3 Aug	Holyhead	16 Sept	Quebec	16 Oct 1854	17 Nov 1854	M. Bridge	" 1854	" 1854
Oregon	3 Aug	Liverpool	14 Jany 1854	San Francisco	29 Mar 1853	24 May	Callao	4 Aug	18 Nov
E. Caroline	9 Aug	– Do –	27 Nov	Aradena	27 Dec	5 Jany 1852	– Do –	15 May	12 Sept
Infanta	24 – • –	M. Bridge	14 Oct 1854	Quebec	1 Nov 1854	2 Dec 1854	M. Bridge	"	"
John Davies	1 Dec 1854	Liverpool	18 Jany	N. Orleans	Mar 11	3 May	Liverpool	"	"
Infanta	22 Mar	M. Bridge	1 May	Boston	22 May	13 June	Quebec	4 July 1855	13 Aug
Lord Stanley	1 Mar	Liverpool	4 July	Geelong	23 July	9 Sept	Callao	10 Nov	12 Mar

604

at	saild	arrived	at	sailed	arrived	at	Length of Voyage	
							Mts. Dys.	
Queenstown	24 Mar	2 Apr	London	.	.	.	11 . 4	
Mt. Bridge	.	.	.	.	.	.	4 . 4	
London	.	.	.	.	.	.	13 . 3	Sold
W	.	.	.	.	.	.	*Lost*	
Queenstown	2 Feby	13 Feby	London	.	.	.	19 . 18	
—Do—	6 Octr	13 Octr	Liverpool	.	.	.	14 . 21	
.	.	.	.	.	.	.	3 . 16	
.	.	.	.	.	.	.	3 . 1	
.	.	.	.	.	.	.	4 . 12	
.	.	.	.	.	.	.	4 . 12	
.	.	.	.	.	.	.	4 . 14	
Quebec	20 July	22 Aug	Mt Bridge	.	.	.	5 . 19	
.	.	.	.	.	.	.	9 . 12	
Queenstown	11 Apr	14 Apr	London	.	.	.	10 . 17	
Callao	6 May	24 Aug	Queenstown	26 Aug	11 Sep	London	14 . 6	
Monte Video	21 Decr	13 Feby	Callao	10 April	23 Aug	—Do—	13 . 12	
Liverpool	.	.	.	.	.	.	5 . 25	
.	.	.	.	.	.	.	3 . 14	
Plymouth	28 Nov	3 Decr	London	.	.	.	16 . 0	
Queenstown	14 Sep	23 Sep	—Do—	.	.	.	13 . 13	
.	.	.	.	.	.	.	3 . 6	
.	.	.	.	.	.	.	5 . 2	
	.	.	.	.	.	.	4 . 22	
Queenstown	13 Mar	16 Mar	Bristol	.	.	.	12 . 15	

Ships

Ships	sailed	From	arrived	at	sailed	arrived	at	sailed	arrived
	1854								
Avon	3 April	M. Bridge	26 May	Quebec	11 July	17 Aug?	Liverpool	..	..
Carlton	26 May	London	5 Sept	Moradura	10 Oct 1855	20 Oct 1855	Callao	15 Dec? 1855	20 Mar 1855
Lady Louisa	8 June	— Do —	23 Oct	Melbourne	6 Jany 1854	2 Mar	Do	25 June	29 Oct
John Davies	22. –..	Liverpool	19 Aug?	Quebec	2. Oct	30 Oct	Liverpool	.	.
Infanta	19 Aug?	M. Bridge	8 Oct 1855	— Do —	28 Oct 1855	1 Dec? 1855	M. Bridge	.	1856
Avon	21 Oct	Liverpool	5 Mar	Callao	1 June	6 Aug	Valparaiso	8 Sept 1856	26 Jany
M. Mary	4 Nov?	London	25 Jany	Port Stanley	2 Feby	12 Mar	Caldera	1 April	9 Apr
Eliza Caroline	9 Dec?	— Do —	30 Dec?	Cardiff	5 Feby	17 July	San Francis	24 Sept	25 Nov
Olivia	29 Dec? 1855	— Do —	21 April	Melbourne	31 May	17 July	Callao	9 Sept	22 Dec? 1856
John Davies	6 Jany	Liverpool	4 May	Moreton Bay	11 June	12 Aug?	— Do —	2 Nov?	3 Apr
Infanta	15 Feby	M. Bridge	22 Apr	Boston	5 May	20 May	Quebec	13 June 1856	14 July
Exodus	21 Apr	Liverpool	26 July	Sydney	27 Sept	24 Nov	Callao	21 Jany	4 May
Carlton	1 May	London	5 May	Swansea	June 8		Wrecked	on	Cape 1865
Lord Stanley	7 – –	Bristol	10 – –	— Do —	25 May	24 Oct	Moradura	23 Nov	3 Dec?
Infanta	26 July 1856	M. Bridge	18 Sept 1856	Quebec	8 Oct	9 Nov?	M. Bridge	. 1856	..
High? Mary	25 Jany	Dundee	26 Jany	New Castle	21 Mar	29 July	Caldera	1 Sept 1857	11 Sept 1857
Lady Louisa	4 Mar	London	2 July	Melbourne	11 Sept	24 Oct	Callao	24 Feby	28 Sept
Avon	1 April	— Do —	27 May	Quebec	18 June	15 July	M. Bridge	.	..
De Salabry	4 May	Liverpool	10 Sept	Melbourne	2 Nov?	20 Dec? 1857	Callao	16 May	27 Sept
Olivia	9 June	London	9 Oct?	— Do —	16 Nov?	3 Jany	— Do —	9 May	4 Sept
John Davies	16 June	Bristol	12 Nov?	Callao	14 Mar	23 July	Queenstown	23 July	29 July
Avon	30 July	M. Bridge	18 Sept Quebec	Quebec	15 Oct?	20 Nov?	M. Bridge	.	..
Eliza Caroline	22 July	Liverpool	15 Nov? 1857	Callao	28 Feby 1858	10 June	Queenstown	13 June	29 June
Exodus	4 Oct?	— Do —	12 Jany	Melbourne	8 Mar	18 Apr	Callao	6 Aug?	31 Oct?

at	sailed	arrived	at	sailed	arrived	at	Length of Voyage
"	1855	"	"	"	"		11 . 14
Queenstown	20 Mar	3 April	London	"	"	"	10 . 8
Do	31 Oct 1855	9 Nov	—Do—	"	"	"	17 . 1
"	"	"	"	"	"	"	11 . 8
"	1856	1856	"	"	"	"	8 . 12
Milf. Haven	4 Feby	10 Feby	London	1855	1855	"	15 . 21
Callao	25 June 1856	6 Nov	Falmouth	12 Nov 1856	28 Nov 1856	Dundee	12 . 24
Do	1 Feby	24 May	Queenstown	26 May	4 June	Liverpool	17 . 27
Queenstown	25 Dec 1856	19 Jany	London	"	"	"	12 . 21
—Do—	8 April	10 Apr	Bristol	"	"	"	15 . 4
M. Bridge	"	"		"	"	"	3 . 30
Queenstown	7 May	12 May	Liverpool	"	"	"	12 . 21
Craysfort		Faulkland Island		"	"	"	Wrecked
Callao	6 Feby	22 June	Queenstown	25 June	7 July	London	14 . 0
"	"	"	"	"	"	"	3 . 14
Callao	28 Nov 1857	1857 31 Mar	Queenstown	1857 3 April	1857 18 Apr	London	14 . 24
Rio de Janeiro	5 Oct	10 Decr	—Do—	19 Decr	24 Dec	London	21 . 20
"	"	"	"	"	"	"	3 . 15
Queenstown	1 Octr	6 Octr	London	"	"	"	17 . 2
—Do—	14 Sept	24 Sept	Bristol	"	"	"	15 . 15
London	"	"		"	"	"	13 . 13
"	"	"		"	"	"	3 . 21
London							11 . 7
Queenstown	5 Nov	8 Nov	Liverpool				13 . 4

Ships	sailed	From	arrived	At	sailed	arrived	At	sailed	arrived
Lord Stanley	13 Aug.	London	11 Dec.	Callao	12 Apr	26 Aug.	Queenstown	28 Aug.	4 Sept.
Wm Wright	10 Apr	Liverpool	10 July	Melbourne	21 Aug.	30 Sept.	Callao	22 Dec.	Apr 4
Avon	6 Apr	M. Bridge	26 May	Quebec	18 June	21 July	M. Bridge	.	.
H. Mary	16 May	London	26 June	7.15 N 24. 30 W	30 W	13 Oct	Coquimbo	3 Nov.	13 Nov
Avon	3 Aug.	M. Bridge	18 Sept	Quebec	9 Oct	23 Nov	M. Bridge	1851	
E. Caroline	7 Aug.	London	21 Aug.	Swansea	11 Sept	31 Dec.	Heradura	Feby 11	25 Feby
John Davies	18 Sept	— Do —	24 Sept	Cardiff	19 Oct	8 Feby	Callao	May 22	7 Oct
Lord Stanley	3 Oct	— Do —	17 Oct	— Do —	14 Nov.	18 Mar	— Do —	June 2	11 Oct
Minnehaha	10 Nov.	Liverpool	17 Mar	Melbourne	13 Apr	11 June	— Do —	Aug. 6	6 Dec.
Olivia	9 Nov.	Bristol	9 Nov.	Cardiff	8 Dec.	30 Mar	Callao	18 June	6 Oct
Exodus	17 Jany	Liverpool	2 Apr	Melbourne	17 May	5 July	Callao	5 Sept	4 Dec.
De Salaberry	17 Feby	London	18 June	— Do —	18 Aug	6 Oct	— Do —	25 Dec.	17 May
Caspian	23 Mar	Liverpool	12 July	— Do —	29 Aug.	13 Oct	— Do —	5 Jany	17 May
Avon	10 April	M. Bridge	15 May	Quebec	7 June	12 July	M. Bridge	.	.
Lady Louisa	14 Apr	London	19 —	— Do —	12 June	14 July	Queenstown	14 July	18 July
Wm Wright	11 May	Bristol	12 —	Newport	18 June	6 Oct	Caldera	6 Nov.	14 Nov
Glen Monarch	9 June	Liverpool	1 Oct	Bombay	17 Dec.	8 Apr	Liverpool	.	.
Avon	29 July	M. Bridge	21 Sept	Quebec	13 Oct	2 Dec.	Liverpool	.	.
Mich. Mary	17 Sept	London	19 Nov.	Savannah	2 Jany	8 Feby	M. Bridge	.	.
E. Caroline	31 Jany	Bristol	1 Feby	Cardiff	19 Feby	1 May	Rio janeiro	12 June	5 Aug
Lady Louisa	5 Mar	M. Bridge	24 Mar	— Do —	18 Apr	21 Aug	Bombay	11 Nov.	29 Mar
John Davies	21 Feby	London	7 Mar	— Do —	4 Apr	9 June	Rio janeiro	7 Aug.	9 Oct
Lord Stanley	16 Mar	— Do —	24 Mar	— Do —	21 Apr	28 Aug	Sydney	23 Oct	20 Dec
H. Mary	26 Mar	M. Bridge	14 May	Boston	28 May	3 June	Miramashi	30 June	27 July

Voyages.

at	Sailed	arrived	at	sailed	arrived	at	Length of Voyage	
							Mos	Days
London							12	22
	1858	1858						
Queenstown	10 Apr	14 Apr	Bristol				12	4
							3	15
	1858	1858		1858	1858			
Callao	10 Jany	26 May	Queenstown	27 May	4 June	London	12	19
							3	20
Callao	7 Apr	3 Aug	Queenstown	3 Aug	8 Aug	Bristol	11	30
Queenstown	9 Oct	14 Oct	London				12	26
_Do_	11 Oct	22 Oct	_Do_				12	19
off Queenstown		21 Dec?	Leith				13	11
_Do_	6 Oct	15 Oct	London				11	6
	1858							
Queenstown	6 Dec	15 Dec	London				12	28
	1859	1859						
_Do_	17 May	28 May	_Do_				15	13
_Do_	17 May	22 May	Liverpool				13	29
							3	2
M. Bridge							3	4
					1859			
Callao	12 Jany	6 May	Queenstown	7 May	13 May	Bristol	12	2
							9	30
							4	3
							4	20
Quebec	25 Aug	21 Sept	Liverpool				7	21
Liverpool							12	24
Quebec	2 Nov	29 Nov	Liverpool				9	8
	1860	1860						
Callao	24 Mar	4 Aug?	Queenstown	6 Aug?	9 Aug?	St Nazaire	16	24
M. Bridge							4	1

Ships	Finished Discharging	Chartering Ports				Commenced Loading	Finished Loading	sailed	from	arrived	at	sailed
		sailed	from	arrived	at							
Caspian	24 Nov	26 Nov arrived at 26 Nov sailed 27 Nov	Rotterdam Rotterdam	4 Dec	C'diff	23 Dec	5 Jany	9 Jany	C'diff	May 6	Callao	June 16
								23 Dec	Barbados	Jany 8	Pensacola	14 Feby
Arizona	29 Nov	"	"	"	"		Jan Ballast	14 Dec	London	16 Dec	Downs	23 Dec
England	12 Jany	20 Jany	Dundee	13 Feby	C'diff	6 Mar		5 Apl	C'diff	Wrecked	off	
Magnificent	15 Jany	26 Jany Feb 11th	Hamburg Leith	7 Mar Roads 26 Feby	C'diff	May 6	May 22	May 21	C'diff	14 Sep	Callao	24 Nov
Bacchus	Jany 11	Jany 26	London	8 Feby	Cardiff	11 Mar	13 Mar		C'diff	14 June	Galle	26 July
Superior	2 Feby	9 Feby	Hamburg	29 Feby	C'diff	24 Feby	20 Apl	22 April	C'diff	27 Aug	Tocanungo	12 Dec saved
Wm Wright	5 Feby	9 Feby arrived	Hamburg	27 Feby 25 Feby	C'diff @ Falmouth	4 Mar sailed 26	July	5 April	C'diff	13 June put in Roddes damaged	Rio	26 June
								11 Jany	Guanape	25 Jany	Callao	30 Jany
Glentilt	Feby 27	29 Feby has sld 21 Mar	Hamburg Auckland C'diff	18 Mar 5 Mar 21 Mar	C'diff Newport		6 May	6 May Mar 31	Newport Callao	15 Sep July 11	Mollendo off Falmouth	Nov 19 11 July
B Princess	6 May	"	"	"	"	20 June	21 June	21 June	L'pool	1865	Valparaiso	
Etta	6 June	10 June	Hamburg	28 June	Newport	9 July		26 July	Newport July	31 Oct	Mollendo	28 Dec
Victory	25 July	"	"	"	"	1 Aug	Aug 22	Aug 22	L'pool	14 Dec	Rangoon	15 Jany
St Emma	31 July	Aug 6	London	16 Aug	C'diff	20 Aug	Sep 20	Sep 22	C'diff	9 Jany	Singapore	28 Jany
Glenmanarch	13 Aug	17 Aug	L'don	23 Aug	Shields		19 Sep	20 Apr July 23	Shields Guanape	Jany 11 Brisham Nov	Valparaiso Falmouth	Jany 11
Mallony	12 Aug	23 Aug	London	28 Aug	Shields		10 Oct	12 Oct	Shields	12 Feby	Singapore	21 Feby
Curlew	28 Aug	31 Aug	Antwerp	5 Sep	Newport		11 Oct	14 Oct	Newport	5 Feby	Iquique	6 Feby
		"	"	"	"			25 Aug	Macabi	20 Dec put in	Falmouth damaged	16 Jany
Dolb Castle	28 Aug	"	"	"	"	1 Sep	23 Sep	24 Sep	London	26 Dec	Melbourne	15 Feby
Minnehaha	30 Oct	4 Nov 8 to 17th	Antwerp Newcastle loading	12 Nov	Shields	27 Nov	5 Dec	12 Dec	Shields 17th Dec 18	12 May Dec 2	Callao	14 June

610

Ships	Harbd Dischargd	Wharf sailed	... Ports from	arrived	at	Commend Loading	Finishd Loading	sailed	from	arrived	at	sailed
Caspian	24 Nov	26 Nov arrived & 26 Nov sailed 27 Nov	Rotterdam	4 Dec Aberdeen	C'diff	23 Dec	5 Jany	9 Jany	C'diff	May 6	Callao	June 11
								23 Dec	Barbados	Jany	Pernambco	17 Feby
Arizona	29 Nov	"	"	"	"		In Ballast	14 Dec	London	16 Dec	Deveno	22 Dec
England	12 Jany	30 Jany	Deemba	13 Feby	C'diff	6 Mar		5 Apl	C'diff	Wrecked		off
Magnificent	15 Jany	26 Jany put out back	Hamburg Leith & London	4 Mar 26 Feby	C'diff	May 6	May 22 sailed Feby	May 21	C'diff	14 Sep	Callao	24 Nov
Bacchus	Jany 11	Jany 28	Elton	8 Feby	Cardiff		Sailed Feby 11 Mar	27 Feby 12 Mar	C'diff	14 June	Galle	26 July
Superior	2 Feby	4 Feby congested at Deal	Hamburg	29 Feby 19 Feby	C'diff	26 Feby	20 Apl	22 April	C'diff	27 Aug	Tucarance	12 Nov finned
Wm Wright	5 Feby	4 Feby arrived	Hamburg	27 Feby 25 May	C'diff @ Falmouth	4 Mar sailed 26 Feby		5 April	C'diff	13 June put in Rudder damaged	Rio	26 June
								11 Jany	Guanape	25 Jany	Callao	30 Jany
Glentilt	Feby 27	29 Feby has set Anchor	Hamburg	18 Mar 5 Mar	C'diff		6 May	6 May	Newport	15 Sep	Mollindo	Nov 19
		21 Mar	C'diff	21 Mar	Newport			Mar 31	Callao	July 11	off Falmouth	11 July
B Princess	6 May	"	"	"	"		20 June	21 June	Lpool	18 Oct	Valpariso	
Etta	6 June	10 June	Hamburg	28 June	Newport	9 July		26 July	NewYork	31 Oct	Mollindo	28 Dec
Victory	25 July	"	"	"	"	2 Aug	Aug 22	Aug 22	Lpool	14 Dec	Rangon	15 Jany
St Emma	31 July	Aug 8	London	16 Aug	C'diff	30 Aug	Sep 20	Sep 22	C'diff	9 Jany	Singapre	28 Jany
Glenmonarch	13 Aug	17 Aug	Lpool	23 Aug	Shields		19 Sep	20 Sepr	Shields	Jany 11	Valpariso	Jany 11
							July 23	Guanape	4 Nov	Falmouth	
Mallony	12 Aug	23 Aug	London	28 Aug	Shields		10 Oct	12 Oct	Shields	12 Feby	Singapre	21 Feby
Curlew	28 Aug	31 Aug	Antwerp	5 Sep	Newport		11 Oct	14 Oct	Newport	5 Feby	Iquique	6 Feby
								25 Aug	Macate	20 Dec put in	Falmouth Lamaged	16 May
Dobb Castle	28 Aug	"	"	"	"	2 Sep	23 Sep	24 Sep	London	26 Dec	Milbourn	15 Feby
Minnehaha	30 Oct	4 Nov 5 Nov	Antwerp West Hartlepool Hauling	12 Nov	Shields	27 Nov	5 Dec	12 Dec	Shields off the Start Dec 21	12 May Dec 21	Callao	14 June

Ships	Finished discharging	Changing Ports				Commenced Loading	Finished Loading	Sailed	From	Arrived	Port
		Sailed	From	Arrived	2nd						
Anglesey	8 Nov [186]	12 Nov Left Flushing	Antwerp 9 Nov	28 Nov Nov 21	Cardiff			2 Dec	Cardiff	7 April	Singapore
Cardiganshire	7 April [187]							7 May	Liverpool	5 Octr	Frisco
Febba	21 June [188]	4 June [1887]	Port ?	17 June	Cardiff						
Dunnerdale	30 June [187]	3 July	Tralee	6 July	Cardiff			26 July	Cardiff	Dec 31	Frisco
Carnarvonshire	4 April 30 July [187]							25 Aug	Liverpool	20 Dec	Frisco
Flintshire	20 Augt [187]							22 Sept	Liverpool	21 Jany	Frisco
Merionith	22 Sep [187]	23 Sept	Dublin	25 Sept	Cardiff			15 Octr	Cardiff	20 Jany	Frisco
Dols Castle	26 Sept [187]	30 Sept	Watsford	1 Octr	Swansea			8 Nov	Swansea	30 Mar	Frisco
Sarah Pimma	25 Octr [187]	4 Nov Passed Gibraltar	Genoa	15 Dec Dec 9	Cardiff			16 Jany	Cardiff	11 May	Rangoon
Montgomeryshire	26 Octr [187]	1 Nov	Bremen Hamburg	12 Nov	Cardiff			29 Nov	Cardiff	25 Mar	Rangoon
Lord Cairns	26 Nov [187]	29 Nov	Limerick	3 Dec	Cardiff			26 Dec	Cardiff	16 April	Frisco
Bacchus	21 Nov [187]	Went to the River Deeiz"						20 Dec	Lpool	22 Apl	Frisco

612

Sailed	Arrived	At	Sailed	Arrived	At	Sailed	Arrived	At	Commenced discharging	Finished discharging	Time at sea		Total length of voyage	
											m. ds		m. ds	
20 April	25 May	Diamond Island	28 May	May 28	Barcelona	Passed Gibraltar Nov 8 11 June 22 Passed St Helena Sept 21	22 Nov	Genoa	187 5 Dec	188 9 Jany	11	1	14	1
20 Nov	8 Mar	L'stown	15 Mar	27 Mar	Middlesbro				188 27 Mar	188 24 April	10	20	12	17
20 Mar	June 3 Put in under damage to rigging	Callao	July 12	11 Nov	Astoria	14 Nov	25 Nov	Hull	188 27 Nov	188 14 Dec	15	30	Sold June 188 14	14
14 Feby	9 June	Falmouth	15 June	23 June	Limerick					188 7 July	9	29	11	4
21 April	27 Augt	L'pool								188 13 Sept	11	5	12	24
4 April	8 July	Queenstown	July 13	16 July	Dublin				188 18 July	188 3 Augt	9	0	10	12
5 May	25 Oct	Astoria	29 Oct	12 Nov Docked 14 Nov	Grimsby				188 15 Nov	188 5 Dec	12	6	14	9
5 June	23 Oct	L'stown	29 Oct	7 Nov	Rotterdam					188 23 Nov	9	22	12	29
2 May	26 Augt	Falmouth	29 Augt	Sept 2	Amsterdam				Sept 4	188 Sept 18	9	4	10	23
7 June	17 Oct	Queenstown	29 Oct	Oct 31	Belfast Lough	1 Nov	Nov 2	Sligo	188 Nov 3	188 Dec 4	10	4	12	8
8 June	20 Oct	Birkenhead								188 31 Oct	10	0	11	10

613

Ships	Finished Discharging	Changing Ports				Commenced Loading	Finished Loading	Sailed	From	Arrived	At
		Sailed	From	Arrived	At						
Dunnerdale	188 / 14 Dec	Jany 22	Hull	Jany 29	North fleet River Thames			5 Feby	London	16 July	Frisco
Denbighshire	189 / 17 Jany	Jany 19	Dunkirk	Lynde off Dover Jany 19							
Anglesey	189 / 4 Feby	Feby 7	Barrow	Feby 8	Liverpool			6 March	Liverpool	27 July	Frisco
Chinsura	189 / 19 Feby	Mar 30	Sunderland	9 Apl	Cardiff			4 May	Cardiff	Aug 16	Coquimbo
Cardiganshire	189 / 16 Apl	Apl 25	Hull	Apl 26	North Shields ?			23 May	North Shields	Oct 2	Frisco
Carnarvonshire	189 / 21 June	June 28	Hull	29 June	North Shields ?			23 July	North Shields	Dec 5	Frisco
Merionetti	189 / 9 Augt	Aug 18	Barmouth Roads	3 Sept	Cardiff	Returned to Barmouth Roads Sept 26		26 Sept	Cardiff	13 Nov	Rio / Sailed Oct 1
Montgomeryshire	189 / 28 Aug							2 May	Rangoon	16 Sept	Rio
								30 Sept	Antwerp	10 Feby	Frisco
Bacchus	88 / 16 Sep	17 Sept Towing	Rotterdam	22 Sept	Cardiff			5 Nov	Cardiff	20 Jany	Cape Town
Flintshire	89 / 19 Sept	29 Sept Towing	Galway	3 Oct	Cardiff			30 Nov	Rio	3rd March	Frisco
								21 Oct	Cardiff	20 Dec	Cape Town
Lord Cairns	89 / 30 Nov	2 Dec	Middlesbro	2 Dec	Shields			15 Sept	Rio	Dec 2	Iquique
								23 Dec off Lizard 28 Dec 7.50 a.m	Shields	20 Apl	Frisco
Dols Castle	189 / 28 Dec	180 / Jany 1 Towing	Cork	Jany 2	Swansea			1 Feby	Swansea	June 12	Frisco

Sailed	Arrived	At	Sailed	Arrived	At	Sailed	Arrived	At	Commenced discharging	Finished discharging	Time at Sea	Total length of voyage
1 Sept	20 Jany	Holyhead	28 Jany	29 Jany	Dublin				90 Jany 30	90 14 Feby	11 24	14 0
24 Sept	7 Feby	Queenstown	14 Feby	18 Feby	Galway Bay		20 Feby 1 March	Galway Roads March		90 Mar 20	11 14	13 - 16
25 Sept	30 Sept	Iquique	Nov 14	7 March	Falmouth	9 March	10 March	London		90 3 April	10 7	13 - 15
26 Dec	27 April	Falmouth	29 Apl	2 May						90 22 May	11 9	13 - 6
29 Jany	2 June	Queenstown	June	June 9	Dublin					28 June	10 17	12 - 7
24 Dec	Mar 25	at Iquals	March 26	4 April	Rangoon							
6 ct 21	14 Feby	Frisco	9 March	17 July	Elston	19 July	27 July	Shields		191 Augt 21	22 - 1	24 - 12
25 April	25 Aug	Falmouth	28 Augt	1 Sept	Dublin					190 16 Sept	11 - 2	12 - 19
21 Feby	May 10	Dismans	May 11	May 14	Rangoon	20 June	27 Oct	Rio		1891 6 ct 14	22 - 14	24 - 28
28 March	Sept 5	Return	12 Sept	19 Sept	West Hartlepool							
24 Jany	Mar 24	Dismans	Mar 25	Mar 28	Rangoon	6 May	12 Aug	Rio		1891 May 16	18 - 13	19 - 19
2 Jany	April 8	off Falmouth	April 30	Dunkirk						190		
20 June	Oct 9	Queenstown	Oct 17	6 ct 20	Sligo				21 Oct	26 Nov	9 27	11 27
19 July	6 ff	Old Head	Kinsale	Nov 30			8 Dec	Galway		191 Jany 6	10 7	12 9

Ships	Finished Discharging	Changing Ports				Commenced Loading	Finished Loading	Sailed	From	arrived	at
		Sailed	From	arr'd	at						
Cardiganshire	— 1893 — Mar 16/93	15 May	Hamburg	29 May	Cardiff			30 June	Cardiff	Aug 9	Rio
Anglesey	May 24/93	16 June	Cork	17 June	Swansea			15 July	Swansea	27 Nov	Frisco
Dunnerdale	July 19/93	24 July	Bristol	24 July	Cardiff			23 Sept	Cardiff	21 Feby '94	Frisco
Chinsura	Aug 29/93	15 Sept	Sunderland	27 Sept	Swansea			31 Oct	Swansea	9 Mar	Frisco
Montgomeryshire	Oct 7/93	12 Oct	Hull	20 Oct	Swansea			22 Nov	Swansea	9 Mar	Frisco
Carnarvonshire	Oct 6/93	13 Oct	Antwerp	29 Oct	Swansea			30 Nov	Swansea	28 Mar	Frisco
Afon Befri	Oct 21/93	Oct 26	Hamburg	16 Nov	Swansea			5 Jany	Swansea	(Lost)	Ship
Flintshire	Oct 27/93	Oct 31	Cork	1 Nov	Swansea			28 Dec	Swansea	7 May	Frisco
Sarah & Emma	Nov 18/93	— Sold —						Sold			
Bacchus	Dec 29/93	(For voyage see February 1896)									
Lord Cairns	— 1894 — Feby 6/94	Mar 26	Middlesbro	27 Mar	Swansea			19 April	Swansea	28 Augt	Frisco
Afon Alaw	Apl 24/94	May 1	Limerick	May 4	Swansea			26 May	Swansea	15 Octr	Frisco

Sailed	arrived	at	Sailed	arrived	at	Sailed	arrived	at	commenced discharging	finished discharging	Time at Sea	Total length of Voyage
23 Sept	5 Dec	Bajagna	23 Dec	10 April	Falmouth	13 April	18 April	Hamburg		May 1/94	9 . 19	13 15
25 Jany.	27 May	Falmouth	31 May	2 June	Cardiff					June 23/94	10. 18	12. 28
3 Nov. ('94)	28 March ('95)	Queenstown	1 April	11 April	Newcastle	— Sold —				May 1/95	18. 19	21. 12 — Sold —
25 Oct.	19 March	Queenstown	25 March	25 March	Cork	— Sold —				Apl 15/95	16. 25	19. 17 — Sold —
19 Oct.	27 Feby	Queenstown	5 March	6 March	Dublin					Mar 22/95	15. 12	17. 15
6 Nov.	19 March	Queenstown	25 March	25 March	Cork					Apl 16/95	15. 25	18. 10
never heard of after this date											Lost	
16 Nov.	10 Apl	Queenstown	18 April	26 April	South Newcastle Shields					May 18/95	15. 29	18. 21
— Sold —						— Sold —						
8 Oct.	26 Feby	Falmouth	1 March	3 March / 4 March	Dunkirk Roads / Dunkirk					March 19/95	10. 13	13. 13
8 March	22 July	Queenstown	2 August	7 August	Fleetwood					Aug 22/95	14. 12	15. 25

Ships	Finished Discharging	Changing Ports				Commenced Loading	Finished Loading	Sailed	From	Arrived	At
		Sailed	From	arr'd	at						
Cardiganshire	1894 May 1	6 May 7 "	Hamburg Cuxhaven	18 May	Swansea			14 June	Swansea	2 Nov	Frisco
Merioneth	June 15	26 June	Dunkirk	29 June	Cardiff			1 Augt	Cardiff	9 Sept	Rio
								13 June	Rio	14 Sept	Frisco
Anglesey	June 23							25 July	Cardiff	30 Nov	Frisco
Dob Castle	Sept 29/94	4 Oct	Mortimer's Point	4 Oct	Penarth		— Sold —				
Lord Cairns	1895 Mar 19/95	2 Apl 8 April	Dunkirk Penarth Roads	7 April 8 April	Penarth Roads Swansea			29 April	Swansea	6 Sept	Frisco
Montgomeryshire	Mar 22/95	26 Mar	Dublin	27 Mar	Cardiff			23 April	Cardiff	28 May	Rio.
								25 Jany	Queenstown	29 Jany 31 Jany	Dunkirk Roads Docked
Carnarvonshire	April 16/95	18 Apl	Cork	20 Apl	Swansea			18 May	Swansea	27 October	Frisco
Flintshire	May 18/95	25 May	South Shields	5 June	Swansea			29 June	Swansea	7 Novr	Frisco
Cardiganshire	May 28/95	1 June	Hull	8 June	Swansea			28 June	Swansea	7 Novr	Frisco
								9 Nov	Off Falmouth	17 Novr	Sunderland
Anglesey	June 15/95	18 June	Fleetwood	19 June	Swansea			6 July	Swansea	7 Novr	Frisco
								8 March	Frisco	22 July	Lpool.
Afon Alaw	Augt 22/95	31 Augt	Fleetwood	2 Sept	Cardiff			25 Octr 7 October	Cardiff Barry Roads	1 February	Singapore
								29 Sept	Falmouth	7 October	Hamburg
Montgomeryshire	1896 Feby 15/96	18 Feby	Dunkirk (Towing)	21 Feby	Cardiff			19 March	Cardiff	1st May	Rio
								13 March	Falmouth	17 March	Middlesbro

Sailed	Arrived	at	Sailed	arrived	at	Sailed	arrived	at	commenced Discharging	finished Discharging	Time at sea	Total length voyage
31 Dec	27 Apl	Falmouth	3 May	10 May	Hull					May 28/95	10.26	12.2?
31 Oct	20 Jany	Diamond Island	22 Jany ⁹⁵·	26 Jany	Rangoon	16 Feby	8 May	Rio				
23 Oct	24 Feby	Falmouth	29 Feby	9 March	Belfast					April 1/96	19.8	21.1?
23 Jany	23 May	Queenstown	3 June	8 June	Fleetwood					June 15/95	10.14	11.2?
— Sold —						— Sold —						
16 Octr	12 Feby	Queenstown	13 Feby	13 Feby	Cork					March 6/?	9.20	11.1?
25 July	3 Sept	Valparaiso	6 Sept	12 Sept	Iquique	21 Octr	21 Jany/?	Queenstown		Feby 15/96	9.8	10.24
11 Decr — Wrecked on Yohane Point, West Coast Ireland, 12.30 A.M. April 11th 1896 —												
9 Jany/96	7 June	Queenstown	14 June	16 June	B'head					June 29/96	11.18	13.11
21 Decr	4 Feby	Sydney	6 March	17 May	Frisco	3 July	9 Novr	Off Falmouth		Decr 9/96	16.19	18.11
24 Decr	9 March	Capetown	21 April	22 May	Newcastle (N.S.W.)	5 Sept	16 Decr	Frisco		Augt 26/?	24.16	26.11
27 Feby	—	Elephant Point — (sailed from Diamond Island, 15 May)	18 April	Bassein	12 May	27 Sept	Falmouth			Octr 27/96	12.2	14.5
13 June	5 Augt	Taltal	10 Augt	11 Octr	Frisco	31 Octr	6 March	Falmouth		Apl 3/97	11.27	13.19

Appendix VII (iii)

Main Ports visited from 1843-1903 by Davies ships

	1843-52	1853-62	1863-72	1873-82	1883-92	1893-1905
Akyab	0	0	8	5	10	0
Antwerp	1	7	35	39	6	8
Bassein	0	0	1	12	9	2
Belfast	2	0	2	0	3	1
Birkenhead	0	3	6	2	10	2
Bombay	1	7	22	5	1	0
Boston	4	3	0	0	0	0
Bristol	0	25	16	3	3	1
Bremerhaven	0	2	0	13	7	0
Browershaven	0	0	12	2	0	0
Caernarvon	12	2	0	0	0	0
Calcutta	0	3	26	10	1	0
Caldera	0	6	1	1	0	0
Capetown	0	0	0	1	4	2
Cardiff	3	24	85	73	68	15
Chincha Is.	1	0	15	1	0	9
Callao	11	55	110	70	1	0
Coquimbo	1	1	7	4	8	0
Cork	7	0	0	0	3	8
Cuxhaven	0	1	6	0	0	0
Diamond Islands	0	0	0	2	0	3
Dublin	1	0	4	3	8	9
Dunkirk	0	0	0	0	7	4
Elephant Point	0	0	0	4	8	0
Falmouth	0	1	15	43	49	16
Fleetwood	1	0	2	3	1	6
Galway	1	0	0	0	6	2
Genoa	0	0	2	0	2	0
Gluckstadt	0	0	7	1	0	0
Glasgow	0	0	5	2	0	0
Gunape Islands	0	0	19	2	0	0
Havre	0	0	0	7	2	0
Hamburg	0	4	24	5	11	5
Holyhead	2	3	4	0	1	0
Huanillo	0	0	0	19	1	0
Hull	2	0	3	5	7	6
Iquique	0	0	0	3	8	1

	1843-52	1853-62	1863-72	1873-82	1883-92	1893-1905
Kingston, Jamaica	0	0	7	0	0	0
Liverpool	85	77	85	106	31	5
Lobos	0	0	0	22	0	0
London	9	61	85	27	11	0
Macabi	0	0	10	13	0	0
Melbourne	0	20	8	0	0	0
Menai Bridge	68	44	13	0	0	0
Mollendo	0	0	8	2	0	0
Monte Video	0	5	19	4	2	0
Moulmein	2	0	0	8	4	0
Newcastle NSW	0	0	0	0	0	10
New Orleans	18	3	0	0	0	0
Newport	0	4	7	5	2	0
New York	11	2	1	0	4	0
Pabellon de Pica	0	0	0	8	0	0
Payta	0	0	4	0	0	0
Penarth Roads	0	0	8	8	7	0
Pensacola	0	2	8	4	0	0
Pt. de Galle, Ceylon	0	0	10	2	0	0
Pisaqua	1	0	0	1	6	2
Quebec	39	45	24	0	0	0
Queenstown	4	50	11	24	45	38
Rangoon	0	0	11	48	20	6
Rio de Janeiro	0	10	13	34	28	8
Rotterdam	0	0	8	1	3	2
San Francisco	1	3	0	22	70	61
Sand Heads	0	4	6	1	2	0
South Shields	0	0	15	14	10	2
St John	9	0	3	0	0	0
St Nazaire	0	2	0	6	0	0
Singapore	1	0	1	30	9	1
Stade	0	0	6	3	0	0
Sunderland	0	1	5	4	4	1
Swansea	0	5	0	0	13	40
Sydney	2	2	0	1	2	8
Valparaiso	0	1	3	4	1	1
Yokohama	0	0	0	0	2	2

Appendix VII (iv)

Examples of voyages by Davies ships.

    (1)   *Eliza Caroline*

    (2)   *Dolbadarn Castle*

    (3)   *Anglesey*

    (4)   *Merioneth*

'Eliza Caroline'

Year	Depart	Port	Arrive	Port	Depart	Arrive	Port
1847	3 May	Liverpool	12 June	Quebec	22 July	1 Sept	Menai Bridge
1847	28 Sept	M. Bridge	26 Oct	St John	27 Nov	25 Dec	Menai Bridge
1848	10 Apr	Liverpool	–	New York	–	22 June	Quebec
1848	8 Nov	Liverpool	21 Dec	New Orleans	21 Feb	2 Apr	Liverpool
1849	11 May	Liverpool	24 June	New York	14 Jly	29 Jly	Quebec
1849	31 Dec	Plymouth	31 Mar	Port Philip	2 May	25 June	Callao
1851	27 May	London	–	Sydney	–	–	Callao
1853	24 Jan	Antwerp	19 Mar	New Orleans	18 Apr	7 June	Liverpool
1853	9 Aug	Liverpool	27 Nov	Heradura	27 Dec	5 Jan	Callao
1854	9 Dec	London	30 Dec	Cardiff	5 Feb	17 July	S. Frans.
1856	22 July	Liverpool	15 Nov	Callao	28 Feb	10 June	Queenstown
1857	7 Aug	London	21 Aug	Swansea	11 Sept	31 Dec	Heradura
1859	31 Jan	Bristol	1 Feb	Cardiff	19 Feb	1 May	Rio de J.
1860	14 Nov	Liverpool	13 Jan	Rio de Jan.	22 Feb	7 Apr	Savannah
1860	7 July	Liverpool	18 Aug	Quebec	3 Sept	1 Oct	Bristol
1860	2 Nov	Bristol	3 Nov	Cardiff	25 Nov	1 Dec	Queenstown
1861	19 July	Menai Br.	1 Sept	Quebec	4 Oct	5 Nov	Liverpool
1862	3 Apr	Liverpool	11 May	Quebec	9 Jne	3 Jly	Menai Brd.
1862	17 Jly	Menai Br.	25 Aug	Quebec	10 Sept	5 Oct	Menai Br.
1862	27 Oct	Menai Br.	1 Nov	Cardiff	25 Nov	12 Jan	Rio de J.
1863	14 July	Menai Br.	17 Aug	Quebec	5 Sept	5 Oct	Menai Br.
1863	21 Oct	Menai Br.	28 Oct	Cardiff	26 Nov	19 Dec	Gibraltar
1864	6 July	Liverpool	14 Aug	Quebec	31 Aug	18 Oct	Bristol
1864	8 Dec	Bristol	13 Dec	Cardiff	21 Dec	1 Feb	Rio de J.
1865	26 July	Cardiff	8 Sept	Quebec	27 Sept	28 Oct	Menai Br.

Depart	Arrive	Port	Depart	Arrive	Port	Time at Sea Mths days		Length of voyage Mths days	
						2	20	3	29
						1	26	2	27
25 Jly	23 Aug	Menai Bridge				3	11	4	9
						2	23	4	25
31 Aug	11 Oct	Liverpool				3	10	5	00
27 Jne	20 Jly	Chinchas	8 Oct	22 Jan	Cork	8	14	12	22
–	–	Payuna	–	22 Sept	Queenstown (1852)				
		(cont'd)	–	6 Dec	Antwerp			18	9
						3	12	4	14
15 May	12 Sept	Queenstown	14 Sept	22 Sept	London	8	4	13	13
24 Sept	25 Nov	Callao (cont'd)	1 Feb 26 May	24 May 4 June	Queenstown Liverpool	12	2	17	27
13 Jne	29 Jne	London				7	22	11	7
11 Feb	25 Feb	Callao (cont'd)	7 Apr 3 Aug	3 Aug 8 Aug	Queenstown Bristol	8	20	11	30
12 Jne	5 Aug	Quebec	25 Aug	21 Sept	Liverpool	5	00	7	21
17 May	28 Jne	Liverpool				4	24	7	14
						2	10	2	21
17 Dec	6 Feb	Rio de J. (cont'd)	22 Mar 8 Jne	11 May 6 Jly	Quebec Menai Bridge	5	6	8	4
						2	16	3	17
						2	1	3	0
						2	3	2	18
21 Feb	11 May	Quebec	27 May	28 Jne	Menai Bridge	5	12	8	1
						2	3	2	21
13 Feb	25 Apr	St John	16 May	14 June	Liverpool	4	7	7	24
						2	27	3	12
24 Mar	10 May	Quebec	13 Jne	8 Jly	Cardiff	3	27	7	00
						2	15	3	02

'Dolbadarn Castle'

Year	Depart	Port	Arrive	Port	Depart	Arrive	Port
1866	8 Dec	Liverpool	2 May	Calcutta	17 June	21 Sept	Passed S. Helena
1868	8 Jan	London	13 May	Calcutta	4 July	7 July	Off Sangor
1869	2 Jan	London	4 May	Sangor	–	6 May	Calcutta
1869	24 Nov	London	18 Mar	Calcutta	22 Apr	7 Sept	London
1870	15 Oct	Sunderland	7 Mar	Rangoon	1 Apr	18 Aug	Falmouth
1871	4 Oct	Liverpool	6 Jan	Pr. de Galle Ceylon	31 Jan	24 Feb	Akyab
1872	24 Sept	London	26 Dec	Melbourne	15 Feb	4 July	London
1873	23 Aug	S. Shields	30 Dec	Pt. de Galle Ceylon	27 Jan	24 Feb	Akyab
1874	12 Nov	Cardiff	11 Mar	Rangoon	14 Apr	9 Sept	Bremerhaven
1875	25 Oct	Bremerhaven	21 Feb	Elephant Pt.	22 Feb	22 Feb	Rangoon
1876	5 Oct	Liverpool	25 Feb	Singapore	10 Mar	31 Mar	Bassein
1877	4 Dec	Cardiff	9 Jan	Rio de Jan.	11 Feb	2 Apr	Mexilliones
1878	25 Nov	Liverpool	29 Mar	Akyab	29 Apr	8 Sept	Falmouth
1879	27 Oct	Cardiff	21 Feb	Singapore	14 Mar	9 Apr	Akyab
1881	28 Jan	Cardiff	26 May	Singapore	12 July	14 Dec	Liverpool
1882	24 Jan	Liverpool	12 Mar	Rio de Jan	13 Apr	17 June	Rangoon
1882	21 Dec	Liverpool	9 May	Rangoon	22 June	3 Nov	Queenstown
1884	5 Feb	Cardiff	13 July	Yokohama	30 July	4 Sept	S. Frans.
1885	4 July	Cardiff	24 Oct	Sydney	27 Nov	20 Feb	Diamond Is.
1886	28 Oct	Liverpool	2 Mar	San Francisco	23 Apr	29 Aug	Falmouth
1887	8 Nov	Swansea	30 Mar	San Francisco	5 May	26 Oct	Queenstown
1889	15 Jan	Cardiff	14 May	San Francisco	12 July	4 Dec	Queenstown
1890	1 Feb	Swansea	12 June	San Francisco	19 July	8 Dec	Galway
1891	13 Feb	Swansea	27 June	San Francisco	10 Aug	21 Dec	Queenstown
1892	17 Feb	Barry	31 Mar	Rio de Jan	10 May	18 July	Iquique
1893	2 Sept	Swansea	5 Feb	San Francisco	7 Apr	1 Sept	Queenstown

Depart	Arrive	Port	Depart	Arrive	Port	Time at Sea Mths days		Length of voyage Mths days	
–	23 Nov	London				10	0	11	15
7 July	16 Nov	Portland Bay	–	23 Nov	London	8	24	10	15
6 June	6 Oct	London				8	1	9	4
							287	9	26
21 Aug	25 Aug	Liverpool					315	11	16
9 Mar	13 Aug	London					314	11	22
							283	10	21
11 Mar	13 Aug	Falmouth	15 Aug	24 Aug	Bremerhaven		366	14	3
							302	12	14
1 Apr	21 Aug	Liverpool					301	10	29
12 Apr	24 Aug	Falmouth	29 Aug	1 Sept	Antwerp		331	12	17
11 June	6 Oct	Birkenhead					306	13	14
8 Sept	3 Sept	Bremerhaven					292	10	26
30 Apr	4 Oct	Queenstown	9 Oct	27 Oct	Antwerp	12	0	13	14
						10	16	13	22
19 July	23 Nov	Liverpool				9	30	11	1
10 Nov	20 Nov	Hamburg				10	30	12	5
30 Oct	5 Apr	Falmouth	15 Apr	23 Apr	S. Shields	14	18	17	5
–	23 Feb	Bassein	27 Mar	9 Sept	Falmouth	14	12	16	9
3 Sept	8 Sept	Waterford				10	11	12	2
29 Oct	12 Nov	Grimsby				12	6	14	9
10 Dec	11 Dec	Cork				10	26	12	23
						10	7	12	9
31 Dec	3 Jan	Dublin				10	21	12	12
7 Sept	27 Dec	Queenstown	3 Jan	20 Jan	Rotterdam	11	3	12	29
10 Sept	13 Sept	Sharpness				12	11	19	13

'Anglesey'

Year	Depart	Port	Arrive	Port	Depart	Arrive	Port
1875	2 Dec	Liverpool	15 Apr	Rangoon	31 May	13 Oct	Liverpool
1876	2 Dec	Liverpool	28 Mar	Rangoon	5 May	2 Sept	Liverpool
1877	26 Oct	Liverpool	14 Feb	Rangoon	16 Mar	27 July	Liverpool
1878	2 Sept	Liverpool	8 Dec	Diamond Is.	–	15 Dec	Bassein
1879	21 Aug	Cardiff	15 Dec	Singapore	7 Jan	11 Feb	Rangoon
1880	21 Sept	Liverpool	12 Jan	Rangoon	16 Mar	12 July	Liverpool
1881	22 Aug	Liverpool	2 Jan	San Francisco	27 Feb	25 June	Queenstown
1882	9 Sept	Cardiff	4 Jan	Singapore	22 Jan	12 Feb	Rangoon
1883	28 Nov	Cardiff	23 Mar	Rangoon	13 Apr	13 Aug	Falmth
1884	10 Oct	Cardiff	9 Feb	Pilot Ground	–	12 Feb	Rangoon
1885	19 Sept	Cardiff	5 Nov	Rio de Janeiro	11 Dec	14 Mar	Elephant Point
1886	21 Dec	Cardiff	7 Apr	Singapore	20 Apr	25 May	Diamond Is.
1888	16 Mar	Swansea	31 July	San Francisco	9 Sept	17 Jan	Barrow
1889	6 Mar	Liverpool	27 July	San Francisco	24 Sept	7 Feb	Queenstown
1890	1 May	Barry	4 Aug	Coquimbo	13 Sept	5 Oct	Pisaqua
1891	18 May	Hamburg	17 Oct	San Francisco	24 Nov	2 May	Queenstown
1892	13 June	Swansea	25 Oct	San Francisco	30 Dec	29 Apr	Falmouth
1893	15 July	Swansea	27 Nov	San Francisco	25 Jan	27 May	Falmouth
1894	25 July	Cardiff	30 Nov	San Francisco	23 Jan	23 May	Queenstown
1895	6 July	Swansea	7 Nov	San Francisco	24 Dec	9 Mar	Capetown
							(cont'd)
1897	30 Sept	Swansea	24 Jan	San Francisco	6 Mar	12 July	Queenstown
1898	27 Oct	Barry	16 Feb	Rangoon	29 Mar	13 Jly	R. de Jan.
1900	29 May	Swansea	10 Nov	San Francisco	29 Dec	6 May	Queenstown
1901	28 June	Swansea	11 Nov	San Francisco	22 Dec	2 Apr	Queenstown
1902	19 June	S. Shields	30 Nov	San Francisco	12 May (1904)	16 Sept	Liverpool
1905	SOLD						

Depart	Arrive	Port	Depart	Arrive	Port	Time at Sea		Length of voyage	
						Mths	days	Mths	days
							316	10	26
							274	10	20
							274	10	27
6 Mar	24 Jne	Queenstown	25 Jne	1 July	Bremerhaven		302	11	5
21 Mar	18 Aug	Liverpool					363	13	7
						9	21	10	26
1 July	3 July	Dublin				10	11	12	15
21 Mar	4 Aug	Queenstown	9 Aug	18 Aug	Hamburg	11	9	13	12
20 Aug	26 Aug	London				8	29	11	23
21 Mar	14 Aug	Liverpool				10	4	11	16
18 Mar	7 Apr	Akyab	13 May	16 Oct	Antwerp	12	27	14	14
28 May	28 May	Bassein	11 Jne	22 Nov	Genoa	11	1	14	1
						10	1	12	26
14 Feb	18 Feb	Galway				11	14	13	16
18 Nov	8 Mar	Hamburg				10	7	12	15
6 Apr	15 Apr	Havre				10	28	12	26
6 May	7 May	Cork				10	24	12	26
31 May	2 June	Cardiff				10	18	12	28
3 June	8 June	Fleetwood				10	14	11	23
21 Apr	22 May	Newcaste NSW	5 Sept	16 Dec	San Francisco				
8 Mar	22 July	Liverpool				24	16	26	11
15 Jly	21 July	Antwerp				9	21	11	17
20 Aug	28 Oct	Caleta Buena	27 Nov	26 Mar	Rotterdam	16	27	20	1
29 Dec	6 May	Queenstown	11 May	13 May	Dublin	11	14	13	17
22 Dec	2 Apr	Queenstown	5 Apr	21 Apr	Sunderland	8	10	11	12
12 May	16 Sept	Liverpool				9	21	28	24
(1904)									

'Merioneth'

Year	Depart	Port	Arrive	Port	Depart	Arrive	Port
1876	13 Jan	Liverpool	29 Apr	Elephant Point	10 May	16 May	Rangoon
1876	14 Dec	Liverpool	13 Apr	Rangoon	29 May	25 Sept	Liverpool
1877	9 Nov	Liverpool	26 Feb	Bombay	4 May	17 Sept	Liverpool
1878	26 Oct	Liverpool	11 Feb	Rangoon	28 Mar	27 July	Falmouth
1879	26 Sept	Cardiff	8 Jan	Singapore	26 Jan	18 Feb	Bassein
1880	19 Nov	Cardiff	17 Apr	Singapore	27 Apr	17 May	Bassein
1882	26 Jan	Cardiff	12 Mar	Rio de Jan.	20 Apr	2 July	Rangoon
1883	5 Feb	Penarth Roads	23 Mar	Rio de Jan.	12 Apr	3 Aug	S. Francisco
1884	16 Apr	Cardiff	24 May	Rio de Jan.	12 July	2 Nov	S. Francisco
1885	22 July	Cardiff	21 Nov	San Francisco	9 Feb	17 June	Falmouth
1886	30 July	Liverpool	20 Dec	San Francisco	16 Apr	23 Aug	Falmouth
1887	15 Oct	Cardiff	20 Jan	San Francisco	4 Apr	8 July	Queenstown
1888	8 Sept	Cardiff	11 Jan	Bombay	31 Jan	2 Mar	Akyab
1889	26 Sept	Cardiff	13 Nov	Rio de Jan. (cont'd)	24 Dec 21 Oct	25 Mar 14 Feb	Akyab S. Francisco
1891	8 Oct	Birkenhead	22 Feb	San Francisco	21 July	3 Dec	Queenstown
1893	5 July	Cardiff	12 Aug	Rio de Jan.	2 Nov	30 Dec	Pisaqua
1894	1 Aug	Cardiff	9 Sept	Rio de Jan. (cont'd)	31 Oct 13 June	20 Jan 14 Sept	Diamond Is. S. Francisco
1896	5 May	Swansea	13 Sept	San Francisco	20 Oct	18 Feb	Queenstown
1897	6 May	Seansea	26 Sept	San Francisco	13 Nov	16 Mar	Falmouth
1898	27 June	Swansea	16 Nov	San Francisco	21 Dec	21 Jan	Astoria
1899	14 Sept	Swansea	24 Jan	San Francisco	3 Mar	19 July	Queenstown
1900	17 Oct	Swansea	25 Feb	San Francisco	29 Mar	18 July	Queenstown
1901	28 Sept	Cardiff	5 Mar	Nagasaki	12 June	1 Aug	S. Francisco
1905	SOLD		(1902)				

Depart	Arrive	Port	Depart	Arrive	Port	Time at Sea		Length of voyage	
						Mths	*days*	*Mths*	*days*
10 June	6 Oct	Liverpool					267	9	7
							285	11	27
							312	11	18
28 July	5 Aug	Bremerhaven					283	10	17
31 Mar	12 Sept	Bremerhaven				11	17	13	14
7 June	8 Nov	Bremerhaven				11	20	14	0
5 Aug	27 Nov	Liverpool				10	1	12	6
20 Sept	9 Feb	Liverpool				12	4	14	7
13 Dec	19 Apr	Falmouth	4 May	14 May	Galway	12	28	15	18
24 June	1 July	Liverpool				11	9	13	3
29 Aug	1 Sept	Dublin				13	2	14	3
13 July	15 July	Dublin				9	0	10	12
4 Mar	7 Mar	Bassein (cont'd)	22 Mar / 17 July	13 July / 22 July	Falmouth / Bremerhaven	10	14	12	6
26 Mar / 9 Mar	4 Apr / 17 July	Rangoon / Queenstown	22 May / 19 July	16 Sept / 27 July	Rio de Jan. / S. Shields	22	1	24	12
10 Dec	16 Dec	Hull				14	8	16	17
14 Jan	14 Jan	Caleta Buena (cont'd)	1 Mar / 28 May	26 May / 1 June	Falmouth / Dunkirk	10	27	17	8
22 Jan / 23 Oct	26 Jan / 24 Feb	Rangoon / Falmouth	16 Feb / 29 Feb	8 May / 9 Mar	Rio de Jan / Belfast	19	8	21	17
27 Feb	8 Mar	Leith				10	3	11	29
19 Mar	21 Mar	Cork				10	15	12	14
8 Feb	21 June	Queenstown	27 June	3 July	Antwerp	12	6	12	14
21 July	24 July	Galway				10	10	12	26
24 July	26 July	Dublin				9	9	11	21
24 June (1904)	16 Oct	Queenstown	24 Oct	26 Oct	Dublin	10	24	38	27

Appendix VIII

Vessels built, owned or managed by Nicholas Treweek, Amlwch (and Liverpool), 1825-1855

As indicated in Chapters V and VII, Nicholas Treweek and his brother, Francis, built a number of vessels at Amlwch with the support of their father, James Treweek, Mona Lodge, who managed the copper mines in the 1820s and 1830s. Following the death of Francis in 1832, Nicholas Treweek continued to build and repair ships at Amlwch, but in his post as 'forwarding agent' for the Anglesey copper mines at Liverpool he extended his activities as a ship-broker. The list of vessels which follows were all registered in the Beaumaris Registers as owned or part owned by Nicholas Treweek during this period; some of them were quickly sold again, others lost soon after their acquisition. After 1855, owing to his early retirement and return to Amlwch, Treweek again concentrated on ship-building with the active co-operation of Captain William Thomas.

Year	Vessel	Rig	Tonnage	At	By	When	Master
1825	Unity	sloop	68	Amlwch	N. Treweek	1825	Robert Jones
1826	Marquis of Anglesey	sloop	65	Amlwch	N. Treweek	1826	Hugh Thomas
1827	Margaret	sloop	43	Amlwch	N. Treweek	1827	John Williams
1829	Eleanor	smack	17	Amlwch	Fr. Treweek	1829	G. Jones
1830	James and Jane	brigantine	130	Amlwch	Treweek Bros.	1830	John Hughes
1832	Amlwch Packet	smack	37	Amlwch	Treweek Bros.	1832	Griffith Jones
1833	Neptune	sloop	48	Emsworth	—	1789	John Griffith

Year	Vessel	Rig	Tonnage	At	By	When	Master
1833	Lydia	sloop	41	Caernarvon	–	1803	John Griffiths
1834	Sarah	smack	18	Amlwch	Treweek Bros.	1834	J. Jones
1834	New Providence	sloop	16	Caernarvon	–	1815	Thomas Hughes
1835	Nimble	sloop	44	Prize in High Court of Admiralty		1809	John Griffiths
1836	Cymraes	sloop	22	Amlwch	Treweek Bros.	1836	Thomas Hughes
1836	Jane and Margaret	sloop	56	Amlwch	Treweek Bros.	1836	Wm. Roberts
1836	Tower	sloop	37	Pwllheli	–	1821	G. Rowlands
1837	Stranger	brig(?)	238	New Yarmouth Nova Scotia	–	1827	?
1839	Marianne	sloop	53	Amlwch	Treweek Bros.	1839	Thomas Hughes
1840	Economy	schooner	60	Amlwch	Treweek Bros.		R. Jones
1840	Providence	sloop	53	Carmarthen	–	1837	William Hughes
1842	Mary	schooner	53	Bangor	N. Treweek		Owen Parry
1844	Cymro	smack	20	Amlwch	N. Treweek	1844	Owen Williams
1845	Resolution	brig	125	Barmouth		1805	William Francis
1845	Havana Packet	snow	210	Liverpool		1818	R. Roberts
1846	Marchioness of Anglesey	schooner	74	St Helens		1815	John Hughes

Year	Vessel	Rig	Tonnage	At	By	When	Master
1846	Active	snow	175	Lancaster		1816	John Hughes
1846	George the Fourth	brig	99	Dumbarton		1829	Ellis Jones
1846	Dasher	schooner	66	Bideford		1805	Hugh Williams
1846	Nottingham	ship	483	Liverpool		1827	Edward Bell
1846	Brothers	sloop	42	Bristol		1820	John Williams
1846	Charlotte	schooner	73	Beaumaris		1841	Owen Williams
1846	White	schooner	91	Miramichi		1845	William Pritchard
1846	Red	schooner	97	'Rouchibougae', New Brunswick		1845	William Thomas
1847	Messenger	barque	536	Miramichi		1840	Magnus Bruce
1847	John and Mary	sloop	18	Chester		1817	John Hughes
1847	Hibernia	brigantine	60	Bristol		1799	John Price
1847	Hope	sloop	18	Cemais		1837	William Owen
1847	Mersey	smack	41	Liverpool		1816	William Jones
1848	Adventure	schooner	75	Cape Breton		1845	Owen Parry
1849	Mary	barque	342	Gage Town, New Brunswick		1842	George McConnell
1849	Confidence	barque	445	Pictou, Nova Scotia		1849	Robert Hogg
1849	Dove	schooner	33	Prince Edward Island		1839	Richard Lemin

Year	Vessel	Rig	Tonnage	At	By	When	Master
1850	Arethusa	ship	712	Quebec		1845	Thomas Morrison / J. Hamilton
1850	Emma	barque	295	Pictou, Nova Scotia		1849	Thomas Morrison
1850	Union	galliot	59	Northwich		1787	William Roose
1851	Anglesey	barque	632	Pictou Nova Scotia		1850	Thomas Morrison / W. E. Bell
1851	Neptune	sloop	42	Emsworth		1789	Robert Hughes
1851	Kendel Castle	schooner	85	Frodsham		1839	William Thomas
1851	Power	sloop	37	Pwllheli		1821	Richard Morgan
1851	Elizabeth	schooner	76	Three Rivers, Prince Edward I.		1838	William Jones
1852	Proteus	brig	225	foreign: wrecked Cemlyn and rebuilt		(1852)	Joseph Whitburn
1852	Rapid	brig	232	Liverpool		1852	James Lindsay
1852	Endeavour	sloop	50	Carreg, Cardigan		1783	Edward Hughes
1853	Naparimi	barque	378	Quebec		1828	W. B. Berrick / J. Jones
1853	Recruit	ship	996	Monkton, New Brunswick		1852	Thomas Morrison
1853	Julia	snow	164	Souris, Prince Edward I.		1848	Henry Jones

Year	Vessel	Rig	Tonnage	At	By	When	Master
1853	Barbara	sloop	46	Rhuddlan		1825	James Jones
1853	Maria	brigantine	76	Little Anchat, Cape Breton		1833	Thomas Owen
1854	Ann Mulvey	schooner	99	Chester		1842	William Jones
1854	Princeton	barque	356	Bath, Maine		1842	Thomas Hughes
1854	Atlas	schooner	66	Northwich		1839	Henry Jones
1854	John	brigantine	88	Prince Edward I.		1849	John Hughes
1854	John Morgan	schooner	78	Caernarvon		1826	John German
1854	Robin Hood	schooner	155	Flint		1854	Owen Parry
1854	Helen	ship	860	Quebec		1840	John Hamilton
1855	Gertrude	brig	230	St Stephens, New Brunswick		1838	Richard Tucker
1855	Iris	snow	277	St Heliers, Jersey		1838	Richard Jones
1855	Village Maid	schooner	92	Miramichi		1852	John Hughes
1855	Joseph	brigantine	109	Three Rivers, Prince Edward I.		1849	Richard Evans

Appendix IX (i)

Ships owned or built by William Thomas and Sons, Amlwch Port, 1849-1914

Built or Acq'd	Name	Rig	Tonnage	When	Built by	at
1849	Clyde	W.Bn.	123	1842		Nova Scotia
1851	Kendal Castle	W.Sr.	85	1839		Frodsham
1854	Anglesea Lass	W.Sr.	99	1854		Rhyl
1858	Mary Catherine	I.Sr.	77	1858	Hughes Thomas & Co.	Amlwch
1859	Alliance	W.Sr.	94	1858	Treweek & Co.	Amlwch
1859	Grace Evans	I.Sr.	89	1859	Treweek & Co.	Amlwch
1859	Lord Willoughby	W.Sr.	69	1840		Preston
1859	Pride of Anglesea	W.Sr.	88	1859		Barnstaple
1860	Jane Pringle	W.Sr.	89	1855		Grimsby
1861	Sea Queen	W.Sr.	82	1861	Treweek & Co.	Amlwch
1861	Albion	W.Sr.	82	1815		Lancaster

Reg. dimensions				
Length	*Breadth*	*Depth*	*Masters*	*Owners*
71.7	19.5	11	W. Thomas 1849 J. Thomas 1851	Lewis Thomas 34, Wm. Thomas 24, Wm. Lewis 8.
			W. Thomas 1851 J. Thomas 1859	N. Treweek and Thomas. Lost 1859.
			W. Thomas	W. Thomas
			J. German	Jones and Company, Amlwch
86.7	19.2	10.0	T. Owens	Palmer and Company?
80	20	9.4	J. Price	Nicholas Treweek, Wm. Thomas, Grace Evans, E. Morgan, etc.
65	17.8	8.9	Roberts?	W. Thomas 64.
74.6	18.5	10.5	R. Jones T. Parry	R. Jones 44, W. Thomas Abandoned off Lizard 15 Dec. 1904.
78.9	16.2	11.1	J. Hughes O. Jones	W. Thomas 48, Owen Owens, Draper, William Morris, Sailmaker. Lost off Bardsey, 9 Dec. 1899.
81.3	19.4	9	David Lewis	N. Treweek 40. Lost, Rhosneigr, 1861.
69.6	20.5	10.0	J. Owens J. Jones W. Parry	W. Thomas, Morcoms.

Built or Acq'd	Name	Rig	Tonnage	When	Built by	at
1862	Coila		133	1860	Hardie	Southwick
1863	Lord Mostyn		46	1844		Rhuddlan
1863	Cymro	W.Sr.	20	1844	Treweek	Amlwch
1863	Woodman	W.Sr.	70	1837		Barmouth
1864	William & Jane	W.Bn.	141	1834		Ostend
1864	Euphemia	W.Sr.	87	1860	Scott	Greenock
1865	Thomas Blythe	W.Bk.	335	1837		Ansi Louis, Is. of Mati
1866	Clara Louisa	W.Bg.	168	1854		Bideford
1866	Amanda	W.Bn.	193	1865	Ross	P. Edwards Is.
1867	Ocean Belle	W.Sr.	62	1865		P. Edwards Is.
1868	Sarah Jane	W.Bn.	56	1856		P. Edwards Is.
1869	John Bright	W.Bk.	498	1847		Dumbarton
1869	William Mellhuish	W.S.	680	1859	Clarke	Jersey

| Reg. dimensions | | | | |
Length	Breadth	Depth	Masters	Owners
89.2	20.8	12.5	H. Jones W. R. Owen	W. Thomas M.O. Wrecked Barrow, repaired 1872.
61.3	17.2	7	J. Williams R. Davies	W. Thomas, Morcoms, W. Lewis Wrecked 1890.
37.3	14.1	6		W. Thomas, Owen Owens, William Williams, Foundry. Lost 8 April 1868.
61	18	9	R. Jones	W. Thomas 64. Sold 1865.
83.5	20.4	12.4		W. Thomas 56, Owen Owens 8.
79	17	9	J. Evans I. Jones W. Gibbon	W. Thomas, Morcoms, D. Edwards, Druggist.
106	26	17		W. Thomas 40, O. Jones and R. Jones, Farmers, Amlwch, 12 each. Sold 1865.
98	21.9	12.6	W. Morgan	W. Thomas 60, W. Thomas, Liv., 4. Sold 1871.
100.5	25.8	12.6	R. Jones	R. Jones 52, W. Thomas 8, W. Thomas, Liv., 4 Sold.
74	20	8	J. Edwards H. Williams	J. Edwards 22, W. Thomas 21. Abandoned 29 Nov. 1896.
65.2	18.4	8		W. Lewis 48, W. Thomas 16. Sold 1873.
				W. Thomas 32, W. Thomas, New- borough, 16, Thomas Morgan and Peake, Cardiff, 8 each. Condemned, Payta, 1870.
179.8	30.3	19.1	D. Jones	W. Thomas, W. Thomas, Liv.

Built or Acq'd	Name	Rig	Tonnage	When	Built by	at
1869	*Welsh Girl*	W.Sr.	99	1869	Thomas	Amlwch
1870	*Lewis and Mary*	W.Sr.	70	1870	Thomas	Amlwch
1871	*Linda*	W.Bk.	311	1865	Duncan	P. Edwards Is.
1871	*Elizabeth Martha*	W.Sr.	70	1857		Rhuddlan
1871	*Anglesea Lass*	W.Bq.	264	1871		Sunderland
1872	*Holy Wath*	W.Sr.	99	1872	Thomas	Amlwch
1873	*Yuca*	W.Bk.	483	1860	Lamport	Workington
1873?	*Toronto*	W.Bk.	689	1872	Anger	Quebec
1873	*Nellie Bywater*	W.Sr.	99	1873	Thomas	Millom
1874	*Cumberland Lassie*	W.Bn.	208	1874	Thomas	Amlwch
1875	*Edith Morgan*	W.Sr.	130	1866	Wilmott	Padstow
1875	*Mersey* (Liverpool Pilot Boat No. 11)	W.Sr.	79	1875	Thomas	Amlwch
1876	*Baron Hill*	W.Bn.	209	1876	Thomas	Amlwch
1876	*Lady Neave*	W.Sr.	89	1876	Thomas	Amlwch
?	*Thomas*	W.Sr.	65	1816		Ulverston

| Reg. dimensions | | | | |
Length	Breadth	Depth	Masters	Owners
86.9	20.9	10.0	T. Jones J. Farrell	W. Thomas 32, W. Thomas, Liv., 4. Lost 21 March 1882.
74.8	20	9.2	E. Pritchard	W. Thomas 56, E. Pritchard 8. Foundered Dec. 1874.
120.3	26.1	14.9	R. Roberts G. Morgan	W. Thomas. Lost Dec. 1880.
			T. Jenkins	W. Thomas, M.O. Lost near Duddon, 12 Feb. 1871.
113.8	26.3	14.9	D. Jones	W. Thomas 64. Lost 1873.
88.4	22.4	10.5	J. Williams W. Griffiths	Morgan & Co., Whitehaven, 1875.
156	27.1	20.5	J. James	W. Thomas, W. Thomas, Liv.
162.5	34.5	19.8	R. H. Roberts	W. Thomas, M.O.
89.7	22.0	10.1	Ellis R. Morgan	W. Postlethwaite.
114.6	24.0	13.8	P. Hodgson	W. Postlethwaite. Wrecked off Start Point, Jan. 1918.
96.8	22.9	12.0	W. Jones	W. Thomas. Wrecked, Sound of Islay.
80.7	19.0	10.3	R. Williams	Sunk near Bar Lightship, 2 Dec. 1885.
119.0	25.4	13.0	J. Hughes	W. Postlethwaite.
87.3	21.0	9.7	I. Jones	W. Thomas 40, W. Owen, farmer, 16, I. Jones, Ma., 8. Lost in collision, 9 July 1911.
61.4	16.8	9.1	R. Evans	

Built or Acq'd	Name	Rig	Tonnage	When	Built by	at
1877	Nantglyn	W.Sr.	103	1877	Thomas	Amlwch
1877	Barbara	I.Bk.	1082	1877	Doxford	Sunderland
1878	Nesta	W.Sr.	104	1878	Thomas	Amlwch
1878	Countess of Lonsdale	W.Sr.	183	1878	Thomas	Duddon
1878	Eilian Hill	W.Sr.	98.7	1878	Thomas	Amlwch
1879	Margaret	W.Sr.	72	1879	Thomas	Amlwch
1879	Glyndwr	W.Sk.	16	1879	Thomas	Amwch
1880?	Countess of Kintore	W.S.	738	1866	Duthie	Aberdeen
1880	Pearl	W.Sr.	100	1880	Thomas	Amlwch
1881	President Garfield	W.Sr.	48	1881	Thomas	Amlwch
1881	Lady Kate	W.Scw. Stm.	78	1881	Thomas	Duddon
1882	Lady Louisa	W.Scw. Stm.	74	1882	Thomas	Duddon
1883	W. S. Caine	I.Scw. Dandy	74	1883	Thomas	Amlwch
1884	Exchange	I.Scw. Stm.	292	1884	Thomas	Amlwch

| Reg. dimensions | | | | |
Length	Breadth	Depth	Masters	Owners
88.6	21.5	10.9	T. Jones	T. Jones and T. Jones, Ma. Supposed foundered October 1881.
220.0	35.1	21.2	R. H. Roberts	W. Thomas, M.O.
88.5	21.3	10.8	J. Hughes	S. R. Platt, Oldham, 64. Sold, 1891, W. Pritchard, Portmadoc.
113.5	25.3	12.6	L. Hughes	Thomas and Postlethwaite.
88	21.3	10.6	L. Thomas	W. Thomas, L. Hughes, Hills, etc. Foundered off Penzance. 15 Dec. 1882.
82.3	20.3	8.3	J. Thomas	W. Thomas.
39.5	13.5	6.5	W. Thomas	W. Thomas. Lengthened 1882. Sold 1886.
182.6	31.4	19.4	W. Edwards	
91.4	21.7	10.0	W. Lewis	T. Fanning Evans 48. Sold to Connah's Quay 1890.
71.7	18	7.3		W. Thomas, Jn. Sold 1897 to Cornish owners.
99.7	21.9	9.8	J. Roberts	G. Farrer & Co., Caernarvon. Engines by De Winton, Caernarvon.
105.0	21.5	9.3	R. Lewis	W. Postlethwaite.
122.4	21.1	7.9	L. Thomas	W. Thomas, then W. Thomas, Liv., M.O., later Manchester, Liverpool and N. Wales S.S. Company.
135	22.3	9.9	A. Grant	W. Thomas & Co., Liv.

Built or Acq'd	Name	Rig	Tonnage	When	Built by	at
1884	*Lady Bessie*	W.Scw. Stm.	79	1884	Thomas	Millom
1885	*Anglesea*	I.Scw. Stm.	149	1885	Thomas	Amlwch
1885	*Elizabeth Peers*	I.Sr.	183	1885	Thomas	Amlwch
1886	*Greyhound*	W.Sr.	191	1886	Thomas	Millom
1887	*Gelert*	I.Sc.	222.9	1887	Thomas	Amlwch
1889	*Eilian*	W.Sr.	116.4	1889	Thomas	Amlwch
1890	*Enterprise*	I.Scw. Stm.	39	1877	Lindsay	Tyne
1890	*Prince Ja Ja*	Steel Sc. 3 Mst.	271	1890	Thomas	Amlwch
1891	*Detlef Wagner*	Scr. I.Bkn.	225	1891	Thomas	Amlwch
1891	*Cygnus*	I.Scw. Stm	355	1891	Thomas	Amlwch
1892	*Maggie Williams*	I.Sr.	226	1892	Thomas	Amlwch
1893	*Cymric*	I.Bkn.	226	1893	Thomas	Amlwch
1894	*Celtic*	I.Sr.	224	1894	Thomas	Amlwch

Reg. dimensions				
Length	Breadth	Depth	Masters	Owners
116.0	22.0	10.6	R. Roberts	G. Farrer & Co., Caernarvon. Engines by De Winton.
95.2	18.4	8.6	W. Gibbon	W. Thomas, Sr., W. Thomas, Jr., L. Thomas, Bilbao, owners 1894.
107.1	23.6	10.4	E. J. Peers	W. Postlethwaite.
120.5	22.8	11.0	– Williams R. Jones	W. Thomas.
124	24	10.9		W. Thomas, Sr., W. Thomas, Jr., L. Thomas. Wrecked, Catalinita Is., 26 April 1890.
98.2	21.6	8.4	R. Griffiths	W. Thomas & Sons 48. R. Griffiths 16. Sunk in collision, English Channel, 1899.
85	20	7		Altered at Amlwch, 1890. W. Thomas & Sons.
140.8	24.3	9.8	J. Richardson	Liverpool & Menai Strait S.S. Co. Ltd.
127	24	10.8	H. Beaumann	Actiesalskobet, Denmark.
148	24	10.8	J. T. Francis	R. J. Francis and A. Evans
123	24	10.8	W. Williams	W. Postlethwaite.
123	24	10.8	R. Jones	W. Thomas & Sons.
123	24	10.6	J. Hughes	W. Thomas & Sons, W. Reney, Connah's Quay.

Built or Acq'd	Name	Rig	Tonnage	When	Built by	at
1894	*Happy Harry*	W.Sr.	142	1894	Duddon S.B. Co.	Duddon
1898	*Gaelic*	I.Bkn.	224	1898	Thomas	Amlwch
1904	*Elizabeth Roberts*	Steel Sr.	134	1904	Thomas	Amlwch
1904	*Meyric*	Steel Sr.	253	1904	Thomas	Amlwch
1905	*Cenric*					
1908	*Eilian*	Steel Sr. (aux. screw)	140	1908	Thomas	Amlwch

Reg. dimensions				
Length	Breadth	Depth	Masters	Owners
101.2	23	10.3	W. Williams	Hodbarrow Mining Company.
126.8	24	10.8	I. Williams	W. Thomas, Jr., 28, L. Thomas 28, I. Williams 8. Sold, 1920, to Connah's Quay.
102	22.1	9.4	E. A. Nielsen	E. O. Roberts, Liv.
129.7	24.8	11.5	W. B. Williams	W. Thomas & Sons.
			M. Parry	W. Thomas & Sons. Lost. Not heard of since leaving Twillingate, Newfoundland, 1906.
102.6	21.9	9.4	H. Hughes	W. Thomas & Sons.

Other vessels managed by Captain Thomas, about which details are uncertain, include *Crystal Palace*, 90 tons, wrecked near Barrow 1871, *Caroline*, Sr., 52 tons, *Dalton*, Flat, 43 tons, *John & Eliza*, Sloop, 26 tons, *Mary Ann*, Sr., 58 tons, *Mary Elizabeth*, Sr., 42 tons, *Mountain Maid*, Sr.(?), 53 tons, *Velocipede*, Bkn., 251 tons. The *Ardri*, *Dunleith* and *Eiliams* belong to the post-1918 period.

Appendix IX (ii)

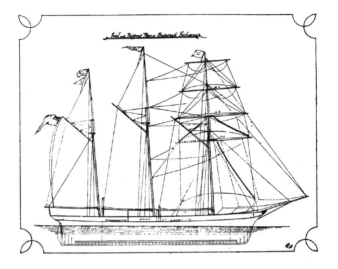

William Thomas's Sail and Rigging Plan for the Schooner to be built, 1892. Thomas's signature and date are in bottom right-hand corner.

Specification dated 3 May 1892, and stamped William Thomas and Sons, Iron and Wood Ship-builder, Amlwch Port.

Specification of an Iron Three Masted Schooner to be built to the order of _____ by Wm. Thomas and Sons, Amlwch Port, Anglesea.

Principal Dimensions: Length 116 Feet
                            Breadth 24   "
                            Depth 10 8/10 Feet

Materials & Workmanship: In all matters not hereafter particularly Specified Materials & Workmanship to be according to the highest class for Lloyds Rules of 100 A 1. The Certificate for Classification to be furnished on delivery at the Builders Expense.

General: The vessel to be built in accordance with this specification and on the same model as the schooner 'Maggie Williams'. The vessel to be delivered to the Owner at Amlwch Port.

Keel: To be of best quality iron and of Dimensions as required by Lloyds Rules in long lengths connected together by good long scarphs.

Stern: Of Best iron connected to the Keel by a good long scarph.

Stern Post: To be of size as required by Lloyds Rules having solid forged rudder braces.

Frames: To be of Angle iron to Dimensions as required by Lloyds Rules to extend in one piece from Keel to Gunwale, Double Frames at the Fore or Watertight Bulkhead. A Doubling piece at least 3'0" long of same size Angles to be fitted back to back with each frame for 3/4ths the vessels length Amidships. All Frames to be carefully fared (?) before riveting of Stringers or plates is started.

Reverse Frames: To be fitted across the top of each Floor and of dimensions as per Lloyds Rules.

Floors: A Floor plate of the dimensions required for a vessel of her class to be fitted to every frame with a hole for water-course to be in each.

Keelsons: To be fitted where required and of sizes equal to the Rules of 100 A 1 Class. to be formed of Double Angle Irons riveted back to back and to Frames & Floors by Lug pieces as required. About 50 Feet of bulb iron 6 & 6/16 to be fitted between the Angles of the Bilge Keelson this to be in addition to the requirements of Lloyds Rules.

Beams: Of sizes and description required by Lloyds Rules to be fitted to every alternate Frame.

Bulkhead: A Collision Bulkhead to be fitted at the Fore end strongly stiffened vertically and horizontally, caulked and made thoroughly watertight.

Plating: All plates except hood plates at Ends of vessel to be at least Four spaces of frames in length and to have their butts properly shifted, no two butts in adjoining strakes to be nearer each other than two spaces of frames and the butts of alternate strakes not to be under each other but to be shifted space of frame.

The garboards and hood plates to be either of B iron or of steel at the Builders option, in order to work these without the risk of cracking.

Riveting: All flush work is to be deeply countersunk by drill, and all holes to be fair or made so by turning, punching to be from the inside leaving the taper outside in each case. All rivets to be in diameter equal to, and spaced according to Lloyds Rules.

Main Deck Stringer: Of Plate iron and of a thickness required by the Rules of Lloyds tapering at the Ends, and connected to the sheer strakes by Angle iron 3 x 3 x 6/16.

Waterway: That on Main Deck to be of the gutter. Form properly cemented.

Tie Plates: To be laid and riveted to Main Deck Beams and to be Diagonally in way of Masts.

Wash Plates: To be fitted between the Floors and connected to them by Angle irons.

Hold Stanchions: Of solid round bar iron 2½" Diam. under each alternate beam for ¾th vessels length Amidship and under Windlass, to have solid welded heads and heels, riveted to the Main Keelson and to the Main Deck Beams with at least two rivets in both head and heel.

Rudder: Strongly framed in one piece, plated with ¼" plates button head rivets; rudder pintles wrought out of the solid.

Cementing: The bottom to be cemented to upper turn of bilge for Entire length of vessel with best Portland Cement mixed with good sand or gravel in proper proportion to set very hard, to be rounded up at side of Floor plates so as to cover rivet heads and Frames.

Ports & Scuppers: Vessel to be fitted with sufficient number of Ports & Scuppers, placed in suitable positions to discharge any large quantity of water that may get on Deck. Bottom of scupper holes to be level with deck. Ports to be hinged from the upper side and Extra strong hinges with brass pins to prevent drooping.

Bulwarks: To be of ¼" iron strongly supported by solid round bar iron of dimensions required by the Rules.

Hatch Coamings: Of iron plate standing at a reasonable height above the Deck, & extending to lower part of beams, having half round iron fitted at its lower edge & a rest bar at the top of sufficient size to receive the hatches, hatch cleats to be spaced about 2 Ft. apart, all necessary battens, etc. etc.

Galley: An iron galley of approved dimensions floored with neat Tiles; well lighted; provided with range locker seat & shelves etc.

Rails: To be of hollow copr iron of suitable size, pin rails to be fitted in the way of each mast for belaying.

Boats: To have two Boats placed on rests on hatches with one pair of wrought iron Davits fitted so that they can be removed from either side of a vessel, with all necessary falls, blocks, oars, etc.

Painting: All ironworks of the Hull to receive 3 coats of good oil paint finished any plain color the inside of the Bulwarks & the galley to be neatly grained and varnished.

Spars: All to be of good selected Timber reasonably free from sap & knots. Fore, Main & Mizen Mast also the Standing Bowsprit to be of P. Pine all the remainder to be of Spruce.

Smithwork: All necessary spar mounting to be of best iron and finished in a good workmanlike manner, all the necessary gearing for Boats, Davits, socket plates, catheads, chain plates, eye & ring bolts, cleats and all other work generally to be of sufficient size and strength for the work for which they are respectively required.

Hatches: Of Dimensions as shown on plan fitted with Centre Fore and Aft wooden Beams carried on iron sockets riveted to hatch coamings for carrying hatch covers.

Hatch covers to be of pattern known as 'half' hatches made in solid about 2¼" thick strongly bolted together with through bolts and fitted with suitable ring bolts to their places and each cover to lock (?).

Ceiling: To be laid in flat of bottom and to extend to turn of bilge, all ceiling to be secured with bolts and nuts and to be about 2" thick.

Deck: To be of well seasoned p. pine reasonably free from strakes and sap with Boundering plank of hard wood. All to be fastened with galvanized bolts and nuts well screwed up, the whole to be caulked payed and made thoroughly watertight. The Deck to be cut for seasoning immediately on Signing Contract.

Companion etc.: To be made of wood, also the skylight of the same material, well varnished, the latter to have glass windows protected with brass gratings. The Forescupper to be made of iron.

Gratings: To be of Hardwood and fitted close to the Companion, the Doors of Galley Forescupper and wheel stand.

Cabin: To be Aft, below the Main Deck, neatly fitted up well lighted and ventilated, 2 Bunks, Table and Sofa. To be made of hardwood and varnished. Linoleum Cloth to be fitted on the Floor. The stairs to be fitted with Ornamental Brass Step Guards and the whole to be finished similar to the cabin of the 'Maggie Williams', 1 good stove and Brass Funnel, 1 Cabin Lamp and 1 Coal Scuttle.

Forecastle: Accomodation to be provided in Forecastle below Main Deck for at least 8 Seamen to be well lighted and ventilated as required by Board of Trade with necessary bunks, seats, lockers, stove lamp, clothes hooks and other usual fittings.

Wheel House: As shewn on plan to be fitted over the steering gear forming Paint Locker and W.C.

Tanks: A large Iron Tank to contain about 800 galls of Water to be fitted under cabin sole with all necessary pipes etc. leading to Main Deck, with a copper Deck Pump.

Steering Gear: To have wheel of best description connected to an ordinary winch Aft, having pitch chain and barrel.

Winches: To have two winches fitted on Main Deck and made of wood or cast iron at Builder's option, one of double and the other of single purchase.

Windlass: A Patent friction windlass to be fitted on Main Deck with all necessary handgear etc.

Hawse Pipes: Of cast iron of sufficient size and strength fitted through bulwarks forward above main Deck fitted on inside of bulwarks with heavy flanges resting on waterway. Outside of Hawse pipe fo be finished with bold half round moulding. One half hawse pipe to be fitted on each quarter of the vessel all properly and secured also a pair of cast iron Fairleads on each side of the stem head.

Mooring Bitts: Two each side to be fitted in most suitable positions well secured through main Deck Stringer Plate and made thoroughly watertight.

Pumps: Two about 5" Diam. cast iron pumps with Brass plungers and having rotary motion.

Chain Locker: To be of sufficient size to contain cables fitted under the floor of the Forecastle.

Castings: Pumps and other pipings to be securely cased in hold.

Chain Plates: Fore, Main and Mizen to be made of Round iron bolted and fitted in their places on the inside of Sheer Strake.

Rigging: The whole of the standing rigging to be of Best Galvd. wire rope parcelled and served all over in the best style. Headstays to have galvanized iron thimbles for the sails – all to be set up with ordinary lanyards or if preferred with Rigging Screws. Deadeyes to be of Lignum-Vitae. Fore and Main Rigging to have 4 Shrounds and the Mizen 3.

Sails: To be made in the best manner and leathered where usual, and to consist of the following

1 Square Sail, 1 Lower Topsail, 1 Upper Topsail, 1 Topgallant Sail, All made of 'Hurricane' Canvas.

1 Fore-Sail, 1 Main-Sail, 1 Mizen Sail, 1 Main Topmast Staysail, 1 Main Gaff Topsail, 1 Mizen Gaff Topsail, 1 Fore Stay-Sail, 1 Standing Jib, 1 Boom Jib, 1 Flying Jib, All to be made of 'Crown' Royal Extra Canvas.

Covers: 1 Wheel Cover, 1 Skylight Cover, 1 Mizen, 1 Mainsail and 1 Foresail cover, covers for Topsails and Topgallant Sail, 1 cover for Forestaysail, 1 for Standing Jib, 1 for Boom Jib and 1 for Flying Jib, also 1 cover for Windlass.

Chains and Anchors: To have a full set of Anchors and Chains, all properly tested and Certtificates of same to be handed to the Owners on completion of the contract.

Ropes: Of Russian Hemp or Manilla of approved size.

Blocks: A complete set of wood and iron blocks of English Elm and Sheaves of Lignum-Vitae with Patent rollers and lashed where usual and necessary.

Lamps: To have complete set of Copper regulation Lamps with Drophic Lenses, consisting of 1 Port Lamp, 1 Starboard Lamp, 2 Anchor Lamps and 2 Globe Lamps. All to pass Board of Trade requirements, side Lamps to be fitted on screens supported by davits in way of Main Rigging with all fittings complete.

Half Rounds: To be supplied and placed where necessary, vessel to have all the necessary ringbolts, cleats, belay pins, hooks and such like of good strength.

Instruments: 1 Good Binnocular Glass in Case, 1 Foghorn, 1 Patent Log and line, 1 Aneroid Barometer in Oak Case, 1 Eight Day Clock to match, 1 Pair parallel rules, 1 Pair Dividers, 1 Log Slate.

Compass: To have one Compass fitted in the After part of the Skylight, to be of the best quality and properly adjusted before vessel is handed over.

Sundries: 1 Deep Sea Lead and Line, 1 Hand Lead and Line, 1 Oil Tin, 2 Paint Tins, 4 Paint Brushes, 2 Deck Scrubbers, 2 Cork Fenders, 1 Cold Chisel, 1 Serving Board & Mallet, 1 Carpenters Maul, 1 Axe, 1 Saw, 1 Oil Feeder, 2 Life Buoys, 2 Hanging Fenders, 1 Hand Hammer, 2 Marline Spikes, 2 Hand Spikes, 3 Galvanized Buckets, 1 Brass Ships Bell with Name and Year Engraved, 1 Mop, 2 Teak Harness Casks with Brass Hoops and padlock, 2 Water Breakers, 3 Saucepans, 1 Stew pan, 2 Tea Kettles, 1 Baking Tin, 1 Frying pan, 1 Soup Ladle, 1 Meat Chopper, 1 doz. Glass Tumblers, 1 quart Decanter, 1 Sugar Basin, 1 Butter Pot, 1 Cream Jug, 1 doz. plates, 1 doz. cups and saucers, ½ doz. mugs, 1 doz. Table knives and Forks, 1 pair Carvers, 2 Ballast Shovels, 1 Iron Crow Bar, 2 Chain hooks, 2 Discharging Gins, 1 Wooden Buoy, 1 Boatswains Chair and 1 Pump hook.

General Clause: This Specification is intended to comprise everything usual and necessary for a complete outfit, with the exception of Bedding Linen Napery and Consumable Stores.

Anything incidentally mentioned twice to be only supplied once. The vessel to be constructed under the Superintendance of Owners representative who shall at all reasonable time have full access to the Builders Yard, to Examine any materials to be used in the construction of same.

Wm. Thomas and Sons
Amlwch Port.
Iron & Wood Ship Builders.
3 May. 92.

Appendix IX (iii)

Summary Accounts of building S.S. *Anglesea* and *Elizabeth Peers*, William Thomas, Amlwch MSS in ARO.

Summary Account of Building the S.S. *Anglesea*

To Iron (Angles & Plates)	493.10. 5
To Chains & Anchors	41.15. 5
To Stern Frame & Keel Bars	49. 9. 9
To Smith Work	140.16. 3
To Blockmaker's Work	24.10.11½
To Timber a/c	169. 3. 1½
To Sawing a/c	16. 8. 0½
To Rivets & Bolts	53.11. 0
To Machineries	1295. 0. 0
To Coals for Furnace	40. 0. 0
To Heth Jones, Foundry a/c	16.12. 0
To Boat	14. 0. 0
To R. Williams & Son, London House, say	7. 0. 0
To Hy. Williams, Cabinet Maker, say	10. 0. 0
To Painting & Patent Filling	10. 0. 0
To Chadburn & Co. Opticians	18. 4. 6
To Brass Name Plate	1.10. 0

'No. 18. New Vessel'
Summary Account of Building The Schooner *'Elizabeth Peers'*
1885

To Iron, (Angles & Plates)	558.16. 3
To Chains & Anchors	71.15. 2
To Stern Frame & Keel Bars, Rudder Frame	29.12. 4
To Smith Work	131. 3. 3
To Block Maker's Work	43.16. 6
To Timber Account	281.13. 0
To Sawing Account	33.12.10
To Rivets & Bolts	69. 4. 0
To Coals for Furnace	30. 0. 0
To Heth Jones, Foundry a/c	14. 0. 0
To Boat	
To R. Williams & Son account	
To Hy. Williams, Cabinet Maker	
To Painting	5.11. 3
To Chadburns Co, Opticians	16. 5. 0
To Patent Windlass & Steering Gear	47.10. 0
To Steering Wheel	4. 0. 0

	£. s. d.
To Patent Windlass & Steering Gear	30.13. 0
To Steering Wheel	2.10. 0
To Lloyd's Surveyors Fees	14. 6. 6
To Use of Machineries	30. 0. 0
To Sailmaking	25. 3. 1½
To Warehouse Sundries	131.17. 9
To Rivetters Wages	95.10. 6½
To Platrs, Carpenters etc. Wages	441. 5. 2
To Towage to Carnarvon (See Sundries a/c)	
To Wm. Jones, Ironmonger's a/c	7. 1. 6
To Samuel Tyzack & Co., Sunderland (Iron)	8.10. 2
To H. Watson & Son, Newcastle, Sluice Valves and Pump	4.16. 6
To Extras per Dewinton & Co.	18. 4.10
To Capt. Lewis Thomas' Expensis to Caernarvon	7. 0. 0
To Hugh Williams Carnarvon, fittings	5. 8. 5
	3223.18.11½
To Sundry Goods as per a/c 1st page	78.13. 4½
	£3302.12. 4

	£. s. d.
To Lloyds Surveyors Fees	14.11. 0
To Use of Machineries	30. 0. 0
To Sailmaking Account	109. 2.10½
To Warehouse Account	138.18. 2
To Rivetters Wages	5. 3. 9
To Plasters, Carpenters etc. Wages	90. 4. 4½
To Wm. Jones, Ironmongers a/c	401.17. 6½
To S Tyzak & Co, Sunderland, Hollow ½ rd. Iron	11. 3. 1
To Sundry Goods as per a/c	19. 2.11
To Female Bust, Figure Head	3. 0. 0
To Ben Gibson & Co., Liverpool Iron	9.12. 6
To Brass Plate	1. 3. 3
To Hy Wilson & Co, Liverpool	10.13. 4
To Hy Watson & Sons, N. Castle on Tyne	15. 6
To H. Williams & O. Roberts, Setting Liners	17. 2. 8½
To Wm. Roberts, contract for making cabin	10. 0. 0
To Harbour Dues	2. 8. 1½
To Colors for New Vessel	9.13. 4
To Insurance on Launching Risk	3. 4.10
Total	£2147.18. 2

Appendix X

Extracts from Accounts of *Heir Apparent* and *Fomalhaut*.
Captain Owen Williams and Captain Williams, Bryn Golau, Ty'n y Gongl.

Schooner 'Heir Apparent' – An Acct. of Earnings
Dr.

1858		
Dec. 31	To Richard Hughes for Smithwork	4.14. 1
"	To James Davies, Blockmaker, Sundry Repairs	10.17. 0
"	To Owen Lewis, Scraping the vessel	10. 6
"	To Rowland Hughes, Repairing figurehead	5. 0
"	To Joseph Rutter, for a Rope	4. 2.11
"	To Matt. Todd, for Smithwork	8. 0
"	To Sundry sums paid by Capt. Owen Williams	
"	for which no bills were given	3.18. 3
1859		
Jan. 10	To Parry & Co. for Paint	13. 2
"	To Bangor Insurance Society's Subs.	5.15. 0
May 1	To Do. Do. 'Call'	11.11. 5
3	To J. Roberts for a Jib-boom	3. 1. 6
"	To J. Jones for Smithwork	16. 9
11	To William R. Ashburner for Carpenter's Work	1. 8. 3
17	To Alexander Broadfoot for Spades	5. 0
June 30	To Owen Williams for Superintending the	
	Carpenters while the Vessel was under Repairs	9. 0. 0
"	To Evan Williams for Oil & Tar	6. 3
July 25	To J. Gribble for Scrubbers	5. 6
Aug. 8	To William Ashburner for new Gaff etc.	10. 2
9	To T. H. Williams for Cordage & Canvas	12. 3
Sept. 29	To William Simpson for Oil & Paint	1.12. 8
Oct. 4	To William Ashburner for Paint & Tar	1.11. 5
Nov. 15	To The Bangor Insurance Society's Call	5.15. 0
"	To William Whitelaw for paint	4. 1
"	To William Morris for Sails	29.11. 7
"	To W. C. Paynter for Sundry Repairs and Carpenters'	
	Wages	113.19. 7
"	To Share of Expences to a meeting of the Society at Bangor	6. 0
"	To Postage Stationery Commission on drafts	5. 0
Dec. 31	To Husbandage	7. 8. 6
"	To Balance for Owners	47.11. 1

£267. 5.11

1858				
July	25	By Moiety of a Freight from Cardiff to Belfast		12.16. 6
Aug.	11	" Do.	Barrow to Briton Ferry	11.14. 1
	23	" Do.	Neath to Liverpool	13. 7. 8
Sept.	24	" Do.	Barrow to Swansea	12.15. 6
Oct.	23	" Do.	Pembrey to Amlwch	13. 7. 8
1859				
Feb.	18	" Do.	Amlwch to Swansea	12.10. 1
	22	" Do.	Swansea to Llanelly	6. 3. 8
March	8	" Do.	Llanelly to Amlwch	15. 3. 4
	28	" Do.	Amlwch to Swansea	12. 3. 0
April	18	" Do.	Swansea to Youghal	18. 5. 9
May	16	" Do.	Youghal to Barrow	9. 0.10
	22	" Do.	Barrow to Swansea	15.12.10
June	4	" Do.	Briton Ferry to Liverpool	17. 3. 5
July	9	" Do.	Barrow to Port Talbot	16. 5 .0
	25	" Do.	Port Talbot to Devoran	11. 4. 6
Aug.	16	" Do.	Devoran to Liverpool	13.16.11
Sept.	6	" Do.	Garston to Waterford	12. 9.11
	28	" Do.	New Ross to Glasson Dock	14. 9.12
Oct.	24	" Do.	Barrow to Briton Ferry	15. 1. 3
Nov.	20	" Do.	Briton Ferry to Liverpool	13.14.10

Division of Balance on the other side,
                    Owen Williams   23.15.6½
                    William Jones   23.15.6½

£267. 5.11

Dr. The Schooner Fomalhaut

1885

Jan.	15	By bills paid for sundry materials		5.15. 8
		Dunage at Ipswich 2.7.5, Cordage at Dublin £1.16.0		4. 3. 5
Apl.	24	W. Hughes 3/ Marquard 14 W. Moore 3.7.0½		4. 4. 0½
Jly	6	J. C. Johnson 4/6 J. A. Hunter 3/4 T. Lewis & Co. 2/		9.10
Aug.	31	Owen & Williams Foundry 12/ W. Parry new funnell 7/3		0.19. 3
Sep.	1	Owen Roberts Shipwright 3.14.0 John Ellis Cordage etc.		
		14/9½		4. 8. 9½
	26	Alex^{er}. Marr 1.2.6 John Lewis 16.6		£1.19. 0
Oct.	21	Lawrence & Timble 8/4 Blacksmith 2/		0.10. 4
		John Lloyd 5		0. 5. 0
Jly	14	J. Ellis new Gafftopsail 56¾ yds No. 5 Coker at 1/7½		4.12. 2½
				27. 7. 6½

Jan.	7	Protection subscription	0.10.10	
Feb.	24	Insurance Call	37. 8. 6	
June	1	Do. Do.	14. 6. 9	
Sep.	4	Do. Do.	7. 8. 9	
			£59.14.10	
				87. 2. 4½
		Balance for Owner		47.14. 1½

£134.16. 6

An Account of Earnings

Cr.

	1885			
Jan.	15	By Freight of Slates	from Bangor to Ipswich	20. 0. 0
Feb.	12	Do.	from Ipswich to Drumore	20. 0. 0
May	29	Do.	from Bangor to Hamburg	26.11. 8
June	16	Do.	from Hamburg to Dunkirk	12.12. 0
July	27	Do.	from London to Newry	12. 7. 6
Sept.	18	Do.	from Bangor to Aberdeen	20.19. 4
Oct.	15	Do.	from Aberdeen to London	8.16. 0
Nov.	10	Do.	from London to Kingstown	13.10. 0

£134.16. 6

Dr. The Schooner Fomalhaut

1886

Jan.	12	Owen Roberts repairing Boat and sundry job	18. 4
May	20	reclassing as pr bill	43. 2. 5½
		Owen & Williams new Iron Knees bolts etc. as pr bill	27.14. 4
	21	Thomas Griffith refitting Rigging	2.15. 0
		John Pritchard scraping vessel twice including deck	2.15. 0
		Mr T. Devonald Lloyd Surveyor	3.14. 6
		W. Parry Ironmonger Galvanised sheet and pan for closet	11. 9
		Parsling canvass 6/3 Rock salt and cartage 11/-	17. 3
		Capn. attending Carpenters	3. 0. 0
Aug.	4	J. Ellis cordage canvass etc. as pr bill	4. 3. 2½
March 4		R. Miller 12/7 T. Ferguson 2/4 T. Lewis 3/ W. T. Samson	
		£3.1.1	3.19. 0
June	17	J. Brown & Son 2/ J. P. Sleightoholme 1.18.9½	2. 0. 9½
	24	R. Miller 18/9 Donald McKay & Son 10/0½	1. 8. 9½
Oct.	1	W. Anderson 5/ Jackson McConnor & Coltart 2.19.3	3. 4. 3
Nov.	17	George Agosti 5/10 R. Starbuck 1.1.0 R. Stocker 4/4	1.11. 2
	23	White & Bros. 7/6 Wm. Kinnaugh & Son new Topsail	
		72 yards £5.14.0	6. 1. 6
Dec.	9	Wire backstay £1.0.4 M. Hexham 3/ New Topmast 1.15.0	2.18. 4

110.15. 8

Jan.	2	Renewal subscription	£0.10.10	
Mar.	24	Insurance Call	5. 5. 0	
Aug.	7	Do. Call	18. 1	6.13.11

£117. 9. 7

An Account of Earnings

1886					
Feb.	26	By Freight of Slates	from Bangor to Nairn	22. 0. 0
Mar.	30	Do.	from Thurso to Londonderry	17. 0. 0
June	12	Do.	from Bangor to Montrose	16. 0. 0
July	5	Do.	from Newcastle to Thurso	10. 0. 0
July	29	Do.	from Thurso to Perth	10. 0. 0
Aug.	21	Do.	from Newcastle to Thurso	10. 0. 0
Sept.	29	Do.	from Thurso to Duddon	10. 2. 6
Nov.	15	Do.	from Liverpool to Burnham	14. 6. 0
Dec.	13	Do.	from London to Whitehaven	15. 0. 0

124. 8. 6

Bills paid   117. 9. 7

Balance for Owners   £6.18.11

Appendix XI

Ships owned and managed by William Thomas, Llanrhuddlad and Liverpool, excluding earlier coastal schooners owned or managed in conjunction with Captain William Thomas, Amlwch, and other merchant schooners owners in Lancashire and Cumberland.

Year acq'd	Name	Rig	Tonnage	When built	Built by	at
1872	North Star	W.Bk.	718	1871	Angers	Quebec
1872	Lady Young	W.Bk.	595	1870	Dinning	Quebec
1873	Sappho	W.Bk.	707	1870	–	Mystic, United States
1874	Malabar	W.S.	1291	1874	Marquis	Quebec
1874	Julia	W.S.	973	1873	Angers	Quebec
1875	Buckhorn	W.Bk.	770	1875	Marquis	Quebec
1875	Havelock	W.S.	1079	1875	Charland	Quebec
1877	County of Flint	I.Bk.	1083	1877	Doxford	Sunderland

Length	Breadth	Depth	Masters	What happened to ship
156.8	32.5	19.5	Jones T. Davies 80	
144.0	32.0	18.5	W. Watkins 80	Lost 1880 'between Plymouth and the Start on her way to Cardiff', WT Liverpool MSS, 29 October 1880.
154.5	34.7	17.3	H. Jones 84	
205.8	33.0	23.8	Roberts 75 D. Evans Griffiths 84	Missing 1888.
132.0	29.5	16.2	W. Evans	Not heard of since 2 September 1874, New York to Liverpool, cargo of rosin and petroleum. Crew of 12 supposed drowned.
164	32.8	20.2		Not heard of since leaving St Helena 8 Nov. 1876, Akyab to England, with cargo of 1,147 tons rice. Crew of 16 supposed drowned.
181.3	37.5	22.4	O. Jones 80 J. Jones 80-84	Sold to Norway 1890. Lost 1896.
219.5	35.1	21.3	Roberts 78 J. Rowlands 84 H. Jones 88-91 D. Davies 92-95 H. Williams 97-98 C. Hughes 00-01 H. Roberts 01-05	Sold Valparaiso, 1907.

Year acq'd	Name	Rig	Tonnage	When built	Built by	at
1877	County of Caernarvon	I.S.	1270	1877	R. & J. Evans	Liverpool
1877	County of Anglesea	I.Bk.	1067	1877	R & J Evans	Liverpool
1877	County of Denbigh	I.Bk.	1082	1877	R & J Evans	Liverpool
1877	County of Cardigan	I.S.	1299?	1877	R. &. J Evans	Liverpool
1880	County of Merioneth	I.Bk.	1065	1880	Doxford	Sunderland
1881	County of Pembroke	I.Bk.	1065	1881	Doxford	Sunderland
1881	S.S. Empire	I.Sc.Sr.	2130	1881	R. &. J. Evans	Liverpool
1882	S.S. Kingdom	I.ScSr.	2176	1882	Doxford	Sunderland
1883	S.S. W. S. Caine	I.S.c. Dandy	183	1883	W. Thomas	Amlwch
1884	S.S. Exchange	I.Sc.Sr.	292	1884	W. Thomas	Amlwch
1883	British Commerce	I.S.	1417	1874	Dobie	Glasgow

Length	Breadth	Depth	Masters	What happened to ship
227.6	37.0	22.5	R. Roberts 78	Lost with all hands on passage from Newcastle, NSW, to West Coast of America, June 1889.
214.4	35.2	21.2	S. Parry 78 R. Wynne 80-91 D. Lewis 94-5 T. Lewis 97-99 R. Edwards 03	Dismasted, ashore Portland, 1905. Sold Russia. 1912 New Zealand.
220.1	35.0	21.3	R. Jones 78	Not heard of sincs spoken to 5˚N 29˚W, 22 Jan. 1880, Astoria to Queenstown, wheat. Crew of 20 supposed drowned.
229.4	37.1	22.7	Hughes 78 Williams 84 W. Richards 88-92 J. Griffiths 93 W. Hughes 95-02 W. Roberts 03-05	Sold France 1911.
221.5	35.1	20.9	E. Davies W. Meredith 90 J. Parry 93-95 D. Davies 98-02 T. J. Thomas 03-05	Sold Norway 1906.
221.5	35.0	20.9	E. Jones 87-91 J. Williams 97-02 W. Hughes 02	Driven ashore and total loss. Algoa Bay, 14 Nov. 1903.
280.0	35.9	24.8	T. Davies 81-85	
280.0	36.0	24.5	H. Roberts 82	
122.4	21.1	7.9	E. Jones 94	
135.0	22.3	9.9	A. Grant 89	
246.2	37.2	21.4		Lost in collision off Isle of Wight 1883.

Year acq'd	Name	Rig	Tonnage	When built	Built by	at
1883?	Portia	I.S.	1434	1868	Palmer Bros & Co.	Newcastle
1884	Ogwen	I.S.	1381	1880	R. Foster	Sunderland
1884?	Menai	I.S.	1434	1880	R. Foster	Sunderland
1885	Kate Thomas	I. 4mst. S.	1748	1885	Doxford	Sunderland
1885	Principality	I. 4mst. Bk.	1758	1885	Doxford	Sunderland
1886	Colony	I. 4mst. S.	1750	1886	Doxford	Sunderland
1886	Province	I. 4mst. Bk.	1842	1886	Doxfod	Sunderland
1887	Metropolis	I. 4mst. S.	1811	1887	R. & J. Evans	Liverpool
1888	Pengwern	I.S.	1648	1882	Russell & Co.	Greenock

Length	Breadth	Depth	Masters	What happened to ship
221.6	36.1	24.7	T. Jones 85 E. Jones 92-5 W. Griffiths 97-9 H. Lewis 99-01	Sold Norway 1901.
231.0	36.1	22.0	H. Evans 84-5	Lost, March 1886. Replaced by *Colony*.
231.1	36.2	22.0	J. Jones 84-85 O. Lewis 85-94 J. Farrell 95	Not heard of since leaving New-castle, NSW, for Tocopilla, 23 February 1895.
258.0	39.5	23.1	T. Williams 85 S. Hughes 89 W. Thomas 93-8 H. Thomas 98-01 J. Williams 01 C. Hughes 01-06	Lost in collision off Land's End, 1910. One survivor.
258.5	39.6	23.1	J. Jones 85 E. Jones 91-02 J. Parry 05	Not heard of since spoken to 23°30'S 22°5'W, 13 July 1905, Junin to Rotterdam, nitrates of soda. Crew of 25 supposed drowned.
250.0	39.5	23.1	J. Owen 86-91 J. Hughes 93-7 J. Thomas 97-9 S. Hughes 99-02	Sold Norway 1915. Sunk by U-boat 1918.
268.5	39.5	23.1	H. R. Jones 87-91 R. Jones 91-8 H. Jones 98-	Wrecked off Norwegian coast 1900.
265.7	40.0	22.9	G. O. Williams 89-91 W. Richards 92-99 T. Williams 01-05	Sold Norway 1914.
256.1	38.2	22.7	D. Davies 88-95 W. W. Griffiths 99-05	Lost with all hands near Elbe Lightship, Jan. 1897.

Year acq'd	Name	Rig	Tonnage	When built	Built by	at
1891	Republic	Steel 4mst. Bk.	2539	1891	W. Doxford & Sons	Sunderland
1891	Dominion	Steel 4mst. Bk.	2539	1891	Doxford	Sunderland
1891	Nation	Steel 4 mst. Bk.	2401	1891	W. Doxford & Sons	Sunderland
1893?	Caernarvon Castle	I.Bk.	752	1870	R. & J. Evans	Liverpool
1894?	S.S. Maritime	Steel Sc.Sr.	2835	1894	Palmers	Newcastle
1896	Annie Thomas	Steel S.	1764	1896	Mackie & Thomson	Glasgow
1896	S.S. Treasury	Steel Sc.Sr.	2956	1896	Palmers	Newcastle
1897?	S.S. Hemisphere	Steel Sc.Sr.	3486	1897	Bartram & Sons	Sunderland
c.1897	Cambrian Hills	Steel S.	1760	1892	A. Rodger & Co.	Pt. Glasgow
c.1897	Cambrian Monarch	Iron S.	1353	1876	T. R. Oswald	S'hampton
c.1897	Cambrian Warrior	S.Bk.	1432	1885	J. Laing	Sunderland

Length	Breadth	Depth	Masters	What happened to ship
294.0	43.0	24.0	J. Owen 91-95	Out of Register, 1897.
294.0	43.0	24.0	W. Meredith 91-6 T. Jones 99-99	Not heard of since sailing, 19 Jan. 1899, from Honolulu for Royal Roads, B. Columbia, in ballast.
294	43	24	R. Wynne 1891-	Not heard of since leaving Rangoon, March 1892. Crew of 30 supposed drowned in hurricane off Mauritius.
186.0	31.3	19.0	W. Roberts 93	Previously owned by D. W. Davies & Co., Blaenau Ffestiniog, 1870-92.
315.0	43.2	20.3	T. Williams 00	
267.0	40.1	23.0	H. Thomas 96-98 W. Meredith 98-	Not heard of since spoken to 57o25'S 70o30'W. 19 Oct. 1899, Cardiff to Acapulco, with coal. Crew of 27 supposed drowned.
325.0	43.0	20.3	O. Davies 99 J. Williams 06	
350.0	46.5	16.2	O. Jones 00 R. Roberts 06	
260.7	38.1	23.1	A. Evans 92-02 O. M. Jones 03 W. Williams 04	Foundered 50o42'N 7o17'W, 1905. Crew saved.
216.5	37.0	23.0	J. Richards 92 D. Thomas 99 R. Griffiths 03	Previously owned by T. Williams and Co., Liverpool.
230.6	37.0	21.8	R. Roberts 97 J. Jones 00 W. Cadwaladr 04	Previously owned by T. Williams and Co., Liverpool.

Year acq'd	Name	Rig	Tonnage	When built	Built by	at
c.1897	Cambrian Prince	I.S.	1393	1876	T. R. Oswald	S'hampton
c.1897	Cambrian Princess(I)	I.S.	1394	1877	T. R. Oswald	S'hampton
c.1897	Cambrian Queen	I.Bk.	1336	1868	Oswald & Co.	Sunderland
1897	Cambrian Chieftain	I.Bk.	1492	1885	Osborne, Graham	Sunderland
1898	S.S. Consols	Steel Sc.Sr.	3493	1898	Bartram & Sons	Sunderland
1900	Marshall (ex Marechal Suchet)	Steel S.	1785	1893	Macmillan	Dumbarton
1900?	Boadicea	Steel +I.S.	1938	1887	R. William-son & Co.	Workington
1900?	Wynnstay	I.S.	1674	1884	Russell & Co.	Pt. Glasgow
1902	S.S. Royal	Steel Sc.Sr.	3833	1902	Palmers	Newcastle
1902	S.S. Imperial	Steel Sc.Sr.	3818	1902	Palmers	Newcastle
1902	James Kerr	Steel 4mst. Bk.	2424	1892	T. Royden & Sons	Liverpool
1903	Afon Alaw	Steel 4mst. Bk.	2050	1891	A. Stephen & Sons	Glasgow
1904	Cambrian Princess (II) (ex Manydown)	I.S.	2437	1884	Oswald Mordant	S'hampton

Length	Breadth	Depth	Masters	What happened to ship
224.7	37.1	22.6	T. Owen 99	Previously owned by T. Williams and Co., Liverpool.
224.7	37.1	22.6	T. Williams 97 W. Roberts 01 W. Owen	Previously owned by T. Williams and Co., Liverpool
221.7	36.8	22.8	D. D. Jones 96	Previously owned by T. Williams and Co., Liverpool.
230.0	37.5	22.5	T. Williams 96 M. Jones 00 T. M. Thomas 04	Previously owned by T. Williams and Co., Liverpool.
350.0	46.5	16.2	H. Jones 06	
267	40.1	23	T. M. Stephens 00	Wrecked, Feb. 1906.
264.0	39.0	23.6	R. Roberts 00 M. Jones P. Jones 09	Sold to Norway 1915.
258.8	38.2	23.1	T. Williams 05	Wrecked Iquique?
365.0	48.3	25.4	T. Williams 02-11	
365.0	48.2	25.5	O. Davies 02-05 H. Pugh 10-11	
293.9	41.2	24.5	C. Powles 92-05 E. Jones 05 M. Jones 07	Sold Germany 1910. Lost 1926.
284.4	41.0	23.7	J. Davies 03 E. Jones 07	Previously owned, R. Hughes & Co., Menai Bridge.
305	41.3	25.0	R. Evans 03 W. Roberts 07	

Year acq'd	Name	Rig	Tonnage	When built	Built by	at
1905	*Rowena* (ex Cluny Castle)	1.4mst. Bk.	1979	1883	Barclay, Curle & Co.	Glasgow
1906	*Crocodile*	Steel 4mst. Bk.	2557	1892	S'hampton Naval Works	S'hampton
1906	*S.S. Crown*	Steel Sc.Sr.	4234	1906	A. Rodger	Pt. Glasgow
1906	*S.S. King*	Steel Sc.Sr.	4144	1906	Russell & Co.	Pt. Glasgow
1906	*S.S. Queen*	Steel Sc.Sr.	4146	1906	Russell & Co.	Pt. Glasgow
1906	*S.S. Trader*	Steel Sc.Sr.	3608	1906	R. Craggs & Son	Middlesboro
1907	*S.S. Transport*	Steel Sc.Sr.	3619	1907	R. Craggs & Son	Middlesboro

Length	Breadth	Depth	Masters	What happened to ship
276.5	41.2	24	W. Cadwaladr 06	Sold 1914 Finland. Hulk Adelaide 1921.
288.4	41.2	24.6	H. Roberts 07	Sold Norway 1915. Sunk by U-boat, 13 June 1917.
384.9	50.0	16.5	W.Richards 06.11	
385.0	50.0	16.5	O. Jones 06-11	
385.0	50.0	16.5	E. Jones 06-11	
346.5	50.7	23.1	J. T. Williams 06-11	
346.5	50.7	23.1	W. Jones 07-11	

Appendix XII

Crew Agreement List – *County of Anglesea*. Dec. 1886 – Aug. 1888.

Name of

					PARTICULARS OF ENGAGEMENT†					
Reference No.	SIGNATURES OF CREW	Year of Birth (Age)	Town or County where born.	If in the Reserve, No. of Commission or R V 2.	Ship in which he last served, and Year of Discharge therefrom. Year.	State Name and Official No. or Port she belonged to.	Date and Place of signing this Agreement. Date.	Place.	In what Capacity engaged, and if Master, Mate, or Engineer,* No. of Certificate.	Time at which he is to be on board.
	1	2	3	4	5	6	7	8	9	10
1	Robert Wynne	40	Conway		1886	Same	10.12.86	Antwerp	O.C. 96904	
2	Master to sign first Ellis Jones	37	Pwllheli		,,	S.S. Iran	10.12.86	,,	O.C. Master 01637 Mate	13.12.86
3	Owen Williams	24	Moelfra		,,	Lady Penrhyn [illegible]	10.12.86	,,	O.C. 01366 2nd Mate	,,
4	Wm. Jno Nash	20	Dublin		,,	Same Ship	10.12.86	,,	3rd Mate	,,
5	Evan Roberts	27	Pwllheli		,,	Same Ship	10.12.86	,,	Steward & Cook	13.12.86
6	Robert [illegible]	26	Amlwch		,,	County of Anglesea	10.12.86	,,	Carpenter	13.12.86
7	John Backstrom	32	Sweden		,,	Balda	13.12.86	,,	AB	When required
8	Anders Nyman	22	Finland		,,	Arbutus	,,	,,	AB	,,
9	Karl Juselius	30	do		,,	Amelia	,,	,,	AB	,,
10	Gustav + Eklblom	28	do		,,	A Leffy	,,	,,	AB	,,
11	Gustav Gerade	28	Germany		,,	Hugh Fortescue	,,	,,	AB	,,
12	A. A. Krook	34	Finland		,,	Foreign	,,	,,	AB	,,
13	Knut Gunggren	27	Sweden		,,	do	,,	,,	AB	,,
14	Alex [illegible]	23	do		,,	do	,,	,,	AB	,,
15	J. Mesins	25	do		,,	do	,,	,,	AB	,,
16	J. W. [illegible]	18	Finland		,,	do	,,	,,	OS	,,
17	John Wynne	18	Liverpool		,,	Same Ship	10.12.86	,,	OS	13.12.86
18	William Ellis	16	Nevin		,,	Same Ship	10.12.86	,,	OS	13.12.86
19	Jacques Smit	29	Holland			Scottie Bay	[illegible]	,,	Carpenter	[illegible]
20										

* Engineers not employed on the Propelling Engines and Boilers

† If any Member of the Crew enters Her Majesty's Service, the Name of the Queen's Ship into which he enters is to be stated under the head of "*Cause of leaving*

Ship "County of Anglesea"

Amount of Wages per Week or Calendar Month.	Advance agreed to.	Amount of weekly monthly Allotment.	Signature or Initials of Superintendent, Consul, or Officer of Customs.	PARTICULARS OF DISCHARGE, &c. To be filled in by the Master upon the Discharge, Death or Desertion of any Member of his Crew.				RELEASE (into M).		No.
				Date, Place, and Cause of leaving this Ship, or of Death.			Balance of Wages paid on Discharge.	We, the undersigned Members of the Crew of this Ship, do hereby release this Ship and the Master and Owner or Owners thereof, from all Claims for Wages, or otherwise in respect of this Voyage. Signatures of Crew made to be on the Line on which he signed in Col. 1.	Signature or In title of Official before whom the Balance of Wages was paid and Release signed.	
11	12	13	14	Date. 15	Place. 16	Cause? 17	18	19	20	
			aug	Remains						1
6 0 0	-	3 0 0	aug	7.4.88	Liverpool	Disd		Ellis Jones	M.N.	2
4 0 0	-	-	aug	do	do	do	564 36	Owen Williams	M.N.	3
2 15 0	-	-	aug	do	do	do	32 19 3	Wm John Nash	M.N.	4
4 0 0	-	2 5 0	aug	do	do	do	32 19 4	Owen Roberts	M.N.	5
4 0 0	-	2 5 0	aug	Never Joined					✓	6
2 10 -	5	-	aug	7.4.88	L'pool	Disd	28 1 76	John Bachstrom	M.N.	7
2 10 -	4	-	aug	do	do	do	37 3 10	Anders Nyman	M.N.	8
2 10 -	4	-	aug	do	do	do	29 8 3	Paul Parvelius	M.N.	9
2 10 -	4	-	aug	do	do	do	29 0 6	Gustaf Stromberg	M.N.	10
2 10 -	4	-	aug	15.4.87	Sydney N.S.W.	Deserted de			✓	11
2 10 -	4	-	aug	7.4.88	L'pool	Disd	26 13 3	A. A. Krook	M.N.	12
2 10 -	4	-	aug	15.4.87	Sydney N.S.W.	Deserted			✗	13
2 10 -	4	-	aug	4.4.87	Sydney N.S.W.	Deserted			✗	14
2 10 -	4	-	aug	4.5.87	Newcastle					15
2 -	3	-	aug	23.3.87	Sydney N.S.W.	Deserted.			✗	16
2 0 0	-	15 -	aug	7.4.88	L'pool	Disd	13 6 4	John Wynn	M.N.	17
1 5 0	-	-	aug	do	do	do	10 8 8	William Ellis	M.N.	18
4 0 0	1 0 0	-		do	do	do	8 0 2	Jacques Smit	M.N.	19
										20

* should be described as Engine Drivers here and in Div. 1.

the Ship," Guns, "H.M.S. Revenge," and the other Causes of leaving the Ship should be briefly stated thus, "Discharged," "Deserted," "Left Sick," "Died."

Turn over.

677

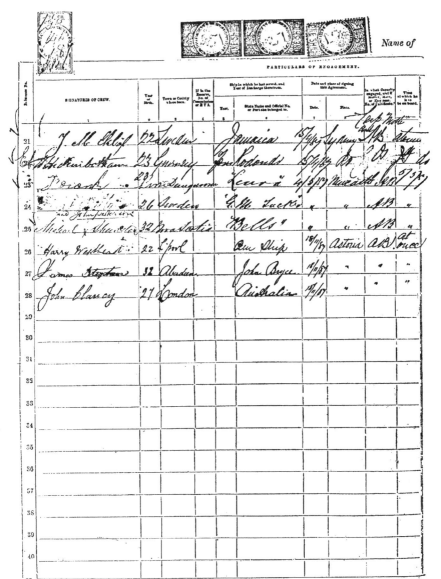

Reference No.	SIGNATURES OF CREW.	Year of Birth.	Town or County where born.	If in the Reserve, No. of Commission or R.V.R.	Ship in which he last served, and Year of discharge therefrom.		Date and place of signing this Agreement.		In what Capacity engaged, and if Master, Mate, or First Mate, No. of Certificate.	Time at which he is to be on board.
					Year.	State Name and Official No. or Port she belonged to.	Date.	Place.		
21	J. Mc Phlof	22	Sweden			Jamaica	15/9/87	Sydney		
22	Hickinbotham	23	Guernsey			Pusladonda	23/9/87			
23	Grant	23				Leno d	4/8/87	Newcastle		
24		26	Sweden			G. Mc. Facho	"	"	AB	"
25	Michael Shandler	32	Nova Scotia			Bells	"	"	AB	"
26	Harry Westheast	22	Lpool			New Ship	18/11/87	Astoria	AB	at once
27	James Stephens	32	Aberdeen			John Bryce	19/11/87	"	"	"
28	John Blancy	27	London			Australian	19/11/87	"	"	"
29										
30										
31										
32										
33										
34										
35										
36										
37										
38										
39										
40										

* Engineers not employed on the Propelling Engines and Boilers
† If any Member of the Crew enters Her Majesty's Service, the Name of the Queen's Ship into which he enters is to be stated under the head of "Cause of leaving"

Ship *County of Anglesea*

Amount of Wages per Week, or Calendar Month.	Advance Agreed to.	Amount of Weekly or Monthly Allotment.	Signature or Initials of Superintendent, Consul, or Officer of Customs.	Date, Place, and Cause of leaving this Ship, or of Death.			Release of Wages paid on Discharge.	We, the undersigned Members of the Crew of this Ship, do hereby renounce this Ship and the Master and Owner or Owners thereof, from all Claims for Wages, or otherwise in respect of this Voyage. Signatures of Crew (each to be on the Line on which he signed in Col. 1).	Signature or Initials of Official before whom the Balance of Wages was paid and Release signed.	Reference No.
				Date.	Place.	Cause.†				
				12.7.87	Wilmington California	Deserted			✗	21
				23.8.87	Wilmington California	Deserted			✓	22
3 10. 3 10.				24.7.87	Wilmington California	Deserted			✓	23
3 10. 3 10.				7.4.88	Lewes Dixel		33 11 11	*John Deverton* Wages received on behalf of undersea. § 132 of Act. 13 & 14 Vict. chap. 16.	Supt. Mercl. Mar. Office	24
3 10. 3 10.				13.7.87	Wilmington California	Deserted			✓	25
6 0 0		£8 0 0	P.L.C.	Chny 9/87	Lewes	Discharged	19 17 6	*Harry Keatley*		26
6 0 0		£8 0 0	P.L.C.	do	do	do	18 4 5	*J Stephen*		27
6 0 0		£8 0 0	P.L.C.	do	do	do	19 9 0	*John Clancy* Wages received on behalf of undersea. § 132 of Act. 13 & 14 Vict. chap. 16.	Supt. Mercl. Mar. Office	28
										29
										30
										31
										32
										33
										34
										35
										36
										37
										38
										39
										40

should be described as Engine Drivers here and in Dis. 1.
the Ship," thus, "H.M.S. Revenge;" and the other Causes of leaving the Ship should be briefly stated thus, "Discharged," "Deserted," "Left Sick," "Died."

Twelve pages.

Index

The Index has been compiled in three sections:

i. Vessels;   ii. Places;   iii. Persons.

Apart from the list of vessels (section i), sections ii and iii are selective. There are two reasons for this: firstly, the 'study' format of each chapter, and, secondly, the sheer bulk of the exhaustive index of places and persons.

i. Vessels

Abbey 395
Abbots Reading 362
Abbotsford 365
Abel 378,379,380,384
Abgeri 542
Abraham 121
Active 348,349
Adelaide 353
Adventure 88
Aerial 361
Afon Alaw 50,260,261,262,275,493
Afon Cefni 260,261,272
Afrique 310
Agnes 239
Ailsie 314,504,505
Air 430,433,439
Ajmeer 248,266
Albion 193,208,234,304,313,314,428
Alert 342
Alexander 354
Alhambra 352
Alice 395
Alice Williams 395
Allegiance 257
Alliance 296,297,298
Alnwick Castle 539
Altair 488,490
Amanda 299,315,405,406,407,492
Amidas 246
Amlwch 204,205
Amlwch Packet 395,401
Andrew of Kylkowberye 28

Anglesea Lass 293,305
Anglesey 257,258,259,261,275,292
Anglesey (1885) 309,310
Anglesey (b.1891) 508
Anglia 534,547
Ann 378
Ann Davies 243,246
Ann Grant 264
Anne 206
Anne of Brest 27
Annie Park 506
Annie Thomas 473
Antelope 45,441
Antelope S.S. 344
Anteros 544
Apapa 542
Archduke Paladino 353
Ardri 310,327
Arfon 476,477
Argus 210
Arion 224
Arizona 248
Arno Merndi 543
Arracan 488,490
Arrogant 175
Assel 391
Assistance 121
Athelstone 400
Aurora 126
Austin of Portinlleyne 121
Avon 249

Twillingate 325
Tŷ Eiddaw, Pwllheli 190
Tŷ Gwyn 131
Tŷ Mawr, Amlwch 190
Tŷ'n Pwll 475
Tynygongl 411-2

Uleaborg 322
Ushant 175

Virginia 106,527,540

Wapping 155
Warrington 203
Waterford 23,27,33,95,191,344,410
Wern y Cwm 44
West Mouse 221,342,352,366
Wexford 75,81,83,96,99,215,348
Whitehaven 115,119,134,207
Wingo Sound 183
Wisconsin 393
Workington 25,210,361,419
Wylfa, Yr 78,365,402

Ynys Faelog 222
Ynys Traws 353
Ynys Wellt 353
'Ynys Wyddel' 341
York 82
Youghal 74,409

iii. Persons

Algeo, Robert 301,465
Allen, William 210
Andrews, *Dr*. K. R. 34
Antonio, Nicolau Mario 325
Archer, *Capt*. G. C. 479
Armstrong, *Lt*. M., R.N.R. 535
Arthur, Hugh 29
Arthur, Mary (*Mrs*) 140
Ashburner, Thomas 300
Ashburner, William 417

Ashong, Amos 325
Ayscue, *Sir* George 97,105

Bacon, Francis 82
Baddiley, *Capt*. 102
Bagwell, Philip 431
Baines, James 266
Baker, J. M. 505
Bangor, *Bp*. of (1906) 366
Banks 92
Banks, Lawrence 133
Baptist, John 510
Barratt 314
'Barti Ddu' (Bartholomew Roberts)
   158
Bartlett, John (Dublin) 75
Bartlett, *Capt*. John 75,81,91,96,107
Bartlett, *Capt*. Thomas 75,81,83,91,
   102,107
Batten, *Capt*. 74,96
Bavand, Richard 30
Bayly, *Adml*. Lewis 538,543,546
Bayly, Lewis (*Bp. of Bangor*) 39,210
Bayly, *Sir* Nicholas 203
Bayne, William 465
Beaver, Hugh 401,443
Beaver, John 174
Beaver, Robert 174
Bedford, *Capt*. 358
Bennett, W. S. 307
Bentham, *Capt*. 185
Berkley, *Capt*. 92
Birchall, *Col*. 443
Bissett, *Sir* James 479,494
Bisson, John P. 414
Blair, Peter 181
Blake, Robert 97ff,541
Bodvel, John 159
Boggie, John 428
Boggie, William 437
Boscawen, *Adml*. Edward 161,166
Bouquet, Michael 223,311,450
Bovis, Amos 325
Bowen, *Capt*. Robert 104

Branwen 22
Brereton 77,85
Bridgman, Orlando 86,107
Briggs, Asa 245,359
Briggs, Henry 44
Brun, Andrew 27
Buckingham, *Earl of* 82
Bulkeley, Blanche (Coytmor) 93
Bulkeley, Charles 31,35
Bulkeley, Daniel 31
Bulkeley, David 35
Bulkeley, Edmund 35
Bulkeley, Edward 35
Bulkeley, *Col.* Richard 93,96,101
Bulkeley, *Sir.* Richard *1st Bt.* 21,47
Bulkeley, *Sir* Richard *3rd Bt.* 26,31, 34,75
Bulkeley, *Sir* Richard Bulkeley Williams (*Bart.*) 251,439
Bulkeley, *Sir* Richard Henry Williams (*Bart.*) 447,451,508
Bulkeley, Thomas, *Viscount* 78,93, 230,436
Bulkeley, William 123,140,142,150, 174,427
Burton, J. H. 449,451
Butler, Rowland 172
Button, *Sir* Thomas 40,105
Byron 91,93

Campbell, *Lt. Cdr.* Gordon, R.N. 536ff
Carlyle, Thomas 381
Carr, Robert 291
Carter, *Col.* 95
Casson, Bros 211
Castlehaven, *Earl of* 84
Cathcart 159
Chadwick, Samuel Taylor 248, 451,508
Chambers, Richard 183
Chappell, Reuben 312,499
Charles I 39,42,71,81,89,107,338
Charles II 107,339,340,434
Charles, Robert 244

Cheadle, *Maj.* Richard 96,101
Cheadle, Thomas 89
Christian, *Capt.* 46
Churchill, Winston Spencer 526, 541,547
Clarendon (*Earl of*) 427
Clarke, *Capt.* Robert 91,105
Clegg, Harry 447
Clough, Richard 24
Coates, *Capt.* 153
Coghlan, Mark 140
Collins, Greenville 24,72,80,339,434
Comenius (Jan Amos Komensky) 82
Condren, James 314
Connor, John 133
Conrad, Joseph 258,477
Cooper, *L./S.* 538
Couch, *Lt. Cdr.* Richard, R.N. 549
Cox, George M. 531
Coytmor, Robert 93
Coytmore, *Capt.* Rowland 93
Cromwell, Oliver 98,107
Cromwell, Thomas 21
Cross, *Lieut.* 134
Craig, Robin 233
Crowe, *Capt.* Albert 262

Dallay, J. 119
Daniell, William 206
Danske, *Capt.* Ralph 77,87
Davies, Beatrice Conway 254
Davies, David 463,496
Davies, David (New Quay) 509
Davies, *Rev.* Evan 464
Davies, *Capt.* (Holyhead) 213
Davies, Henry Rees (Treborth) 237, 255,261,275,448,451,493
Davies, John (M. Bridge) 231ff-245ff, 291
Davies, *Prof.* J. Glyn 258,378,412
Davies, J. R. 451
Davies, Owen 122
Davies, *Prof.* Ralph 23,119
Davies, Richard, *Sen.* 230ff,378,446

**More Maritime Titles
from Gwasg Carreg Gwalch**

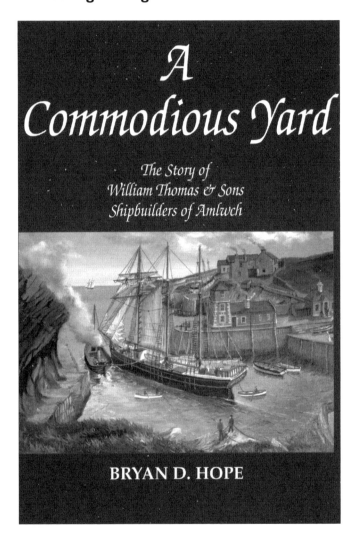

A
Commodious Yard

The Story of
William Thomas & Sons
Shipbuilders of Amlwch

BRYAN D. HOPE

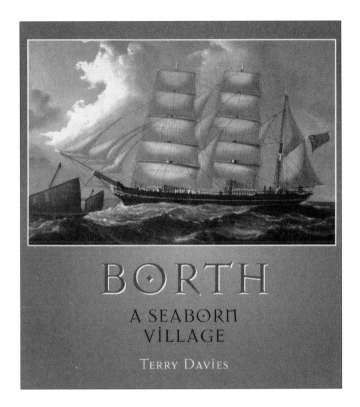

BORTH

A SEABORN VILLAGE

TERRY DAVIES

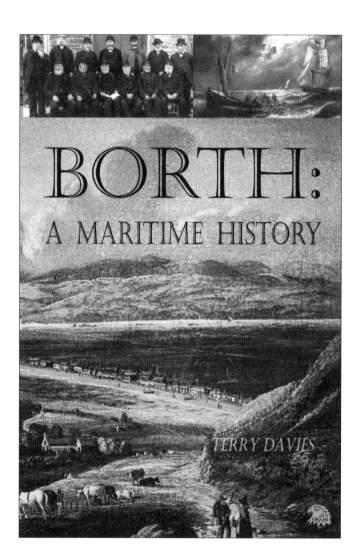

BORTH:
A MARITIME HISTORY

TERRY DAVIES

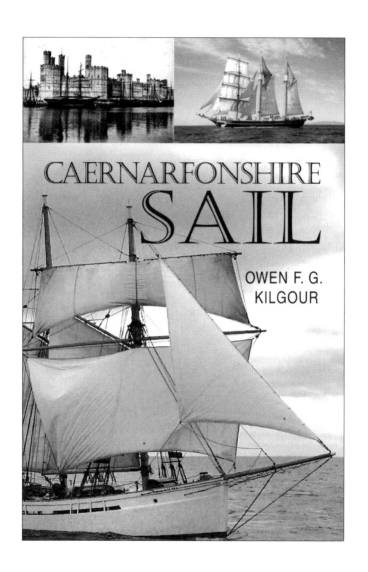

CAERNARFONSHIRE SAIL

OWEN F. G. KILGOUR

HEARTS OF OAK, NERVES OF STEEL

Shipwrecks and heroism in the Celtic Sea

Ian Skidmore

THE STORY OF COXSWAIN DICK EVANS BEM

LIFEBOAT VC

IAN SKIDMORE

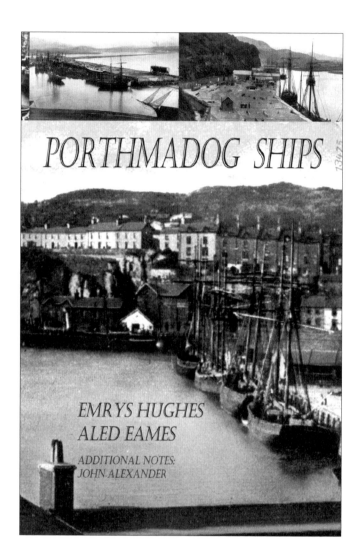

PORTHMADOG SHIPS

EMRYS HUGHES
ALED EAMES

ADDITIONAL NOTES:
JOHN ALEXANDER

THE RAILS AND SAILS
OF WELSH SLATE

Alun John Richards

Sentenced to Hell

The story of men and women
transported from north Wales
1730-1878

J Richard Williams

Voyages of the Celtic Saints

Graham Panes

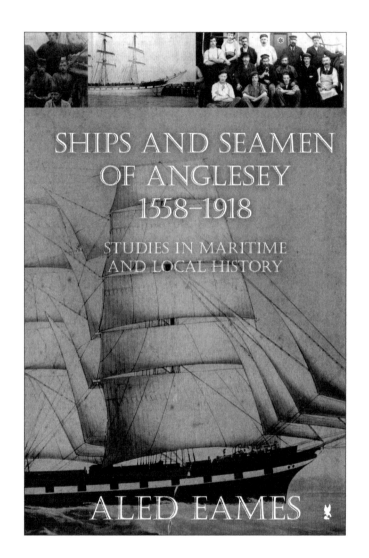

SHIPS AND SEAMEN OF ANGLESEY 1558–1918

STUDIES IN MARITIME AND LOCAL HISTORY

ALED EAMES

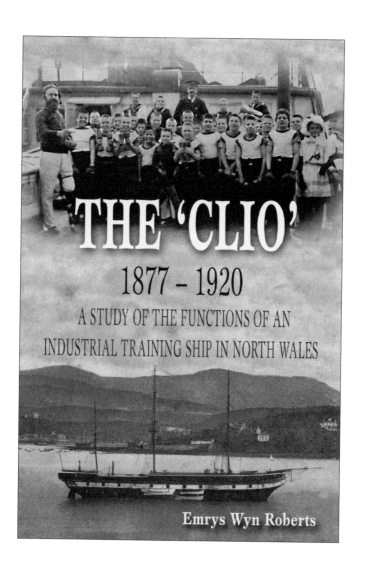

THE 'CLIO'

1877 – 1920

A STUDY OF THE FUNCTIONS OF AN
INDUSTRIAL TRAINING SHIP IN NORTH WALES

Emrys Wyn Roberts